Ella Fitzgerald
(and Chick Webb)

Ella Fitzgerald

An Annotated Discography;

Including a Complete Discography of Chick Webb

J. WILFRED JOHNSON

McFarland & Company, Inc., Publishers
Jefferson, North Carolina, and London

Library of Congress Cataloguing-in-Publication Data

Johnson, J. Wilfred, 1920–
Ella Fitzgerald: An annotated discography; including a complete
discography of Chick Webb / J. Wilfred Johnson.
p.   cm.
Includes index.
ISBN 0-7864-0906-1 (illustrated case binding : 50# alkaline papers) ∞
1. Fitzgerald, Ella — Discography.   [2. Webb, Chick —
Discography.]   2. [i.e., 3.] Sound recordings — catalogs.   I. Title.
ML156.7.F594 J64 2001   016.78242165'092 — dc21   00-53706

British Library cataloguing data are available

Manufactured in the United States of America

Cover image ©2000 Corbis Images

*McFarland & Company, Inc., Publishers
Box 611, Jefferson, North Carolina 28640
www.mcfarlandpub.com*

This book is dedicated to
Mr. Norman Granz
and
to the Memory of
Miss Ella Fitzgerald
(1917–1996)
and
to the Memory of
William Henry ("Chick") Webb, Jr.
(1909–1939)
without whom…

Acknowledgments

Since I first began collecting data for this book in 1988, I have received hundreds of letters supporting and encouraging the production of this discography, especially from the members of the Ella Fitzgerald Music Appreciation Society, many of whom contributed information contained in their collections, as well as research to ensure the accuracy of the information contained herein.

I am particularly grateful:

• in the United States, to Marcy Belfer, James W. Blackman, Michael Carrafiello, Frank Constanzo, Joseph Del Popolo, Tony DiGiacomo, Mike Farrace, Joan Gillen, Edward Jablonski, Mark B. Jorgensen, Lawrence Katz, Bernard J. Klug, Donald B. Little, Kenny Lucas, Maurice M. Manown, Wayne L. Martin, Charles G. Myers, Ed O'Brien, Barbara J. Pearson, Charles Pignone, Alan B. Richer, Ric Ross, Michael B. Schnurr, Roger Schore, Oded Z. Shulsinger, Dan Singer, and Bob Yeager

• in Canada, to Tom Lord

• in the United Kingdom, to Gerry Atkinson, Sarah Attwood, Ken Bailey, Mrs. O. Bannister, J.D. Bare, T.D. Barnard, M.S. Blackwell, R.J. Buckett, June E. Coleman, Stanley A. Colk, John B. Currall, Angela M. Darling, A. D'Auria, E. Ken Deacon, Brian Deverill, Victor Donson, Graeme Dowling, Edwin Edwards, Joanne Ellis, R.L. Forman, Caroline Fraser, B. Gastrell, Patience Gent, Manuel Gosano, Millicent Gowland, Mrs. S.B. Graham, Gordon Gray, Greig W.W. Hill, Jim Houghton, Les Hurley, Stephen Jones, Graham S. Langley, P.A. Long, Mrs. Marion Lord, John B. Mackie, Harold Martin, Jean McCarthy, Philip Mead, Christopher Reynolds, Chris Shackell, Ian Sharp, Roger Smith, Mrs. Margaret Solari, Margaret Thomas, Paul Thompson, W.G. Tuffey, Fred J. Wadsworth, John Meredith Williams, and Jean Wilson

• in France, to R. Demilien, Danièle Lostanlen, J.P. Mittay, Evan Orensten Frank Tenot, and Alain Tercinet

• in the Netherlands, to J.E. Broers, Wim de Boois, C. de Pater, J.K. Froger, Jan Gort, Henk Groeneveld, Mw. C. Hartmans, W. Heemstra, Frans Maas, Dick Schwartz, Jan van de Ruit, M.A. van Olderen, and Jeanne van Zundert

• in Germany, to René de Vries and Dirk Meyer

• in Denmark, to Michael P. Krog

• in Portugal, to Mário Diaz

• in Belgium, to G. Schrijvers.

Most especially, I wish to express my deepest gratitude to Michel Macaire, of Tours, France, for standing by to take over the publication of our quarterly, **ELLA!**, when it became impossible for me to continue, and for his vast contribution to the data contained in this volume.

For permission to reprint the essays in Part One, I am grateful to John McDonough and Bruce Crowther.

For invaluable support and assistance, I am very grateful to Mike Lang, Ben Young, and Tom Greenwood, Verve Records; Eric Miller, Terri Hinte, and Stuart Kremsky of Fantasy, Inc.; Jerald Dotson and Joan A. Sturgis, Capitol Records; Steve Lang, Reprise Records; Michael Kapp, Warner Special Products; Mandana Eidgah, Buddha Records; and Orrin Keepnews, San Francisco.

My special thanks to the wonderful people at Central Branch, Multnomah County Library, Portland, Oregon.

Contents

Preface

The Ella Fitzgerald Music Appreciation Society was founded in 1989 for the purpose of researching, collecting, and promulgating information concerned with the recorded works of Miss Ella Fitzgerald. The quarterly publication, **ELLA!**, began publication in October with short articles, recording session information, and LP and CD listings. Today the publication is no longer a quarterly, but issued as new information presents itself. Recently published is Issue No. 30, a tribute to the continuing interest in the legacy of the First Lady of Song.

This volume represents the combined efforts of many people who submitted information, news clippings, programs, photocopies of their personal collections, and a mountain of relevant material, so that short of compiling a "bio-discography," we have, at least, a rather complete discography. I say "rather complete," for it would not surprise me to hear, once again, that Orrin Keepnews, Phil Schaap, or even Norman Granz has "discovered" more concert tapes and that GRP Decca Jazz or Verve or Pablo is issuing newly discovered material in more Ella albums. One can only hope this will be the case. The fact that Dave Grusin, Orrin Keepnews, and Joel Dorn of GRP Decca Jazz just in time for Christmas 1997 issued a beautiful 4-CD boxed set with much material heretofore unavailable on CD should encourage others with access to Ella's recording session tapes. (Did Warner Bros. take a chance on the $500 Sinatra briefcase? No! It sold out.)

While researching this volume, I consulted the works of experts in the field, particularly those of the legendary deans of jazz discography, Brian Rust and Walter Bruyninckx, as well as their disciples Roger Kinkel and Jorgen Grunnet Jepsen. And though I admire and applaud the work of all these gentlemen, I found that I had to consult additional references for supplemental and incremental information. I therefore determined that, should our work come to fruition, its contents would contain everything possible that I could accumulate relevant to the music and recordings of Miss Fitzgerald. Thus, the extent of this volume.

However, I expect that as soon as this book reaches the hands of Ella's collectors, there will be criticism for having omitted this concert or that recording session that I was unable to unearth before publication. We who enter the field of discography must be concerned not only with the discs issued, but also with the tapes, acetates, and records that are buried in New Jersey and California tape vaults from which discs might possibly be issued in the future. I still have dreams of coming upon a warehouse of dusty files and boxes of tapes of all those *Jazz At The Philharmonic* concerts that Norman Granz has forgotten he recorded. When a company such as the British Flyright Records can, in 1994, give us a 1971 concert in Tilburg, Holland, who knows what's in store for the future — and from what quarter! And this does not even address the existence of all those radio broadcast sessions that lie ignored in NBC and CBS (and Mutual?) warehouses. What treasures there must be!

This discography is complete, insofar as I presently can determine, but what I don't know might possibly warrant a supplemental volume.

After publishing its final newsletter early in 2000, the Ella Fitzgerald Music Appreciation Society closed its doors, chiefly because its original purpose has been fulfilled: You hold it in your hand. Acknowledgment of the vast amount of information members contributed to this volume seems woefully insufficient compared with the appreciation I feel. I want to express my thanks to all of you.

Information that does not appear in this volume about Ella's recording sessions, concerts, or tours is most welcome. Please write to me in care of the publisher whose address appears in the front of this book. Such information (and your comments) will be greatly appreciated by the many to whom it will be made accessible; and if there are future editions of this volume, the information will be included, with due credit.

And, please, may I take here an opportunity:

The Society of Singers is a nonprofit organization "dedicated to providing compassionate understanding, counseling, financial and case management services to persons who are, or have been, professional singers." The founder-leader of the society is Ginny (Mrs. Henry)

Mancini, who did a lot of singing herself. In 1989 the society awarded its first lifetime achievement award to Ella Fitzgerald. The award itself, a handsome crystal trophy designed by Tiffany & Co., was immediately dubbed the "Ella." Among other recipients have been Frank Sinatra (1990), Tony Martin (1992), Peggy Lee (1994), Steve Lawrence and Eydie Gorme (1995), Lena Horne (1997), Rosemary Clooney (1998), Joe Williams (1999, awarded posthumously), and Tony Bennett (2000). You do not have to be a singer to join the society, nor do you have to join the society to contribute. So look into your heart and think about the singer who sang the song you first fell in love to, and please send a contribution, however small, to The Society of Singers, 8242 West Third Street, Suite 250, Los Angeles, California 90048, and tell them that Ella inspired you to send the check. You may also call them at (323) 651 1696 and make your contribution with your credit card. Visit them at www.singers.com on the Internet. They have many nice gifts for sale with the Society of Singers logo, not to mention two wonderful and unique compact discs that are real treasures, and even a Christmas disc. A major goal of the society is to establish a retirement residence facility for professional singers.

Finally, the information contained in this volume includes all known Ella Fitzgerald recordings released to June 2000. Moreover, where there is a schedule for future releases, such as those of the French Classics label, that information is also included, but, of course, is subject to change. I will continue to update the material in my personal files. If you should seek further information, or have information you would like to contribute, please write to me in care of the publisher.

J. Wilfred Johnson
Portland, Oregon
July 2000

How to Use This Book

Two abbreviations are the keys to the information contained in this book: DRN and LPD. With these in mind, you have before you all that you want to know about the recording careers of Chick Webb and Ella Fitzgerald.

THE DRN (DISCOGRAPHER REFERENCE NUMBER)

This is a simple way to identify a specific recording of a performance by an artist. An invention of this discographer, it is a variation of similar designations used by other discographers. I hope that its use in this book will encourage standardization.

Here is a sample DRN with song title:

350612-1 I'll Chase the Blues Away

The numbers reveal that this session took place on 12 June 1935. The date translates, binomially, to 35 (for the year), 06 (for the month), and 12 (for the date). The added tag "-1" indicates that it is the first song to be recorded in that session. Thus, with this simple numeric phrase, we can identify a specific recording. In a book covering recordings by many artists, an artist's initials could be added to the numeric phrase for clarity: CW350612-1 would signify a Chick Webb recording. This volume, however, deals only with the recordings of Chick Webb and Ella Fitzgerald, and therefore the artists' initials are not included, since it is clear that we are listing only the recordings of Chick Webb and His Orchestra from 1927 to 1939 (including all of his work with other bands) and of Ella Fitzgerald from 1939 to 1992.

Occasionally, a record company will release a take other than the designated master take, an alternative take. In such a case, the day's Discographer Reference Number must be adjusted to reflect this new addition.

During some recording sessions, the artist has chosen to sing a medley of songs. A good example is Ella's Capitol record *30 by Ella* (LPD-92). On each track she records a medley of five songs. The DRN identifies each alphabetically, e.g., as 680521-1a, 680521-1b, 680521-1c, etc.

When the date of a recording is unknown, the DRN reflects this lack of information with "00." An example is the entry for the *Jazz At The Philharmonic* film soundtrack recorded during September 1950. We do not know the actual date the recordings took place, so we indicate this with 500900-1, 500900-2, etc.

When other artists are involved in a session that includes songs in which Ella does not participate (e.g., the many concert sessions with Duke Ellington, Count Basie, et al.), no DRN is given for performances without Ella, but the song titles are included for information.

THE LPD (LONG-PLAY DISC)

This abbreviation is used to preclude listing the title of an album every time there is a reference to it. For example, in **Part One: The Recording Sessions — A Discography**, each performance is followed by a notation of the record(s) and album(s) in which it may be found. Ella's performance of "A-Tisket, A-Tasket" recorded on 2 May 1938 (DRN 380501-1) appears on a 78rpm Decca single, as well as in seven albums or album sets:

Ella Fitzgerald/The Early Years, Part 1 (1935-1938) (a 2-CD set)
Ella Fitzgerald/75th Birthday Anniversary Celebration (a 2-CD set)
ELLA: The Legendary Decca Recordings (a 4-CD set)
The Chronological Ella Fitzgerald/1937-1938 (a CD)
Ella and Her Fellas (an LP)
Ella Fitzgerald/Golden Favorites (an LP)
The Best of Ella... (a 2-LP set)

Instead of listing the titles of all these albums, we simply refer to them by their respective LPD numbers: LPD-1, LPD-3, LPD-5, LPD-9, LPD-22, LPD-35, and LPD-40.

Note that LPD may stand for one LP, a set of LPs, a CD, a set of CDs, an 8-track tape, or simply a cassette tape. Each release, regardless of format(s) or the number of units contained therein, is assigned an LPD number.

THE PARTS OF THE BOOK

Part One: The Recording Sessions — A Discography is a chronological listing of all known recorded performances (released or not yet released) of both Chick Webb and Ella Fitzgerald. The information given in these recording sessions is as follows:

The title performer. The name given for each session is the name that appears on the initially released record.

The composition of the orchestra or accompanying group or the name of the accompanist. This information has been researched carefully and is believed to be correct. Where uncertainties exist, they are identified as such. In some cases accompanying groups are not known, and research has failed to identify the musicians. If a reader has confirmed identification for these musicians, the author will be grateful for the information.

The recording venues and dates. These, too, have been diligently researched. Further information is solicited.

The Discographer Reference Number (DRN), the recording company matrix (master) number, and the title of the recording. The DRN is explained above. The matrix (or master) number is assigned by the recording company to identify the single title being recorded. More often than not, during a recording session, a performance (or part of a performance) is repeated — perhaps because a mistake was made, or because the leader, conductor or soloist simply wants to try again in the hope of a better performance or interpretation. Each of these is known as a "take." In the end, one take is chosen for the master, and is so designated. In this discography, the master take is identified by a hyphenated number following the matrix number. For example, 14325-3 indicates that when recording title number 14325, the third performance of the song was chosen for the master take. The choosing is usually done by consensus of the producer, the orchestra leader, and the soloist (if the soloist is of star status).

Titles of songs have been researched, and in a few cases, the record is mis-titled in some respect, either in a misspelling (or other anomaly) of a word or words, or by its designation with an alternative title. An example of the former is "Stardust," used occasionally for the correct title, "Star Dust." An example of the latter is "Mr. Paganini," usually given on Chick's and Ella's recordings as "(If You Can't Sing It) You'll Have To Swing It." Composer-lyricist Sam Coslow in his autobiography, *Cocktails for Two: The Many Lives of Giant Songwriter Sam Coslow* (Arlington House, 1977), refers to it only as "Mr. Paganini." When "swing" as a description of a musical form became popular, songs with "swing" in the title were thought to sell more copies of sheet music and phonograph records. Thus "Mr. Paganini" acquired a more "saleable" title, and Ella's recording took off and became a major hit.

Following the numerical and title information, one finds the record company and the disc number (in the case of 78s and EPs) and/or the LPD number(s) of the albums in which the song appears. Look up the LPD number in **Part Two: Ella's Records** to find the title of the album.

Abbreviations used in this discography will be, for the most part, obvious to the reader. For example: v = vocals by, EF = Ella Fitzgerald, CL = Charles Linton, and instr = instrumental (no vocals), etc. For each recording session entry, full participant information is given.

For information regarding methods of recording in this era, see the excellent *Brian Rust's Guide to Discography* by Brian Rust (Greenwood, 1980), Appendix I, "Glossary of Terms Used in Discography."

Occasionally, there is a note concerning "charts." This indicates the popularity of the record. Briefly, here is a history of these popularity rankings: In 1934, *Billboard* magazine and *Variety* newspaper began regularly to publish two charts, one for best-selling records and one for recordings of the most popular radio airplay and sheet-music songs. In April 1935, "Your Hit Parade," a popular weekly radio program, began broadcasting, and the songs were incorporated into the radio airplay charts. In November of the same year, *Billboard* incorporated best-seller listings as reported by the record companies themselves. Early in 1938, *Billboard* stopped running the listings, which were carried by *Metronome* until the end of the year.

Late in 1938, *Billboard* began listing the thirty most popular records in jukeboxes around the country. Finally, on 20 July 1940, *Billboard* listed its first comprehensive "Best Sellers in Stores" records chart, discounting "Your Hit Parade," radio airplay, and sheet-music sales data, but retaining its separate chart for jukeboxes. It is from *Billboard* that the information in this volume is taken. All records reaching the "Best Sellers in Stores" charts are indicated with a special note immediately following the listing in the discography.

Part Two: Ella's Records gives complete contents of Ella's LPs and CDs, including track listings, titles (with lyricists and composers), timings, and the DRN for each performance. Other details, such as formats, playing times, release dates, and the names of producers, engineers, and authors of liner notes, are also given. The records are listed chronologically in terms of the dates the performances thereon were recorded, not of the dates when the albums were released. Part Two closes with an alphabetical index to the LPDs.

Part Three: The Songs Ella Sings offers an annotated, alphabetical listing of all the songs contained on all of Ella's records. The lyricist and composer are given, as well as the year of copyright, and a short note about the first or otherwise notable performances of the song. Since all songs were sung by Ella, her performances are not mentioned except where her record introduced the song to the public, or where the performance was especially noteworthy. The DRN is given for all of Ella's known performances, whether released (in bold text) or not yet released (in standard text). The DRN can be used to locate the song in **Part One: The Recording Sessions — A Discography**. For example:

Laura (1945)

Lyrics by Johnny Mercer, music by David Raksin

The music is from David Raksin's score for the 1944 20th Century-Fox film **Laura**. Lyrics were added several months after the release of the film, by which time the melody had become popular. Introduced on radio by Johnny Johnston, who recorded it for Capitol. Woody Herman's 1945 Columbia recording sold over a million copies.

500900-2, **641021-2**

So, we see that Ella recorded it twice, the first time for the soundtrack of the film *Jazz At The Philharmonic*, which was never released either as a film or on a record. This DRN is therefore listed in standard text. We know that it was recorded in September 1950, but we do not know the exact day; we have therefore used "00" in lieu. If you look up this DRN in Part One, you will find it grouped with the other selections for *Jazz At The Philharmonic* in September 1950.

We see that the second recording was made on 21 October 1964. When you look up that date in Part One, you will find that it was recorded for and released on *Ella Fitzgerald Sings the Johnny Mercer Song Book* (LPD-80), the entire contents of which may be found in **Part Two: Ella's Records.**

Following the Annotated Song Index in Part Three is a brief list (an imaginary "album," if you will) of songs that Ella recorded that you've never heard her sing — because the recordings have yet to be released.

The book closes with five appendices of interest to the dedicated aficionado of Ella's songs and her career:

Appendix A: They Wrote the Songs Ella Sings is an alphabetical list of composers and lyricists. Under each name is an alphabetical list of the songs to which that person made a contribution.

Appendix B: They Play While Ella Sings is an alphabetical list of all musicians appearing in Part One, and identifies the years when they recorded with Ella. At the end of this list, you will also find, **…And They Sang with Ella**, a list of those groups and individuals who accompanied Ella in song.

Appendix C: Ella's Movies gives information and reviews of the four movies in which Ella appeared.

Appendix D: Do-It-Yourself Ella Fitzgerald Song Books is a list of interesting suggestions for compiling your own personal "albums."

Appendix E: Some Recommended Reading is just that.

Because access to song titles, musicians' names, and the names of the composers and lyricists is provided though the appendices, the **General Index** does not include this information but indexes miscellaneous information found largely in the front matter, such as the names of persons mentioned in the introductory essays. The titles section of the book are also indexed, so that, for example, a reader may quickly locate a summary of Chick Webb's recordings, or of Ella's recordings with a particular company.

Introduction

The first of these essays, a beautiful and discerning tribute to Miss Ella Fitzgerald, appeared in the September 1996 issue of Down Beat *magazine. With the kind permission of its distinguished author, we have chosen it to introduce this volume concerned with the art and the achievements of the First Lady of Song.*
Following this tribute are essays on the careers of Chick Webb and Norman Granz, also provided by the gracious permission of their authors.

Ella: A Voice We'll Never Forget
by John McDonough

Of all the sad thoughts that have seen print since Ella Fitzgerald's not entirely unexpected passing on June 15, none seems sadder than the fact that we have lost a living link to a smarter, more literate, more courtly time in our cultural history. It was an era that coalesced between the wars, respected elitism, honored craft, imitated elegance, rewarded quality and expired sometime in the 1960s. As long as there were originals of the period like Ella around, though, the spirit of those times had its voices. It all seems the more precious nowadays with every new obituary.

Fitzgerald outlived her era by nearly 30 years, but long enough to pass her musical wisdom to a younger, less fortunate musical generation. But she had been in complete retirement for more than three years at the time of her death. In the '80s and early '90s, her concert schedule was disrupted by frequent hospitalizations. She underwent open-heart surgery in the summer of 1986, and that curtailed her performance schedule, despite her mightiest efforts to maintain her pace. 1990 was to have been a busy year, with nearly 30 concerts scheduled, including performances in Europe. But much of it had to be canceled before May. She performed several concerts in 1991 to generally excellent reviews. By then she had grown frail-looking and audiences seemed amazed that such a slight lady could still command such a powerful voice.

In 1992 diabetes resulted in surgery to remove a toe. Her final concert appearance was in December 1992 in Palm Beach, Florida. She was flown out on a private jet and performed sitting down. Though she continued to have a great will to perform, according to sources close to the singer, the amputation of both legs below the knees in 1993 ended any possibility of future appearances.

The dimensions of her reputation, which transcended all categories and demographics, can be gauged by the massive obituary profile published by the *New York Times.*

The work that lies behind the enormous Fitzgerald reputation is divided among three principle record labels: Decca, Verve and Pablo. Her last released recording to date was "All That Jazz" (Pablo) in 1990. It won her 12th Grammy. A subsequent session made in 1991 with her trio plus Harry Edison awaits release. And there are reportedly numerous club and concert tapes from the '50s, '60s and '70s in the vaults.

If the clear, youthful voice was nature's gift to her art, the musicianship that drove it was all hers. Born April 25, 1918 (more recent evidence suggests 1917), in Newport News, Va., it was fate, not training, that led her into singing after an attempt at dancing failed. Benny Carter was among the first to recognize her talent in 1934, and he alerted talent scout John Hammond. But Hammond passed, a decision he would regret but not deny.

She joined the Chick Webb band at 17 in 1935 and quickly made it her appendage. Decca saw to it that most of Webb's records featured her vocals. Today they hold up moderately well, interesting principally because of where they led. Her sound is a bit nasal and adolescent. Her style follows period swing conventions. And for every good tune she gets ("Don't Worry 'Bout Me"), there are a dozen pieces of trash ("Chew Your Bubble Gum"). If this was all there was, Ella Fitzgerald today would be a lively, somewhat interesting period artifact.

After Webb's death in 1939, she took over as leader of Webb's band. Decca and her manager Moe Gale built her as a single, and for the next 17 years she muddled along as a moderately interesting pop singer who sang what she was told and seldom got out of second gear.

By the late '40s, though, another Ella began to flower, one nurtured and managed by Norman Granz on the Jazz At The Philharmonic concert circuit. This Ella sang only the best songs. And in Granz's open-ended JATP concerts she had the space and freedom to meet the finest musicians of her generation outside of the Decca hit factory. Fitzgerald always had a knack for mimicking other singers. In the JATP concerts she began mimicking the musicians.

It's important to note that she came of age in a time when jazz had moved to the center of popular music and brought with it the jazz musician's respect for and pursuit of technique and virtuosity. With swing and bebop, these values reached a nirvana of fulfillment in the work of Tatum, Eldridge, Goodman, Young, Christian, Hampton, Peterson, Parker, Gillespie and many others. In targeting her mimicry on musicians like these (and probably Illinois Jacquet and Flip Phillips as well), Fitzgerald trained her sights on some of the most extravagantly gifted virtuosos jazz has produced.

Singers had scatted before Fitzgerald, of course, and she picked up fragments from Armstrong, Leo Watson and a couple of others. But those debts were minor. The origins of Fitzgerald's vocal improvising were rooted primarily in instrumental models, not vocal ones. And particularly the instrumental models at that point where swing and bebop met. She coined an uncanny and remarkably abstract vocabulary of semi-verbal onomatopoeia that expressed the most subtle nuances of jazz improvisation — its attack, smears, curves, phrasing, vibrato and pulse. Coupled with an overdrive falsetto reserve, she met the greatest musicians on their terms and dazzled audiences. In mimicking virtuosity, she came to possess it.

"She set the standard for scatting, not only with the way she soloed, but with her tone," says vocalist Kevin Mahogany, who noted that he studied Fitzgerald long before he listened to male jazz singers. "That's why the instrumentalists respected her so much."

As early as "Flying Home" (1945) and "Lady Be Good" (1947), both for Decca, it was clear how firmly she grasped instrumental vocalizing. But they are mere miniatures compared to the concert performances *Ella Fitzgerald at the Opera House* (Verve/Polygram), a 1957 magnum opus from JATP performances in Chicago and Los Angeles.

By the early '50s, however, there was a problem. Granz may have managed her performing career, but Decca still managed her recordings, which were less than distinguished. For 10 years she was partitioned between two sovereigns. Then late in 1955 fate handed Granz powerful leverage. Decca, which had owned Universal Pictures since 1952, was expecting large profits from the soundtrack album of Universal's *The Benny Goodman Story*. When Granz produced exclusive contracts with most of the film's star musicians, however, Decca had to choose between Goodman and Fitzgerald. The company readily surrendered the singer's contract to Granz.

On the strength of having acquired Fitzgerald's services for recording, Granz set up Verve Records with a view toward reaching the pop as well as jazz market. On Tuesday, Feb. 7, 1956, Fitzgerald joined with arranger conductor Buddy Bregman to begin the first of the masterworks that would put her among the immortals, *Ella Fitzgerald Sings the Cole Porter Song Book* (Verve/Polygram). The other famous song books followed — Rodgers and Hart, Ellington, Berlin, Gershwin, Arlen, Kern and Mercer.

"When I recorded Ella, I always wanted her to be way out front," says Granz. "I didn't want a blend, as if she were a band singer. The reason was that I frankly didn't care what happened to the music. The music supported Ella. I've had arrangers tell me that in bar 23 a trumpet hit a wrong note. I didn't care. I wasn't interested in making perfect records. If they were perfect, fine. But I wanted to make records in which Ella sounded best. If I thought she sounded great on a first take, I wasn't interested in wasting time doing six more, only to come back to the first one. I couldn't care less if there were clams here and there.

"There were times when I would walk into a studio and they'd have everyone walled off for stereo. I would always see that Ella was in the middle of the musicians. The engineers would go up the wall because they couldn't get any separation. I wanted singing, not separation.

"The issue many people missed when the song books came out was that, with all due respect to Ella, in my mind the writers had to be of equal stature to the performer. Otherwise, it would have come out simply as another collection of songs that Ella did. That's why in every instance I insisted that she do the verse.

"When we did the Porter album, we came to some verses that were difficult or really didn't work. Ella would get uptight and say, 'Why do I have to do this?' Translation: She had to spend time working on them. Usually Ella would go in and do her songs very fast. We never laid down tracks or anything like that. Everything was live with the band. We would do two takes, three at most, because that's how she worked.

"As the Ella song books became successful, certain composers wanted her to do their work. Irving Berlin actually called up and said his daughters were driving him crazy playing the Porter album. 'When are you going to do me?' he asked. I told him I was researching him now, and he was gassed when the album was finished. He was so anxious to have Ella do his songs, he offered a 50 per cent cut in mechanical royalties after he heard the session acetates. It was a very nice gesture."

But the barbarians were already at the gates. As Fitzgerald recorded the Porter album, Elvis Presley made his first network appearances on the CBS Dorsey Brothers Stage Show. As if to italicize the astonishing timing of this confluence, four days after the Porter session, Miss Fitzgerald actually appeared as a guest with Presley on the Dorsey program. The Presley phenomenon and the rock & roll revolution that issued from it would signal the collapse of the composer's place in American popular music. That it should happen at precisely the moment Miss Fitzgerald offered a new perspective on its appreciation and demonstrated that their work could be treated in a definitive manner as a body of literary work seems an astonishing irony. The song book project would become an unexpected and historic elegy to a vanishing age of literacy, intelligence and elitism in American music.

During the time Granz left the record business from 1960 to 1972, he continued to be her principal producer, though she ventured to Capitol for several albums. Finally came the long Pablo era in the '70s and '80s, when Granz resumed recording and paired her with everyone from Count Basie to André Previn to Nelson Riddle, plus a series of intimate duet albums with guitarist Joe Pass. During this period, in 1979, Fitzgerald was inducted into the Down Beat Hall of Fame.

Salle Productions, formed around 1960, was devoted to Fitzgerald's business, professional and performing interests. Its offices were (and still are) at 451 N. Cañon Drive in Beverly Hills, home of Granz's original JATP and Clef Records operations.

Fitzgerald made two major motion picture appearances, *Pete Kelly's Blues* (Warner Bros., 1955) and *St. Louis Blues* (Paramount, 1958). There were also numerous television appearances. Among the best: the *Swing Into Spring* programs of 1958 and '59 and a superb PBS-WTTW Chicago production mounted by Granz in November 1979. The latter teamed her with Count Basie and His Orchestra, Roy Eldridge, Zoot Sims, Joe Pass and many others.

Fitzgerald married bassist Ray Brown in 1947. The couple was divorced six years later but continued to work together. She is survived by Brown and their adopted son, Ray Brown, Jr.

Fortunately for the rest of us, Ella Fitzgerald will be remembered for generations to come — through personal recollections and numerous CDs of her recordings. As Mahogany says, "It's a voice that you never forget. When you're a vocalist, that's what you aspire to. I don't know if any of us ever will attain it, but it's a goal worth reaching toward."

The Ella Fitzgerald Legacy

What does this body of work tell us about Ella Fitzgerald and her contributions? First, the song books helped change the way we thing about our classic popular standards. She treated our grandest songwriters as composers; their music, as a canon. Some say her style tended to favor the composer over the lyricist. Perhaps, though no poet could ask for a more perfect recitation of a lyric than Fitzgerald bequeathed to "Suppertime" (Berlin) and "Love for Sale" (Porter). Much of the reverence accorded the so-called "American Popular Song" today is because Ella Fitzgerald sang it in the way she did.

She served both art and commerce without pandering. Her commercial albums (those done under Granz, at least) showed a respect for the mass market rare in popular culture. And her jazz albums were so consistently good, critics gave up long ago finding fault, save perhaps for a certain redundancy in the Pablo releases.

Though the elements of her vocabulary are familiar, her technique and sense of proportion held them in balance. Fifty-six years of recorded work — more than 30 of them as an icon — never came between Ella and the kind of artist she was.

This may also tell us something about the woman behind the artist. She was said to be shy and inarticulate, with not an introspective bone in her body. She had little to say about the processes, methodologies and nuances of her interpretations, why she did this and not that, etc. People who aren't given to analysis of such things are often blessed with a natural immunity to that most fatal virus that can strike an intuitive artist — self-consciousness, leading to self-imitation.

Few singers were as dependent upon pure musicianship as she was. Or had such extraordinary reserves of it. She didn't sing songs. She played them. She could not call on the skills of an actress the way Billie Holiday, Lena Horne, Judy Garland or Barbra Streisand could (and can). This is why some have accused her of a certain emotional neutrality, especially on ballads. It is also why she never "sold" (or oversold) her material. She was a songwriter's dream. She let the song speak for itself and seek its own emotional level.

She was never compelled to bother with nostalgia, because she never attached herself to the cycles of fashion that nostalgia feeds on. She had one great pop hit in her career, "A-Tisket, A-Tasket," and over the last 45 years of her career she seemed to avoid it like the plague, as if that's the one she might end up being remembered for.

The standards that Granz underwrote for her between 1956 and 1989 gave her distance from pop without isolation in the protected sanctuary of mainstream jazz; so far, they seem eternally youthful and relatively undated. The work of her arrangers has worn well, too: Billy May, Nelson Riddle, Paul Weston, Marty Paich and Buddy Bregman, who has been, perhaps, too unfairly dismissed. Bregman, after all, arranged and conducted the seminal Cole Porter and Rodgers & Hart song books. Each has become a classic of American popular music and helped establish Ella Fitzgerald as one of the two or, at most, three most important and influential singers of the 20th century.

Let's hope the 21st can do as well.

Down Beat,
Volume 63, Number 9,
September 1996

Chick Webb and the Home of Happy Feet

by Bruce Crowther

The Savoy Ballroom opened in 1926 on Lenox Avenue between 140th and 141st Streets in Harlem, and quickly earned a reputation as the nation's greatest dance center, partly through the excellent facilities offered, not least of which was a 10,000 square foot polished maple dance floor, and partly because the dancers who flocked there most nights were skilled far beyond the standards of many professionals. The ballroom used "The Home of Happy Feet" as a highly appropriate publicity tag, although the ballroom's regulars referred to it affectionately as "The Track."

Through the late 1920s and into the 1930s, most of the "name" black bands played at the Savoy, some of them enjoying extended engagements if they pleased the demanding dancers. Among the less well-known bands which played there in 1927 was The Harlem Stompers, a medium-sized group led by a diminutive drummer named Chick Webb. In 1931, now leading a big band, Chick became a fixture at the ballroom and, so far as the dancers were concerned, he was soon the undisputed King of the Savoy.

William Henry Webb was born in Baltimore, Maryland, probably in 1909. He was a sickly child and developed tuberculosis of the spine. Crippled and destined for a life of pain and immobility, he underwent an operation at Johns Hopkins Hospital, Baltimore, and was thereafter able to walk. However, he remained small in stature, hunchbacked, and was incapable of free and easy movement in his legs and shoulders. Any one of Chick Webb's disabilities should have put a career as a drummer into the realm of dreams, but Chick was tough, energetic, and absolutely determined to fulfill his twin ambitions of becoming a drummer and a band leader.

By 1920, at age 11, Chick was playing drums with a local band of youngsters and showed enough promise to be hired by the Jazzola Orchestra, with whom he played on pleasure boats until 1925 when he decided to head for New York City.

In New York, Chick first joined the Edgar Dowell band, but was eager to lead his own band. In 1926 at age 17I, he formed a quintet for which he secured a residency at the Black Bottom Club, from where he moved to the Paddocks Club before his first engagement at the Savoy with his Harlem Stompers in 1927.

The next few years found Chick working only intermittently. When he was able to find work, it was sometimes at such prestigious venues as the Cotton Club and Roseland, but engagements of this stature were usually only fleeting. It was not until 1931 at age 22I, when he became resident at the Savoy with a big band, that the switchback times were over. Apart from the financial stability from this point onwards, Chick Webb's was the band by which all others at the Savoy were measured. More often than not, especially when matched with Webb in a band "battle," the others were found wanting.

From the start of his bandleading career, Chick was always able to attract good musicians to his band. Comments made in later years by former sidemen suggest that their willingness to play with Chick derived from a combination of his infectious enthusiasm for his music and the fact that he was a kind and likable man.

Among early sidemen were pianist-arranger Don Kirkpatrick and Don's brother-in-law, alto saxophonist Johnny Hodges. A measure of Chick's generosity can be gained from the fact he encouraged Johnny to take a potentially more rewarding job. Other early sidemen who stayed longer than most include trumpeter Bobby Stark and guitarist John Trueheart. Stark was a strong, if occasionally wayward, trumpeter with much more solo talent than he was usually allowed to display. Trueheart, who had worked with Chick in the Jazzola Orchestra, remained a close friend to the end of the drummer's life.

By 1931 the band included such solid soloists as trumpeter Louis Bacon and trombonist Jimmy Harrison, while the reed section showcased the exceptional talents of Benny Carter and Hilton Jefferson. Chick also hired Bardu Ali, a smooth and sophisticated character, to front the band, baton in hand; but no one was ever in any doubt that the driving force was little Chick.

From the band's handful of 1931 recordings it is possible to hear something of the reason for the enthusiasm of the Savoy's patrons, especially from the fine solos played by Harrison, but it was when the band returned to the recording studios two years later that Chick Webb's full flowering was heard. By this time, the band was playing arrangements specially written for them, even if the cost to Chick was sometimes disproportionate. In his memoirs, *The Night People*, Dicky Wells observes: "Chick went hungry a lot just to keep the band in music. He would live on hamburgers so he could buy arrangements."

Don Kirkpatrick was still writing for the band (he was replaced on piano by Joe Steele and later by Tommy Fulford), although the principal contributor to the excellence of the band's book was alto saxophonist-violinist Edgar Sampson.

Sampson's scores for the band proved to be a great asset. Direct and simple though they are, Sampson's charts are imbued with great swing and have an enviable looseness of structure which encouraged the soloists to show off their paces. A good example is "Clap Hands! Here Comes Charlie!" which includes some searing trumpet from Taft Jordan, another new arrival whose solo skills became a highlight of the band (and further inhibited Bobby Stark's potential in this area).

Sampson's work for the band included arrangements on several of his own compositions, among them such soon-to-be jazz standards as "Blue Lou," "Don't Be That Way," and "Stompin' at the Savoy." The band's 1934 recordings of these tunes are particularly rewarding, perhaps because they were fresh material and had yet to acquire a weary patina of overworked familiarity. "Blue Lou" is taken at a relaxed tempo, with good solos from Mario Bauza, trumpet, Sampson, and Steele, while on the up-tempo "Don't Be That Way," Williams, Sampson, Jordan, and trombonist Claude Jones all shine. "Stompin' at the Savoy" crackles with vibrant urgency and includes fine solo work by trumpeters Bauza and Reunald Jones and long-term tenor saxophonist Elmer Williams.

Another arranger who served the band well was Charlie Dixon, and some of his charts are among the best of the band's 1937 recordings. These include a dynamic "Harlem Congo," featuring Jordan, Williams, and clarinetist Louis Jordan; a deceptively lazy version of Fats Waller's "Squeeze Me"; and the excellent "That Naughty Waltz," with fine solos by Chauncey Haughton on clarinet, and Taft Jordan.

An occasional arranger for the band was Benny Carter, who was responsible for an outstanding version of Gershwin's "Liza," recorded in 1938.

From around 1933 onwards, the regularity of the band's employment at the Savoy allowed Chick to employ and keep top-flight soloists and sidemen. Apart from those already mentioned, there were such sound performers as saxophonists Ted McRae and Wayman Carver. Carver joined fellow reed section member Chauncey Haughton in

a "band within the band," The Little Chicks, which employed the unusual instrumentation of flute (Carver), clarinet (Haughton), and rhythm section. The Little Chicks can be heard on such engaging excursions as "I Got Rhythm" and "Sweet Sue, Just You."

For all the undoubted qualities of his sidemen and arrangers, however, on every instrumental number the band recorded, Chick's personal musical contribution is never in doubt. On the evidence of records, whether from studio sessions or from the handful of radio remotes that are available, Chick was one of the best three or four big band drummers around at the time (other qualifiers would include Sid Catlett and Jo Jones). On slow and medium tempo numbers, Chick's drumming is imbued with fluid grace, while on up-tempo tunes he drives the band with great flair and exuberance.

When he takes solos, they are usually brief, to the point, and beautifully shaded. Such examples as "Spinnin' the Webb" and "In the Groove at the Grove" (from 1938 and 1939, respectively), both of which number among his handful of compositions, demonstrate his ability to make a telling impact with much less fuss and drama than many more famous drummers. On his occasional extended solos, for example, on the unlikely "My Wild Irish Rose," from a 1939 airshot, he displays intelligence and wit, qualities in short supply among his inferiors. In some instances, "Liza" and "Harlem Congo" among them, it is hard to imagine how Chick's work, whether solo or in ensemble, could have been bettered. Indeed, "Liza," which appears in the form of a small concerto for drums and orchestra, is exemplary and might well contain the best example of Chick's drumming on record.

The high regard with which Chick was viewed within the jazz world can be gleaned from comments made by musicians, especially drummers. Most often quoted is Gene Krupa, who consciously changed his own playing style after first hearing Chick. Given the number of big band drummers who subsequently copied Krupa, there must be many hundreds who, consciously or not, continued to develop the legacy of Chick Webb for many years after his death. Krupa, at least, gave credit to his idol, and for the rest of his life never tired of telling anyone that the little man from Baltimore was the finest drummer he had ever heard: "That man was dynamic; he could reach the most amazing heights." And Krupa was always happy to acknowledge that the best lesson in drumming he ever had occurred when he was with the Benny Goodman band which tangled with Chick's boys at the Savoy on 11 May 1937, declaring, "I was never cut by a better man."

For all his undoubted merits as a drummer and bandleader, however, to say nothing of the rapturous esteem with which he was regarded by the dancers at the Savoy, Chick Webb is almost forgotten today. When he is remembered it is usually for none of the reasons suggested above, but because of a young singer he employed in 1934 — Ella Fitzgerald.

As Ella's fame grew, so there was a proportionate increase in the numbers of those claiming to have "discovered" her. Among the claimants, and possibly more likely than most, is Bardu Ali, front man for the Chick Webb band. Whoever heard Ella first, Bardu Ali certainly took her along to meet his boss, who was impressed despite the fact that he didn't need a singer, least of all one with no experience. But Ella's voice captivated him and everyone in the band, and she was hired, at first being paid by Chick because the band's manager was notably unenthusiastic.

Ella was 17 and might well consider herself lucky to have been hired by a man who was much more careful with her undeveloped talent than many other bandleaders might have been. Chick urged Ella to take things slowly, telling her. "There's lots to learn … you never want to be someone who goes up fast, because you come down the same way." Under Chick's tutelage Ella carefully developed her latent talent and, under his watchful eye, the band learned to respect her. Later, when Ella's mother died, Chick became her guardian.

Ella's first recordings for the band, "I'll Chase the Blues Away" and "Love and Kisses," came in June 1935, and if they proved to be an inauspicious debut, a session in October the same year brought a marked improvement with "Rhythm and Romance" and other popular songs of the moment. By the following year, Ella's contributions had become a significant part of the band's recording sessions. One of these songs, "If You Can't Sing It, You'll Have To Swing It" (better known as "Mr. Paganini"), became very popular, as did "A-Tisket, A-Tasket," a nonsense song to which Ella helped contribute the lyric. Apparently "A-Tisket, A-Tasket" was composed to bring some cheer to Chick who was undergoing one of his periods of hospitalization; certainly, the boost the record gave to the band's bank balance must have helped everyone. "Undecided," recorded early in 1939, is a better song and is superbly performed by Ella while Chick boosts the band into a dynamic performance. By this time, almost every record the band made was a vocal (only "In the Groove at the Grove" from the band's 1939 released output is an instrumental), and no one was in any doubt about Ella's vital role in the band's success.

However, time was running out; frail and constantly in pain, Chick took the band on tour in mid-summer 1939 and was rushed to a hospital when he collapsed while play-

ing on a riverboat near Washington. He was taken to Johns Hopkins Hospital, Baltimore, where, 30 years earlier, he had undergone the operation that had enabled him to walk. Chick was suffering from pleurisy and a resurgence of tuberculosis of the spine. Doctors decided that his condition was too grave to warrant further surgery, and he was taken to his parents' home. Chick hung on for a week, as friends and relatives gathered to support him in his last hours. On 16 June 1939, he asked to be raised up in his bed. He said, "I'm sorry. I gotta go," and died.

Assessing a musician's place in jazz history on the basis of a few records and the reminiscences of not always impartial observers is difficult. It would be an overstatement to suggest that Chick Webb's band was on a par with those of Ellington, Basie, or Lunceford, even though, on occasion, he defeated them all in band battles at the Savoy. Nevertheless, a few such giants apart, there are not many bands which displayed so much simple straight-ahead swing in performances that are liberally peppered with excellent hot solos. Undoubtedly, Chick's was one of the best dozen or so black bands of its time.

As a drummer, Chick knew few peers, and even fewer betters. Listening to records in chronological sequence in an attempt to decide upon a drummer's influence is a method of dubious accuracy. However, there is a noticeable change in big band drumming style in the mid-1930s which appears directly attributable to Chick Webb. By the end of the decade, another, perhaps greater, influence appears with the work of Jo Jones and, to some extent, this has obscured the importance of Chick Webb in the development of big band drumming.

Setting aside rank and status, there is no doubt about the vitality and excitement of Chick's band, and there is much enjoyment to be gained from listening to the band's recordings.

Certainly, for eight glorious years, Chick Webb, King Of The Savoy, ensured that Harlem's greatest ballroom truly was the home of happy feet.

Jazz Journal International,
Volume 42, Issue 3,
March 1989

Bruce Crowther is the author of Singing Jazz: The Singers and Their Styles, *and, with Mike Pinfold, is co-author of* The Jazz Singers: From Ragtime to the New Wave, *and* The Big Band Years. *He has also written biographies of Gene Krupa, Michelle Pfeiffer, and Robert Mitchum.*

The Norman Granz Story

by John McDonough

It was 1944 and 21 Chicanos had been arrested during rioting in Los Angeles and convicted of murder. Dubbed the "Zoot Suiters" by the press, their appeal case had become one of the more lively liberal Southern California causes of the decade—a kind of West Coast Sacco and Vanzetti. There was a committee to run the defense and a series of benefit shows to raise the money.

One fund raiser was a jazz concert pulled together in July by a young, politically active UCLA student named Norman Granz. A born iconoclast, he booked the Los Angeles Philharmonic Auditorium for the affair. Imagine! Jazz At The Philharmonic! But it raised over $500 for the cause and Granz went on to become a millionaire.

That was how it all started for the world famous Jazz At The Philharmonic empire, which at its height in the mid-'50s embraced the most elite corps of jazzmen ever assembled under one corporate command, a group of record labels (remember Clef, Norgran, and Verve?) that generated one of the most prolific catalogs in record history, and a series of world-wide concert tours that grossed millions. Not only Granz became rich; many of the musicians who were part of it made the biggest money of their careers.

Today Granz, at 60, is anything but retired. Five years ago he returned to the record business after a sabbatical of more than a decade and established Pablo Records, which, like its ancestors, was created in its founder's image without doubt, apology or compromise. With over 150 albums in release, six Grammys on its trophy shelf, and a roster of contract artists, including Ella Fitzgerald, Oscar Peterson, Count Basie, Dizzy Gillespie and Roy Eldridge, Pablo is among the most distinguished jazz labels in the world today.

Granz's contribution to recorded jazz goes back 35 years. Because of him we have today monuments in vinyl to Art Tatum, Lester Young, Charlie Parker, Billie Holiday, Duke Ellington and many more, often with dozens of albums each to their credit. The depth of Granz's coverage is extraordinary. It is a body of work which, taken in toto, is utterly unique.

It might never have happened if Granz hadn't been weaned off the fashionable big bands by Coleman Hawkins' famous record of "Body and Soul" in 1939. Yet his career as an impresario was launched as much out of a sense of social outrage as a love of music.

"Black musicians were playing all over Los Angeles in the early '40s," Granz recalls, "but almost entirely to white audiences. This was because there were very few places that welcomed blacks as patrons. I was particularly aware of this because in addition to my day job as a film editor at MGM I had been putting on occasional jam sessions at the Trou-ville Club in the Beverly Fairfax area. One day Billie Holiday came to me and complained that Billy Berg, who owned the club, wouldn't admit some of her black friends."

Granz went to Berg with a proposal. "Give me Sunday nights when the club is dark and the house band is off," he said, "and I'll give you a jam session and a crowd of paying customers." Berg was interested. But Granz attached four conditions to his offer: one, integrate the audiences; two, pay the musicians; three, put tables on the dance floor so people would listen instead of dance; and four, allow integrated crowds the other six nights of the week. When Sundays quickly became Berg's most lucrative night of the week, Granz's sessions became both a precedent and a lever. Other clubs came to Granz ready to accept similar conditions. Pretty soon he and his band of traveling players (which included a minor West Coast pianist who later decided that singing was more lucrative than playing—Nat King Cole) had built a little weekly circuit for themselves.

The next step was the concert stage. Early in 1944 he started a series of jazz concerts at Music Town in South L.A. In addition to his regulars Granz would add any other musicians he could recruit from bands temporarily in the area. One of them was the volcanic tenor sax star of the Lionel Hampton and Cab Calloway bands, Illinois Jacquet. He became a regular on the concerts, and by the time the troupe moved into the L.A. Philharmonic Auditorium he was the most exciting and inciting factor in the shows. "The kids went wild over the screaming harmonics produced by Jacquet," reported *down beat* in the summer of 1944, "who registered presumably 'hot' facial expressions for the benefit of the galleries." Thus, Jazz At The Philharmonic and its image were born.

JATP (as it soon came to be known) had tapped an exposed nerve among young audiences with its jam sessions juggernauts. Despite the sensual ballad medleys and the probing subtleties of Coleman Hawkins and Thelonious Monk (who played JATP concerts in 1945), its reputation and principal attraction came to rest on excitement—the explosive, incendiary excitement of a revival meeting—that sometimes spilled over into rowdiness. In the fall of 1945 Granz hit the road for a limited tour under the JATP banner. "Concerts Rock the Coast," headlined one report. Early in 1946, after being banned from the L.A. Philharmonic Auditorium, the concert rolled out on its first national tour, and into Carnegie Hall in New York by June.

For the audiences who cheered it wildly, it was heaven on earth. But for many of the critics who wrote about it, it was hell on wheels, a gratuitous pandering to the worst elements and instincts of the jazz teeny bopper. It was a view that would cling stubbornly (and for the most part unfairly) to the JATP image for years, despite the regular presence of such modern messiahs as Charlie Parker and Dizzy Gillespie in the lineups.

"The critics used to review the audience almost as harshly as the musicians," recalls Granz. "They criticized them for cheering too loud, whistling too much and so on. And they accused the musicians and myself of soliciting this kind of behavior from the crowds. I used to answer reviews like that, because they ignored so many other aspects of the presentation. They said Illinois Jacquet and Flip Phillips played differently in the jam sessions than they did with Hampton and Woody Herman. That was nonsense. Critics would ignore a set by Lennie Tristano, hardly a panderer to public tastes; a set by Ella Fitzgerald, who did mostly ballads; or a set by Oscar Peterson or The Modern Jazz Quartet."

The quality of the audience was often related to the quality of the hall. The best crowds were in Chicago and New York, where the Civic Opera House and Carnegie Hall were centrally located and well managed. The worst were in Baltimore where a lack of an unsegregated auditorium facility forced Granz into a fight arena where the owner insisted on having hot dogs and peanuts hawked during the concert.

"Ella might be in the middle of a ballad," says Granz, "and someone would yell up, 'Work with it, girl.' She'd get scared and whip into a fast "How High the Moon." When the concerts were drawing their biggest crowds in the late '40s and early '50s I used to have handbills handed out with the ticket stubs explaining 'How to act at a jazz concert.' Unfortunately, all it took was a few exhibitionists in an audience to set things off. But we gradually did change the public. And at least they were happy concerts. In the '60s jazz got terribly serious and the fun went out of it. I think that's changing now."

Granz may or may not have helped civilize the American jazz audience. But he certainly helped integrate it. When JATP became a big earner, he threw its weight around freely in the cause of social justice, which remained his first after-profit priority. Promoters who wanted Granz and the money he could bring had to accept his iron-clad clauses against discrimination at the door. JATP played the first mixed dance in Kansas City and the first mixed concert in Charleston, S.C. A sold-out performance in New Orleans was canceled over Jim Crow seating policies. Granz hit a restaurant in Jackson, Michigan, with a lawsuit when it refused to seat him, Helen Humes, and a party of musicians. No institution was too far removed to get a scolding. In 1947 Spencer's Department Store in Dayton, Ohio, invited Granz to an autographing party in its record department. When he showed up accompanied by several black musicians from the tour the store disapproved. Granz not only refused to do the autographing by himself, he yanked his entire record inventory from the store and ordered his distributor to quit selling his albums to its buyers.

By the late '40s records had become an important part of the Granz music machine. But it wasn't until the '50s that he emerged as a major force in the relatively minor leagues of jazz recording. From the start Granz had been recording his concerts regularly with a view toward commercial albums. It's hard to imagine the dimension of that innovation in those far-off pre-LP days of the '40s. Today, many albums in all genres are concert recordings. But back then, it had never been done. Granz was the first. (Benny Goodman's famous 1938 concert at Carnegie Hall was indeed recorded before the first JATP concerts, but not for commercial release. Albert Marx had it recorded privately as a souvenir for his wife, Helen Ward, who had sung with the first Goodman band. Several weeks later Goodman borrowed the acetate discs and had a dub made for himself. This was the set that was discovered years later in his Park Avenue apartment — in 1950, by which time Granz's JATP records had established the live jazz concert as fair game for commercial recording.)

The initial release was a 1945 version of "How High the Moon," which along with "Perdido" became an early JATP anthem. Illinois Jacquet wailed on tenor and Gene Krupa (called only "Chicago Flash" for contractual reasons) banged artfully on drums. Without a record company to release his concerts, Granz at first relied on Stinson (the original JATP Volume One is still available on that label) and then Disc Records, which released performances from the original "Zoot Suit" benefit concert of 1944. In 1947 he formed Clef Records and set up an extensive distribution agreement with Chicago-based Mercury Records. David Stone Martin, the artist who had created the original JATP symbol for Stinson, signed on as house artist and began turning out distinctive looking cover artwork for the new label (as he does today for Progressive Records). The Clef (and later Verve) record covers remain today among the most attractive ever created.* The empire expanded. In

---

*Editor's Note: *David Stone Martin: Jazz Graphics*, by Manek Daver (Graphic-sha Publishing Co., Ltd., Tokyo, February 1991), is an outstanding book of photographs of the album cover art of David Stone Martin. It contains, as well, incisive essays on Martin's work for Moses Asch and Norman Granz, and many heretofore unpublished drawings. In March 1994, Mr. Daver published his second work, *Jazz Album Covers/The Rare and the Beautiful*, which includes photographs of more than 400 original issue jackets demonstrating the lettering, the colors and the designs of Martin and many other artists specializing in this fascinating field. With a foreword by Norman Granz. (The publisher is the same.)—JWJ

1948 Granz issued a lavish, prestigiously priced limited edition package called *The Jazz Scene*. Reviews were excellent, although with one reservation. At $25 a set, some suggested Granz was pricing himself out of his own market.

"I always thought that was a silly criticism," says he. "I saw evidence of what the jazz audience could afford at my concerts. They weren't poor. Traditionally they embraced three main groups in about equal proportions: young blacks, young Italians, and young Jews. They had come of age in time to catch the tail end of the big band era and get a taste of bop. They had much more of an awareness of jazz than young people seem to have today, which is understandable since kids have grown up largely on junk for the last 25 years. Anyone under 30 today who has an awareness of jazz now probably had to go out of his way to get it."

Clef broke off from Mercury in 1951 and went independent, which was the way Granz wanted it from the start, although Mercury had no artist or repertoire influence on Clef. Other labels soon popped up. Norgran became his modern jazz banner, meaning Lester Young, Gillespie, Parker, et al. Down Home Records came along when he began recording traditional musicians like Kid Ory and Red Allen. Then in 1956 Verve was born out of a dispute over a movie sound track.

"Ella had recorded for Decca exclusively since the '30s," Granz recalls. "This meant I could never include her in any of the JATP concert albums, which was very frustrating. But it would have been tolerable if I could have produced the albums she did for Decca. But even this was impossible, despite the fact that I had been her manager since 1954. Early in 1956 Decca was hot to issue the sound track of *The Benny Goodman Story*. But Benny's band included several artists under contract to me. Now I had Decca over a barrel. They asked me what I wanted. I said I wanted to buy Ella's contract, and they said okay. I immediately formed Verve because I felt I needed a broader label for her. Call it a 'pop' label, I guess. Pretty soon I decided it was silly to have four labels, so in '57 I consolidated them all under Verve.

"From the beginning in the '40s records had never been a money making proposition. The profits from the concert receipts always subsidized the records, which after 1949 were overwhelmingly studio-made sessions and not concert recordings. We put out a tremendous number of albums, but none of them ever sold. Some writers thought I was churning out a lot of records to make millions, as if they were rock hits. Quite the opposite. The concerts were our bread and butter. They made up for the losses the records ran up."

Buddy Rich once said of his years with Granz that he would receive quarterly statements on his financial standing in terms of record sales. "I'd get this letter that would inform me that I had sold so many records in the past three months and that I owed the company $20,000 or something like that. I owed the company $20,000! It was a joke."

The debts were only on paper, however. Granz explains: "We would give an advance on royalties to the artist, and that was his to keep regardless of sales. If the record sold enough to make back that advance plus basic production costs, additional royalties theoretically would be paid. But that almost never happened. They usually lost money. So a deficit would be entered in the books. Six months later I might do another record with that artist and it would be the same thing. He'd get an advance, the record wouldn't earn back its investment, and another deficit would be added to the artist's statement. If I did a third LP, let's say, and it was successful, the artist would start getting additional royalties at the point where its profits not only paid off its own advance and production costs but the accumulated deficits of the artist's first two records. That's what Rich meant when he said he "owed" me whatever it was. But it was only on paper.

"No artist was ever personally responsible for those losses. We were very generous in our terms, actually. Most other labels charged an artist's account for publicity and all sorts of extras. And today, companies load studio time and editing costs as well — understandable, I suppose, since most rock musicians can't play shit and have to be beefed up in a lot of post production hocus pocus."

Granz's Clef and Verve LPs also attracted the attention of high fidelity press for the quality of their sound and the revolutionary recording process first introduced by Granz — Muenster Dummel High Fidelity. One leading component magazine did a story on the process. What was Muenster Dummel High Fidelity?

"It was a complete put-on," laughs Granz. "I've always been skeptical of a lot of stuff I read about sound production. Today it's utter nonsense. The entire back of a sleeve is full of credits. The kid who goes for the coffee even gets a credit line. Well, back in the '50s high fidelity was the big thing, but I considered it something of a con by the record companies, especially when they began putting 'high fidelity' stickers on LPs that had been in their catalogs for several years. Moreover, there were all kinds of strange, technical sounding names for this system or that. They were all coined by advertising types, no doubt. So I decided to put everybody on. Muenster was my favorite cheese, and Ernie Dummel was one of my engineers. So we came up with Muenster Dummel Hi Fi. No one knew what it meant, but it sounded impressive. We really had the last laugh when some sound magazine wrote it up."

"After I formed Verve things began to change. Almost immediately we had the biggest seller I've ever been involved with, Ella's *Cole Porter Song Book* set. It was the 11th biggest LP of the year. That was insane for me. Then came the Ella/Louis Armstrong duets and they were pretty good sellers. Verve put me in the commercial music market for the first time, so I brought in some producers who could handle that sort of stuff. I'm not especially proud of everything we did, but we were a big company now putting out 150 albums a year. Buddy Bregman, who arranged the orchestrations for the Ella/Cole Porter album, got involved in recording people like Jane Powell, Mitzi Gaynor and Conrad Sallenger. We did a very nice Bing Crosby session right after he left Decca. I remember Barney Kessel, the guitarist, came to me once and said he wanted to do some production work in the commercial field. So he came up with Ricky Nelson, believe it or not. Ricky became another big seller for Verve.

"I got the company involved in spoken word albums—did a lot of strange things, like Alice B. Toklas, Evelyn Waugh, Linus Pauling and Dorothy Parker. But we had some tremendous sellers too. I did Mort Sahl's first LPs. But the biggest sellers were the Shelley Berman and Jonathan Winters albums. I offered to record Lenny Bruce too, but when he said he wanted to sing and control the cover art and all the rest, I decided it wasn't worth the aggravation."

Bruce would send his reviews to Granz later on with angry notes attached. "Dear M.F.," he would say. "Read this and eat your heart out." The letters were written on butcher paper in blood, presumably not Bruce's own.

"As the fortunes of Verve rose, the concert tours began to be less successful. The artists were the best, and they were paid accordingly. We always traveled first class and expenses were getting high. Some performers were getting to be headliners. I couldn't afford Ella after 1957, even though I continued to be her manager. I still recorded a lot of jazz sessions, but after 1957 the subsidies came entirely from the sales of the commercial stuff on Verve."

Granz made his last JATP tour in the United States in the fall of 1957. He continued to tour in Europe, but America would not see another Granz concert until 1967 when he came out of retirement briefly for an encore tour. He spent more and more time on the Continent. The bigger Verve got, the less interested he seemed in running it. By 1959 he decided it was time to sell. Frank Sinatra, who was leaving Capitol and looking for a going company to buy, made an offer. But Granz would have to stay on to run it, so the deal fell through. Another offer came from Holland, but they wanted Granz too. The best of the offers finally came from MGM—$2.8 million with Granz serving as a consultant for one year. The new owners promptly brought in new a&r chief Creed Taylor, who found he had no need of Granz's advice and immediately fired every Verve jazz artist except Ella, Oscar Peterson, Johnny Hodges and Stan Getz. Most of the 1200 albums Granz had done were soon collectors' items.

"It would have been foolish of me to expect the company to have continued as before under the new owners," Granz recalls. "I had been personally involved in the making of every jazz record in that accumulated catalog since 1944. For better or worse the company stood for something when I left. But the new owners were lawyers and marketing people. I can't blame them for not caring as much as I did. It wasn't their work.

"My biggest regrets are over what I didn't record when I could have. A session was set up for Art Tatum and Charlie Parker. Parker showed up but Art didn't. I rented Carnegie Hall for the date, which was to have been a duet with no rhythm section. I would love to have done Tatum with Dizzy too. I'm sorry I didn't do more Armstrong. I don't know why but without exception I always got him under the worst possible conditions. We'd work for months to set everything up and then—like on the *Porgy and Bess* LP with Ella—at the last minute we'd find he'd have a concert somewhere that evening. Everything would have to be rushed. There were some other albums with Ella or just quartet accompaniment. They were simple, but his lip was in terrible shape. There was one session with orchestra backgrounds where it was so bad he practically had to sing the whole thing. I felt so sorry. He was playing almost entirely from one side of his mouth.

"Duke Ellington was another misfortune. The Ellington Song Book album with Ella was done under the worst conditions. He was under contract to Columbia, but I had Johnny Hodges. When Hodges rejoined the band in 1956 I managed to force a few concessions. I would have Duke for one LP or two if I used Ella. We planned far in advance, but in the end Duke failed to do a single arrangement. Ella had to use the band's regular arrangements. She'd do a vocal where an instrumental chorus would normally go. To stretch it to four LPs, we padded it with various small group things with Hodges, Ben Webster and so on.

"I never was able to record Ella with Sinatra either. In the late '50s they were both at their peaks, but a meeting was contractually impossible. Later on in the early '60s they started an album together but never finished it. Frank didn't think it was right. I had nothing to do with it.

"Sometimes I'd read a critic who'd say I overrecorded artists. But if you took away all the albums I did with Billie, Parker, Lester, Art Tatum, Ben Webster, and even Ella in the '50s, many would have gone totally unrecorded and most wouldn't have had more than a couple of records. For all the people who say I overrecorded artists, my most profound regret is that I may not have recorded them enough. Now it's too late in many cases."

In 1959 Granz moved to Lugano, Switzerland, where he confined his activities to occasional European JATP tours, managed Ella and Oscar, and assembled one of the world's more impressive private modern art collections. He was almost totally absent from recording studios, however, and the familiar "Supervised by Norman Granz" insignia vanished from the scene. The 1967 U.S. JATP tour was successful and suggested there was still a market for jazz in the height of the rock era, but without Granz to sustain the effort the point was soon forgotten. Then in 1972 he put on an Ella/Basie concert in Santa Monica.

"I don't know what possessed me to do it, but I decided to record it. While I was at it I decided to add a few surprise guests. Oscar was in town, and I brought in Stan Getz, Roy Eldridge, Harry Edison, Ray Brown and some others. It was a lot of fun and went well, so afterwards I thought I'd see how it might go as a record. I put out a small mail order thing and it was a disaster. Sold about 150. But a few got over to Europe and I got a call from Polydor saying they would give me world-wide distribution if I went back in the record business. It was too good to refuse. I had bought all the Art Tatum sessions from MGM in 1972 and I also had a number of old JATP concert tapes that had not been part of the Verve sale in 1959. Since the musicians hadn't been paid, they were not mine to sell. Anyway, at least I had something to release until I could do some new sessions. I lined up a group of independent distributors to cover the U.S. market, and they served well until I went with RCA in 1975. I named the label Pablo for my favorite artist, Pablo Picasso."

From among the accumulated concert tapes have come mid-'50s JATP blowing sessions from Tokyo and Stockholm that remind us how really exciting jazz can be and how much the excitement was taken for granted during the halcyon years when it was so plentiful. I find that excitement is now an endangered species in jazz with so many of its progenitors gone or past their peak. And from a 1961 Granz concert tour came *Afro Blue Impressions*, one of the finest John Coltrane-McCoy Tyner collaborations currently available. "I had known Coltrane since he was a protégé of Johnny Hodges and playing rock and roll on the side," says Granz. "Unlike some of the current instant successes who think they are playing jazz — I guess they call it fusion — Trane had a firm grasp of what jazz was all about, where it came from, and who the people were before him who created it. I didn't see him much in the late '50s. In 1960 I presented Miles Davis on his first extended European tour, and Trane was in the group. Then in 1961 he asked me to handle his first European tour as leader. The *Afro Blue* album was from that tour."

But the vast majority of the Pablo catalog is new, which was a principal reason Granz set it up in the first place. He wanted to record his favorite artists and issue albums when the mood struck him. He wanted a one man company that wouldn't get too big. And that's pretty much what he has today.

"There have been more artists to record than I originally thought," he says, "and perhaps Pablo has grown a bit faster than I would have liked. I have favored a small number of players with repeated albums, and you sometimes feel like you're playing musical chairs using many of the same people. But they're the best. It's been a special kick recording Basie away from his band. I've done him in trios and quartets, with Zoot Sims, in several jam sessions and now with Dizzy Gillespie. I think these shifting combinations bring out fresh dimensions in an established artist. There's a lot more I want to do along that line. I approached Buddy Rich, who was a regular on the old JATP circuit, but he refused on the ground of economics. I've been after Lionel Hampton for more than a year. I'd love to mix him up with some players worthy of his talent, but it's funny. He's still smarting from a 25-year-old injury. Can you believe this: I did an album with Hampton, Gene Krupa and Teddy Wilson and for no particular reason, the art director put Krupa's name first on the album cover. Incredible!"

Granz confesses that it hasn't all been fun. He is impatient with the burdens of production trivia — proofreading, pressing, contracts and the like. But he plays the game of artistic politics well. Most of the Pablo family has been able to shine on at least one solo album, thus keeping all the artists happy. It keeps Granz happy too, because it keeps him doing what he likes best.

"After 35 years in the business, I'm still happiest in the studio."

Down Beat,
Volume 46, Numbers 16 and 17,
October and November 1979

Part One

THE RECORDING SESSIONS —
A DISCOGRAPHY

The Chick Webb Recording Sessions, 1927–1934

Chick Webb first entered the recording studio in August 1927, at age eighteen, with his own band, Chick Webb's Harlem Stompers, to cut a side that unfortunately was never released, and the master of which has seemingly disappeared. It was almost two years later, in June 1929, that the new band of ten musicians, The Jungle Band (Africa-oriented band titles were popular among jazz aficionados in the Twenties), recorded their first release. During the next four years, his fame grew, and his extraordinary talent led him to the podium of the Savoy Ballroom, Harlem's most popular venue for dancers, going dancing rating very high on the scale of mass entertainment, exceeded only by going to the movies. By 1935, Chick Webb and His Orchestra was firmly ensconced and he was popularly crowned "King of the Savoy." During the six intervening years, Webb had recorded thirty-one additional sides, with his own and other orchestras. (From his final five months, January to May, 1939, there are forty-six released sides.)

On 12 June 1935, at Decca Recording Company studios, 50 West 57th Street, New York City, Chick Webb and His Orchestra made the first recordings with their vocalist Ella Fitzgerald. Their second recording session took place on 12 October, the same year, and so popular were the results from this session that until the demise of Mr. Webb in 1939 and, three years later, the breakup of the band, relatively few records were produced by the orchestra without Miss Fitzgerald's vocals.

Chick Webb's last studio recording session with his orchestra took place on 21 April 1939, with one additional personal appearance recorded on 4 May 1939, less than four years after Miss Fitzgerald's first recording with the orchestra. In the interests of an historic record, all recordings made by Chick Webb from the beginning of his career are included in this discography chronologically. A survey of Webb's records in the pre–Ella period is found on page 23.

CHICK WEBB'S HARLEM STOMPERS

Leader, Drums: Chick Webb; Trumpet: Bobby Stark; Alto Saxophone: Johnny Hodges; Piano: Don Kirkpatrick; Guitar: John Trueheart. Recorded at Brunswick Studios, New York, Thursday, 25 August 1927

270825-1   E6358-6 Low Levee — High Water (*Not yet released*)

THE JUNGLE BAND

Leader, Drums: Chick Webb; Trumpets: Ward Pinkett, Edwin Swayzee; Trombone: Robert Horton; Clarinets: Hilton Jefferson, Louis Jordan, Elmer Williams; Alto Saxophones: Hilton Jefferson, Louis Jordan; Tenor Saxophone: Elmer Williams; Piano: Don Kirkpatrick; Banjo-Guitar: John Trueheart; Double Bass: Elmer James; Vocalist: Ward Pinkett. Recorded at Brunswick Studios, New York, Friday, 14 June 1929.

290614-1   E30039-A Dog Bottom (vWard Pinkett) (78: Brunswick 4450/CWLPD-1, CWLPD-2, CWLPD-3)

THE JUNGLE BAND

Leader: Chick Webb; Same personnel as on 14 June, except omit drums. Recorded at Brunswick Studios, New York, Monday, 27 June 1929.

290627-1   E30091-A Jungle Mama (Jungle Blues) (78: Brunswick 4450/CWLPD-2, CWLPD-3)

CHICK WEBB AND HIS ORCHESTRA

Leader, Drums: Chick Webb; Trumpets: Louis Bacon, Shelton Hemphill, Louis Hunt; Trombone: Jimmy Harrison; Clarinets: Benny Carter, Hilton Jefferson, Elmer Williams; Alto Saxophones: Benny Carter, Hilton Jefferson; Tenor Saxophone:

Elmer Williams; Piano: Don Kirkpatrick; Banjo-Guitar: John Trueheart; Double Bass-String Bass: Elmer James; Vocalist: Louis Bacon. Recorded at Brunswick Studios, New York, Monday, 30 March 1931

310330-1   E36432-A   Heebie Jeebies (78: Vocalion 1607/CWLPD-2, CWLPD-3)

310330-2   E36433-A   Blues in My Heart (Louis Bacon) (78: Brunswick 6156/CWLPD-2, CWLPD-3)

310330-3   E36434-A   Soft and Sweet* (78: Vocalion 1607/CWLPD-2, CWLPD-3)

A rare collector's item is the British issue Brunswick 02079, a few of which are correctly labeled SOFT AND SWEET, but play HEEBIE JEEBIES in error.

LOUIS ARMSTRONG WITH CHICK WEBB AND HIS ORCHESTRA

Leader, Drums: Chick Webb; Trumpets: Louis Armstrong, Louis Bacon, Billy Hicks, Louis Hunt; Trombone: Charlie Green; Clarinet: Pete Clark; Alto Saxophones: Pete Clark, Edgar Sampson; Tenor Saxophone: Elmer Williams; Piano: Don Kirkpatrick; Guitar: John Trueheart; String Bass: Elmer James; Bells: Mezz Mezzrow*; Vocalist: Louis Armstrong. Recorded at RCA Victor Studios, Camden, New Jersey, Thursday, 8 December 1932.

321208-1   74820-1   That's My Home (vLouis Armstrong) (78: Vocalion 24200/CWLPD-4)

321208-2   74820-2   That's My Home (vLouis Armstrong) 78: Victor 40-0102/LP: RCA Victor LPM 2322)

321208-3   74821-1   Hobo, You Can't Ride on This Train* (vLouis Armstrong) (78: Victor 24200/CWLPD-4)

321208-4   74821-2   Hobo, You Can't Ride on This Train* (vLouis Armstrong) (CD: Bluebird 9759-2-RB)

321208-5   74822-1   I Hate to Leave You Now (vLouis Armstrong) (78: Victor 24204/CWLPD-4)

321208-6   74822-2   I Hate To Leave You Now (vLouis Armstrong) (78: Bluebird B10236/LP: RCA Victor LPM 2322)

321208-7   74823-1   You'll Wish You'd Never Been Born (vLouis Armstrong) (78: Victor 24204/CWLPD-4)

CHICK WEBB'S SAVOY ORCHESTRA

Leader, Drums: Chick Webb; Trumpets: Mario Bauza, Reunald Jones, Taft Jordan; Trombone: Sandy Williams; Alto Saxophones: Pete Clark, Edgard Sampson; Tenor Saxophone: Elmer Williams; Piano: Joe Steele; Banjo-Guitar: John Trueheart; String Bass: John Kirby; Vocalist: Taft Jordan. Recorded at Columbia Studios, New York, Wednesday, 20 December 1933.

331220-1   152658-1   On the Sunny Side of the Street (vTaft Jordan) (78: Vocalion 3246/CWLPD-2)

331220-2   152659-2   The Darktown Strutters' Ball (Never released on 78 *see* 15 January 1934 for additional takes. LP: Columbia CL-2639)

CHICK WEBB AND HIS ORCHESTRA

Leader, Drums: Chick Webb. Same personnel as on 20 December except no vocalist. Recorded at Columbia Studios, New York, Monday, 15 January 1934.

340115-1   152659-4   The Darktown Strutters' Ball (78: Columbia CB-754/CWLPD-2)

340115-2   152686-3   If Dreams Come True (78: Columbia CB-754/CWLPD-2)

340115-3   152687-2   Let's Get Together* (78: Columbia CB-741/CWLPD-1, CWLPD-2)

This became the orchestra's theme song shortly after this recording.

MEZZ MEZZROW AND HIS ORCHESTRA

Leader, Clarinet, Alto Saxophone: Mezz Mezzrow; Trumpets: Reunald Jones, Max Kaminsky, Chelsea Quealey; Trombone: Floyd O'Brien; Alto Saxophone: Benny Carter; Tenor Saxophone: Bud Freeman; Piano: Willie "The Lion" Smith; String Bass: John Kirby; Drums: Chick Webb. Recorded at RCA Victor Studios, New York, Monday, 7 May 1934

340507-1   82392-1   Old Fashioned Love (arranged by Alex Hill) (78: Victor 25202/CWLPD-5)

340507-2   82393-1   Apologies (arranged by Mezz Mezzrow) (78: Victor 25019/CWLPD-1, CWLPD-5)

340507-3   82394-1   Sendin' the Vipers (arranged by Mezz Mezzrow) (78: Victor 25019/CWLPD-5)

340507-4   82395-1   35th and Calumet (arranged by Floyd O'Brien) (78: Victor 25202/CWLPD-5)

CHICK WEBB AND HIS ORCHESTRA

Leader, Drums: Chick Webb. Same personnel as 15 January 1934 except add vocalists Taft Jordan and Chuck Richards. Recorded at Columbia Studios, New York, Wednesday, 9 May 1934.

340509-1   152733-2   I Can't Dance (I Got Ants in My Pants) (vTaft Jordan) (78: Columbia 2920-D/CWLPD-2)

340509-2   152734-2   Imagination (vChuck Richards) (78: Columbia 2920-D/CWLPD-2)

340509-3   152735-1   Why Should I Beg for Love? *Not yet released* (vTaft Jordan) (Arranged by Edgar Sampson)

340509-4   152735-2   Why Should I Beg for Love? *Not yet released* (vTaft Jordan) (Arranged by Edgar Sampson)

CHICK WEBB AND HIS ORCHESTRA

Leader, Drums: Chick Webb. Personnel, same as on 9 May 1934, except no vocals by Chuck Richards. Recorded at Columbia Studios, New York, Friday, 18 May 1934.

340518-1 152735-4 Why Should I Beg for Love? (vTaft Jordan) (arranged by Edgar Sampson) (78: Columbia 2926-D/CWLPD-2)

340518-2 152740-2 Stompin' at the Savoy (78: Columbia 2926-D/CWLPD-1, CWLPD-2)

CHICK WEBB AND HIS ORCHESTRA

Leader, Drums: Chick Webb; Trumpets: Mario Bauza, Taft Jordan, Bobby Stark; Trombone: Fernando Arbello, Sandy Williams; Flute: Wayman Carver; Alto Saxophones: Pete Clark, Edgar Sampson; Tenor Saxophones: Wayman Carver, Elmer Williams; Piano: Joe Steele; Banjo-Guitar: John Trueheart; Bass: John Kirby; Vocalists: Taft Jordan, Charles Linton. Recorded at Columbia Studios, New York, Friday, 6 July 1934.

340706-1 152769-2 Blue Minor* (78: Okeh 41572/CWLPD-2, CWLPD-3)

340706-2 152770-2 True (vCharles Linton) (78: Okeh 41571/CWLPD-2)

340706-3 152771-2 Lonesome Moments* (vTaft Jordan) (78: Okeh 41572/CWLPD-2)

340706-4 152772-2 If It Ain't Love (vCharles Linton) (78: Okeh 41571/CWLPD-2)

Arranged by Edgar Sampson

CHICK WEBB AND HIS ORCHESTRA

Leader, Drums: Chick Webb; Trumpets: Mario Bauza, Taft Jordan, Bobby Stark; Trombones: Claude Jones, Sandy Williams; Flute: Wayman Carver; Clarinet: Pete Clark; Alto Saxophones: Pete Clark, Edgar Sampson; Tenor Saxophones: Wayman Carver, Elmer Williams; Tuba: John Kirby; Piano: Joe Steele; Banjo-Guitar: John Trueheart; Bass: John Kirby; Vocalist: Charles Linton. Recorded at Decca Recording Company, Monday, 10 September 1934.

340910-1 38593-A That Rhythm Man (vTaft Jordan) (78: Decca 173/CWLPD-2)

340910-2 38594-A On the Sunny Side of the Street (vTaft Jordan) (78: Decca 172/CWLPD-2)

340910-3 38595-A Lona* (78: Decca 173/CWLPD-2, CWLPD-3)

340910-4 38595-A Blue Minor* (78: Decca 172/CWLPD-2, CWLPD-3)

340910-5 38595-B Blue Minor* (Not released on 78/LP: Decca DL9222)

Arranged by Edgar Sampson

CHICK WEBB AND HIS ORCHESTRA

Leader, Drums: Chick Webb. Personnel, same as on 10 September 1934. Recorded at Decca Recording Company, New York, Monday, 19 November 1934.

341119-1 39138-A It's Over Because We're Through (vTaft Jordan) (78: Decca 483/CWLPD-2)

341119-2 39140-A Don't Be That Way (78: Decca 483/CWLPD-1, CWLPD-2, CWLPD-3)

341119-3 39141-A What a Shuffle* (78: Decca 1087/CWLPD-1, CWLPD-2, CWLPD-3)

341119-4 391412-A Blue Lou (78: Decca 1065/CWLPD-2, CWLPD-3)

Arranged by Edgar Sampson
Note: Matrix 39139 still remains untraced.

✄

The next recording session for **Chick Webb and His Orchestra** occurred on the historic Wednesday, 12 June 1935, at Decca Recording Company, New York, that included Ella Fitzgerald in her debut recording. All Chick Webb recording sessions from that date are included chronologically in this section, and all Chick Webb albums from that period are included in ELLA'S RECORDS.

A Survey of Chick Webb Long-Play and Compact Discs

When the 33⅓ rpm long-playing record began to dominate the field of record releases, virtually all record companies hurried to release collections of artists' works previously available only on 78rpm records. Among them was Decca Recording Company. When it came to releasing LPs of Chick Webb recordings, they seem to have forgotten that there was a Chick Webb band prior to Ella Fitzgerald's having become a member in 1934. In fact, so successful had the band become, that practically no LPs were released of Mr. Webb's recordings that did not include Miss Fitzgerald's vocals. Consequently, relatively few of the great Chick Webb bands recordings prior to 1935 were released. Thanks to M. Gilles Pétard and his "Chronological" series on the Classics label, we now have the entire output of the early recordings of Chick Webb on compact disc. From 1929, when Webb's first record was released, until 1934, his year with Miss Fitzgerald, Webb recorded a dozen sessions that produced 41 sides: 34 are released on CD (16 vocals, 18 instrumentals); 4 of the remaining may be found on LP (3 vocals, 1 instrumental); 3 remain unreleased (2 vocals, 1 instrumental).

CWLPD-1   An Introduction to Chick Webb: His Best Recordings, 1929–1939

1. Dog Bottom (Webb) 2:36   290614-1
2. Hobo, You Can't Ride This Train (Armstrong) 2:58   321208-3
3. Let's Get Together (Webb) 3:01   340115-3
4. Apologies (Mezzrow) 3:10   340507-2
5. Stompin' at the Savoy (Razaf-Goodman-Sampson-Webb) 3:08   340518-2
6. Don't Be that Way (Sampson) 2:35   341119-2
7. What a Shuffle (Kirkpatrick) 2:54   341119-3
8. Vote for Mr. Rhythm (Robin-Rainger-Siegel) 2:27   361029-5
9. Clap Hands! Here Comes Charley (Meyer-Rose-Mc-Donald) 2:30   370324-5
10. My Honey's Lovin' Arms (Rudy-Meyer) 2:46   370325-1
11. I Got a Guy (Sunshine) 3:20   371027-2
12. Sweet Sue, Just You (Harris-Young) 2:43   371101-2
13. Rock It for Me (Werner-Werner) 3:10   371101-3
14. Harlem Congo (White) 3:12   371101-5
15. Hallelujah! (Youmans-Robin-Grey) 4:00   371217-5
16. A-Tisket, A-Tasket (Fitzgerald-Alexander) 2:36   380502-1
17. Liza (All the Clouds'll Roll Away) (Gershwin-Kahn) 2:45   380503-7
18. Wacky Dust (Adams-Levant) 3:03   380817-1
19. Gotta Pebble in My Shoe (Feldman) 2:52   380817-2
20. Franklin D. Roosevelt Jones (Rome) 2:53   381006-1
21. Undecided (Shavers) 3:15   390217-1
22. In the Groove at the Grove (Webb) 2:43   390217-3

CD: Best of Jazz 4015 (released 1994). Total playing time, 66:37. Produced by Gilles Pétard. Liner notes by Graham Colombé.

CWLPD-2   The Chronological Chick Webb and His Orchestra, 1929–1934

1. Dog Bottom (Webb) 2:35   290614-1
2. Jungle Mama (Webb) 3:10   290627-1
3. Heebie Jeebies (Atkins) 3:06   310330-1
4. Blues in My Heart (Carter-Mills) 3:05   310330-2
5. Soft and Sweet (Sampson) 3:04   310330-3
6. On the Sunny Side of the Street (Fields-McHugh) 2:55   331220-1
7. The Darktown Strutters' Ball (Brooks) 2:48   331220-2
8. If Dreams Come True (Mills-Sampson-Goodman) 3:20   340115-2
9. Let's Get Together (Webb) 3:00   340115-3
10. I Can't Dance (I Got Ants in My Pants) (Gaines-Williams) 2:55   340509-1
11. Imagination (Van Heusen) 3:51   340509-2

12. Why Should I Beg for Love? (Sampson) 3:02   340518-1
13. Stompin' at the Savoy (Razaf-Goodman-Sampson-Webb) 3:10   340518-2
14. Blue Minor (Sampson) 2:50   340706-1
15. True (Sampson) 2:41   340706-2
16. Lonesome Moments (Sampson-Webb) 2:45   340706-3
17. If It Ain't Love (Razaf-Redman-Waller) 2:57   340706-4
18. That Rhythm Man (Razaf-Waller-Brooks) 2:53   340910-1
19. On the Sunny Side of the Street (Fields-McHugh) 2:48   340910-2
20. Lona (Bauza) 2:47   340910-3
21. Blue Minor (Sampson) 3:023   40910-4
22. It's Over Because We're Through (Bryant) 3:14   341119-1
23. Don't Be That Way (Sampson) 2:35   341119-2
24. What a Shuffle (Kirkpatrick) 3:02   341119-3
25. Blue Lou (Mills-Sampson) 3:02   341119-4

CD: Classics 502 (released December 1989). Total playing time, 75:27. Produced by Gilles Pétard. Liner notes by Anatol Schenker.

*Note: The second volume of this series, **The Chronological Chick Webb and His Orchestra/1935-1938** (Classics 517), appears in ELLA'S RECORDS, as LPD-8, since it falls in the Ella Fitzgerald period.*

CWLPD-3   Spinnin' the Webb: Chick Webb and His Orchestra

1. Dog Bottom (Webb) 2:36   290614-1
2. Jungle Mama (Webb) 3:13   290627-1
3. Heebie Jeebies (Atkins) 3:05   310330-1
4. Blues in My Heart (Carter-Mills) 3:06   310330-2
5. Lona (Bauza) 2:44   340910-3
6. Blue Minor (Sampson) 3:00   340910-4
7. Don't Be That Way (Parish-Sampson-Goodman) 2:36   341119-2
8. What a Shuffle (Kirkpatrick) 2:50   341119-3
9. Blue Lou (Mills-Sampson) 2:59   341119-4
10. Go Harlem (Razaf-Johnson) 2:18   360602-1
11. Clap Hands! Here Comes Charley (Meyer-Rose-Mc-Donald) 2:26   370324-5
12. That Naughty Waltz (Levy-Stanley) 2:54   370324-8
13. I Got Rhythm (Gershwin-Gershwin) 2:30   370921-2
14. Squeeze Me (Waller-Williams) 3:06   371101-4
15. Harlem Congo (White) 3:14   371101-5
16. Midnite in a Madhouse (Clinton) 2:29   371217-6
17. Spinnin' the Webb (Webb-Fitzgerald) 3:00   380503-6
18. Liza (Gershwin-Kahn) 2:37   380503-7
19. Who Ya Hunchin'? (Webb-Fitzgerald) 3:49   390109-7
20. In the Groove at the Grove (Webb) 2:54   390217-3

CD: Decca Jazz GRD-635 (released February 1994). Total playing time, 57:12. Original sessions produced by Jack Kapp/This collection produced by Orin Keepnews. Liner notes by Loren Schoenberg.

These next two discs are not primarily of Chick Webb recordings, although Webb tracks appear on them that are unavailable elsewhere on compact disc.

CWLPD-4   The Chronological Louis Armstrong, 1931–1932

Louis Armstrong and His Orchestra

1. Lazy River (Arodin-Carmichael) 3:05   311103-1
2. Chinatown, My Chinatown (Jerome-Schwartz) 3:18 311103-2
3. Wrap Your Troubles in Dreams (Koehler-Moll-Barris) 3:39   311104-1
4. Star Dust (Parish-Carmichael) 3:36   311104-4
5. You Can Depend on Me (Carpenter-Dunlap-Hines) 3:17   311105-1
6. Georgia on My Mind (Gorrell-Carmichael) 3:19 311105-2
7. The Lonesome Road (Shilkret-Austin)* 3:31 311106-1
8. I Got Rhythm (Gershwin-Gershwin) 3:05   311106-2
9. Between the Devil and the Deep Blue Sea (Koehler-Arlen) 3:00   320125-1
10. Kickin' the Gong Around (Koehler-Arlen) 3:17 320125-3
11. Home (Armstrong) 4:03   320127-1
12. All of Me (Simons-Marks) 2:57   320127-2
13. Love, You Funny Thing (Turk-Ahlert) 3:38 320302-1
14. The New Tiger Rag (DeCosta-Morton-Carey-Miller) 3:20   320302-2
15. Keepin' Out of Mischief Now (Razaf-Waller) 3:30 320311-1
16. Lawd, You Made the Night Too Long (Lewis-Young) 3:20   320311-2

Chick Webb and His Orchestra, with Guest Louis Armstrong

17. That's My Home (Armstrong) 3:10   321208-1
18. Hobo, You Can't Ride This Train (Armstrong) 3:01 321208-3
19. I Hate To Leave You Now (Dick-Link-Waller) 3:12 321208-5
20. You'll Wish You'd Never Been Born (Armstrong) 3:19 321208-7

Louis Armstrong and His Orchestra

21. Medley of Armstrong Hits (Part 1) 3:44   321221-1 When You're Smiling (Fisher-Goodwin-Shay)/Saint James Infirmary (Mills)/Dinah (Murphy-Marshall)

*On "The Lonesome Road," comments by trio McKendrick, Randolph, and Joe Lindsey (not the same as bass player John Lindsay).

CD: Classics 536 (released 1990). Total playing time, 70:21. Produced by **Gilles Pétard**. Liner notes by Anatol Schenker.

Tracks 1–16: **Louis Armstrong and His Orchestra**, Louis with trumpet and vocals on all tracks, and Trumpet: Zilmer Randolph; Trombone: Preston Jackson; Clarinet: Lester Boone; Alto saxophones: Lester Boone, George James; Tenor Saxophone: Al Washington; Piano: Charlie Alexander; Banjo-Guitar: Mike McKendrick; Bass: John Lindsay; Drums: Tubby Hall. All tracks recorded in Chicago.

Tracks 17–20: See **The Chick Webb Recording Sessions, 1927–1934**.

Track 21: **Louis Armstrong and His Orchestra**, Louis on trumpet and vocals, with Trumpets: Charlie Gaines + one unknown; Trombone: unknown; Alto Saxophones: Arthur Davy, Louis Jordan; Tenor Saxophone: Ellworth Blake; Piano: Wesley Robinson; Banjo-Guitar: unknown; Tuba: Ed Hayes; Drums: Benny Hill. This track recorded in New York.

CWLPD-5   Mezz Mezzrow, 1928–1936

The Chicago Rhythm Kings

1. There'll Be Some Changes Made (Overstreet-Higgins) 2:50   280406-1
2. I've Found a New Baby (Williams-Palmer) 3:05 280406-2

The Jungle Kings

3 Friars Point Shuffle (Condon-McKenzie) 2:52 280409-3
4. Darktown Strutters' Ball (Brooks) 2:30   280409-4

Frank Teschmacher's Chicagoans

5. Jazz Me Blues (Delaney) 2:38   280428-2

The Louisiana Rhythm Kings

6. Baby, Won't You Please Come Home (Williams-Warfield) 2:36   280428-1

Mezz Mezzrow and His Orchestra

7. Free Love (Carter-Mezzrow-Sampson) 2:49   331106-1
8. Dissonance (Mezzrow) 2:50   331106-2
9. Swingin' with Mezz (Hill-Mezzrow) 3:01   331106-3
10. Love, You're Not the One for Me (Carter-Mezzrow) 3:06   331106-4
11. Old Fashioned Love (Mack-Johnson/arr. Hill)* 3:02 340507-1
12. Apologies (Mezzrow)* 3:18   340507-2
13. Sendin' the Vipers (Mezzrow)* 2:52   340507-3
14. 35th and Calumet* 2:47   340507-4

Art Karle and His Boys

15. Moon Over Miami (Leslie-Burke) 3:09   360113-1
16. I Feel Like a Feather in the Breeze (Gordon-Revel) 2:34   360113-2

17. Suzannah (Brown-Akst-Richmn) 2:48   360113-3
18. Lights Out (Hill) 3:08   360113-4

Mezz Mezzrow and His Swing Band

19. A Melody from the Sky (Mitchell-Alter) 3:00
    360312-1
20. Lost (Ohman-Mercer-Teetor) 2:26   360312-2

Tracks with Chick Webb, drums.

CD: Classics 713 (released 1993). Total playing time, 58:59. Produced by **Gilles Pétard.** Liner notes by Anatol Schenker.

Tracks 1–2, Cornet: Muggsy Spanier; Clarinet: Frank Teschmacher; Tenor Saxophone: Mezz Mezzrow; Piano: Joe Sullivan; Banjo: Eddie Condon; Bass: Jim Lannigan; Drums: Gene Krupa; Vocalist: Red McKenzie. Recorded in Chicago.

Tracks 3–4, Clarinet: Frank Teschmacher, Tenor Saxophone: Mezz Mezzrow; Alto Saxophone: Rod Cless; Piano: Joe Sullivan; Banjo: Eddie Condon; Bass: Jim Lannigan; Drums: Gene Krupa; Vocalist: Red McKenzie. Recorded in Chicago.

Track 5, same as on Tracks 3–4, except Vocalist: Elinor Charler replaces Red McKenzie. Recorded in Chicago.

Track 6, Cornet: Muggsy Spanier, Clarinet: Frank Teschmacher, Tenor Saxophone: Mezz Mezzrow; Piano: Joe Sullivan; Banjo: Eddie Condon; Bass: Jim Lannigan; Drums: Gene Krupa

Tracks 7–10, Trumpets: Freddy Goodman, Ben Gusick, Max Kaminsky; Trombone: Floyd O'Brien; Clarinet: Mezz Mezzrow; Alto Saxophones: Benny Carter, Mezz Mezzrow; Tenor Saxophones: Benny Carter, Johnny Russell; Piano: Teddy Wilson; Guitar: Clayton Duerr; Bass: Pops Foster; Drums: Jack Maisel; Vocalist: Benny Carter on Track 10 only. Recorded in New York City.

*Tracks 11–14, See **The Chick Webb Recording Sessions, 1927–1934**

Tracks 15–18, Trumpet: Frank Newton; Clarinet: Mezz Mezzrow; Tenor Saxophone: Art Karle; Piano: Joe Bushkin; Guitar: Ted Tonisen; Bass: Louis Thompson; Drums: George Stafford; Vocalist: Chick Bullock. Recorded in New York City.

Tracks 19–20, Trumpet Frank Newton; Clarinet: Mezz Mezzrow; Tenor Saxophone: Bud Freeman; Piano: Willie "The Lion" Smith; Guitar: Al Casey; Bass: Wellman Braud; Drums: George Stafford; Vocalist: Lucille Stewart. Recorded in New York City.

☙

Decca released two LP collections in the 1950s, and they stand among the more important releases of Chick Webb's work:

Chick Webb: A Legend, Volume One (1929–1936). Decca DL 9222

1. Dog Bottom/2. Jungle Mama/3. Heebie Jeebies/4. Soft and Sweet/5. That Rhythm Man/6. Blue Minor/7. It's All Over Because We're Through/8. Don't Be That Way/9. What a Shuffle/10. Blue Lou/11. Down Home Rag/12. Facts and Figures/13. Go Harlem/14. A Little Bit Later On

Chick Webb: King of Swing, Volume Two (1937–1939), Decca DL 9223

1. Clap Hands! Here Comes Charley/2. That Naughty Waltz/3. I Got Rhythm/4. Squeeze Me/5. Harlem Congo/6. The Dipsy Doodle/7. Hallelujah!/ 8. Midnite in a Madhouse/9. A-Tisket, A-Tasket/10. Spinnin' the Webb/11. Liza/12. Who Ya Hunchin'/13. Undecided/14. In the Groove at the Grove

☙

In the 1960s, MCA issued a 2-LP set, most tracks featuring Ella:

The Best of Chick Webb, MCA 2-4107

Disc One: 1. A-Tisket, A-Tasket/2. Undecided/3. The Dipsy Doodle/4. Blue Lou/5. Harlem Congo/6. Don't That Way/7. 'Tain't What You Do/8. I Want To Be Happy/9. Sweet Sue, Just You/10. If Dreams Come True

Disc Two: 1. Rock It for Me/2. Liza/3. Franklin D. Roosevelt Jones/4. Squeeze Me/5. Strictly Jive/6. The Organ Grinder's Swing/7. MacPherson Is Rehearsin'/8. I Got Rhythm/9. On the Sunny Side of the Street/10. Hallelujah!

☙

The Jazz Anthology label released two LPs worth noting, since the second contains rare broadcast tracks.

Chick Webb and His Orchestra, 1936, Featuring Ella Fitzgerald Jazz Anthology JA5199

1. Stompin' at the Savoy/2. Don't Be That Way/3. Nitwit Serenade/4. King Porter Stomp/5. Shine/6. The Darktown Strutters' Ball/7. Big John's Special/8. You Hit the Spot/9. Rhythm and Romance/10. Keepin' Out of Mischief Now/11. Go Harlem!/12 When Dreams Come True

Chick Webb and His Orchestra, 1937–1939, Jazz Anthology JA 5113

1. Tea for Two/2. How Am I To Know?/3. One O'Clock Jump/4. A Blue Room/5. Crazy Rhythm/6. Grand Terrace Rhythm/7. Sugarfoot Stomp/8. Blue Skies/9. By Heck/10. Dinah/11. Poor Little Rich Girl/12. Breakin' It Down/13. My Wild Irish Rose/14. The Stars and Stripes Forever

The Ella Fitzgerald Recording Sessions

(Including the Chick Webb Recording Sessions, 1935–1939)

——— THE DECCA YEARS (1935–1955) ———

CHICK WEBB AND HIS ORCHESTRA

Chick Webb, Leader/Drums; Trumpets: Mario Bauza, Taft Jordan, Bobby Stark; Trombones: Claude Jones, Sandy Williams; Clarinet: Pete Clark; Flute: Wayman Carver; Alto Saxophones: Pete Clark, Edgar Sampson; Tenor Saxophones: Wayman Carver, Elmer Williams; Piano: Don Kirkpatrick; Banjo-Guitar: John Trueheart; String Bass: Bill Thomas; Vocals: Ella Fitzgerald, Charles Linton; Arrangements: Edgar Sampson (except "Down Home Rag"). Recorded at Decca Recording Company, New York, Wednesday, 12 June 1935

(350612-1) 39614-A I'll Chase the Blues Away (vEF) (78: Brunswick (E) 02602); LPD-1, LPD-7, LPD-121)

350612-2 39615-A Down Home Rag (instr) (Arr: Wayman Carver) (78: Decca 785B; LPD-8)

350612-3 39616-A Are You Here To Stay? (vCL) (78: Decca 494B; LPD-8)

(350612-4) 39617-A Love and Kisses (vEF) (78: Decca 494A; LPD-1, LPD-7, LPD-121)

Note: 350612-1 was not released in the U.S. until the advent of the CD. "Love and Kisses" was Miss Fitzgerald's first U.S. released recording.

CHICK WEBB AND HIS ORCHESTRA

Chick Webb, Leader/Drums; Trumpets: Mario Bauza, Taft Jordan, Bobby Stark; Trombones: Claude Jones, Sandy Williams; Clarinet: Pete Clark; Flute: Wayman Carver; Alto Saxophones: Pete Clark, Edgar Sampson; Tenor Saxophones: Wayman Carver, Elmer Williams; Piano: Don Kirkpatrick; Banjo and Guitar: John Trueheart; String Bass: Bill Thomas; Vocals: Ella Fitzgerald, Charles Linton, Taft Jordan; Arrangements: Edgar Sampson. Recorded at Decca Recording Company, New York, Saturday, 12 October 1935

(351012-1) 60054-A Rhythm and Romance (vEF) (78: Decca 588A; LPD-1, LPD-7, LPD-121)

351012-2 60055-A Moonlight and Magnolias (vCL) (78: Decca 588B; LPD-8)

(351012-3) 60056-A I'll Chase the Blues Away (vEF) (78: Decca 640B; LPD-7, LPD-121)

351012-4 60057-A I May Be Wrong (But I Think You're Wonderful) (vTJ) (78: Decca 640A; LPD-8)

351012-5 60058-A Facts and Figures (instr) (78: Decca 830B; LPD-8)

CHICK WEBB AND HIS ORCHESTRA

Chick Webb, Leader/Drums; Trumpets: Mario Bauza, Taft Jordan, Bobby Stark; Trombones: Claude Jones, Sandy Williams; Clarinet: Pete Clark; Flute: Wayman Carver; Alto Saxophones: Pete Clark, Edgar Sampson; Tenor Saxophones: Wayman Carver, Elmer Williams; Piano: Don Kirkpatrick; Banjo-Guitar: John Trueheart; String Bass: Bill Thomas; Vocals: Ella Fitzgerald, Charles Linton; Arrangements: Edgar Sampson. Recorded at World Broadcasting Systems Studio (711 Fifth Avenue), New York, Wednesday, 19 February 1936 (2:30–5:30 p.m.)

360219-1 W-1249 Big John's Special (instr)

360219-2 W-1250 You Hit the Spot (vEF)

360219-3 W-1251 Stompin' at the Savoy (instr)

360219-4 W-1252 Don't Be That Way (instr)

360219-5 W-1265 Shine (vEF)

360219-6 W-1266 Go Harlem (instr)

360219-7 W-1267 The Darktown Strutters' Ball (vEF)

360219-8 W-1268 Keepin' Out of Mischief Now (instr)

360219-9 W-1269 Nitwit Serenade (instr)

360219-10 W-1270 King Porter Stomp (instr)

360219-11 W-1271 If Dreams Come True (vCL)

360219-12 W-1272 Rhythm and Romance (vEF)

Note: These recordings were released on 78 rpm 16" recordings for use in radio station broadcasts, and were never released on 78 rpm 10" discs for sale to the public. Because of contractual agreements, the transcriptions were credited to artists Chuck Warner and His Orchestra, with vocals by Evelyn Fields and Carl Landon. The original contract guaranteed Chick Webb, his vocalists, and twelve musicians. (All selections on LPD-6)

TEDDY WILSON AND HIS ORCHESTRA

Teddy Wilson, Leader/Piano; Trumpet: Frank Newton; Trombone: Benny Norton; Clarinet-Alto Saxophone: Jerry Blake; Tenor Saxophone: Ted McRae; Guitar: John Trueheart; String Bass: Lennie Stanfield; Drums: Cozy Cole; Vocals: Ella Fitzgerald. Recorded at Decca Recording Company, New York, Tuesday 17 March 1936

(360317-1) B18830-1 My Melancholy Baby (vEF) (78: Brunswick 7729B; LPD-7, LPD-121)

Note: Charted 19 September 1936; weeks, 8; peak, #6

(360317-2) B18832-1 All My Life (vEF) (78: Brunswick 7640A; LPD-7, LPD-121)

Note: Charted 25 April 1936; weeks, 2; peak, #13

CHICK WEBB AND HIS ORCHESTRA

Chick Webb, Leader/Drums; Trumpets: Mario Bauza, Taft Jordan, Bobby Stark; Trombones: Claude Jones, Sandy Williams; Clarinet: Pete Clark; Flute: Wayman Carver; Alto Saxophones: Pete Clark, Edgar Sampson; Tenor Saxophones: Wayman Carver, Elmer Williams; Piano: Don Kirkpatrick; Banjo and Guitar: John Trueheart; String Bass: Bill Thomas; Vocals: Ella Fitzgerald; Arrangements: Edgar Sampson. Recorded at Decca Recording Company, New York, Tuesday, 7 April 1936

360407-1 60999-A Love, You're Just a Laugh (vEF) Rejected

360407-2 60999-B Love, You're Just a Laugh (vEF) Rejected

(360407-3) 61000-A Crying My Heart Out for You (vEF) (78: Decca 785A; LPD-7, LPD-121)

(360407-4) 61001-A Under the Spell of the Blues (vEF) (78: Decca 831B; LPD-1, LPD-7, LPD-121)

(360407-5) 61002-A When I Get Low, I Get High (vEF) (78: 1123B; LPD-1; LPD-7, LPD-121)

CHICK WEBB AND HIS ORCHESTRA

Chick Webb, Leader/Drums; Trumpets: Mario Bauza, Taft Jordan, Bobby Stark; Trombones: Nat Story, Sandy Williams; Clarinet: Pete Clark; Flute: Wayman Carver; Alto Saxophones: Pete Clark, Edgar Sampson; Tenor Saxophones: Wayman Carver, Ted McRae; Piano: Don Kirkpatrick; Banjo and Guitar: John Trueheart; String Bass: Bill Thomas; Vocals: Ella Fitzgerald; Arrangements: Edgar Sampson. Recorded at Decca Recording Company, New York, Tuesday, 2 June 1936

360602-1 61123-A Go Harlem (instr) (78: Decca 995A; LPD-8)

(360602-2) 61124-A Sing Me a Swing Song (and Let Me Dance) (vEF) (78: Decca 830A; LPD-1, LPD-7, LPD-121)

Note: Charted 25 July 1936; weeks, 1; peak #18

(360602-3) 61125-A A Little Bit Later On (vEF) (78: Decca 831A; LPD-1, LPD-7, LPD-121)

(360602-4) 61126-A Love, You're Just a Laugh (vEF) (78: Decca 1114B; LPD-1, LPD-7, LPD-121)

(360602-5) 61127-A Devoting My Time to You (vEF) (78: Decca 995B; LPD-7, LPD-121)

CHICK WEBB AND HIS ORCHESTRA

Chick Webb, Leader/Drums; Trumpets: Mario Bauza, Taft Jordan, Bobby Stark; Trombones: Nat Story, Sandy Williams; Flute: Wayman Carver; Alto Saxophones: Pete Clark, Louis Jordan; Tenor Saxophones: Wayman Carver, Ted McRae; Piano: Tommy Fulford; Guitar: John Trueheart; String Bass: Beverley Peer; Vocals: Ella Fitzgerald. Recorded at Decca Recording Company, New York, Thursday, 29 October 1936

(361029-1) 61361-A Mister Paganini (You'll Have To Swing It) (vEF) (78: Decca 1032A; LPD-7, LPD-121)

Note: Charted 19 December 1936; weeks, 1; peak, #20

(361029-2) 61361-B Mister Paganini (You'll Have To Swing It) (vEF) (LPD-1)

(361029-3) 61362-A Swinging on the Reservation (vEF) (78: Decca 1065A; LPD-7, LPD-121)

(361029-4) 61363-A I Got the Spring Fever Blues (vEF) (78: Decca 1087A; LPD-7, LPD-121)

(361029-5) 61364-A Vote for Mr. Rhythm (vEF) (78: Decca 1032B; LPD-1, LPD-7, LPD-121)

BENNY GOODMAN AND HIS ORCHESTRA

Benny Goodman, Leader; Clarinet; Trumpets: Ziggy Elman, Chris Griffin, Zeke Zarchey; Trombones: Red Ballard Murray McEachern; Alto Saxophones: Bill DePew, Hymie Schertzer; Tenor Saxophones: Vido Musso, Art Rollini; Piano: Jess Stacy; Guitar: Allan Reuss; String Bass: Harry Goodman; Drums: Gene Krupa; Vocals: Ella Fitzgerald. Recorded at RCA Victor Studios, New York, Thursday, 5 November 1936

(361105-1) BS02463-1 Goodnight, My Love (vEF) (78: Victor 25461A; LPD-7, LPD-121)

Note: Charted 16 January 1937; weeks, 13; peak, #1 (4 weeks)

(361105-2) BS02464-1 Oh, Yes, Take Another Guess (vEF) (78: Victor 25461B; LPD-7, LPD-121)

(361105-3) BS02465-1 Did You Mean It? (vEF) (78: Victor 25469B; LPD-7, LPD-121)

Note: Decca protested vehemently when these Ella-BG records hit the stores ("Did You Mean It?" was released on 25 November 1936), so they were withdrawn, eventually. ("Did You Mean It?" was pulled from the Victor catalog on 20 January 1937). Something had to be done, and this is what happened: The original issue of Victor 25461-A is matrix BS02453-1, "Goodnight, My Love," coupled with Victor 25461-1, "Oh, Yes, Take Another Guess." The original issue of

Victor 25469-A is matrix BS02459-1, "'Tain't No Use," coupled with Victor 25469-B, matrix BS02465-1, "Did You Mean It?" Catalog number 25461 was then re-used. The second issue is Victor 25461-A, matrix BS042351, "Goodnight, My Love," vocal by Frances Hunt, recorded 14 January 1937; confusingly the second issue couples the A side with the original Victor 25461-B, matrix BS02459-1, "'Tain't No Use." Catalog number 25461 was then used a third time. The third issue is Victor 25461-A, matrix BS02463-1, "Goodnight, My Love," the original Ella vocal, coupled with Victor 25461-B, matrix BS 02459-1, "'Tain't No Use." Catalog number 25469 was not re-used—for which all thanks. Until the reissues of the BG-Ella sides in the 1960s, the originals were collectors' prizes—and still are, for that matter. But latter-day collectors now find the Frances Hunt release hard to find, which must prove something!

To wind up the caducous entente cordiale of Miss Fitzgerald and Mr. Goodman, Ella sang with the band on the "Camel Caravan" broadcast of 10 November 1936. Unfortunately, no air checks of this program are extant. If there were, they might provide "live" Ella with Benny, AND Lionel Hampton's first date with the band as a regular member. (The Hamp drove East in a battered Chevy, with his vibes in the trunk, and arrived in New York that very day, Tuesday, 10 November 1936.)

ELLA FITZGERALD AND HER SAVOY EIGHT

Ella Fitzgerald, Leader/Vocals; Trumpet: Taft Jordan; Trombone: Sandy Williams; Clarinet: Pete Clark; Tenor and Baritone Saxophones: Ted McRae; Piano: Tommy Fulford; Guitar: John Trueheart; String Bass: Beverley Peer; Drums: Chick Webb. Recorded at Decca Recording Company, New York, Wednesday, 18 November 1936

361118-1 61419-A   My Last Affair (vEF) (78: Decca 1061B; LPD-1, LPD-7, LPD-11, LPD-16, LPD-121)

361118-2 61420-A   The Organ Grinder's Swing (vEF) (78: Decca 1062A; LPD-1, LPD-7, LPD-11, LPD-16, LPD-121)

ELLA FITZGERALD AND HER SAVOY EIGHT

Ella Fitzgerald, Leader/Vocals; Trumpet: Taft Jordan; Trombone: Sandy Williams; Clarinet: Pete Clark; Tenor and Baritone Saxophones: Ted McRae; Piano: Tommy Fulford; Guitar: John Trueheart; String Bass: Beverley Peer; Drums: Chick Webb. Recorded at Decca Recording Company, New York, Thursday, 19 November 1936

361119-1 61421-A   Shine (vEF) (78: Decca 1062B; LPD-1, LPD-7, LPD-11, LPD-121)

361119-2 61420-A   The Darktown Strutters' Ball (vEF) (78: Decca 1061A; LPD-1, LPD-7, LPD-121)

CHICK WEBB AND HIS ORCHESTRA

Chick Webb, Leader/Drums; Trumpets: Mario Bauza, Taft Jordan, Bobby Stark; Trombones: Nat Story, Sandy Williams; Clarinet: Pete Clark; Alto Saxophones: Pete Clark, Louis Jordan, Ted McRae; Tenor Saxophone, Flute: Wayman Carver; Piano: Tommy Fulford; Guitar: John Trueheart; String Bass: Beverley Peer; Vocals: Ella Fitzgerald, Louis Jordan, Charles Linton. Recorded at Decca Recording Company, New York, Thursday, 14 January 1937

370114-1 61527-A   Oh, Yes, Take Another Guess (vEF) (78: Decca 1123A; LPD-1, LPD-7, LPD-121)

370114-2 61528-A   Love Marches On (vTrio: EF-LJ-CL) (78: Decca 1115B; LPD-8)

THE MILLS BROTHERS-ELLA FITZGERALD

First Tenor: Herbert Mills; Second Tenor: Donald Mills; Baritone: Harry Mills; Bass: John Mills, Sr.; Alto: Ella Fitzgerald; Accompanied by Guitar: Bernard Addison. Recorded at Decca Recording Company, New York, Thursday, 14 January 1937

370114-3 61529-A   Big Boy Blue (vMB-EF) (78: Decca 1148B; LPD-9, LPD121, LPD-122, LPD-123)

Note: Charted 24 April 1937; weeks, 1; peak, #20

CHICK WEBB AND HIS ORCHESTRA

Chick Webb, Leader/Drums; Trumpets: Mario Bauza, Taft Jordan, Bobby Stark; Trombones: Nat Story, Sandy Williams; Clarinet: Pete Clark; Alto Saxophones: Pete Clark, Louis Jordan, Ted McRae; Tenor Saxophone, Flute: Wayman Carver; Piano: Tommy Fulford; Guitar: John Trueheart; String Bass: Beverley Peer; Vocals: Ella Fitzgerald, Louis Jordan, Charles Linton. Recorded at Decca Recording Company, New York, Friday, 15 January 1937

370115-1 61529-A*   There's Frost on the Moon (vTrio: EF-LJ-CL) (78: Decca 1114A; LPD-8)

370115-2 61530-A   Gee, But You're Swell (vLJ) (78: Decca 1115A; LPD-8)

*Due to an error in Decca's ledger-keeping, matrix 61529 was used twice, for the last session of 14 January, and the first session of 15 January 1937.

THE MILLS BROTHERS-ELLA FITZGERALD

First Tenor: Herbert Mills; Second Tenor: Donald Mills; Baritone: Harry Mills; Bass: John Mills, Sr.; Alto: Ella Fitzgerald; Accompanied by Guitar: Bernard Addison. Recorded at Decca Recording Company, New York, Wednesday, 3 February 1937

370203-1 61576-A   Dedicated to You (vMB-EF) (78: Decca 1148A; LPD-9, LPD-121, LPD-123)

Note: Charted 10 April 1937; weeks, 1; peak, #19

CHICK WEBB AND HIS ORCHESTRA

Chick Webb, Leader/Drums; Trumpets: Mario Bauza, Taft Jordan, Bobby Stark; Trombones: Nat Story, Sandy Williams; Clarinet: Pete Clark; Alto Saxophones: Pete Clark, Louis Jordan, Ted McRae; Tenor Saxophone, Flute: Wayman Carver; Piano: Tommy Fulford; Guitar: John Trueheart; String Bass: Beverley Peer; Vocals: Ella Fitzgerald. Radio WJZ broadcast from Radio City, New York, Monday, 8 February 1937

370208-1   Have a Good Night, Folks! (instr)
370208-2   Open 'Em Up, Chick! (instr)
370208-3   Swing, Mr. Charlie, Swing! (instr)
370208-4   Vote for Mr. Rhythm (vEF)
370208-5   Wanton Rhythm Man (instr)
370208-6   Big Boy Blue (vEF)

(All selections on LPD-149)

JIMMY MUNDY AND HIS SWING CLUB SEVEN

Jimmy Mundy, Leader/Tenor Saxophone; Trumpet: Walter Fuller; Trombone: Trummy Young; Clarinet-Alto Saxophone: Omer Simeon; Piano: Billy Kyle; Guitar: Dick Palmer; String Bass: Quinn Wilson; Drums: Chick Webb; Vocals: Walter Fuller; Arrangements: Jimmy Mundy. Recorded at Decca Recording Company, New York, Wednesday, 3 March 1937

370303-1   M159-1 I Surrender, Dear (vWF) (78: Variety 598)
370303-2   M160-1 Ain't Misbehavin' (vWF) (78: Variety 598)

CHICK WEBB AND HIS ORCHESTRA

Chick Webb, Leader/Drums; Trumpets: Mario Bauza, Taft Jordan, Bobby Stark; Trombones: Nat Story, Sandy Williams; Clarinet: Pete Clark; Alto Saxophones: Pete Clark, Louis Jordan, Ted McRae; Tenor Saxophone-Flute: Wayman Carver; Piano: Tommy Fulford; Guit2ar: John Trueheart; String Bass: Beverley Peer; Vocals: Ella Fitzgerald, Louis Jordan, Charles Linton. Recorded at Decca Recording Company, New York, Wednesday, 24 March 1937

370324-1   62064-A   Rusty Hinge (vLJ) (78 Decca 1273A; LPD-8)
370324-2   62065-A   Wake Up and Live (vTrio: EF-LJ-CL) (78 Decca 1213A; LPD 8, LPD-120)
370324-3   62066-A   It's Swell of You (vLJ) (78: Decca 1213A; LPD-8)
370324-4   62067-A   You Showed Me the Way (vEF) (78: Decca 1220A; LPD-9, LPD-121)
370324-5   62067-B   You Showed Me the Way (vEF) (LPD-1)
370324-6   62067-A   Clap Hands! Here Comes Charlie (instr) (78: Decca 1220B; LPD-8)
370324-7   62069-A   Cryin' Mood (vEF) (78: Decca 1273B; LPD-1, LPD-9, LPD-11, LPD-121)
370324-8   62072-A   Love Is the Thing (So They Say) (vEF) (78: Decca 1356B; LPD-9, LPD-121)
370324-9   62073-A   That Naughty Waltz (instr) (Arr: Charlie Dixon) (78: Decca 1356A; LPD-8)

THE GOTHAM STOMPERS

Trumpet: Cootie Williams; Trombone: Sandy Williams; Clarinet: Barney Bigard; Alto Saxophone: Johnny Hodges;

Baritone Saxophone: Harry Carney; Piano: Tommy Fulford; Guitar: Bernard Addison; String Bass: Billy Taylor; Drums: Chick Webb; Vocals: Ivie Anderson; Arrangements: Wayman Carver. Recorded at Decca Recording Company, New York, Thursday 25 March 1937

370325-1   M301-1 My Honey's Lovin' Arms (vIA) (78: Variety 629)
370325-2   M302-1 Did Anyone Ever Tell You? (vIA) (78: Variety 541)
370325-3   M303-1 Alabamy Home (instr) (78: Variety 629)
370325-4   M304-1 Where Are You? (vIA) (78: Variety 541)

ELLA FITZGERALD AND HER SAVOY EIGHT

Ella Fitzgerald, Leader/Vocals; Trumpet: Taft Jordan; Trombone: Sandy Williams; Alto Saxophone: Louis Jordan; Tenor and Baritone Saxophones: Ted McRae; Piano: Tommy Fulford; Guitar: Bobby Johnson; String Bass: Beverley Peer; Drums: Chick Webb. Recorded at Decca Recording Company, New York, Monday, 24 May 1937

370524-1   62213-A   All Over Nothing at All (vEF) (78: Decca 1339A; LPD-9, LPD-16, LPD-121)

Note: Charted 14 August 1937; weeks, 1; peak, #20

370524-2   62214-A   If You Ever Should Leave (vEF) Rejected
370524-3   62214-B   If You Ever Should Leave (vEF) (78: Decca 1302A; LPD-1, LPD-9, LPD-16, LPD-121)
370524-4   62215-A   Everyone's Wrong but Me (vEF) (78: Decca 1302B; LPD-1, LPS-9, LPD-16, LPD-121)

Note: Charted 10 July 1937; weeks, 4; peak, #12

370524-5   62216-A   Deep in the Heart of the South (vEF) (78: Decca 1339B; LPD-9, LPD-121)

CHICK WEBB AND HIS LITTLE CHICKS

Chick Webb, Leader/Drums; Clarinet: Chauncey Haughton; Flute: Wayman Carver; Piano: Tommy Fulford; String Bass: Beverley Peer. Recorded at Decca Recording Company, New York, Tuesday, 21 September 1937

370921-1   62618-A   In a Little Spanish Town (instr) (78: Decca 1513A; LPD-8)
370921-2   62619-A   I Got Rhythm (instr) (78: Decca 1759B; LPD-8)
370921-3   62620-A   I Ain't Got Nobody (instr) (78: Decca 1513B; LPD-8)

CHICK WEBB AND HIS ORCHESTRA

Chick Webb, Leader/Drums; Trumpets: Mario Bauza, Taft Jordan, Bobby Stark; Trombones: Nat Story, Sandy Williams; Clarinet: Chauncey Haughton; Flute: Wayman

Carver; Alto Saxophones: Chauncey Haughton, Louis Jordan; Tenor Saxophones: Wayman Carver, Ted McRae; Piano: Tommy Fulford; Guitar: Bobby Johnson; String Bass: Beverley Peer; Vocals: Ella Fitzgerald. Recorded at Decca Recording Company, New York, Wednesday, 27 October 1937

(371027-1)   62725-A   Just a Simple Melody (vEF) (78: Decca 1521B; LPD-1, LPD-9, LPD-11, LPD-121)

(371027-2)   62726-A   I Got a Guy (vEF) (78: Decca 1681B; LPD-1, LPD-9, LPD-121)

Note: Charted 11 June 1938; weeks, 2; peak, #18

371027-3   62727-A   Strictly Jive (instr) (78: Decca 1586B; LPD-8)

(371027-4)   62728-A   Holiday in Harlem (vEF) (78: Decca 1521A; LPD-9, LPD-11, LPD-121)

CHICK WEBB AND HIS LITTLE CHICKS

Chick Webb, Leader/Drums; Clarinet: Chauncey Haughton; Flute: Wayman Carver; Piano: Tommy Fulford; String Bass: Beverley Peer. Recorded at Decca Recording Company, New York, Monday, 1 November 1937

371101-1   62737-A   Sweet Sue, Just You (instr) Rejected

371101-2   62737-B   Sweet Sue, Just You (instr) (78: Decca 1759A; LPD-8)

CHICK WEBB AND HIS ORCHESTRA

Chick Webb, Leader/Drums; Trumpets: Mario Bauza, Taft Jordan, Bobby Stark; Trombones: Nat Story, Sandy Williams; Clarinet: Chauncey Haughton; Flute: Wayman Carver; Alto Saxophones: Chauncey Haughton, Louis Jordan; Tenor Saxophones: Wayman Carver, Ted McRae; Piano: Tommy Fulford; Guitar: Bobby Johnson; String Bass: Beverley Peer; Vocals: Ella Fitzgerald. Recorded at Decca Recording Company, New York, Monday, 1 November 1937

(371101-3)   62738-A   Rock It for Me (vEF) (78: Decca 1586A; LPD-1, LPD-9, LPD-121)

Note: Charted 19 February 1938; weeks, 1; peak, #19

371101-4   62739-A   Squeeze Me (instr) (78: Decca 1716B; LPD-8)

371101-5   62740-A   Harlem Congo (instr) (Arr: Charlie Dixon) (78: Decca 1681A; LPD-8)

CHICK WEBB AND HIS ORCHESTRA

Chick Webb, Leader/Drums; Trumpets: Mario Bauza, Taft Jordan, Bobby Stark; Trombones: Nat Story, Sandy Williams; Clarinet: Chauncey Haughton; Flute: Wayman Carver; Alto Saxophones: Chauncey Haughton, Louis Jordan; Tenor Saxophones: Wayman Carver, Ted McRae; Piano: Tommy Fulford; Guitar: Bobby Johnson; String Bass: Beverley Peer; Vocals: Ella Fitzgerald. Recorded at Decca Recording Company, New York, Tuesday, 2 November 1937

(371102-1)   62743-A   Hallelujah! (vEF) Rejected

(371102-2)   62743-B   Hallelujah! (vEF) Rejected

(371102-3)   62744-A   I Want To Be Happy (vEF) Rejected

(371102-4)   62744-B   I Want To Be Happy (vEF) Rejected

CHICK WEBB AND HIS ORCHESTRA

Chick Webb, Leader/Drums; Trumpets: Mario Bauza, Taft Jordan, Bobby Stark; Trombones: Nat Story, Sandy Williams; Clarinet: Garvin Bushell; Flute Wayman Carver; Alto Saxophones: Garvin Bushell, Louis Jordan; Tenor Saxophones: Wayman Carver, Ted McRae; Piano: Tommy Fulford; Guitar: Bobby Johnson; String Bass: Beverley Peer; Vocals: Ella Fitzgerald. NBC radio broadcast from Savoy Ballroom, New York, Friday, 10 December 1937

371210-1   Bronzeville Stomp (instr) (LPD-147)

(371210-2)   He's Tall, He's Tan, He's Terrific (vEF) (LPD-147)

(371210-3)   Honeysuckle Rose (vEF) (LPD-147)

CHICK WEBB AND HIS ORCHESTRA

Chick Webb, Leader/Drums; Trumpets: Mario Bauza, Taft Jordan, Bobby Stark; Trombones: Nat Story, Sandy Williams; Clarinet: Garvin Bushell; Flute: Wayman Carver; Alto Saxophones: Garvin Bushell, Louis Jordan; Tenor Saxophones: Wayman Carver, Ted McRae; Piano: Tommy Fulford; Guitar: Bobby Johnson; String Bass: Beverley Peer; Vocals: Ella Fitzgerald. Recorded at Decca Recording Company, New York, Friday, 17 December 1937

(371217-1)   62886-A   I Want to Be Happy (vEF) (Arr: Van Alexander) (78: Decca 15039; LPD-1, LPD-9, LPD-121)

(371217-2)   62886-B   I Want to Be Happy (vEF) (Arr: Van Alexander) (78: Decca Z-778) (Australian)

(371217-3)   62887-A   The Dipsy Doodle (vEF) (78: Decca 1587A; LPD-1, LPD-9, LPD-121)

(371217-4)   62888-A   If Dreams Come True (vEF) (78: Decca 1716-A; LPD-1, LPD-9, LPD-121)

(371217-5)   62889-A   Hallelujah! (vEF) (78: Decca 15039; LPD-1, LPD-9, LPD-121)

371217-6   62890-A   Midnite in a Madhouse (Midnite in Harlem) (instr) (78: Decca 1587B; LPD-8)

371217-7   62890-B   Midnite in a Madhouse (Midnite in Harlem) (instr) (78: Decca Y-5208) (New Zealand)

ELLA FITZGERALD AND HER SAVOY EIGHT

Ella Fitzgerald, Leader/Vocals; Trumpet: Taft Jordan; Trombone: Sandy Williams; Alto Saxophone: Louis Jordan; Tenor and Baritone Saxophones: Ted McRae; Piano: Tommy Fulford; Guitar: Bobby Johnson; String Bass: Beverley Peer; Drums: Chick Webb. Recorded at Decca Recording Company, New York, Tuesday, 21 December 1937

371221-1 62896-A Bei Mir Bist Du Schoen (vEF) (78: Decca 1596A; LPD-1, LPD-9, LPD-121)

371221-2 62897-A It's My Turn Now (vEF) (78: Decca 1596B; LPD-1, LPD-9, LPD-121)

ELLA FITZGERALD AND HER SAVOY EIGHT

Ella Fitzgerald, Leader/Vocals; Trumpet: Taft Jordan; Trombone: Sandy Williams; Alto Saxophone: Louis Jordan; Tenor and Baritone Saxophones: Ted McRae; Piano: Tommy Fulford; Guitar: Bobby Johnson; String Bass: Beverley Peer; Drums: Chick Webb. Recorded at Decca Recording Company, New York, Tuesday, 25 January 1938

380125-1 63225-A It's Wonderful (vEF) (78: Decca 1669B; LPD-1, LPD-9, LPD-121)

380125-2 63226-A I Was Doing All Right (vEF) (78: Decca 1669A; LPD-1, LPD-9, LPD-16, LPD-121)

CHICK WEBB AND HIS ORCHESTRA

Chick Webb, Leader/Drums; Trumpets: Mario Bauza, Taft Jordan, Bobby Stark; Trombones: George Matthews Nat Story, Sandy Williams; Clarinet: Garvin Bushell; Flute: Wayman Carver; Alto Saxophones: Garvin Bushell, Louis Jordan; Tenor Saxophones: Wayman Carver, Ted McRae; Piano: Tommy Fulford; Guitar: Bobby Johnson; String Bass: Beverley Peer; Vocals: Ella Fitzgerald. Recorded at Decca Recording Company, New York, Thursday, 2 May 1938

380502-1 63693-A A-Tisket, A-Tasket (vEF and band members) (78: Decca 1840A; LPD-1, LPD-3, LPD-5, LPD-9, LPD-22, LPD-35, LPD-40, LPD-121)

Note: Charted 18 June 1938; weeks, 19; peak, #1 (10 weeks). This recording was selected for the National Association of Recording Arts and Sciences Hall of Fame

380502-2 63694-A Heart of Mine (vEF) (78: Decca 2721B; LPD-1, LPD-10, LPD-121)

380502-3 63695-A I'm Just a Jitterbug (vEF) (78: Decca 1899B; LPD-1, LPD-10, LPD-121)

380502-4 63696-C Azure (instr) (78: Decca 1899A; LPD-8)

ELLA FITZGERALD AND HER SAVOY EIGHT

Ella Fitzgerald, Leader; Vocals; Trumpet: Taft Jordan; Trombone: Sandy Williams; Alto Saxophone: Louis Jordan; Tenor and Baritone Saxophones: Ted McRae; Piano: Tommy Fulford; Guitar: Bobby Johnson; String Bass: Beverley Peer; Drums; Chick Webb. Recorded at Decca Recording Company, New York, Friday, 3 May 1938

380503-1 63703-A This Time It's Real (vEF) (78: Decca 1806A; LPD-10, LPD-121)

380503-2 63704-A (Oh, Oh) What Do You Know About Love? (vEF) (78: Decca 1967A; LPD-10, LPD-121)

380503-3 63705-A You Can't Be Mine (and Somebody Else's Too) (vEF) Rejected

380503-4 63705-B You Can't Be Mine (and Someone Else's Too) (vEF) (78: Decca 1806B; LPD-1, LPD-10, LPD-16, LPD-121)

380503-5 63706-A We Can't Go On This Way (vEF) (78: Decca 1846B; LPD-10, LPD-121)

CHICK WEBB AND HIS ORCHESTRA

Chick Webb, Leader/Drums; Trumpets: Mario Bauza, Taft Jordan, Bobby Stark; Trombones: George Matthews, Nat Story, Sandy Williams; Clarinet: Garvin Bushell; Flute: Wayman Carver; Alto Saxophones: Garvin Bushell, Louis Jordan; Tenor Saxophones: Wayman Carver, Ted McRae; Piano: Tommy Fulford; Guitar: Bobby Johnson; String Bass: Beverley Peer. Recorded at Decca Recording Company, New York, Friday, 3 May 1938

380503-6 63707-A Spinnin' the Webb (instr) (78: Decca 2021B; LPD-8)

380503-7 63708-A Liza (All the Cloud'll Roll Away) (instr) (78: Decca 1840B; LPD-8)

ELLA FITZGERALD AND HER SAVOY EIGHT

Ella Fitzgerald, Leader/Vocals; Trumpet: Taft Jordan; Trombone: Sandy Williams; Alto Saxophone: Louis Jordan; Tenor and Baritone Saxophones: Ted McRae; Piano: Tommy Fulford; Guitar: Bobby Johnson; String Bass: Beverley Peer; Drums: Chick Webb. Recorded at Decca Recording Company, New York, Friday, 3 May 1938

380503-8 63709-A Saving Myself for You (vEF) Rejected

380503-9 63709-B Saving Myself for You (vEF) (78: Decca 1846B; LPD-10, LPD-121)

380503-10 63710-A If You Only Knew (vEF) (78: Decca 1967B; LPD-10, LPD-121)

380503-11 63710-B If You Only Knew (vEF) (LPD-1)

CHICK WEBB AND HIS ORCHESTRA

Chick Webb, Leader/Drums; Trumpets: Mario Bauza, Taft Jordan, Bobby Stark; Trombones: George Matthews, Nat Story, Sandy Williams; Clarinet: Garvin Bushell; Flute: Wayman Carver; Alto Saxophones: Garvin Bushell, Hilton Jefferson; Tenor Saxophones: Wayman Carver, Ted McRae; Piano: Tommy Fulford; Guitar: Bobby Johnson; String Bass: Beverley Peer; Vocals: Ella Fitzgerald. WNEW-AM radio broadcast, Concert, Randall's Island Stadium, New York, Sunday, 29 May 1938

Note: A short portion of silent newsreel exists from this event. The audio portion was broadcast on WNEW-AM in New York City, and was recorded off the air by Bill Savory. Hosted by Martin Block, the concert was a benefit performance for unemployed musicians.

CHICK WEBB AND HIS ORCHESTRA

Chick Webb, Leader/Drums; Trumpets: Mario Bauza, Taft Jordan, Bobby Stark; Trombones: George Matthews, Nat Story, Sandy Williams; Clarinet: Garvin Bushell; Flute: Wayman Carver; Alto Saxophones: Garvin Bushell, Hilton Jefferson; Tenor Saxophones: Wayman Carver, Ted McRae; Piano: Tommy Fulford; Guitar: Bobby Johnson; String Bass: Beverley Peer; Vocals: Ella Fitzgerald, Taft Jordan. Recorded at Decca Recording Company, New York, Thursday, 9 June 1938

(380609-1) 63934-A Pack Up Your Sins and Go to the Devil (vEF) (78: Decca 1894B; LPD-1, LPD-10, LPD-11, LPD-121)

(380609-2) 63935-A MacPherson Is Rehearsin' (To Swing) (vEF) (78: Decca 2080B; LPD-1, LPD-10, LPD-121)

Note: Charted 12 November 1938; weeks, 1; peak, #14

(380609-3) 63936-A Everybody Step (vEF) (78: Decca 1894A; LPD-1, LPD-10, LPD-121)

(380609-4) 63937-A Ella (vEF-TJ) (78: Decca 2148A; LPD-10, LPD-121)

CHICK WEBB AND HIS ORCHESTRA

Chick Webb, Leader/Drums; Trumpets: Mario Bauza, Taft Jordan, Bobby Stark; Trombones: George Matthews, Nat Story, Sandy Williams; Clarinet: Garvin Bushell; Flute: Wayman Carver; Alto Saxophones: Garvin Bushell, Hilton Jefferson; Tenor Saxophones: Wayman Carver, Ted McRae; Piano: Tommy Fulford; Guitar: Bobby Johnson; String Bass: Beverley Peer; Vocals: Ella Fitzgerald. WNEW-AM radio broadcast, NBC Studios, Radio City, "Saturday Night Swing Club," Saturday, 13 August 1938

(380813-1) Saving Myself for You (vEF) (LPD-148)

CHICK WEBB AND HIS ORCHESTRA

Chick Webb, Leader/Drums; Trumpets: Mario Bauza, Taft Jordan, Bobby Stark; Trombones: George Matthews, Nat Story, Sandy Williams; Clarinet: Garvin Bushell; Flute: Wayman Carver; Alto Saxophones: Garvin Bushell, Hilton Jefferson; Tenor Saxophones: Wayman Carver, Ted McRae; Piano: Tommy Fulford; Guitar: Bobby Johnson; String Bass: Beverley Peer; Vocals: Ella Fitzgerald. Recorded at Decca Recording Company, New York, Wednesday, 17 August 1938

(380817-1) 64459-A Wacky Dust (vEF) (78: Decca 2021A; LPD-1, LPD-10, LPD-11, LPD-121)

Note: Charted 12 November 1938; weeks, 4; peak, #13

(380817-2) 64460-A Gotta Pebble in My Shoe (vEF) (78: Decca 2231A; LPD-10, LPD-121)

(380817-3) 64461-A I Can't Stop Loving You (vEF) (78: Decca 2310B; LPD-10, LPD-121)

ELLA FITZGERALD AND HER SAVOY EIGHT

Ella Fitzgerald, Leader/Vocals; Trumpet: Taft Jordan; Trombone: Sandy Williams; Alto Saxophone: Hilton

Jefferson; Tenor and Baritone Saxophones: Ted McRae; Piano: Tommy Fulford; Guitar: Bobby Johnson; String Bass: Beverley Peer; Drums: Chick Webb. Recorded at Decca Recording Company, New York, Thursday, 18 August 1938

(380818-1) 64462-A Strictly from Dixie (vEF) (78: Decca 2202B; LPD-1, LPD-10, LPD-121)

(380818-2) 64463-A Woe Is Me (vEF) (78: Decca 2202A; LPD-10, LPD-121)

CHICK WEBB AND HIS ORCHESTRA

Chick Webb, Leader/Drums; Trumpets: Mario Bauza, Taft Jordan, Bobby Stark; Trombones: George Matthews, Nat Story, Sandy Williams; Clarinet: Garvin Bushell; Flute: Wayman Carver; Alto Saxophones: Garvin Bushell, Hilton Jefferson; Tenor Saxophones: Wayman Carver, Ted McRae; Piano: Tommy Fulford; Guitar: Bobby Johnson; String Bass: Beverley Peer; Vocals: Ella Fitzgerald. Recorded at Decca Recording Company, New York, Thursday, 18 August 1938

380818-3 64464-A Who Ya Hunchin'? (instr) (78: Decca 2231B)

(380818-4) 64465-A I Let a Tear Fall in the River (vEF) (78: Decca 2080A; LPD-10, LPD-121)

CHICK WEBB AND HIS ORCHESTRA

Chick Webb, Leader/Drums; Trumpets: Taft Jordan, Bobby Stark, Dick Vance; Trombones: George Matthews, Nat Story, Sandy Williams; Clarinet: Garvin Bushell; Flute: Wayman Carver; Alto Saxophones: Garvin Bushell, Hilton Jefferson; Tenor Saxophones: Wayman Carver, Ted McRae; Piano: Tommy Fulford; Guitar: Bobby Johnson; String Bass: Beverley Peer; Vocals: Ella Fitzgerald. Recorded at Decca Recording Company, New York, Thursday, 6 October 1938

(381006-1) 64573-A Franklin D. Roosevelt Jones (vEF) (78: Decca 2105A; LPD-1, LPD-10, LPD-121)

Note: Charted 26 November 1938; weeks, 6; peak, #8

(381006-2) 64574-A I Love Each Move You Make (vEF) (78: Decca 2105B; LPD-10, LPD-121)

(381006-3) 64575-A It's Foxy (vEF) (78: Decca 2309A; LPD-1, LPD-10, LPD-121)

(381006-4) 64576-A I Found My Yellow Basket (vEF-band members) (78: Decca 2148B; LPD-1, LPD-10, LPD-121)

Note: Charted 12 November 1938; weeks, 6; peak, #3

CHICK WEBB AND HIS ORCHESTRA

Chick Webb, Leader/Drums; Trumpets: Taft Jordan, Bobby Stark, Dick Vance; Trombones: George Matthews, Nat Story, Sandy Williams; Clarinet: Garvin Bushell; Flute: Wayman Carver; Alto Saxophones: Garvin Bushell, Hilton Jefferson; Tenor Saxophones: Wayman Carver, Ted McRae; Piano: Tommy Fulford; Guitar: Bobby Johnson; String Bass: Beverley Peer; Vocals: Ella Fitzgerald. Commercial transcriptions, recorded at Radio City, New York, Monday, 9 January 1939

390109-1   Tea for Two (instr)
390109-2   How Am I To Know? (instr)
390109-3   One O'Clock Jump (instr)
390109-4   A Blue Room (instr)
390109-5   Crazy Rhythm (instr)
390109-6   Sugarfoot Stomp (instr)
390109-7   Grand Terrace Rhythm (instr)
390109-8   By Heck! (instr)
390109-9   Blue Skies (instr)
390109-10   Dinah (instr)
390109-11   Who Ya Hunchin' (instr)
390109-12   Liza (All the Clouds'll Roll Away) (instr)

(All selections on LPD-150)

CHICK WEBB AND HIS QUINTET

Chick Webb, Leader/Drums; Clarinet: Chauncey Haughton; Flute: Wayman Carver; Piano: Tommy Fulford; String Bass: Beverley Peer; Vocals: Ella Fitzgerald. WNEW-AM radio broadcast, Radio City, New York, "Saturday Night Swing Club," Saturday, 21 January 1939

390121-1   I Let a Tear Fall in the River (vEF) (LPD-148)

CHICK WEBB AND HIS ORCHESTRA

Chick Webb, Leader/Drums; Trumpets: Taft Jordan, Bobby Stark, Dick Vance; Trombones: George Matthews, Nat Story, Sandy Williams; Clarinet: Garvin Bushell; Flute: Wayman Carver; Alto Saxpophones: Garvin Bushell, Hilton Jefferson; Tenor Saxophones: Wayman Carver, Ted McRae; Piano: Tommy Fulford; Guitar: Bobby Johnson; String Bass: Beverley Peer; Vocals: Ella Fitzgerald. WNEW-AM radio broadcast from The Blue Room, Lincoln Hotel, New York, Friday, 10 February 1939

390210-1   Blue Lou (instr)
390210-2   Deep in a Dream (vEF)
390210-3   One O'Clock Jump (instr)
390210-4   That Was My Heart (vEF)

(All selections on LPD-149)

CHICK WEBB AND HIS ORCHESTRA

Chick Webb, Leader/Drums; Trumpets: Taft Jordan, Bobby Stark, Dick Vance; Trombones: George Matthews, Nat Story, Sandy Williams; Clarinet: Garvin Bushell; Flute: Wayman Carver; Alto Saxophones: Garvin Bushell, Hilton Jefferson; Tenor Saxophones: Wayman Carver, Ted McRae; Piano: Tommy Fulford; Guitar: Bobby Johnson; String Bass: Beverley Peer; Vocals: Ella Fitzgerald. Recorded at Decca Recording Company, New York, Friday, 17 February 1939

390217-1   65039-A Undecided (vEF) (78: Decca 2323A; LPD-2, LPD-3, LPD-5, LPD-10, LPD-16, LPD-40, LPD-121)

Note: Charted 18 March 1939; weeks, 4; peak, #8

390217-2   65040-A 'Tain't What You Do (It's the Way That 'Cha Do It) (vEF) (78: Decca 2310A; LPD-2, LPD-12, LPD-121)

Note: Charted 25 March 1939; weeks, 1; peak, #19

390217-3   65041-A In the Groove at the Grove (instr) (78: Decca 2323B; CWLPD-3)
390217-4   65042-A One Side of Me (vEF) (78: Decca 2556B; LPD-11, LPD-12, LPD-121)
390217-5   65043-A My Heart Belongs to Daddy (vEF) (78: Decca 2309B; LPD-2, LPD-11, LPD-12, LPD-121)

ELLA FITZGERALD AND HER SAVOY EIGHT

Ella Fitzgerald, Leader/Vocals; Trumpet: Taft Jordan; Trombone: Sandy Williams; Alto Saxophone: Hilton Jefferson; Tenor and Baritone Saxophones: Ted McRae; Piano: Tommy Fulford; Guitar: John Trueheart; String Bass: Beverley Peer; Drums: Chick Webb. Recorded at Decca Recording Company, New York, Thursday, 2 March 1939

390302-1   65092-A Once Is Enough for Me (vEF) (78: Decca 2451B; LPD-12)
390302-2   65093-A I Had To Live and Learn (vEF) (78: Decca 2581A; LPD-12)

CHICK WEBB AND HIS ORCHESTRA

Chick Webb, Leader/Drums; Trumpets: Taft Jordan, Bobby Stark, Dick Vance; Trombones: George Matthews, Nat Story, Sandy Williams; Clarinet: Garvin Bushell; Flute: Wayman Carver; Alto Saxophones: Garvin Bushell, Hilton Jefferson; Tenor Saxophones: Wayman Carver, Ted McRae; Piano: Tommy Fulford; Guitar: John Trueheart; String Bass: Beverley Peer; Vocals: Ella Fitzgerald. Recorded at Decca Recording Company, New York, Thursday, 2 March 1939

390302-3   65094-A Sugar Pie (vEF) (78: Decca 2665-A; LPD-11, LPD-12)
390302-4   65095-A (When It's) Slumbertime Along the Swanee (vEF) (78: Decca 2389B; LPD-11, LPD-12)
390302-5   65096-A I'm Up a Tree (vEF) (78: Decca 2468B; LPD-12)
390302-6   65097-A Chew, Chew, Chew (Your Bubble Gum) (vEF) (78: Decca 2389A; LPD2, LPD-12)

Note: Charted 6 May 1939; weeks, 1; peak, #14

ELLA FITZGERALD AND HER SAVOY EIGHT

Ella Fitzgerald, Leader/Vocals; Trumpet: Taft Jordan; Trombone: Sandy Williams; Alto Saxophone: Hilton Jefferson; Tenor and Baritone Saxophones: Ted McRae; Piano: Tommy Fulford; Guitar: John Trueheart; String Bass: Beverley Peer; Drums: Chick Webb. Recorded at Decca Recording Company, New York, Friday, 21 April 1939

390421-1   65441-A Don't Worry 'Bout Me (vEF) (78: Decca 2451A; LPD-2, LPD-3, LPD-12, LPD-16)

390421-2   65442-A   If Anything Happened to You (vEF) (78: Decca 2481B; LPD-12)

390421-3   65443-A   If That's What You're Thinking (You're Wrong) (vEF) (78: Decca 2581B; LPD-12)

390421-4   65444-A   If You Ever Change Your Mind (vEF) (78: Decca 2481A; LPD-2, LPD-12)

CHICK WEBB AND HIS ORCHESTRA

Chick Webb, Leader/Drums; Trumpets: Taft Jordan, Bobby Stark, Dick Vance; Trombones: George Matthews, Nat Story, Sandy Williams; Clarinet: Garvin Bushell; Flute: Wayman Carver; Alto Saxophones: Garvin Bushell, Hilton Jefferson; Tenor Saxophones: Wayman Carver, Ted McRae; Piano: Tommy Fulford; Guitar: John Trueheart; String Bass: Beverley Peer; Vocals: Ella Fitzgerald. Recorded at Decca Recording Company, New York, Friday, 21 April 1939

390421-5   65445-A   Have Mercy (vEF) (78: Decca 2468A; LPD-12)

390421-6   65446-A   Little White Lies (vEF) (78: Decca 2556A; LPD-2, LPD-11, LPD-12)

390421-7   65447-A   Coochi-Coochi-Coo (vEF) (78: Decca 2803B; LPD-2, LPD-11, LPD-12)

390421-8   65448-A   That Was My Heart (vEF) (78: Decca 2665B; LPD-12)

Note: This was Chick Webb's last studio recording session.

CHICK WEBB AND HIS ORCHESTRA

Chick Webb, Leader/Drums; Trumpets: Taft Jordan, Bobby Stark, Dick Vance; Trombones: George Matthews, Nat Story, Sandy Williams; Clarinet; Garvin Bushell; Flute: Wayman Carver; Alto Saxophones: Garvin Bushell, Hilton Jefferson; Tenor Saxophones: Wayman Carver, Ted McRae; Piano: Tommy Fulford; Guitar: John Trueheart; String Bass: Beverley Peer; Vocals: Ella Fitzgerald. NBC radio broadcast from The Southland Cafe, Boston, Thursday, 4 May 1939

390504-1   Let's Get Together (signature theme)

390504-2   Poor Little Rich Girl (instr)

390504-3   A New Moon and an Old Serenade (vEF)

390504-4   Breakin' 'Em Down (instr)

390504-5   If I Didn't Care (vEF)

390504-6   The Stars and Stripes Forever (instr)

390504-7   I Never Knew Heaven Could Speak (vEF)

390504-8   My Wild Irish Rose (instr)

390504-9   Chew, Chew, Chew (Your Bubble Gum) (vEF)

390504-10   Let's Get Together (signature theme)

(All selections on LPD-150)

Note: This is the last known recorded session with Chick Webb. After the Southland Café gig, the band embarked on a series of one nighters, none of which is known to have been recorded, or, if so, if any recordings exist. Chick Webb died at Johns Hopkins Hospital, Baltimore, Maryland, 16 June 1939.

✍

On the following two pages the reader will find a listing, in alphabetical order by title, of all Chick Webb records without vocals by Ella Fitzgerald. Following that list, the discography of Ella's recording sessions will resume.

An Alphabetical Listing of Chick Webb Records Without Ella Fitzgerald Vocals

Recordings released are in bold type; those not yet released in standard type.

Ain't Misbehavin' (Razaf-Waller-Brooks) **370303-2**

Alabamy Home (Ringle-Ellington) **370325-3**

Apologies (Mezzrow) **340507-2**

Are You Here To Stay? (Sampson-Harrison) **350612-3**

Azure (Mills-Ellington) **380502-4**

Big John's Special (Henderson) **360219-1**

Blue Lou (Sampson-Mills) **341119-4**

Blue Minor (Sampson) **340706-1, 340910-4, 340910-5**

A Blue Room (Rodgers-Hart) **390109-4, 390210-1**

Blue Skies (Berlin) **390109-9**

Blues in My Heart (Carter-Mills) **310330-2**

Breakin' 'Em Down (Sampson) **390504-4**

Bronzeville Stomp (Sampson) **371210-2**

By Heck (Gilbert-Henry) **390109-8**

Clap Hands! Here Comes Charlie! (Rose-Macdonald-Meyer) **370324-5**

Crazy Rhythm (Ceasar-Meyer-Kahn) **390109-5**

The Darktown Strutters' Ball (Brooks) **331220-2, 340115-1**

Did Anyone Ever Tell You? **370325-2**

Dinah (Lewis-Young-Akst) **390109-10**

Dog Bottom (Webb) **290614-1**

Don't Be That Way (Parish-Sampson) **341119-2, 360219-4**

Down Home Rag (Lewis-Seatman) **350612-2**

Facts and Figures (Sampson) **351012-5**

Gee, But You're Swell (Tobias-Baer) **370115-2**

Go Harlem (Razaf-Johnson) **360219-6, 360602-1**

Grand Terrace Rhythm (Cahn-Chaplin) **390109-7**

Harlem Congo (White) **371101-5**

Have a Good Night, Folks! (Webb) **370208-1**

Heebie Jeebies (Atkins) **310330-1**

Hobo, You Can't Ride This Train (Armstrong) **321208-3, 321208-4**

How Am I To Know? (Parker-King) **390109-2**

I Ain't Got Nobody (Graham-Williams) **370921-3**

I Can't Dance (I Got Ants in My Pants (Gaines-Williams) **340509-1**

I Got Rhythm (Gershwin-Gershwin) **370921-2**

I Hate To Leave You Now (Dick-Link-Waller) **321208-5, 321208-6**

I May Be Wrong (But I Think You're Wonderful) (Ruskin-Sullivan) **351012-4**

I Surrender, Dear (Clifford-Barris) **370303-1**

If Dreams Come True (Mills-Sampson-Goodman) **340115-2, 360219-11**

If It Ain't Love (Razaf-Redman-Waller) **340706-4**

Imagination (Burke-Van Heusen) **340509-2**

In a Little Spanish Town (Wayne-Lewis-Young) **370921-1**

In the Groove at the Grove (Webb) **390217-3**

It's Over Because We're Through (Bryant) **341119-1**

It's Swell of You (Gordon-Revel) **370324-3**

Jungle Mama (Jungle Blues) (Webb) **290627-1**

Keepin' Out of Mischief Now (Razaf-Waller) **360219-8**

King Porter Stomp (Morton) **360219-10**

Let's Get Together (Webb) **340115-3, 390504-1, 390504-10**

Liza (Gershwin-Gershwin-Kahn) **380503-7, 390109-12**

Lona (Bauza) **340910-3**

Lonesome Moments (Sampson-Webb) **340706-3**

Low Levee — High Water (Webb) **270825-1**

Midnite in a Madhouse (Midnite in Harlem) (Clinton) **371217-6, 371217-7**

Moonlight and Magnolias (DeRose-Gillespie) **351012-2**

My Honey's Lovin' Arms (Rudy-Meyer) **370325-1**

My Wild Irish Rose (Olcott) **390504-8**

Nit Wit Serenade (Hudson-Webb) **360219-9**

Old-Fashioned Love (Mack-Johnson) **340507-1**

On the Sunny Side of the Street (Fields-McHugh) **331220-1, 340910-2**

One O'Clock Jump (Basie) **390109-3, 390210-3**

Open 'Em Up, Chick! (Sampson) **370208-2**

Poor Little Rich Girl (Coward) **390504-2**

Rusty Hinge (LaFremiere-Brown) **370324-1**

Sendin' the Vipers (Mezzrow) **340507-3**

Soft and Sweet (Sampson) **310330-3**

Spinnin' the Webb (Webb-Fitzgerald) **380503-6**

(continued)

(continued from previous page)

Squeeze Me (Waller-Williams) **371101-4**

The Stars and Stripes Forever (Souza) **390504-6**

Stompin' at the Savoy (Razaf-Sampson-Webb) **340518-2, 360219-3**

Strictly Jive (Webb) **371027-3**

Sugarfoot Stomp (Melrose-Oliver) **390109-6**

Sweet Sue, Just You (Harris-Young) 371101-1, **371101-2**

Swing, Mr. Charlie, Swing (Sampson) **370208-3**

Tea for Two (Caesar-Youmans) **390109-1**

That Naughty Waltz (Levy-Stanley) **370324-8**

That Rhythm Man (Razaf-Waller-Brooks) **340910-1**

That's My Home (Armstrong) **321208-1, 321208-2**

35th and Calumet (O'Brien-Mezzrow) **340507-4**

True (Sampson) **340706-2**

Wanton Rhythm Man **370208-5**

What a Shuffle (Kirkpatrick) **341119-3**

Where Are You? (Adamson-McHugh) **370325-4**

Who Ya Hunchin' (Fitzgerald-Webb) **380818-3, 390109-11**

Why Should I Beg for Love? (Sampson) 340509-3, **340509-4, 340518-1**

You'll Wish You'd Never Been Born (Armstrong) **321208-7**

For the period, 1927 to 1934,
    41 studio recordings were made, of which
        21 were with vocal refrains, of which
            16 are are on compact disc,
            3 may be found on LP records, and
            2 are not yet released.
        20 were instrumentals, of which
            18 may be found on compact disc,
            3 may be found on LP records, and
            1 is not yet released.
For the period, 1935 to 1939
    51 studio recordings were made, of which
        31 were commerical releases, of which
            10 were with vocal refrains, of which
                6 may be found on compact disc,and
                4 may be found only on 78rpm records;
            21 were instrumentals, of which
                17 may be found on compact disc,

                3 may be found only on 78rpm records, and
                1 is not yet released
        20 were commercial transcriptions, not for sale, of which
            1 was with vocal refrain,
            19 were instrumentals, and all
                20 may be found on compact disc
        13 were radio transcriptions taken from broadcasts, of which all
            13 were instrumentals, of which
                6 may be found on compact disc, and
                7 may be found on LP records
To recapitulate, Chick Webb made (without Ella), 105 recordings, of which
    83 may be found on compact discs,
    11 may be found on LP records,
    7 may be found only on 78rpm recordings, and
    4 are not yet released.

ELLA FITZGERALD AND HER FAMOUS ORCHESTRA

    Ella Fitzgerald, Leader/Vocals; Trumpets: Taft Jordan, Bobby Stark, Dick Vance; Trombones: George Matthews, Nat Story, Sandy Williams; Clarinet: Garvin Bushell; Flute: Wayman Carver; Soprano Saxophone: Garvin Bushell; Alto Saxophones: Wayman Carver, Hilton Jefferson; Tenor Saxophones: Wayman Carver, Ted McRae; Baritone Saxophone: Ted McRae; Piano: Tommy Fulford; Guitar: John Trueheart; String Bass: Beverley Peer; Drums: Bill Beason. Recorded at Decca Recording Company, New York, Thursday, 29 June 1939

390629-1   65903-A Betcha Nickel(vEF) (78: Decca 2904A; LPD-2, LPD-12, LPD-122)

390629-2   65904-A Stairway to the Stars (vEF) (78: Deccaa 2598A; LPD-2, LPD-3, LPD-5, LPD-12, LPD-16, LPD-35, LPD-40)

390629-3   65905-A I Want the Waiter (with the Water) (vEF) (78: Decca 2628A; LPD-2, LPD-12)

Note: Charted 2 September 1939; weeks, 3; peak, #9

390629-4   65906-A That's All, Brother (vEF) (78: Decca 2628B; LPD-12)

390629-5   65907-A Out of Nowhere (vEF) (78: Decca 2598B; LPD-2, LPD-12)

ELLA FITZGERALD AND HER FAMOUS ORCHESTRA

Ella Fitzgerald, Leader/Vocals; Trumpets: Taft Jordan, Bobby Stark, Dick Vance; Trombones: George Matthews, Nat Story, Sandy Williams; Clarinet: Garvin Bushell; Flute: Wayman Carver; Soprano Saxophone: Garvin Bushell; Alto Saxophones: Wayman Carver, Hilton Jefferson; Tenor Saxophones: Wayman Carver, Ted McRae; Baritone Saxophone: Ted McRae; Piano: Tommy Fulford; Guitar: John Trueheart; String Bass: Beverley Peer; Drums: Bill Beason. WNEW-AM radio broadcast from Savoy Ballroom, New York, Sunday, 16 July 1939

390716-1   Betcha Nickel (vEF)
390716-2   That's All, Brother (vEF)

These selections are from a 15-minute sustaining broadcast, the remainder of which has never been released.

(Both selections on LPD-162)

ELLA FITZGERALD AND HER FAMOUS ORCHESTRA

Ella Fitzgerald, Leader/Vocals; Trumpets: Taft Jordan, Bobby Stark, Dick Vance; Trombones: George Matthews, Nat Story, Sandy Williams; Clarinet: Garvin Bushell; Flute: Wayman Carver; Soprano Saxophone: Garvin Bushell; Alto Saxophones: Wayman Carver, Hilton Jefferson; Tenor Saxophones: Wayman Carver, Ted McRae; Baritone Saxophone: Ted McRae; Piano: Tommy Fulford; Guitar: John Trueheart; String Bass: Beverley Peer; Drums: Bill Beason. WNEW-AM radop brpadcast from Savoy Ballroom, New York, Thursday, 20 July 1939

390720-1   The Lamp Is Low (vEF)
390720-2   Little White Lies (vEF)
390720-3   St. Louis blues (vEF)

These selections are from a 15-minute sustaining broadcast, the remainder of which has never been released. (These selections on LPD-162)

ELLA FITZGERALD AND HER FAMOUS ORCHESTRA

Ella Fitzgerald, Leader/Vocals; Trumpets: Taft Jordan, Bobby Stark, Dick Vance; Trombones: George Matthews, Nat Story, Sandy Williams; Clarinet: Garvin Bushell; Flute: Wayman Carver; Soprano Saxophone: Garvin Bushell; Alto Saxophones: Wayman Carver, Hilton Jefferson; Tenor Saxophones: Wayman Carver, Ted McRae; Baritone Saxophone: Ted McRae; Piano: Tommy Fulford; Guitar: John Trueheart; String Bass: Beverley Peer; Drums: Bill Beason. WNEW-AM radio broadcast from Savoy Ballroom, New York, Tuesday, 15 August 1939

390815-2   A-Tisket-A-Tasket (Opening Theme) (vEF)
390815-2   Please Tell Me the Truth (vEF)
390815-3   Stairway to the Stars (vEF)

These selections are from a 15-minute sustaining broadcast, the remainder of which has never been released.

(All selections on LPD-162)

ELLA FITZGERALD AND HER FAMOUS ORCHESTRA

Ella Fitzgerald, Leader/Vocals; Trumpets: Taft Jordan, Bobby Stark, Dick Vance; Trombones: George Matthews, Nat Story, Sandy Williams; Clarinet: Garvin Bushell; Flute: Wayman Carver; Soprano Saxophone: Garvin Bushell; Alto Saxophones: Wayman Carver, Hilton Jefferson; Tenor Saxophones: Wayman Carver, Ted McRae; Baritone Saxophone: Ted McRae; Piano: Tommy Fulford; Guitar: John Trueheart; String Bass: Beverley Peer; Drums: Bill Beason. Recorded at Decca Recording Company, New York, Friday, 18 August 1939

390818-1   66134-A   My Last Goodbye (vEF) (78: Decca 2721A; LPD-2, LPD-13)
390818-2   66135-A   (I Always Dream of) Billy (vEF) (78: Decca 2769A; LPD-2, LPD-13)
390818-3   66136-A   Please Tell Me the Truth (vEF) (78: Decca 2769B; LPD-13)
390818-4   66137-A   I'm Not Complainin' (vEF) (78: Decca 3005B; LPD-13)
390818-5   66138-A   Betcha Nickel (vEF) Rejected

ELLA FITZGERALD AND HER FAMOUS ORCHESTRA

Ella Fitzgerald, Leader/Vocals; Trumpets: Taft Jordan, Bobby Stark, Dick Vance; Trombones: George Matthews, Nat Story, Sandy Williams; Clarinet: Garvin Bushell; Flute: Wayman Carver; Soprano Saxophone: Garvin Bushell; Alto Saxophones: Wayman Carver, Hilton Jefferson; Tenor Saxophones: Wayman Carver, Ted McRae; Baritone Saxophone: Ted McRae; Piano: Tommy Fulford; Guitar: John Trueheart; String Bass: Beverley Peer; Drums: Bill Beason. WNEW-AM radio broadcast from Savoy Ballroom, New York, Thursday, 24 August 1939

390824-1   To You (vEF)
390824-2   (Hep! Hep!) The Jumpin' Jive (vEF)

These selections are from a 15-minute sustaining broadcast, the remainder of which has never been released.

(Both selections on LPD-162)

ELLA FITZGERALD AND HER FAMOUS ORCHESTRA

Ella Fitzgerald, Leader/Vocals; Trumpets: Taft Jordan, Bobby Stark, Dick Vance; Trombones: George Matthews, Nat Story, Sandy Williams; Clarinet: Garvin Bushell; Flute: Wayman Carver; Soprano Saxophone: Garvin Bushell; Alto Saxophones: Wayman Carver, Hilton Jefferson; Tenor Saxophones: Wayman Carver, Ted McRae; Baritone Saxophone: Ted McRae; Piano: Tommy Fulford; Guitar: John Trueheart; String Bass: Beverley Peer; Drums: Bill Beason. WNEW-AM radio broadcast from Savoy Ballroom, New York, Saturday, 26 August 1939

390826-1   Day In — Day Out (vEF)
390826-2   (I Always Dream of) Billy (vEF)

These selections are from a 15-minute sustaining broadcast, the remainder of which has never been released.

(Both selections on LPD-162)

ELLA FITZGERALD AND HER FAMOUS ORCHESTRA

Ella Fitzgerald, Leader/Vocals; Trumpets: Taft Jordan, Bobby Stark, Dick Vance; Trombones: George Matthews, Nat Story, Sandy Williams; Clarinet: Garvin Bushell; Flute: Wayman Carver; Soprano Saxophone:Garvin Bushell; Alto Saxophones: Wayman Carver, Hilton Jefferson; Tenor Saxophones: Wayman Carver, Ted McRae; Baritone Saxophone: Ted McRae; Piano: Tommy Fulford; Guitar: John Trueheart; String Bass: Beverley Peer; Drums: Bill Beason. Radio broadcast from Grand Terrace Ballroom, Chicago (Illinois), Thursday, 21 September 1939

390921-1   Oh Boy! I'm in the Groove (vEF)
390921-2   Baby, What Else Can I Do? (vEF)
390921-3   Well All Right (vEF)

These selections are from a broadcast, the remainder of which has never been released.

(These Selections on LPD-162)

ELLA FITZGERALD AND HER FAMOUS ORCHESTRA

Ella Fitzgerald, Leader/Vocals; Trumpets: Taft Jordan, Bobby Stark, Dick Vance; Trombones: George Matthews, Nat Story, Sandy Williams; Clarinet: Garvin Bushell; Flute: Wayman Carver; Soprano Saxophone:Garvin Bushell; Alto Saxophones: Wayman Carver, Hilton Jefferson; Tenor Saxophones: Wayman Carver, Ted McRae; Baritone Saxophone: Ted McRae; Piano: Tommy Fulford; Guitar: John Trueheart; String Bass: Beverley Peer; Drums: Bill Beason. Recorded at Decca Recording Company, New York, Thursday, 12 October 1939

391012-1   91836-A   You're Gonna Lose Your Gal (vEF) (78: Decca 2816B; LPD-2, LPD-13)
391012-2   91837-A   (What Can I Say) After I Say I'm Sorry (vEF) (78: Decca 2826B; LPD-2, LPD-13)
391012-3   91838-A   Baby, What Else Can I Do? (vEF) (78: Decca 2826A; LPD-13)
391012-4   91839-A   My Wubba Dolly (vEF) (78: Decca 2826A; LPD-13)

Note: Charted 28 October 1939; weeks, 1; peak, #16

391012-5   91840-A   Lindy Hopper's Delight (instr) (78: Decca 3186A; LPD-13)
391012-6   91841-A   Moon Ray (vEF) (78: Decca 2904B; LPD-2, LPD-13)

ELLA FITZGERALD AND HER FAMOUS ORCHESTRA

Ella Fitzgerald, Leader/Vocals; Trumpets: Taft Jordan, Bobby Stark, Dick Vance; Trombones: George Matthews, Nat Story, Sandy Williams; Clarinet: Garvin Bushell; Flute: Wayman Carver; Soprano Saxophone: Garvin Bushell; Alto Saxophones: Wayman Carver, Hilton Jefferson; Tenor Saxophones: Wayman Carver, Ted McRae; Baritone Saxophone: Ted McRae; Piano: Tommy Fulford; Guitar: John Trueheart; String Bass: Beverley Peer; Drums: Bill Beason. WNEW-AM radio broadcast from Savoy Ballroom, New York, Thursday, 14 December 1939

391214-1   My Wubby Dolly (vEF)
391214-2   My Prayer (vEF)

This is part of a 15-minute sustaining broadcast, the remainder of which has never been released.

(Both selections on LPD-162)

ELLA FITZGERALD AND HER FAMOUS ORCHESTRA

Ella Fitzgerald, Leader/Vocals; Trumpets: Taft Jordan, Bobby Stark, Dick Vance; Trombones: George Matthews, Nat Story, Sandy Williams; Clarinet, Garvin Bushell; Flute: Wayman Carver; Soprano Saxophone: Garvin Bushell; Alto Saxophones: Wayman Carver, Hilton Jefferson; Tenor Saxophones: Wayman Carver, Ted McRaie; Baritone Saxophone: Ted McRae; Piano: Tommy Fulford; Guitar: John Trueheart; String Bass: Beverley Peer; Drums: Bill Beason; Vocals: Taft Jordan. WNEW-AM radio broadcast from Savoy Ballroom, New York, Monday, 22 January 1940

400122-1   A-Tisket-A-Tasket (signature theme) (vEF)
400122-2   Traffic Jam (instr)
400122-3   A Lover Is Blue (vEF)
400122-4   Dodging the Dean (instr)
400122-5   'Tain't What You Do (It's the Way That 'Cha Do It) (vEF)
400122-6   I'm Confessin' (vJT)
400122-7   Blue Lou (instr)
400122-8   What's the Matter with Me? (vEF)
400122-9   I Want the Waiter (with the Water) (vEF)
400122-10   Let's Get Together (closing theme)

(All selections on LPD-151)

ELLA FITZGERALD AND HER FAMOUS ORCHESTRA

Ella Fitzgerald, Leader/Vocals; Trumpets: Taft Jordan, Bobby Stark, Dick Vance; Trombones: George Matthews, Nat Story, Sandy Williams; Clarinets, Garvin Bushell; Flute: Wayman Carver; Soprano Saxophone: Garvin Bushell; Alto Saxophones: Wayman Carver, Hilton Jefferson; Tenor Saxophones: Wayman Carver, Ted McRae; Baritone Saxophone: Ted McRae; Piano: Tommy Fulford; Guitar: John Trueheart; String Bass: Beverley Peer; Drums: Bill Beason. WNEW-AM radio broacast from SavoyBallroom, New York, Thursday, 25 January 1940

400125-1 A-Tisket, A-Tasket (signature theme) (vEF)
400125-2 Limehouse Blues (instr)
400125-3 This Changing World (vEF)
400125-4 Oh! Johnny! Oh! Johnny! Oh! (vEF)
400125-5 Diga Diga Doo (instr)
400125-6 Thank Your Stars (vEF)
400125-7 Take It from the Top (instr)
400125-8 Vagabond Dreams (vEF)
400125-9 Breakin' 'Em Down (instr)
400125-10 Let's Get Together (closing theme) (instr)

(All selections on LPD-151)

ELLA FITZGERALD AND HER FAMOUS ORCHESTRA

Ella Fitzgerald, Leader/Vocals; Trumpets: Taft Jordan, Bobby Stark, Dick Vance; Trombones: George Matthews, Nat Story, Sandy Williams; Clarinet, Garvin Bushell; Flute: Wayman Carver; Soprano Saxophone: Garvin Bushell; Alto Saxophones: Wayman Carver, Hilton Jefferson; Tenor Saxophones: Wayman Carver, Ted McRae; Baritone Saxophone: Ted McRae; Piano: Tommy Fulford; Guitar: John Trueheart; String Bass: Beverley Peer; Drums: Bill Beason. Recorded at Decca Recording Company, New York, Friday, 26 January 1940

400126-1 67119-A Is There Somebody Else? (vEF) (78: Decca 2988B; LPD-13)

400126-2 67120-A Sugar Blues (vEF) (78: Decca 3078A; LPD-2, LPD-13)

Note: Charted 1 June 1940; weeks, 1; peak, #27

400126-3 67121-A The Starlit Hour (vEF) (78: Decca 2988A; LPD-2, LPD-13)

Note: Charted 20 April 1940; weeks, 3; peak, #17

400126-4 67122-A What's the Matter with Me? (vEF) (78: Decca 3005A; LPD-2, LPD-13)

ELLA FITZGERALD AND HER FAMOUS ORCHESTRA

Ella Fitzgerald, Leader/Vocals; Trumpets: Taft Jordan, Irving Randolph, Dick Vance; Trombones:John Haughton, George Matthews, Sandy Williams; Clarinets-Alto Saxophones: Chauncey Haughton, Eddie Barefield; Tenor Saxophones: Ted McRae, Sam Simmons; Baritone Saxophone: Ted McRae; Piano:Roger Ramirez; Guitar: John Trueheart; String Bass: Beverley Peer; Drums: Bill Beason. Recorded at Decca Recording Company, New York, Thursday, 15 February 1940

400215-1 67195-A Baby, Won't You Please Come Home? (vEF) (78: Decca 3186B; LPD-2, LPD-13, LPD-15)

400215-2 67196-A If It Weren't for You (vEF) (78: Decca 3026A; LPD-2, LPD-13)

400215-3 67197-A Sing Song Swing (vEF) (78: Decca 3026B; LPD-13)

Note: charted 27 April 1940; weeks, 2; peak, #23

400215-4 67198-A Imagination (vEF) (78: Decca 3078B; LPD-2, LPD-13)

Note: Charted 18 May 1940; weeks, 3; peak, #15

ELLA FITZGERALD WITH THE CHICK WEBB ORCHESTRA

Ella Fitzgerald, Leader/Vocals; Trumpets: Taft Jordan, Irving Randolph, Dick Vance; Trombones: John Haughton, George Matthews, Sandy Williams; Clarinets-Alto Saxophones: Chauncey Haughton, Eddie Barefield; Tenor Saxophones: Ted McRae, Sam Simmons; Baritone Saxophone: Ted McRae; Piano: Roger Ramirez; Guitar: John Trueheart; String Bass: Beverley Peer; Drums: Bill Beason. WNEW-AM radio broadcast from Roseland Ballroom, New York, 26 February 1940

400226-1 A-Tisket, A-Tasket (vEF)
400226-2 Royal Garden Blues (instr)
400226-3 Sing Song Swing (vEF)
400226-4 Sugar Blues (vEF)
400226-5 Make Believe (instr)
400226-6 Sweet Sue, Just You (instr)
400226-7 It's a Blue World (vEF)
400226-8 Is There Somebody Else? (vEF)
400226-9 One Moment, Please (instr)
400226-10 I Wanna Be a Rug-Cutter (instr)

(All selections on LPD-151)

ELLA FITZGERALD WITH THE CHICK WEBB ORCHESTRA

Ella Fitzgerald, Leader/Vocals; Trumpets: Taft Jordan, Irving Randolph, Dick Vance; Trombones: John Haughton, George Matthews, Sandy Williams; Clarinets-Alto Saxophones: Chauncey Haughton, Eddie Barefield; Tenor Saxophones: Ted McRae, Sam Simmons; Baritone Saxophone: Ted McRae; Piano: Roger Ramirez; Guitar: John Trueheart; String Bass: Beverley Peer; Drums: Bill Beason. WNEW-AM radio broadcast from Roseland Ballroom, New York, 4 March 1940

400304-1 A-Tisket, A-Tasket (signature theme) (vEF)
400304-2 I Got Rhythm (instr)
400304-3 One Cigarette for Two (vEF)
400304-4 Chewin' Gum (vEF)
400304-5 Lover, Come Back to Me (instr)
400304-6 Who Ya Hunchin'? (instr)
400304-7 The Starlit Hour (vEF)
400304-8 Sing Song Swing (vEF)
400304-9 Goin' and Gettin' It (instr)
400304-10 Let's Get Together (closing theme) (instr)

(All selections on LPD-151)

ELLA FITZGERALD AND HER FAMOUS ORCHESTRA

Ella Fitzgerald, Leader/Vocals; Trumpets: Taft Jordan, Irving Randolph, Dick Vance; Trombones: John Haughton, George Matthews, Sandy Williams; Clarinets-Alto Saxophones: Chauncey Haughton, Eddie Barefield; Tenor Saxophones: Ted McRae, Sam Simmons; Baritone Saxophone: Ted McRae; Piano: Roger Ramirez; Guitar: John Trueheart; String Bass: Beverley Peer; Drums: Bill Beason. WNEW-AM radio broadcast from Roseland Ballroom, New York, early 1940

400000-1		Sing Song Swing (vEF)
400000-2		The Starlit Hour (vEF)
400000-3		The Yodelin' Jive (vEF)
400000-4		Careless

These selections are from one or more radio broadcasts more details of which are not available.

(All selections on LPD-162)

ELLA FITZGERALD AND HER FAMOUS ORCHESTRA

Ella Fitzgerald, Leader/Vocals; Trumpets: Taft Jordan, Irving Randolph, Dick Vance; Trombones: John Haughton, George Matthews, Sandy Williams; Clarinets-Alto Saxophones: Chauncey Haughton, Eddie Barefield; Tenor Saxophones: Ted McRae, Sam Simmons; Baritone Saxophone: Ted McRae; Piano: Tommy Fulford; Guitar: John Trueheart; String Bass: Beverley Peer; Drums: Bill Beason. Recorded at Decca Recording Company, New York, Wednesday, 20 March 1940

400320-1 67358-A Take It from the Top (instr) (78: Decca 3236B; LPD-13)

400320-2 67359-A Tea Dance (instr) (78: Decca 3441B; LPD-13)

400320-3 67360-A Jubilee Swing (instr) (78: Decca 3236A; LPD-13)

400320-4 67361-A (untitled) (instr) (LPD-13)

ELLA FITZGERALD AND HER FAMOUS ORCHESTRA

Ella Fitzgerald, Leader/Vocals; Trumpets: Taft Jordan, Irving Randolph, Dick Vance; Trombones: John Haughton, George Matthews, Sandy Williams; Clarinets-Alto Saxophones: Chauncey Haughton, Eddie Barefield; Tenor Saxophones: Ted McRae, Sam Simmons; Baritone Saxophone: Ted McRae; Piano: Tommy Fulford; Guitar: John Trueheart; String Bass: Beverley Peer; Drums: Bill Beason. Recorded at Decca Recording Company, New York, Thursday, 9 May 1940

400509-1 67699-A Deedle-De-Dum (vEF) (78: Decca 3324B; LPD-2, LPD-13)

400509-2 67700-A Shake Down the Stars (vEF) (78: Decca 3199A; LPD-2, LPD-14)

Note: Charted 6 July 1940; weeks, 2; peak, #18

400509-3 67701-A Gulf Coast Blues (vEF) (78: Decca 3324A; LPD-2, LPD-14)

400509-4 67706-A I Fell in Love with a Dream (vEF) (78: Decca 3199B; LPD-14)

ELLA FITZGERALD AND HER FAMOUS ORCHESTRA

Ella Fitzgerald, Leader/Vocals; Trumpets: Taft Jordan, Irving Randolph, Dick Vance; Trombones: Earl Hardy, George Matthews, John McConnell; Clarinets-Alto Saxophones: Pete Clark, Chauncey Haughton; Tenor Saxophones: Ted McRae, Sam Simmons; Baritone Saxophone: Ted McRae; Piano: Tommy Fulford; Guitar: Ulysses Livingston; String Bass: Beverley Peer; Drums: Bill Beason. Recorded at Decca Recording Company, New York, Wednesday, 25 September 1940

400925-1 68146-A The Five O'Clock Whistle (vEF) (78: Decca 3420B; LPD-2, LPD-3, LPD-5, LPD-14, LPD-16)

400925-2 68147-A So Long (vEF) (78: Decca 3420A; LPD-14, LPD-26)

400925-3 68148-A Louisville, K-Y (vEF) (78: Decca 3441A; LPD-2, LPD-14)

400925-4 68148-B Louisville, K-Y *Not yet released*

ELLA FITZGERALD AND HER FAMOUS ORCHESTRA

Ella Fitzgerald, Leader/Vocals; Trumpets: Taft Jordan, Irving Randolph, Dick Vance; Trombones: Earl Hardy, George Matthews, John McConnell; Clarinets-Alto Saxophones: Pete Clark, George Dorsey; Tenor Saxophones: Ted McRae, Sam Simmons; Baritone Saxophone: Ted McRae; Piano: Tommy Fulford; Guitar: Ulysses Livingston; String Bass: Beverley Peer; Drums: Bill Beason. Recorded at Decca Recording Company, New York, Friday, 8 November 1940

401108-1 68329-A Taking a Chance on Love (vEF) (78: Decca 3490B; LPD-2, LPD-14)

401108-2 68330-A Cabin in the Sky (vEF) (78 Decca 3490A; LPD-2, LPD-14, LPD-15)

401108-3 68331-A I'm the Lonesomest Gal in Town (vEF) (78 Decca 3666A; LPD-2, LPD-14, LPD-15)

ELLA FITZGERALD AND HER FAMOUS ORCHESTRA

Ella Fitzgerald, Leader/Vocals; Trumpets: Taft Jordan, Irving Randolph, Dick Vance; Trombones: Earl Hardy, George Matthews, John McConnell; Clarinets-Alto Saxophones: Pete Clark, George Dorsey; Tenor Saxophones: Ted McRae, Sam Simmons; Baritone Saxophone: Ted McRae; Piano: Tommy Fulford; Guitar: Ulysses Livingston; String Bass: Beverley Peer; Drums: Bill Beason. Recorded at Decca Recording Company, New York, Wednesday, 8 January 1941

410108-1 68558-A Three Little Words (vEF) (78 Decca 3608B; LPD-2, LPD-14)

410108-2   68559-A   Hello, Ma! I Done It Again (vEF) (78: Decca 3612B; LPD-14)

Note: Charted 15 March 1941; weeks, 1; peak, #26

410108-3   68560-A   Wishful Thinking (vEF) (78: Decca 3612A; LPD-14)

410108-4   68561-A   The One I Love (Belongs to Somebody Else) (vEF) (78: Decca 3608A; LPD-2, LPD-14, LPD-15)

410108-5   68562-A   The Muffin Man (vEF) (78: Decca 3666B; LPD-2, LPD-14)

Note: Charted 2 August 1941; weeks, 1; peak, #23

ELLA FITZGERALD AND HER FAMOUS ORCHESTRA

Ella Fitzgerald, Leader/Vocals; Trumpets: Taft Jordan, Irving Randolph, Dick Vance; Trombones: George Matthews, John McConnell, Earl Murphy; Clarinets-Alto Saxophones: Pete Clark, Chauncey Haughton; Tenor Saxophones: Ted McRae, Lonnie Simmons; Piano: Tommy Fulford; Guitar: Ulysses Livingston; String Bass: Beverley Peer; Drums: Bill Beason. Recorded at Decca Recording Company, New York, Monday, 31 March 1941

410331-1   68894-A   Keep Cool, Fool (vEF) (78: Decca 3754A; LPD-2, LPD-14)

410331-2   68895-A   No Nothing (vEF) (78: Decca 3754B; LPD-2, LPD-14)

410331-3   68896-A   My Man (Mon Homme) (vEF) (78: Decca 4291A; LPD-2, LPD-14)

ELLA FITZGERALD AND HER FAMOUS ORCHESTRA

Ella Fitzgerald, Leader/Vocals; Trumpets: Taft Jordan, Irving Randolph, Dick Vance; Trombones: George Matthews, John McConnell, Earl Murphy; Clarinets-Alto Saxophones: Pete Clark, Chauncey Haughton; Tenor Saxophones: Ted McRae, Lonnie Simmons, Elmer Williams; Piano: Tommy Fulford; Guitar: Ulysses Livingston; String Bass: Beverley Peer; Drums: Jesse Price. Recorded at Decca Recording Company, Los Angeles, Thursday, 31 July 1941

410731-1   DLA2607-A   I Can't Believe That You're in Love with Me (vEF) (78: Decca 18421; LPD-2, LPD-14, LPD-15)

410731-2   DLA2608-A   I Must Have That Man (vEF) (78: Decca 18530; LPD-2, LPD-14, LPD-15)

410731-3   DLA2609-A   When My Sugar Walks Down the Street (vEF) (78 Decca 18587; LPD-2, LPD-14)

Note: Charted 11 March 1944; weeks, 1; peak, #27

410731-4   DLA2610-A   I Got It Bad (and That Ain't Good) (vEF) (78: Decca 3968A; LPD-2, LPD-14, LPD-15, LPD-35)

410731-5   DLA2611-A   Melinda, the Mousie (vEF) (78: Decca 3968B; LPD-14)

410731-6   DLA2612-A   Can't Help Lovin' Dat Man (vEF) (78: Decca 18421; LPD-2, LPD-14, LPD-15)

*Note: This was the final recording session of "Ella Fitzgerald and Her Famous Orchestra," and thus ends Miss Fitzgerald's career as a band singer. From this point on in this discography, "(vEF)" following the title of the recording is omitted, since each recording listed hereinafter with a DRN is a vocal by Miss Fitzgerald, and, as such, is part of her **oeuvre**. There are entries without Miss Fitzgerald's vocals (and not assigned DRNs); these are given because they were a part of her recording session or a recorded concert in which she participated, and, therefore, may be of interest to the reader.*

ELLA FITZGERALD, vocals

Accompanied by Tenor Saxophone: Ted McRae; Piano: Tommy Fulford; Guitar: Ulysses Livingston; String Bass: Beverley Peer; Drums: Kenny Clarke. Recorded at Decca Recording Company, New York, Monday, 6 October 1941

411006-1   69784-A   Jim (78: Decca 4007A; LPD-4, LPD-17, LPD-124)

411006-2   69785-A   This Love of Mine (78: Decca 4007B; LPD-4, LPD-17, LPD-124)

ELLA FITZGERALD, vocals

Accompanied by Alto Saxophone: Eddie Barefield; Piano: Tommy Fulford; Guitar: Ulysses Livingston; String Bass: Beverley Peer; Drums: Bill Beason. Recorded at Decca Recording Company, New York, Tuesday, 28 October 1941

411028-1   69875-A   Somebody Nobody Loves (78: Decca 4082B; LPD-4, LPD-17, LPD-124)

411028-2   69876-A   You Don't Know What Love Is (78: Decca 4082A; LPD-4, LPD-16, LPD-17, LPD-32)

ELLA FITZGERALD, vocals

Accompanied by Alto Saxophone: Eddie Barefield; Piano: Tommy Fulford; Guitar: Ulysses Livingston; String Bass: Beverley Peer; Drums: Bill Beason. Recorded at Decca Recording Company, New York, Wednesday, 5 November 1941

411105-1   69905-A   Who Are You? (78: Decca 4291B; LPD-17, LPD-124)

411105-2   69906-A   I'm Thrilled (78: Decca 4073A; LPD-17)

411105-3   69907-A   Make Love to Me (78: Decca 4073B; LPD-4, LPD-17, LPD-124)

ELLA FITZGERALD, vocals

Accompanied by **The Four Keys** (Piano-vocals: Bill Furness; Guitar-vocals: Slim Furness; Bass-vocals: Peck Furness; Drums-vocals: Ernie Hatfield). Recorded at Decca Recording Company, New York, Wednesday, 11 March 1942

420311-1   70470-A   I'm Getting Mighty Lonesome for You (78: Decca 4315A; LPD-17)

420311-2   70471-A   When I Come Back Crying (Will You Be Laughing at Me?) (78: Decca 4315B; LPD-17)

ELLA FITZGERALD, vocals

Accompanied by The Four Keys (Piano-vocals: Bill Furness; Guitar-vocals: Slim Furness; Bass-vocals: Peck Furness; Drums-vocals: Ernie Hatfield) and Piano: Tommy Fulford*. Recorded at Decca Recording Company, New York, Friday, 10 April 1942

420410-1   70652-A   All I Need Is You (78: Decca 18347; LPD-17)

420410-2   70653-A   Mama, Come Home (78: Decca 18347; LPD-4, LPD-17, LPD-123)

ELLA FITZGERALD, vocals

Accompanied by **The Four Keys** (Piano-vocals: Bill Furness; Guitar-vocals: Slim Furness; Bass-vocals: Peck Furness; Drums-vocals: Ernie Hatfield) and Piano: Tommy Fulford#. Recorded at Decca Recording Company, New York, Friday, 31 July 1942

420731-1   71286-A   My Heart and I Decided (78: Decca 18530; LPD-4, LPD-17)

420731-2   71287-A   (I Put) A Four-Leaf Clover in Your Pocket (78: Decca 18472; LPD-17, LPD-123)

420731-3   71288-A   He's My Guy (78: Decca 18472; LPD-4, LPD-17, LPD-124)

Note: Tommy Fulford is listed as pianist for the above two sessions. It is likely that he replaced Bill Furness, since the recordings do not feature two pianos.

☌

The American Federation of Musicians (AFM), by far the largest organization of union musicians in the United States, reached a peak in its membership with 146,326 members in 1929, a figure not reached again until 1944. The economic depression of the era resulted in reduced employment opportunities for musicians, as it did for almost every other occupational group. Even more serious in the long term was the challenge produced by technological changes in the industry. The introduction of sound movies eliminated thousands of jobs musicians had held in movie theaters. Recorded, or "canned," music was an even greater threat. Relations with the film industry were largely resolved by intricate contract negotiations, but the issue of musical records was a much more serious problem. After several attempts to resolve the issue, the AFM finally issued a directive under which, after midnight, 31 July 1942, union members were prohibited from making records, transcriptions, or any other type of mechanically reproduced music, unless the companies concerned could guarantee that they wouldn't be played in juke boxes or over the radio. Since the courts ruled that the companies have no control over their products after they have been sold, the order meant, in effect, that no new recordings at all could be made. After a twenty-seven-month dispute, the strike was lifted, effective 1 November 1944, when the AFM won a royalty on each record union musicians made. The royalty was placed in a trust fund to provide relief for unemployed musicians, and to provide employment of musicians in live performances to offset any loss of employment stemming from the burgeoning sales of phonograph records and other forms of recorded performances. However, Decca Recording Company, in September 1943, reached an agreement with the AFM, although recording was still restricted, pending a complete settlement.

☌

ELLA FITZGERALD–THE INK SPOTS, vocals

Accompanied by Trumpet: John McGhee; Piano: Bill Doggett; Guitar: Bernie Mackay; Bass: Bob Haggartt; Drums: Johnny Blowers. (**The Ink Spots**: Bill Kenny, counter tenor; Ivory "Deke" Watson, tenor; Charles Fuqua, baritone; Orville "Hoppy" Jones, bass and talking chorus.) Recorded at Decca Recording Company, New York, Wednesday, 3 November 1943

431103-1   71482-A   Cow-Cow Boogie (78: Decca 18587/LPD-3, LPD-4, LPD-5, LPD-17, LPD-32. LPD-35, LPD-122)

Note: Charted 11 March 1944; weeks, 8; peak, #10

ELLA FITZGERALD, vocals

Accompanied by Trumpet: John McGhee; Piano: Bill Doggett; Guitar: Bernie Mackay; Bass: Bob Haggart; Drums: Johnny Blowers. Recorded at Decca Recording Company, Chicago, Tuesday, 21 March 1944

440321-1   C25135   Time Alone Will Tell (78: Decca 18605; LPD-4, LPD-17)

440321-2   CC25136   Once Too Often (78: Decca 18605; LPD-4, LPD-17)

Note: Charted 8 July 1944; weeks, 2; peak, #24

ELLA FITZGERALD, and members of the Cootie Williams orchestra, vocals. Accompanied by Cootie Williams and His Orchestra Cootie Williams, Leader

Trumpets: Ermit V. Perry-Tommy Stevenson-George Treadwell-Lamar Wright; Trombones: Ed Burke-Ed Glover-Bob Horton; Soprano Saxophone: Eddie Vinson; Alto Saxophones: Rupert Cole-Frank Powell; Tenor Saxophones: Lee Pope-Sam Taylor; Baritone Saxophone: Ed de Verteuil; Piano: Bud Powell; Guitar: Leroy Kirkland; Bass: Carl Pruitt; Drums: Sylvester Payne. Recorded at NBC Studio, Hollywood, California, 1 May 1944

440501-1   D6TC5173   A-Tisket, A-Tasket (78: AFRS Jubilee 78; V-Disc 661-B; LPD-161)

440410-2   Do Nothing Till You Hear from Me* (LP: BIAC-BRAD 10540)

*This track was never released on V-Disc. Reputedly, pianist Bud Powell replaced Bill Doggett on this track.

THE INK SPOTS-ELLA FITZGERALD, vocals

Accompanied by Piano: Bill Doggett; Guitar: Bernie Mackay; Bass: Bob Haggart (**The Ink Spots**: Bill Kenny, counter tenor; Ivory "Deke" Watson, tenor; Charles Fuqua, baritone; Orville "Hoppy" Jones, bass and talking chorus.) Recorded at Decca Recording Company, New York, Wednesday, 30 August 1944

440830-1   72370-A   Into Each Life Some Rain Must Fall (78: Decca 23356; LPD-3, LPD-4, LPD-5, LPD-17. LPD-40, LPD-122, LPD-123)

Note: Charted 11 November 1944; weeks, 17; peak, #1 (2 weeks)

440830-2   72371-A   I'm Making Believe (78 Decca 23356; LPD-4, LPD-5, LPD-17)

Note: Charted 4 November 1944; weeks, 17; peak, #1 (2 weeks)

ELLA FITZGERALD, vocals. Accompanied by **Claude Hopkins and His Orchestra** Claude Hopkins, Leader (personnel unknown)

Recorded at NBC Studios, New York, October 1944

441000-1   Is You Is or Is You Ain't My Baby (78: AFRS Jubilee 100; LPD-161)
441000-2   St. Louis Blues (78: AFRS Jubilee 100; LPD-161)

(Both selections are AFRS Jubilee Transcriptions, never commercially released.)

ELLA FITZGERALD, vocals. Accompanied by **Johnny Long and His Orchestra** Johnny Long, Leader

Trumpets: 1—2; Trombone: 1; Alto Saxophones: 1—2; Tenor Saxophone: 1; Piano: 1; Guitar: 1; String Bass: 1; Drums: 1; Vocals: **The Song Spinners**; Arr: Johnny Long. Recorded at Decca Recording Company, New York, Monday, 6 November 1944

441106-1   72483-A   And Her Tears Flowed Like Wine (78 Decca 18633; LPD-4, LPD-17, LPD-123)

Note: Charted 6 January 1945; weeks, 5; peak, #10

441106-2   72484-A   I'm Confessin' (78: Decca 18633; LPD-4, LPD-17, LPD-23)

ELLA FITZGERALD, vocals.

Accompanied by Claude Hopkins and His Orchestra Claude Hopkins, Leader. Personnel unknown. Recorded at WNEW-AM radio broadcast from Café Zanzibar, New York City, for the "Let's Go Nightclubbing" program, Wednesday, 28 February 1945

450228-1   A-Tisket, A-Tasket (LPD-161)

THE INK SPOTS-ELLA FITZGERALD, vocals

Accompanied by Piano: Bill Doggett; Guitar; Bernie Mackay; Bass: Bob Haggart (**The Ink Spots**: Bill Kenny,

countertenor; Ivory "Deke" Watson, tenor; Charles Fuqua, baritone; Herb Kenny, bass and talking chorus). Recorded at Decca Recording Company, New York, Monday, 26 February 1945

450226-1   72746-A   I'm Beginning To See the Light (78: Decca 23399; LPD-4, LPD-5, LPD-18, LPD-123)

Note: Charted 28 April 1945; weeks, 6; peak, #5

450226-2   72747-A   That's the Way It Is (78: Decca 23399; LPD-4, LPD-18, LPD-22, LPD-24)

ELLA FITZGERALD–THE DELTA RHYTHM BOYS, vocals

Accompanied by Piano: René Knight; Guitar: Hy White; Bass: Haig Stephens; Drums: George Wettling. (**The Delta Rhythm Boys**: Carl Jones, first tenor; Traverse Crawford, second tenor; Kelsey Pharr, baritone; Otho Gaines, bass). Recorded at Decca Recording Company, New York, Tuesday 27 March 1945

450327-1   72798-A   (It's Only a) Paper Moon (78: Decca 23425; LPD-3, LPD-5, LPD-18, LPD-22, LPD-40, LPD-122, LPD-123)

Note: Charted 25 August 1945; weeks, 3; peak, #9

450327-2   72798-B   (It's Only a) Paper Moon (LPD-4)
450327-3   72799 (I'm Gonna Hurry You Out of My Mind and) Cry You Out of My Heart. *Not yet released*

ELLA FITZGERALD-THE DELTA RHYTHM BOYS, vocals

Accompanied by Piano: René Knight; Guitar: Hy White; Bass: Haig Stephens; Drums: George Wettling (**The Delta Rhythm Boys**: Carl Jones, first tenor; Traverse Crawford, second tenor; Kelsey Pharr, baritone; Otho Gaines, bass). Recorded at Decca Recording Company, New York, Wednesday, 28 March 1945

450328-1   72800-A   (I'm Gonna Hurry You Out of My Mind and) Cry You Out of My Heart (78: Decca 23425; LPD-4, LPD-5, LPD-18)

ELLA FITZGERALD, vocals

Accompanied by **Randy Brooks and His Orchestra** Randy Brooks, Leader; Trumpet; Trumpets: George Bardon-Ernie Englund; Trombone: Harry Brooks; Alto Saxophones: Paul Bardon-Eddie Caine; Tenor Saxophones: Stuart Anderson-John Lesko; Baritone Saxophone: Eddie Shomer; Piano: Shorty Allen; String Bass: Paul Lajoie; Drums: Sonny Mann; Arr: Randy Brooks. Recorded at Decca Recording Company, New York, Wednesday, 29 August 1945

450829-1   73020-A   A Kiss Goodnight (78: Decca 18713; LPD-4, LPD-18, LPD-32)

450829-2   73021-A   Benny's Coming Home on Saturday (78: Decca 18713; LPD-4, LPD-18)

ELLA FITZGERALD, vocals

Accompanied by **Vic Schoen and His Orchestra**Vic Schoen, Leader; Trumpets: Charles Genduso-Ralph Mussilo-Louis Ruggiero; Trombone: William Pritchard; Alto Saxophones: Sid Cooper-Bernie Kaufman; Tenor Saxophones: Harry Feldman-Sid Rubin; Piano: Moe Wechsler; Guitar: Hy White; Bass: Felix Giobbe; Drums: Irv Kluger; Arr: Vic Schoen. Recorded at Decca Recording Company, New York, Thursday, 4 October 1945

451004-1   73066-A   Flying Home (78: Decca 23956; LPD-3, LPD-5, LPD-18, LDP-36, LPD-37, LPD-40)
451004-2   73066-B   Flying Home (LPD-4)

ELLA FITZGERALD-LOUIS JORDAN, vocals

Accompanied by **Louis Jordan and His Tympany Five** Louis Jordan, Leader; Alto Saxophone. Trumpet: Aaron Izenhall; Tenor Saxophone: Josh Jackson; Piano: Bill Davis; Guitar: Carl Hogan; Bass: Jesse Simpkins; Drums: Eddie Byrd; Maraccas: Harry Dial; Claves: Vic Lourie; Arr: Louis Jordan. Recorded at Decca Recording Company, New York, Monday, 8 October 1945

451008-1   73073-A   Stone Cold Dead in de Market (78: Decca 23546; LPD-3, LPD-4, LPD-5, LPD-18, LPD-22, LPD-32, LPD-35)

Note: Charted 6 July 1946; weeks, 6; peak, #7

451008-2   73074-A   Petootie Pie (78: Decca 233546; LPD-4, LPD-5, LPD-18, LPD-121)

ELLA FITZGERALD AND HER V-DISC JUMPERS

Ella Fitzgerald, Leader; Vocals. Trumpet: Charlie Shavers; Trombone: Lou McGarity; Clarinet: Peanuts Hucko; Tenor Saxophone: Al Sears; Piano: Buddy Weed; Guitar: Remo Palmieri; Bass: Trigger Alpert; Drums: Buddy Rich. Recorded at Columbia Broadcasting System studio, New York, Friday, 12 October 1945

451012-1   1596   That's Rich (78: V-Disc 603; LPD-18, LPD-161)
451012-2   1599   I'll Always Be in Love with You (Arr Jack Mathias) (78: V-Disc 569A; LPD-18, LPD-161)
451012-3   1600   I'll See You in My Dreams. *Not yet released*
451012-4   1601   I'll See You in My Dreams (78: V-Disc 730A; LPD-18, LPD-161)

ELLA FITZGERALD-LOUIS JORDAN, vocals

Accompanied by **Louis Jordan and His Tympany Five**Louis Jordan, Leader; Alto Saxophone. Trumpet: Aaron Izenhall; Tenor Saxophone: Josh Jackson; Piano: Bill Davis;

Guitar: Carl Hogan; Bass: Jesse Simpkins; Drums: Eddie Byrd; Maraccas: Harry Dial; Claves: Vic Lourie. Recorded at Decca Recording Company, New York, Monday, 15 October 1945

451015-1   73081-A   Petootie Pie (LPD-18, LPD-124)

Note: By chance, Jack Kapp heard the 8 October recording of "Petootie Pie" in Milt Gabler's office before its release. He insisted that, since he could not understand a word of what was being sung, that the side be remade. Gabler complied at this session, but, listening to both, decided he preferred the original recording, which he ordered be released in July 1946, unknown to Kapp. When the record became a hit, charting at #7 for six weeks, Kapp crowed, "See, ain't you glad you remade that record?"

LOUIS ARMSTRONG–ELLA FITZGERALD, vocals

Accompanied by **Bob Haggart and His Orchestra**Bob Haggart, Leader. Trumpets: Louis Armstrong-Billy Butterfield; Clarinet: Bill Stegmeyer; Alto Saxophones: George Koenig-Bill Stegmeyer; Tenor Saxophones: Art Drellinger-Jack Greenberg; Baritone Saxophone: Milton Chatz; Piano: Joe Bushkin; Guitar: Danny Perri; Bass: Trigger Alpert; Drums: Cozy Cole; Arr: Bob Haggart. Recorded at Decca Recording Company, New York, Friday 18 January 1946

460118-1   73285-A   You Won't Be Satisfied (78: Decca 18814; LPD-3, LPD-4, LPD-5, LPD-18, LPD-22)

Note: Charted 6 April 1946; weeks, 2; peak, #10

460118-2   73286-A   The Frim Fram Sauce (78: Decca 18814; LPD-4, LPD-5, LPD-18, LPD-22)

ELLA FITZGERALD, vocals

Accompanied by **Cootie Williams and His Orchestra** Cootie Williams, Leader. Trumpets: Bob Merrill-Ermit V. Perry-Clarence "Gene" Redd-George Treadwell; Trombones: Ed Burke-Bob Horton-Edward Johnson; Alto Saxophones: Rupert Cole-John Jackson; Tenor Saxophones: Everett Gaines-Sam Taylor; Baritone Saxophone: Bob Ashton; Piano: Arnold Jarvis; Guitar: Napoleon "Snags" Allen; Bass: Norman Keenan; Drums: Butch Ballard. Recorded at WNEW-AM broadcast from Café Zanzibar, New York City, for the "Let's Go Nightclubbing" program, Monday, 21 January 1946

460121-1   The Honeydripper (LPD-161)

ELLA FITZGERALD, vocals

Accompanied by Piano: Billy Kyle; Guitar: Jimmy Shirley; Bass: Junior Raglan; Drums: Sylvester Payne. Recorded at Decca Recording Company, New York, Thursday, 21 February 1946

460221-1   73388-A   I'm Just a Lucky So-and-So (78: Decca 18814; LPD-3, LPD-4, LPD-5, LPD-18, LPD-30, LPD-122)
460221-2   73389-A   I Didn't Mean a Word I Said (78: Decca 18814; LPD-3, LPD-4, LPD-5, LPD-18, LPD-30)

ELLA FITZGERALD-THE DELTA RHYTHM BOYS, vocals

Accompanied by Piano: René Knight; Guitar: Jimmy Shirley; Bass: Lamont Moten; Drums: Eddie Bourne (**The Delta Rhythm Boys**: Carl Jones, first tenor; Traverse Crawford, second tenor; Kelsey Pharr, baritone; Otho Gaines, bass). Recorded at Decca Recording Company, New York, Thursday, 29 August 1946

460829-1 73669-A (I Love You) For Sentimental Reasons (78: Decca 23670; LPD-4, LPD-5, LPD-18, LPD-23, LPD-24, LPD-40, LPD-122)

Note: Charted 7 December 1946; weeks, 14; peak, #8

460829-2 73670-A It's a Pity To Say Goodnight (78: Decca 23670; LPD-4, LPD-5, LPD-18, LPD-123)

ELLA FITZGERALD, vocals

Accompanied by **Eddie Heywood and His Orchestra** EddieHeywood, Leader; Piano. Trumpet; Leonard Graham; Trombone: Al King; Alto Saxophone: Jimmy Powell; Bass: Billy Taylor; Drums; William "Keg" Purnell. Recorded at Decca Recording Company, New York, Friday, 24 January 1947

470124-1 73786-A Guilty (78: Decca 23844; LPD-4, LPD-18, LPD-23, LPD-24, LPD-32, LPD-122)

Note: Charted 12 April 1947; weeks, 4; peak, #11

470124-2 73787-A Sentimental Journey (78: Decca 23844; LPD-4, LPD-18, LPD-22, LPD-32, LPD-122)

ELLA FITZGERALD, vocals

Accompanied by **Tommy Dorsey and His Orchestra** Tommy Dorsey, Leader; Trombone Trumpets: Irving Goodman-Johnny Martel-Andy Peretti-Charlie Shavers; Trombones: Larry Hall-Alex Mastren-Sol Train; Calinet: Abe Most; Alto Saxophones: Sid Cooper-Abe Most; Tenor Saxophones: Gail Curtis-Boomie Richman; Baritone Saxophone: Marty Berman; Piano: Johnny Potaker; Guitar: Carmen Mastren; Bass: Sid Bloch; Drums: Alvin Stoller. Recorded at and broadcast from station WOR Radio, New York, on the occasion of the celebration of the station's 25th anniversary, Saturday, 22 February 1947

470222-1 Guilty (LPD-161)

ELLA FITZGERALD-BUDDY RICH, vocals

Accompanied by Accordian: Joe Mooney; Piano: Nick Tagg; Drums: Sidney Catlett. Recorded in performance, "Saturday Night Swing Show," Radio WNEW, Studio 1, New York, 1 March 1947

470301-1 JD432 Budella (scat version of Irving Berlin's "Blue Skies") (78: V-Disc 775A; LPD-18, LPD-161)

ELLA FITZGERALD, vocals

Accompanied by **Bob Haggart and His Orchestra** Bob Haggart, Leader; Bass. Trumpets: Andy Ferretti-Chris Griffin-Bob Peck; Trombones: Will Bradley- Freddie Ohms-Jack Satterfield; Baritone Saxophone: Ernie Caceres; Piano: Stan Freeman; Guitar: Dan Perri; Drums: Morey Feld; Vocals: **The Andy Love Quintet**; Arr: Bob Haggart. Recorded at Decca Recording Company, New York, Wednesday, 19 March 1947

470319-1 73818-A A Sunday Kind of Love (78 Decca 23866; LPD-4, LPD-5, LPD-19, LPD-23, LPD-24, LPD-33, LPD-35)

470319-2 73819-A That's My Desire (78: Decca 23866; LPD-4, LPD-5, LPD-19, LPD-24, LPD-32, LPD-39)

470319-3 73820-A Oh! Lady, Be Good!* (78: Decca 23956; LPD-3,LPD-4,LPD-5,LPD-19,LPD-30,LPD-36,LPD-37,LPD-40)

*Note: The Andy Love Quintet does not sing on this track.

ELLA FITZGERALD, vocals

Accompanied by **Bob Haggart and His Orchestra** Bob Haggart, Leader; Bass. Trumpet: Andy Ferretti; Trombones: Will Bradley-Freddie Ohms-Billy Rauch- Seymour Shaffer; Clarinet: Art Drellinger; Alto Saxophone: Toots Mondello; Tenor Saxophone: Hymie Schertzer; Piano: Stan Freeman; Guitar: Dan Perri; Drums: Norris Shawker; Arr: Bob Haggart. Recorded at Decca Recording Company, New York, Friday, 11 July 1947

470711-1 74000-A You're Breakin' in a New Heart. *Not yet released*

ELLA FITZGERALD, vocals

Accompanied by **Bob Haggart and His Orchestra** Bob Haggart, Leader; Bass. Trumpet: Andy Ferretti; Trombones: Will Bradley-Freddie Ohms-Billy Rauch- Seymour Shaffer; Clarinet: Art Drellinger; Alto Saxophone: Toots Mondello; Tenor Saxophone: Hymie Schertzer; Piano: Stan Freeman; Guitar: Dan Perri; Drums: Norris Shawker; Arr: Bob Haggart. Recorded at Decca Recording Company, New York, Tuesday, 22 July 1947

470722-1 74013-A Don't You Think I Ought To Know? (78: Decca 24157; LPD-4, LPD-19, LPD-23)

470722-2 74014-A You're Breakin' in a New Heart (78: Decca 24157; LPD-4, LPD-19)

ELLA FITZGERALD, vocals

Accompanied by **Cootie Williams and His Orchestra** Cootie Williams, Leader. Trumpets: Otis Gamble-Bob Merrill-Ermit V. Perry-Clarence "Gene" Redd; Trombones: Ed Burke-Edward Johnson-Julius Watson; Alto Saxophones: Rupert Cole-Daniel Williams; Tenor Saxophones: Chuck Clark-Eddie Johnson; Bariton Saxophone: Bob Ashton; Piano: Ray Tunia; Guitar: Pee Wee Tinney; Bass: Norman Keenan; Drums: Butch Ballard. Recorded in performance at the

Howard Theatre, Washington, D.C., Wednesday, 6 August 1947

470806-1   Across the Alley from the Alamo (LPD-161)
470806-2   Oh! Lady, Be Good! (LPD-161)

DIZZY GILLESPIE AND HIS ORCHESTRA,
with Ella Fitzgerald Dizzy Gillespie, Leader; Trumpet

Jazz At The Philharmonic

Trumpets: Dave Burns-Ray Orr-Matthew McKay-Elmon Wright; Trombones: Taswell Baird; Bill Shepherd; Alto Saxophones: John Brown-Howard Johnson; Tenor Saxophones: Joe Gayles-James Moody (or George Nicholas); Baritone Saxophone: Cecil Payne; Vibraphone: Milt Jackson; Piano: John Lewis; Bass: Al McKibbon; Drums: Joe Harris. Recorded in performance at Carnegie Hall, New York, Monday, 29 September 1947.

470929-1   (It's) Almost Like Being in Love
470929-2   Stairway to the Stars
470929-3   Lover Man

ELLA FITZGERALD, vocals, accompanied by Piano: John Lewis; Bass: Al McKibbon; Drums: Joe Harris

470929-4   Flying Home
470929-5   Oh! Lady, Be Good!
470929-6   How High the Moon*

*with Trio and Dizzy Gillespie, trumpet.

(All selections on LPD-50, LPD-161)

Note: This was Ella Fitzgerald's Carnegie Hall debut.

ELLA FITZGERALD, vocals

Accompanied by **The Day Dreamers.** Recorded at Decca Recording Company, New York, Thursday, 18 December 1947.

471218-1   74300-A I Want to Learn About Love (78: Decca 24581; LPD-4, LPD-19)
471218-2   74301-A That Old Feeling (78 Decca 28049; LPD-4, LPD-19, LPD-23, LPD-32)

ELLA FITZGERALD, vocals

Accompanied by Trumpet: Leonard Graham; Bass: Ray Brown, et al. Recorded at Decca Recording Company, New York, Saturday 20 December 1947

471220-1   74322-A My Baby Likes to Be-Bop (78: Decca 24232; LPD-4, LPD-19, LPD-124)
471220-2   74323-A No Sense (78: Decca 24538; LPD-4, LPD-19, LPD-124)
471220-3   74324-A How High the Moon (LPD-4)
471220-4   74324-B How High the Moon (78: Decca 24387; LPD-3, LPD-5, LPD-19, LPD-36, LPD-37, LPD-40, LPD-122)
471220-5   74324-C How High the Moon (LPD-4)

ELLA FITZGERALD, vocals

Accompanied by Tenor Saxophone: Illinois Jacquet; Organ: Sir Charles Thompson; Piano: Hank Jones; Guitar: Hy White; Bass: John Simmons; Drums: J.C. Heard. Recorded at Decca Recording Company, New York, Tuesday, 23 December 1947

471223-1   74386-A I've Got a Feelin' I'm Fallin' (78: Decca 24232; LPD-19, LPD-123)
471223-2   74387-A You Turned the Tables on Me (78 Decca 24387; LPD-19, LPD-32, LPD-39, LPD-122, LPD-123)
471223-3   74392-A I Cried and Cried and Cried (78: Coral 6.22178; LPD 19, LPD-124)
471223-4   74393-A Robbins' Nest (78: Decca 24538; LPD-19, LPD-122, LPD-124)

ELLA FITZGERALD, vocals

Accompanied by **The Song Spinners.** Recorded at Decca Recording Company, New York, Thursday, 29 April 1948

480429-1   74537-A Tea Leaves (78: Decca 24446; LPD-19)

Note: Charted 19 June 1948; weeks, 2; peak, #24

ELLA FITZGERALD, vocals

Accompanied by **The Song Spinners.** Recorded at Decca Recording Company, New York, Friday, 30 April 1948

480430-1   74538-A My Happiness (78: 24446; LPD-3, LPD-5, LPD-19, LPD-35)

Note: Charted 19 June 1948; weeks, 2; peak, #6

ELLA FITZGERALD, vocals

Recorded at NBC Studios, New York, Tuesday, 25 May 1948

480525-1   Have Mercy! (78: AFRS Jubilee Transcriptions 281)
480525-2   Oh! Lady, Be Good! (78: AFRS Jubilee Transcriptions 281)

ELLA FITZGERALD, vocals

Recorded at NBC Studios, New York, Tuesday, 1 June 1948

480601-1   My Baby Likes to Be-Bop (78: AFRS Jubilee Transcriptions 282)
480601-2   The Gentleman Is a Dope (78: AFRS Jubilee Transcriptions 282)

ELLA FITZGERALD, vocals

Accompanied by unknown instrumental group and a male quartet. Recorded at Decca Recording Company, New York, Friday, 20 August 1948

480820-1   74590-A   It's Too Soon To Know (78: Decca 24497; LPD-19, LPD-23, LPD-26. LPD-40)
480820-2   74591-A   I Can't Go on Without You* (78: Decca 24497; LPD-19)

Musicians on this track include Illinois Jacquet, tenor saxophone.

ELLA FITZGERALD, vocals

Accompanied by mixed chorus and rhythm. Recorded at Decca Recording Company, NewYork, Wednesday, 10 November 1948.

481110-1   74621-A   To Make a Mistake Is Human (78: Decca 24529; LPD-19)
481110-2   74622-A   In My Dreams (78: Decca 24529; LPD-19)

ELLA FITZGERALD, vocals

Accompanied by **The Ray Brown Trio**. Piano: Hank Jones; Bass: Ray Brown; Drums Charlie Smith. Recorded in performance at The Royal Roost, New York, Saturday, 27 November 1948

481127-1   Ool-Ya-Koo
481127-2   Love That Boy
481127-3   Mr. Paganini (You'll Have To Swing It)
481127-4   It's Too Soon to Know

Accompanied by **The Ray Brown Quintet**. Trombone: Kai Winding; Tenor Saxophone: Allan Eager; Piano: Hank Jones; Bass: Ray Brown; Drums: Charlie Smith

481127-5   I Never Knew (I Could Love Anybody)

Jam Session with **The Ray Brown Quintet** and **The Lester Young Quartet**. Trumpet: Jesse Drakes; Trombone; Ted Kelly; Tenor Saxophone: Lester Young; Piano: Fred Jefferson; Drums: Roy Haynes

481127-6   How High the Moon

(All selections on LPD-152)

ELLA FITZGERALD, vocals

Accompanied by **The Ray Brown Trio**. Piano: Hank Jones; Bass: Ray Brown; Drums: Charlie Smith. Recorded in performance at The Royal Roost, New York, Saturday, 4 December 1948

481204-1   Heat Wave
481204-2   Old Mother Hubbard

Accompanied by **The Ray Brown Quintet**. Trombone: Kai Winding; Tenor Saxophone: Allan Eager; Piano: Hank Jones; Bass: Ray Brown; Drums: Charlie Smith

481204-3   Bop Goes the Weasel
481204-4   Bebop Boogie (Boppin' Boogie)*
481204-5   I Cover the Waterfront*
481204-6   How High the Moon**
481204-7   Sunday**

481204-8   I'm Confessin'*
Accompanied by **The Ray Brown Trio**

481204-9   Ool-Ya-Koo
481204-10   Flyin' Home

*(All selections, except * and ** on LPD-152)*

* These three tracks purportedly on LP Session SR 103, and ** these two tracks purportedly on LP Charlie Parker PLP 409, neither of which is known to the author.

ELLA FITZGERALD, vocals

Accompanied by **Sy Oliver and His Orchestra**. Sy Oliver, Leader; Arrangements. Recorded at Decca Recording Company, New York, Friday, 14 January 1949

490114-1   74686   I Couldn't Stay Away (78: Decca 24562; LPD-19a)
490114-2   74687   Old Mother Hubbard (78: Decca 24581; lLPD-19a)
490114-3   74688   Someone Like You (78: Decca 24562; LPD-19a, LPD-26)

ELLA FITZGERALD, vocals

Jazz At The Philharmonic

Accompanied by **The Ray Brown Trio**. Piano: Hank Jones; Bass: Ray Brown; Drums: Roy Haynes, with Tenor Saxophone: Flip Phillips.* Recorded in performance at Carnegie Hall, New York, Friday, 11 February 1949

490211-1   Robbins' Nest *Not yet released*
490211-2   I Got a Guy *Not yet released*
490211-3   Old Mother Hubbard *Not yet released*
490211-4   Flying Home* *Not yet released*
490211-5   Lover Man *Not yet released*
490211-6   Ool-Ya-Koo *Not yet released*

ELLA FITZGERALD, vocals

Accompanied by **The Ray Brown Trio**. Piano: Hank Jones; Bass: Ray Brown; Drums: Roy Haynes. Recorded in performance at the opening of Bop City, New York, Friday, 15 April 1949

490415-1   Old Mother Hubbard
490415-2   Mr. Paganini (You'll Have To Swing It)
490415-3   There's a Small Hotel
490415-4   How High the Moon
490415-5   Oh, Lady, Be Good! *Not yet released*

(All selections, except the last, on LPD-152)

ELLA FITZGERALD, vocals

Accompanied by **The Ray Brown Trio**. Piano: Hank Jones; Bass: Ray Brown; Drums: Roy Haynes. Recorded in performance at Bop City, New York, Saturday, 23 April 1949

490423-1   Robbins' Nest

490423-2   As You Desire Me
490423-3   Thou Swell
    Accompanied by **The Ray Brown Trio** with Trumpet: Howard McGhee; Tenor Saxophones: Brew Moore-Flip Phillips; **Machito's Rhythm**

490423-4   Flyin' Home
(All selections on LPD-152)

ELLA FITZGERALD, vocals

Miss Ella Fitzgerald and Mr. Gordon Jenkins Invite You to Listen and Relax

Accompanied by orchestra and chorus conducted by **Gordon Jenkins.** Recorded at Decca Recording Company, New York, 28 April 1949

490428-1   74862 Happy Talk (78: Decca 24639; LPD-5, LPD-19a, LPD-24, LPD-27)
490428-2   74863 I'm Gonna Wash That Man Right Outa My Hair (78: Decca 24639; LPD-5, LPD-19a, LPD-24, LPD-27)
490428-3   74864 Black Coffee (78: Decca 24646; LPD-3, LPD-5, LPD-19a, LPD-27)
490428-4   74865 Lover's Gold (78: Decca 24646; LPD-19a, LPD-27)

ELLA FITZGERALD-LOUIS JORDAN, vocals

Accompanied by **Louis Jordan and His Tympany Five** Louis Jordan, Leader; Alto Saxophone. Trumpet: Aaron Izanhall; Tenor Saxophone: Eddie Johnson; Piano: Bill Davis; Guitar: Carl Hogan; Bass: Dallas Bartley; Drums: Christopher Columbus. Recorded at Decca Recording Company, New York, Thursday, 28 April 1949

490428-5   74866 Baby, It's Cold Outside (78: Decca 24644; LPD-5, LPD-19a, LPD-22, LPD-122)
Note: Charted 11 June 1949; weeks, 13; peak, #9

490428-6   74867 Don't Cry, Cry-Baby (78: Decca 24644; LPD-5, LPD-19a, LPD-124)

ELLA FITZGERALD, vocals

Accompanied by **The Ray Brown Trio.** Piano: Hank Jones; Bass: Ray Brown; Drums: Roy Haynes. Recorded in performance at the Royal Roost, New York, Saturday, 30 April 1949

490430-1   Someone Like You
490430-2   Again
490430-3   In a Mellow Tone (In a Mellotone)
490430-4   Lemon Drop
490430-5   I Hadn't Anyone Till You
(All selections on LPD-152)

ELLA FITZGERALD, vocals

Accompanied by orchestra under the direction of **Sonny Burke.** Recorded at Decca Recording Company, Los Angeles, Wednesday, 20 July 1949

490720-1   L5097 Crying (78: Decca 34708; LPD-19a, LPD-24, LPD-26)
490720-2   L5098 A New Shade of Blue (78: Decca 34708; LPD-19a)

ELLA FITZGERALD, vocals

Jazz At The Philharmonic

Accompanied by **The Ray Brown Trio.** Piano: Hank Jones; Bass: Ray Brown; Drums: Buddy Rich. Recorded in performance at Carnegie Hall, New York, Sunday, 18 September 1949

FIRST SET

490918-1   Robbins' Nest (LPD-20, LPD-31)
490918-2   A New Shade of Blue (LPD-20)
490918-3   Old Mother Hubbard (LPD-20)
490918-4   I'm Just a Lucky So-and-So (LPD-20, LPD-31)
490918-5   Somebody Loves Me (LPD-20, LPD-31)
490918-6   Basin Street Blues (LPD-20, LPD-31)

    Accompanied by **The JATP All-Stars.** Trumpet: Roy Eldridge; Trombone: Tommy Turk; Alto Saxophone: Charlie Parker; Tenor Saxophones: Flip Phillips-Lester Young and **The Ray Brown Trio**

490918-7   Flyin' Home (LPD-20, LPD-31)

SECOND SET

Accompanied by **The Ray Brown Trio**

490918-8   Oh! Lady, Be Good! (LPD-20)
490918-9   Black Coffee (LPD-20, LPD-31)
490918-10   A-Tisket, A-Tasket (LPD-20)

    Accompanied by **The JATP All-Stars** and **The Ray Brown Trio**

490918-11   How High the Moon (LPD-20)
490918-12   Perdido (LPD-20, LPD-86)

ELLA FITZGERALD, vocals

Accompanied by orchestra under the direction of **Sy Oliver.** Recorded at Decca Recording Company, New York, Tuesday, 20 September 1949

490920-1   75279 In the Evening (When the Sun Goes Down) (78: Decca 24780; LPD-3, LPD-5, LPD-19a, LPD-24, LPD-28, LPD-121, LPD-124)
490920-2   75280 Talk Fast, My Heart, Talk Fast (78: Decca 24780; LPD-19a, LPD-124)
490920-3   75281 I'm Waitin' for the Junk Man (78: Decca 24868; LPD-19a, LPD-124)
490920-4   75282 Basin Street Blues (78: Decca 24868; LPD-3, LPD-5, LPD-19a, LPD-28, LPD-36, LPD-37, LPD-40)

ELLA FITZGERALD, vocals

Miss Ella Fitzgerald and Mr. Gordon Jenkins Invite You To Listen and Relax

Accompanied by orchestra and chorus under the direction of **Gordon Jenkins**. Recorded at Decca Recording Company, New York, Wednesday, 21 September 1949

490921-1   75287 I Hadn't Anyone Till You (78: Decca 24900; LPD-19a, LPD-24, LPD-26, LPD-27, LPD-40)

490921-2   75288 Dream a Little Longer (78: Decca 24900; LPD-19a, LPD-24, LPD-27)

490921-3   75289 Foolish Tears (78: Decca 24773; LPD-19a, LPD-24, LPD-27)

490921-4   75290 A Man Wrote a Song (78: Decca 24773; LPD-19a, LPD-27)

ELLA FITZGERALD–

THE MILLS BROTHERS, vocals

The Mills Brothers: Herbert Mills, first tenor; Donald Mills, second tenor; Harry Mills, baritone; John Mills, Sr., bass. Recorded at Decca Recording Company, Los Angeles, Monday, 7 November 1949

491107-1   L5191 Fairy Tales (78: Decca 24813; LPD-5, LPD-19a)

491107-2   L5192 I Gotta Have My Baby Back (78; Decca 24813; LPD-5, LPD-19a, LPD-22)

ELLA FITZGERALD, vocals

The Kraft Radio Show

Accompanied by **The John Scott Trotter Orchestra**. Recorded in performance at NBC Studios, Los Angeles, Wednesday, 9 November 1949

491109-1   A Dreamer's Holiday (duet with Bing Crosby)

491109-2   My Happiness

491109-3   'Way Back Home (sextet with Bing Crosby and The Mills Brothers)

(All selections on LPD-153)

ELLA FITZGERALD, vocals

The Kraft Radio Show

Accompanied by **The John Scott Trotter Orchestra**. Recorded in performance at NBC Studios, Los Angeles, Wednesday, 23 November 1949

491123-1   Everything I Have Is Yours (duet with **Bing Crosby**) (LPD-153)

ELLA FITZGERALD, vocals

Accompanied by **Sy Oliver and His Orchestra**. Sy Oliver, Leader; Arrangements. Recorded at Decca Recording Company, New York, Thursday, 2 February 1950

500202-1   75801 Baby, Won't You Say You Love Me? (78: Decca 24917; LPD-19b)

500202-2   75802 Don'cha Go 'Way Mad (78: Decca 24917; LPD-19b, LPD-22, LPD-122)

ELLA FITZGERALD, vocals

Accompanied by **Sy Oliver and His Orchestra**. Sy Oliver, Leader/Arrangements. Trumpets: Tony Faso, Bernie Privin, Paul Webster; Trombone: Henderson Chambers; Alto Saxophones: Sid Cooper, Milt Yaner; Tenor Saxophones: Al Klink, Jerry Jerome; Piano: Hank Jones; Guitar: Everett Barksdale; Bass: Ray Brown; Drums: Jimmy Crawford. Recorded at Decca Recording Company, New York, Monday, 6 March 1950

500306-1   75936 Solid as a Rock (78: Decca 24958; LPD-19b, LPD-28, LPD-122, LPD-125)

500306-2   75937 I've Got the World on a String (78: Decca 27120; LPD-3, LPD-5, LPD-19b, LPD-28, LPD-39, LPD-40)

500306-3   75938 Sugarfoot Rag (78: Decca 24958; LPD-19b, LPD-122, LPD-125)

500306-4   75939 Peas and Rice (78: Decca 27120; LPD-19b)

ELLA FITZGERALD, vocals

The Kraft Radio Show

Accompanied by orchestra conducted by **John Scott Trotter**. Recorded in performance at NBC Studios, Los Angeles, Wednesday, 3 May 1950

500503-1   Stay with the Happy People (duet with **Bing Crosby**)

500503-2   I Hadn't Anyone Till You

(Both tracks on LPD-153)

ELLA FITZGERALD, vocals

Accompanied by **Four Hits and a Miss**. Recorded at Decca Recording Company, Los Angeles, Tuesday, 9 May 1950

500509-1   L5594 M-i-s-s-i-s-s-i-p-p-i (78: Decca 27061; LPD-19b, LPD-121, LPD-123)

500509-2   L5595 I Don't Want the World (78: Decca 27061; LPD-19b, LPD-123)

ELLA FITZGERALD, vocals

Accompanied by **Louis Jordan and His Tympany Five**. Louis Jordan, Leader/Alto Saxophone; Trumpet: Aaron Izenhall; Tenor Saxophone: Josh Jackson; Piano: Bill Doggett; Guitar: Bill Jennings; Bass: Bob Bushnell; Drums: Joe Morris. Recorded at Decca Recording Company, New York, Tuesday, 15 August 1950

500815-1   76731 Ain't Nobody's Business but My Own (78: Decca 27200; LPD-3, LPD-5, LPD-19b, LPD-124)

500815-2 76732 I'll Never Be Free (78: Decca 27200; LPD-5, LPD-19b)

ELLA FITZGERALD– LOUIS ARMSTRONG, vocals

Accompanied by orchestra conducted by **Sy Oliver.** Trumpet: Paul Webster; Clarinet: Hank D'Amico; Tenor Saxophone: Frank Ludwig; Piano: Hank Jones; Guitar: Everett Barksdale; Bass: Ray Brown; Drums: Johnny Blowers; Arr: Sy Oliver. Recorded at Decca Recording Company, New York, Friday, 25 August 1950

500825-1 76750 Dream a Little Dream of Me (78: Decca 27209; LPD-3, LPD-5, LPD-19b, LPD-22, LPD-28)

500825-2 76751 Can Anyone Explain? (78: Decca 27209; LPD-5, LPD-19b, LPD-28)

Note: Charted 18 November 1950; weeks, 1; peak, #30

ELLA FITZGERALD, vocals

Ella Sings Gershwin

Accompanied by Piano: **Ellis Larkins.** Recorded at Decca Recording Company, New York, Monday, 11 September 1950

500911-1 76823 Looking for a Boy (78: Decca 27369; LPD-5, LPD-19b, LPD-21, LPD-30)

500911-2 76824 My One and Only (78: Decca 27368; LPD-5, LPD-19b, LPD-21, LPD-30)

500911-3 76825 How Long Has This Been Going On? (78: Decca 27370; LPD-5, LPD-19b, LPD-21, LPD-30)

500911-4 76826 I've Got a Crush on You (78: Decca 27370; LPD-5, LPD-19b, LPD-21, LPD-30)

ELLA FITZGERALD, vocals

Ella Sings Gershwin

Accompanied by Piano: **Ellis Larkins.** Recorded at Decca Recording Company, New York, Tuesday, 12 September 1950

500912-1 76834 But Not for Me (78: Decca 27369; LPD-5, LPD-19b, LPD-21, LPD-30)

500912-2 76835 Soon (78: Decca 27371; LPD-5, LPD-19b, LPD-21, LPD-30)

500912-3 76836 Someone to Watch Over Me (78: Decca 27368; LPD-5, LPD-19b, LPD-21, LPD-30)

500912-4 76837 Maybe (78: Decca 27371; LPD-5, LPD-19b, LPD-21, LPD-30)

ELLA FITZGERALD, vocals

Jazz At The Philharmonic (film soundtrack)

Accompanied by **Jazz At The Philharmonic All-Stars.** Trumpet: Harry Edison; Alto Saxophone: Charlie Parker; Tenor Saxophones: Coleman Hawkins, Flip Phillips; Piano: Hank Jones; Bass: Ray Brown; Drums: Buddy Rich. Recorded at New York, Mid-September 1950

500900-1 Don't Cry, Joe *Not yet released*
500900-2 Laura *Not yet released*
500900-3 You Go to My Head *Not yet released*
500900-4 I'll Remember April *Not yet released*
500900-5 Run, Joe, Run *Not yet released*
500900-6 The Boy Next Door *Not yet released*
500900-7 My Old Flame *Not yet released*
500900-8 Night and Day *Not yet released*
500900-9 The Way You Look Tonight *Not yet released*
500900-10 The Huckle Buck *Not yet released*
500900-11 Body and Soul *Not yet released*

Note: These studio sessions were recorded for use in an unreleased motion picture short subject, Jazz At The Philharmonic. For a number of years it was presumed that this film, shot by Gjon Mili, was lost; nevertheless, a copy does exist, but, as of this date, there are, sadly, no plans for its release.

ELLA FITZGERALD, vocals

Accompanied by **The Ray Brown Quintet.** Trumpet: Charlie Shavers; Piano: Hank Jones; Guitar: John Collins; Bass: Ray Brown; Drums: Charlie Smith. Recorded at Decca Recording Company, New York, Tuesday, 26 September 1950

500926-1 76899 Santa Claus Got Stuck in My Chimney (78: Decca 27255; LPD-19b)

500926-2 76900 Molasses, Molasses (78: Decca 27255; LPD-19b)

ELLA FITZGERALD, vocals

The Kraft Music Hall

Accompanied by orchestra conducted by **John Scott Trotter.** Recorded at NBC Studios, Los Angeles, Wednesday, 29 November 1950

501129-1 Basin Street Blues (duet with **Bing Crosby**; Trumpet: **Red Nichols**)

501129-2 Can Anyone Explain?

501129-3 Silver Bells (duet with **Bing Crosby**)

501129-4 A Marshmallow World

501129-5 Memphis Blues (accompanied by **The Firehouse Five +2**)

(All titles on LPD-153)

ELLA FITZGERALD–THE INK SPOTS, vocals

Accompanied by ? (**The Ink Spots**: Bill Kenny, countertenor; Ivory "Deke" Watson, tenor; Charles Fuqua, baritone; Herb Kenny, bass and talking chorus). Recorded at Decca Recording Company, New York, Wednesday, 20 December 1950

501220-1 80291 Little Small Town Girl (78: Decca 27419; LPD-19b)

501220-2   80292 I Still Feel the Same About You (78: Decca 27419; LPD-5, LPD-19b, LPD-123)

ELLA FITZGERALD, vocals

Accompanied by Piano: Hank Jones; Bass: Ray Brown; Drums: Charles Smith. Recorded in performance at Birdland (night club), New York, Saturday evening, 30 December 1950

501230-1   Old Mother Hubbard
501230-2   These Foolish Things
501230-3   In a Mellow Tone
501230-4   Flying Home
501230-5   Back in Your Own Back Yard
501230-6   Jumping with Symphony Syd
501230-7   How High the Moon

(All selections on LPD-163)

ELLA FITZGERALD, vocals

Accompanied by **The Skylarks** (Gilda Maiken, Lead; George Becker, Lead; Jackie Gershwin, First Tenor; Joe Hamilton, Second Tenor; Earl Brown, Baritone) and orchestra conducted by **Sy Oliver** Arr: Sy Oliver. Recorded at Decca Recording Company, New York, Friday, 12 January 1951

510112-1   80337-4A Lonesome Gal (78: 27453; LPD-19c)
510112-2   80338-3A The Bean Bag Song (78: 27453; LPD19c, LPD-123)

ELLA FITZGERALD, vocals

Accompanied by orchestra conducted by **Sy Oliver**. Trumpets: Tony Faso, Bernie Privin, Paul Webster; Trombone: Mort Bullman; Saxophones: Artie Baker, George Dorsey, Bill Holcomb, Al Klink; Piano: Hank Jones; Guitar: Everett Barksdale; Bass: Sandy Block; Drums: Jimmy Crawford; Arr: Sy Oliver. Recorded at Decca Recording Company, New York, Tuesday, 27 March 1951

510327-1   80745-A The Chesapeake and Ohio (78: Decca 27602; LPD-19c, LPD-125)
510327-2   80746-A Little Man in a Flying Saucer (78: Decca 27578; LPD-19c, LPD-125)
510327-3   80747-A Because of Rain (78: Decca 27602; LPD-19c, LPD-23, LPD-24, LPD-28)
510327-4   80748-A The Hot Canary (78: Decca 27578; LPD-19c, LPD-24, LPD-125)

ELLA FITZGERALD, vocals

Accompanied by Piano: Hank Jones; Bass: Clyde Lombardi; Drums: Charles Smith. Recorded in performance at Birdland (night club), New York, Saturday evening, 19 May 1951

510519-1   Show Me the Way to Get Out of This World
510519-2   Imagination *Not yet released*
510519-3   Old Mother Hubbard *Not yet released*

510519-4   Lemon Drop *Not yet released*
510519-5   How Long Has This Been Going On?
510519-6   Love, Come Back to Me *Not yet released*
510519-7   Someone to Watch Over Me
510519-8   Jumping with Symphony Syd

(All released selections on LPD-163)

ELLA FITZGERALD, vocals

Accompanied by Piano: Hank Jones; Guitar: Everett Barksdale; Bass: Sandy Block; Drums: Jimmy Crawford. Recorded at Decca Recording Company, New York, Thursday, 24 May 1951

510524-1   81075 Even as You and I (78: Decca 27634; LPD-19c, LPD-26)
510524-2   81076 Do You Really Love Me? (78: Decca 27634; LPD-19c, LPD-26)
510524-3   81077 Love You Madly (78: Decca 27693; LPD-19c)

ELLA FITZGERALD, vocals

Accompanied by Organ: Bill Doggett; Piano: Hank Jones; Guitar: Everett Barksdale; Bass: Arnold Fishkin; Drums: Johnny Blowers, and **The Ray Charles Singers**. Recorded at Decca Recording Company, New York, Tuesday, 26 June 1951

510626-1   81214 Mixed Emotions (78: Decca 27680; LPD-19c, LPD-23, LPD-24, LPD-26, LPD-40)
510626-2   81215-A Smooth Sailing (78: Decca 27693; LPD-3, LPD-5, LPD-19c, LPD-36, LPD-37, LPD-40)

Note: Charted 8 September 1951; weeks, 6; peak, #23

510626-3   81216-A Come On-a My House (78: 27680; LPD-19c)

ELLA FITZGERALD, vocals

Accompanied by orchestra conducted by **Sy Oliver**. Trumpets: Taft Jordan, Carl Poole, Bernie Privin; Trombones: Henderson Chambers, Frank Saracco; Alto Saxophones: Hymie Schertzer, Milt Yaner; Tenor Saxophones: Al Klink, Fred Williams; Baritone Saxophone: Stewart Blake; Piano: Hank Jones; Guitar: Everett Barksdale; Bass: Sandy Block; Drums: Johnny Blowers; Arr: Sy Oliver. Recorded at Decca Recording Company, New York, Wednesday, 18 July 1951

510718-1   81286 It's My Own Darn Fault (78: Decca 27948; LPD-19c)
510718-2   81287 I Don't Want to Take a Chance (78: Decca 27948; LPD-19c, LPD-28, LPD-125)
510718-3   81288 There Never Was a Baby (Like My Baby) (78: Decca 27724; LPD-19c, LPD-23, LPD-24, LPD-28, LPD-32)
510718-4   81289 Give a Little, Get a Little (Love) (78: Decca 27724; LPD-19c, LPD-24, LPD-28, LPD-39)

LOUIS ARMSTRONG AND
ELLA FITZGERALD, vocals

Accompanied by **Dave Barbour and His Orchestra.** Dave Barbour, Leader-Guitar; Trumpets: Louis Armstrong, Larry Neil; Trombone: Frank Howard; Saxophones: Heinie Beau, Jack Dumont, Chuck Gentry; Piano: Hank Jones; Bass: Ray Brown; Drums: Alvin Stoller; Arr: Dave Barbour. Recorded at Decca Recording Company, Los Angeles, Friday, 23 November 1951

511123-1   L6526 Necessary Evil (78: Decca 27901; LPD-19c, LPD-126)

511123-2   L6527 Oops! (78: Decca 27901; LPD-19c, LPD-126)

511123-3   L6528 Would You Like to Take a Walk? (78: Decca 28552; LPD-5, LPD-19c, LPD-22, LPD-126)

511123-4   L6529 Who Walks in When I Walk Out? (78: Decca 28552; LPD-5, LPD-19c, LPD-126)

ELLA FITZGERALD AND
LOUIS ARMSTRONG

The Bing Crosby Show

Accompanied by orchestra conducted by **John Scott Trotter.** Recorded in performance at CBS Studios, Los Angeles, Wednesday, 28 November 1951

511128-1   Undecided (vEF)

511128-2   Memphis Blues (vTrio: **Bing Crosby, Ella Fitzgerald, Louis Armstrong**)

511128-3   Chesterfield Cigarette Commercial (**Bing, Ella, Louis**)

(All titles on LPD-153)

ELLA FITZGERALD, vocals

Accompanied by orchestra conducted by **Sonny Burke.** Trumpets: Pete Candoli, Mickey Mangano, Carlton McBeath, Oliver Mitchell; Trombones: Milt Bernhart, John Halliburton, Jim Priddy, Paul Tanner; Saxophones: Chuck Gentry, Hugo Lowenstern, Don Raffell, Hammond Russum; Piano: Hank Jones; Guitar: Laurindo Almeida; Bass: Joe Mondragon; Drums: Tommy Rowles; Arr: Sonny Burke. Recorded at Decca Recording Company, Los Angeles, Monday, 26 November 1951

511126-1   L6533-A Baby Doll (78: Decca 27900; LPD-19c, LPD-23, LPD-26, LPD-32)

511126-2   L6534-A What Does It Take? (78: Decca 28034; LPD-19c)

511126-3   L6535-A Lady Bug (78: Decca 27900; LPD-19c)

511126-4   L6536-A Lazy Day (78: Decca 28034; LPD-19c)

ELLA FITZGERALD, vocals

Accompanied by **The Ray Brown Quintet.** Organ: Bill Doggett; Piano: Hank Jones; Bass: Ray Brown; Drums: Rudy Taylor; Bells: Dick Jacobs, and **The Ray Charles Singers.** Recorded at Decca Recording Company, New York, Friday, 4 January 1952

520104-1   82075 Air Mail Special (78: Decca 28126; LPD-3, LPD-5, LPD-19d, LPD-36, LPD-37, LPD-123)

520104-2   82076 Rough Ridin' (78: Decca 27948; LPD-3, LPD-19d, LPD-36, LPD-37)

ELLA FITZGERALD, vocals

Accompanied by orchestra conducted by **Sy Oliver.** Trumpets: Taft Jordan, James Nottingham, Bernie Privin; Trombones: Mort Bullman, Al Grey; Alto Saxopones: Sid Cooper, Milt Yaner; Tenor Saxophones: Dick Jacobs, Sam Taylor; Baritone Saxophones: Dave McRae; Piano: Hank Jones; Guitar: Everett Barksdale; Bass: Sandy Block; Drums: Jimmy Crawford; Arr: Sy Oliver. Recorded at Decca Recording Company, New York, Monday, 25 February 1952

520225-1   82319 A Guy Is a Guy (78: Decca 28049; LPD-19d, LPD-28)

520225-2   82320 Nowhere Guy (78: Decca 28707; LPD-19d, LPD-125)

520225-3   82321 Gee, Baby, But I'm Glad to Know You Love Me (78: Decca 28131; LPD-19d, LPD-24, LPD-26)

520225-4   82322-A Goody Goody (78: Decca 28126; LPD-3, LPD-5, LPD-19d, LPD-28, LPD-32, LPD-35, LPD-122, LPD-125)

ELLA FITZGERALD, vocals

Accompanied by Piano: Hank Jones; Bass: Sandy Block; Drums: Jimmy Crawford. Recorded in performance at Birdland (night club), New York, Saturday evening, 7 June 1952

520607-1   Show Me the Way to Get Out of This World

520607-2   Angel Eyes

520607-3   Walkin' My Baby Back Home

520607-4   Goody Goody

520607-5   Air Mail Special

Accompanied by Piano: Hank Jones; Bass: Sandy Block; Drums: Jimmy Crawford; Vibraphone: Terry Gibbs; Mellophone: Don Elliot

520607-6   How High the Moon

(All selections on LPD-163)

ELLA FITZGERALD, vocals

Accompanied by orchestra conducted by **Sy Oliver.** Trumpets: Taft Jordan, James Nottingham, Bernie Privin; Trombones: Mort Bullman, Al Grey; Alto Saxophones: Sid Cooper, Milt Yaner; Tenor Saxophones: Dick Jacobs, Sam Taylor; Baritone Saxophone: Dave McRae; Piano: Hank Jones; Guitar: Everett Barksdale; Bass: Sandy Block; Drums: Jimmy Crawford; Arr: Sy Oliver. Recorded at Decca Recording Company, New York, Thursday, 26 June 1952

520626-1   83008 Preview* (78: Decca 28321; LPD-3, LPD-19d, LPD-28, LPD-37, LPD-124)

520626-2   83009 Ding-Dong Boogie* (78: Decca 28321; LPD-19d, LPD-125)

520626-3   83010-A Mr. Paganini (You'll Have To Swing It), Part 1 (78: Decca 28774; LPD-3, LPD-5, LPD-19d, LPD-28, LPD-34, LPD-40, LPD-122)

520626-4   83011-A Mr. Paganini (You'll Have To Swing It), Part 2 (78: Decca 28774; LPD-3, LPD-5, LPD-19d, LPD-28. LPD-34, LPD-40, LPD-122)

520626-5   83012 Angel Eyes (78: Decca 28707; LPD-3, LPD-5, LPD-19d, LPD-28, LPD-32, LPD-35, LPD-36, LPD-37)

520626-6   83013 Early Autumn (78: Decca 29810; LPD-19d, LPD-28, LPD-122, LPD-125)

*Accompanied by Tenor Saxophone Sam Taylor; Piano: Hank Jones; Guitar: Everett Barksdale; Bass: Sandy Block; Drums: Jimmy Crawford, only

ELLA FITZGERALD, vocals

Accompanied by orchestra conducted by **Leroy Kirkland.** Vibraphone: Phil Kraus; Piano: Hank Jones; Guitar: Hy White; Bass: George Duvivier; Drums: Stan Kane; Arr: Leroy Kirkland. Recorded at Decca Recording Company, New York, Friday, 11 August 1952

520811-1   83243-1 Trying (78: Decca 28375; LPD-19d)

Note: Charted 27 September 1952; weeks, 4; peak, #21

520811-2   83244 The Greatest There Is (78: Decca 28930; LPD-19d, LPD-122)

520811-3   83247 My Bonnie (78: Decca 28375; LPD-19d)

520811-4   83248 Ella's Contribution to the Blues (78: Decca 29810; LPD-19d, LPD-39, LPD-122)

ELLA FITZGERALD, vocals

Accompanied by Piano: Hank Jones; Bass: Nelson Boyd; Drums: Roy Haynes. Recorded in performance at Birdland (night club), New York, Saturday evening, 16 August 1952

520816-1   (It's Only a) Paper Moon
520816-2   Be Anything (but Be Mine)
520816-3   Preview
520816-4   You're Driving Me Crazy
520816-5   Lemon Drop
520816-6   The Frim Fram Sauce

(All selections on LPD-163)

ELLA FITZGERALD, vocals

Jazz At The Philharmonic

Accompanied by the **Jazz At The Philharmonic All-Stars.** Trumpets: Roy Eldridge, Charlie Shavers; Alto Saxophone: Benny Carter; Tenor Saxophones: Flip Phillips, Lester Young; Piano: Oscar Peterson; Guitar: Barney Kessel; Bass: Ray Brown; Drums: Gene Krupa, Buddy Rich. Recorded in performance at Carnegie Hall, New York, Saturday, 13 September 1952

520913-1   Perdido (LPD-127)

ELLA FITZGERALD, vocals

Accompanied by orchestra conducted by **Leroy Kirkland.** Vibraphone; Phil Kraus; Piano: Hank Jones; Guitar: Hy White; Bass: George Duvivier; Drums: Stan Kane; Arr: Leroy Kirkland. Recorded at Decca Recording Company, New York, Friday, 19 September 1952

520919-1   83429 My Favorite Song (78: Decca 28433; LPD-19d)

520919-2   83430 Walking by the River (78: Decca 28433; LPD-19d, LPD-23, LPD-24, LPD-26, LPD-40)

Note: Charted 29 November 1952; weeks, 1; peak, #29

ELLA FITZGERALD, vocals

Accompanied by **The Lawson-Haggart Jazz Band.** Trumpet: Yank Lawson; Trombone-Violin: Lou McGarity; Clarinet: Bill Stegmeyer; Piano: Lou Stein; Bass: Bob Haggart; Drums: Cliff Leeman. Recorded at Decca Recording Company, New York, Wednesday, 15 October 1952

521015-1   83496 Basin Street Blues *Not yet released*

ELLA FITZGERALD, vocals

Accompanied by orchestra conducted by **Jerry Gray.** Trumpets: John Best, Conrad Gozzo, Tom Patton, Whitey Thomas; Trombones: George Arus, Milt Bernhart, John Halliburton, Jim Priddy; Alto Saxophones, Baritone Saxophones, Clarinets: Dale Brown, John Rotella, Riley Weston; Tenor Saxophones: Bob Cooper; Ronny Perry; Piano: Hank Jones; Guitar: Bobby Gibbons; Bass: Bob Stone; Drums: Alvin Stoller; Arr: Jerry Gray. Recorded at Decca Recording Company, Los Angeles, Sunday, 30 November 1952

521130-1   L6955 I Can't Lie to Myself (78: Decca 28589; LPD-19d)

521130-2   L6956 Don't Wake Me Up (78: Decca 28589; LPD-19d)

ELLA FITZGERALD, vocals

The Bing Crosby Show

Accompanied by orchestra conducted by **John Scott Trotter.** Recorded in performance at CBS Studios, Los Angeles, Thursday, 18 December 1952

521218-1   Medley: a. Trying; b. My Favorite Song; c. Between the Devil and the Deep Blue Sea

521218-2   Rudolph, the Red Nosed Reindeer (duet with **Bing Crosby**)

(Both selections on LPD-153)

ELLA FITZGERALD, vocals

The Bing Crosby Show

Accompanied by orchestra conducted by **John Scott Trotter**. Recorded in performance at CBS Studios, Los Angeles, Thursday, 1 January 1953

530101-1 Medley: a. I Hadn't Anyone Till You; b. If You Ever Should Leave; c. I Can't Give You Anything But Love
530101-2 Chicago Style (duet with **Bing Crosby**)
(Both selections on LPD-153)

ELLA FITZGERALD, vocals

Accompanied by orchestra conducted by **Sy Oliver**. Trumpets: Taft Jordan, Jimmy Nottingham, Charlie Shavers; Trombones: Henderson Chambers, Frank Saracco; Alto Saxophones: Art Baker, George Dorsey; Tenor Saxophones: Mel Tait; Sam Taylor; Baritone Saxophone: Manny Albam; Piano: Hank Jones; Guitar: Everett Barksdale; Bass: George Duvivier; Drums: Jimmy Crawford; Arr: Sy Oliver. Recorded at Decca Recording Company, New York, Friday 13 February 1953

530213-1 83951-A Careless (78: Decca 28671; LPD-19e, LPD-24, LPD-28, LPD-32, LPD-39)
530213-2 83952-A Blue Lou (78: Decca 28671; LPD-3, LPD-5, LPD-19e, LPD-28, LPD-32, LPD-39, LPD-122)
530213-3 83953-A I Wondered What Kind of a Guy You'd Be (78: Decca 28930; LPD-19e, LPD-125)

ELLA FITZGERALD, vocals

Accompanied by Trumpet: Taft Jordan; Organ: Bill Doggett; Bass: Sandy Bloch; Drums: Jimmy Crawford, and **The Ray Charles Singers**. Recorded at Decca Recording Company, New York, Thursday, 11 June 1953

530611-1 84694 When the Hands of the Clock Pray at Midnight (78: Decca 28762; LPD-19e)
530611-2 84695-A Crying in the Chapel (78: Decca 28762; LPD-19e)

Note: Charted 5 September 1953; weeks, 4; peak, #15

ELLA FITZGERALD, vocals

Jazz At The Philharmonic

Accompanied by Piano: Ray Tunia; Bass: Ray Brown; Guitar: Herb Ellis; Drums: J.C. Heard. Recorded in performance at Bushnell Memorial Auditorium, Hartford, Connecticut, Friday, 11 September 1953

530911-1 S'posin' *Not yet released*
530911-2 Bill (LPD-31)
530911-3 Lover, Come Back to Me *Not yet released*
530911-4 The Birth of the Blues *Not yet released*
530911-5 Angel Eyes *Not yet released*
530911-6 Love You Madly *Not yet released*

530911-7 Babalu *Not yet released*
530911-8 Why Don't You Do Right? (LPD-31)
530911-9 One O'Clock Jump *Not yet released*

ELLA FITZGERALD, vocals

Jazz At The Philharmonic in Tokyo: Live at the Nichigeki Theatre, 1953

Recorded in performance at the Nichigeki Theatre, Tokyo, Japan, Wednesday, 18 November 1953

ELLA FITZGERALD AND HER QUARTET

Piano: Raymond Tunia; Guitar: Herb Ellis; Bass: Ray Brown; Drums: J.C. Heard

531118-1 On the Sunny Side of the Street
531118-2 Body and Soul
531118-3 Why Don't You Do Right?
531118-4 Oh, Lady, Be Good!
531118-5 I Got It Bad (and That Ain't Good)
531118-6 How High the Moon
531118-7 My Funny Valentine
531118-8 Smooth Sailing
531118-9 The Frim Fram Sauce

ELLA FITZGERALD WITH JAZZ AT THE PHILHARMONIC ALL-STARS

Trumpets: Roy Eldridge, Charlie Shavers; Trombone: Bill Harris; Alto Saxophones: Benny Carter, Willie Smith; Tenor Saxophones: Flip Phillips, Ben Webster; Piano: Oscar Peterson; Guitar: Herb Ellis; Bass: Ray Brown; Drums: J.C. Heard

531118-10 Perdido
531118-11 After Hours Session: a. Sweethearts on Parade, b. Dixie *Not yet released*
(All selections, except After Hours Session, on LPD-25, LPD-118)

ELLA FITZGERALD, vocals

The Bing Crosby General Electric Show

Accompanied by orchestra conducted by **John Scott Trotter**. Trumpets: Ziggy Elman, Robert Guy, Red Nichols; Trombones: Joe Howard, Wendell Mayhew, Ted Vesely; Saxophones: Warren Baker, Dave Harris, Matty Matlock, Phil Sundel, Larry Wright; Piano: Buddy Cole; Guitar: Perry Botkin; Bass: Phil Stephens; Drums: Nick Fatool + String Section. Recorded in performance at CBS Studios, Los Angeles, Sunday, 13 December 1953

531213-1 White Christmas (duet with **Bing Crosby**)
531213-2 Moanin' Low
(Both selections appear on LPD-153)

ELLA FITZGERALD, vocals

Accompanied by orchestra conducted by **Sy Oliver**. Trumpets: Taft Jordan, Jimmy Nottingham, Charlie Shavers;

Trombones: Frank Saracco, Jack Satterfield; Alto Saxophones: George Dorsey, Bill Holcomb; Tenor Saxophones: Sam Taylor; Baritone Saxophone: Dave McRae; Piano: Dave Martin; Guitar: Everett Barksdale; Bass: Sandy Bloch; Drums: Jimmy Crawford; Bongo: Lawrence Rivera; Arr: Sy Oliver. Recorded at Decca Recording Company, New York, Wednesday, 23 December 1953

531223-1   85590 An Empty Ballroom (78: Decca 29259; LPD-19e, LPD-39, LPD-40)

531223-2   85591 If You Don't, I Know Who Will (78: Decca 29259; LPD-19e, LPD-125)

531223-3   85592-1 Melancholy Me (78: Decca 29008; LPD-19e, LPD-26, LPD-28)

Note: Charted 6 March 1954; weeks, 1; peak, #25

531223-4   85593-1 Somebody Bad Stole de Weddin' Bell (78: Decca 29008; LPD-19e)

ELLA FITZGERALD, vocals

The Bing Crosby General Electric Show

Accompanied by orchestra conducted by **John Scott Trotter**. Trumpets: Ziggy Elman, Robert Guy, Red Nichols; Trombones: Joe Howard, Wendell Mayhew, Ted Vesely; Saxophones: Warren Baker, Dave Harris, Matty Matlock, Phil Sundel, Larry Wright; Piano: Buddy Cole; Guitar: Perry Botkin; Bass Phil Stephens; Drums: Nick Fatool + String Section. Recorded in performance at CBS Studios, Los Angeles, Sunday, 27 December 1953

531227-1   Someone to Watch Over Me
531227-2   Istanbul (duet with **Bing Crosby**; Trumpet Solo: Ziggy Elman)
531227-3   Looking for a Boy

(All selections on LPD-153)

ELLA FITZGERALD, vocals

The Bing Crosby General Electric Show

Accompanied by orchestra conducted by **John Scott Trotter**. Trumpets: Ziggy Elman, Robert Guy, Red Nichols; Trombones: Joe Howard, Wendell Mayhew, Ted Vesely; Saxophones: Warren Baker, Dave Harris, Matty Matlock, Phil Sundel, Larry Wright; Piano: Buddy Cole; Guitar: Perry Botkin; Bass: Phil Stephens; Drums: Nick Fatool + String Section. Recorded in performance at CBS Studios, Los Angeles, Thursday, 31 December 1953

531231-1   L7519-1 Moanin' Low (78: Decca 29475; LPD-19e, LPD-33, LPD-34)
531231-2   L7520-1 Taking a Chance on Love (78: Decca 29475; LPD-19e, LPD-32, LPD-34, LPD-35)

ELLA FITZGERALD, vocals

The Bing Crosby General Electric Show

Accompanied by orchestra conducted by **John Scott Trotter**. Trumpets: Ziggy Elman, Robert Guy, Red Nichols;

Trombones: Joe Howard, Wendell Mayhew, Ted Vesely; Saxophones: Warren Baker, Dave Harris, Matty Matlock, Phil Sundel, Larry Wright; Piano: Buddy Cole; Guitar: Perry Botkin; Bass: Phil Stephens; Drums: Nick Fatool + String Section. Recorded in performance at CBS Studios, Los Angeles, Sunday, 14 February 1954

540214-1   That's A-Plenty (duet with **Bing Crosby**)
540214-2   Taking a Chance on Love

(Both selections on LPD-153)

ELLA FITZGERALD, vocals

Miss Ella Fitzgerald and Mr. Gordon Jenkins Invite You to Listen and Relax

Accompanied by orchestra and chorus conducted by **Gordon Jenkins**. Arr: Gordon Jenkins. Recorded at Decca Recording Company, New York, Thursday, 25 March 1954

540325-1   86079-1 I Wished on the Moon (78: Decca 29137; LPD-3, LPD-5, LPD-19e, LPD-27, LPD-40)
540325-2   86080-1 Baby (78: Decca 29108; LPD-19e, LPD-27)
540325-3   86081-1 I Need (78: Decca 29108; LPD-19e, LPD-27)
540325-4   86082-1 Who's Afraid? (Not I, Not I) (78: Decca 29137; LPD-19e, LPD-27)

ELLA FITZGERALD, vocals

Songs in a Mellow Mood

Accompanied by Piano: **Ellis Larkins**. Recorded at Decca Recording Company, New York, Monday, 29 March 1954

540329-1   86087 I'm Glad There Is You (LPD-5, LPD-19e, LPD-29)
540329-2   86088 Baby, What Else Could I Do? (LPD-LPD-5, LPD-19e, LPD-29, LPD-33)
540329-3   86089 What Is There To Say? (LPD-5, LPD-19e, LPD-29)
540329-4   86090 Makin' Whoopee (LPD-5, LPD-19e, LPD-29, LPD-33)
540329-5   86091 Until the Real Thing Comes Along (LPD-3, LPD-5, LPD-19e, LPD-29)
540329-6   86092 People Will Say We're in Love (LPD-5, LPD-19e, LPD-29)

ELLA FITZGERALD, vocals

Songs in a Mellow Mood

Accompanied by piano: **Ellis Larkins**. Recorded at Decca Recording Company, New York, Tuesday, 30 March 1954

540330-1   86093 Please Be Kind (LPD-5, LPD-19e, LPD-29, LPD-33)
540330-2   86094 Imagination (LPD-5, LPD-19f, LPD-29, LPD-122)

540330-3   86095 My Heart Belongs to Daddy (LPD-5, LPD-19f, LPD-29, LPD-122)

540330-4   86096 You Leave Me Breathless (LPD-5, LPD-19f, LPD-29, LPD-33)

540330-5   86097 Nice Work if You Can Get It (LPD-5, LPD-19f, LPD-29, LPD-30)

540330-6   86098 Star Dust (LPD-5, LPD-19f, LPD-29, LPD-33)

ELLA FITZGERALD, vocals

Accompanied by orchestra conducted by **Sy Oliver**. Recorded at Decca Recording Company, New York, Friday, 4 June 1954

540604-1   86356 Lullaby of Birdland (78: Decca 29198; LPD-3, LPD-5, LPD-19f, LPD-28, LPD-32, LPD-36, LPD-37, LPD-124)

540604-2   86357 Later (78: Decca 29198; LPD-19f, LPD-36, LPD-37)

ELLA FITZGERALD, vocals

Jazz At The Philharmonic: The Ella Fitzgerald Set

Accompanied by **The Ray Brown Quartet**. Piano: Raymond Tunia; Guitar: Herb Ellis; Bass: Ray Brown; Drums: Buddy Rich. Recorded in performance at Bushnell Memorial Auditorium, Hartford, Connecticut, Friday, 17 September 1954

540917-1   A Foggy Day (in London Town) (LPD-31)

540917-2   Lullaby of Birdland (LPD-86)

540917-3   The Man That Got Away (LPD-31)

540917-4   Hernando's Hideaway (LPD-31)

540917-5   Later (LPD-31)

ELLA FITZGERALD, vocals

Accompanied by **The JATP All-Stars**. Trumpets: Roy Eldridge, Dizzy Gillespie; Trombone: ? ; Alto Saxophone: ? ; Tenor Saxophones: Flip Phillips, ? ; Piano: Raymond Tunia; Guitar: Herb Ellis; Bass: Ray Brown; Drums: Buddy Rich

540917-6   Perdido *Not yet released*

ELLA FITZGERALD, vocals

Jazz At The Philharmonic: The Ella Fitzgerald Set

Accompanied by **The Ray Brown Quartet**. Piano: Raymond Tunia; Guitar: Herb Ellis; Bass: Ray Brown; Drums: Buddy Rich. Recorded in performance at Carnegie Hall, New York, Saturday, 18 September 1954

540918-1   That Old Black Magic *Not yet released*

540918-2   Hey, There! *Not yet released*

ELLA FITZGERALD, vocals

Accompanied by Piano: Raymond Tunia, and **Apollo Theater Orchestra** (personnel unknown). Recorded in performance at Apollo Theater, New York, in late fall, 1954

540000-1   I Can't Get Started (with You) (LPD-163)

FRANK SINATRA AND ELLA FITZGERALD, vocals

Finian's Rainbow film soundtrack*

Accompanied by Piano: Oscar Peterson; Guitar: Herb Ellis; Bass: Ray Brown; Drums: Frank Flynn. Recorded at M-G-M Studio, Los Angeles, Saturday, 20 November 1954

541120-1   Necessity (duet) (LPD-128)

*This animated-feature film by Distributors Corporation of America was never produced, and the soundtrack, although recorded by Ella, Sinatra, Ella Logan, and Louis Armstrong, was never officially released.

ELLA FITZGERALD, vocals

U.S. All Stars in Berlin

Accompanied by **U.S. All Stars**. Recorded at Armed Forces Radio, Berlin (Germany), Thursday, 10 February 1955

550210-1   Papa Loves Mambo

550210-2   Perdido

(Both selections on LPD-154)

ELLA FITZGERALD, vocals

Accompanied by orchestra conducted by **André Previn**. Arr: André Previn. Recorded at Decca Recording Company, Los Angeles, Friday, 1 April 1955

550401-1   L8280 Thanks for the Memory (LPD-5, LPD-19f, LPD-33, LPD-34)

550401-2   L8281 It Might As Well Be Spring (LPD-5, LPD-19f, LPD-32, LPD-34)

550401-3   L8282 You'll Never Know (LPD-5, LPD-19f, LPD-33, LPD-34)

550401-4   L8283 I Can't Get Started (LPD-5, LPD-19f, LPD-32, LPD-34)

ELLA FITZGERALD, vocals

Accompanied by orchestra conducted by **Benny Carter**. Arr: Benny Carter. Recorded at Decca Recording Company, Los Angeles, Wednesday, 27 April 1955

550427-1   L8362 Between the Devil and the Deep Blue Sea (LPD-3, LPD-5, LPD-19f, LPD-33, LPD-34, LPD-122)

550427-2   L8363 That Old Black Magic (LPD-3, LPD-5, LPD-19f, LPD-34, LPD-40, LPD-122)

550427-3   L8364 Ol' Devil Moon (78: Decca 29580; LPD-3, LPD-5, LPD-19f, LPD-33, LPD-34, LPD-35, LPD-122)

550427-4   L8365 Lover, Come Back to Me (78: Decca 29580; LPD-3, LPD-5, LPD-19f, LPD-34, LPD-35, LPD-40, LPD-122)

ELLA FITZGERALD, vocals

Pete Kelly's Blues; film soundtrack

Accompanied by Quartet: Recorded at Warner Brothers Studio, Burbank, California, Tuesday, 3 May 1955

550503-1 L8379 Hard Hearted Hannah (78: Decca 29689; LPD-3, LPD-5, LPD-19f, LPD-38, LPD-122)

550503-2 K8380 Pete Kelly's Blues (78: Decca 29689; LPD-19f, LPD-38, LPD-122)

550503-3 L8381 Ella Hums the Blues (LPD-19f, LPD-36, LPD-37, LPD-38)

Note: The album **Pete Kelly's Blues Peggy Lee and Ella Fitzgerald**, *on which these tracks appear, as well as those of Peggy Lee who recorded nine others for the film, was produced by Milt Gabler on the Decca label. These recordings are the actual soundtrack recordings, the rights to which were purchased from Warner Brothers. The album was charted 17 September 1955; weeks, 10; peak, #7.*

ELLA FITZGERALD, vocals

Accompanied by orchestra and chorus conducted by **Toots Camarata.** Trombones: Will Bradley, Cutty Cutshall, Frank Saracco; Flügelhorns: Dick Moore, Lester Salomon; Alto Saxophone: Hymie Schertzer; Cello: Don Abney; Piano: Dick Hyman; Guitar: Barry Galbraith; Bass: Sandy Bloch; Drums: Phil Kraus. Recorded at Decca Recording Company, New York, Monday, 1 August 1955

550801-1 88435 Soldier Boy (78: Decca 29648; LPD-19f)

550801-2 88436 A Satisfied Mind (78: Decca 29648; LPD-19f, LPD-39)

ELLA FITZGERALD, vocals

One Night Stand with Stan Kenton and Music '55

Accompanied by **Stan Kenton and His Orchestra** Stan Kenton, Leader; Piano. Trumpets: Bob Clark, Ed Leddy, Sam Noto, Al Porcino, Stu Williamson; Trombones: Gus Chapell, Bob Fitzpatrick, Carl Fontana, Kent Larsen; Baritone Trombone: Don Kelly; Alto Saxophones: Lennie Neihaus, Charlie Mariano; Tenor Saxophones: Bill Perkins, Dave Van Kreidt; Baritone Saxophone: Don Davidson; Guitar: Ralph Blaze; Bass: Max Bennett; Drums: Mel Lewis. Recorded in performance at CBS Television, New York, Tuesday, 2 August 1955

550802-1 How High the Moon
550802-2 Someone to Watch Over Me
550802-3 Skylark
550802-4 Star Dust (duet with Hoagy Carmichael)

(All selections on LPD-155)

ELLA FITZGERALD, vocals

Accompanied by Piano: Don Abney; Bass: unknown; Drums: unknown. Recorded in performance at Basin Street (night club), New York, Wednesday evening, 3 August 1955, (or Sunday evening, 7 August 1955)

550803-1 Later
550803-2 That Old Black Magic

(Both selections on LPD-163)

ELLA FITZGERALD, vocals

Accompanied by **Stan Kenton and His Orchestra with The JATP All-Stars.** Personnel in the Kenton orchestra*, same as on 2 August 1955; added are: Trumpet: Dizzie Gillespie; Tenor Saxophones: Coleman Hawkins, Illinois Jacquet; Piano: Lou Stein; Bass: Oscar Pettiford; Drums: Buddy Rich. Recorded in performance at CBS Studios, New York, Tuesday, 13 September 1955

550913-1 B-flat Blues (LP Issue: This track appears in an Italian 21-LP collection, titled **Bean and the Boys: Coleman Hawkins' Live and Uncommercial Recordings, 1940–1965** (Bean 01).

*Kenton (piano), Perkins and Van Kreidt (tenor saxophones), Bennett (bass), and Lewis (drums) are not heard on this track.

ELLA FITZGERALD, vocals

Accompanied by orchestra and chorus conducted by **Toots Camarata.** Trumpets: Dale McMickle, Jimmy Nottingham, Charlie Shavers; Trombones: Will Bradley, Cutty Cutshall, Frank Saracco, Ward Silloway; Alto Saxophones: Al Howard, Hymie Schertzer; Tenor Saxophones: Hal Feldman, Al Klink; Piano: Don Abney; Guitar: Al Casamenti; Bass: Eddie Safranski; Drums: Jimmy Crawford; Harp: Janet Putman + Violins. Recorded at Decca Recording Company, New York, Friday, 5 August 1955

550805-1 88456 My One and Only Love (78: Decca 29746; LPD-3, LPD-5, LPD-19f, LPD-39, LPD-40)

550805-2 88457 The Impatient Years (78: Decca 29665; LPD-19f, LPD-39)

550805-3 88458 But Not Like Mine (78: Decca 29665; LPD-19f, LPD-39)

550805-4 88459 (Love Is) The Tender Trap (78: Decca 29746; LPD-5, LPD-19f, LPD-40)

∅

Thus ends Ella's 21-year career with Decca Recording Company, during which time she recorded the 582 performances found in these sessions, and an unknown number that still lie undisturbed in the archives of radio and television.

The Decca Years: A Survey

During her years with Chick Webb and His Orchestra (1935-1939),

60 vocals with the orchestra were released,

27 vocals were released with Ella Fitzgerald and Her Savoy Eight,

2 vocals were released with Teddy Wilson and His Orchestra,

2 vocals were released with The Mills Brothers,

3 vocals were released (RCA) with Benny Goodman and His Orchestra,

4 vocal commercial transcriptions with Chick Webb and His Orchestra were released, and

11 vocal radio transcriptions with Chick Webb and His Orchestra were released.

6 vocals with Chick Webb and His Orchestra were rejected, and

3 vocals by Ella Fitzgerald and Her Savoy Eight were rejected.

During 1939–1941, Ella Fitzgerald and Her Famous Orchestra recorded,

47 vocals that were released,

5 instrumentals that were released (part of her *oeuvre*),

41 vocal radio transcriptions were released, and

1 radio transcription with vocal by Taft Jordan was released, and

19 instrumental radio transcriptions were released.

1 vocal has not yet been released.

From 1941, after the demise of her orchestra, until 1955,

199 vocals were released by Decca, of which

3 were from a film soundtrack (**Pete Kelly's Blues**), and

2 were from radio transcriptions.

5 vocals were released on V-Discs,

1 vocal recorded for V-Disc was released on a commercial LP,

38 vocals of concert performances (JATP) were released,

4 vocal commercial transcriptions were released,

56 cabaret performances were released from radio transcriptions,

38 radio performances were released from radio transcriptions, and

1 performance for the soundtrack of the unproduced film, **Finian's Rainbow**, was released.

3 vocal studio recordings have not yet been released,

1 V-Disc vocal was rejected,

4 cabaret performances from radio transcriptions have not yet been released,

18 JATP performances have not yet been released, and

12 performances for a film, **Jazz At The Philharmonic**, have not yet been released.

To recapitulate, of the

612 recordings made by Ella during The Decca Years,

478 may be found on compact discs, and of the remaining,

50 may be found on LP records, and

36 may be found only on 78rpm records; and the remaining

48 have not yet been released.

THE VERVE YEARS (1956–1966)

ELLA FITZGERALD, vocals

Recorded in performance at Shrine Auditorium, Los Angeles, Saturday, 21 January 1956

560121-1 And the Angels Sing *Not yet released*
560121-2 Joe Williams' Blues *Not yet released*
560121-3 Air Mail Special *Not yet released*
560121-4 'S Wonderful *Not yet released*
560121-5 Cry Me a River *Not yet released*
560121-6 Lullaby of Birdland *Not yet released*
560121-7 Medley: a. Fools Rush In; b. Glad to Be Unhappy *Not yet released*

ELLA FITZGERALD, vocals

Accompanied by orchestra conducted by **Buddy Bregman.** Trumpets: Pete Candoli, Harry Edison, Conrad Gozzo, Ray Linn; Trombones: Milt Bernhardt, Joe Howard, Lloyd Ulyate; Bass Trombone: George Roberts; Alto Saxophones: Herb Geller, Bud Shank; Tenor Saxophones: Bob Cooper, Ted Nash; Baritone Saxophone: Chuck Gentry; Piano: Paul Smith; Guitar: Barney Kessel; Bass: Joe Mondragon; Drums: Alvin Stoller; Arrangements: Buddy Bregman. Recorded at Capitol Studios, Los Angeles, Wednesday, 25 January 1956

560125-1 20054-6* Stay There (78: Verve 2012; 45: Verve 10021)
560125-2 20055-7* The Sun Forgot to Shine This Morning (78: Verve 2021; 45: Verve 10021)
560125-3 20056-7* Too Young for the Blues (LPD-86)
560125-4 20056-8* Too Young for the Blues (78: Verve 2002; 45: Verve 10002; LPD-128)
560125-5 20057-5* It's Only a Man (78: Verve 2002; 45: Verve 10002; LPD-128)

Note: These masters were transferred from Clef Mx 2718-6, 2719-7, 2720-7, 2720-8, and 2721-5, respectively.

ELLA FITZGERALD, vocals

Accompanied by Piano: Don Abney; Bass: Vernon Alley; Drums: Frankie Capp. Recorded in performance at Zardi's (nightclub), Los Angeles, Thursday evening, 2 February 1956

560202-1 It All Depends on You *Not yet released*
560202-2 Tenderly *Not yet released*
560202-3 Why Don't You Do Right? *Not yet released*
560202-4 In a Mellow Tone Not Yet released
560202-5 Joe Williams' Blues *Not yet released*
560202-6 A Fine Romance *Not yet released*
560202-7 How High the Moon *Not yet released*
560202-8 Gone with the Wind *Not yet released*
560202-9 Bernie's Tune *Not yet released*
560202-10 'S Wonderful *Not yet released*
560202-11 Glad to Be Unhappy *Not yet released*
560202-12 Lullaby of Birdland Not Yet released
560202-13 (Love Is) The Tender Trap *Not yet released*
560202-14 And the Angels Sing *Not yet released*
560202-15 I Can't Give You Anything but Love *Not yet released*
560202-16 Little Boy *Not yet released*
560202-17 A-Tisket, A-Tasket *Not yet released*
560202-18 My Heart Belongs to Daddy *Not yet released*
560202-19 Air Mail Special *Not yet released*
560202-20 I've Got a Crush on You *Not yet released*

ELLA FITZGERALD, vocals

Ella Fitzgerald Sings the Cole Porter Song Book

Orchestra conducted by **Buddy Bregman.** Trumpets: Pete Candoli-Harry "Sweets" Edison-Maynard Ferguson-Conrad Gozzo; Trombones: Milt Bernhart, Joe Howard, Lloyd Ulyate; Bass Trombone: George Roberts; Alto Saxophones: Herb Geller, Bud Shank; Tenor Saxophones: Bob Cooper, Ted Nash; Baritone Saxophone: Chuck Gentry; Piano: Paul Smith; Guitar: Barney Kessel; Bass: Joe Mondragon; Drums: Alvin Stoller; Arrangements: Buddy Bregman. Recorded at Capitol Records, Los Angeles, Tuesday, 7 February 1956

560207-1 20066-15 Ridin' High (EP: Verve EPV-5011; LPD-41)
560207-2 20067-3 It's All Right with Me (45: Verve 10077; EP: Verve EPV-5006; LPD-41)
560207-3 20068-5 From This Moment On (EP: Verve EPV-5006; LPD-41)
560207-4 20069-1 Just One of Those Things (EP: Verve EPV-5008; LPD-41)
560207-5 20070-5 Too Darn Hot (EP: Verve EPV-5005; LPD-41, LPD-86) Accompanied by Piano: Paul Smith
560207-6 20071-2 Miss Otis Regrets (EP: Verve EPV-5005; LPD-41, LPD-86)

Orchestra conducted by **Buddy Bregman.** Violins: Misha Russell (concertmaster), eleven unknown others; Violas: two unknown; Cellos: Robert La Marchina, Edgar Lustgarten; Flute: Ted Nash; Oboe: Bob Cooper; Harp: Corky Hale; Piano-Celeste: Paul Smith; Guitar: Barney Kessel; Bass: Joe Mondragon; Drums: Alvin Stoller; Arrangements: Buddy Bregman

560207-7 20061-5 Why Can't You Behave? (EP: Verve EPV-5010; LPD-41)
560207-8 20062-3 I Love Paris (EP: Verve EPV-5010; LPD-41)
560207-9 20063-4 Do I Love You? (EP: Verve EPV-5006; LPD-41)

560207-10 20064-6 Ev'ry Time We Say Goodbye (EP: Verve EPV-5007; LPD-41)

560207-11 20065-5 I Am in Love (EP: Verve EPV-5008; LPD-41)

> Accompanied by Piano: Paul Smith; Guitar: Barney Kessel; Bass: Joe Mondragon; Drums: Alvin Stoller; Arrangements: Buddy Bregman

560207-12 20072-2 Get Out of Town (EP: Verve EPV-5005; LPD-41)

560207-13 20073-2 Easy To Love (EP: Verve EPV-5011; LPD-41)

ELLA FITZGERALD, vocals

Ella Fitzgerald Sings the Cole Porter Song Book, etc.

> Accompanied by orchestra conducted by **Buddy Bregman.** Violins: Misha Russell (concertmaster), eleven unknown others; Violas: two unknown; Cellos: Robert La Marchina, Edgar Lustgarten; Trumpets: Pete Candoli, Harry "Sweets" Edison, Maynard Ferguson, Conrad Gozzo; Trombones: Milt Bernhart, Joe Howard, Lloyd Ulyate; Bass Trombone: George Roberts; Flutes: Ted Nash, Bud Shank; Clarinets: Bob Cooper, Herb Geller, Ted Nash, Bud Shank*; Alto Saxophones: Herb Geller, Bud Shank; Tenor Saxophones: Bob Cooper, Ted Nash; Baritone Saxophone Bass Clarinet: Chuck Gentry; Harp: Corky Hale; Piano: Paul Smith; Guitar: Barney Kessel; Bass: Joe Mondragon; Drums: Alvin Stoller; Arrangements: Buddy Bregman, except as noted. Recorded at Capitol Records, Los Angeles, Wednesday, 8 February 1956

*Mr. Shank's clarinet is heard only on "You Do Something to Me," "(I'm) Always True to You in My Fashion," and "Ace in the Hole."

560208-1 20074 Beale Street Blues (arr. Nelson Riddle) (45: Verve 10128)

560208-2 20076-4 You Do Something to Me (EP: Verve EPV-5010; LPD-41)

560208-3 20078-4 Begin the Beguine (EP: Verve EPV-5008; LPD-41)

560208-4 20079-7 All Through the Night (EP: Verve EPV-5004; LPD-41)

560208-5 20080-4 (I'm) Always True to You in My Fashion (EP: Verve EPV-5011; LPD-41)

560208-6 20090-1 You're the Top (EP: Verve EPV 5007; LPD-41)

560208-7 20082-2 Ace in the Hole (EP: Verve EPV-5008; LPD-41)

560208-8 20083-8 Love for Sale (EP: Verve EPV-5007; LPD-41)

560208-9 20084-11 Anything Goes (EP: Verve EPV-5004; LPD-41)

ELLA FITZGERALD, vocals

Ella Fitzgerald Sings the Cole Porter Song

> Accompanied by orchestra conducted by **Buddy Bregman.** Violins: Misha Russell (concertmaster), eleven unknown

others; Violas: four unknown; Cellos: Robert La Marchina, Edgar Lustgarten, two unknown others; Trumpets: Pete Candoli, Harry "Sweets" Edison, Maynard Ferguson, Conrad Gozzo; Trombones: Milt Bernhart, Joe Howard, Lloyd Ulyate; Bass Trombone: George Roberts; Flutes: Ted Nash, Bud Shank; Clarinets: Bob Cooper, Herb Geller, Ted Nash, Bud Shank*; Alto Saxophones: Herb Geller, Bud Shank; Tenor Saxophones: Bob Cooper, Ted Nash; Baritone Saxophone-Bass Clarinet: Chuck Gentry; Harp: Corky Hale; Piano: Paul Smith; Guitar: Barney Kessel; Bass: Joe Mondragon; Drums: Alvin Stoller; Arrangements: Buddy Bregman. Recorded at Capitol Records, Los Angeles, Thursday, 9 February 1956

*Mr. Shank's clarinet is heard only on "It's De-Lovely."

560209-1 20075-2 So in Love (EP: Verve EPV-5009; LPD-41)

560209-2 20077-3 In the Still of the Night (EP: Verve EPV-5009; LPD-41)

560209-3 20081-8 It's De-Lovely (EP: Verve EPV-5004; LPD-41)

560209-4 20085-4 I Concentrate on You (EP: Verve EPV 5009; LPD-41)

> Accompanied by Piano: Paul Smith; Guitar: Barney Kessel; Bass: Joe Mondragon; Drums: Alvin Stoller; Arrangement: Buddy Bregman

560209-5 20086-1 Let's Do It (45: Verve 10050; EP: Verve EPV-5006; LPD-41)

ELLA FITZGERALD, vocals

Ella Fitzgerald Sings the Cole Porter Song Book

> Accompanied by Piano: Paul Smith; Guitar: Barney Kessel; Bass: Joe Mondragon; Drums: Alvin Stoller; Arrangement: Buddy Bregman. Recorded at Capitol Records, Los Angeles, Thursday, 9 February 1956

560209-6 20089-1 I Get a Kick Out of You (EP: Verve EPV-5004; LPD-41)

> Accompanied by orchestra conducted by **Buddy Bregman.** Trombones: Milt Bernhart, Joe Howard, Lloyd Ulyate; Bass Trombone: George Roberts; Piano: Paul Smith; Guitar: Barney Kessel; Bass: Joe Mondragon; Drums: Alvin Stoller; Arrangements: Buddy Bregman

560209-7 20091-2 I've Got You Under My Skin (EP: Verve EPV-5009; LPD-41)

560209-8 20092-2 What Is This Thing Called Loved? (EP: Verve EPV-5010; LPD-41)

560209-9 20093-5 All of You (45: Verve 10077; EP: Verve EPV 5007; LPD-41)

560209-10 20094-2 Don't Fence Me In (EP: Verve EPV-5011; LPD-41)

ELLA FITZGERALD, vocals

Ella Fitzgerald Sings the Cole Porter Song Book, etc.

> Accompanied by orchestra conducted by **Buddy Bregman.** Violins: Misha Russell (concertmaster), seven others unknown;

Violas: two unknown; Cellos: Robert La Marchina, Edgar Lustgarten; Trumpets: Pete Candoli, Harry "Sweets" Edison, Maynard Ferguson, Conrad Gozzo; Trombones: Milt Bernhart, Joe Howard, Lloyd Ulyate; Bass Trombone: George Roberts; Alto Saxophones: Herb Geller, Bud Shank; Tenor Saxophones: Bob Cooper, Ted Nash; Baritone Saxophone: Chuck Gentry; Harp: Corky Hale; Piano: Paul Smith; Guitar: Barney Kessel; Bass: Joe Mondragon; Drums: Alvin Stoller; Arrangements: Buddy Bregman. Recorded at Capitol Records, Tuesday, 27 March 1956

560327-1   20121-10 Night and Day (EP: Verve EPV-5005; LPD-41)

560327-2   20122-3 (The End of) A Beautiful Friendship (78: Verve 2012; 45: Verve 10012; LPD-73, LPD-128)

Note: Charted 28 July 1956; weeks, 5; peak, #74

Accompanied by Piano: Paul Smith; Guitar: Barney Kessel; Bass: Joe Mondragon; Drums: Alvin Stoller; Arrangements: Buddy Bregman

560327-3   20123-3 You're the Top (LPD-41)

560327-4   20124-8 I Concentrate on You (LPD-41)

560327-5   20125-10 I Had to Find Out for Myself *Not yet released*

560327-6   20125-11 I Had to Find Out for Myself *Not yet released*

560327-7   20126-3 Let's Do It (LPD-41)

*Note: The 2-LP album, **Ella Fitzgerald Sings the Cole Porter Song Book**, charted 28 July 1956; weeks, 15; peak, #1 (the first multi-LP album to achieve this distinction.*

ELLA FITZGERALD, vocals

METRONOME All Star Date (Metronome All Stars, 1956)

Accompanied by **Count Basie and His Orchestra.** Count Basie, Leader/Piano.* Trumpets: Wendell Culley, Reunald Jones, Thaddeus "Thad" Jones, Joe Newman; Trombones: Henry Coker, Bill Hughes, Benny Powell; Flute: Frank Wess; Clarinet: Marshall Royal; Alto Saxophones: Bill Graham, Marshall Royall; Tenor Saxophones: Frank Foster, Frank Wess; Baritone Saxophone: Charlie Fowlkes; Piano: Ralph Burns*; Guitar: Freddie Green; Bass: Eddie Jones; Drums: Percival "Sonny" Payne; Arrangement: William B. Davis, Ralph Burns. Recorded at Fine Sound Studio, New York, Monday, 25 June 1956

560625-1   2900-4 April in Paris (78: Columbia LX-1621 (12"); 45: Clef 89172; EP: Clef EPC-303; LPD-42, LPD-86)

ELLA FITZGERALD–
JOE WILLIAMS, vocal duet

560625-2   2901-1 Too Close for Comfort (EP: Verve 74047, EPV-5161; LPD-129)

560625-3   2902-1 Salty Lips Rejected

560625-4   2903-2 Every Day I Have the Blues (EP: Clef EPC-303; LPD-42)

Count Basie is replaced at piano by Ralph Burns on "April in Paris" and "Every Day I Have the Blues."

Accompanied by **The Count Basie Octet** (Trumpets: Thaddeus "Thad" Jones, Joe Newman; Trombone: Henry Coker; Tenor Saxophone: Frank Wess; Piano: William "Count" Basie; Guitar: Freddie Green; Bass: Eddie Jones; Drums: Percival "Sonny" Payne

560625-5   2904-5 Party Blues (78: Columbia LX-1621 (12"); 45: Clef 89172; EP: Clef EPC-303; LPD-42)

ELLA FITZGERALD, vocals

Jazz at the Hollywood Bowl

Accompanied by Piano: Paul Smith; Guitar: Barney Kessel; Bass: Joe Mondragon; Drums: Alvin Stoller. Recorded in performance at The Hollywood Bowl, Los Angeles, Wednesday evening, 15 August 1956

560815-1   This Can't Be Love *Not yet released*

560815-2   (The End of) A Beautiful Friendship *Not yet released*

560815-3   I Could Have Danced All Night *Not yet released*

560815-4   Oh, Lady, Be Good! *Not yet released*

560815-5   Love for Sale (EP: Verve EPV-5063; LPD-43)

560815-6   Just One of Those Things (LPD-43)

560815-7   Angel Eyes *Not yet Released*

560815-8   Little Girl Blue (EP: Verve EPV-5063; LPD-43)

560815-9   Too Close for Comfort (LPD-43)

560815-10   I Can't Give You Anything but Love (EP: Verve EPV-5063; LPD-43)

560815-11   Air Mail Special (EP: Verve EPV-5063; LPD-43)

VOCAL DUETS WITH LOUIS ARMSTRONG

Accompanied by Trumpet: Louis Armstrong; Trombone: Trummy Young; Clarinet: Ed Hall; Piano: Billy Kyle; Bass: Dale Jones; Drums: Barrett Deems

560815-12   You Won't Be Satisfied (EP: Verve EPV-5064; LPD-43)

560815-13   Undecided (EP: Verve EPV-5064; LPD-43, LPD-86)

Accompanied by the **Jazz At The Philharmonic All-Stars**: Trumpets: Louis Armstrong, Harry "Sweets" Edison, Roy Eldridge; Tenor Saxophones: Illinois Jacquet, Flip Phillips; Trombone: Trummy Young; Clarinet: Ed Hall; Piano: Billy Kyle; Guitar: Herb Ellis; Bass: Ray Brown; Drums: Alvin Stoller

560815-14   Finale: When the Saints Go Marching In (EP: Verve EPV-5064; LPD-43)

Ella Fitzgerald and
Louis Armstrong, vocals

Ella and Louis

Accompanied by Trumpet: Louis Armstrong; Piano: Oscar Peterson; Guitar: Herb Ellis; Bass: Ray Brown; Drums: Buddy Rich. Recorded at Capitol Records, Thursday, 16 August 1956

560816-1   20207-2 They Can't Take That Away from Me (EP: Verve EPV-5014; LPD-44)

560816-2   20208-8 Isn't This a Lovely Day? (EP: Verve EPV-5012; LPD-44)

560816-3   20209-5 Tenderly (EP: Verve EPV-5013; LPD-44)

560816-4   20210-2 Stars Fell on Alabama (78: Verve 2023; 45: Verve 10023; EP: Verve EPV-5015; LPD-44)

560816-5   20222-2 Can't We Be Friends? (78: Verve 2023; 45: Verve 10023; EP: Verve EPV5047; LPD-44, LPD-86)

560816-6   20211-5 Cheek to Cheek (EP: Verve EPV-5012; LPD-44)

560816-7   20212-10 Under a Blanket of Blue (EP: Verve EPV 5015; LPD-44)

560816-8   20213-7 Moonlight in Vermont (EP: Verve EPV 5015; LPD-44)

560816-9   20214-6 A Foggy Day (in London Town) (EP: Verve EPV 5015; LPD-44)

560816-10   20215-6 April in Paris (EP: Verve EPV 5013; LPD-44)

560816-11   20216-1 The Nearness of You (EP: Verve EPV 5014; LPD-44)

Note: This album, **Ella and Louis,** *charted 15 December 1956; weeks, 2; peak #12*

Ella Fitzgerald, vocals

Ella Fitzgerald Sings the
Rodgers and Hart Song Book, etc.

Orchestra conducted by **Buddy Bregman.** Trumpets: Pete Candoli, Maynard Ferguson, Conrad Gozzo, Ray Linn; Trombones: Milt Bernhart, Joe Howard, Lloyd Ulyate; Bass Trombone: George Roberts; Alto Saxophones: Bud Shank, Maurice Stein; Tenor Saxophones: Bob Cooper, Ted Nash; Baritone Saxophone: Chuck Gentry; Piano: Paul Smith; Guitar: Barney Kessel; Bass: Joe Mondragon; Drums: Alvin Stoller; Arrangements: Buddy Bregman. Recorded at Studio A, Capitol Records, Los Angeles, Tuesday, 21 August 1956

560821-1   20217-5 This Can't Be Love (EP: Verve EPV-5033; LPD-45)

560821-2   20218-5 The Lady Is a Tramp (EP: Verve EPV-5032; LPD-45)

560821-3   20219-7 I've Got Five Dollars (EP: Verve EPV-5028; LPD-45)

560821-4   20220-alt Lover (LPD-45)

560821-5   20220-3 Lover (EP: Verve EPV-5029; LPD-45)

560821-6   20221-3 The Silent Treatment (78: Verve 2021; 45: Verve 10021; LPD-128)

Ella Fitzgerald, vocals

Ella Fitzgerald Sings the
Rodgers and Hart Song Book

Orchestra conducted by **Buddy Bregman.** Violins: Misha Russell (concertmaster) and eleven unknown others; Violas: two unknown; Cellos: Robert La Marchina, Edgar Lustgarten; Trumpets: Pete Candoli, Maynard Ferguson, Conrad Gozzo, Ray Linn; French Horn: Vincent DeRosa, one unknown; Trombones: Milt Bernhart, Joe Howard, Lloyd Ulyate; Bass Trombone: George Roberts; Soprano Saxophones: Bub Shank, Willie Schwartz; Alto Saxophones: Bud Shank, Willie Schwartz; Tenor Saxophones: Bob Cooper, Ted Nash; Baritone Saxophone: Chuck Gentry; Flutes: Ted Nash, Bud Shank; Clarinets: Bob Cooper, Ted Nash, Bud Shank, Willie Schwartz; Bass Clarinet: Chuck Gentry; Piano: Paul Smith; Guitar: Barney Kessel; Bass: Joe Mondragon; Drums: Alvin Stoller; Arrangements: Buddy Bregman. Recorded in Studio B, Capitol Records, Los Angeles, Tuesday, 28 August 1956

560828-1   20223-3 Ten Cents a Dance (EP: Verve EPV-5028; LPD-45)

560828-2   20224-3 I Wish I Were in Love Again (EP: Verve EPV-5032; LPD-45)

560828-3   20225-2 Mountain Greenery (EP: Verve EPV-5027; LPD-45)

560828-4   20226-7 Johnny One Note (EP: Verve EPV-5032; LPD-45)

560828-5   20227-10 Give It Back to the Indians (EP: Verve EPV-5034; LPD-45)

Ella Fitzgerald, vocals

Ella Fitzgerald Sings the
Rodgers and Hart Song Book

Orchestra conducted by **Buddy Bregman.** Violins: Misha Russell (concertmaster) eleven unknown others; Violas: two unknown; Cellos: Robert La Marchina, Edgar Lustgarten, two unknown others; French Horns: Vincent DeRosa, two unknown others; Flutes: Ted Nash, Willie Schwartz, Bud Shank; Oboe: Arnold Koblentz; English Horn: Arnold Koblentz; Bassoons: Chuck Gentry, two unknown others; Baritone Saxophone: Chuck Gentry; Bass Clarinet: Chuck Gentry; Harp: Corky Hale; Piano: Paul Smith; Guitar: Barney Kessel; Bass: Joe Mondragon; Glockenspiel-Marimbas-Timpani-Tubular Bells-Vibraphone-Xylophone: Milt Holland; Drums: Alvin Stoller; Arrangements: Buddy Bregman. Recorded at Studio B, Capitol Records, Los Angeles, Wednesday, 29 August 1956

560829-1   20228-3 Blue Moon (EP: Verve EPV-5029; LPD-45)

560829-2   20229-3 Thou Swell (EP: Verve EPV-5031; LPD-45)

560829-3   20230-1 Manhattan (45: Verve V10050; EP: Verve EPV-5031; LPD-45)

560829-4   20231-4 There's a Small Hotel (EP: Verve EPV-5034; LPD-45)

560829-5   20232-3 I Didn't Know What Time It Was (EP: Verve EPV-5034; LPD-45)

> Accompanied by Piano: Paul Smith; Guitar: Barney Kessel; Bass: Joe Mondragon; Drums: Alvin Stoller

560829-6   20233-6 With a Song in My Heart (EP: Verve EPV-5030; LPD-45)

560829-7   20234-4 To Keep My Love Alive (EP: Verve EPV-5030; LPD-45)

560829-8   20235-3 Bewitched (Bothered and Bewildered) (EP: Verve EPV-5027; LPD-45, LPD-86)

> Accompanied by Guitar: Barney Kessel

560829-9   20236-4 Wait Till You See Her (EP: Verve EPV 5027; LPD-45)

ELLA FITZGERALD, vocals

Ella Fitzgerald Sings the Rodgers and Hart Song Book

> Accompanied by orchestra conducted by **Buddy Bregman**. Violins: Misha Russell (concertmaster) eleven unknown others; Violas: four unknown; Cellos: Robert La Marchina, Edgar Lustgarten, two unknown others; Harp: Corky Hale; Piano-Celeste: Paul Smith; Guitar: Barney Kessel; Bass: Joe Mondragon; Drums: Alvin Stoller; Glockenspiel-Percussion: Milt Holland; Arrangements: Buddy Bregman. Recorded in Studio B, Capitol Records, Los Angeles, Thursday, 30 August 1956

560830-1   20237-2 My Romance (EP: Verve EPV-5034; LPD-45)

560830-2   20237-3 My Heart Stood Still (EP: Verve EPV-5028; LPD-45)

> Accompanied by orchestra conducted by **Buddy Bregman**. Violins: Misha Russell (concertmaster) seven unknown others; Violas: two unknown; Cellos: Robert La Marchina, Edgar Lustgarten; French Horn: Vincent DeRosa; Flute: Ted Nash; Oboe-English Horn: Bob Cooper; Harp: Corky Hale; Piano-Celeste: Paul Smith; Guitar: Barney Kessel; Bass: Joe Mondragon; Glockenspiel-Vibraphone: Milt Holland; Drums: Alvin Stoller; Arrangements: Buddy Bregman

560830-3   20239-1 A Ship Without a Sail (EP: Verve EPV-5031; LPD-45)

560830-4   20240-1 Have You Met Sir (Miss) Jones? (EP: Verve EPV-5030; LPD-45)

560830-5   20242-2 It Never Entered My Mind (EP: Verve EPV-5033; LPD-45)

560830-6   20243-2 Little Girl Blue (EP: Verve EPV-5033; LPD-45)

560830-7   20244-6 Spring Is Here (EP: Verve EPV-5032; LPD-45)

> Accompanied by orchestra conducted by **Buddy Bregman**. Violins: Misha Russell (concertmaster) eleven unknown others; Violas: four unknown; Cellos: Robert La Marchina, Edgar Lustgarten, two unknown others; Harp: Corky Hale; Piano-Celeste: Paul Smith; Guitar: Barney Kessel; Bass: Joe Mondragon; Drums: Alvin Stoller; Glockenspiel-Percussion: Milt Holland; Arrangements: Buddy Bregman

560830-8   20245-2 My Funny Valentine (EP: Verve EPV-5035; LPD-45)

560830-9   20246-1 I Could Write a Book (EP: Verve EPV-5035; LPD-45)

ELLA FITZGERALD, vocals

Ella Fitzgerald Sings the Rodgers and Hart Song Book

> Accompanied by orchestra conducted by **Buddy Bregman**. Trumpet: Ray Linn*; French Horn: Vincent DeRosa; Flute: Jule Kinzler; Clarinet: Abe Most; Oboe: Arnold Koblentz; English Horn: Bob Cooper; Bass Clarinet-Bassoon: Chuck Gentry; Piano: Paul Smith; Guitar: Barney Kessel; Bass: Joe Mondragon; Drums: Alvin Stoller; Arrangements: Paul Smith. Recorded in Studio A, Capitol Records, Los Angeles, Friday, 31 August 1956

*Mr. Linn's trumpet is heard only on "Where or When" and "You Took Advantage of Me."

560831-1   20241-2 Here in My Arms (EP: Verve EPV-5029; LPD-45)

560831-2   20247-4 A Blue Room (EP: Verve EPV-5035; LPD-45)

560831-3   20248-3 Dancing on the Ceiling (He Dances on My Ceiling) (EP: Verve EPV-5031; LPD-45)

560831-4   20249-6 Where or When (EP: Verve EPV-5033; LPD-45)

560831-5   20250-1 Isn't It Romantic? (EP: Verve EPV-5029; LPD-45)

560831-6   20251-2 You Took Advantage of Me (EP: Verve EPV-5030; LPD-45)

*Note: This album, **Ella Fitzgerald Sings the Rodgers and Hart Song Book**, charted 16 March 1957; weeks, 4; peak, #11*

ELLA FITZGERALD, vocals

Ella Fitzgerald Sings the Duke Ellington Song Book, etc.

> Accompanied by Violin: Stuff Smith; Tenor Saxophone: Ben Webster; Piano: Paul Smith; Guitar: Barney Kessel; Bass: Joe Mondragon; Drums: Alvin Stoller. Recorded at Radio Recorders, Los Angeles, Tuesday, 4 September 1956

560904-1   20252-4 I Let a Song Go Out of My Heart (EP: Verve EPV-5016; LPD-51)

560904-2   20253-1 Rocks in My Bed (EP: Verve EPV-5019; LPD-51)

560904-3   20254-3 Cotton Tail (EP: Verve EPV-5016; LPD-51)

560904-4   20255-1 Just Squeeze Me (EP: Verve EPV-5019; LPD-51)

560904-5   20256-4 Do Nothin' Till You Hear from Me (EP: Verve EPV-5016; LPD-51)

560904-6   20257-2 Solitude* (EP: Verve EPV-5018; LPD-51)

560904-7   20258-6 Sophisticated Lady (EP: Verve EPV-5018; LPD-51)

560904-8   20259-2 Just A-Sittin' and A-Rockin' (EP: Verve EPV-5018; LPD-51, LPD-86)

560904-9   20260-1 It Don't Mean a Thing (If It Ain't Got That Swing) (EP: Verve EPV-5017; LPD-51)

560904-10   20261-4 Prelude to a Kiss (EP: Verve EPV-5017; LPD-51)

560904-11   20262-1 Don't Get Around Much Anymore (EP: Verve EPV-5018; LPD-51)

560904-12   20263-3 Satin Doll (EP: Verve EPV-5019; LPD-51)

560904-13   20264-2 Azure* (EP: Verve EPV-5017; LPD-51)

560904-14   20265-5 In a Sentimental Mood* (EP: Verve EPV-5019; LPD-51)

560904-15   20266-2 Ev'rything I've Got Belongs to You** (EP: Verve EPV-5035; LPD-45)

*Accompanied by Guitar: Barney Kessel, only.

This track, with accompaniment of Piano: Paul Smith; Guitar: Barney Kessel; Bass: Joe Mondragon; and Drums: Alvin Stoller, only, is a part of **Ella Fitzgerald Sings the Rodgers and Hart Song Book.

ELLA FITZGERALD, vocals

Accompanied by orchestra conducted by Russ Garcia (personnel unknown). Arrangements: Russ Garcia. Recorded at Capitol Records, Los Angeles, Monday, 14 January 1957

570114-1   20575-9 Hear My Heart (45: Verve V-10031)

570114-2   20576-8 Hotta Chocolata (45: Verve V-10031)

ELLA FITZGERALD, vocals

Jazz At The Philharmonic: "Americans in Sweden"

Accompanied by Piano: Don Abney; Guitar: Herb Ellis; Bass: Ray Brown; Drums: Jo Jones. Recorded in performance at the Konserthuset, Stockholm (Sweden), Monday, 28 April 1957

570428-1   You Got Me Singin' the Blues

570428-2   Angel Eyes

570428-3   Lullaby of Birdland

570428-4   Tenderly

570428-5   Do Nothin' Till You Hear from Me

570428-6   April in Paris

570428-7   I Can't Give You Anything but Love

(All titles on LPD-46, LPD-50)

Recorded in performance at The Circus, Stockholm (Sweden), Tuesday, 29 April 1957. Accompanied by Piano: Don Abney; Guitar: Herb Ellis; Bass: Ray Brown; Drums: Jo Jones

570429-1   Love for Sale

Accompanied by Trumpet: Roy Eldridge; Violin: Stuff Smith; Piano: Oscar Peterson; Guitar: Herb Ellis; Bass: Ray Brown; Drums: Jo Jones

570429-2   It Don't Mean a Thing (if It Ain't Got That Swing)

(Both titles on LPD-46, LPD-50)

ELLA FITZGERALD, vocals

Ella Fitzgerald Sings the Duke Ellington Song Volume

Accompanied by **Duke Ellington and His Orchestra. Duke Ellington,** Leader/Piano. Trumpets: Cat Anderson, Willie Cook, Dizzy Gillespie,* Ray Nance, Clark Terry; Trombones: Quentin Jackson, John Sanders, Britt Woodman; Clarinets: Harry Carney, Jimmy Hamilton, Russel Procope; Bass Clarinet: Harry Carney; Alto Saxophones: Johnny Hodges, Russell Procope; Tenor Saxophones: Frank Foster, Jimmy Hamilton; Baritone Saxophone: Harry Carney; Piano: Billy Strayhorn*; Bass: Jimmy Woode; Drums: Sam Woodyard; Vocals: Ray Nance; Arrangements: Billy Strayhorn. Recorded at Fine Recording Studios, New York, Monday, 24 June 1957

570624-1   21033-6 Day Dream (LPD-51)

570624-2   21034-6 Take the A Train* (LPD-51)

570624-3   21035 I'm Just a Lucky So-and-So Rejected

*Mr. Gillespie is heard only on "Take the A Train," on which also Duke Ellington replaces Billy Strayhorn at piano.

ELLA FITZGERALD, vocals

Ella Fitzgerald Sings the Duke Ellington Song Book

Accompanied by **Duke Ellington and His Orchestra. Duke Ellington,** Leader/Piano. Trumpets: Cat Anderson, Willie Cook, Ray Nance (or Harold "Shorty" Baker), Clark Terry; Trombones: Quentin Jackson, John Sanders, Britt Woodman; Clarinets: Harry Carney, Jimmy Hamilton, Russell Procope; Bass Clarinet: Harry Carney; Alto Saxophones: Johnny Hodges, Russell Procope; Tenor Saxophones: Paul Gonsalves, Jimmy Hamilton; Baritone Saxophone: Harry Carney; Piano: Duke Ellington; Bass: Jimmy Woode; Drums: Sam Woodyard; Clave: Mercer Ellington*; Cowbell: Clark Terry.* Recorded at Fine Recording Studios, New York, Tuesday, 25 June 1957

570625-1 21036-6 Everything But You (LPD-51)

570625-2 21037-6 I Got It Bad (and That Ain't Good) (LPD-51)

570625-3 21038-3 Drop Me Off in Harlem (LPD-51)

570625-4 21039-4 Lost in Meditation (LPD-51)

570625-5 21040-4 I Ain't Got Nothin' but the Blues (LPD-51)

The clave and cowbell are heard only on "Lost in Meditation."

ELLA FITZGERALD, vocals

Ella Fitzgerald Sings the Duke Ellington Song Book

Accompanied by **Duke Ellington and His Orchestra. Duke Ellington**, Leader/Piano Trumpets: Cat Anderson, Willie Cook-, Ray Nance (or Harold "Shorty" Baker), Clark Terry; Trombones: Quentin Jackson, John Sanders, Britt Woodman; Clarinets: Harry Carney, Jimmy Hamilton, Russell Procope; Bass Clarinet: Harry Carney; Alto Saxophones: Johnny Hodges, Russell Procope; Tenor Saxophones: Frank Foster, Jimmy Hamilton; Baritone Saxophone: Harry Carney; Piano: Duke Ellington, Billy Strayhorn*; Bass: Jimmy Woode; Drums: Sam Woodyard. Recorded at Fine Recording Studios, New York, Wednesday, 26 June 1957

570626-1 21049-2 Clementine* (LPD-51)

570626-2 21050 I'm Just a Lucky So-and-So (LPD-51, LPD-86)

570626-3 21051-12 I'm Beginning to See the Light (LPD-51)

570626-4 21052 I Didn't Know About You (LPD-51)

570626-5 21053-3 Rockin' in Rhythm (LPD-51)

*Billy Strayhorn replaces Ellington at piano on "Clementine."

ELLA FITZGERALD, vocals

Ella Fitzgerald Sings the Duke Ellington Song Book

Accompanied by **Duke Ellington and His Orchestra. Duke Ellington**, Leader/Piano; Trumpets: Cat Anderson, Harold "Shorty" Baker (or Ray Nance), Willie Cook, Clark Terry; Trombones: Quentin Jackson, John Sanders, Britt Woodman; Clarinets: Harry Carney, Jimmy Hamilton, Russell Procope; Bass Clarinet: Russell Procope; Alto Saxophones: Johnny Hodges, Russell Procope; Tenor Saxophones: Paul Gonsalves, Jimmy Hamilton; Piano: Duke Ellington, Billy Strayhorn*; Bass: Jimmy Woode; Drums: Sam Woodyard. Recorded at Fine Recording Studios, New York, Thursday, 27 June 1957

570627-1 21062-5 Lush Life** *Not yet released*

570627-2 21063-3 All Too Soon (LPD-51)

570627-3 21064-8 Caravan (LPD-51)

570627-4 21065-7 Bli-Blip (LPD-51)

570627-5 Rehearsal Chelsea Bridge* (LPD-51)

570627-6 Rehearsal Chelsea Bridge* (LPD-51)

570627-7 Rehearsal Chelsea Bridge* (LPD-51)

570627-8 Rehearsal Chelsea Bridge* (LPD-51)

570627-9 Rehearsal Chelsea Bridge* (LPD-51)

570627-10 21066-alt Chelsea Bridge* (LPD-51)

570627-11 21066-8 Chelsea Bridge* (LPD-51)

570627-12 21067-4 Perdido (LPD-51)

570627-13 21068-2 The E and D Blues (E for Ella, D for Duke) (LPD-51)

*Billy Strayhorn replaces Ellington at piano on "Chelsea Bridge" tracks

**Accompanied by Piano: Billy Strayhorn, only

ELLA FITZGERALD, vocals

Jazz At The Philharmonic; The Newport Jazz Festival, 1957 (Ella Fitzgerald, Billie Holiday and Carmen McRae at Newport)

Accompanied by Piano: Don Abney; Bass: Wendell Marshall; Drums: Jo Jones. Recorded in performance at Freebody Park, Newport, Rhode Island, Thursday, 4 July 1957

570704-1 This Can't Be Love

570704-2 I Got It Bad (and That Ain't Good)

570704-3 Body and Soul

570704-4 Too Close for Comfort

570704-5 Lullaby of Birdland

570704-6 I'm Gonna Sit Right Down and Write Myself a Letter

570704-7 April in Paris

570704-8 I've Got a Crush on You

570704-9 Air Mail Special (LPD-86)

570704-10 I Can't Give You Anything by Love

(All titles on LPD-47)

*For information on other recordings made at the 1957 Newport Jazz Festival on this LP and CD, see page 219.

ELLA FITZGERALD AND LOUIS ARMSTRONG, vocals

Ella and Louis Again

Accompanied by Trumpet: Louis Armstrong; Piano: Oscar Peterson; Guitar: Herb Ellis; Bass: Ray Brown; Drums: Louis Bellson. Recorded at Capitol Records, Los Angeles, Tuesday, 23 July 1957

570723-1 21132-2 Our Love Is Here To Stay (vEF-LA) (EP: Verve EPV-5054; LPD-48)

570723-2 21133-2 Learnin' the Blues (vEF-LA) (EP: Verve EPV-5053; LPD-48)

570723-3 21134-8 Autumn in New York (vEF-LA) (EP: Verve EPV-5049; LPD-48)

570723-4 21135-9 Let's Call the Whole Thing Off (vEF-LA) (EP: Verve EPV-5053; LPD-48)

570723-5 21136-9 They All Laughed (vEF-LA)* (EP: Verve EPV-5050; LPD-48)

570723-6 21137-5 Gee, Baby, Ain't I Good to You (vEF-LA) (EP: Verve EPV-5051; LPD-48)

570723-7   21138-1 Stompin' at the Savoy (vEF-LA) (EP: Verve EPV-5050; LPD-48)

At this point in the session, Mr. Armstrong left, and the session continued with Miss Fitzgerald, solo, accompanied by the rhythm section.

570723-8   21139-3 These Foolish Things (EP: Verve EPV-5052; LPD-48)

570723-9   21140-3 Comes Love (EP: Verve EPV-5049; LPD-48)

570723-10   21141-6 Ill Wind (EP: Verve EPV-5053; LPD-48)

*No trumpet on this track.

ELLA FITZGERALD, vocals

Hello, Love; Get Happy!, etc.

Accompanied by Orchestra conducted by **Frank DeVol.** Violins: Sam Albert, Lou Raderman, Israel Baker, Robert Barene, Harold Dictorow, Sam Freed, Jr., David Frisina, Benny Gill, Mort Herbert, Henry Hill, Anatole Kaminsky, Dan Lube, Alfred Lustgarten, Bill Miller, Ambrose Russo, Albert Saparoff; Violas: G.R. Henhennick, Jan Hlinka, Virginia Majewski, Robert Ostrowsky, Sandford Schonback, Milton Thomas; Cellos: Justin Di Tullio, Armand Kaproff, Raphael Kramer, Nino Rosso; Trumpets: Pete Candoli, Harry "Sweets" Edison, Ray Linn, George Werth; Trombones: Milt Bernhardt, George Roberts, Lloyd Ulyate; Flutes: Martin Ruderman, Sylvia Ruderman; Alto Saxophone: Clint Neagley; Tenor Saxophone: Ben Webster; Woodwinds: Skeets Herfurt, Joseph Koch, Ernest Romersa; Oboes: Bert Gassman, Arnold Koblentz, Gordon Schoneberg; Bassoons: Norman Herzberg, Kenneth Lowman, Jack Marsh; Piano: Arnold Ross; Harp: Dorothy Remsen; Guitar: Barney Kessell; Bass: Abe Luboff, Joe Mondragon, Philip Stephens; Drums: Alvin Stoller; Percussion: Milt Howard; Arrangements: Frank DeVol. Recorded at Capitol Records, Los Angeles, Tuesday, 24 July 1957

570724-1   21162-5 Tenderly (LPD-56)

570724-2   21163-3 Moonlight in Vermont (LPD-56)

570724-3   21164-2 Stairway to the Stars (45: Verve 10171; LPD-56)

570724-4   21165-3 How Long Has This Been Going On? *Not yet released*

570724-5   21166-3 A-Tisket, A-Tasket (45: Verve 10079; LPD-60, LPD-73, LPD-86)

570724-6   21167-4 You Turned the Tables on Me (LPD-60)

570724-7   21168-4 The Gypsy in My Soul (LPD-60)

570724-8   21169-4 Goody Goody (45: Verve 10079; LPD-60)

570724-9   21170-2 St. Louis Blues (45: Verve 10128; LPD-60)

570724-10   21171-6 (Baby,) Don'cha Go 'Way Mad

Four takes were made, at which point Ella suggests fleshing out the introduction. She sings it, and then the instrumentalists rehearse it, and two further takes were made. (Phil Schaap) (LPD-86).

Accompanied by Guitar: Barney Kessel

570724-11   21172-1 Angel Eyes (LPD-86)

ELLA FITZGERALD AND LOUIS ARMSTRONG, vocals

Ella and Louis Again

Accompanied by Trumpet: Louis Armstrong; Piano: Oscar Peterson; Guitar Herb Ellis; Bass: Ray Brown; Drums: Louis Bellson. Recorded at Capitol Records, Los Angeles, Tuesday, 13 August 1957

570813-1   21267-6 I Won't Dance (vEF-LA)* (EP: Verve EPV-5054; LPD-48, LPD-86)

570813-2   21268-5 A Fine Romance (vEF-LA) (EP: Verve EPV-5054; LPD-48)

570813-3   21269-9 Don't Be That Way (vEF-LA)* (EP: Verve EPV-5049; LPD-48, LPD-77)

570813-4   21270-7 I'm Putting All My Eggs in One Basket (vEF-LA)* (EP: Verve EPV-5052; LPD-48)

570813-5   21271-12 I've Got My Love to Keep Me Warm (vEF-LA)* (EP: Verve EPV-5051; LPD-48)

*No trumpet on these tracks.

ELLA FITZGERALD AND LOUIS ARMSTRONG, vocals

Porgy and Bess

Accompanied by orchestra conducted by **Russ Garcia** (personnel, consisting of Strings, Piano, Guitar, Bass, Drums, and Choir, unknown); Arrangements: Russ Garcia. Recorded at Capitol Records, Los Angeles, Sunday, 18 August 1957

570818-1   21290-3 Summertime (vEF-LA) (LPD-86)

570818-2   21291-6 Bess, You Is My Woman Now (vEF-LA)

570818-3   21292-10 I Got Plenty o' Nuttin' (vEF-LA)

570818-4   21293-2 It Ain't Necessarily So (VEF-LA)

(All titles on LPD-57)

ELLA FITZGERALD AND LOUIS ARMSTRONG, vocals

Porgy and Bess

Accompanied by orchestra conducted by **Russ Garcia** (personnel, consisting of Strings, Piano, Guitar, Bass, Drums, and Choir, unknown); Arrangements: Russ Garcia. Recorded at Capitol Records, Los Angeles, Monday, 19 August 1957

570819-1
21294-6 There's a Boat Dat's Leavin' Soon for New York (vEF-LA)
570819-2
21295-9 A Woman Is a Sometime Thing (vLA)
570819-3
21296-9 O Lawd, I'm on My Way (vLA-Choir)
570819-4
21297-9 They Pass By (vEF-LA)*Not yet released
570819-5
21298-11 Bess, Oh Where Is My Bess? (vLA)**

*Armstrong does not play trumpet on this track.

**Remade 14 October 1957, q.v.

(All titles, except "They Pass By," on LPD-57)

ELLA FITZGERALD, vocals

Porgy and Bess

Accompanied by orchestra conducted by **Russ Garcia** (personnel, consisting of Strings, Piano, Guitar, Bass, Drums, and Choir, unknown); Arrangements: Russ Garcia. Recorded at Capitol Records, Los Angeles, Wednesday, 28 August 1957

570828-1   21360-1 I Wants to Stay Here
570828-2   21361-4 My Man's Gone Now
570828-3   21362-14 What You Want Wid Bess?
570828-4   21363-7 The Buzzard Song
570828-5   21364-4 Oh, Doctor Jesus
570828-6   21365-1 Here Comes de Honey Man
570828-7   21366-2 Oh, Dey's So Fresh an' Fine (Strawberry Woman)
21367-1   Medley Music (no vocal)* Not yet released

*Remade 14 October 1957, q.v.

(All titles, except "Medley Music," on LPD-57)

☙

The following entry is included for information of those interested. These are the final tracks on **Ella Fitzgerald Sings the Duke Ellington Song Book**, but contain no vocals by Miss Fitzgerald.

DUKE ELLINGTON AND HIS ORCHESTRA

Conducted by **Duke Ellington.** Trumpets: Cat Anderson, Harold "Shorty" Baker, Willie Cook, Clark Terry; Trombones: Quentin Jackson, John Sanders, Britt Woodman; Clarinets: Harry Carney, Jimmy Hamilton, Russel Procope; Bass Clarinet: Harry Carney; Alto Saxophones: Johnny Hodges, Russell Procope; Tenor Saxophones: Paul Gonsalves, Jimmy Hamilton; Pianos: Duke Ellington,** Billy Strayhorn*; Bass: Jimmy Woode; Drums: Sam Woodyard; Narrators: Duke Ellington,* Billy Strayhorn** (Narration was dubbed in October 1957). Recorded at Universal Recording Studio, Chicago, Tuesday, 3 September 1957

570903-1   21380-13 Portrait of Ella, First Movement: Royal Ancestry*

570903-2   21381-1 Portrait of Ella, Second Movement: All Heart*
570903-3   21381-3 Portrait of Ella, Second Movement: All Heart*
570903-4   21381-6 Portrait of Ella, Second Movement: All Heart*
570903-5   21381-8 Portrait of Ella, Second Movement: All Heart*
570903-2   21381-12 Portrait of Ella, Second Movement: All Heart*
570903-3   21382-7 Portrait of Ella, Third Movement: Beyond Category*
570903-4   21383-4 Portrait of Ella, Fourth Movement: Total Jazz* **

(All titles on LPD-51)

ELLA FITZGERALD, vocals

Jazz At The Philharmonic (Ella Fitzgerald at the Opera House)

Accompanied by Piano: Oscar Peterson; Guitar: Herb Ellis; Bass: Ray Brown; Drums: Jo Jones. Recorded in performance at Chicago Civic Opera, Chicago (Illinois), Sunday, 29 September 1957

570929-1   It's All Right with Me (early concert) Not yet released
570929-2   It's All Right with Me
570929-3   Don'cha Go 'Way Mad
570929-4   Bewitched (Bothered, and Bewildered)
570929-5   These Foolish Things
570929-6   Ill Wind
570929-7   Goody Goody
570929-8   Moonlight in Vermont
570929-9   Them There Eyes

Accompanied by J.A.T.P. All-Stars. Trumpet: Roy Eldridge; Trombone: J.J. Johnson; Alto Saxophone: Sonny Stitt; Tenor Saxophones: Stan Getz, Coleman Hawkins, Illinois Jacquet, Flip Phillips, Lester Young; Piano: Oscar Peterson; Guitar: Herb Ellis; Bass: Ray Brown; Drums: Connie Kay

570929-10   Stompin' at the Savoy (45: Verve 89187)
570929-11   Oh, Lady, Be Good!**

*Connie Kay replaces Jo Jones

**Jo Jones replaces Connie Kay

(All titles on LPD-49)

ELLA FITZGERALD, vocals

Jazz At The Philharmonic (Ella Fitzgerald at the Opera House)

Accompanied by Piano: Oscar Peterson; Guitar: Herb Ellis; Bass: Ray Brown; Drums: Joe Jones. Recorded in performance at the Shrine Auditorium, Los Angeles, Wednesday, 9 October 1957

571009-1   It's All Right with Me
571009-2   Don'cha Go 'Way Mad
571009-3   Bewitched (Bothered, and Bewildered) (LPD-50)
571009-4   These Foolish Things (LPD-50)
571009-5   Ill Wind
571009-6   Goody Goody (LPD-73)
571009-7   Moonlight in Vermont

    Accompanied by J.A.T.P. All-Stars. Trumpet: Roy Eldridge; Trombone: J.J. Johnson; Alto Saxophone: Sonny Stitt; Tenor Saxophones: Stan Getz, Coleman Hawkins, Illinois Jacquet, Flip Phillips, Lester Young; Piano: Oscar Peterson; Guitar: Herb Ellis; Bass: Ray Brown; Drums: Connie Kay,* Jo Jones**

571009-8   Stompin' at the Savoy* (LPD-50)
571009-9   Oh! Lady, Be Good!** (LPD-86)

(All titles on LPD-49)

✌

    The following entry is made for the information of interested readers. There are no Ella Fitzgerald vocals, although the titles appear on **Ella Fitzgerald; Louis Armstrong; Porgy and Bess**

LOUIS ARMSTRONG, VOCALS

    Accompanied by orchestra conducted by **Russ Garcia** (personnel not known). Recorded at Capitol Records, Los Angeles, Monday, 14 October 1957

21708   Porgy and Bess: Overture (no vocals)
21367-2   Medley Music (no vocals)
21714-1   Crab Man (vLA)
21715   Bess, You Is My Woman Now*

*Additional orchestration recorded on this date was intercut with master 21291-6 recorded on 18 August 1957 (q.v.)

(All titles on LPD-57)

ELLA FITZGERALD, vocals

Like Someone in Love

    Accompanied by orchestra conducted by **Frank DeVol**, featuring Tenor Saxophone: Stan Getz*; Arrangements: Frank DeVol. Recorded at Capitol Records, Los Angeles, Tuesday, 15 October 1957

571015-1   21728-6 There's a Lull in My Life* (EP: Verve EPV-5058; LPD-52)
571015-2   21729-5 You're Blasé* (EP: Verve EPV 5060; LPD-52)
571015-3   21730-3 More Than You Know (EP: Verve EPV-5058; LPD-52, LPD-86)
571015-4   21731-1 Like Someone in Love (EP: Verve EPV-5059; LPD-52)
571015-5   21732-1 What Will I Tell My Heart?* (45: Verve 10111; EP: Verve EPV-5058; LPD-52)

571015-6   21733-4 We'll Be Together Again (EP: Verve EPV-5059; LPD-52)
571015-7   21734-2 Then I'll Be Tired of You (EP: Verve EPV-5059; LPD-52)
571015-8   21735-6 Close Your Eyes (EP: Verve EPV-5059; LPD-52)
571015-9   21736-8 I Thought About You (EP: Verve EPV-5060; LPD-52)
571015-10   21737-4 I Never Had a Chance (EP: Verve EPV-5058; LPD-52)
571015-11   21738-6 Midnight Sun* (45: Verve 10111; EP: Verve EPV-5060; LPD-52)
571015-12   21739 How Long Has This Been Going On? *Not yet released*

(This title was remade on 28 October 1957)

ELLA FITZGERALD, vocals

Ella Fitzgerald Sings the Duke Ellington Song Book

    Accompanied by Tenor Saxophone: Ben Webster; Piano: Oscar Peterson; Guitar: Herb Ellis; Bass: Ray Brown; Drums: Alvin Stoller. Recorded at Capitol Records, Los Angeles, Thursday, 17 October 1957

571017-1   21773-5 In a Mellow Tone
571017-2   21774-6 Mood Indigo*
571017-3   21775-8 Love You Madly
571017-4   21776-11 Lush Life** (LPD-86)
571017-5   21777-9 Squatty Roo

*Tenor Saxophone: Ben Webster is not heard on this track

**Accompanied by Guitar: Oscar Peterson, only

(All titles appear on LPD-51)

ELLA FITZGERALD, vocals

Like Someone in Love; Hello, Love

    Accompanied by orchestra conducted by **Frank DeVol**, featuring Tenor Saxophone: Stan Getz*; Arrangements: Frank DeVol. Recorded at Capitol Records, Los Angeles, Monday, 28 October 1957

571028-1   21792-3 I'll Never Be the Same (LPD-52, LPD-56)
571028-2   21793-5 Night Wind (LPD-52)
571028-3   21794-4 Hurry Home* (EP: Verve EPV-5061; LPD-52)
571028-4   21795-3 How Long Has This Been Going On?* (EP: Verve EPV-5061; LPD-52)
571028-5   21796-2 Lost in a Fog (LPD-50, LPD-56)
571028-6   21797-3 Everything Happens to Me (LPD-50, LPD-56)
571028-7   21798-2 What's New?* (EP: Verve EPV-5061; LPD-52)
571028-8   21799-1 So Rare (LPD-50, LPD-56)

ELLA FITZGERALD, vocals

Ella Fitzgerald Sings the Irving Berlin Song Book

Accompanied by orchestra conducted by **Paul Weston**. Trumpet: Don Fagerquist; Clarinet: Fred Stulce; Trombones: Ted Nash, Babe Russin; Baritone Saxophone: Chuck Gentry; Woodwinds: Gene Cipriano; Piano: Paul Smith; Guitar: Barney Kessel; Bass: Jack Ryan; Drums: Alvin Stoller; Arrangements: Paul Weston. Recorded at Radio Recorders, Los Angeles, Thursday, 13 March 1958

580313-1 22119-4 Isn't This a Lovely Day (To Be Caught in the Rain)
580313-2 22120-2 All By Myself in the Morning
580313-3 22121-3 (Let's Go) Slumming on Park Avenue
580313-4 22122-3 I'm Putting All My Eggs in One Basket
580313-5 22123-5 Always

(All tracks on LPD-53)

ELLA FITZGERALD, vocals

Ella Fitzgerald Sings the Irving Berlin Song Book

Accompanied by orchestra conducted by **Paul Weston**. Trumpet: Don Fagerquist; Clarinet: Julian Matlock; Trombones: Ted Nash, Babe Russin; Baritone Saxophone: Chuck Gentry; Woodwinds: Gene Cipriano; Piano: Paul Smith; Guitar: Barney Kessel; Bass: Jack Ryan; Drums: Alvin Stoller; Arrangements: Paul Weston. Recorded at Radio Recorders, Los Angeles, Friday, 14 March 1958

580314-1 22124-2 I Used to Be Color Blind
580314-2 22125-2 You Can Have Him
580314-3 22126-4 How's Chances?
580314-4 22127-3 No Strings (I'm Fancy Free)

(All tracks on LPD-53)

ELLA FITZGERALD, vocals

Ella Fitzgerald Sings the Irving Berlin Song Book

Accompanied by orchestra conducted by **Paul Weston**. Trumpets: John Best, Pete Candoli, Harry "Sweets" Edison, Don Fagerquist, Mannie Klein; Trombones: Edward Kusby, Dick Noel, William Schaefer; Valve Trombone: Juan Tizol; Reeds: Chuck Gentry, Matty Matlock, Ted Nash, Babe Russin, Fred Stulce; Piano: Paul Smith; Guitar: Barney Kessel; Bass: Joe Mondragon; Drums: Alvin Stoller; Arrangements: Paul Weston. Recorded at Radio Recorders, Los Angeles, Monday 17 March 1958

580317-1 22128-2 You Keep Coming Back Like a Song
580317-2 22129-2 Supper Time
580317-3 22130-1 How Deep Is the Ocean
580317-4 22131-2 You're Laughing at Me
580317-5 22132-4 Russian Lullaby*
580317-6 22133-2 Change Partners
580317-7 22134-2 Now It Can Be Told

580317-8 22135-4 How About Me?
580317-9 22136-6 Get Thee Behind Me, Satan
580317-10 22137-5 Reaching for the Moon

*Accompanied by unknown Viola and Harp, only.
(All tracks on LPD-53)

ELLA FITZGERALD, vocals

Ella Fitzgerald Sings the Irving Berlin Song Book

Accompanied by orchestra conducted by **Paul Weston**. Personnel same as that on Monday, 17 March 1958. Recorded at Radio Recorders, Los Angeles, Tuesday, 18 March 1958

580318-1 22138-3 I've Got My Love to Keep Me Warm
580318-2 22139-3 Heat Wave
580318-3 22140-2 Cheek to Cheek
580318-4 22141-4 The Song Is Ended
580318-5 22142-2 Blue Skies (Trumpet solo: Harry "Sweets" Edison) (LPD-60, LPD-86)
580318-6 22143-3 Lazy
580318-7 22144-3 Let's Face the Music and Dance
580318-8 22145-6 It's a Lovely Day Today
580318-9 22146-3 Puttin' on the Ritz
580318-10 22147-5 (You Forgot To) Remember

(All tracks on LPD-53)

ELLA FITZGERALD, vocals

Ella Fitzgerald Sings the Irving Berlin Song Book, etc.

Accompanied by orchestra conducted by **Paul Weston**. Trumpet: Harry "Sweets" Edison; Flutes: Leonard Hartman-Matty Mattlock-Ted Nash (or Fred Stulce); Piano: Paul Smith; Guitar: Barney Kessel; Bass: Joe Mondragon; Drums: Alvin Stoller; Arrangements: Paul Weston. Recorded at Radio Recorders Annex, Los Angeles, Wednesday, 19 March 1958

580319-1 22148-5 Alexander's Ragtime Band
580319-2 22149-2 Let Yourself Go
580319-3 22150-2 Top Hat, White Tie, and Tails

(The above tracks on LPD-53)

580319-4 22151-2 Teach Me How To Cry (45: Verve 10130)

Accompanied by Trumpet: Harry "Sweets" Edison; Flute; Piano; Guitar; Bass; Drums

580319-5 22152-3 Swingin' Shepherd Blues (45: Verve 10130; LPD-86)
580319-6 22152-alt Swingin' Shepherd Blues (LPD-60)

ELLA FITZGERALD, vocals

The Texaco Star Theatre; "Swing Into Spring"

Accompanied by **Benny Goodman and His Orchestra**, Benny Goodman, Leader; Clarinet. Trumpets: Billy Butterfield,

Buck Clayton, Bernie Glow, Doc Severinsen; Trombones: Eddie Bert, Urbie Green, Lou McGarity; Alto Saxophones: Walt Levinsky, Hymie Schertzer; Tenor Saxophones: Al Klink, Zoot Sims; Baritone Saxophone: Sol Schlinger; Piano: Hank Jones; Guitar: Kenny Burrell; Bass: Russ Sanders; Drums: Leroy Burnes. Televised and recorded at NBC Studios, New York, Wednesday, 9 April 1958

580409-1   Ridin' High

Accompanied by **The Benny Goodman Quintet with Harry James.** Trumpet: Harry James; Clarinet: Benny Goodman; Vibraphone: Red Norvo; Piano: Teddy Wilson; Bass: Arvell Shaw; Drums: Leroy Burnes

580409-2   Medley (with **Jo Stafford**): a. I Gotta Right To Sing the Blues (vEF); b. Limehouse Blues (vJS); c. How Come You Do Me Like You Do (vJS); d. Poor Butterfly (vEF); e. Hard Hearted Hannah (vEF); f. I Got It Bad (and That Ain't Good) (vJS); g. St. Louis Blues (duet EF-JS)

Accompanied by **Benny Goodman and His Orchestra** (as above), including Vibraphone: Red Norvo; Piano: Teddy Wilson (replaces Hank Jones)

580409-3   Gotta Be This or That (vEF-BG-JS-The McGuire Sisters)

(All tracks on LPD-155)

ELLA FITZGERALD, vocals

Jazz At The Philharmonic; (Ella in Rome)

Accompanied by Piano: Lou Levy; Bass: Max Bennett; Drums: Gus Johnson. Recorded in performance at Teatro Sistina, Rome (Italy), Thursday, 24 April 1958

580424-1   St. Louis Blues (LPD-52)

Accompanied by Piano: Oscar Peterson; Guitar: Herb Ellis; Bass: Ray Brown; Drums: Gus Johnson

580424-2   Stompin' at the Savoy *Not yet released*

Note: This concert comprises all those titles listed for 25 April; however, these are the only two known to have been recorded on this date. In fact, the artists were unaware of being recorded on either of these dates.

ELLA FITZGERALD, vocals

Ella in Rome

Accompanied by Piano: Lou Levy; Bass: Max Bennett; Drums: Gus Johnson. Recorded in performance at Teatro Sistina, Rome (Italy), Friday **afternoon**, 25 April 1958

580425-1   When You're Smiling
580425-2   A Foggy Day (in London Town)
580425-3   Midnight Sun
580425-4   The Lady Is a Tramp
580425-5   Just Squeeze Me *Not yet released*
580425-6   That Old Black Magic *Not yet released*
580425-7   Sophisticated Lady

580425-8   Caravan
580425-9   Angel Eyes *Not yet released*
580425-10   St. Louis Blues *Not yet released*

Accompanied by Piano: Oscar Peterson; Guitar: Herb Ellis; Bass: Ray Brown; Drums: Gus Johnson

580425-11   Stompin' at the Savoy *Not yet released*

Accompanied by Piano: Lou Levy; Bass: Max Bennett; Drums: Gus Johnson. Recorded in performance at Teatro Sistina, Rome (Italy), Friday **evening**, 25 April 1958

580425-12   When You're Smiling *Not yet released*
580425-13   A Foggy Day (in London Town) *Not yet released*
580425-14   These Foolish Things (LPD-86)
580425-15   Midnight Sun *Not yet released*
580425-16   The Lady Is a Tramp *Not yet released*
580425-17   Just Squeeze Me
580425-18   Angel Eyes
580425-19   That Old Black Magic
580425-20   Just One of Those Things
580425-21   Sophisticated Lady *Not yet released*
580425-22   Caravan *Not yet released*
580425-23   I Wants to Stay Here (I Loves You, Porgy)
580425-24   It's All Right with Me
580425-25   I Can't Give You Anything but Love
580425-26   St. Louis Blues *Not yet released*

Accompanied by Piano: Oscar Peterson; Guitar: Herb Ellis; Bass: Ray Brown; Drums: Gus Johnson

580425-27   Stompin' at the Savoy

(All released titles on LPD-54)

ELLA FITZGERALD, vocals

The Frank Sinatra Show

Telecast and recorded at ABC Studios, Los Angeles, Friday, 9 May 1958

580509-1   April in Paris *Not yet released*
580509-2   Angel Eyes *Not yet released*
580509-3   When You're Smiling *Not yet released*
580509-4   Medley (duet with Frank Sinatra): a. Moonlight in Vermont; b. I May Be Wrong (But I Think You're Wonderful); c. Party Blues; d. Put Your Dreams Away *Not yet released*

(Three "Medley" tracks, a., b., and c. on LPD-157)

ELLA FITZGERALD, vocals

Accompanied by Celesta: Lou Levy; Organ: Dick Hyman; Bass: Max Bennett; Drums: Gus Johnson. Recorded at Fine Studios, New York, Tuesday, 1 July 1958

580701-1   22290 Your Red Wagon (45: Verve 10143; LPD-131)

Accompanied by Piano: Lou Levy; Bass: Max Bennett; Drums: Gus Johnson

580701-2 22291 Trav'lin' Light (45: Verve 10143; LPD-86)

ELLA FITZGERALD, vocals

Jazz At The Philharmonic Festival du Jazz, Cannes, 1958

Accompanied by Piano: Lou Levy; Bass: Max Bennett; Drums: Gus Johnson. Recorded in performance at Palais des Festivals, Cannes (France), Wednesday, 9 July 1958

580709-1 I'm Beginning to See the Light
580709-2 My Heart Belongs to Daddy
580709-3 Just One of Those Things
580709-4 I Can't Give You Anything but Love
(All tracks on LPD-143)

Note: There were, no doubt, other performances at this concert, but this is the only known release of recordings this editor has been able to discover.

ELLA FITZGERALD, vocals

Accompanied by Piano: Lou Levy; Bass: Max Bennett; Drums: Gus Johnson. Recorded in performance at Mr. Kelly's (nightclub), London House, Chicago (Illinois), Sunday, 10 August 1958 (three performances)

580810-1 22335 Your Red Wagon *Not yet released*
580810-2 22336 Nice Work If You Can Get It *Not yet released*
580810-3 22337 I'm Glad There Is You *Not yet released*
580810-4 22338 How Long Has This Been Going On? *Not yet released*
580810-5 22339 Across the Alley from the Alamo *Not yet released*
580810-6 22340 Perdido *Not yet released*
580810-7 22341 The Lady Is a Tramp *Not yet released*
580810-8 22342 Witchcraft *Not yet released*
580810-9 22343 Bewitched (Bothered, and Bewildered) *Not yet released*
580810-10 22344 Summertime *Not yet released*
580810-11 22345 In the Wee Small Hours (of the Morning) *Not yet released*
580810-12 22346 St. Louis Blues *Not yet released*
580810-13 22347 Lover *Not yet released*
580810-14 22348 On the Sunny Side of the Street *Not yet released*
580810-15 22349 Willow, Weep for Me *Not yet released*
580810-16 22350 My Heart Belongs to Daddy *Not yet released*
580810-17 22341-RE The Lady Is a Tramp (second version) *Not yet released*
580810-18 22351 Too Close for Comfort *Not yet released*

580810-19 22352 (unknown title) *Not yet released*
580810-20 22342-RE Witchcraft (second version) *Not yet released*
580810-21 22353 Love Me or Leave Me *Not yet released*
580810-22 22354 St. Louis Blues *Not yet released*
580810-23 22355 Porgy and Bess Medley (titles unknown) *Not yet released*
580810-24 22356 How High the Moon *Not yet released*
580810-25 22357 Exactly Like You *Not yet released*
580810-26 22358 Come Rain or Come Shine *Not yet released*
580810-27 22359 Star Dust *Not yet released*
580810-28 22360 'S Wonderful *Not yet released*
580810-29 22361 Oo-Bop-Sh'Bam *Not yet released*
580810-30 22362 You Don't Know What Love Is *Not yet released*
580810-31 22342-RE Witchcraft (third version) *Not yet released*
580810-32 22340-RE Perdido (second version) *Not yet released*
580810-33 22345-RE In the Wee Small Hours (second version) *Not yet released*
580810-34 22363 My Funny Valentine *Not yet released*

ELLA FITZGERALD, vocals

Ella Swings Lightly

Accompanied by The Marty Paich Dek-Tette, conducted by **Marty Paich.** Trumpets: Don Fagerquist, Al Porcino; Valve Trombone: Bob Enevoldsen; French Horn: Vince De Rosa; Tuba: John Kitzmiller; Alto Saxophone: Bud Shank; Tenor Saxophones: Bob Enevoldsen-Bill Holman; Baritone Saxophone: Med Flory; Piano: Lou Levy; Bass: Joe Mondragon; Drums: Mel Lewis; Arrangements: Marty Paich. Recorded at Radio Recorders, Los Angeles, Saturday, 22 November 1958

581122-1 22563-8 You Hit the Spot
581122-2 22564-2 Blues in the Night
581122-3 22565-7 What's Your Story, Morning Glory?
581122-4 22566-6 Just You, Just Me
581122-5 22567-2 My Kinda Love
581122-6 22568-3 If I Were a Bell
581122-7 22569-3 Teardrops from My Eyes (45: 10166 [mono]; VS-702 [stereo])
581122-8 22570-alt You're an Old Smoothie (LPD-86)

(All tracks, except the last, "You're an Old Smoothie," on LPD-55)

ELLA FITZGERALD, vocals

Ella Swings Lightly

Accompanied by The Marty Paich Dek-tette, conducted by **Marty Paich.** Trumpets: Don Fagerquist, Al Porcino; Valve

Trombone: Bob Enevoldsen; French Horn: Vince De Rosa; Tuba: John Kitzmiller; Alto Saxophone: Bud Shank; Tenor Saxophones: Bob Enevoldsen-Bill Holman; Baritone Saxophone: Med Flory; Piano: Lou Levy; Bass: Joe Mondragon; Drums: Mel Lewis; Arrangements: Marty Paich. Recorded at Radio Recorders, Los Angeles, Sunday, 23 November 1958

581123-1   22570-3 You're an Old Smoothie
581123-2   22571-3 As Long As I Live
581123-3   22572-1 Knock Me a Kiss
581123-4   22573-4 Gotta Be This or That
581123-5   22574-3 720 in the Books
581123-6   22575-3 Moonlight on the Ganges
581123-7   22575-alt Oh, What a Night for Love!
581123-8   22576-4 Oh, What a Night for Love! (45: Verve 10158 (edited))
581123-9   22577-1 Little Jazz
581123-10   22577-2 Little Jazz (45: Verve 10166)
581123-11   22578-2 Little White Lies
581123-12   22579-3 You Brought a New Kind of Love to Me
581123-13   22580-1 Dreams Are Made for Children (45: Verve 10158)

(All tracks on LPD-55)

ELLA FITZGERALD, vocals

Ella Fitzgerald Sings Sweet Songs for Swingers

Accompanied by orchestra conducted by **Frank DeVol**. Trumpets: Harry "Sweets" Edison-four others unknown; Trombones: 3–4 unknown; Reeds: 5 unknown; Piano: unknown; Guitar: unknown; Bass: unknown; Drums: unknown. Recorded at Radio Recorders, Los Angeles, Monday, 24 November 1958

581124-1   22581-6 East of the Sun
581124-2   22582-4 Lullaby of Broadway
581124-3   22583-2 Let's Fall in Love
581124-4   22584-4 I Remember You
581124-5   22585-3 Sweet and Lovely
581124-6   22586-1 Can't We Be Friends?
581124-7   22587-7 Out of This World
581124-8   22588-1 Makin' Whoopee (LPD-86)

(All tracks on LPD-58)

ELLA FITZGERALD, vocals

Ella Fitzgerald Sings the George and Ira Gershwin Song Book

Accompanied by orchestra conducted by **Nelson Riddle**. Violins: Israel Baker, Victor Bay, Alex Beller, Walter Edelstein, James Getzoff, Ben Gill, Murray Kellner, Nat Ross, Marshall Sosson, Gerald Vinci; Violas: Alvin Dinken, Paul Robyn, Barbara Simons; Cellos: Elizabeth Greenschpoon, George Neikrug, Kurt Reher; French Horn: Vincent DeRosa; Trumpets: Don Fagerquist, Mannie Klein, Dale McMickle, Shorty Sherock; Trombones: Milton Bernhart, Richard Noel,

Tommy Pederson; Bass Trombone: Karl DeKarske; Tenor Saxophone: Ted Nash; Woodwinds: Buddy Collette, Harry Klee, Joe Koch, Champ Webb; Harp: Katherine Julyie; Piano: Paul Smith; Guitar: Herb Ellis; Bass: Joe Comfort; Drums: Frank Flynn, Alvin Stoller; Arrangements: Nelson Riddle. Recorded at Capitol Records, Los Angeles, Monday, 5 January 1959

590105-1   22617-5 Soon
590105-2   22618-8 I Got Rhythm
590105-3   22619-3 Our Love Is Here to Stay
590105-4   22619-7 Our Love Is Here to Stay
590105-5   22620-9 They Can't Take That Away from Me
590105-6   22621-2 How Long Has This Been Going On? (LPD-86)

Accompanied by orchestra conducted by **Nelson Riddle**. Violins: Felix Slatkin (concertmaster), Victor Bay, Alex Beller, Jacques Gasselin, James Getzoff, Ben Gill, Murray Kellner, Nat Ross, Eunice Shapiro, Marshall Sosson; Violas: Alvin Dinken, Stanley Harris, Barbara Simons; Cellos: Armand Kaproff, Kurt Reher, Eleanor Slatkin; French Horn: Vincent DeRosa; Trumpets: Caroll Lewis, Vito Mangano, Dale McMickle, Shorty Sherock; Trombones: Milton Bernhart, Richard Noel, Tommy Pederson; Bass Trombone: George Roberts; Tenor Saxophone: Ted Nash; Woodwinds: Buddy Collette, Harry Klee, Joe Koch, Champ Webb; Harp: Katherine Julyie; Piano: Paul Smith; Guitar: Herb Ellis; Bass: Joe Comfort; Drums: Frank Flynn, Alvin Stoller; Arrangements: Nelson Riddle

590105-7   22622-3 A Foggy Day (in London Town)
590105-8   22623-5 The Man I Love
590105-9   22624-2 (I'm) Bidin' My Time
590105-10   22625-6 He Loves and She Loves
590105-11   22626-5 (I've Got) Beginner's Luck

(All tracks on LPD-59)

ELLA FITZGERALD, vocals

Ella Fitzgerald Sings the George and Ira Gershwin Song Book

Accompanied by orchestra conducted by **Nelson Riddle**. Trumpets: Conrad Gozzo, Carroll Lewis, Vito Mangano, Shorty Sherock; Trombones: Richard Noel, Tommy Pederson; Valve Trombone: Juan Tizol; Bass Trombone: George Roberts; Tenor Saxophones: Benny Carter, Plas Johnson, Ted Nash; Woodwinds: Justin Gordon, Joe Koch; Piano: Paul Smith; Guitar: Herb Ellis; Bass: Joe Mondragon; Drums: Bill Richmond; Arrangements: Nelson Riddle. Recorded at Capitol Records, Los Angeles, Wednesday, 7 January 1959

590107-1   22627-7 Somebody Loves Me (LPD-60, LPD-68)
590107-2   22628-3 Slap That Bass
590107-3   22629-3 Clap Yo' Hands
590107-4   22630-3 Cheerful Little Earful (LPD-60, LPD-68)
590107-5   22631-6 You've Got What Gets Me

(All tracks on LPD-59)

ELLA FITZGERALD, vocals

Ella Fitzgerald Sings the George and Ira Gershwin Song Book

Accompanied by orchestra conducted by **Nelson Riddle.** Violins: Misha Russell (concertmaster) Victor Arno, Victor Bay, Alex Beller, Jacques Gasselin, Ben Gill, Harry Hill, Murray Kellner, Erno Neufeld, Paul Shure, Marshall Sosson, Gerald Vinci; Violas: Alvin Dinken, Paul Robyn, Barbara Simons, David Sterkin; Cellos: James Arkatov, Elizabeth Greenschpoon, George Neikrug, Kurt Reher; Harp: Katherine Julyie; Piano: Paul Smith; Guitar: Herb Ellis; Bass: Joe Mondragon; Drums: Bill Richmond; Arrangements: Nelson Riddle. Recorded at Capitol Records, Thursday, 8 January 1959

590108-1	22632-5	Embraceable You
590108-2	22633-3	I've Got a Crush on You
590108-3	22634-3	But Not for Me
590108-4	22635-2	Oh! Lady, Be Good!
590108-5	22635-8	Oh! Lady, Be Good!
590108-6	22635-9	Oh! Lady, Be Good!
590108-7	22635-10	Oh! Lady, Be Good!

(All tracks on LPD-59)

ELLA FITZGERALD, vocals

Ella Fitzgerald Sings the George and Ira Gershwin Song Book

Accompanied by orchestra conducted by **Nelson Riddle.** Violins: Felix Slatkin (concertmaster) Victor Arno, Victor Bay, Alex Beller, Harold Dicterow, Benn Gill, Murray Kellner, Erno Neufeld, Paul Shure, Marshall Sosson, Gerald Vinci; Violas: Alvin Dinken, Stanley Harris, Paul Robyn; Cellos: Elizabeth Greenschpoon, Armand Kaproff, Eleanor Slatkin; French Horns: James Decker, Vincent DeRosa; Trumpets: Pete Candoli, Dale McMickle, Shorty Sherock, Joe Triscari; Trombones: Dick Nash, Tommy Pederson, James Priddy; Bass Trombone: Karl DeKarske; Tuba: Ed Gilbert; Tenor Saxophone: Ted Nash; Woodwinds: Gene Cipriano, Jewell Grant, William Green, Harry Klee, Champ Webb; Harp: Katherine Julyie; Piano: Lou Levy; Guitar: Herb Ellis; Bass: Joe Comfort; Drums: Frank Flynn, Mel Lewis; Arrangements: Nelson Riddle. Recorded at Capitol Records, Los Angeles, Wednesday, 18 March 1959

590318-1	22749-5	I Can't Be Bothered Now
590318-2	22750-5	Of Thee I Sing
590318-3	22751-9	I Was Doing All Right
590318-4	22752-6	Funny Face
590318-5	22753-6	Fascinating Rhythm

(All tracks are on LPD-59)

ELLA FITZGERALD, vocals

Hello, Love, etc.

Accompanied by orchestra conducted by **Frank DeVol** (Piano: Lou Levy; Guitar: Herb Ellis; other personnel not known). Recorded at Capitol Records, Los Angeles, Wednesday, 25 March 1959

590325-1	22759-4	You Go to My Head
590325-2	22760-4	Willow, Weep for Me
590325-3	22761-4	I've Grown Accustomed to His Face
590325-4	22762-4	Spring Will Be a Little Late This Year
590325-5	22763-6	I'm Through with Love

(All tracks on LPD-56)

Accompanied by Piano: Lou Levy; Guitar: Herb Ellis; Bass: unknown; Drums: unknown

590325-6	22764-4	Pennies from Heaven *Not yet released*
590325-7	22765-4	It's a Good Day *Not yet released*

Accompanied by Guitar: Herb Ellis

590325-8	22766-3	Detour Ahead (LPD-86)

No accompaniment

590325-9	22767	Voicetracks (speech, streetcalls) for **Porgy and Bess**

(Intercut and dubbed with Medley Music recorded on [LPD-57] 14 October 1957, q.v.)

ELLA FITZGERALD, vocals

Ella Fitzgerald Sings the George and Ira Gershwin Song Book

Accompanied by orchestra conducted by **Nelson Riddle.** Violins: Felix Slatkin (concertmaster) Victor Arno, Victor Bay, Alex Beller, Harold Dicterow, Ben Gill, Murra Kellner, Erno Neufeld, Nathan Ross, Paul Shure; Violas: Alvin Dinken, Stanley Harris, Paul Robyn; Cellos: Dave Filerman, Elizabeth Greenschpoon, George Neikrug, Eleanor Slatkin; French Horns: James Decker, Vincent DeRosa; Trumpet: Don Fagerquist; Trombones: Dick Nash, Tommy Pederson, James Priddy; Bass Trombone: George Roberts; Tuba: Ed Gilbert; Alto Saxophone: Ronnie Lang; Woodwinds: Jewell Grant, William Green, Jules Jacob, Wilbur Schwartz, Champ Webb; Harp: Katherine Julyie; Piano: Paul Smith; Guitar: Barney Kessel; Bass: Joe Comfort; Drums: Larry Bunker, Mel Lewis, Alvin Stoller; Arrangements: Nelson Riddle. Recorded at Capitol Records, Los Angeles, Thursday, 26 March 1959

590326-1	22768-4	My One and Only
590326-2	22769-2	Someone to Watch Over Me
590326-3	22770-7	Nice Work If You Can Get It
590326-4	22771-3	Love Walked In
590326-5	22772-10	But Not for Me (45: Verve 10180 [mono]-Verve VS-717 [stereo])

*It is most likely that this spliced master, or another of the takes at this session, was used on the soundtrack of the 1959 Paramount film, **But Not for Me**, which Ella sang under the titles. The film, starring Clark Gable and Caroll Baker, was a success, and the song gained a new popularity.*

590326-6   22773-15 Let's Call the Whole Thing Off
590326-7   22774-6 Looking for a Boy
590326-8   22775-7 The Lorelei
(This title was remade on 15 July 1959)

590326-9   22776-3 Let's Kiss and Make Up
590326-10   22777-8 They All Laughed
(All tracks on LPD-59)

ELLA FITZGERALD, vocals

The Texaco Star Theatre; "Swing Into Spring"

Accompanied by **Benny Goodman and His Orchestra**, Benny Goodman, Leader; Clarinet. Trumpets: Irwin Berger, Buck Clayton, John Frosk, Allen Smith; Trombones: Buster Cooper, Urbie Green, Hale Rood; Clarinet: Benny Goodman; Alto Saxophones: Gerald Sanfino, Hymie Schertzer; Tenor Saxophones: Babe Clark, Herb Geller; Baritone Saxophone: Pepper Adams; Piano: Hank Jones; Guitar: Kenny Burrell; Bass: Jack Lesberg; Drums: Roy Burnes; Percussion: Phil Kraus; Vocalist: Donna Musgrove; Arrangements: Ralph Burns. Telecast and recorded at CBS Television Studio, Los Angeles, 10 April 1959

590410-1   Medley (with **Peggy Lee**): a. 'S Wonderful (vEF); b. Things Are Swingin' (vPL); c. 'S Wonderful (duet EF-PL)
590410-2   Mountain Greenery

Accompanied by Piano: **André Previn**

590410-3   Ah! Men! Ah! Women! (trio EF-PL-BG)

Accompanied by **The Benny Goodman Quartet** (Clarinet: Benny Goodman; Piano: André Previn; Bass: Jack Lesberg; Drums: Shelley Manne)

590410-4   I Must Have That Man
590410-5   Medley (with **Benny Goodman** and **Peggy Lee**): a. Sweet Georgia Brown (vBG); b. I'm Just Wild About Harry (vPL); c. Sweet Lorraine (vBG); d. The Gentleman Is a Dope (vEF); e. When a Woman Loves a Man (vPL); f. The Glory of Love (BG-PL-EF)
590410-6   Swing Into Spring; 'S Wonderful (vEF-PL-TheHi-Lo's-Chorus)
(All tracks on LPD-156)

ELLA FITZGERALD, vocals

Sweet Songs for Swingers and Get Happy!

Accompanied by orchestra conducted by **Frank DeVol**. Trumpets: Frank Beach, Pete Candoli, Carroll "Cappy" Lewis, Al Procino; Trombones: Harry Betts, Dick Noel, George Roberts, Lloyd Ulyate; Woodwinds: Gene Cipriano, Buddy Collette, Chuck Gentry, Plas Johnson, Ron Langinger; Vibraphone: Victor Feldman; Piano: Lou Levy; Guitar: Herb Ellis; Bass: Joe Mondragon; Drums: Alvin Stoller; Arrangements: Frank DeVol, Russell Garcia. Recorded at Capitol Records, Los Angeles, 11 July 1959

590711-1   26413-5 My Old Flame (LPD-58)

590711-2   26414-2 Gone with the Wind (LPD-58)
590711-3   26415-8 That Old Feeling (LPD-58)
590711-4   26416-3* Moonlight Becomes You (LPD-60)
590711-5   26417-2 Moonlight Serenade (LPD-58)
590711-6   26418-3 You Make Me Feel So Young (45: Verve 10180; LPD-60)
*Spliced master

ELLA FITZGERALD, vocals

Ella Fitzgerald Sings the George and Ira Gershwin Song Book

Accompanied by orchestra conducted by **Nelson Riddle**; Trumpet: Carroll Lewis; Trombones: Richard Noel, Tommy Pederson, James Priddy; Bass Trombone: George Roberts; Alto Saxophone: Ronnie Lang; Baritone Saxophone: Chuck Gentry; Woodwinds: Buddy Collette, Harry Klee, Champ Webb; Piano: Lou Levy; Guitar: Herb Ellis; Bass: Ralph Peña; Drums: Frank Flynn, Alvin Stoller; Arrangements: Nelson Riddle. Recorded at Capitol Records, Los Angeles, Wednesday, 15 July 1959

590715-1   26433-7 Shall We Dance
590715-2   26434-3 That Certain Feeling
590715-3   26435-7 Boy! What Love Has Done to Me
590715-4   26436-7 Boy Wanted
590715-5   26437-3 "The Half of It, Dearie" Blues
590715-6   22775-16 The Lorelei
(All tracks on LPD-59)

ELLA FITZGERALD, vocals

Ella Fitzgerald Sings the George and Ira Gershwin Song Book

Accompanied by orchestra conducted by **Nelson Riddle**. Violins: Misha Russell (concertmaster) Victor Bay, Alex Beller, Jacques Gasselin, Ben Gill, Joseph Livoti, Dan Lube, Paul Shure, Marshall Sosson, Gerald Vinci; Violas: Alvin Dinken, Lou Kievman, Barbara Simons; Cellos: Armand Kaproff, Edgar Lustgarten, Kurt Reher; Trumpets: Pete Candoli, Carroll Lewis, Dale McMickle, Shorty Sherock; Trombones: Richard Noel, Tommy Pederson, James Priddy; Bass Trombone: George Roberts; Tuba: Red Callender; Alto Saxophone: Ronnie Lang; Baritone Saxophone: Chuck Gentry; Woodwinds: Buddy Collette, Harry Klee, Champ Webb; Harp: Katherine Julyie; Piano: Lou Levy; Guitar: Herb Ellis; Bass: Joe Comfort; Drums: Frank Flynn, Alvin Stoller; Arrangements: Nelson Riddle. Recorded at Capitol Records, Los Angeles, Thursday, 16 July 1959

590716-1   26438-6 'S Wonderful
590716-2   26439-3 Who Cares?
590716-3   26440-8 Treat Me Rough
590716-4   26441-3 Strike Up the Band
590716-5   26442-12 Sam and Delilah
590716-6   26443-3 By Strauss
(All tracks on LPD-59)

ELLA FITZGERALD, vocals

Ella Fitzgerald Sings the George and Ira Gershwin Song Book

Accompanied by orchestra conducted by **Nelson Riddle.** Trumpets: Pete Candoli, Carroll Lewis, Dale McMickle, Shorty Sherock; Trombones: Richard Noel, Tommy Pederson, James Priddy; Bass Trombone: George Roberts; Alto Saxophone: Ronnie Lang; Woodwinds: Buddy Collette, Harry Klee, Joe Koch, Buck Skalak; Piano: Lou Levy; Guitar: Herb Ellis; Bass: Joe Comfort; Drums: Frank Flynn, Alvin Stoller; Arrangements: Nelson Riddle. Recorded at Capitol Records, Los Angeles, Friday, 17 July 1959

590717-1   26444-11 My Cousin in Milwaukee
590717-2   26445-9 Things Are Looking Up
590717-3   26446-5 Stiff Upper Lip
590717-4   26447-12 Oh, So Nice
590717-5   26448-5 Just Another Rhumba

(All tracks on LPD-59)

ELLA FITZGERALD, vocals

Ella Fitzgerald Sings the George and Ira Gershwin Song Book

Accompanied by orchestra conducted by **Nelson Riddle.** Violins: Victor Arno, Victor Bay, Alex Beller, Harold Dicterow, Ben Gill, Murray Kellner, Marvin Limonick, Dan Lube, Lou Raderman, Marshall Sosson, Gerald Vinci; Violas: Alvin Dinken, Ralph Lane, Alex Neimann, Barbara Simons; Cellos: Elizabeth Greenschpoon, Edgar Lustgarten, Kurt Reher, Eleanor Slatkin; Harp: Katharine Julyie; Piano: Lou Levy, Lou Busch*; Guitar: Herb Ellis; Bass: Joe Comfort; Drums: Alvin Stoller; Arrangements: Nelson Riddle. Recorded at Capitol Records, Los Angeles, Saturday 18 July 1959

590718-1   26449-6 Somebody from Somewhere
590718-2   26450-4 Love Is Sweeping the Country
590718-3   26451-6 For You, for Me, for Evermore
590718-4   26452-6 Aren't You Kinda Glad We Did?
590718-5   26453-4 Isn't It a Pity?
590718-6   26454-6 The Real American Folk Song (Is a Rag)*

*Lou Busch replaces Lou Levy at piano on this track.

(All tracks on LPD-59)

ELLA FITZGERALD, vocals

Cannes Jazz Festival*

Accompanied by Lou Levy Trio. Piano: Lou Levy; Bass: Max Bennett; Drum: Gus Johnson. Recorded in performance at Cannes Jazz Festival, Cannes (France), on Wednesday, 1 July 1959

590701-1   I'm Beginning to See the Light
590701-2   My Heart Belongs to Daddy
590701-3   Just One of Those Things
590701-4   I Can't Give You Anything but Love

*There were undoubtedly more songs recorded at this concert, but as far as is known to the compiler, these are the only tracks to be released on any format.

(All tracks on LPD-143)

Ella Fitzgerald Sings the George and Ira Gershwin Song Book

These tracks contain no vocals. The information is given for interested readers. Orchestra conducted by **Nelson Riddle.** Arrangements: Nelson Riddle. Recorded at Capitol Records, Los Angeles, Wednesday 20 August 1959

AMBULATORY SUITE (Gershwin):

26492-10   March of the Swiss Soldiers
26493-8   Promenade (Walking the Dog)
26494-9   Fidgety Feet
26495-10   Prelude I (Gershwin)
26496-19   Prelude III (Gershwin)
26497-2   Prelude II (Gershwin)

(All tracks on LPD-59)

ELLA FITZGERALD, vocals

Get Happy!, etc.

Accompanied by orchestra conducted by **Marty Paich.** Violins: Felix Slatkin (concertmaster), David Frisina, Dan Lube, William Miller, Eunice Shapiro; Trumpets: Pete Candoli, Philip Candreva, Buddy Childers, Stu Williamson; Trombones: Murray MacEachern, George Roberts, Tommy Shepard, Lloyd Ulyate; Woodwinds: Jay Corre, Chuck Gentry, Bill Holman, Ted Nash; Piano: Claude Williamson, Jr.; Harp: Mary Jane Barton; Guitar: Herb Ellis; Bass: Red Mitchell; Drums: Jack Sperling; Arrangements: Marty Paich (except Track 3, 4 and 5, Russell Garcia). Recorded at United Recorders, Los Angeles, Thursday, 3 September 1959

590903-1   22892-6 Like Young (LPD-60)
590903-2   22893-6 Cool Breeze (LPD-60)
     Accompanied by Guitar: Herb Ellis
590903-3   22894-4 Beat Me, Daddy, Eight to the Bar (LPD-60)
     Accompanied by orchestra conducted by Russ Garcia
590903-4   22895-4 The Christmas Song (45: Verve 10186)
590903-5   22896-4 The Secret of Christmas (45: Verve 10186; LPD-131)

ELLA FITZGERALD, vocals

An Afternoon with Frank Sinatra

Accompanied by Red Norvo and His Jazz Group. Telecast and recorded at ABC Television Studios, Los Angeles, Sunday, 13 December 1959

591213-1   There's a Lull in My Life *Not yet released*

591213-2   Just You, Just Me *Not yet released*
591213-3   He Loves and She Loves *Not yet released*
591213-4   Can't We Be Friends? (duet with Frank Sinatra) (LPD-157)

ELLA FITZGERALD, vocals

Jazz At The Philharmonic (Ella in Berlin; Mack the Knife)

Accompanied by Piano: Paul Smith; Guitar: Jim Hall; Bass: Wilfred Middlebrooks; Drums: Gus Johnson. Recorded in performance at Deutschlandhalle, Berlin (Germany), Sunday, 13 February 1960

600213-1   That Old Black Magic
600213-2   Our Love Is Here to Stay
600213-3   26607 Gone with the Wind (45: Verve VK-109; LPD-77)
600213-4   26608 Misty
600213-5   26609 The Lady Is a Tramp
600213-6   26610 The Man I Love
600213-7   26611 Summertime
600213-8   26612 Too Darn Hot
600213-9   26613 The Lorelei (LPD-73)
600213-10   26614 Mack the Knife (45: Verve 10209, Verve VK-109; LPD-73, LPD-86)

Note: Charted 30 May 1960; weeks, 7; peak, #27

600213-11   26615 How High the Moon (45: Verve 10220, Verve VK-110; LPD-73, LPD-86)

Note: Charted 15 August 1960; weeks, 5; peak, #76

(All tracks on LPD-61)

*Note: Two other performances appear on these albums ("Love for Sale" and "Just One of Those Things") which were **not** recorded at this concert, but which, in fact, were performances from **Jazz at the Hollywood Bowl**, 15 August 1956. See 560815-7 and 560815-8.*

*This album, **Ella in Berlin; Mack The Knife**, charted 12 December 1960; weeks, 20; peak, #11*

ELLA FITZGERALD, vocals

Ella Fitzgerald Sings Songs from Let No Man Write My Epitaph/The Intimate Ella

Accompanied by Piano: Paul Smith. Recorded at Capitol Records, Los Angeles, Thursday, 14 April 1960

600414-1   26587-4 My Melancholy Baby
600414-2   26588-4 Angel Eyes
600414-3   26589-8 Black Coffee (LPD-86)
600414-4   26590-2 I Hadn't Anyone Till You
600414-5   26591-2 I Cried for You
600414-6   26592-6 Misty

(All tracks on LPD-62)

ELLA FITZGERALD, vocals

Ella Fitzgerald Sings Songs from Let No Man Write My Epitaph/The Intimate Ella

Accompanied by Piano: Paul Smith. Recorded at Capitol Records, Los Angeles, Tuesday, 19 April 1960

600419-1   26593-4 Who's Sorry Now?
600419-2   26594-2 I Can't Give You Anything but Love
600419-3   26495-4 I'm Getting Sentimental Over You
600419-4   26596-6 Then You've Never Been Blue
600419-5   26597-8 September Song
600419-6   26598-9 Reach for Tomorrow
600419-7   26599-3 One for My Baby

(All tracks on LPD-62)

ELLA FITZGERALD, vocals

Ella Wishes You a Swinging Christmas, etc.

Accompanied by orchestra conducted by **Frank DeVol.** Arrangements: Frank DeVol. Recorded at Fine Sound studio, New York, Friday, 15 July 1960

600715-1   26717-9 Santa Claus Is Coming to Town (LPD-63)
600715-2   26718-5 Jingle Bells (LPD-63)
600715-3   26719-6 Frosty, the Snowman (LPD-61)
600715-4   26720-3 Medley: a. We Three Kings of Orient Are; b. O Little Town of Bethlehem (45: HMV 45POP817 [English])
600715-5   26721-4 Christmas Island *Not yet released*
600715-6   26722-7 Rudolph, the Red Nosed Reindeer (LPD-63)
600715-7   26723-5 The Christmas Song *Not yet released*

(This track was remade on 5 August 1960, q.v.)

ELLA FITZGERALD, vocals

Ella Wishes You a Swinging Christmas, etc.

Accompanied by orchestra conducted by **Frank DeVol.** Recorded at Fine Sound studio, New York, Saturday, 16 July 1960

600716-1   26724-3 Winter Wonderland (LPD-63)
600716-2   26725-7 Let It Snow! Let It Snow! Let It Snow! (LPD-63, LPD-86)
600716-3   26726-3 What Are You Doing New Year's Eve? (LPD-63)
600716-4   26727-4 White Christmas (LPD-132)
600716-5   26728-4 Have Yourself a Merry Little Christmas (LPD-63)

ELLA FITZGERALD, vocals

Ella Fitzgerald Sings the Harold Arlen Song Book

Accompanied by orchestra conducted by **Billy May.** Including Trumpet: Don Fagerquist; Tenor Saxophones: Plas

Johnson, Ted Nash; Piano: Paul Smith; Guitar: Al Hendrickson or John Collins; Bass: Joe Mondragon; Drums: Alvin Stoller; Arrangements: Billy May. Recorded at Capitol Records, Los Angeles, Monday, 1 August 1960

600801-1 26729-6 Hooray for Love
600801-2 26730-7 When the Sun Comes Out
600801-3 26731-6 As Long as I Live
600801-4 26732-4 (It's Only a) Paper Moon
600801-5 26733-7 The Man That Got Away
600801-6 26734-5 Ac-Cent-Tchu-Ate the Positive
600801-7 26735-4 This Time the Dream's on Me
Rejected
600801-8 26736-1 I've Got the World on a String

(All tracks, except "This Time the Dream's on Me," on LPD-64)

ELLA FITZGERALD, vocals

Ella Fitzgerald Sings the Harold Arlen Song Book

Accompanied by orchestra conducted by **Billy May.** Including Tenor Saxophone: Ted Nash; Piano: Paul Smith; Guitar: Al Hendrickson or JohnCollins; Bass: Joe Mondragon; Drums: Alvin Stoller; Arrangements: Billy May. Recorded at Capitol Records, Los Angeles, Tuesday, 2 August 1960

600802-1 26737-1 Get Happy! (LPD-86)
600802-2 26738-4 Sing, My Heart
600802-3 26738-alt Sing, My Heart
600802-4 26739-3 Ding-Dong! The Witch Is Dead!
600802-5 26740-3 Let's Take a Walk Around the Block
600802-6 26740-alt Let's Take a Walk Around the Block

(All tracks on LPD-64)

ELLA FITZGERALD, vocals

Ella Wishes You a Swinging Christmas

Accompanied by orchestra conducted by **Frank DeVol.** Recorded at Capitol Records, Los Angeles, Friday, 5 August 1960

600805-1 26741-5 Good Morning Blues
600805-2 26742-13 Sleigh Ride
600805-3 26723-9 The Christmas Song (remake)
600805-4 26727-9 White Christmas (remake)

(All tracks on LPD-63)

ELLA FITZGERALD, vocals

Ella Fitzgerald Sings the Harold Arlen Song Book

Accompanied by orchestra conducted by **Billy May.** Trumpets: Frank Beach, Don Fagerquist, Conrad Gozzo, Joe Triscari; Trombones: Milton Bernhart, Edward Kusby, Richard Noel; Bass Trombone: George Roberts; Alto Saxophone: Benny Carter; Tenor Saxophone: Plas Johnson; Baritone Saxophone: Chuck Gentry; Woodwinds: Justin Gordon, Wilbur

Schwartz; Piano: Lou Levy; Guitar: Herb Ellis; Basses: Wilfred Middlebrooks, Joe Mondragon; Drums: Alvin Stoller; Arrangements: Billy May. Recorded at Radio Recorders, Los Angeles, Saturday, 14 January 1961

610114-1 26909-5 That Old Black Magic
610114-2 26910-5 Blues in the Night (EP: Verve EP 5073)
610114-3 26911-4 I Gotta Right to Sing the Blues
610114-4 26912-5 Stormy Weather
610114-5 26913-2 One for My Baby (EP: Verve EP 5073)

(All tracks on LPD-64)

ELLA FITZGERALD, vocals

Ella Fitzgerald Sings the Harold Arlen Song Book

Accompanied by orchestra conducted by **Billy May.** Violins: Misha Russell (concertmaster) Israel Baker, Jacques Gasselin, Ben Gill, Murray Kellner, Dan Lube, Erno Neufeld, Lou Raderman, Nathan Ross, Marshall Sosson, Joseph Stepansky, Gerald Vinci; Violas: Alvin Dinken, Lou Kievman, Virginia Majewski, Paul Robyn; Cellos: Armand Kaproff, Ray Kramer, Edgar Lustgarten, Eleanor Slatkin; Trumpet: Don Fagerquist; Trombone: Milton Barnhart; Alto Saxophone: Benny Carter; Tenor Saxophone: Plas Johnson; Baritone Saxophone: Chuck Gentry; Harp Verlye Brilhart; Piano:Lou Levy; Guitar: Herb Ellis; Basses: Wilfred Middlebrooks, Joe Mondragon; Drums: Alvin Stoller; Arrangers: Billy May, Russ Garcia,* Walter Sheets.** Recorded at Radio Recorders Annex, Los Angeles, Sunday, 15 January 1961

610115-1 26915-3 My Shining Hour
610115-2 26916-3 Ill Wind
610115-3 26917-7 Over the Rainbow
610115-4 26918-6 This Time the Dream's on Me
610115-5 26919-1 It Was Written in the Stars** (spliced take)
610115-6 26920-2 Heart and Soul (LPD-86)

(All tracks, except the last, "Heart and Soul," on LPD-64)

Note: Some discographies list a title "Lost It for Me" as having been recorded at this session, assigning it the master number, 26914-2. The author can find no evidence of this recording, nor, indeed, a song with this title by Harold Arlen or any other composer.

ELLA FITZGERALD, vocals

Ella Fitzgerald Sings the Harold Arlen Song Book

Accompanied by orchestra conducted by **Billy May.** Trumpet: Don Fagerquist; Trombone: Milton Bernhart; Alto Saxophone: Benny Carter; Baritone Saxophone: Chuck Gentry; Woodwinds: Henry Beau, Justin Gordon, Jules Jacob; Vibraphone: Emil Richards; Piano: Lou Levy; Guitar: Herb Ellis; Basses: Wilfred Middlebrooks, Joe Mondragon; Drums: Alvin Stoller; Arrangements: Billy May. Recorded at Radio Recorders Annex, Los Angeles, Monday, 16 January 1961

610116-1 26921-4 Between the Devil and the Deep Blue Sea

610116-2 26922-4 Let's Fall in Love

610116-3 26923-5 Happiness Is (Just) a Thing Called Joe

610116-6 26924-6 Out of This World

610116-5 26925-2 Come Rain or Come Shine (EP: Verve EP 5073)

(All tracks on LPD-64)

ELLA FITZGERALD, vocals

Clap Hands! Here Comes Charlie!

Accompanied by Piano: Lou Levy; Guitar: Herb Ellis; Bass: Wilfred Middlebrooks; Drums: Gus Johnson. Recorded at New York, Monday 23 January 1961

610123-1 26926-6 On a Slow Boat to China *Not yet released*

610123-2 26927-7 You're Driving Me Crazy *Not yet released*

610123-3 26928-4 Spring Can Really Hang You Up the Most *Not yet released*

610123-4 26929-4 This Year's Kisses *Not yet released*

610123-5 26930-5 'Round Midnight *Not yet released*

610123-6 26931-4 The One I Love Belongs to Somebody Else (LPD-67)

610123-7 26932-5 I Got a Guy (LPD-67)

610123-8 26932-8 I Got a Guy *Not yet released*

610123-9 26933-32 This Could Be the Start of Something Big (LPD-67)

610123-10 26934-4 Stella by Starlight *Not yet released*

(This track was remade on 23 June 1961)

ELLA FITZGERALD, vocals

Jazz At The Philharmonic/(Ella Returns to Berlin)

Accompanied by Piano: Lou Levy; Guitar: Herb Ellis; Bass: Wilfred Middlebrooks; Drums: Gus Johnson. Recorded in performance at Deutschlandhalle, Berlin (Germany), Saturday, 11 February 1961

610211-1 Give Me the Simple Life

610211-2 Take the "A" Train

610211-3 On a Slow Boat to China

610211-4 Medley: a. Why Was I Born?; b. Can't Help Lovin' Dat Man; c. People Will Say We're in Love

610211-5 You're Driving Me Crazy

610211-6 Rock It for Me

610211-7 Witchcraft

610211-8 Anything Goes

610211-9 Cheek to Cheek

610211-10 Misty

610211-11 Caravan

610211-12 Mr. Paganini (You'll Have To Swing It)

610211-13 Mack the Knife

610211-14 'Round Midnight

610211-15 Joe Williams' Blues

Accompanied by Piano: Oscar Peterson; Guitar: Herb Ellis; Bass: Ray Brown; Drums: Ed Thigpen

610211-16 This Can't Be Love

(All tracks on LPD-65)

ELLA FITZGERALD, vocals

The Lady Is a Tramp

Accompanied by **The Lou Levy Quartet.** Piano: Lou Levy; Guitar: Herb Ellis; Bass: Wilfred Middlebrooks; Drums: Gus Johnson. Recorded in performance at Sportspalast (?), Belgrade (Yugoslavia), Tuesday, 21 February 1961

610221-1 Too Close for Comfort

610221-2 A Foggy Day (in London Town)

610221-3 Cole Porter Medley: a. Get Out of Town; b. Easy to Love

610221-4 You're Driving Me Crazy

610221-5 Cheek to Cheek

610221-6 Caravan

610221-7 Oh! Lady, Be Good!

610221-8 'Round Midnight

610221-9 The Lady Is a Tramp

610221-10 Mr. Paganini (You'll Have To Swing It)

(All tracks on LPD-143)

ELLA FITZGERALD, vocals

Ella in Hollywood

Accompanied by Piano: Lou Levy; Guitar: Herb Ellis; Bass: Wilfred Middlebrooks; Drums: Gus Johnson. Recorded in performance at Crescendo (nightclub), Los Angeles, Thursday, 11 May 1961

SECOND SET

610511-1 Mr.Paganini (You'll Have To Swing It) *Not yet released*

ELLA FITZGERALD, vocals

Ella in Hollywood

Accompanied by Piano: Lou Levy; Guitar: Herb Ellis; Bass: Wilfred Middlebrooks; Drums: Gus Johnson. Recorded in performance at Crescendo (nightclub), Los Angeles, Friday, 12 May 1961

FIRST SET

610512-1 27036 Mr. Paganini (You'll Have To Swing It) (LPD-66, LPD-73, LPD-86)

SECOND SET

610512-2 Lover, Come Back to Me *Not yet released*

610512-3 You Brought a New Kind of Love to Me *Not yet released*

610512-4   Across the Alley from the Alamo *Not yet released*

610512-5   I'm Glad There Is You *Not yet released*

610512-6   'Round Midnight *Not yet released*

610512-7   Take the "A" Train *Not yet released*

THIRD SET

610512-8   A-Tisket, A-Tasket (LPD-132)

ELLA FITZGERALD, vocals

Ella in Hollywood

Accompanied by Piano: Lou Levy; Guitar: Herb Ellis; Bass: Wilfred Middlebrooks; Drums: Gus Johnson. Recorded in performance at Crescendo (nightclub), Los Angeles, Saturday, 13 May 1961

FIRST SET

610513-1   I Found a New Baby *Not yet released*

610513-2   On the Sunny Side of the Street *Not yet released*

610513-3   Am I Blue? *Not yet released*

610513-4   I've Got a Crush on You *Not yet released*

610513-5   It's All Right with Me *Not yet released*

610513-6   Caravan *Not yet released*

610513-7   Blue Moon *Not yet released*

610513-8   Lullaby of Birdland *Not yet released*

610513-9   A-Tisket, A-Tasket *Not yet released*

610513-10   Imagination *Not yet released*

610513-11   Mack the Knife *Not yet released*

610513-12   Joe Williams' Blues *Not yet released*

THIRD SET

610513-13   Give Me the Simple Life *Not yet released*

610513-14   Mr. Paganini (You'll Have To Swing It) *Not yet released*

610513-15   'Round Midnight *Not yet released*

610513-16   Just Squeeze Me *Not yet released*

610513-17   This Could Be the Start of Something Big *Not yet released*

610513-18   'S Wonderful *Not yet released*

610513-19   In the Wee Small Hours (of the Morning) *Not yet released*

610513-20   Mack the Knife *Not yet released*

610513-21   How High the Moon *Not yet released*

ELLA FITZGERALD, vocals

Ella in Hollywood

Accompanied by Piano: Lou Levy; Guitar: Herb Ellis; Bass: Wilfred Middlebrooks; Drums: Gus Johnson. Recorded in performance at Crescendo (nightclub), Los Angeles, Sunday, 14 May 1961

FIRST SET

610514-1   27040 Just in Time (LPD-66)

610514-2   Rock It for Me *Not yet released*

610514-3   'S Wonderful *Not yet released*

610514-4   St. Louis Blues *Not yet released*

SECOND SET

610514-5   27038 I've Got the World on a String (LPD-66)

610514-6   It's All Right with Me *Not yet released*

610514-7   Mr. Paganini (You'll Have To Swing It) *Not yet released*

ELLA FITZGERALD, vocals

Ella in Hollywood

Accompanied by Piano: Lou Levy; Guitar: Herb Ellis; Bass: Wilfred Middlebrooks; Drums: Gus Johnson. Recorded in performance at Crescendo (nightclub), Los Angeles, Tuesday, 16 May 1961

FIRST SET

610516-1   I Found a New Baby *Not yet released*

610516-2   Deep Purple *Not yet released*

610516-3   27039 You're Driving Me Crazy (LPD-66)

610516-4   27042 Blue Moon (LPD-66)

SECOND SET

610516-5   27044 This Could Be the Start of Something Big (LPD-66)

610516-6   27045 Baby, Won't You Please Come Home (LPD-66)

610516-7   27043 On a Slow Boat to China *Not yet released*

610516-8   Take the "A" Train *Not yet released*

610516-9   Li'l Darlin' *Not yet released*

610516-10   27046 Caravan *Not yet released*

610516-11   In the Wee Small Hours (of the Morning) *Not yet released*

610516-12   Mack the Knife *Not yet released*

610516-13   27047 Joe Williams' Blues *Not yet released*

Note: "On a Slow Boat to China," "Caravan," and "Joe Williams' Blues" were assigned master numbers and were intended for use in **Ella in Hollywood,** *but were deleted before release.*

ELLA FITZGERALD, vocals

Ella in Hollywood

Accompanied by Piano: Lou Levy; Guitar: Herb Ellis; Bass: Wilfred Middlebrooks; Drums: Gus Johnson. Recorded in performance at Crescendo (nightclub), Los Angeles, Wednesday, 17 May 1961

FIRST SET

610517-1   Mr. Paganini (You'll Have To Swing It) *Not yet released*

SECOND SET

610517-2   27051 Satin Doll (LPD-66)

610517-3   'S Wonderful *Not yet released*
610517-4   27052 Air Mail Special (LPD-66)

ELLA FITZGERALD, vocals

Ella in Hollywood

Accompanied by Piano: Lou Levy; Guitar: Herb Ellis; Bass: Wilfred Middlebrooks; Drums Gus Johnson. Recorded in performance at Crescendo (nightclub), Los Angeles, Thursday, 18 May 1961

610518-1   The Lady's in Love with You* *Not yet released*
610518-2   Our Love Is Here to Stay* *Not yet released*
610518-3   Come Rain or Come Shine* *Not yet released*
610518-4   Anything Goes* *Not yet released*
610518-5   This Could Be the Start of Something Big* *Not yet released*
610518-6   Candy* *Not yet released*
610518-7   Little Girl Blue* *Not yet released*
610518-8   You're Driving Me Crazy* *Not yet released*

*These eight tracks, although never released commercially, are on a 10" sound tape reel (analog, 15 ips, 2-track, stereo) in the Wally Heider Collection in the Library of Congress.

610518-9   Mack the Knife *Not yet released*
610518-10   Blue Moon *Not yet released*
610518-11   Joe Williams' Blues *Not yet released*
610518-12   'S Wonderful *Not yet released*

SECOND SET

610518-13   Give Me the Simple Life *Not yet released*
610518-14   On a Slow Boat to China *Not yet released*
610518-15   Am I Blue? *Not yet released*
610518-16   Lullaby of Birdland *Not yet released*
610518-17   But Not for Me *Not yet released*
610518-18   Take the "A" Train *Not yet released*
610518-19   In the Wee Small Hours (of the Morning) *Not yet released*
610518-20   Witchcraft *Not yet released*
610518-21   A-Tisket, A-Tasket *Not yet released*
610518-22   Mack the Knife *Not yet released*
610518-23   I've Got a Crush on You *Not yet released*
610518-24   Joe Williams' Blues *Not yet released*

ELLA FITZGERALD, vocals

Ella in Hollywood

Accompanied by Piano: Lou Levy; Guitar: Herb Ellis; Bass: Wilfred Middlebrooks; Drums: Gus Johnson. Recorded in performance at Crescendo (nightclub), Los Angeles, Friday, 19 May 1961

FIRST SET

610519-1   This Could Be the Start of Something Big *Not yet released*

610519-2   Witchcraft *Not yet released*
610519-3   Gone with the Wind *Not yet released*
610519-4   27048 It Might as Well Be Spring (LPD-64)
610519-5   Happiness Is (Just) a Thing Called Joe *Not yet released*
610519-6   It's De-Lovely *Not yet released*
610519-7   The Lady Is a Tramp *Not yet released*
610519-8   That Old Black Magic *Not yet released*
610519-9   Lullaby of Birdland *Not yet released*

SECOND SET

610519-10   Just Squeeze Me *Not yet released*
610519-11   Mr. Paganini (You'll Have To Swing It) *Not yet released*
610519-12   Stompin' at the Savoy *Not yet released*

THIRD SET

610519-13   'S Wonderful *Not yet released*
610519-14   Nice Work if You Can Get It *Not yet released*
610519-15   I Can't Get Started with You *Not yet released*
610519-16   Give Me the Simple Life *Not yet released*
610519-17   Caravan *Not yet released*
610519-18   Little Girl Blue *Not yet released*
610519-19   One for My Baby *Not yet released*
610519-20   This Could Be the Start of Something Big *Not yet released*
610519-21   The Lorelei *Not yet released*
610519-22   Across the Alley from the Alamo *Not yet released*
610519-23   A-Tisket, A-Tasket *Not yet released*

ELLA FITZGERALD, vocals

Ella in Hollywood

Accompanied by Piano: Lou Levy; Guitar: Herb Ellis; Bass: Wilfred Middlebrooks; Drums: Gus Johnson. Recorded in performance at Crescendo (nightclub), Los Angeles, Saturday, 20 May 1961

FIRST SET

610520-1   You're Driving Me Crazy *Not yet released*
610520-2   A-Tisket, A-Tasket *Not yet released*
610520-3   How Long Has This Been Going On? *Not yet released*
610520-4   Mack the Knife *Not yet released*
610520-5   I've Got a Crush on You *Not yet released*
610520-6   Blue Moon *Not yet released*
610520-7   Joe Williams' Blues *Not yet released*
610520-8   This Could Be the Start of Something Big *Not yet released*
610520-9   Witchcraft *Not yet released*
610520-10   Lullaby of Birdland *Not yet released*
610520-11   Happy Birthday *Not yet released*

610520-12 Oh, Lady, Be Good! *Not yet released*

610520-13 Come Rain or Come Shine *Not yet released*

610520-14 The Lady Is a Tramp *Not yet released*

Note: These 14 tracks, although never released commercially, are on a 10" sound tape reel (analog, 15 ips, 2-track, stereo) in the Wally Heider Collection in the Library of Congress.

SECOND SET

610520-15 Lover, Come Back to Me *Not yet released*

610520-16 Too Close for Comfort *Not yet released*

610520-17 Little White Lies *Not yet released*

610520-18 On the Sunny Side of the Street *Not yet released*

610520-19 Ac-Cent-Tchu-Ate the Positive *Not yet released*

610520-20 Little Girl Blue *Not yet released*

610520-21 Anything Goes *Not yet released*

610520-22 Take the "A" Train *Not yet released*

610520-23 Mr. Paganini (You'll Have To Swing It) *Not yet released*

Note: The tape ran out close to the end of the performance, and the ending is presumably lost.

THIRD SET

610520-24 This Could Be the Start of Something Big *Not yet released*

610520-25 I Found a New Baby *Not yet released*

610520-26 On a Slow Boat to China *Not yet released*

610520-27 Medley: a. Am I Blue?; b. Blue and Sentimental; c. Baby, Won't You Please Come Home?* *Not yet released*

610520-28 Baby, Won't You Please Come Home? *Not yet released*

610520-29 My Heart Belongs to Daddy *Not yet released*

610520-30 Perdido *Not yet released*

610520-31 Witchcraft *Not yet released*

610520-32 In the Wee Small Hours (of the Morning) *Not yet released*

*This medley was a novelty or a novel way of getting into "Baby, Won't You Please Come Home?" Ella's laughter leads to her halting the performance, quickly followed with another "Baby, Won't You Please Come Home?" this time without the other songs interpolated as an introduction.

ELLA FITZGERALD, vocals

Ella in Hollywood

Accompanied by Piano: Lou Levy; Guitar: Herb Ellis; Bass: Wilfred Middlebrooks; Drums: Gus Johnson. Recorded in performance at Crescendo (nightclub), Los Angeles, Sunday, 21 May 1961

SECOND SET

610521-1 Love for Sale *Not yet released*

610521-2 27050 Stairway to the Stars (LPD-66)

610521-3 Mr. Paganini (You'll Have To Swing It) *Not yet released*

610521-4 27049 Take the "A" Train (LPD-66)

610521-5 Mack the Knife *Not yet released*

610521-6 Exactly Like You *Not yet released*

*Note: This album, **Ella in Hollywood**, charted 6 January 1962; weeks, 1; peak, #35*

ELLA FITZGERALD, vocals

Clap Hands! Here Comes Charlie!

Accompanied by Piano: Lou Levy; Guitar: Herb Ellis; Bass: Joe Mondragon; Drums: Stan Levey. Recorded at Radio Recorders, Los Angeles, Thursday, 22 June 1961

610622-1 27022-2 Stella by Starlight

610622-2 27023-4 This Year's Kisses

610622-3 27024-8 Spring Can Really Hang You Up the Most

610622-4 27025-12 The Jersey Bounce

610622-5 27026-4 You're My Thrill

610622-6 27027-2 Good Morning, Heartache

(All tracks on LPD-67)

ELLA FITZGERALD, vocals

Clap Hands! Here Comes Charlie!

Accompanied by Piano: Lou Levy; Guitar: Herb Ellis; Bass: Joe Mondragon; Drums: Stan Levey. Recorded at Radio Recorders, Los Angeles, Friday, 23 June 1961

610623-1 27028-6 Born to Be Blue

610623-2 27029-1 'Round Midnight

610623-3 27030-6 My Reverie

(All tracks on LPD-67)

ELLA FITZGERALD, vocals

Clap Hands! Here Comes Charlie!

Accompanied by Piano: Lou Levy; Guitar: Herb Ellis; Bass: Joe Mondragon; Drums: Stan Levey. Recorded at Radio Recorders, Los Angeles, Saturday, 24 June 1961

610624-1 27031-3 Cry Me a River

610624-2 27032-4 Signing Off

610624-3 27033-5 Clap Hands! Here Comes Charlie!

610624-4 27034-4 A Night in Tunisia (LPD-86)

610624-5 27035-1 The Music Goes 'Round and 'Round

(All tracks on LPD-67)

ELLA FITZGERALD, vocals

Accompanied by Piano: Knud Jorgensen; Bass: Jimmy Woode; Drums William Schiöpffe. Recorded at studio, Copenhagen (Denmark), Friday, 25 August 1961

610825-1 Mr. Paganini (You'll Have To Swing It) (45: Verve 90012 [Germany])
610825-2 You're Driving Me Crazy (Ich Fühle Mich Crazy) (45: Verve 90012 [Germany])

Note: Ella sings these two tracks in German.

ELLA FITZGERALD, vocals

Ella Swings Brightly/Gently with Nelson

Accompanied by orchestra conducted by **Nelson Riddle.** Arrangements: Nelson Riddle. Recorded at Capitol Records, Los Angeles, Monday, 13 November 1961

611113-1 61VK597 Darn That Dream (LPD-70)
611113-2 61VK598 Mean to Me (LPD-68)
611113-3 61VK599 Georgia on My Mind (LPD-70)
611113-4 61VK600 I Can't Get Started (with You) (LPD-70, LPD-86)

ELLA FITZGERALD, vocals

Ella Swings Brightly/Gently with Nelson

Accompanied by orchestra conducted by **Nelson Riddle.** Recorded at Capitol Records, Los Angeles, Tuesday, 14 November 1961

611114-1 61VK601 What Am I Here For? (LPD-68)
611114-2 61VK602 Alone Together (LPD-68)
611114-3 61VK603 I Only Have Eyes for You (LPD-68)
611114-4 61VK604 It's a Pity to Say Goodnight (LPD-70)
611114-5 61VK605 I Hear Music (LPD-68)
611114-6 61VK606 When Your Lover Has Gone (LPD-68, LPD-77)

ELLA FITZGERALD, vocals

Ella Swings Brightly/Gently with Nelson

Accompanied by orchestra conducted by **Nelson Riddle.** Recorded at Capitol Records, Los Angeles, Wednesday, 15 November 1961

611115-1 61VK607 Pick Yourself Up (LPD-68)
611115-2 61VK608 The Gentleman Is a Dope (LPD-68)
611115-3 61VK609 Call Me Darling (LPD-68)
611115-4 61VK609-alt Call Me Darling (LPD-70)
611115-5 61VK610 Love Me or Leave Me (LPD-68)
611115-6 61VK611 All of Me (LPD-70)

ELLA FITZGERALD, vocals

Ella Swings Brightly with Nelson

Accompanied by orchestra conducted by **Nelson Riddle.** Arrangements: Nelson Riddle. Recorded at Capitol Records, Los Angeles, Wednesday, 27 December 1961

611227-1 61VK656 Don't Be That Way (LPD-68, LPD-86)
611227-2 61VK657 I Won't Dance (LPD-68, LPD-77)
611227-3 61VK658 I'm Gonna Go Fishin' (LPD-68)

ELLA FITZGERALD, vocals

Rhythm Is My Business

Accompanied by orchestra conducted by **Bill Doggett.** Trumpets: Ray Copeland, Taft Jordan, Ernie Royal, Joe Wilder; Trombones: Melba Liston, Kai Winding, Britt Woodman; Reeds: Carl Davis, Jerry Dodgion, Wilmer Shakesnider, Les Taylor, Phil Woods; Piano: Hank Jones; Guitar: Mundell Lowe; Bass: Lucille Dixon; Drums: Gus Johnson; Arrangements: Bill Doggett. Recorded at Webster Hall, New York, Monday, 29 January 1962

620129-1 62VK272 I'll Always Be in Love with You (45: Verve VK 10259; LPD-69)

ELLA FITZGERALD, vocals

Rhythm Is My Business

Accompanied by orchestra conducted by **Bill Doggett**, organ. Trumpets: Ray Copeland, Taft Jordan, Ernie Royal, Joe Wilder; Trombones: Melba Liston, Kai Winding, Britt Woodman; Reeds: Carl Davis, Jerry Dodgion, Wilmer Shakesnider, Les Taylor, Phil Woods; Piano: Hank Jones; Guitar: Mundell Lowe; Bass: Lucille Dixon; Drums: Gus Johnson; Arrangements: Bill Doggett. Recorded at Webster Hall, New York, Tuesday, 30 January 1962

620130-1 62VK296-1 After You've Gone (LPD-86)
620130-2 62VK290 Broadway (LPD-77)
620130-3 62VK293 I Can't Face the Music
620130-4 62VK295 You Can Depend on Me
620130-5 62VK297 Hallelujah, I Love Him So
620130-6 62VK300 If I Could Be with You (One Hour Tonight)

(All tracks on LPD-69)

ELLA FITZGERALD, vocals

Rhythm Is My Business

Accompanied by orchestra conducted by **Bill Doggett**, organ. Trumpets: Ray Copeland, Taft Jordan, Ernie Royal, Joe Wilder; Trombones: Melba Liston, Kai Winding, Britt Woodman; Reeds: Carl Davis, Jerry Dodgion, Wilmer Shakesnider, Les Taylor, Phil Woods; Piano: Hank Jones; Guitar: Mundell Lowe; Bass: George Duvivier; Drums: Gus Johnson; Arrangements: Bill Doggett. Recorded at Webster Hall, New York, Wednesday, 31 January 1962

620131-1 62VK291 Laughing on the Outside
620131-2 62VK292 Show Me the Way to Get Out of This World
620131-3 62VK294 No Moon at All
620131-4 62VK301 Runnin' Wild
620131-5 62VK298 Rough Ridin'
620131-6 62VK299 Taking a Chance on Love

(All tracks on LPD-69)

ELLA FITZGERALD, vocals

Ella Swings Gently with Nelson

Accompanied by orchestra conducted by **Nelson Riddle**. Arrangements: Nelson Riddle. Recorded at Capitol Records, Los Angeles, Monday, 9 April 1962

620409-1 62VK414 It's a Blue World
620409-2 62VK415 He's Funny That Way
620409-3 62VK416 Street of Dreams
620409-4 62VK417 Body and Soul

(All tracks on LPD-70)

ELLA FITZGERALD, vocals

Ella Swings Gently with Nelson

Accompanied by orchestra conducted by **Nelson Riddle**. Recorded at Capitol Records, Los Angeles, Tuesday, 10 April 1962

620410-1 62VK418 I Wished on the Moon
620410-2 62VK419 Imagination
620410-3 62VK420 My One and Only Love
620410-4 62VK421 The Very Thought of You
620410-5 62VK422 Sweet and Slow (LPD-77)

(All tracks on LPD-70)

ELLA FITZGERALD, vocals

Accompanied by Piano: Paul Smith; Bass: Wilfred Middlebrooks; Drums: Stan Levey. Recorded in performance at Crescendo (nightclub), Los Angeles, Friday, 29 June 1962

FIRST SET

620629-1 Misty (incomplete) *Not yet released*
620629-2 Hallelujah, I Love Him So *Not yet released*
620629-3 Joe Williams' Blues *Not yet released*
620629-4 Bill Bailey, Won't You Please Come Home? *Not yet released*
620629-5 Mack the Knife *Not yet released*

LATER SETS

620629-6 All of Me *Not yet released*
620629-7 62VK710 It Might As Well Be Spring *Not yet released*
620629-8 The Lady Is a Tramp *Not yet released*
620629-9 Little Girl Blue *Not yet released*

620629-10 On the Sunny Side of the Street *Not yet released*
620629-11 62VK712 My Heart Belongs to Daddy *Not yet released*
620629-12 62VK713 Hard Hearted Hannah *Not yet released*
620629-13 Broadway *Not yet released*
620629-14 He's My Kind of Boy *Not yet released*
620629-15 It Had to Be You *Not yet released*
620629-16 All of Me (second version) *Not yet released*
620629-17 Bewitched (Bothered and Bewildered) *Not yet released*
620629-18 Exactly Like You *Not yet released*
620629-19 I've Got a Crush on You *Not yet released*
620629-20 How Long Has This Been Going On? *Not yet released*
620629-21 62VK709 C'est Magnifique *Not yet released*
620629-22 62VK711 On the Sunny Side of the Street *Not yet released*
620629-23 62VK785 Bill Bailey, Won't You Please Come Home? (45: Verve VK 10288; LPD-75)

Note: Charted 6 April 1963; weeks, 3; peak, #75

ELLA FITZGERALD, vocals

Accompanied by Piano: Paul Smith; Bass: Wilfred Middlebrooks; Drums: Stan Levey. Recorded in performance at Crescendo (nightclub), Los Angeles, Saturday, 30 June 1962

FIRST SET

620630-1 62VK715 He's My Kind of Boy *Not yet released*
620630-2 62VK716 Teach Me Tonight *Not yet released*
620630-3 62VK719 Exactly Like You *Not yet released*
620630-4 C'est Magnifique *Not yet released*

LATER sets

620630-5 On the Sunny Side of the Street *Not yet released*
620630-6 When Your Lover Has Gone *Not yet released*
620630-7 Teach Me Tonight *Not yet released*
620630-8 62VK717 Taking a Chance on Love *Not yet released*
620630-9 Good Morning, Heartache *Not yet released*
620630-10 Clap Hands! Here Comes Charlie! *Not yet released*
620630-11 C'est Magnifique (second version) *Not yet released*
620630-12 It Had to Be You *Not yet released*

620630-13 62VK719 Exactly Like You *Not yet released*

620630-14 Hallelujah, I Love Him So *Not yet released*

620630-15 Exactly Like You (second version) *Not yet released*

620630-16 62VK718 Perdido *Not yet released*

620630-17 Angel Eyes *Not yet released*

620630-18 62VK714 Ol' Man Mose (45: Verve VK 10288)

620630-19 Bill Bailey, Won't You Please Come Home? *Not yet released*

620630-20 Bill Bailey, Won't You Please Come Home? (encore) *Not yet released*

620630-21 All of Me *Not yet released*

620630-22 He's My Kind of Boy *Not yet released*

620630-23 My Heart Belongs to Daddy (incomplete) *Not yet released*

620630-24 Too Close for Comfort *Not yet released*

620630-25 Teach Me Tonight (second version) *Not yet released*

620630-26 Too Darn Hot (incomplete) *Not yet released*

Note: The Crescendo had an upstairs room with dancing. Although it doesn't bleed on to the tape, the upstairs dancing to different music was distracting Ella (note the false start before "Too Close for Comfort"). So she created an impromptu parody, which I've arbitrarily entitled "Ella's Twist." The twist was very big during the 1962 rock 'n' roll scene. — Phil Schaap, in Stuart Nicholson's **Ella Fitzgerald: A Biography of the First Lady of Jazz.**

620630-27 "Ella's Twist" *Not yet released*

620630-28 Too Darn Hot *Not yet released*

620630-29 Bewitched (Bothered and Bewildered) *Not yet released*

ELLA FITZGERALD, vocals

Accompanied by orchestra conducted by **Marty Paich**. Arrangements: Marty Paich. Recorded at Capitol Records, Los Angeles, Monday, 1 October 1962

621001-1 62VK631 Desafinado (45: Verve VK 10274; LPD-73)

621001-2 62VK632 Star Dust Bossa Nova (45: Verve VK 10274)

621001-3 62VK659 Steam Heat (LPD-71)

621001-4 62VK658 A Felicidade *Not yet released*

ELLA FITZGERALD, vocals

Ella Sings Broadway

Accompanied by orchestra conducted by **Marty Paich**. Arrangements: Marty Paich. Recorded at Capitol Records, Los Angeles, Tuesday, 2 October 1962

621002-1 62VK660 I Could Have Danced All Night

621002-2 62VK661 Whatever Lola Wants

621002-3 62VK662 Guys and Dolls

621002-4 62VK663 Hernando's Hideaway (LPD-86)

(All tracks on LPD-71)

ELLA FITZGERALD, vocals

Ella Sings Broadway

Accompanied by orchestra conducted by **Marty Paich**. Arrangements: Marty Paich. Recorded at Capitol Records, Los Angeles, Wednesday, 3 October 1962

621003-1 62VK720 Somebody, Somewhere

621003-2 62VK721 No Other Love

621003-3 62VK722 Dites-Moi

621003-4 62VK723 Warm All Over

(All tracks on LPD-71)

ELLA FITZGERALD, vocals

Ella Sings Broadway

Accompanied by orchestra conducted by **Marty Paich**. Arrangements: Marty Paich. Recorded at Capitol Records, Los Angeles, Thursday, 4 October 1962

621004-1 62VK724 Almost Like Being in Love

621004-2 62VK725 If I Were a Bell

621004-3 62VK726 Show Me (LPD-77)

(All tracks on LPD-71)

ELLA FITZGERALD, vocals

Ella Fitzgerald Sings the Jerome Kern Song Book

Accompanied by orchestra conducted by **Nelson Riddle**. Violins: Felix Slatkin (concertmaster) Victor Arno, Israel Baker, Victor Bay, Alex Beller, Erno Neufeld, Lou Raderman, Nathan Ross, Marshall Sosson, Gerald Vinci; Violas: Alex Neimann, Paul Robyn, Barbara Simons; Cellos: Armand Kaproff, Edgar Lustgarten, Eleanor Slatkin; Trumpets: Don Fagerquist, Carroll Lewis, George Seaberg, Shorty Sherock; Trombones: Dick Nash, Tommy Pederson, Tommy Shepard; Bass Trombone: George Roberts; Tenor Saxophone: Plas Johnson; Woodwinds: Harry Klee, Joe Koch, Wilbur Schwartz, Chap Webb; Harp: Ann Stockton; Piano: Paul Smith; Guitar: Robert Bain; Bass: Joe Comfort; Drums: Frank Flynn, Alvin Stoller; Arrangements: Nelson Riddle. Recorded at Studio 10H, Radio Recorders, Los Angeles, Saturday, 5 January 1963

630105-1 63VK204 I'm Old Fashioned

630105-2 63VK205 A Fine Romance (LPD-86)

630105-3 63VK206 I'll Be Hard To Handle

(All tracks on LPD-72)

ELLA FITZGERALD, vocals

Ella Fitzgerald Sings the Jerome Kern Song Book

Accompanied by orchestra conducted by **Nelson Riddle**. Cellos: Justin Ditullio, Armand Kaproff, Ray Kramer, George

Neikrug, David Pratt, Kurt Reher, Emmet Sergeant, Joseph Saxon, Eleanor Slatkin, William Vandenberg; French Horns: John Cave, James Decker, Vincent DeRosa, William Hinshaw, Arthur Maebe; Trumpets: Carroll Lewis, Vito Mangano, Shorty Sherock; Trombones: Tommy Pederson, Tommy Shepard; Bass Trombone: George Roberts; Alto Saxophone: Ronnie Lang; Tenor Saxophone: Ted Nash; Woodwinds: Buddy Collette, Harry Klee, Wilbur Schwartz; Harp: Ann Stockton; Piano: Paul Smith; Guitar: Robert Bain; Bass: Joe Comfort; Drums; Frank Flynn, Alvin Stoller; Arrangements: Nelson Riddle.. Recorded at Studio 10H, Radio Recorders, Los Angeles, Sunday, 6 January 1963

630106-1   63VK207 The Way You Look Tonight
630106-2   63VK208 Can't Help Lovin' Dat Man
630106-3   63VK209 Yesterdays
630106-4   63VK210 Why Was I Born?

(All the above tracks are on LPD-72)

ELLA FITZGERALD, vocals

Ella Fitzgerald Sings the Jerome Kern Song Book

Accompanied by orchestra conducted by **Nelson Riddle.** Violins: Victor Arno, Israel Baker, Victor Bay, Alex Beller, Dan Lube, Erno Neufeld, Lou Raderman, Nathan Ross, Sidney Sharp, Gerald Vinci; Cellos; Armand Kaproff, Ray Kramer, Eleanor Slatkin; Violas: Alex Neimann, Paul Robyn, Barbara Simons; Trumpets: Don Fagerquist, Carroll Lewis, George Seaberg, Shorty Sherock; Trombones: Dick Nash, Tommy Pederson, Tommy Shepard; Bass Trombone: George Roberts; Tenor Saxophone: Plas Johnson; Woodwinds: Harry Klee, Joe Koch, Wilbur Schwartz, Champ Webb; Piano: Paul Smith; Guitar: Robert Bain; Bass: Joe Comfort; Drums: Frank Flynn, Alvin Stoller; Arrangements: Nelson Riddle. Recorded at Studio 10H, Radio Recorders, Los Angeles, Monday, 7 January 1963

630107-1   63VK211 You Couldn't Be Cuter
630107-2   63VK212 She Didn't Say Yes
630107-3   63VK213 Let's Begin
630107-4   63VK214 Remind Me
630107-5   63VK215 All the Things You Are

(All the above tracks are on LPD-72)

ELLA FITZGERALD, vocals

Ella and Basie!/On the Sunny Side of the Street

Accompanied by **Count Basie and His Orchestra.** Count Basie, Conductor/Piano. Trumpets: Al Aarons, George "Sonny" Cohn, Joe Newman, Don Rader, Fortunatus "Flip" Ricard; Trombones: Henry Coker, Urban "Urbie" Green, Grover Mitchell, Benny Powell; Clarinet: Marshall Royal; Flutes: Eric Dixon, Frank Wess; Alto Saxophones: Marshall Royal, Frank Wess; Tenor Saxophones: Eric Dixon, Frank Foster, Frank Wess; Baritone Saxophone: Charlie Fowlkes; Guitar: Freddie Green; Bass: George "Buddy" Catlett; Drums: Percival "Sonny" Payne; Arrangements: Quincy Jones. Recorded at A & R Studio, New York, Monday, 15 July 1963

630715-1   63VK505 I'm Beginning to See the Light

630715-2   63VK506 'Deed I Do (LPD-86)
630715-3   63VK509 On the Sunny Side of the Street
630715-4   63VK510 Satin Doll
630715-5   63VK512 Honeysuckle Rose (LPD-77)

(All tracks on LPD-74)

ELLA FITZGERALD, vocals

Ella and Basie!/On the Sunny Side of the Street

Accompanied by **Count Basie and His Septet**: Trumpet: Joe Newman; Trombone: Urban "Urbie" Green; Tenor Saxophone: Frank Foster; Guitar: Freddie Green; Bass: George "Buddy" Catlett; Drums: Percival "Sonny" Payne; Piano-Organ: William "Count" Basie. Recorded at A & R Studio, New York, Tuesday, 16 July 1963

630716-1   63VK513 Them There Eyes (head arrangement) (Basie on piano)
630716-2   63VK514 Dream a Little Dream of Me (Basie on organ)

Accompanied by **Count Basie and His Orchestra.** Count Basie, Conductor/Piano. Trumpets: Al Aarons, George "Sonny" Cohn, Joe Newman, Don Rader, Fortunatus; Flip Ricard; Trombones: Henry Coker, Urban "Urbie" Green, Grover Mitchell, Buddy Powell; Clarinet: Marshall Royal; Flutes: Eric Dixon, Frank Wess; Alto Saxophones: Marshall Royal, Frank Wess; Tenor Saxophones: Eric Dixon, Frank Foster, Frank Wess; Baritone Saxophone: Charlie Fowlkes; Guitar: Freddie Green; Bass: George "Buddy" Catlett; Drums: Percival "Sonny" Payne; Arrangements: Quincy Jones. Recorded at A & R Studio, New York, Tuesday, 16 July 1963

630716-3   63VK504 Shiny Stockings (Arr: Frank Foster, Quincy Jones) (LPD-73)
630716-4   63VK507 My Last Affair
630716-5   63VK507-1 My Last Affair (alternative take)
630716-6   63VK507-2 My Last Affair (alternative take)
630716-7   63VK508 Ain't Misbehavin'
630716-8   63VK511 Into Some Life Some Rain Must Fall
630716-9   63VK515 Tea for Two
630716-10   Unnumbered-1 Robbins' Nest (breakdown)
630716-11   Unnumbered-5 Robbins' Nest (complete take)
630716-12   Unnumbered-6 Robbins' Nest (complete take)
630716-13   Unnumbered-13 Robbins' Nest (complete take)

(All tracks on LPD-74)

ELLA FITZGERALD, vocals

These Are the Blues

Accompanied by Trumpet: Roy Eldridge; Organ: "Wild Bill" Davis; Guitar: Herb Ellis; Bass: Ray Brown; Drums: Gus

Johnson. Recorded at A & R Studio, New York, Monday, 28 October 1963

631028-1 63VK674 How Long, How Long Blues
631028-2 63VK675 See See Rider (C.C. Rider)
(LPD-77)
631028-3 63VK676 Trouble in Mind
631028-4 63VK677 Jailhouse Blues
631028-5 63VK678 Heah Me Talkin' To Ya (LPD-86)
631028-6 63VK679 Cherry Red

(All the above tracks are on LPD-75)

ELLA FITZGERALD, vocals

These Are the Blues

Accompanied by Trumpet: Roy Eldridge; Organ: "Wild Bill" Davis; Guitar: Herb Ellis; Bass: Ray Brown; Drums: Gus Johnson. Recorded at A & R Studio, New York, Tuesday, 29 October 1963

631029-1 63VK680-6 You Don't Know My Mind
631029-2 63VK681-4 Down-Hearted Blues
631029-3 63VK682-1 St. Louis Blues
631029-4 63VK683-2 In the Evening (When the Sun Goes Down)
631029-5 Private Jam Session *Not yet released*

(All tracks, except "Private Jam Session," on LPD-75)

ELLA FITZGERALD, vocals

Accompanied by **The Roy Eldridge Quartet**. Trumpet: Roy Eldridge; Piano: Tommy Flanagan; Bass: Bill Yancey; Drums: Gus Johnson. Recorded at 3 February 1964

640203-1 You'd Be So Nice To Come Home To *Not yet released*
640203-2 I'm Beginning to See the Light *Not yet released*
640203-3 My Last Affair *Not yet released*
640203-4 Dream a Little Dream of Me *Not yet released*
640203-5 Goody Goody *Not yet released*
640203-6 I Love Being Here with You *Not yet released*
640203-7 Ten Cents a Dance *Not yet released*
640204-8 Deep Purple *Not yet released*
640203-9 Witchcraft *Not yet released*
640203-10 Them There Eyes *Not yet released*
640203-11 Shiny Stockings *Not yet released*
640203-12 The Lady Is a Tramp *Not yet released*
640203-13 Bill Bailey, Won't You Please Come Home? *Not yet released*
640203-14 Perdido *Not yet released*
640203-15 Mack the Knife *Not yet released*

ELLA FITZGERALD, vocals

Hello, Dolly!

Accompanied by orchestra conducted by **Frank DeVol**. Tenor Saxophone: Zoot Sims; Arrangements: Frank DeVol. Recorded at A & R Studio, New York, Tuesday, 3 March 1964

640303-1 64VK281-4 There! I've Said It Again *Not yet released*
640303-2 64VK282-4 How High the Moon
640303-3 64VK283-2 Pete Kelly's Blues
640303-4 64VK284-11 Memories of You

(All tracks, except "There! I've Said It Again," on LPD-76)

ELLA FITZGERALD, vocals

Hello, Dolly!

Accompanied by orchestra conducted by **Frank DeVol**. Arrangements: Frank DeVol. Recorded at A & R Studio, New York, Wednesday, 4 March 1964

640304-1 64VK285-4 Lullaby of the Leaves
640304-2 64VK286-5 I'll See You in My Dreams *Not yet released*
640304-3 64VK287-2 My Man (Mon Homme)
640304-4 64VK288-7 The Thrill Is Gone (LPD-77)
640304-5 64VK289-5 There Are Such Things *Not yet released*
640304-6 64VK290-6 Miss Otis Regrets
640304-7 64VK291-3 Volare

(All tracks, except "I'll See You in My Dreams" and "The Thrill Is Gone," on LPD-76)

ELLA FITZGERALD, vocals

Hello, Dolly!

Accompanied by orchestra conducted by **Johnny Spence**. Arrangements: Johnny Spence. Recorded at Olympic Studio, London (England), Tuesday, 7 April 1964

640407-1 64VK335 Can't Buy Me Love (LPD-86)
640407-2 64VK336 Hello, Dolly!
640407-3 64VK385 People (LPD-77)
640407-4 64VK386 The Sweetest Sounds

(All tracks on LPD-76)

ELLA FITZGERALD, vocals

The Fifth Festival Mondial du Jazz Antibes —Juan-les Pins (Ella at Juan-les Pins)

Accompanied by **The Roy Eldridge Quartet**. Trumpet: Roy Eldridge; Piano: Tommy Flanagan; Bass: Bill Yancey; Drums: Gus Johnson. Recorded in performance at Pinède Gould Amphithéâtre, Antibes-Juan-les Pins (France), Tuesday, 28 July 1964

640728-1 Hello, Dolly! *Not yet released*

640728-2	Just A-Sittin' and A-Rockin'	
640728-3	Day In, Day Out (LPD-86)	
640728-4	I Love Being Here with You *Not yet released*	
640728-5	People *Not yet released*	
640728-6	Someone to Watch Over Me *Not yet released*	
640728-7	Can't Buy Me Love *Not yet released*	
640728-8	Them There Eyes *Not yet released*	
640728-9	The Lady Is a Tramp	
640728-10	Summertime	
640728-11	Cutie Pants	
640728-12	I'm Putting All My Eggs in One Basket *Not yet released*	
640728-13	St. Louis Blues	
640728-14	Perdido *Not yet released*	
640728-15	Mack the Knife *Not yet released*	
640728-16	Honeysuckle Rose	

(All released tracks on LPD-78)

ELLA FITZGERALD, vocals

The Fifth Festival Mondial du Jazz Antibes Juanles Pins (Ella at Juanles Pins)

Accompanied by **The Roy Eldridge Quartet**. Trumpet: Roy Eldridge; Piano: Tommy Flanagan; Bass: Bill Yancey; Drums: Gus Johnson. Recorded in performance at Pinède Gould Amphithéâtre, Antibes-Juan-les Pins (France), Wednesday, 29 July 1964

640729-1	Hello, Dolly!
640729-2	Day In, Day Out
640729-3	Just A-Sittin' and A-Rockin'
640729-4	I Love Being Here with You
640729-5	People
640729-6	Someone to Watch Over Me
640729-7	Can't Buy Me Love
640729-8	Them There Eyes
640729-9	The Lady Is a Tramp
640729-10	Summertime
640729-11	Cutie Pants
640729-12	I'm Putting All My Eggs in One Basket
640729-13	St. Louis Blues (laughing throughout, no vocal)
640729-14	Perdido

(All tracks on LPD-79)

640729-15	Goody Goody
640729-16	The Boy from Ipanema
640729-17	They Can't Take That Away from Me
640729-18	You'd Be So Nice to Come Home To
640729-19	Shiny Stockings *Not yet released*
640729-20	Somewhere in the Night
640729-21	I've Got You Under My Skin
640729-22	Blues in the Night *Not yet released*
640729-23	Too Close for Comfort *Not yet released*
640729-24	Mack the Knife *Not yet released*
640729-25	The Cricket Song
640729-26	How High the Moon

(All released tracks on LPD-78)

ELLA FITZGERALD, vocals

Ella in Nippon; not yet released

Accompanied by **The Roy Eldridge Quartet**. Trumpet: Roy Eldridge; Piano: Tommy Flanagan; Bass: Bill Yancey; Drums: Gus Johnson. Recorded in performance at Tokyo (Japan), 1963

PRODUCED FOR ISSUE

630000-1	Cheek to Cheek *Not yet released*
630000-2	Deep Purple *Not yet released*
630000-3	Too Close for Comfort *Not yet released*
630000-4	I Love Being Here with You *Not yet released*
630000-5	Fly Me to the Moon *Not yet released*
630000-6	'S Wonderful *Not yet released*
630000-7	I've Got You Under My Skin *Not yet released*
630000-8	Hallelujah, I Love Him So *Not yet released*
630000-9	Misty *Not yet released*
630000-10	Whatever Lola Wants *Not yet released*
630000-11	Bill Bailey, Won't You Please Come Home? *Not yet released*
630000-12	Ella's Blues *Not yet released*

(Other material recorded at same concerts)

630000-13	Cheek to Cheek *Not yet released*
630000-14	Can't Help Lovin' Date Man *Not yet released*
630000-15	Shiny Stockings *Not yet released*
630000-16	Bill Bailey, Won't You Please Come Home? *Not yet released*
630000-17	Take the "A" Train *Not yet released*
630000-18	A-Tisket, A-Tasket *Not yet released*
630000-19	Hallelujah, I Love Him So *Not yet released*
630000-20	Ella's Blues *Not yet released*
630000-21	Mack the Knife *Not yet released*
630000-22	Ain't Misbehavin' *Not yet released*
630000-23	My Last Affair *Not yet released*

Accompanied by large Japanese big band, featuring Roy Eldridge, trumpet

630000-24	Perdido *Not yet released*

ELLA FITZGERALD, vocals

Ella Fitzgerald Sings the Johnny Mercer Song Book, etc.

Accompanied by **Nelson Riddle.** French Horns: John Cave, James Decker, William Hinshaw; Trumpets: Carroll Lewis, Vito Mangano, George Seaberg, Shorty Sherock; Trombones: Dick Nash, Tommy Pederson, Tommy Shepard; Bass Trombone: George Roberts; Flutes: Buddy Collette, Harry Klee; Clarinets: Abe Most, Buddy DeFranco; Tenor Saxophones: Plas Johnson, Babe Russin; Oboes: Norman Benno, Seymour Schoneberg; Bassoons: Lloyd Hildebrand, Howard Terry; Woodwinds: Joe Koch, Wilbur Schwartz, William Smith; Harp: Katharine Julyie; Piano: Paul Smith; Guitar: Barney Kessel; Bass: Joe Comfort; Percussion: Emil Raddochia; Drums: Irving Cottler. Recorded at Radio Recorders, Los Angeles, Monday, 19 October 1964

641019-1 64VK538 Trav'lin' Light (45: Verve VK 10337; LPD-80)

641019-2 64VK502 I've Grown Accustomed to His Face (45: Verve VK 10337)

641019-2 64VK507 All the Livelong Day (45: Verve VK 10388)

641019-3 64VK508 I'm a Poached Egg (45: Verve VK 10388)

641019-4 64VK531 Early Autumn (LPD-80)

641019-5 64VK540 Dream (When You're Feeling Blue) (LPD-80)

ELLA FITZGERALD, vocals

Ella Fitzgerald Sings the Johnny Mercer Song Book

Accompanied by orchestra conducted by **Nelson Riddle.** French Horns: William Hinshaw, Robert Perissi, George Price; Trumpets: John Audino, Carroll Lewis, Vito Mangano, George Seaberg; Trombones: Milton Bernhart, Gilbert Falco, Tommy Shepard; Bass Trombone: George Roberts; Flutes: Buddy Collette, Henry Klee; Clarinets: Buddy DeFranco, George Smith; Tenor Saxophone: Babe Russin; Oboes: Norman Benno, Seymour Schoneberg; Bassoons: Lloyd Hildebrand, Howard Terry; Woodwinds: Gene Cipriano, Joe Koch, Wilbur Schwartz, William Smith; Harp: Katharine Julyie; Piano: Paul Smith; Guitar: Robert Bain; Bass: Joe Comfort; Percussion: Frank Flynn; Drums: Irving Cottler; Arrangements: Nelson Riddle. Recorded at Radio Recorders, Los Angeles, Tuesday 20 October 1964

641020-1 64VK532 Day In, Day Out

641020-2 64VK534 This Time the Dream's on Me

641020-3 64VK535 Skylark

641020-4 64VK536 Single-O

641020-5 64VK539 Midnight Sun

(All the above tracks are on LPD-80)

ELLA FITZGERALD, vocals

Ella Fitzgerald Sings the Johnny Mercer Song Book

Accompanied by orchestra conducted by **Nelson Riddle.** French Horns: John Cave, James Decker, William Hinshaw; Trumpets: Carroll Lewis, Vito Mangano, George Seaberg, Shorty Sherock; Trombones: Milton Bernhart, Tommy Ped-

erson, Tommy Shepard; Bass Trombone: George Roberts; Flutes: Buddy Collette, Harry Klee; Clarinets: Buddy DeFranco, George Smith; Tenor Saxophones: Plas Johnson, Babe Russin; Oboes: Norman Benno, Seymour Schoneberg; Bassoons: Lloyd Hildebrand, Howard Terry; Woodwinds: Joe Koch, Wilbur Schwartz, William Smith; Harp: Katharine Julyie; Piano: Paul Smith; Guitar: Barney Kessel; Bass: Joe Comfort; Percussion: Emil Raddochia; Drums: Irving Cottler; Arrangements: Nelson Riddle. Recorded at Radio Recorders, Los Angeles, Wednesday, 21 October 1964

641021-1 64VK530 Too Marvelous for Words

641021-2 64VK533 Laura

641021-3 64VK537 Something's Gotta Give (LPD-86)

641021-4 64VK541 I Remember You

641021-5 64VK542 When a Woman Loves a Man

(All the above tracks are on LPD-80)

ELLA FITZGERALD, vocals

Accompanied by orchestra conducted by **Marty Paich.** Arrangements: Marty Paich. Recorded at Radio Recorders, Los Angeles, Thursday, 22 October 1964

641022-1 64VK545-11 Ol' MacDonald *Not yet released*

641022-2 64VK546-3 I Said No *Not yet released*

641022-3 64VK547-5 When Sunny Gets Blue *Not yet released*

641022-4 64VK543 I've Got Your Number *Not yet released*

641022-5 64VK544 Thanks for the Memory *Not yet released*

641022-6 64VK548 Spring Can Really Hang You Up the Most *Not yet released*

641022-7 64VK549 Melancholy Serenade *Not yet released*

ELLA FITZGERALD, vocals

Accompanied by Guitar: Barney Kessel; and others. Recorded at Radio Recorders, Los Angeles, Friday, 23 October 1964

641023-1 64VK518 That Ringo Beat (45: Verve VK 10340)

641023-2 64VK519 I'm Fallin' in Love (45: Verve VK 10340)

ELLA FITZGERALD, vocals

Ella in Hamburg

Accompanied by Piano: Tommy Flanagan; Bass: Keter Betts; Drums: Gus Johnson. Recorded in performance at Musikhalle, Hamburg (Germany), Friday, 26 March 1965

650326-1 65VK444 Walk Right In

650326-2 65VK445 That Old Black Magic

650326-3 65VK446 Body and Soul

650326-4   65VK447 Here's That Rainy Day (LPD-86)
650326-5   65VK448 And the Angels Sing
650326-6   65VK449 Ellington Medley: a. Mood Indigo; b. Do Nothin' Till You Hear from Me; c. It Don't Mean a Thing
650326-7   65VK450 Don't Rain on My Parade
650326-8   65VK451 Angel Eyes
650326-9   65VK452 Smooth Sailing
650326-10   65VK453 Ol' MacDonald Had a Farm
650326-11   65VK454 The Boy from Ipanema
650326-12   65VK508 A Hard Day's Night

(All tracks on LPD-81)

ELLA FITZGERALD, vocals

Accompanied by orchestra conducted by **Marty Paich**. Arrangements: Marty Paich. Recorded at Radio Recorders, Los Angeles, Friday, 25 June 1965

650625-1   65VK401 Time After Time *Not yet released*
650625-2   65VK402 Whisper Not *Not yet released*
650625-3   65VK403 You've Changed *Not yet released*
650625-4   65VK404 Lover Man *Not yet released*

ELLA FITZGERALD, vocals

Accompanied by orchestra conducted by **Marty Paich**. Arrangements: Marty Paich. Recorded at Radio Recorders, Los Angeles, Saturday, 26 June 1965

650626-1   65VK412 Wives and Lovers *Not yet released*
650626-2   65VK413 Matchmaker, Matchmaker Not yet Released
650626-3   65VK414 Sweet Georgia Brown *Not yet released*
650626-4   65VK415 Don't Rain on My Parade *Not yet released*

ELLA FITZGERALD, vocals

Accompanied by orchestra conducted by **Marty Paich**. Arrangements: Marty Paich. Recorded at Radio Recorders, Los Angeles, Tuesday, 6 July 1965

650706-1   65VK399 She's Just a Quiet Girl (45: Verve VK 10359)
650706-2   65VK400 We Three (My Echo, My Shadow and Me) (45: Verve VK 10359)

ELLA FITZGERALD, vocals

Ella at Duke's Place

Accompanied by **Duke Ellington and His Orchestra**. Duke Ellington, Leader/Piano; Trumpets: Cat Anderson, Mercer Ellington, Herbie Jones, Cootie Williams; Trombones: Lawrence Brown, Buster Cooper; Bass Trombone: Chuck Connors; Clarinets: Harry Carney, Jimmy Hamilton, Russell Procope; Bass Clarinet: Harry Carney; Alto Saxophones: Johnny Hodges, Russell Procope; Tenor Saxophones: Paul Gonsalves, Jimmy Hamilton; Baritone Saxophone: Harry Carney; Piano: Jimmy Jones*; Bass: John Lamb; Drums: Louis Bellson; Arrangements: Duke Ellington, Gerald Wilson, Jimmy Jones. Recorded at United Recording Studios, Los Angeles, Sunday, 17 October 1965

651017-1   65VK5533-1-1 Imagine My Frustration (arr. Wilson) *Not yet released*
651017-2   65VK5533-1-2 Imagine My Frustration (arr. Wilson) (LPD-82)
651017-3   65VK5533-1-3 Imagine My Frustration (arr. Wilson) *Not yet released.*

Recorded at United Recording Studios, Los Angeles, Monday, 18 October 1965

651018-1   65VK5533-2 What Am I Here For? (arr. Ellington) (LPD-82)
651018-2   65VK5533-2 Duke's Place (arr. Ellington)

(This track reportedly appears on an Azure [label] album)

651018-3   65VK5533-3-2 Duke's Place (arr. Ellington) (45: V-10408 [edited]; LPD-82)
651018-4   65VK5533-4 Azure* (arr. Jones)

*Jimmy Jones replaces Ellington on piano (LPD-82). Recorded at United Recording Studios, Los Angeles, Tuesday, 19 October 1965

651019-1   65VK5533-5 I Like the Sunrise* (arr. Jones) (LPD-82)
651019-2   65VK5533-6 Cotton Tail (arr. Ellington) (Ellington and Jones at pianos) (LPD-82)
651019-3   65VK5533-7 Something To Live For* (arr. Jones) (LPD-82, LPD-86)
651019-4   65VK5533-8 A Flower Is a Lovesome Thing* (arr. Jones) (LPD-82)

*Jimmy Jones replaces Ellington at piano. Recorded at United Recording Studios, Los Angeles, Wednesday, 20 October 1965

651020-1   65VK5533-9-1 Passion Flower* (arr. Jones) *Not yet released*
651020-2   65VK5533-9-2 Passion Flower* (arr. Jones) (LPD-82)
651020-3   65VK5533-10 The Brown Skinned Gal in the Calico Gown* *Not yet released*
651020-4   65VK5533-10 The Brown Skinned Gal in the Calico Gown* (LPD-82) (arr. Ellington)

*Jimmy Jones replaces Ellington at piano

ELLA FITZGERALD, vocals

Duke & Ella in Concert

Accompanied by Piano: Jimmy Jones; Bass: Joe Comfort; Drums: Gus Johnson. Recorded in performance at Teatro Lirico, Milan (Italy), 30 January 1966

660130-1   How High the Moon
660130-2   Lover Man
660130-3   Mack the Knife
    Accompanied by **The Jimmy Jones Trio with Duke Ellington and His Orchestra**. Duke Ellington, Leader/Piano; Trumpets: Cat Anderson, Mercer Ellington, Herbie Jones, Cootie Williams; Trombones: Lawrence Brown, Chuck Connors, Buster Cooper; Clarinets: Harry Carney, Jimmy Hamilton, Russell Procope; Alto Saxophones: Johnny Hodges, Russell Procope; Tenor Saxophones: Paul Gonsalves, Jimmy Hamilton; Baritone Saxophone: Harry Carney; Bass: Joe Comfort; Drums: Gus Johnson

660130-4   Cotton Tail

(All tracks on LPD-142)

    Accompanied by Duke Ellington, piano

660130-5   I'm Just a Lucky So-and-So *Not yet released*. (This recording was made backstage at the Teatro Lirico)

ELLA FITZGERALD, vocals

Ella Fitzgerald and Duke Ellington/ The Stockholm Concert, 1966

    Accompanied by **The Jimmy Jones Trio with Duke Ellington and His Orchestra**. Duke Ellington, Leader/Piano*; Trumpets: Cat Anderson, Mercer Ellington, Herbie Jones, Cootie Williams; Trombones: Lawrence Brown, Chuck Connors, Buster Cooper; Clarinets: Harry Carney, Jimmy Hamilton, Russell Procope; Alto Saxophones: Johnny Hodges, Russell Procope; Tenor Saxophones: Paul Gonsalves, Jimmy Hamilton; Baritone Saxophone: Harry Carney; Piano: Jimmy Jones; Bass: Joe Comfort; Drums: Gus Johnson. Recorded in performance at The Circus, Stockholm (Sweden), Monday, 8 February 1966

660208-1   Sweet Georgia Brown *Not yet released*
660208-2   So Danò Samba *Not yet released*
660208-3   Medley: a. How High the Moon *Not yet released*; b. A Hard Day's Night; c. Smoke Gets in Your Eyes
660208-4   Imagine My Frustration* (LPD-118)
660208-5   Duke's Place (Ellington and Jones at pianos) (LPD-118)
660208-6   Satin Doll (LPD-118)
660208-7   Something to Live For (LPD-118)
660208-8   Wives and Lovers
660208-9   So Danò Samba (LPD-118)
660208-10   Let's Do It
660208-11   Lover Man
660208-12   How High the Moon*
660208-13   Mr. Paganini (You'll Have To Swing It)*
660208-14   Cotton Tail*

*Duke Ellington replaces Jimmy Jones on these tracks

(All tracks on LPD-83)

ELLA FITZGERALD, vocals

Só Danò Samba

    Accompanied by Piano: Jimmy Jones; Bass: Joe Comfort; Drums: Gus Johnson. Recorded in performance at Théâtre Americain, Brussels (Belgium), Tuesday, 22 February 1966

660222-1   Satin Doll
660222-2   Wives and Lovers
660222-3   Something to Live For
660222-4   Let's Do It
660222-5   Sweet Georgia Brown
660222-6   Midnight Sun
660222-7   How High the Moon
660222-8   I'm Just a Lucky-So-and-So
660222-9   Só Danò Samba
660222-10   Mack The Knife

(All tracks on LPD-140)

ELLA FITZGERALD, vocals

    Accompanied by orchestra conducted by Gordon Jenkins. Arrangements: Gordon Jenkins. Recorded at United Recording Studios, Los Angeles, Tuesday, 5 April 1966

660406-1   L1 The Shadow of Your Smile (45: Verve VK10408)
660406-2   L2 You're Gonna Hear from Me *Not yet released*

ELLA FITZGERALD, vocals

Whisper Not

    Accompanied by orchestra conducted by **Marty Paich**. Trumpet: Harry "Sweets" Edison, Stu Williamson; Tenor Saxophone: Bill Perkins; Piano: Jimmy Rowles; Bass: Joe Mondragon; Drums: Shelley Manne; and others; Arrangements: Marty Paich. Recorded at United Recording Studios, Los Angeles, Wednesday, 20 July 1966

660720-1   100669 Sweet Georgia Brown
660720-2   100670 Whisper Not
660720-3   100671 I Said No
660720-4   100672 Thanks for the Memory
660720-5   100673 Spring Can Really Hang You Up the Most
660720-6   100674 Ol' MacDonald Had a Farm
660720-7   100675 Time After Time
660720-8   100676 You've Changed (LPD-86)
660720-9   100677 I've Got Your Number
660720-10   100678 Lover Man
660720-11   100679 Wives and Lovers
660720-12   100680 Matchmaker, Matchmaker

(All tracks on LPD-84)

DUKE ELLINGTON AND HIS ORCHESTRA WITH ELLA FITZGERALD

The Sixth Festival Mondial du Jazz Antibes-Juan-les Pins (Ella and Duke at the Côte d'Azur)

Duke Ellington, Leader/Piano Trumpets: Cat Anderson, Mercer Ellington, Herbie Jones, Cootie Williams; Trombones: Lawrence Brown, Chuck Connors, Buster Cooper; Clarinet: Jimmy Hamilton; Alto Saxophones: Johnny Hodges, Russell Procope; Tenor Saxophones: Paul Gonsalves, Jimmy Hamilton; Baritone Saxophone: Harry Carney; Bass: John Lamb; Drums: Sam Woodyard. Recorded in performance at Pinède Gould Amphithéâtre, Antibes-Juan-les Pins (France), Wednesday, 27 July 1966

660727-1   Azure (LPD-85)

Accompanied by **The Jimmy Jones Trio**. Piano: Jimmy Jones; Bass: Jim Hughart; Drums: Grady Tate

660727-2   Só Danò Samba (Jazz Samba) *Not yet released*

660727-3   You Go to My Head; Goin' Out of My Head *Not yet released*

660727-4   How Long Has This Been Going On? *Not yet released*

660727-5   Misty *Not yet released*

660727-6   The More I See You *Not yet released*

660727-7   Lullaby of Birdland *Not yet released*

Accompanied by **Duke Ellington and His Orchestra with The Jimmy Jones Trio**. Duke Ellington, Leader; Piano Trumpets: Cat Anderson, Mercer Ellington, Herbie Jones, Cootie Williams; Trombones: Lawrence Brown, Chuck Connors, Buster Cooper; Clarinet: Jimmy Hamilton; Alto Saxophones: Johnny Hodges, Russell Procope; Tenor Saxophones: Paul Gonsalves, Jimmy Hamilton; Baritone Saxophone: Harry Carney; Piano: Jimmy Jones; Bass: Jim Hughart; Drums: Grady Tate

660727-8   Let's Do It

660727-9   Satin Doll

660727-10   Cotton Tail*

*Duke Ellington replaces Jimmy Jones at piano

(All released tracks on LPD-85)

ELLA FITZGERALD, vocals

The Sixth Fesitval Mondial du Jazz Antibes-Juan-les Pins (Ella and Duke at the Côte d'Azur)

Accompanied by **Duke Ellington and His Orchestra with The Jimmy Jones Trio**, Duke Ellington, Leader; Trumpets: Cat Anderson, Mercer Ellington, Herbie Jones, Cootie Williams; Trombones: Lawrence Brown, Chuck Connors, Buster Cooper; Clarinet: Jimmy Hamilton; Alto Saxophones: Johnny Hodges, Russell Procope; Tenor Saxophones: Paul Gonsalves, Jimmy Hamilton; Baritone Saxophone: Harry Carney; Piano: Jimmy Jones; Bass: Jim Hughart; Drums: Grady Tate. Recorded in performance at Pinède Gould Amphithéâtre, Antibes-Juan-les Pins (France), Thursday, 28 July 1966

660728-1   Who/Thou Swell

660728-2   Satin Doll

660728-3   Wives and Lovers

660728-4   Something to Live For

660728-5   Let's Do It

660728-6   Sweet Georgia Brown *Not yet released*

Accompanied by **The Jimmy Jones Trio**. Piano: Jimmy Jones; Bass: Jim Hughart; Drums: Grady Tate

660728-7   101599 The More I See You

660728-8   101596 You Go to My Head; Goin' Out of My Head

660728-9   101595 Só Danò Samba [Jazz Samba] (LPD-84)

660728-10   101600 Lullaby of Birdland

660728-11   101597 How Long Has This Been Going On?

Accompanied by **Duke Ellington and His Orchestra with The Jimmy Jones Trio**, Duke Ellington, Leader; Trumpets: Cat Anderson, Mercer Ellington, Herbie Jones, Cootie Williams; Trombones: Lawrence Brown, Chuck Connors, Buster Cooper; Clarinet: Jimmy Hamilton; Alto Saxophones: Johnny Hodges, Russell Procope; Tenor Saxophones: Paul Gonsalves, Jimmy Hamilton; Baritone Saxophone: Harry Carney; Piano: Jimmy Jones; Bass: Jim Hughart; Drums: Grady Tate

660728-12   Mack the Knife

660728-13   Cotton Tail *Not yet released*

660728-14   Imagine My Frustration *Not yet released*

(All released tracks on LPD-85)

ELLA FITZGERALD, vocals

The Sixth Festival Mondial du Jazz Antibes-Juan-les Pins (Ella and Duke at the Côte d'Azur)

Accompanied by **Duke Ellington and His Orchestra with The Jimmy Jones Trio**, Duke Ellington, Leader/Piano; Trumpets: Cat Anderson, Mercer Ellington, Herbie Jones, Cootie Williams; Trombones: Lawrence Brown, Chuck Connors, Buster Cooper; Clarinet: Jimmy Hamilton; Alto Saxophones: Johnny Hodges, Russel Procope; Tenor Saxophones: Paul Gonsalves, Jimmy Hamilton; Baritone Saxophone: Harry Carney; Piano: Jimmy Jones; Bass: Jim Hughart; Drums: Grady Tate. Recorded in performance at Pinède Gould Amphithéâtre, Antibes-Juan-les Pins (France), Friday, 29 July 1966

660729-1   Who?/Thou Swell

660729-2   Satin Doll

660729-3   Wives and Lovers

660729-4   Something to Live For

660729-5   Let's Do It

660729-6   Sweet Georgia Brown

Accompanied by The Jimmy Jones Trio. Piano: Jimmy Jones; Bass: Jim Hughart; Drums: Grady Tate

660729-7   You Go to My Head; Goin' Out of My Head

660729-8   Só Danò Samba
660729-9   Lullaby of Birdland
660719-10   The Moment of Truth
660729-11   Misty

Accompanied by **Duke Ellington and His Orchestra with The Jimmy Jones Trio**, Duke Ellington, Leader/Piano; Trumpets: Cat Anderson, Mercer Ellington, Herbie Jones, Cootie Williams; Trombones: Lawrence Brown, Chuck Connors, Buster Cooper; Clarinet: Jimmy Hamilton; Alto Saxophones: Johnny Hodges, Russell Procope; Tenor Saxophones: Paul Gonsalves, Jimmy Hamilton; Baritone Saxophone: Harry Carney; Piano: Jimmy Jones; Bass: Jim Hughart; Drums: Grady Tate

660729-12   Mack the Knife
660729-13   Cotton Tail*

*Duke Ellington replaces Jimmy Jones

Accompanied by **Duke Ellington and His Orchestra**. Duke Ellington, Leader/Piano; Trumpets: Cat Anderson, Mercer Ellington, Herbie Jones, Ray Nance; Trombones: Lawrence Brown, Chuck Connors, Buster Cooper; Clarinet: Jimmy Hamilton; Alto Saxophones: Johnny Hodges, Russell Procope; Tenor Saxophones: Paul GonsalvesBen Webster; Baritone Saxophone: Harry Carney; Bass: John Lamb; Drums: Sam Woodyard; Vocals: Ray Nance

660729-14   It Don't Mean a Thing (vDuet EF-RN) (LPD-86)

Accompanied by **The Duke Ellington Quintet**. Tenor Saxophones: Paul Gonsalves, Ben Webster; Piano: Duke Ellington; Bass: John Lamb; Drums: Sam Woodyard; Vocals: Ray Nance

660729-15   101603 Just Squeeze Me (vDuet EF-RN)

(All tracks on LPD-85)

The Verve Years: A Survey

During Ella's reign at Verve Records, from 21 January 1956, when she appeared in concert at Shrine Auditorium, Los Angeles, until she returned from the Côte d'Azur in late summer, 1966, she recorded 1,191 titles, of which,

611 were studio recordings, of which
506 may be found on compact discs; of the remaining 105 recordings,
39 may be found on long-play releases,
22 may be found only on 45 rpm records, and
44 have not yet been released.

309 tracks are known to have been recorded at concerts, of which
202 may be found on compact discs; of the remaining 107 recordings
14 may be found on long-play releases, and
93 have not yet been released.

246 tracks are known to have been recorded in cabarets, of which
13 may be found on compact discs; of the remaining 233 recordings,
1 may be found on a long-play record,
1 was released only on a 45 rpm record, and
231 have not yet been released.

25 titles from televison performances, of which
10 may be found on compact discs; of the remaining 15 recordings,

8 may be found on on an long-play record, and
7 have not yet been released.

To recapitulate, of the 1,191 recordings made,
731 may be found on compact discs; of the remaining 460 recordings,
62 may be found only on long-play records,
23 may be found on a 45 rpm release, and
375 titles have not yet been released.

To date, Ella's discography reveals that, combined with her Decca years,
1,803 recordings were made, of which
1,209 may be found on compact discs; of the 594 remaining recordings,
112 may be found on long-play records,
23 may be found only on 45 rpm records,
36 may be found only on 78 rpm records, and
423 remain as yet unreleased.

THE CONCERT YEARS (1966–1971)

ELLA FITZGERALD, vocals

Frank & Dean's Party by the Bay

Accompanied by orchestra conducted by **Nelson Riddle**. Recorded in performance at Civic Auditorium, San Francisco (California), Wednesday evening, 7 September 1966

660907-1   Something's Gotta Give
660907-2   Body and Soul
660907-3   Too Marvelous for Words

(All tracks on LPD-159)

ELLA FITZGERALD, vocals

Accompanied by **The Jimmy Jones Trio**, and **Cat Anderson**; Trumpet: Cat Anderson; Piano: Jimmy Jones; Bass: Jim Hughart; Drums: Ed Thigpen. Recorded in performance at The Greek Theatre, Los Angeles, Wednesday, 14 September 1966, and telecast Sunday, 25 September 1966

660914-1   Star Dust (45: Stateside SS 569; EP: Stateside SE 1044)
660914-2   I'm Just a Lucky So-and-So (45: Stateside SS 569; EP: Stateside SE 1044)

Accompanied by **The Jimmy Jones Trio with Duke Ellington and His Orchestra**. Duke Ellington, Leader/Piano; Trumpets: Cat Anderson, Mercer Ellington, Herbie Jones, Cootie Williams; Trombones: Lawrence Brown, Chuck Connors, Buster Cooper; Clarinet: Jimmy Hamilton; Alto Saxophones: Johnny Hodges, Russell Procope; Tenor Saxophones: Paul Gonsalves, Jimmy Hamilton; Baritone Saxophone: Harry Carney; Piano: Jimmy Jones; Bass: Jim Hughart; Drums: Ed Thigpen

660914-3   The Moment of Truth (EP: Stateside SE 1044)
660914-4   Satin Doll *Not yet released* on audio disc
660914-5   These Boots Are Made for Walking (45: Stateside SS 569; EP: Stateside SE 1044)
660914-6   Something to Live For *Not yet released* on audio disc
660914-7   Let's Do It *Not yet released* on audio disc
660914-8   Sweet Georgia Brown *Not yet released* on audio disc
660914-9   Baby, Bye-Bye *Not yet released* on audio disc
660914-10   Mack the Knife *Not yet released* on audio disc
660914-11   Cotton Tail *Not yet released* on audio disc

(These performances were telecast, but never committed to LP or CD; however, the following performances were released on CD in 1995.)

ELLA FITZGERALD, vocals

Duke Ellington and Ella Fitzgerald/ Live at the Greek Theatre, Los Angeles

Accompanied by **The Jimmy Jones Trio with Duke Ellington and His Orchestra**. Duke Ellington, Leader/Piano; Trumpets: Cat Anderson, Mercer Ellington, Herbie Jones, Cootie Williams; Trombones: Lawrence Brown, Chuck Connors, Buster Cooper; Clarinet: Jimmy Hamilton; Alto Saxophones: Johnny Hodges, Russell Procope; Tenor Saxophones: Paul Gonsalves, Jimmy Hamilton; Baritone Saxophone: Harry Carney; Piano: Jimmy Jones; Bass: Jim Hughart; Drums: Ed Thigpen. Recorded in performance at the Greek Theatre, Los Angeles, Friday, 23 September 1966

660923-1   Sweet Georgia Brown

Accompanied by **The Jimmy Jones Trio**. Piano: Jimmy Jones; Bass: Jim Hughart; Drums: Ed Thigpen

660923-2   Star Dust
660923-3   Só Danò Samba
660923-4   How Long Has This Been Going On?

Accompanied by **The Jimmy Jones Trio with Duke Ellington and His Orchestra**. Duke Ellington, Leader; Piano

660923-5   St. Louis Blues

Accompanied by **The Jimmy Jones Trio**

660923-6   Misty

Accompanied by **The Jimmy Jones Trio with Duke Ellington and His Orchestra**

660923-7   Mack the Knife
660923-8   Cotton Tail

Accompanied by **The Jimmy Jones Trio**

660923-9   Things Ain't What They Used to Be (45-second version)

(All tracks on LPD-87)

ELLA FITZGERALD, vocals

Duke Ellington Live in Europe/ Guest Star Ella Fitzgerald

Accompanied by **The Jimmy Jones Trio**. Piano: Jimmy Jones; Bass: Bob Cranshaw; Drums: Sam Woodyard. Recorded in performance at De Doelen, Rotterdam (Netherlands), Saturday, 28 January 1967

670128-1   On the Sunny Side of the Street
670128-2   You've Changed
670128-3   Mack The Knife

Accompanied by **The Jimmy Jones Trio with Duke Ellington and His Orchestra**. Duke Ellington, Leader; Piano (replaces Jimmy Jones on this track). Trumpets: Cat Anderson, Mercer Ellington, Money Johnson, Herbie Jones, Cootie Williams; Trombones: Lawrence Brown, Chuck Connors,

Buster Cooper; Clarinets: Harry Carney, Jimmy Hamilton, Russell Procope; Alto Saxophones: Johnny Hodges, Russell Procope; Tenor Saxophones: Paul Gonsalves, Jimmy Hamilton; Bass: Bob Cranshaw; Drums: Sam Woodyard

670128-4   Cotton Tail

(All tracks on LPD-141)

ELLA FITZGERALD, vocals

Brighten the Corner

Accompanied by orchestra and chorus conducted by **Ralph Carmichael.** Arrangements: Ralph Carmichael. Recorded at Capitol Records, Los Angeles, February 1967

670200-1   L56900 God Will Take Care of You
670200-2   L56901 What a Friend We Have in Jesus
670200-3   L56902 (God Be with You) Till We Meet Again
670200-4   L56903 Abide with Me
670200-5   L56904 In the Garden
670200-6   L56905 Brighten the Corner (Where You Are)
670200-7   L56906 I Shall Not Be Moved
670200-8   L56907 Just a Closer Walk with Thee
670200-9   L56912 Throw Out the Lifeline
670200-10   L56913 The Old Rugged Cross
670200-11   L56914 Rock of Ages
670200-12   L56915 I Need Thee Every Hour
670200-13   L56916 Let the Lower Light Be Burning
670200-14   L56917 The Church in the Wildwood

(All tracks on LPD-88)

ELLA FITZGERALD, vocals

Jazz At The Philharmonic
(The Greatest Jazz Concert in the World)

Accompanied by **The Jimmy Jones Trio with Duke Ellington and His Orchestra.** Duke Ellington, Leader; Trumpets: Cat Anderson, Mercer Ellington, Herbie Jones, Cootie Williams; Trombones: Lawrence Brown, Chuck Connors, Buster Cooper; Clarinet: Jimmy Hamilton; Alto Saxophones: Johnny Hodges, Russell Procope; Tenor Saxophones: Paul Gonsalves, Jimmy Hamilton; Baritone Saxophone: Harry Carney; Piano: Jimmy Jones; Bass: Bob Cranshaw; Drums: Sam Woodyard. Recorded in performance at Carnegie Hall, New York, Sunday, 26 March 1967

670326-1   Don't Be That Way
670326-2   You've Changed
670326-3   Let's Do It
670326-4   On the Sunny Side of the Street

(These four tracks on LPD-118)

Accompanied by **The Jimmy Jones Trio.** Piano: Jimmy Jones; Bass: Bob Cranshaw; Drums: Sam Woodyard

670326-5   (It's Only a) Paper Moon

670326-6   Day Dream
670326-7   If I Could Be with You
670326-8   Between the Devil and the Deep Blue Sea

Accompanied by **The Jimmy Jones Trio with Duke Ellington and His Orchestra.** Duke Ellington, Leader; Piano (Ellington replaces Jimmy Jones on this track)

670326-9   Cotton Tail* (LPD-118)

*There were two concerts on this date, afternoon and evening, and there are two released versions of his track, one on the LP, and and a different one on the CD, with no explanation in the liner notes. It is believed that the LP set contains the the above track; it is not known when the CD version was recorded, since the tour played in several cities, in all of which the concerts were recorded.

(All tracks on LPD-89)

ELLA FITZGERALD, vocals

Ella Fitzgerald's Christmas

Accompanied by orchestra anc chorus conducted by **Ralph Carmichael.** Arrangements: Ralph Carmichael. Recorded at Capitol Records, Los Angeles, Monday, 17 July 1967

670717-1   L57998 Silent Night
670717-2   L57999 Hark! The Herald Angels Sing
670717-3   L58000 Angels We Have Heart on High
670717-4   L58001 We Three Kings of Orient Are

(All tracks on LPD-90)

ELLA FITZGERALD, vocals

Ella Fitzgerald's Christmas

Accompanied by orchestra and chorus conducted by **Ralph Carmichael.** Arrangements: Ralph Carmichael. Recorded at Capitol Records, Los Angeles, Tuesday, 18 July 1967

670718-1   L58006 O Little Town of Bethlehem
670718-2   L58007 Away in a Manger [Luther's Cradle Hymn]
670718-3   L58008 It Came Upon the Midnight Clear
670718-4   L58009 Sleep, My Little Jesus
670718-5   L58010 Joy to the World
670718-6   L58011 O Holy Night
670718-7   L58012 O Come, All Ye Faithful [Adeste Fideles]
670718-8   L58013 God Rest Ye Merry, Gentlemen
670718-9   L58033 The First Noël

(All tracks on LPD-90)

ELLA FITZGERALD, vocals

A Place for Lovers (film soundtrack)

Accompanied by orchestra conducted by (?) **Ralph Carmichael.** Recorded at Capitol Records, Los Angeles, Saturday, 21 October 1967

671021-1   L58524-5 A Place for Lovers
671021-2   L58525-11 Lonely Is* (45: Verve; Polydor
L58524) (France)

*This does not appear on the film soundtrack

ELLA FITZGERALD, vocals

Misty Blue
Accompanied by orchestra conducted by **Sid Feller**.
Arrangements: Sid Feller. Recorded at Capitol Records, Los
Angeles, Wednesday, 20 December 1967

671220-1   L58921 I Taught Him Everything He Knows
671220-2   L58922 Don't Touch Me
671220-3   L58923 Turn the World Around (the
Other Way)
671220-4   L58924 Walking in the Sunshine
(All tracks on LPD-91)

ELLA FITZGERALD, vocals

Misty Blue
Accompanied by orchestra conducted by **Sid Feller**.
Arrangements: Sid Feller. Recorded at Capitol Records, Los
Angeles, Thursday, 21 December 1967

671221-1   L58936 It's Only Love
671221-2   L58937 Born to Lose
671221-3   L58938 The Chokin' Kind
671221-4   L58939 Misty Blue
(All tracks on LPD-91)

ELLA FITZGERALD, vocals

Misty Blue
Accompanied by orchestra conducted by **Sid Feller**.
Arrangements: Sid Feller. Recorded at Capitol Records, Los
Angeles, Friday, 22 December 1967

671222-1   L58944 Evil on Your Mind
671222-2   L58945 Don't Let That Doorknob Hit You
671222-3   L58946 This Gun Don't Care
(All tracks on LPD-91)

ELLA FITZGERALD, vocals

Accompanied by orchestra conducted by **Benny Carter**.
Arrangement: Benny Carter. Recorded at A & R Recording
Studio, New York, Friday, 10 May 1968

680510-1   It's Up to Me and You (45: Capitol 2212;
LPD-134)

ELLA FITZGERALD, vocals

Ella Fitzgerald Live from the Cave Supper Club
Accompanied by **Fraser McPherson and His Orchestra**.
Recorded in performance at The Cave (supper club), Van-
couver, B.C. (Canada), Sunday evening, 19 May 1968

680518-1   I'm Beginning to See the Light
680518-2   Medley: a. Blue Skies; b. On a Clear Day;
c. A Foggy Day (in London Town)
680518-3   Girl Talk
680518-4   Sweet Georgia Brown
Accompanied by **The Tee Carson Trio** (Piano: Tee Carson; Bass: Keter Betts; Drums: Joe Harris

680518-5   Gone with the Wind
680518-6   Sunny
680518-7   Goin' Out of My Head
680518-8   For Once in My Life
680518-9   One Note Samba
680518-10   Satin Doll
680518-11   I Can't Stop Loving You
680518-12   Just One of Those Things
(All tracks on LPD-160)

ELLA FITZGERALD, vocals

30 by Ella
Accompanied by **Benny Carter's Magnificent Seven**.
Benny Carter, Leader; Alto Saxophone; Trumpet: Harry
"Sweets" Edison; Tenor Saxophone; Georgie Auld; Piano:
Jimmy Jones; Guitar: John Collins; Bass: Bob West; Drums:
Panama Francis; Arrangements: Benny Carter. Recorded at
Capitol Records, Los Angeles, Tuesday, 28 May 1968

680528-1   L59798 Medley: a. No Regrets; b. I've Got
a Feelin' You're Foolin'; c. Don't Blame Me (instrumental); d. Deep Purple; e. Rain; f. You're a Sweetheart
680528-2   L59799 Medley: a. On Green Dolphin
Street; b. How Am I To Know?; c. Just Friends (instrumental); d. I Cried for You; e. Seems Like Old
Times; f. You Stepped Out of a Dream
(All tracks on LPD-92)

ELLA FITZGERALD, vocals

30 by Ella
Accompanied by **Benny Carter's Magnificent Seven**.
Benny Carter, Leader; Alto Saxophone; Trumpet: Harry
"Sweets" Edison; Tenor Saxophone: Georgie Auld; Piano:
Jimmy Jones; Guitar: John Collins; Bass: Bob West; Drums:
Louis Bellson. Arrangements: Benny Carter. Recorded at
Capitol Records, Los Angeles, Wednesday, 29 May 1968

680529-1   L59819 Medley: a. If I Give My Heart to
You; b. Once in a While; c. Ebb Tide (instrumental);
d. The Lamp Is Low; e. Where Are You?; f. Thinking
of You
680529-2   L59820 Medley: a. My Mother's Eyes; b.
Try a Little Tenderness; c. I Got It Bad (and That Ain't
Good) (instr); d. Everything I Have Is Yours; e. I Never
Knew (I Could Love Anybody); f. Goodnight, My Love
(All tracks on LPD-92)

ELLA FITZGERALD, vocals

30 by Ella

Accompanied by **Benny Carter's Magnificent Seven**. Benny Carter, Leader; Alto Saxophone; Trumpet: Harry "Sweets" Edison; Tenor Saxophone: Georgie Auld; Piano: Jimmy Jones; Bass: Bob West; Guitar: John Collins; Drums: Louis Bellson; Arrangements: Benny Carter. Recorded at Capitol Records, Los Angeles, Monday, 3 June 1968

680603-1 L59892 Medley: a. Candy; b. All I Do Is Dream of You; c. Spring Is Here (instr); d. 720 in the Books; e. It Happened in Monterey; f. (What Can I Say) After I Say I'm Sorry (LPD-92)

680603-2 L59893 Hawaiian War Chant (LPD-92, LPD-133)

680603-3 L59894 Medley: a. Four or Five Times; b. Maybe; c. Taking a Chance on Love (instr); d. Elmer's Tune; e. At Sundown; f. It's a Wonderful World (LPD-92)

ELLA FITZGERALD, vocals

Sunshine of Your Love

Accompanied by **Ernie Hecksher's Big Band**. Ernie Hecksher, Leader. Arrangements: *Marty Paich; **Frank DeVol; ***Tee Carson; ****Bill Holman. Recorded in performance at The Venetian Room, Fairmont Hotel, San Francisco, 00 Feburary 1969

690200-1 Hey, Jude!*
690200-2 Sunshine of Your Love*
690200-3 This Girl's in Love with You**
690200-4 Watch What Happens***
690200-5 Alright, Okay, You Win*
690200-6 Give Me the Simple Life****

(All tracks on LPD-93)

ELLA FITZGERALD, vocals

Sunshine of Your Love

Accompanied by **The Tommy Flanagan Trio**. Piano: Tommy Flanagan; Bass: Frank De La Rosa; Drums: Ed Thigpen. Recorded in performance at The Venetian Room, Fairmont Hotel, San Francisco, 00 February, 1969

690200-7   Useless Landscape (Inútil Paisagem)
690200-8   Ol' Devil Moon
690200-9   Don'cha Go 'Way Mad
690200-10 A House Is Not a Home
690200-11 Trouble Is a Man
690200-12 Love You Madly

(All tracks on LPD-93)

ELLA FITZGERALD, vocals

Ella

Accompanied by orchestra conducted by **Richard Perry**. Arrangements: Richard Perry. Recorded at Olympic Sound Studio, London (England), Monday, 26 May 1969

690526-1 M7365 I'll Never Fall in Love Again
690526-2 M7362 Open Your Window
690526-3 M7363 Yellow Man

(All tracks on LPD-94)

ELLA FITZGERALD, vocals

Ella

Accompanied by orchestra conducted by **Richard Perry**. Personnel: Same as 26 May 1969; Arrangements: Richard Perry. Recorded at Olympic Sound Studio, London (England), Wednesday, 28 May 1969

690528-1 M7371 Knock on Wood
690528-2 M7370 Savoy Truffle
690528-3 M7369 Got to Get You Into My Life

(All tracks on LPD-94)

ELLA FITZGERALD, vocals

Ella

Accompanied by orchestra conducted by **Richard Perry**. Personnel: Same as on 26 May 1969; Arrangements: Richard Perry. Recorded at Olympic Sound Studio, London (England), Wednesday, 29 May 1969

690529-1 M7364 I Wonder Why (LPD-94)

ELLA FITZGERALD, vocals

Ella

Accompanied by orchestra conducted by **Richard Perry**. Personnel: Same as on 26 May 1969; Arrangements: Richard Perry. Recorded at Olympic Sound Studio, London (England), Friday, 30 May 1968

690530-1 M7366 Get Ready
690530-2 M7367 The Hunter Get Captured by the Game
690530-3 M7368 Ooo Baby, Baby

(All tracks on LPD-94)

ELLA FITZGERALD, vocals

Ella Fitzgerald with The Tommy Flanagan Trio

Accompanied by Tommy Flanagan Trio. Piano: Tommy Flanagan; Bass: Frank De La Rosa; Drums: Ed Thigpen. Recorded in performance at Pinède Gould Amphithéâtre, Antibes-Juan-les Pins (France), Tuesday, 29 July 1969

690729-1 I Won't Dance
690729-2 That Old Black Magic
690729-3 Medley: a. It Happened in Monterey; b. No Regrets; c. It's a Wonderful World
690729-4 Cabaret
690729-5 Love You Madly
690729-6 A Man and a Woman (Un Homme et Une Femme)

690729-7 Alright, Okay, You Win
690729-8 People
690729-9 I Concentrate on You
690729-10 Mr. Paganini (You'll Have To Swing It)
(All tracks on LPD-143)

ELLA FITZGERALD, vocals

Things Ain't What They Used to Be (And You Better Believe It)

Accompanied by orchestra conducted by **Gerald Wilson**. Trumpets: Bobby Bryant, Harry "Sweets" Edison, Paul Hubinon, Larry McGuire, Alex Rodriguez; Trombones: James Cleveland, Thurman Green, J.J. Johnson, Alexander Thomas, William Tole, Mike Wimberly, Britt Woodman; Flutes: William Green, Marshall Royal, Anthony Ortega, Ernest Watts; Piccolos: William Green, Anthony Ortega, Ernest Watts; Clarinet: Marshall Royal; French Horn-Tubular Bells: Arthur Maebe; Alto Saxophones: Henry De Vega, Marshall Royal; Tenor Saxophones: Ray Bojorquez, Harold Land; Baritone Saxophone: Richard Alplenalp; Piano: Tommy Flanagan; Organ-Electric Piano: Joe Sample; Vibraphones: Vic Feldman, Bobby Hutcherson; Solo Guitar: Dennis Budamir; Rhythm Guitar: Herb Ellis; Fender Bass, Double Bass: Ray Brown; Drums: Louis Bellson; Bongos-Congas: Modesto Duran, Francisco DeSouza; Arrangements: Gerald Wilson. Recorded at Crystal-Sound Recording Studio, Los Angeles, Thursday, 23 October 1969

691023-1 M17767 I Don't Know Why (I Love You Like I Do) *Not yet released*
691023-2 M17768 Try a Little Bit (45: Reprise 0922)

ELLA FITZGERALD, vocals

Things Ain't What They Used to Be (and You Better Believe It)

Accompanied by orchestra conducted by **Gerald Wilson**. Personnel: Same as on 23 October 1969; Arrangements: Gerald Wilson. Recorded at Western Recording Studio, Los Angeles, Sunday, 4 January 1970

700104-1 N19299 Willow, Weep for Me
700104-2 N19374 Have Mercy *Not yet released*
700104-3 N19301 Tuxedo Junction
700104-4 N19302 Black Coffee

(All tracks, except "Have Mercy," on LPD-96)

ELLA FITZGERALD, vocals

Things Ain't What They Used to Be (and You Better Believe It)

Accompanied by orchestra conducted by **Gerald Wilson**. Personnel: Same as on 23 October 1969; Arrangements: Gerald Wilson. Recorded at Western Recording Studio, Los Angeles, Monday, 5 January 1970

700105-1 N19300 In the Mood *Not yet released*

700105-2 N19303 Sunny
700105-3 N19305 A Man and A Woman (Un Homme et Une Femme)
(Released titles on LPD-96)

ELLA FITZGERALD, vocals

Things Ain't What They Used to Be (and You Better Believe it)

Accompanied by orchestra conducted by **Gerald Wilson**. Personnel: Same as on 23 October 1969; Arrangements: Gerald Wilson. Recorded at Western Recording Studio, Los Angeles, Tuesday, 6 January 1970

700106-1 N19319 Manteca *Not yet released*
700106-2 N19320 Mas Que Nada (LPD-96)

ELLA FITZGERALD, vocals

Things Ain't What They Used to Be (and You Better Believe It)

Accompanied by orchestra conducted by **Gerald Wilson**. Personnel: Same as on 23 October 1969; Arrangements: Gerald Wilson. Recorded at Western Recording Studio, Los Angeles, Friday, 23 January 1970

700123-1 N18189 Once It Was All Right, Now [Farmer Joe] *Not yet released*

ELLA FITZGERALD, vocals

Things Ain't What They Used to Be (and You Better Believe It)

Accompanied by orchestra conducted by **Gerald Wilson**. Personnel: Same as on 23 October 1969. Arrangements: Gerald Wilson. Recorded at Western Recording Studio, Los Angeles, Saturday, 24 January 1970

700124-1 N18190 Lucky *Not yet released*
700124-2 N18191 Hands Off the Man [The Flim Flam Man] *Not yet released*
700124-3 N18192 Timer *Not yet released*

ELLA FITZGERALD, vocals

Ella Fitzgerald in Budapest

Accompanied by **The Tommy Flanagan Trio**: Piano: Tommy Flanagan; Bass: Frank De la Rosa; Drums: Ed Thigpen. Recorded in performance at National Theatre, Budapest (Hungary), Wednesday evening, 20 May 1970

700520-1 Crazy Rhythm
700520-2 Medley: a. This Guy's in Love with You; b. I'm Gonna Sit Right Down and Write Myself a Letter
700520-3 Open Your Window
700520-4 Satin Doll
700520-5 Spinning Wheel

700520-6 As Time Goes By
700520-7 You'd Better Love Me
700520-8 I'll Never Fall in Love Again
700520-9 Hello, Young Lovers
700520-10 Medley: a. I Concentrate on You; b. You Go to My Head
700520-11 The Girl from Ipanema
700520-12 Cabaret
700520-13 Dancing in the Dark
700520-14 Raindrops Keep Falling on My Head
700520-15 The Lady Is a Tramp
700520-16 Summertime
700520-17 Mr. Paganini ([If You Can't Sing It] You'll Have To Swing It)
700520-18 Mack the Knife
700520-19 People

(All tracks on LPD-95)

ELLA FITZGERALD, vocals

Things Ain't What They Used to Be (and You Better Believe It)

Accompanied by orchestra conducted by **Gerald Wilson**. Arrangements: Gerald Wilson. Recorded at Western Recording Studio, Los Angeles, Friday, 6 November 1970

701106-1 N19319 Manteca (LPD-96)
701106-2 N19320 Mas Que Nada *Not yet released*

ELLA FITZGERALD, vocals

Things Ain't What They Used to Be (and You Better Believe It)

Accompanied by orchestra conducted by **Gerald Wilson**. Arrangements: Gerald Wilson. Recorded at Western Recording Studio, Los Angeles, Monday 21 December 1970

701221-1 N19514 Just When We're Falling in Love
701221-2 N19512 Don't Dream of Anybody but Me
701221-3 N19513 Days of Wine and Roses

(All tracks on LPD-96)

ELLA FITZGERALD, vocals

Things Ain't What They Used to Be (and You Better Believe It)

Accompanied by orchestra conducted by **Gerald Wilson**. Arrangements: Gerald Wilson. Recorded at Western Recording Studio, Los Angeles, Tuesday, 22 December 1970

701222-1 N19304 I Heard It Through the Grapevine
7012222-2 N19530 Things Ain't What They Used to Be

(Both tracks are on LPD 96)

ELLA FITZGERALD, vocals

Count Basie Orchestra/Live from Tilburg, Holland/ Featuring Ella Fitzgerald

Accompanied by **The Tommy Flanagan Trio with Count Basie and His Orchestra**. William "Count" Basie, Leader; Trumpets: Paul Cohen, George "Sonny" Cohn, George "Pete" Minger, Waymon Reed; Flügelhorn: Waymon Reed; Trombones: Al Grey, Melvin Wanzo, John Watson; Bass Trombone: Bill Hughes; Flutes: Eric Dixon, Cecil Payne, Bobby Plater; Alto Saxophones: Curtis Peagler, Bobby Plater; Tenor Saxophones: Eddie "Lockjaw" Davis, Eric Dixon; Baritone Saxophone: Cecil Payne; Piano: Tommy Flanagan; Bass: Frank De La Rosa; Drums: Ed Thigpen. Recorded in performance at (place), Tilburg (Holland), Friday, 7 May 1971

710507-1 St. Louis Blues
710507-2 Willow, Weep for Me
710507-3 Close to You
710507-4 Mas Que Nada
710507-5 Things Ain't What They Used to Be

Accompanied by **The Tommy Flanagan Trio**

710507-6 They Can't Take That Away from Me

Accompanied by **The Tommy Flanagan Trio with Count Basie and His Orchestra**. Count Basie, Leader (as above)

710507-7 Li'l Darlin'
710507-8 Manteca

Accompanied by **Count Basie and His Orchestra**. William "Count" Basie, Leader/Piano; Trumpets: Paul Cohen, George "Sonny" Cohen, George "Pete" Minger, Waymon Reed; Flügelhorn: Waymon Reed; Trombones: Al Grey, Melvin Wanzo, John Watson; Bass Trombone: Bill Hughes; Flutes: Eric Dixon, Cecil Payne, Bobby Plater; Alto Saxophones: Curtis Peagler, Bobby Plater; Tenor Saxophones: Eddie "Lockjaw" Davis, Eric Dixon; Baritone Saxophone: Cecil Payne; Piano: William "Count" Basie; Guitar: Freddie Green; Bass: Norman Keenan; Drums: Harold Jones

710507-8 C Jam Blues

(All tracks on LPD-145)

ELLA FITZGERALD, vocals

The Lady Is a Tramp

Accompanied by Piano: Tommy Flanagan; Bass Frank De La Rosa; Drums: Ed Thigpen. Recorded in performance at the Sportspalast(?), Belgrade (Yugoslavia), Tuesday, 18 May 1971

710518-1 Lullaby of Birdland
710518-2 Ellington Medley: a. Mood Indigo; b. It Don't Mean a Thing
710518-3 Days of Wine and Roses
710518-4 Something
710518-5 Summertime
710518-6 Mack the Knife

710518-7   Hello, Dolly!
710518-8   Put a Little Love in Your Heart
710518-9   How High the Moon

(All tracks on LPD-144)

ELLA FITZGERALD, vocals

International Jazz Festival on the Côte d'Azur (Ella à Nice)

Accompanied by Piano: Tommy Flanagan; Bass: Frank De La Rosa; Drums: Ed Thigpen. Recorded in performance at Théâtre de Verdure, Nice (France), Wednesday, 21 July 1971

710721-1   Night and Day (LPD-118)
710721-2   The Many Faces of Cole Porter: a. Get Out of Town; b. Easy to Love; c. You Do Something to Me (LPD-118)
710721-3   The Ballad Medley: a. Body and Soul; b. The Man I Love; c. I Wants to Stay Here (I Loves You, Porgy) (LPD-118)
710721-4   The Bossa Scene: a. The Girl from Ipanema; b. Fly Me to the Moon; c. O Nossa Amor (Carnival Samba); d. Cielito Lindo; e. Madalena; f. Agua de Beber (Water To Drink) (LPD-118)
710721-5   Summertime
710721-6   They Can't Take That Away from Me (LPD-118)
710721-7   Aspects of Duke: a. Mood Indigo; b. Do Nothin' Till You Hear from Me; c. It Don't Mean a Thing (if It Ain't Got That Swing)
710721-8   Something
710721-9   St. Louis Blues (LPD-118)
710721-10   Close to You
710721-11   Put a Little Love in Your Heart

(All tracks on LPD-97)

The Concert Years: A Survey

*During **"The Concert Years,"** from the summer of 1966 to 21 July 1971, so-called because for the only time in her career Ella was not under exclusive contract to a recording company; however, from 1956 until her death, she was personally managed only by Norman Granz. During this five-year period Ella is known to have made 284 recordings, of which*

116 were studio recordings, of which
104 may be found on compact discs,
  1 may be found on a long-play record,
  2 may be found only on 45 rpm records, and
  9 are not yet released.

101 titles are known to have been recorded at concerts, of which
  99 may be found on compact discs, and
  4 may be found on a 45rpm EP, and
  7 have not yet been released.

14 recordings were made during cabaret performances, of which all
14 may be found on compact discs,

To recapitulate,
240 titles were recorded, of which
217 may be found on compact discs,
  1 may be found on a long-play record,
  2 may be found only on 45 rpm records
  4 may be found on an extended play 45rpm record, and
16 titles have not yet been released.

🙰

To date, Ella's discography reveals that, until 21 July 1971,
2,043 titles were recorded, of which
1,426 may be found on compact discs; of the remaining,
  113 may be found only on long-play records,
    4 may be found on an extended play 45rpm record,
  25 may be found only on 45 rpm records,
  36 may be found only on 78 rpm records, and
439 have not as yet been released.

THE PABLO YEARS (1972–1992)

ELLA FITZGERALD, vocals

Jazz At The Philharmonic (Jazz at the Santa Monica Civic '72)

Accompanied by **The Tommy Flanagan Trio with Count Basie and His Orchestra.** William "Count" Basie, Leader; Trumpets: Paul Cohen, George "Sonny" Cohn, George "Pete" Minger, Waymon Reed; Flügelhorn: Waymon Reed; Trombones: Al Grey, Frank Hooks, Melvin Wanzo; Bass Trombone: Bill Hughes; Flutes: Eric Dixon, Bobby Plater; Alto Saxophones: Curtis Peagler, Bobby Plater; Tenor Saxophones: Eric Dixon, Jimmy Forrest; Baritone Saxophone: John C. Williams; Piano: Tommy Flanagan; Guitar: Freddie Green; Bass: Keter Betts; Drums: Bobby Durham. Recorded in performance at Santa Monica Civic Center Auditorium, Santa Monica (California), Friday, 2 June 1972

720602-1	L.O.V.E (LPD-118)
720602-2	Begin the Beguine (LPD-118)
720602-3	Indian Summer (LPD-118)
720602-4	You've Got a Friend (LPD-118)
720602-5	What's Going On?

Accompanied by **The Tommy Flanagan Trio.** Piano: Tommy Flanagan; Bass: Keter Betts; Drums: Bobby Durham

720602-6	Night and Day
720602-7	Spring Can Really Hang You Up the Most (LPD-118)
720602-8	Little White Lies
720602-9	Madalena (LPD-118)

Accompanied by **The Tommy Flanagan with Count Basie and His Orchestra,** William "Count" Basie, Leader (as above)

720602-10	Shiny Stockings (LPD-118)
720602-11	Cole Porter Medley: a. Too Darn Hot (Intro: Big Noise from Winnetka); b. It's All Right with Me
720602-12	Street Beater ("Sanford and Son" Theme)
720602-13	I Can't Stop Loving You (LPD-118)

Accompanied by **The Count Basie Orchestra and the JATP All-Stars,** William "Count" Basie, Director; Piano Trumpets: Paul Cohen, George "Sonny" Cohn, Harry "Sweets" Edison, David "Roy" Eldridge, George "Pete" Minger, Waymon Reed; Flügelhorn: Waymon Reed; Trombones: Al Grey, Frank Hooks, Melvin Wanzo; Bass Trombone: Bill Hughes; Flutes: Eric Dixon, Bobby Plater; Alto Saxophones: Curtis Peagler, Bobby Plater; Tenor Saxophones: Eddie "Lockjaw" Davis, Eric Dixon, Jimmy Forrest, Stan Getz; Baritone Saxophone: John C. Williams; Guitar: Freddie Greene; Bass: Ray Brown; Drums: Ed Thigpen

720602-14	C Jam Blues

(All tracks on LPD-98)

ELLA FITZGERALD, vocals

Ella Loves Cole

Accompanied by orchestra conducted by **Nelson Riddle.** Arrangements: Nelson Riddle. Recorded at MGM Studio, Culver City, Los Angeles, Monday, 12 June 1972

720612-1	25409	I Get a Kick Out of You
720612-2	25410	Down in the Depths (on the Ninetieth Floor)
720612-3	25411	At Long Last Love
720612-4	25412	I've Got You Under My Skin
720612-5	25413	So Near and Yet So Far
720612-6	25414	All of You
720612-7	25415	Without Love
720612-8	25416	My Heart Belongs to Daddy
720612-9	25417	Love for Sale
720612-10	25418	Just One of Those Things
720612-11	25419	I Concentrate on You
720612-12	25420	Anything Goes
720612-13	25421	C'est Magnifique

(All tracks on LPD-99, LPD-108)

ELLA FITZGERALD, vocals

Ella Fitzgerald/Newport Jazz Festival/ Live at Carnegie Hall, July 5, 1973

Accompanied by **The Chick Webb Orchestra, Eddie Barefield,** Leader. Trumpets: Taft Jordan, Frank Lo Pinto, Dick Vance, Francis "Franc" Williams; Trombones: Garnett Brown, Al Cobb, Jack Jeffers, George Matthews; Clarinets-Alto Saxophones: Eddie Barefield, Chauncey Haughton, Pete Clark; Tenor Saxophones: Arthur Clarke, Bob Ashton; Baritone Saxophone: Haywood Henry; Piano: Cliff Smalls; Guitar: Lawrence Lucie; Drums: Beverley Peer. Recorded in performance at Carnegie Hall, New York, Friday, 5 July 1973

730705-1	A-Tisket, A-Tasket
730705-2	Indian Summer
730705-3	Smooth Sailing

Accompanied by Piano: **Ellis Larkins**

730705-4	You Turned the Tables on Me
730705-5	Nice Work if You Can Get It
730705-6	I've Got a Crush on You

Accompanied by **The Tommy Flanagan Quartet.** Piano: Tommy Flanagan; Guitar: Joe Pass; Bass: Keter Betts; Drums: Freddie Waits

730705-7	I've Gotta Be Me
730705-8	Down in the Depths (on the Ninetieth Floor)
730705-9	Good Morning, Heartache
730705-10	What's Going On?

730705-11 Miss Otis Regrets
 Accompanied by Guitar: **Joe Pass**
730705-12 Don't Worry 'Bout Me
730705-13 These Foolish Things
 Accompanied by **The Tommy Flanagan Quartet**. Piano: Tommy Flanagan; Guitar: Joe Pass; Bass: Keter Betts; Drums: Freddie Waits
730705-14 Any Old Blues
730705-15 Taking a Chance on Love
730705-16 I'm in the Mood for Love
730705-17 Lemon Drop
730705-18 A-Tisket, A-Tasket (excerpt)
730705-19 Some of These Days
730705-20 People
730705-21 A-Tisket, A-Tasket (excerpt)
(All tracks on LPD-100)

ELLA FITZGERALD, vocals

Take Love Easy

 Accompanied by Guitar: **Joe Pass**. Recorded at Metro-Goldwyn-Mayer Studio, Los Angeles, Tuesday, 28 August 1973

730828-1 5030 Take Love Easy
730828-2 5031 Once I Loved
730828-3 5032 Don't Be That Way
730828-4 5033 You're Blasé
730828-5 5034 Lush Life
730828-6 5035 A Foggy Day (in London Town)
730828-7 5036 Gee, Baby, Ain't I Good to You?
730828-8 5037 You Go to My Head
730828-9 5038 I Want To Talk About You
(All tracks on LPD-101)

ELLA FITZGERALD, vocals

"Fine and Mellow"/Ella Fitzgerald Jams

 Accompanied by Trumpets: Harry "Sweets" Edison, Clark Terry; Flügelhorn: Clark Terry; Tenor Saxophones: Eddie "Lockjaw" Davis, Zoot Sims; Guitar: Joe Pass; Piano: Tommy Flanagan; Bass: Ray Brown; Drums: Louis Bellson. Recorded at Metro-Goldwyn-Mayer Studios, Los Angeles, Tuesday, 8 January 1974

740108-1 5235 Fine and Mellow
740108-2 5236 (I Don't Stand) A Ghost of a Chance (with You)
740108-3 5237 I Can't Give You Anything but Love
740108-4 5238 Polkadots and Moonbeams
740108-5 5239 I'm in the Mood for Love
740108-6 5240 The Man I Love
740108-7 5241 I'm Just a Lucky So-and-So
740108-8 5242 'Round Midnight
740108-9 5253 Rockin' in Rhythm
(All tracks are on LPD-102)

ELLA FITZGERALD, vocals

Ella in London

 Accompanied by Piano: Tommy Flanagan; Guitar: Joe Pass; Bass: Keter Betts; Drums: Bobby Durham. Recorded in performance at Ronnie Scott's Jazz Club, London (England), Thursday, 11 April 1974

740411-1 Sweet Georgia Brown (LPD-118)
740411-2 They Can't Take That Away from Me (LPD-118)
740411-3 Ev'ry Time We Say Goodbye (LPD-118)
740411-4 The Man I Love (LPD-118)
740411-5 It Don't Mean a Thing (if It Ain't Got That Swing)
740411-6 Happy Blues
740411-7 You've Got a Friend (LPD-118)
740411-8 Lemon Drop (LPD-118)
740411-9 The Very Thought of You (LPD-118)
(All the above tracks are on LPD-103)

ELLA FITZGERALD, vocals

 Accompanied by orchestra conducted by **Marty Paich**. Recorded at Metro-Goldwyn-Mayer Studios, 18 October 1974

741018-1 Roxie (45: Pablo 10273)
741018-2 My Own Best Friend (45: Pablo 10273)

ELLA FITZGERALD, vocals

Ella and Oscar

 Accompanied by Piano: **Oscar Peterson**. Recorded at Metro-Goldwyn-Mayer Studios, Los Angeles, Monday, 19 May 1975

750519-1 5728 Mean to Me
750519-2 5729 How Long Has This Been Going On?
750519-3 5730 When Your Lover Has Gone
750519-4 5731 More Than You Know
750519-5 5732 There's a Lull in My Life

 Accompanied by Piano: **Oscar Peterson**; Bass: **Ray Brown**

750519-6 5733 Midnight Sun
750519-7 5734 I Hear Music
750519-8 5735 Street of Dreams
750519-9 5736 April in Paris
(All tracks on LPD-104)

ELLA FITZGERALD, vocals

Jazz Montreux/9th Montreux International Festival (Montreux Jazz Festival, 1975/Ella)

 Accompanied by Piano: Tommy Flanagan; Bass: Keter Betts; Drums: Bobby Durham. Recorded in performance at Festival Hall, Montreux (Switzerland), Thursday, 17 July 1975

750717-1   5890 Caravan (LPD-118)
750717-2   5891 Satin Doll (LPD-118)
750717-3   5892 Teach Me Tonight (LPD-118)
750717-4   5893 Wave (LPD-118)
750717-5   5894 It's All Right with Me (LPD-118)
750717-6   5895 Let's Do It (LPD-118)
750717-7   5896 The Man I Love (LPD-137)
750717-8   5897 How High the Moon (LPD-118)
750717-9   5898 The Girl from Ipanema
750717-10   5899 T'ain't Nobody's Biz-Ness (LPD-118)

(All tracks, except "The Man I Love," on LPD-105)

ELLA FITZGERALD, vocals

Fitzgerald and Pass ... Again

Accompanied by Guitar: **Joe Pass**. Recorded at RCA Victor's Music Center of the World, Los Angeles, Thursday, 29 January 1976

760129-1   6008 I Didn't Know About You
760129-2   6009 One Note Samba
760129-3   6010 'Tis Autumn
760129-4   6011 The One I Love (Belongs to Somebody Else)
760208-5   6012 Nature Boy

Recorded at RCA Victor's Music Center of the World, Los Angeles, Friday, 30 January 1976

760130-1   6013 All Too Soon
760130-2   6014 I Ain't Got Nothin' but the Blues
760130-3   6015 You Took Advantage of Me
760130-4   6016 I've Got the World on a String
760130-5   6017 The Tennessee Waltz.

Recorded at RCA Victor's Music Center of the World, Los Angeles, Sunday, 8 February 1976

760208-1   6020 My Old Flame
760208-2   6021 That Old Feeling
760208-3   6022 Rain
760208-4   6023 Solitude

(All tracks on LPD-106)

ELLA FITZGERALD, vocals

Jazz Montreux/10th Montreux International Festival (Ella Fitzgerald with The Tommy Flanagan Trio/Montreux '77)

Accompanied by **The Tommy Flanagan Trio**. Piano: Tommy Flanagan; Bass: Keter Betts; Drums: Bobby Durham. Record in performance at Festival Hall, Montreux (Switzerland), Thursday, 14 July 1977

770714-1   6409 Too Close for Comfort (LPD-118)
770714-2   6410 I Ain't Got Nothin' but the Blues (LPD-118)
770714-3   6411 My Man [Mon Homme]
770714-4   6412 Come Rain or Come Shine

770714-5   6413 Day by Day (LPD-118)
770714-6   6414 Ordinary Fool (LPD-118)
770714-7   6415 One Note Samba
770714-8   6416 I Let a Song Go Out of My Heart
770714-9   6417 Billie's Bounce (LPD-118)
770714-10   6418 You Are the Sunshine of My Life

(All tracks on LPD-107)

ELLA FITZGERALD, vocals

Dream Dancing/Ella Fitzgerald & Cole Porter

Accompanied by orchestra conducted by **Nelson Riddle**. Trumpets: Al Aarons, Carl Lewis, Shorty Sherock, Charles Turner; Trombones: J.J. Johnson, Dick Noel, Billy Watrous; Bass Trombone: Christopher Riccle; Bassoons: Don Christlieb, Bobby Tricarico; Clarinets: Mahlon Clark, Bill Green; Oboes: Norman Benno, Gordon Schoneberg; Flutes: Harry Klee, Wilbur Schwartz; Piano: Paul Smith; Guitar: Ralph Grasso; Bass: John Heard; Drums: Louis Bellson; Arrangements: Nelson Riddle. Recorded at Group IV Studios, Los Angeles, Monday, 13 February 1978

780213-1   EF14 Dream Dancing
780213-2   EF15 After You — Who?

(Both tracks are on LPD-106)

ELLA FITZGERALD, vocals

Lady Time/Ella

Accompanied by Organ: Jackie Davis; Drums: Louis Bellson. Recorded at Wally Heide Studio, Los Angeles, Monday, 19 June 1978

780619-1   6637 I Never Had a Chance
780619-2   6638 I'm Confessin' (that I Love You)
780619-3   6639 All or Nothing at All
780619-4   6640 Since I Fell for You

Recorded at Wally Heide Studio, Los Angeles, Tuesday, 20 June 1978

780620-1   6642 That's My Desire
780620-2   6643 Mack the Knife
780620-3   6644 I'm in the Mood for Love
780620-4   6645 What Will I Tell My Heart?
780620-5   6646 I'm Walkin'
780620-6   6647 And the Angels Sing
780620-11   6648 I Cried for You

(All tracks on LPD-109)

ELLA FITZGERALD, vocals

"A Classy Pair"/Ella Fitzgerald Sings/Count Basie Plays

Accompanied by **Count Basie and His Orchestra**. William "Count" Basie, Leader; Piano Trumpets: Ray Brown, George "Sonny" Cohn, George "Pete" Minger, Nolan Smith; Trombones: Melvin Wanzo, Dennis Wilson, Mitchell "Booty"

Wood; Bass Trombone: Bill Hughes; Flutes: Eric Dixon, Danny Turner; Alto Saxophones: Bobby Plater, Danny Turner; Tenor Saxophones: Eric Dixon, Kenny Hing; Baritone Saxophone: Charlie Fowlkes; Guitar: Freddie Green; Bass: John Clayton; Drums: Charles "Butch" Miles; Arrangements: Benny Carter. Recorded at Group IV Studios, Los Angeles, Thursday, 15 February 1979

790215-1   6739 Just A-Sittin' and A-Rockin'
790215-2   6740 I'm Getting Sentimental Over You
790215-3   6741 Sweet Lorraine
790215-4   6742 (Title not known)
790215-5   6743 Ain't Misbehavin'.

Recorded at Group IV Studios, Los Angeles, Friday, 16 February 1979

790216-   6744 My Kind of Trouble Is You
790216-2   6745 Don't Worry 'Bout Me
790216-3   6746 Teach Me Tonight
790216-4   6747 Honeysuckle Rose
790216-5   6748 (Title not known)
790216-6   6749 The Organ Grinder's Song

(All tracks on LPD-110)

ELLA FITZGERALD, vocals

Jazz Montreux/11th Montreux International Festival (A Perfect Match/Ella and Basie

Accompanied by **The Ella Fitzgerald Trio with Count Basie and His Orchestra.** William "Count" Basie, Leader; Piano* Trumpets Ray Brown, Paul Cohen, George "Sonny" Cohn, George "Pete" Minger; Trombones: Melvin Wanzo, Dennis Wilson, Mitchell "Booty" Wood; Bass Trombone: Bill Hughes; Flutes: Eric Dixon, Danny Turner; Alto Saxophones: Bobby Plater, Danny Turner; Tenor Saxophones: Eric Dixon, Kenny Hing; Baritone Saxophone: Charlie Fowlkes; Piano: Paul Smith; Guitar: Freddie Green; Bass: Keter Betts; Drums: Mickey Roker. Recorded in performance at Festival Hall, Montreux (Switzerland), Thursday, 12 July 1979

790712-1   7131 Please Don't Talk About Me When I'm Gone (LPD-110, LPD-118)
790712-2   7132 Sweet Georgia Brown
790712-3   7133 Some Other Spring (LPD-110)
790712-4   7134 Make Me Rainbows (LPD-118)
790712-5   7135 After You've Gone (LPD-118)

(All tracks on LPD-111)

Accompanied by Flute: Danny Turner; Piano: Paul Smith; Bass: Keter Betts; Drums: Mickey Roker

790712-6   7136 'Round Midnight (LPD-111, 118)

Accompanied by Piano: Paul Smith; Bass: Keter Betts; Drums: Mickey Roker

790712-7   7137 Fine and Mellow (LPD-111)
790712-8   7141 (I Don't Stand) A Ghost of a Chance (with You) (LPD-112)
790712-9   7142 Flying Home (LPD-112)

790712-10   Bill Bailey, Won't You Please Come Home
Not yet released

Accompanied by **The Ella Fitzgerald Trio with Count Basie and His Orchestra**, as above

790712-11   7138 You've Changed (LPD-111, LPD-118)
790712-12   7143 Honeysuckle Rose (LPD-111)
790712-13   7139 St. Louis Blues (LPD-111)
790712-14   7140 Basella (C Jam Blues) (LPD-111, LPD-118)

Accompanied by Piano: Paul Smith; Bass: Keter Betts; Drums: Mickey Roker

790712-15   I've Got a Crush on You *Not yet released*

ELLA FITZGERALD, vocals

Ella Abraça Jobim/Ella Fitzgerald Sings the Antonio Carlos Jobim Song Book

Accompanied by orchestra conducted by **Eric Bulling**. Trumpet: Clark Terry; Tenor Saxophone: Zoot Sims; Harmonica: Toots Thielemans; Rhythm Guitars: Roland Bautista, Oscar Castro-Neves, Paul Jackson, Mitch Holer; Solo Electric Guitar: Joe Pass; Solo Acoustic Guitar: Oscar Castro-Neves; Keyboards: Mike Lang, Clarence McDonald, Terry Trotter; Bass: Abraham Laboriel; Drums: Alex Acuna; Percussion: Paulinho da Costa. Recorded at Group IV Studios, Los Angeles, Wednesday, 17 September 1980

800917-1
7078 Dreamer [Vivo Sonhando]
800917-2
7079 Wave
800917-3
7080 A Felicidade.

Recorded at Group IV Studios, Los Angeles, Thursday, 18 September 1980

800918-1   7081 Water to Drink [Agua de Beber]
800918-2   7082 Quiet Nights of Quiet Stars [Corcovado]
800918-3   7083 Bonita.

Recorded at Group IV Studios, Los Angeles, Friday, 19 September 1980

800919-1   7084 Dindi
800919-2   7085 How Insensitive [Insensatez]
800919-3   7086 Useless Landscape [Inútil Paisagem]
800919-4   7087 One Note Samba [Samba de Uma Nota Só]
800919-5   7088 Photograph [Fotografia]
800919-6   7089 Triste

Recorded at Group IV Studios, Los Angeles, Tuesday, 23 September 1980

800923-1   7090 This Love That I've Found [Só Tinha de Ser Com Você]

Recorded at Group IV Studios, Los Angeles, Wednesday, 18 March 1981

810318-1 7091 The Girl from Ipanema [Garôta de Ipanema]
810318-2 7092 Off-Key [Desafinado]
810318-3 7093 He's a Carioca [Ele É Carioca]

Recorded at Group IV Studios, Los Angeles, Thursday, 19 March 1981

810319-1 7094 Somewhere in the Hills [Favela]

Recorded at Group IV Studios, Los Angeles, Friday, 20 March 1981

810320-1 7095 Song of the Jet [Samba do Avio]
810320-2 7096 Don't Ever Go Away [Por Causa de Você]

(All tracks on LPD-113)

ELLA FITZGERALD, vocals

Ella Fitzgerald in Edinburgh

Accompanied by **The Jimmy Rowles Trio with the BBC Concert Orchestra**, conducted by **Joseph Doakes**. The **Jimmy Rowles Trio**. Piano: Jimmy Rowles; Bass: Keter Betts; Drums: Bobby Durham. Recorded in performance at Edinburgh Playhouse, Sunday, 26 July 1981

810726-1 From This Moment On
810726-2 Satin Doll
810726-3 Ain't Misbehavin'
810726-4 Manhattan
810726-5 It's All Right with Me
810726-6 Oh! Lady, Be Good!
810726-7 Let's Do It
810726-8 Blue Moon
810726-9 People
810726-10 St. Louis Blues
810726-11 Hard Hearted Hannah
810726-12 Meditation
810726-13 Summertime *Not yet released*
810726-14 'S Wonderful *Not yet released*
810726-15 Let's Fall in Love *Not yet released*
810726-16 Medley: a. Them There Eyes *Not yet released*; b. Body and Soul; c. Oh! Lady, Be Good!

(Tracks 1–12 on LPD 146)

ELLA FITZGERALD, vocals

The Best Is Yet to Come

Accompanied by orchestra conducted by **Nelson Riddle**. Cellos: Christine Ermacoff, Barbara Jane Hunter, Dennis Karmazyn, Jerome Kessler, Robert L. Martin, Judy Perett, Frederick Seykora, Nancy Stein; Trumpet: Al Aarons; Trombone: Bill Watrous; Flügelhorns: David Allen Duke, Richard Klein, Joe Meyer, Gale Robinson; Flutes: Bill Green, Ronnie Lang, Hubert Laws, Wilbur Schwartz; Alto Saxophone: Marshall Royal; Tenor Saxophone: Bob Cooper; Piano: Jimmy Rowles; Organ: Art Hillery; Guitars: Joe Pass, Tommy Tedesco*; Bass: Jim Hughart; Drums: Shelley Manne; Arrangements: Nelson

Riddle. Recorded at Ocean Way Studios, Los Angeles, Thursday, 4 February 1982

820204-1 Don't Be That Way
820204-2 God Bless the Child
820204-3 You're Driving Me Crazy
820204-4 Any Old Time
820204-5 The Best Is Yet to Come

Recorded at Ocean Way Studios, Los Angeles, Friday, 5 February 1982

820205-1 I Wonder Where Our Love Has Gone*
820205-2 Good-Bye*
820205-3 Autumn in New York*
820205-4 Deep Purple*
820205-5 Somewhere in the Night*

(All tracks on LPD-114)

ELLA FITZGERALD, vocals

"Speak Love"

Accompanied by **Joe Pass**, piano. Recorded at Group IV Recording Studios, Los Angeles, Monday, 21 March 1983

830321-1 7392 Speak Low
830321-2 7393 Girl Talk
830321-3 7394 At Last
830321-4 7395 (Title not known) *Not yet released*
830321-5 7396 (Title not known) *Not yet released*
830321-6 7399 Gone with the Wind

Recorded at Group IV Recording Studios, Los Angeles, Tuesday, 22 March 1983

830322-1 7397 Blue and Sentimental
830322-2 7398 (Title not known) *Not yet released*
830322-3 7400 (Title not known) *Not yet released*
830322-4 7401 There's No You
830322-5 7402 Georgia on My Mind
830322-6 7403 (Title not known) *Not yet released*
830322-7 7404 (Title not known) *Not yet released*
830322-8 7405 I May Be Wrong (But I Think You're Wonderful)
830322-9 7406 Comes Love
830322-10 7407 The Thrill Is Gone

(All tracks on LPD-115)

ELLA FITZGERALD, vocals

Nice Work if You Can Get It/Ella Fitzgerald and André Previn Do Gershwin

Accompanied by **André Previn**, piano, and **Niels-Henning Orsted Pederson**, bass. Recorded at RCA Studios, New York, Monday, 23 May 1983

830523-1 7418 A Foggy Day (in London Town)
830523-2 7419 Nice Work if You Can Get It
830523-3 7420 Medley: a. I've Got a Crush on You; b. Someone to Watch Over Me; c. Embraceable You

830523-4 7421 Who Cares?
830523-5 7422 Let's Call the Whole Thing Off
830523-6 7423 (Title not known) *Not yet released*
830523-7 7424 They Can't Take That Away from Me
830523-8 7425 But Not for Me
830523-9 7426 How Long Has This Been Going On?

(All tracks on LPD-116)

ELLA FITZGERALD, vocals

"Return to Happiness"/Jazz At The Philharmonic/ Yoyogi National Stadium, Tokyo, 1983

Accompanied by Piano: Paul Smith; Bass: Keter Betts; Drums: Bobby Durham. Recorded in performance at Yoyogi National Stadium, Tokyo (Japan), October 1983

831000-1 Manteca
831000-2 Willow, Weep for Me
831000-3 All of Me
831000-4 Blue Moon
831000-5 Night and Day
831000-6 They Can't Take That Away from Me
831000-7 Medley: a. The Man I Love; b. Body and Soul
831000-8 'Round Midnight

Accompanied by **The JATP All-Stars**. Trumpets: Harry "Sweets" Edison, Clark Terry; Trombones: Al Grey, J.J. Johnson; Tenor Saxophone: Eddie "Lockjaw" Davis, Zoot Sims; Piano: Oscar Peterson; Bass: Niels Henning, Orsted Pedersen; Drums: Louis Bellson

831000-9 Flyin' Home

(All tracks on LPD-117)

ELLA FITZGERALD, vocals

"Easy Living"

Accompanied by **Joe Pass**, guitar. Recorded at Group IV Recording Studio, Los Angeles, Tuesday; Friday, 25; 28 February 1986

860228-1 My Ship
860228-2 On Green Dolphin Street
860228-3 Why Don't You Do Right?
860228-4 Don't Be That Way
860228-5 My Man (Mon Homme)
860228-6 Don't Worry 'Bout Me
860228-7 Days of Wine and Roses
860228-8 Easy Living
860228-9 (I Don't Stand) A Ghost of a Chance (with You)
860228-10 Moonlight in Vermont
860228-11 Love for Sale
860228-12 By Myself
860228-13 I Want a Little Girl
860228-14 I'm Making Believe

860228-15 (I'd Like to Get You) On a Slow Boat to China

(All tracks on LPD-119)

ELLA FITZGERALD, vocals

All That Jazz

Accompanied by Trumpet: Clark Terry; Trombone: Al Grey; Piano: Mike Wofford; Bass: Ray Brown; Drums: Bobby Durham. Recorded at Group IV Recording Studio, Los Angeles, Wednesday, 15 March 1989

890315-1 That Old Devil Called Love
890315-2 Just When We're Falling in Love (Robbins' Nest)
890315-3 Little Jazz

Recorded at Group IV Recording Studio, Los Angeles, Thursday, 16 March 1989

890316-1 Dream a Little Dream of Me
890316-2 Oh, Look at Me Now
890316-3 When Your Lover Has Gone
890316-4 Good Morning, Heartache

(All tracks on LPD-120)

ELLA FITZGERALD, vocals

All That Jazz

Accompanied by Trumpet: Harry "Sweets" Edison; Alto Saxophone: Benny Carter; Piano: Kenny Barron; Bass: Ray Brown; Drums: Bobby Durham. Recorded at Group IV Recording Studio, Los Angeles, Monday, 20 March 1989

890320-1 My Last Affair
890320-2 Baby, Don't Quit Now
890320-3 The Jersey Bounce

Recorded at Group IV Recording Studio, Los Angeles, Wednesday, 22 March 1989

890322-1 All That Jazz
890322-2 The Nearness of You

ELLA FITZGERALD, vocals

Back on the Block

Ella adds her voice by dubbing a multi-track with a Quincy Jones ensemble, with contributions from Sarah Vaughan, Miles Davis, Take 6, Bobby McFerrin, Al Jarreau, Dizzy Gillespie, James Moody, George Benson, and many others. Recorded at Los Angeles, 1989

890000-1 Wee B. Doinit
890000-2 Birdland
890000-3 Jazz Corner of the World

(All tracks on LPD-138)

ELLA FITZGERALD, vocals

Ella and Joe/Not yet released

Accompanied by Guitar: Joe Pass. Recorded at Group IV Recording Studios, Los Angeles, Spring 1991

910000-1 What a Difference a Day Makes *Not yet released*

(Others, unknown)

Note: This album was not released because Ella was unhappy with the quality of her voice. She wanted to redo some of the numbers and record more, but became too ill to continue.

ELLA FITZGERALD, vocals

The Setting Sun film Soundtrack

Accompanied by orchestra conducted by Billy May. Recorded at Warner Brothers Studio, Burbank, California, January 1992

920100-1 The Setting Sun (LPD-139)

The Pablo Years: A Survey

*Included here are the tracks purportedly done for Quincy Jones on his Warner Bros./Quest record, **Back on the Block**, her one known recording for her proposed **Ella and Joe** album, and her last recording for the sound track of the Japanese film, **The Setting Sun**. During this period Ella is known to have recorded 266 titles, of which*

159 were studio recordings, of which
154 may be found on compact discs; of the remaining 5 recordings,
2 may be found only on long-play records,
2 may be found only on 45 rpm records, and
1 is not yet released.

98 titles are known to have been recorded at concerts, of which
79 may be found on compact discs; of the remaining 19 recordings,
12 may be found only on a cassette tape; and
7 remain as yet unreleased.

9 recordings were made at cabaret performances, and all
9 titles may be found on compact discs.

To recapitulate:
266 titles were recorded, of which
242 may be found on compact discs; of the remaining,
2 may be found on long-play records
2 may be found only on 45 rpm records,
12 may be found only on a cassette tape, and
8 titles remain as yet unreleased.

Ella's Complete Discography: A Survey

Ella's complete discography reveals that during her career, a total of

2,309 recordings are known to exist, of which
1,668 may be found on compact discs; of the remaining,
115 may be found on long-play records,
4 may be found on an extended play 45rpm record,
27 may be found only on 45 rpm records,
36 may be found only on 78 rpm records,

12 may be found only on a cassette tape, and
447 titles remain as yet unreleased.

℘

All of these statistics are thought to be world's records for any performer in the history of the recording industry.

Part Two

Ella's Records

The Long-Play Albums and Compact Discs: A Collector's Checklist

The discs listed here are those that have been released in the United States. A number of foreign releases are included where the material does not duplicate U.S. releases, notably those of the **Classics** label and of concerts in Belgium, Britain, France, and Italy which, although marketed in the U.S. in some cases, were never released here.

The albums are listed chronologically, using the date of the latest track on the record as a reference point. An exception is the listing of the first five albums, those Decca releases which have been remastered and issued by GRP Decca Jazz during the past few years, and which comprise a good basic library of the recordings of Ella's Decca years (1935–1955).

The album number in this list is that of the latest issue. Since many have been issued a number of times in several formats, details of all the albums follow.

This check list groups Ella's albums and CDs into five "collections" for convenience:

- The "A" Collection (Ella Fitzgerald albums)
- The "B" Collection (other albums with Ella Fitzgerald tracks not found on albums in the "A" Collection)
- The "Radio and Television" Collection
- The Ella Collections (albums of previously issued tracks; to avoid repetition in the listing of contents, no LPD numbers have been assigned to these albums)
- Chick Webb Albums, 1929–1936

Sections I–V offer quick reference to the titles in each collection. Sections VI–X list the complete contents of each LP or CD.

An alphabetical list of the LPs and CDs is found on page 198.

I. The "A" Collection: Titles

(For "A" Collection contents, see page 116.)

LPD-1 Ella Fitzgerald/The Early Years/Part 1 (1935–1938)
(GRP Decca Jazz GRD-2-618) (2CD)

LPD-2 Ella Fitzgerald/The Early Years/Part 2 (1939–1941)
(GRP Decca Jazz GRD-2-623) (2CD)

LPD-3 Ella Fitzgerald/75th Birthday
Anniversary Celebration
(GRP Decca Jazz GRD-2-619) (2CD)

LPD-4 Ella Fitzgerald/The War Years (1941–1947)
(GRP Decca Jazz GRD-2-628) (2CD)

LPD-5 ELLA: The Legendary Decca Recordings
(GRP Decca Jazz GRD 4-648) (4CD)

LPD-6 Chick Webb and His Orchestra —1936
(Circle CCD-72) (CD)

LPD-7 The Chronological Ella Fitzgerald/1935–1937
(Classics 500) (CD)

LPD-8 The Chronological Chick Webb and His Orchestra/1935–1938
(Classics 517) (CD)

LPD-9 The Chronological Ella Fitzgerald/1937–1938
(Classics 506) (CD)

LPD-10 The Chronological Ella Fitzgerald/1938–1939
(Classics 518) (CD)

LPD-11 Chick Webb 4/Ella Swings the Band, 1936–1939
(MCA 1327) (LP)

LPD-12 The Chronological Ella Fitzgerald/1939
(Classics 525) (CD)

LPD-13 The Chronological Ella Fitzgerald/1939–1940
(Classics 566) (CD)

LPD-14 The Chronological Ella Fitzgerald/1940–1941
(Classics 644) (CD)

LPD-15 Ella Fitzgerald/Souvenir Album
(Decca DL 5084) (LP)

LPD-16 Ella Fitzgerald/Stairway to the Stars
(Decca DL 4446) (LP)

LPD-17 The Chronological Ella Fitzgerald/1941–1944
(Classics 840) (CD)

LPD-18 The Chronological Ella Fitzgerald/1945–1947
(Classics 998) (CD)

LPD-19 The Chronological Ella Fitzgerald/1947–1948
(Classics 1049) (CD)

LPD-19a The Chronological Ella Fitzgerald/1949
(Classics 1115) (CD)

LPD-19b The Chronological Ella Fitzgerald/1950
(Classics — To be released *ca.* April 2001) (CD)

LPD-19c The Chronological Ella Fitzgerald/1951
(Classics — To be released *ca.* April 2002) (CD)

LPD-19d The Chronological Ella Fitzgerald/1952
(Classics — To be released *ca.* April 2003 (CD)

LPD-19e The Chronological Ella Fitzgerald/1953–1954
(Classics — To be released *ca.* June 2004) (CD)

LPD-19f The Chronological Ella Fitzgerald/1954–1955
(Classics — To be released *ca.* October 2005 (CD)

LPD-20 The Complete Jazz At The Philharmonic on
Verve, 1944 –1949
(Verve 314 523 893) (10CD)

LPD-21 Ella Sings Gershwin/Ella Fitzgerald with Ellis
Larkins at the Piano / Pure Ella
(GRP Decca Jazz GRD-636) (CD)

LPD-22 Ella and Her Fellas
(Decca DL 8477) (LP)

LPD-23 Ella Fitzgerald/For Sentimental Reasons
(Decca DL 8832) (LP)

LPD-24 Ella Fitzgerald/That's My Desire
(Blue Moon BMCD 3012) (CD)

LPD-25 Jazz At The Philharmonic in Tokyo/
Live at the Nichigeki Theatre,1953
(Pablo 2620104-2) (2CD)

LPD-26 Early Ella/Great Ballads by Ella Fitzgerald
(Decca DL 4447) (LP)

LPD-27 Miss Ella Fitzgerald and Mr. Gordon Jenkins
Invite You to Listen and Relax
(MCA MVCJ-19222) (CD)

LPD-28 Ella Fitzgerald/The Last Decca Years, 1949–1954
(GRP Decca Jazz GRD-1110 6822) (CD)

LPD-29 Ella Fitzgerald/Songs in a Mellow Mood: Pure Ella
(GRP Decca Jazz GRD-636) (CD)

LPD-30 Ella Sings Gershwin (with an Assist by Duke
Ellington and Jimmy McHugh)
(Decca DL 4451) (LP)

LPD-31 Jazz At The Philharmonic/The Ella Fitzgerald
Set
(Verve 815 147-1) (LP)

LPD-32 The Best of Ella Fitzgerald, Volume II
(MCA 2-4016) (2LP)

LPD-33 Ella Fitzgerald/Memories
(MCA 734) (LP)

LPD-34 Ella Fitzgerald/Sweet and Hot
(MCA/Universal MCLD 19365) (CD)

LPD-35 Ella Fitzgerald/Golden Favorites
(Decca DL 4129) (LP)

LPD-36 Ella Fitzgerald/Lullabies of Birdland
(MCA Universal MCLD 19365) (CD)

LPD-37 Ella Fitzgerald/Smooth Sailing
(Decca DL 4887) (LP)

LPD-38 *Pete Kelly's Blues*/Peggy Lee and Ella Fitzgerald
(MCA MCVJ-19223) (CD)

LPD-39 Ella Fitzgerald/First Lady of Song
(MCA MVCJ-19221) (CD)

LPD-40 The Best of Ella…
(MCA 2-2047) (2LP)

LPD-41 Ella Fitzgerald Sings The Cole Porter Song Book
(Verve Master Edition 314 537 257) (2CD)

LPD-42 Metronome All Stars, 1956
(Verve MG V-8030) (LP)

LPD-43 Jazz at the Hollywood Bowl
(Verve MG V-8231) (LP)

LPD-44 Ella Fitzgerald and Louis Armstrong/
Ella and Louis
(Verve Master Edition 314 537 2842) (CD)

LPD-45 Ella Fitzgerald Sings the
Rodgers and Hart Song Book
(Verve Master Edition 314 537 258) (2CD)

LPD-46 Jazz At The Philharmonic/Stockholm 1957
(Tax 3703) (CD)

LPD-47 Ella Fitzgerald, Billie Holiday
and Carmen McRae at Newport
(Verve 314 559 809) (CD)

LPD-48 Ella Fitzgerald and Louis Armstrong/
Ella and Louis Again
(Verve Master Edition 314 537 284) (CD)

LPD-49 Ella at the Opera House
(Verve 821 269) (CD)

LPD-50 Ella Fitzgerald/18 Top Tracks/CD Jazz
(Frequenz 044-006) (CD)

LPD-51 Ella Fitzgerald Sings the
Duke Ellington Song Book
(Verve Master Edition 314 559 248) (3CD)

LPD-52 Ella Fitzgerald/Like Someone in Love
(Verve 835 647) (CD)

LPD-53 Ella Fitzgerald Sings the Irving Berlin Song Book
(Verve 314 519 841) (2CD)

LPD-54 Ella in Rome/The Birthday Concert

(Verve 835 454) (CD)

LPD-55 Ella Swings Lightly
(Verve 847 392) (CD)

LPD-56 Ella Fitzgerald/Hello, Love
(Polygram POCJ-2760) (CD)

LPD-57 Porgy and Bess/Ella Fitzgerald
and Louis Armstrong
(Verve Master Edition 314 537 284) (CD)

LPD-58 Ella Fitzgerald Sings Sweet Songs for Swingers
(Verve MG V-4032) (LP)

LPD-59 Ella Fitzgerald Sings the
George and Ira Gershwin Song Book
(Verve Master Edition 314 539 759) (4CD)

LPD-60 Ella Fitzgerald/Get Happy!
(Verve 523 321) (CD)

LPD-61 Mack The Knife/The Complete Ella in Berlin
(Verve 314 519 564) (CD)

LPD-62 Ella Fitzgerald Sings Songs from *Let No Man
Write My Epitaph* (Verve MG V-4043)/
The Intimate Ella (Verve 839838) (CD)

LPD-63 Ella Wishes You a Swinging Christmas
(Verve 827 150) (CD)

LPD-64 Ella Fitzgerald Sings the Harold Arlen Song Book
(Verve Master Edition 314 519 845) (2CD)

LPD-65 Ella Returns to Berlin
(Verve 837 758) (CD)

LPD-66 Ella in Hollywood with the Lou Levy Quartet
(Verve POCJ-2647) (CD)

LPD-67 Ella Fitzgerald/Clap Hands! Here Comes Charlie!
(Verve 835 646) (CD)

LPD-68 Ella Swings Brightly with Nelson
(Verve 314 519 347) (CD)

LPD-69 Ella Fitzgerald/Rhythm Is My Business
(Verve 314 559 513) (CD)

LPD-70 Ella Swings Gently with Nelson
(Verve 314 519 348) (CD)

LPD-71 Ella Sings Broadway
(Verve MG V-4059) (LP)

LPD-72 Ella Fitzgerald Sings the Jerome Kern Song Book
(Verve 825 669) (CD)

LPD-73 Verve's Choice: The Best of Ella Fitzgerald
(Verve MG V-4063) (LP)

LPD-74 Ella and Basie!/On the Sunny Side of the Street
(Verve Master Edition 314 539 059) (CD)

LPD-75 Ella Fitzgerald/These Are the Blues
(Verve 829 536) (CD)

LPD-76 Ella Fitzgerald/Hello, Dolly!
(Verve MG V-4064) (LP)

LPD-77 The Best of Ella Fitzgerald
(Verve V6-8720) (LP)

LPD-78 Ella at Juan-les Pins
(Verve MG V-4065) (LP)

LPD-79 Ella Fitzgerald in Concert with Roy Eldridge

and the Tommy Flanagan Trio (JCD 01) (CD)

LPD-80 Ella Fitzgerald Sings the Johnny Mercer Song Book
(Verve Master Edition 314 539 057) (CD)

LPD-81 Ella in Hamburg
(Verve POCJ 2649) (CD)

LPD-82 Ella at Duke's Place
(Verve 314 529 700) (CD)

LPD-83 Ella Fitzgerald/Duke Ellington/
The Stockholm Concert, 1966
(Jazz World JWD 102.213) (CD)

LPD-84 Whisper Not
(Verve V-4071) (LP)

LPD-85 The Ella and Duke at the Côte d'Azur
(Verve 314 539 033) (8CD)

LPD-86 Ella Fitzgerald/First Lady of Song
(Verve 314 517 898-2) (3CD)

LPD-87 Duke Ellington and Ella Fitzgerald/
Live at the Greek Theatre, Los Angeles
(Status 1013) (CD)

LPD-88 Ella Fitzgerald/Brighten the Corner
(Capitol CDP 7 95151) (CD)

LPD-89 The Greatest Jazz Concert in the World:
Duke Ellington/Ella Fitzgerald/Oscar Peterson
(Pablo 2625 704) (3CD)

LPD-90 Ella Fitzgerald's Christmas
(Capitol CDP 7 94452) (CD)

LPD-91 Ella Fitzgerald/Misty Blue
(Capitol CDP 7 95152) (CD)

LPD-9230 by Ella
(Capitol CDP 7 48333 2) (CD)

LPD-93 Ella Fitzgerald/Sunshine of Your Love
(Verve 314 533 102) (CD)

LPD-94 Ella Fitzgerald/Ella
(Reprise 9 20623) (CD)

LPD-95 Ella Fitzgerald in Budapest
(Pablo PACD 5308) (CD)

LPD-96 Things Ain't What They Used To Be
(and You Better Believe It)
(Reprise 9 26023) (CD)

LPD-97 Ella à Nice
(Fantasy OJCCD 442) (CD)

LPD-98 Jazz at the Santa Monica Civic, 1972
(Pablo 2625-701) (3CD)

LPD-99 Ella Loves Cole
(Atlantic SD 1631) (LP)

LPD-100 Ella Fitzgerald/Newport Jazz Festival/
Live at Carnegie Hall, 5 July 1973
(Legacy/Columbia C2K 66809)

LPD-101 Ella Fitzgerald/Take Love Easy
(Pablo PACD 2310 702) (CD)

LPD-102 Ella Fitzgerald Jams/Fine and Mellow
(Pablo PACD 2310 829) (CD)

LPD-103 Ella in London

(Pablo PACD 2310 711) (CD)

LPD-104 Ella and Oscar
(Pablo PACD 2310 759) (CD)

LPD-105 Montreux Jazz Festival, 1975/Ella
(Fantasy OJCCD 789) (CD)

LPD-106 Ella and Pass … Again
(Pablo PACD 2310 772) (CD)

LPD-107 Ella Fitzgerald with The Tommy Flanagan Trio/
Montreux '77
(Fantasy OJCCD 376) (CD)

LPD-108 Dream Dancing/Ella Fitzgerld & Cole Porter
(Pablo PACD 2310 814) (CD)

LPD-109 Ella Fitzgerald/Lady Time
(Pablo PACD 2310 825) (CD)

LPD-110 "A Classy Pair"/Ella Fitzgerald Sings/
Count Basie Plays
(Pablo Today PACD 2310 132) (CD)

LPD-111 A Perfect Match/Ella and Basie
(Pablo Today PACD 2312 110) (CD)

LPD-112 Joe Pass-Ella Fitzgerald-Count Basie/
Digital III at Montreux

(Pablo Live PACD 2308 223) (CD)

LPD-113 Ella Abraça Jobim/
The Antonio Carlos Jobim Song Book
(Pablo PACD 2630 201) (CD)

LPD-114 Ella Fitzgerald/The Best Is Yet to Come
(Pablo Today PACD 2312 138) (CD)

LPD-115 "Speak Love"/Ella Fitzgerald and Joe Pass
(Pablo PACD 2310 888) (CD)

LPD-116 Nice Work If You Can Get It/
Ella Fitzgerald and André Previn
Do Gershwin (Pablo 2312 140) (CD)

LPD-117 Return to Happiness/Jazz At The Philhar-
monic/ Yoyogi National Stadium, Tokyo, 1983
(Pablo PACD 2620 117) (2CD)

LPD-118 Ella/The Concert Years
(Pablo 4CD-4414) (4CD)

LPD-119 Ella Fitzgerald and Joe Pass/"Easy Living"
(Pablo PACD 2310 921) (CD)

LPD-120 Ella Fitzgerald/All That Jazz
(Pablo PACD 2310 938) (CD)

II. The "B" Collection: Titles

*(Albums with Ella Fitzgerald tracks not released on albums in
the "A" Collection. For "B" Collection contents, see page 179.)*

LPD-121 Ella Fitzgerald/The Complete Recordings
1935–1939
(Affinity AFS-1020-3) (3CD)

LPD-122 Ella Fitzgerald/"The First Lady of Song"
(MCA 510.184/195) (French) (2LP)

LPD-123 Ella, Volume 4, 1937–1952, and the Vocal Groups
(MCA Coral 6.22065 (PCO 7665)) (LP)

LPD-124 Ella, Volume 5, 1941–1955
(MCA Coral 6.22178 (PCO 7666)) (LP)

LPD-125 Ella, Volume 6, 1949–1954
(MCA Coral 6.22179 (PCO 7667)) (LP)

LPD-126 Louis Armstrong/"Because of You"
(Ambassador CLA 1918) (CD)

LPD-127 Gene Krupa and Buddy Rich/
The Drum Battle at JATP
(Verve 314 559 810) (CD)

LPD-128 Sinatra/The Soundtrack Sessions
(Bravura BRCD 7106) (CD)

LPD-129 Here Come the Girls!
(Verve MG V-2036) (LP)

LPD-130 One O'Clock Jump/
Ella Fitzgerald-Count Basie-Joe Williams
(Verve 314 559 806) (CD)

LPD-131 The Essential American Singers
(Verve 314 517 176) (CD)

LPD-132 Have Yourself a Jazzy Little Christmas
(Verve 840 501) (CD)

LPD-133 Compact/Walkman Jazz/Ella Fitzgerald
(Verve 831 367) (CD)

LPD-134 Verve Elite Edition Collector's Disc
(Verve 314 547 265) (CD)

LPD-135 Route 66/Capitol Sings Coast to Coast
(Capitol D103060) (CD)

LPD-136 The Big Bands' Greatest Vocalists/Ella
Fitzgerald with Skitch Henderson and His Orchestra
(Joyce 6045) (LP)

LPD-137 The Montreux Collection
(Pablo PACD 5306) (CD)

LPD-138 Back on the Block
(QWest/Warner Bros. 26020) (CD)

LPD-139 The Setting Sun (Japanese film soundtrack)
(RCA Japan VICP 8084) (CD)

LPD-140 Ella Fitzgerald/Só Danço Samba
(Jazz Birdies of Paradise) (CD)

LPD-141 Duke Ellington/Live in Europe/
Guest Star: Ella Fitzgerald
(Mucica Jazz MJCD 1099) (CD)

LPD-142 Duke and Ella in Concert/
Milan, 30 January 1966
(Jazz-Blues-Soul JBS 93B2b) (CD)

LPD-143 Ella Fitzgerald with The Tommy Flanagan Trio
(Laserlight 17 109) (CD)
LPD-144 Ella Fitzgerald/The Lady Is a Tramp
(Jazz Door 1268) (CD)
LPD-145 Count Basie Orchestra/Live from Tilburg, Hol-

land, 1971/Featuring Ella Fitzgerald & Live from La
Cabaret Casino, Paradise Island, Nassau, Bahamas, 1969
(Jazz Band EBCD 2121) (CD)
LPD-146 Ella Fitzgerald in Edinburgh
(CT only/no number)

III. The "Radio and Television" Collection: Titles

(For "Radio and Television" Collection contents, see page 185.)

LPD-147 Bronzeville Stomp/Chick Webb in the 1930's
(Jazz Archives JA 33) (LP)
LPD-148 The Saturday Night Swing Club Is on the Air
(Fanfare 17-117) (LP)
LPD-149 Chick Webb and His Orchestra/
Ella Fitzgerald — The Ink Spots
(Twinkgost Rogo CWIS 37) (LP)
LPD-150 The King of Drums: Chick Webb
and His Savoy Ballroom Orchestra, 1939
(Tax CD 3706) (CD)
LPD-151 Ella Fitzgerald/On the Air/
The Complete 1940 Broadcasts
(Masters of Jazz MJCD 137/138) (2CD)
LPD-152 Ella Fitzgerald/Royal Roost Sessions
with The Ray Brown Trio and Quintet
(Cool N' Blue 9117) (CD)
LPD-153 Ella Fitzgerald and Bing Crosby/My Happiness
(Parrot PARCD 002) (CD)
LPD-154 U.S. All-Stars in Berlin
(Jazz Band EBCD 2113-2) (CD)
LPD-155 One Night Stand with

Stan Kenton and Music '55
(Joyce 1130) (LP)
LPD-156 Swing into Spring/
The Classic NBC Broadcast of April 9, 1958
(Sandy Hook 2057) (CD)
LPD-157 Swing into Spring/
The Classic NBC Broadcast of April 10, 1959
(A&R 2000/2001) (LP)
LPD-158 Sinatra: The Television Years
(Bravura BRCD 105) (CD)
LPD-159 Frank and Dean's Party by the Bay
(BMD 2260) (Privately Issued CD)
LPD-160 Ella Fitzgerald/Live from The Cave Supper Club
(Jazz Band EBCD 2144) (CD)
LPD-161 Ella Fitzgerald/On the Air/Volume 3/1944–1947
(Masters of Jazz MJCD 169) (CD)
LPD-162 Ella Fitzgerald in the Groove
(Buddha Records 74465 99702 2) (CD)
LPD-163 The Enchanting Ella Fitzgerald/
Live at Birdland, 1950–1952
(Baldwin Street Music BJH 309) (CD)

IV. The Ella Collections: Titles

(Albums of previously issued tracks. For contents, see page 193.)

THE DECCA YEARS

The Best of Ella Fitzgerald
(GRP Decca Jazz GRD 659) (CD)
Ella and Friends
(GRP Decca Jazz GRD 663) (CD)
Pure Ella
(GRP Decca Jazz GRD 636) (CD)
Ella Fitzgerald with Chick Webb/Swingsation
(GRP Decca Jazz GRD 9921) (CD)
Priceless Jazz Collection/Ella Fitzgerald
(GRP GRD 9870) (CD)
Priceless Jazz Collection/More Ella Fitzgerald
(GRP GRD 9916) (CD)

THE VERVE YEARS

The Best of Ella and Louis
(Verve 314 537 909) (CD)
The Best of Ella Fitzgerald: First Lady of Song
(Verve 314 523 382) (CD)
The Best of the Song Books
(Verve 314 519 804 (CD)
The Best of the Song Books: The Ballads
(Verve 314 521 867) (CD)
Love Songs: The Best of the Verve Song Books
(Verve 831 762) (CD)
Compact Jazz/Ella Fitzgerald Live!
(Verve 833 294) (CD)

Compact Jazz/Ella Fitzgerald and Louis Armstrong
(Verve 835 313) (CD)
Compact Jazz/Ella Fitzgerald and Duke Ellington
(Verve 314 517 953) (CD)
Day Dream: Best of the Duke Ellington Song Book
(Verve 314 527 223) (CD)
Ella Fitzgerald/Verve Jazz Masters 6
(Verve 314 519 822) (CD)
Ella Fitzgerald and Louis Armstrong/
Verve Jazz Masters 24
(Verve 314 521 851) (CD)
The Essential Ella Fitzgerald/The Great Songs
(Verve 314 517 170) (CD)
Jazz 'Round Midnight/Ella Fitzgerald
(Verve 314 511 035) (CD)
Jazz 'Round Midnight Again/Ella Fitzgerald
(Verve 314 527 032) (CD)
Jazz 'Round Midnight/
Ella Fitzgerald and Louis Armstrong
(Verve 314 557 352) (CD)
The Jazz Sides/Ella Fitzgerald/Jazz Masters 46
(Verve 314 527 655) (CD)

Oh! Lady, Be Good! Best of the Gershwin Song Book
(Verve 314 529 581) (CD)
Our Love Is Here To Stay/
Ella Fitzgerald and Louis Armstrong
Sing Gershwin (Verve 314 539 679) (CD)
Pure Ella
(Verve 314 539 206) (CD)
Quiet Now/Ella's Moods
(Verve 314 559 736) (CD)
The Silver Collection/The Song Books
(Verve 823 445) (CD)
The Ultimate Ella Fitzgerald (Selected by Joe Williams)
(Verve 314 539 054) (CD)
Ella Fitzgerald: Something to Live For
(Verve 314 547 800) (2CD)

THE PABLO YEARS

The Best of Ella Fitzgerald
(Pablo PACD 2405-421) (CD)
Bluella: Ella Fitzgerald Sings the Blues
(Pablo PACD 2310-960) (CD)

V. Chick Webb Albums, 1929–1936

(All other of Webb's albums are included with those of Ella Fitzgerald, above.)

CWLPD-1 An Introduction to Chick Webb/His Best
Recordings/1929–1939
(Best of Jazz 4015) (CD)
CWLPD-2 The Chronological Chick Webb
and His Orchestra/1929–1934
(Classics 502) (CD)
CWLPD-3 Spinnin' the Webb/
Chick Webb and His Orchestra
(Decca Jazz GRD-635) (CD)
CWLPD-4 The Chronological Louis Armstrong/1931–1932
(Classics 536) (CD)
CWLPD-5 Mezz Mezzrow/1928–1936
(Classics 713) (CD)
Chick Webb: A Legend, Volume 1 (1929–1936)
(Decca DL 9222) (LP)

Chick Webb: King of Swing, Volume 2 (1937–1939)
(Decca DL 9223) (LP)
The Best of Chick Webb
(MCA 2-4107) (2LP)
Chick Webb and His Orchestra, Featuring Ella Fitzgerald
(Jazz Anthology JA 5199) (LP)
Chick Webb and His Orchestra, 1937–1939
(Jazz Anthology JA 5113) (LP)
Bronzeville Stomp/Chick Webb in the 1930's
See LPD-147 (Jazz Archives JA 33) (LP)*

(See pages XXX for the details on all the above albums.)

VI. The "A" Collection: Contents

The Decca Years (1935–1939)

LPD-1 ELLA FITZGERALD/
THE EARLY YEARS/PART 1

With Chick Webb & His Orchestra (1935–1939)

1. I'll Chase the Blues Away (Sampson-Harrison) 2:30
350612-1

2. Love and Kisses (Curtis) 3:15   350612-4
3. Rhythm and Romance (Johnson-Whiting-Burton)
3:02   351012-1
4. Under the Spell of the Blues (Sampson-Harrison)
2:56   360407-4
5. When I Get Low, I Get High (Sunshine) 2:23
360407-5
6. Sing Me a Swing Song (Carmichael-Adams) 2:33
360602-2

7. A Little Bit Later On (Levinson-Nieberg) 3:00 360602-3
8. Love, You're Just a Laugh (Gardner-Cahn-Chaplin) 3:07 360602-4
9. Mr. Paganini [You'll Have To Swing It] (Coslow) 2:52 361029-2
10. Vote for Mr. Rhythm (Robin-Rainger-Siegel) 2:24 361029-5
11. My Last Affair (Johnson) 2:41 361118-1
12. The Organ Grinder's Swing (Hudson-Parish-Mills) 2:47 361118-2
13. Shine (Dabney-Brown-Mack) 2:47 361119-1
14. The Darktown Strutters' Ball (Brooks) 3:00 361119-2
15. Oh, Yes, Take Another Guess (Mencher-Newman-Sherman) 2:40 370114-1
16. You Showed Me the Way(Green-McRae-Fitzgerald-Webb) 3:16 370324-2
17. Cryin' Mood (Razaf-Webb) 2:35 370324-7
18. If You Ever Should Leave (Cahn-Chaplin) 3:02 370524-3
19. Everyone's Wrong But Me (Cahn-Chaplin) 3:01 370524-4
20. Just a Simple Melody (Cahn-Chaplin) 2:55 371027-1
21. I Got a Guy (Sunshine) 3:18 371027-2
22. Rock It for Me (Werner-Werner) 3:06 371101-3
23. I Want To Be Happy (Youmans-Caesar-Harbach) 4:28 371217-1
24. The Dipsy Doodle (Clinton) 3:07 371217-3
25. If Dreams Come True (Sampson-Mills-Goodman) 3:32 371217-4
26. Hallelujah! (Youmans-Robin-Grey) 4:02 371217-5
27. Bei Mir Bist Du Schoen (Secunda-Jacobs-Cahn-Chaplin) 3:00 371221-1
28. It's My Turn Now (Cahn-Chaplin) 2:52 371221-2
29. It's Wonderful (Wells-Parish-Smith) 2:53 380125-1
30. I Was Doing All Right (Gershwin-Gershwin) 2:51 380125-2
31. A-Tisket, A-Tasket (Fitzgerald-Alexander) 2:36 380502-1
32. Heart of Mine (Webb-Heyman) 2:51 380502-2
33. I'm Just a Jitterbug (David-Livingston) 3:13 380502-3
34. You Can't Be Mine(Johnson-Webb) 2:55 380503-4
35. If You Only Knew (Beal-Webb) 2:42 380503-11
36. Pack Up Your Sins and Go to the Devil (Berlin) 2:52 380609-1
37. MacPherson Is Rehearsin' (To Swing) (Sunshine) 3:04 380609-2
38. Everybody Step (Berlin) 2:40 380609-3
39. Wacky Dust (Adams-Levant) 3:00 380817-1
40. Strictly from Dixie (Cavanaugh-Webb-Brooks-Brooks) 2:44 380818-1
41. Franklin D. Roosevelt Jones (Rome) 2:49 381006-1
42. It's Foxy (Bishop-Webb) 2:56 381006-3
43. I Found My Yellow Basket (Fitzgerald-Webb) 2:33 381006-4

CD: GRP Decca Jazz GRD-2-618 (2 discs) (released October 1992). Disc 1, Tracks 1-21 (61:16)/Disc 2, Tracks 22-43 (67:02). Total playing time: 2:08:18. Original sessions produced by Jack Kapp/Reissue produced by **Orin Keepnews**. Liner notes by Will Friedwald. Reviewed by Bruce Crowther, **Jazz Journal International**, Volume 46, Issue 4, April 1993. This set was repackaged in 1995 with Part 2, and released as a 4-CD set, **Ella Fitzgerald/The Early Years (1935–1941)** (GRP Decca Jazz GRD-654).

The Decca Years (1939–1941)

LPD-2 ELLA FITZGERALD/ THE EARLY YEARS/PART 2

Featuring Ella Fitzgerald & Her Famous Orchestra (1939–1941)

1. Undecided (Robin-Shavers) 3:17 390217-1
2. 'Tain't What You Do (It's the Way That Cha Do It) (Oliver-Young) 2:56 390217-2
3. My Heart Belongs to Daddy (Porter) 2:59 390217-5
4. Chew-Chew-Chew (Your Bubble Gum) (Ram-Fitzgerald-Webb) 2:58 390302-6
5. Don't Worry 'Bout Me (Koehler-Bloom) 3:05 390421-1
6. If You Ever Change Your Mind (Watts-Green-Sigler) 3:02 390421-4
7. Little White Lies (Donaldson) 2:50 390421-6
8. Coochi-Coochi-Coo (Werner-Werner) 2:59 390421-7
9. Betcha Nickel (Fitzgerald-Webb) 2:51 390629-1
10. Stairway to the Stars (Parish-Malneck-Signorelli) 3:15 390629-2
11. I Want the Waiter (with the Water) (Werner-Werner) 3:05 390629-3
12. Out of Nowhere (Heyman-Gree) 2:56 390629-5
13. My Last Goodbye (Howard) 3:14 390818-1
14. (I Always Dream of) Billy (Kendis-Paley-Godwin) 2:37 390818-2
15. You're Gonna Lose Your Gal (Young-Monaco) 3:05 391012-1
16. After I Say I'm Sorry (Donaldson-Lyman) 2:49 391012-2
17. Moon Ray (Shaw-Madison-Quenzer) 2:57 391012-6
18. Sugar Blues (Fletcher-Williams) 2:44 400126-2

19. The Starlit Hour (Parish–DeRose) 3:04   400126-3
20. What's the Matter with Me? (Shand–Lewis) 2:53 400126-4
21. Baby, Won't You Please Come Home? (Warfield–Williams) 2:32   400215-1
22. If It Weren't for You (Mizzy–Taylor) 2:56   400215-2
23. Imagination (Burke–Van Heusen) 2:55   400215-4
24. Deedle-Dee-Dum (Fitzgerald–Kahn–Wynn–Waters) 2:35   400509-1
25. Shake Down the Stars (DeLange–Van Heusen) 2:43 400509-2
26. Gulf Coast Blues (Williams) 2:54   400509-3
27. The Five O'Clock Whistle (Myrow–Gannon–Irwin) 3:07   400925-1
28. Louisville, K-Y (Skylar) 3:05   400925-3
29. Taking a Chance on Love (Latouche–Fetter–Duke) 3:03   401108-1
30. Cabin in the Sky (Latouche–Duke) 2:43   401108-2
31. I'm the Lonesomest Girl in Town (Brown–Von Tilzer) 2:38   401108-3
32. Three Little Words (Kalmar–Ruby) 3:02   410108-1
33. The One I Love Belongs to Somebody Else (Kahn–Jones) 3:02   410108-4
34. The Muffin Man (Fitzgerald) 3:23   410108-5
35. Keep Cool, Fool (Myrow–Rhythm) 2:58   410331-1
36. No Nothing (Ryan–Handman–Kurtz) 3:04   410331-2
37. My Man [Mon Homme] (Yvain–Pollock) 2:58 410331-3
38. I Can't Believe That You're in Love with Me (Gaskill–McHugh) 2:32   410731-1
39. I Must Have That Man (Fields–McHugh) 3:07 410731-2
40. When My Sugar Walks Down the Street (Austin–McHugh–Mills) 2:41   410731-3
41. I Got It Bad (and That Ain't Good) (Webster–Ellington) 2:54   410731-4
42. Can't Help Lovin' Dat Man (Hammerstein II–Kern) 2:46   410731-6

CD: GRP Decca Jazz GRD-2-623 (2 discs) (released October 1993). Disc 1, Tracks 1-21 (63:01)/Disc 2, Tracks 22-42 (60:24). Total playing time: 2:03:25. Original sessions produced by **Jack Kapp**/Reissue produced by **Orrin Keepnews**. The liner notes are by **Geoffrey Mark Fidelman**. Reviewed by **Bruce Crowther**, *Jazz Journal International*, Volume 47, Issue 2, February 1994. This set was repackaged in 1995 with Part 1 and issued as a 4-CD set, GRP/Decca Jazz GRD-654.

The Decca Years (1938–1955)

LPD-3 ELLA FITZGERALD/ 75TH BIRTHDAY CELEBRATION

1. A-Tisket, A-Tasket (Fitzgerald–Alexander) 2:36 380502-1
2. Undecided (Shavers–Robin) 3:17   390217-1
3. Don't Worry 'Bout Me (Koehler–Bloom) 3:05 390421-1
4. Stairway to the Stars (Parish–Malneck–Signorelli) 3:16   390629-2
5. The Five O'Clock Whistle (Gannon–Myrow–Irwin) 3:07   400925-1
6. Cow-Cow Boogie (Carter–DePaul–Raye) 2:52 431103-1
7. Into Each Life Some Rain Must Fall (Fisher–Roberts) 3:07   440830-1
8. (It's Only) A Paper Moon (Rose–Harburg–Arlen) 2:34   450327-1
9. Flying Home (Hampton–Goodman–Robin) 2:27 451004-1
10. Stone Cold Dead in de Market (Hendricks) 2:38 451008-1
11. You Won't Be Satisfied (James–Stock) 2:52   460118-1
12. I'm Just a Lucky So-and-So (Ellington–David) 2:54 460221-1
13. I Didn't Mean a Word I Said (Adamson–McHugh) 3:17   460221-2
14. Oh! Lady, Be Good! (Gershwin–Gershwin) 3:05 470319-3
15. How High the Moon (Hamilton–Lewis) 3:13 471220-3
16. My Happiness (Peterson–Bergantine) 3:15   480430-1
17. Black Coffee (Burke–Webster) 3:03   490428-3
18. In the Evening When the Sun Goes Down (Carr–Raye) 2:37   490920-1
19. Basin Street Blues (Williams) 3:06   490920-4
20. I've Got the World on a String (Koehler–Arlen) 3:17 500306-2
21. Ain't Nobody's Business but My Own (Taylor) 3:13 500815-1
22. Dream a Little Dream of Me (Kahn–Schwandt–Andrée) 3:04   500825-1
23. Smooth Sailing (Cobb) 3:04   510626-2
24. Air Mail Special (Goodman–Mundy–Christian) 3:00 520104-1
25. Rough Ridin' (Fitzgerald–Jones–Tennyson) 3:12 520104-2
26. Goody-Goody (Mercer–Malneck) 2:23   520225-4
27. Angel Eyes (Brent–Dennis) 2:53   520626-4
28. Mr. Paganini [You'll Have To Swing It] (Coslow) 5:09   520626-1/2

29. Preview (Quinchette) 3:02   520626-6
30. Blue Lou (Sampson-Mills) 2:45   530213-2
31. I Wished on the Moon (Parker-Rainger) 3:08
    540325-1
32. Until the Real Thing Comes Along (Cahn-Chaplin-
    Holliner-Nichols-Freeman) 2:55   540329-5
33. Lullaby of Birdland (Shearing-Weiss) 2:49
    540604-1
34. That Old Black Magic (Mercer-Arlen) 2:30
    550427-1
35. Ol' Devil Moon (Harburg-Lane) 2:57   550427-2
36. Lover, Come Back to Me (Hammerstein II-
    Romberg) 1:59   550427-3
37. Between the Devil and the Deep Blue Sea (Koehler-
    Arlen) 2:15   550427-4
38. Hard Hearted Hannah (Bates-Bigelow-Yeller-Ager)
    2:58   550503-1
39. My One and Only Love (Wood-Mellin) 3:18
    550805-1

CD: GRP Decca Jazz GRD-2-619 (2 discs in hard-bound book) (released March 1993) Disc 1, Tracks 1-20 (60:38)/Disc 2, Tracks 21-39 (57:28). Total playing time: 1:58:06. Original sessions produced by **Jack Kapp** (Tracks 1-7) and **Milt Gabler**. Reissue produced by **Milt Gabler** and **Orrin Keepnews**; repertoire selected by Gabler. The "liner notes" is a 36-page hard-bound book comprising three parts: Chapter 1, THE FIRST LADY OF SONG, by **Dan Morgenstern**; Chapter 2, FOR ELLA, by Milt Gabler; and Chapter 3, REMEMBERING MILT GABLER, by **Bud Katzel**; and a discography. The discs are lodged inside the front cover of this beautiful presentation. Reviewed by **Bruce Crowther**, *Jazz Journal International*, Volume 46, Issue 7, July 1993.

The Decca Years (1941–1947)

LPD-4 ELLA FITZGERALD/ THE WAR YEARS (1941–1947)

1. Jim (Petrillo-Samuels-Shawn) 2:58   411006-1
2. This Love of Mine (Sinatra-Parker-Sanicola) 2:52
   411006-2
3. Somebody Nobody Loves (Miller) 3:09   411028-1
4. You Don't Know What Love Is (Raye-De Paul) 3:22
   411028-2
5. Make Love to Me (Gannon-Mann-Weiss) 2:45
   411105-3
6. Mama, Come Home (Battle-Gannon-Myrow) 2:40
   420410-2
7. My Heart and I Decided (Donaldson) 2:58
   420731-1
8. He's My Guy (Raye-De Paul) 3:16   420731-3

9. Cow Cow Boogie (Carter-Ray-De Paul) 2:52
   431103-1
10. Time Alone Will Tell (Gordon-Monaco) 3:05
    440321-1
11. Once Too Often (Gordon-Monaco) 2:55   440321-2
12. Into Each Life Some Rain Must Fall (Fisher-Roberts)
    3:06   440830-1
13. I'm Making Believe (Gordon-Monaco) 3:09
    440830-2
14. And Her Tears Flowed Like Wine (Greene-Kenton-
    Lawrence) 3:13   441106-1
15. I'm Confessin' (That I Love You) (Neiberg-
    Dougherty-Reynolds) 3:22   441106-2
16. I'm Beginning to See the Light (James-Ellington-
    Hodges-George) 2:42   450226-1
17. That's the Way It Is (Whitney-Kramer) 3:15
    450226-2
18. (It's Only a) Paper Moon (Rose-Harburg-Arlen)
    2:39   450327-2
19. Cry You Out of My Heart (Heath-Lange-Loring)
    2:44   450328-1
20. A Kiss Goodnight (Victor-Herman-Slack) 3:05
    450829-1
21. Benny's Coming Home on Saturday (Fisher-Roberts)
    3:23   450829-2
22. Flying Home (Goodman-Hampton-Robin) 2:25
    451004-2
23. Stone Cold Dead in de Market (Hendricks) 2:37
    451008-1
24. Petootie Pie (Leveen-Pack-Paparelli) 2:35   451008-2
25. You Won't Be Satisfied (James-Stock) 2:52   460118-1
26. The Frim Fram Sauce (Ricardel-Evans) 3:11
    460118-2
27. I'm Just a Lucky So-and-So (David-Ellington) 2:53
    460221-1
28. I Didn't Mean a Word I Said (Adamson-McHugh)
    3:16   460221-2
29. For Sentimental Reasons (Watson-Best) 3:07 460819-1
30. It's a Pity to Say Goodnight (Reid) 2:37   460819-2
31. Guilty (Kahn-Akst-Whiting) 3:10   470124-1
32. Sentimental Journey (Green-Brown-Homer) 3:15
    470124-2
33. A Sunday Kind of Love (Belle-Prima-Leonard-
    Rhodes) 3:12   470319-1
34. That's My Desire (Kresa-Loveday) 2:59   470319-2
35. Oh! Lady, Be Good! (Gershwin-Gershwin) 3:13
    470319-3
36. Don't You Think I Ought to Know (Johnson-Wet-
    tergreen) 3:06   470722-1
37. You're Breakin' in a New Heart (Drake-Shirl) 2:25
    470722-2
38. I Want to Learn About Love (Lee-Roberts) 2:21
    471218-1

39. That Old Feeling (Brown-Fain) 2:24   471218-2

40. My Baby Likes to Bebop (And I Like to Bebop Too) (Bishop) 2:39   471220-1

41. No Sense (Fitzgerald-Brown) 2:56   471220-2

42. How High the Moon (Lewis-Hamilton) 3:18 471220-3

43. How High the Moon (Lewis-Hamilton) 3:13 471220-5

CD: GRP Decca Jazz GRD-2-628 (2 discs) (released September 1994). Disc I, Tracks 1-21 (64:42)/Disc II, Tracks 22-43 (64:59). Total playing time: 2:09:41. Original sessions produced by **Milt Gabler.** Reissue produced by **Orrin Keepnews.** Liner notes by **Gino Falzarano.** Reviewed by **Larry Birnbaum,** *Down Beat,* Volume 62, Number 2, February 1995.

The Decca Years (1938-1955)

LPD-5 ELLA: THE LEGENDARY DECCA RECORDINGS

Disc 1/The Very Best of Ella

1. A-Tisket, A-Tasket (Fitzgerald-Alexander) 2:36 380502-1

2. Undecided (Shavers-Robin) 3:17   390217-1

3. Stairway to the Stars (Malneck-Parish-Signorelli) 3:16   390629-2

4. The Five O'Clock Whistle (Gannon-Irwin-Myrow) 3:07   400925-1

5. Cow-Cow Boogie (Carter-DePaul-Raye) 2:52 431103-1

6. Flying Home (Goodman-Hampton-Robin) 2:27 451004-1

7. Stone Cold Dead in de Market (Hendricks) 2:38 451008-1

8. You Won't Be Satisfied (James-Stock) 2:52   460118-1

9. I'm Just a Lucky So-and-So (David-Ellington) 2:54 460221-1

10. I Didn't Mean a Word I Said (Adamson-McHugh) 3:16   460221-2

11. Oh! Lady, Be Good! (Gershwin-Gershwin) 3:06 470319-3

12. How High the Moon (Lewis-Hamilton) 3:13 471220-4

13. My Happiness (Peterson-Bergantine) 3:16   480430-1

14. In the Evening (When the Sun Goes Down) (Carr-Raye) 2:37   490920-1

15. Smooth Sailing (Cobb) 3:04   510626-2

16. Air Mail Special (Goodman-Christian-Mundy) 3:00 520104-1

17. Mr. Paganini [You'll Have To Swing It] (Coslow) 5:09   520626-2/3

18. Blue Lou (Mills-Sampson) 2:45   530213-2

19. Lullaby of Birdland (Shearing-Weiss) 2:49 540604-1

20. Hard Hearted Hannah (Bates-Bigelow-Ager-Yellen) 2:58   550503-1

Total playing time, 61:14

Disc 2/Ella & Friends

WITH LOUIS ARMSTRONG

1. The Frim Fram Sauce (Ricardel-Evans) 3:11 460118-2

2. Dream a Little Dream of Me (Kahn-Schwandt-André) 3:04   500825-1

3. Can Anyone Explain? (Benjamin-Weiss) 3:09 500825-2

4. Would You Like To Take a Walk? (Dixon-Rose-Warren) 3:15   511123-3

5. Who Walks In When I Walk Out (Goodhart-Hoffman-Freed) 2:16   511123-4

WITH THE INK SPOTS

6. Into Each Life Some Rain Must Fall (Roberts-Fisher) 3:07   440830-1

7. I'm Making Believe (Gordon-Monaco) 3:09 440830-2

8. I'm Beginning to See the Light (George-Hodges-James-Ellington) 2:42   450226-1

9. I Still Feel the Same About You (Reed-Manning) 3:15   501220-2

WITH LOUIS JORDAN

10. Petootie Pie (Leveen-Paparelli-Pack) 2:35   451008-2

11. Baby, It's Cold Outside (Loesser) 2:40   490428-5

12. Don't Cry, Cry-Baby (Unger-Bernie-Johnson) 2:56 490428-6

13. Ain't Nobody's Business (but My Own) (Taylor) 3:12 500815-1

14. I'll Never Be Free (Benjamin-Weiss) 3:09   500815-2

WITH THE DELTA RHYTHM BOYS

15. (It's Only a) Paper Moon (Harburg-Rose-Arlen) 2:34 450327-1

16. (Gonna) Cry You Out of My Heart (Lange) 2:44 450328-1

17. (I Love You) For Sentimental Reasons (Watson-Best) 3:07   460819-1

18. It's a Pity to Say Goodnight (Reid) 2:37   460819-2

WITH THE MILLS BROTHERS

19. Fairy Tales (Reitz) 2:51   491107-1

20. I Gotta Have My Baby Back (Tillman) 3:21 491107-2

Total playing time, 58:56

Disc 3/Ella Sings Gershwin & Others

1. Someone to Watch Over Me (Gershwin-Gershwin) 3:13   500912-3
2. My One and Only (Gershwin-Gershwin) 3:13 500911-2
3. But Not for Me (Gershwin-Gershwin) 3:12 500912-1
4. Looking for a Boy (Gershwin-Gershwin) 3:06 500911-1
5. I've Got a Crush on You (Gershwin-Gershwin) 3:13 500911-4
6. How Long Has This Been Going On? (Gershwin-Gershwin) 3:14   500911-3
7. Maybe (Gershwin-Gershwin) 3:24   500912-4
8. Soon (Gershwin-Gershwin) 2:44   500912-2
9. I'm Glad There Is You (Madeira-Dorsey) 3:06 540329-1
10. What Is There to Say? (Harburg-Duke) 3:19 540329-3
11. People Will Say We're in Love (Hammerstein-Rodgers) 3:08   540329-6
12. Please Be Kind (Cahn-Chaplin) 3:32   540330-1
13. Until the Real Thing Comes Along (Cahn-Chaplin-Freeman-Holiner-Nichols) 2:54   540329-5
14. Makin' Whoopee (Kahn-Donaldson) 3:03 540329-4
15. Imagination (Burke-Van Heusen) 2:34   540330-2
16. Star Dust (Parish-Carmichael) 3:58   540330-6
17. My Heart Belongs to Daddy (Porter) 2:36   540330-3
18. You Leave Me Breathless (Freed-Holander) 3:02 540330-4
19. Baby, What Else Can I Do? (Hirsch-Marks) 3:46 540329-2
20. Nice Work If You Can Get It (Gershwin-Gershwin) 2:37   540330-5

Total playing time, 64:02

Disc 4/Ella & the Arrangers

SY OLIVER

1. Basin Street Blues (Williams) 3:06   490920-4
2. I've Got the World on a String (Koehler-Arlen) 3:17 500306-2
3. Goody Goody (Mercer-Malneck) 2:23   520225-4
4. Angel Eyes (Brent-Dennis) 2:53   520626-4

GORDON JENKINS

5. Happy Talk (Hammerstein-Rodgers) 2:26 490428-1
6. I'm Gonna Wash That Man Right Outa My Hair (Hammerstein-Rodgers) 2:54   490428-2
7. Black Coffee (Webster-Burke) 3:03   490428-3
8. I Wished on the Moon (Parker-Rainger) 3:08 540525-1

BOB HAGGART

9. A Sunday Kind of Love (Belle-Prima-Leonard-Rhodes) 3:12   470319-1
10. That's My Desire (Loveday-Kress) 2:59   470319-2

ANDRÉ PREVIN

11. Thanks for the Memory (Robin-Rainger) 2:26 550401-2
12. It Might As Well Be Spring (Hammerstein-Rodgers) 2:39   550401-3
13. You'll Never Know (Gordon-Warren) 3:07 550401-1
14. I Can't Get Started (Gershwin-Duke) 3:04 550401-4

BENNY CARTER

15. That Old Black Magic (Mercer-Arlen) 2:30 550427-4
16. Ol' Devil Moon (Harburg-Lane) 2:56 550427-1
17. Lover, Come Back to Me (Hammerstein-Romberg) 1:59 550427-2
18. Between the Devil and the Deep Blue Sea (Koehler-Arlen) 2:16 550427-3

TOOTS CAMARATA

19. (Love Is) The Tender Trap (Cahn-Van Heusen) 2:59 550805-4
20. My One and Only Love (Mellin-Wood) 3:16 550805-1

Total playing time, 56:35

CD: Decca Jazz DRG 4-648 (September 1995) Total playing time, 4:00:47 (4 CD). Original sessions produced by **Jack Kapp** (1938–1944) and **Milt Gabler**. Re-Issue produced by **Orrin Keepnews** and **Joel Dorn**. The "liner notes," two essays, by **James Gavin** and **Geoffrey Mark Fidelman**, are contained in a 43-page booklet, along with a discography.

The Decca Years (1936)

LPD6 CHICK WEBB AND HIS ORCHESTRA—1936*

Chick Webb and His Orchestra, 1936

1. Big John Special (Henderson) (instr) 3:34   360219-1
2. Shine (Dabney-Mack-Brown) (vEF) 3:05   360219-5
3. Stompin' at the Savoy (Webb-Goodman-Sampson) (instr) 2:58   360219-3
4. Keepin' Out of Mischief Now (Waller-Razaf) (instr) 2:14   360219-8
5. You Hit the Spot (Revel-Gordon) (vEF) 2:24 360219-2
6. Go, Harlem (Johnson-Razaf) (instr) 2:10   360219-6

7. Don't Be That Way (Sampson-Goodmn-Parish)
    (instr) 2:24   360219-4

8. The Darktown Strutters' Ball (Brooks) (vEF) 1:37
    360219-7

9. If Dreams Come True (Sampson-Goodman-Mills)
    (vCL) 2:34   360219-11

10. Nit Wit Serenade (Hudson-Webb) (instr) 2:45
    360219-9

11. Rhythm and Romance (Johnson-Whiting-Schwartz)
    (vEF) 2:20   360219-12

12. King Porter Stomp (Morton) (instr) 3:14   360219-10

    BILL CHALLIS AND HIS ORCHESTRA, 1936

13. Diga Diga Doo (McHugh-Fields) (instr) 2:35

14. Dear Old Southland (Layton-Creamer) (instr) 2:28

15. Rhythm in My Nursery Rhymes (Lunceford-Chap-
    lin-Cahn-Raye) (vBea Wain and the Bachelors) 1:35

16. Let's Face the Music and Dance (Berlin) (instr) 2:38

    WOODY HERMAN AND HIS ORCHESTRA, 1937

17. Davenport Blues (Beiderbecke) (instr) 3:15

18. Things Are Looking Up (Gershwin-Gershwin)
    (instr) 3:08

19. Sweet Someone (Revel-Gordon) (vWoody Herman)
    3:07

20. Apache Dance (Offenbach) (instr) 2:50

21. You're a Sweetheart (McHugh-Adamson) (vWoody
    Herman) 3:02

22. Queen Isabella (Thomas-Denniker) (instr) 2:19

*The CD is mislabeled, **Chick Webb and His Orchestra — 1937**

LP: Circle 17 (released 1985). Side 1, Tracks 1–6
(16:25)/Side 2, Tracks 6–12 (14:54). Total playing time,
31:19 (Tracks 13–22 do not appear on LP). CD: Circle
CCD-72 (released 1995). Total playing time, 60:51 (Chick
Webb portion, Tracks 1–12, 31:19). Produced by **George H.
Buck, Jr.** Liner notes by **Frank Driggs**. Because of the
brevity of the Chick Webb portion of this album, Mr. Buck
has generously allowed us a preview of two other of his recent compact discs: **Bill Challis and His Orchestra, 1936**
(Circle CCD-71), featuring Bea Wain, Artie Shaw, Manny
Klein, Will Bradley, Jack Jenny, and Frank Signorelli; and
Woody Herman and His Orchestra, 1937 (Circle CCD-
95), the formative years of "The Band That Plays the Blues."

The Decca Years (1935–1937)

LPD-7 THE CHRONOLOGICAL ELLA FITZGERALD/1935–1937

1. I'll Chase the Blues Away (Sampson-Harrison) 2:32
    350612-1

2. Love and Kisses (Curtis) 3:17   350612-4

3. Rhythm and Romance (Johnson-Whiting-Schwartz)
    3:04   351012-1

4. I'll Chase the Blues Away (Sampson-Harrison) 2:44
    351012-3

5. My Melancholy Baby (Norton-Burnett) 2:58
    360317-1

6. All My Life (Mitchell-Stept) 3:11   360317-2

7. Crying My Heart Out for You (Hopkins-Johnson)
    3:04   360407-3

8. Under the Spell of the Blues (Sampson-Harrison)
    3:02   360407-4

9. When I Get Low, I Get High (Sunshine) 2:27
    360407-5

10. Sing Me a Swing Song (and Let Me Dance)
    (Carmichael-Adams) 2:58   360603-2

11. A Little Bit Later On (Levinson-Nieburg) 3:07
    360602-3

12. Love, You're Just a Laugh (Gardner-Cahn-Chaplin)
    3:07   360602-4

13. Devoting My Time to You (Webb-Williams) 2:24
    360602-5

14. Mr. Paganini (You'll Have To Swing It) (Coslow)
    2:58 361029-1

15. Swinging on the Reservation (Carver-Webb) 3:05
    361029-3

16. I've Got the Spring Fever Blues (Werner-Bauer) 3:01
    361029-4

17. Vote for Mr. Rhythm (Robin-Rainger-Siegal) 2:28
    361029-5

18. Goodnight, My Love (Revel-Gordon) 3:08
    361105-1

19. Oh, Yes, Take Another Guess (Mencher-Newman-
    Sherman) 2:28   361105-2

20. Did You Mean It? (Greer-Dixon) 2:19   361105-3

21. My Last Affair (Johnson) 3:02   361118-1

22. The Organ Grinder's Swing (Hudson-Parish-Wells)
    2:40   361118-2

23. Shine (Mack-Brown-Dant) 2:54   361119-1

24. The Darktown Strutters' Ball (Brooks) 2:57   361119-2

25. Oh, Yes, Take Another Guess (Mencher-Newman-
    Sherman) 2:43   370114-1

CD: Classics 500 (released April 1990). Total playing
time: 72:16. Original sessions produced by **Jack Kapp**. Reissue produced by **Gilles Pétard** from shellac 78rpm
recordings using modern technology. Liner notes by Anatol Schenker. Reviewed by **Bruce Crowther**, *Jazz Journal
International*, Volume 43, Issue 8, August 1990.

The Decca Years (1935–1938)

LPD-8 THE CHRONOLOGICAL CHICK WEBB AND HIS ORCHESTRA/1935–1938

1. Down Home Rag (Lewis-Seatman) 2:52   350612-2
2. Are You Here To Stay? (Sampson-Harrison) 3:11   350612-3
3. Moonlight and Magnolias (DeRose-Gillespie) 2:51   351012-2
4. I May Be Wrong (but I Think You're Wonderful) (Sullivan-Ruskin) 3:03   351012-4
5. Facts and Figures (Sampson) 2:33   351012-5
6. Go Harlem (Razaf-Johnson) 2:20   360602-1
7. Love Marches On (Loeb-Tobias) 2:52   370114-2
8. There's Frost on the Moon (Young-Ahlert) 2:49   370115-1
9. Gee, But You're Swell (Tobias-Baer) 2:37   370115-2
10. Rusty Hinge (LaFremiere-Brown) 3:06   370324-1
11. Wake Up and Live (Gordon-Revel) 2:37   370324-2
12. It's Swell of You (Gordon Revel) 3:12   370324-3
13. Clap Hands! Here Comes Charlie (Meyer-Rose-Mc-Donald) 2:31   370324-6
14. That Naughty Waltz (Levy-Stanley) 3:01   370324-9
15. In a Little Spanish Town (Wayne-Lewis-Young) 2:40   370921-1
16. I Got Rhythm (Gershwin-Gershwin) 2:31   370921-2
17. I Ain't Got Nobody (Graham-Williams) 3:02   370921-3
18. Strictly Jive (Webb) 3:17   371027-3
19. Sweet Sue, Just You (Harris-Young) 2:44   371101-1
20. Squeeze Me (Waller-Williams) 3:10   371101-4
21. Harlem Congo (White) 3:14   371101-5
22. Midnite in a Madhouse (Clinton) 2:33   371217-6
23. Azure (Ellington) 3:12   380502-4
24. Spinnin' the Webb (Fitzgerald-Webb) 3:04   380503-6
25. Liza (All the Clouds'll Roll Away) (Gershwin-Gershwin-Kahn) 2:45   380503-7

CD: Classics 517 (released August 1990). Total playing time, 73:01. Original sessions produced by **Jack Kapp**/Re-issue produced by **Giles Pétard**. Liner notes by **Anatol Schenker**. Reviewed by **Bruce Crowther**, *Jazz Journal International*, Volume 43, Issue 10, October 1990.

The Decca Years (1937–1938)

LPD-9 THE CHRONOLOGICAL ELLA FITZGERALD/1937–1938

1. Big Boy Blue (Lawrence-Howell-Tinturin) 2:46   370114-3
2. Dedicated to You (Cahn-Chaplin) 3:10   370203-1
3. You Showed Me the Way (Green-McRae) 3:09   370324-4
4. Cryin' Mood (Razaf-Webb) 2:35   370324-7
5. Love Is the Thing (So They Say) (Werner-Werner) 2:51   370324-8
6. All Over Nothing at All (Tinturin-Lawrence) 2:40   370524-1
7. If You Ever Should Leave (Cahn-Chaplin) 3:13   370524-3
8. Everyone's Wrong But Me (Cahn-Chaplin) 3:06   370524-4
9. Deep in the Heart of the South (Tinturin-Lawrece) 3:16   370524-5
10. Just a Simple Melody (Cahn-Chaplin) 2:56   371027-1
11. I Got a Guy (Sunshine) 3:20   371027-2
12. Holiday in Harlem (Reed-Webb) 3:10   371027-4
13. Rock It for Me (Werner-Werner) 3;10   371101-1
14. I Want To Be Happy (Youmans-Caesar-Harbach) 4:27   371217-1
15. The Dipsy Doodle (Clinton) 3:14   371217-3
16. If Dreams Come True (Sampson) 3:27   371217-4
17. Hallelujah! (Youmans-Robin-Grey) 4:00   371217-5
18. Bei Mir Bist du Schoen (Secunda-Jacobs-Cahn-Chaplin) 3:06   371221-1
19. It's My Turn Now (Cahn-Chaplin) 2:56   371221-2
20. It's Wonderful (Wells-Parish-Smith) 2:57   380125-1
21. I Was Doing All Right (Gershwin-Gershwin) 2:56   380125-2
22. A-Tisket, A-Tasket (Fitzgerald-Alexander) 2:35   380502-1

CD: Classics 506 (released May 1990). Total playing time, 69:16. Original sessions produced by **Jack Kapp**/Re-issue produced by **Gilles Pétard**. Liner notes by **Anatol Schenker**. Reviewed by **Bruce Crowther**, *Jazz Journal International*, Volume 43, Issue 8, August 1990.

The Decca Years (1938–1939)

LPD-10 THE CHRONOLOGICAL ELLA FITZGERALD/1938–1939

1. Heart of Mine (Webb-Heyman) 2:55   380502-2
2. I'm Just a Jitterbug (David-Livingstone) 3:18   380502-3
3. This Time It's Real (Shivers-Bernier-Emmerich) 3:08   380503-1
4. (Oh, Oh) What Do You Know About Love? (Livingstone-David) 3:03   380503-2
5. You Can't Be Mine (and Someone Else's Too) (Johnson-Webb) 3:04   380503-3

6. We Can't Go On This Way (LaFreniere-Butterfield-Post-Bishop) 3:00   380503-4

7. Saving Myself for You (Cahn-Chaplin) 2:49   380503-9

8. If You Only Knew (Beal-Webb) 2:47   380503-10

9. Pack Up Your Sins and Go to the Devil (Berlin) 2:55   380609-1

10. MacPherson Is Rehearsin' (To Swing) (Sunshine) 3:07 380609-2

11. Everybody Step (Berlin) 2:43   380609-3

12. Ella (Ellsworth-Webb) 2:46   380609-4

13. Wacky Dust (Adams-Levant) 3:04   380817-1

14. Gotta Pebble in My Shoe (Feldman) 2:53   380817-2

15. I Can't Stop Loving You (Jones-Webb) 3:05   380817-3

16. Strictly from Dixie (Cavanaugh-Webb-Pierce) 2:50   380818-1

17. Woe Is Me (Daniel-Lawrence) 2:50   380818-2

18. I Let a Tear Fall in the River (David-Livingstone-Webb) 3:11   380818-4

19. Franklin D. Roosevelt Jones (Rome) 2:54   381006-1

20. I Love Each Move You Make (Grumble-Webb) 3:01   381006-2

21. It's Foxy (Bishop-Webb) 3:03   381006-3

22. I Found My Yellow Basket (Fitzgerald-Webb) 2:35   381006-4

23. Undecided (Shavers) 3:15   390217-1

CD: Classics 518 (released May 1990). Total playing time, 69:28. Original sessions produced by **Jack Kapp**/Reissue produced by **Gilles Pétard**. Liner notes by **Anatol Schenker**. Reviewed by **Bruce Crowther**, *Jazz Journal International*, Volume 43, Issue 8, August 1990.

The Decca Years (1936–1939)

LPD-11 CHICK WEBB 4/ELLA SWINGS THE BAND, 1936–1939

1. The Organ Grinder's Swing (Parish-Mills-Hudson) 2:53   361118-2

2. Shine (Mack-Brown-Dabney) 2:52   361119-1

3. My Last Affair (Johnson) 2:42   361118-1

4. Cryin' Mood (Razaf-Webb) 2:36   370324-7

5. Just a Simple Melody (Cahn-Chaplin) 2:58   371027-1

6. Holiday in Harlem (Reed-Webb) 3:09   371027-4

7. Pack Up Your Sins and Go to the Devil (Berlin) 2:55   380609-1

8. Wacky Dust (Adams-Levant) 3:04   380817-1

9. One Side of Me (Sunshine) 3:21   390217-4

10. My Heart Belongs to Daddy (Porter) 3:07   390217-5

11. Sugar Pie (Beal-Webb) 3:11   390302-3

12. (When It's) Slumbertime Along the Swanee (Tinturin-Sacco) 2:49   390302-4

13. Little White Lies (Donaldson) 2:56   390421-6

14. Coochi-Coochi-Coo (Werner-Werner) 3:08   390421-7

LP: MCA 1327 (released 1972). Side One, Track 1–7 (20:35)/Side Two, Tracks 8–14 (22:06). Total playing time: 42:41. Original sessions produced by **Jack Kapp**. All the tracks on this LP, included here for the record, appear elsewhere on compact disc.

The Decca Years (1939)

LPD12 THE CHRONOLOGICAL ELLA FITZGERALD/1939

1. 'Tain't What You Do (It's the Way That Cha Do It) (Young-Oliver) 3:02   390217-2

2. One Side of Me (Sunshine) 3:21   390217-4

3. My Heart Belongs to Daddy (Porter) 3:07   390217-5

4. Once Is Enough for Me (Fitzgerald-Webb) 3:01   390302-1

5. I Had to Live and Learn (Johnson-May-Webb) 3:07   390302-2

6. Sugar Pie (Beal-Webb) 3:11   390302-3

7. (When It's) Slumbertime Along the Swanee (Tinturin-Sacco) 2:49   390302-4

8. I'm Up a Tree (Stillman-Webb-Cooke) 3:04   390302-5

9. Chew-Chew-Chew (Your Bubble Gum) (Webb-Ram-Fitzgerald) 3:02   390302-6

10. Don't Worry 'Bout Me (Koehler-Bloom) 3:09   390421-1

11. If Anything Happened to You (Van Heusen) 3:06   390421-2

12. If That's What You're Thinking (You're Wrong) (Lawrence-Gans) 3:05   390421-3

13. If You Ever Change Your Mind (Watts-Green-Sigler) 3:02   390421-4

14. Have Mercy (Ram-Webb) 3:07   390421-5

15. Little White Lies (Donaldson) 2:56   390421-6

16. Coochi-Coochi-Coo (Werner-Werner) 3:03   390421-7

17. That Was My Heart (Webb-Johnson) 3:02   390421-8

18. Betcha Nickel (Fitzgerald-Webb) 2:57   390629-1

19. Stairway to the Stars (Signorelli-Malneck-Parish) 3:12   390629-2

20. I Want the Waiter (with the Water) (Werner-Werner) 3:08   390629-3

21. That's All, Brother (Livingstone-David-Hager) 3:04   390629-4
22. Out of Nowhere (Green-Heyman) 2:54   390629-5

CD: Classics 525 (released June 1990). Total playing time, 69:15. Original sessions produced by **Jack Kapp**/Reissue produced by **Gilles Pétard.** Liner notes by **Anatol Schenker.** Reviewed by **Bruce Crowther,** *Jazz Journal International*, Volume 44, Issue 2, February 1991.

The Decca Years (1939–1940)

LPD-13 THE CHRONOLOGICAL ELLA FITZGERALD/1939–1940

1. My Last Goodbye (Howard) 3:20   390818-1
2. (I Always Dream of) Billy (Kendis-Paley-Godwin) 2:42   390818-2
3. Please Tell Me the Truth (Fitzgerald-Sampson) 3:15   390818-3
4. I'm Not Complainin' (Sampson-Stillman) 3:07   390818-4
5. You're Gonna Lose Your Gal (Monaco-Young) 3:06   391012-1
6. (What Can I Say) After I Say I'm Sorry (Donaldson-Lyman) 2:48   391012-2
7. Baby, What Else Can I Do? (Marks-Hirsch) 3:04   391012-3
8. My Wubba Dolly (Werner-Werner) 3:01   391012-4
9. Lindy Hoppers' Delight (Barefield-McRae) (instr)* 2:51   391012-5
10. Moon Ray (Shaw-Madison-Quenzer) 3:03   391012-6
11. Is There Somebody Else? (Robertson) 2:35   400126-1
12. Sugar Blues (Williams-Fletcher) 2:50   400126-2
13. The Starlit Hour (Parish-DeRose) 3:09   400126-3
14. What's the Matter with Me? (Shand-Lewis) 2:58   400126-4
15. Baby, Won't You Please Come Home (Warfield-Williams) 2:31   400215-1
16. If It Weren't for You (Mizzy-Taylor) 3:00   400215-2
17. Sing Song Swing (Cook-Garrett) 3:02   400215-3
18. Imagination (Van Heusen-Burke) 2:59   400215-4
19. Take It from the Top (McRae) (instr) 2:55   400320-1
20. Tea Dance (Vance) (instr) 3:17   400320-2
21. Jubilee Swing (McRae-Hale-Fields) (instr) 3:16   400320-3
22. (Untitled) (Composer unknown) (instr) 3:04   400320-4
23. Deedle-De-Dum (Fitzgerald-Kahn-Wynn-Waters) 2:40   400509-1

*Five instrumentals are included here, their being a part of Ella's oeuvre, since she was nominally the leader of the band.

CD: Classics 566 (released February 1991). Total playing time, 69:54. Original sessions produced by **Jack Kapp**/Re-issue produced by **Gilles Pétard.** Liner notes by **Anatol Schenker.** Reviewed by **Ian Crosbie,** *Jazz Journal International*, Volume 44, Issue 7, July 1991.

The Decca Years (1940–1941)

LPD-14 THE CHRONOLOGICAL ELLA FITZGERALD/1940–1941

1. Shake Down the Stars (Van Heusen-DeLange) 2:48   400509-2
2. Gulf Coast Blues (Williams) 3:01   400509-3
3. I Fell in Love with a Dream(Fitzgerald-Skye-Goldsmith) 3:10   400509-4
4. The Five O'Clock Whistle (Myrow-Gannon-Irwin) 2:53   400925-1
5. So Long (Morgan-Harris-Melcher) 3:04   400925-2
6. Louisville, K-Y (Skylar) 3:06   400925-3
7. Taking a Chance on Love (Duke-Latouche-Fetter) 3:06   401108-1
8. Cabin in the Sky (Duke-Latouche) 2:44   401108-2
9. I'm the Lonesomest Gal in Town (Von Tilzer-Brown) 2:36   401108-3
10. Three Little Words (Kalmar-Ruby) 2:36   410108-1
11. Hello, Ma! I Done It Again (Rainger-Robin) 2:30   410108-2
12. Wishful Thinking (Rainger-Robin) 3:00   410108-3
13. The One I Love Belongs to Somebody Else (Jones-Kahn) 3:01   410108-4
14. The Muffin Man (Fitzgerald) 2:26   410108-5
15. Keep Cool, Fool (Myrow-Rhythm) 3:03   410331-1
16. No Nothing (Ryan-Handman-Kurtz) 3:08   410331-2
17. My Man [Mon Homme] (Yvain-Pollock) 3:06   410331-3
18. I Can't Believe That You're in Love with Me (Gaskill-McHugh) 2:30   410731-1
19. I Must Have That Man (McHugh-Fields) 3:05   410731-2
20. When My Sugar Walks Down the Street (Austin-McHugh-Mills) 2:38   410731-3
21. I Got It Bad (and That Ain't Good) (Ellington-Webster) 2:53   410731-4
22. Melinda, the Mousie (Irvin-Gannon-Myrow) 2:49   410731-5
23. Can't Help Lovin' Dat Man (Kern-Hammerstein) 2:45   410731-6

CD: Classics 644 (released May 1992). Total playing time, 66:55. Original sessions produced by **Jack Kapp**/Reissue produced by **Gilles Pétard.** Liner notes by **Anatol Schenker.** Note: The first six discs of *The Chronological Ella Fitzgerald* are available as a 6-CD boxed set, **The Chronological Ella Fitzgerald, Volume 1, 1935–1941,** (Classics 63) containing 138 tracks.

The Decca Years (1940–1941)

LPD-15 ELLA FITZGERALD
SOUVENIR ALBUM

1. I'm the Lonesomest Gal in Town (Von Tilzer-Brown) 2:36   401108-3
2. The One I Love Belongs to Somebody Else (Jones-Kahn) 3:01   410108-4
3. Baby, Won't You Please Come Home? (Warfield-Williams) 2:31   400215-1
4. I Can't Believe That You're in Love with Me (Gaskill-McHugh) 2:30   410731-1
5. I Got It Bad (and That Ain't Good) (Ellington-Webster) 2:53   410731-4
6. Cabin in the Sky (Duke-Latouche) 2:44   401108-2
7. I Must Have That Man (McHugh-Fields) 3:05   410731-2
8. Can't Help Lovin' Dat Man (Kern-Hammerstein) 2:45   410731-6

LP: Decca DL 5084 (10") (released 23 January 1950). Side 1, Tracks 1–4 (10:59)/Side 2, Tracks 5–8 (11:45). Total playing time: 22:44. Original sessions produced by **Jack Kapp**/This album produced by **Milt Gabler.** The liner notes are uncredited. Reviewed by **Sinclair Traill,** *Jazz Journal,* Volume 6, Issue 6, June 1953.

The Decca Years (1936–1941)

LPD-16 ELLA FITZGERALD/
STAIRWAY TO THE STARS

1. Stairway to the Stars (Parish-Malneck-Signorelli) 3:15   390629-2
2. I Was Doing All Right (Gershwin-Gershwin) 2:51   380125-2
3. All Over Nothing at All (Tinturin-Lawrence) 2:40   370524-1
4. You Can't Be Mine (and Someone Else's Too) (J.C. Johnson-Webb) 2:55   380503-4
5. My Last Affair (Haven Johnson) 2:42   361118-1

6. The Organ Grinder's Swing (Parish-Mills-Hudson) 2:53   361118-2
7. The Five O'Clock Whistle (Myrow-Gannon-Irwin) 3:07   400925-1
8. You Don't Know What Love Is (Raye-De Paul) 3:22   411028-2
9. Undecided (Shavers-Robin) 3:02   390217-1
10. Everyone's Wrong but Me (Cahn-Chaplin) 3:06   370524-4
11. Don't Worry 'Bout Me (Koehler-Bloom) 3:09   390421-1
12. If You Ever Should Leave (Cahn-Chaplin) 3:13   370524-3

LP: Decca DL-4446 (mono)/DL-74446 (stereo) (released 20 January 1964). Side One, Tracks 1–6 (17:41)/Side Two, Tracks 7–12 (19:24). Total playing time: 37:05. Original sessions produced by **Jack Kapp.** This album produced by **Milt Gabler.** Liner notes by **Stanley Dance.** Reviewed by **John A. Tynan,** *Down Beat,* Volume 31, Number 13, 4 June 1964.

The Decca Years (1941–1944)

LPD-17 THE CHRONOLOGICAL
ELLA FITZGERALD/1941–1944

1. Jim (Samuels-Shawn-Petrillo) 2:57   411006-1
2. This Love of Mine (Sinatra-Parker-Sanicola) 2:52   411006-2
3. Somebody Nobody Loves (Miller) 3:09   411028-1
4. You Don't Know What Love Is (Raye-DePaul) 3:22   411028-2
5. Who Are You? (Worth-Cowan) 2:55   411105-1
6. I'm Thrilled (Lippan-Dee) 3:04   411105-2
7. Make Love to Me (Gannon-Mann-Weiss) 2:45   411105-3
8. I'm Getting Mighty Lonesome for You (Ram) 2:42   420311-1
9. When I Come Back Crying (Lawnhurst-Seymour) 2:54   420311-2
10. All I Need Is You (DeRose-Davis-Parish) 2:58   420410-1
11. Mama, Come Home (Battle-Gannon-Myrow) 2:40   420410-2
12. My Heart and I Decided (Donaldson) 2:59   420731-1
13. (I Put) A Four-Leaf Clover in Your Pocket (Loeb-Davis) 2:53   420731-2
14. He's My Guy (Raye-DePaul) 3:16   420731-3
15. Cow Cow Boogie [Cuma-Ti-Yi-Ti-Ay] (Carter-Raye-DePaul) 2:52   431103-1

16. Once Too Often (Gordon-Monaco) 2:55   440321-2
17. Time Alone Will Tell (Gordon-Monaco) 3:05 440321-1
18. Into Each Life Some Rain Must Fall (Fisher-Roberts) 3:06 440830-1
19. I'm Making Believe (Gordon-Monaco) 3:09 440830-2
20. And Her Tears Flowed Like Wine (Greene-Kenton-Lawrence) 3:21 441106-1
21. I'm Confessin' (That I Love You) (Nieberg-Daugherty-Reynolds) 3:21 441106-2

    CD: Classics 840 (released September 1995). Total playing time, 64:23. Original sessions produced by **Jack Kapp**. This CD produced by **Gilles Pétard**. Liner notes by **Anatol Schenker**.

The Decca Years (1945–1947)

LPD-18 THE CHRONOLOGICAL ELLA FITZGERALD/1945–1947

1. I'm Beginning to See the Light (James-Ellington-Hodges-George) 2:41 450226-1
2. That's the Way It Is (Whitney-Kramer) 3:15 450226-2
3. (It's Only a) Paper Moon (Rose-Harburg-Arlen) 2:33 450327-1
4. Cry You Out of My Heart (Heath-Lange-Loring) 2:43 450328-1
5. A Kiss Goodnight (Victor-Herman-Slack) 3:04 450829-1
6. Benny's Coming Home on Saturday (Fisher-Roberts) 3:22 450829-2
7. Flying Home (Goodman-Hampton-Robin) 2:26 451004-1
8. Stone Cold Dead in de Market (Hendricks) 2:38 451008-1
9. Petootie Pie (Leveen-Pack-Paparelli) 2:32 451008-2
10. That's Rich (Oliver) 3:16 451012-1
11. I'll Always Be in Love with You (Ruby-Green-Stept) 4:24 451012-2
12. I'll See You in My Dreams (Jones-Kahn) 4:04 451012-4
13. Petootie Pie (Leveen-Pack-Paparelli) 2:28   451015-1
14. You Won't Be Satisfied (James-Stock) 2:51 460118-1
15. The Frim Fram Sauce (Ricardel-Evans) 3:10 460118-2
16. I'm Just a Lucky So-and-So (David-Ellington) 2:52 460221-1
17. I Didn't Mean a Word I Said (Adamson-McHugh) 3:16 460221-2

18. (I Love You) For Sentimental Reasons (Watson-Best) 3:07 460829-1
19. It's a Pity To Say Goodnight (Reid) 2:37 460829-2
20. Guilty (Kahn-Akst-Whiting) 3:10 470124-1
21. Sentimental Journey (Green-Brown-Homer) 3:15 470124-2
22. Budella (Blue Skies) (Janak-Berlin) 4:18 470301-1

    CD: Classics 998 (released April 1998). Total playing time, 69:21. Original sessions produced by **Jack Kapp**. This CD produced by **Gilles Pétard**. Liner notes by **Anatol Schenker**.

The Decca Years (1947–1948)

LPD-19 THE CHRONOLOGICAL ELLA FITZGERALD/1947–1948

1. A Sunday Kind of Love (Belle-Prima-Leonard-Rhodes) 3:12 470319-1
2. That's My Desire (Kresa-Loveday) 2:59 470319-2
3. Oh! Lady, Be Good! (Gershwin-Gershwin) 3:13 470319-3
4. Don't You Think I Ought to Know? (Johnson-Wettergreen) 3:05 470722-1
5. You're Breakin' in a New Heart (Drake-Shirl) 2:25 470722-2
6. I Want to Learn About Love (Lee-Roberts) 2:21 471218-1
7. That Old Feeling (Brown-Fain) 2:24 471218-2
8. My Baby Likes to Be-Bop (Bishop) 2:39 471220-1
9. No Sense (Fitzgerald-Brown) 2:56 471220-2
10. How High the Moon (Lewis-Hamilton) 3:13 471220-4
11. I've Got a Feelin' I'm Fallin' (Link-Waller-Rose) 2:31 471223-1
12. You Turned the Tables on Me (Alter-Mitchell) 2:54 471223-2
13. I Cried and Cried and Cried (Kuhn) 2:52 471223-3
14. Robbins' Nest (Thompson-Jacquet) 2:31 471223-4
15. Tea Leaves (Berk-Capano-Freedman) 2:39 480429-1
16. My Happiness (Bergantine-Peterson) 3:13 480430-1
17. It's Too Soon to Know (Chessler) 2:35 480820-1
18. I Can't Go On (Without You) (Glover-Nix) 2:47 480820-2
19. To Make a Mistake Is Human (Drake-Shirl) 3:04 481110-1
20. In My Dreams (Shearer) 2:56 481110-2

    CD: Classics 1049 (released January 1999). Total playing time, 57:40. Original sessions produced by **Jack Kapp**. This CD produced by **Gilles Pétard**. Liner notes by **Anatol Schenker**.

The Decca Years (1949)

LPD-19A THE CHRONOLOGICAL ELLA FITZGERALD/1949

1. I Couldn't Stay Away (Raleigh-Wayne) 2:48 490114-1
2. Old Mother Hubbard (Tobias-Poll) 3:12 490114-2
3. Someone Like You (Blane-Warren) 3:05 490414-3
4. Happy Talk (Hammerstein-Rodgers) 2:25 490428-1
5. I'm Gonna Wash That Man Right Outa My Hair (Hammerstein-Rodgers) 2:52 490428-2
6. Black Coffee (Webster-Burke) 3:03 490428-3
7. Lover's Gold (Merrill-Nevins) 3:07 490428-4
8. Baby, It's Cold Outside (Loesser) 2:27 490428-5
9. Don't Cry, Cry-Baby (Unger-Berni-Johnson) 2:56 490428-6
10. Crying (Rose-Chernis) 3:06 490720-1
11. A New Shade of Blue (Poll-Ackers-Farrow) 2:53 490720-2
12. In the Evening (When the Sun Goes Down) (Carr) 2:37 490920-1
13. Talk Fast, My Heart, Talk Fast (Raye-DePaul 2:41 490920-2
14. I'm Waitin' for the Junk Man 3:02 490920-3
15. Basin Street Blues (Williams) 3:04 490920-4
16. I Hadn't Anyone Till You (Noble) 2:57 490921-1
17. Dream a Little Longer (Kahn-Kahn) 2:58 490921-2
18. Foolish Tears (Carson) 2:56 490921-3
19. A Man Wrote a Song (Franklin) 3:04 490921-4
20. Fairy Tales (Reitz) 2:56 491107-1
21. I Gotta Have My Baby Back (Tillman) 3:17 491107-2

CD: Classics 1114 (released November 2000). Total playing time, 64:26. Original sessions produced by **Jack Kapp**. This CD produced by **Gilles Pétard**. Liner notes by **Anatol Schenker**.

The Decca Years (1950)

LPD-19B THE CHRONOLOGICAL ELLA FITZGERALD/1950

1. Baby, Won't You Say You Love Me? (Gordon-Myrow) 2:52 500202-1
2. Don'cha Go 'Way Mad (Stillman-Mundy-Jacquet) 3:13 500202-2
3. Solid As a Rock (Hilliard-Mann) 2:57 500306-1
4. I've Got the World on a String (Koehler-Arlen) 3:16 500306-2
5. Sugarfoot Rag (Vaughan-Garland) 2:53 500306-3
6. Peas and Rice (Larkin) 2:47 500306-4
7. M-I-S-S-I-S-S-I-P-P-I (Hanlon-Ryan-Tierney) 2:20 500509-1

8. I Don't Want the World (Heath-Lange) 2:11 500509-2
9. Ain't Nobody's Business but My Own (Taylor) 3:12 500815-1
10. I'll Never Be Free (Benjamin-Weiss) 3:09 500815-2
11. Dream a Little Dream of Me (Kahn-Schwandt-André) 3:04 500825-1
12. Can Anyone Explain? (Benjamin-Weiss) 3:09 500825-2
13. Looking for a Boy (Gershwin-Gershwin) 3:06 500911-1
14. My One and Only (Gershwin-Gershwin) 3:13 500911-2
15. How Long Has This Been Going On? (Gershwin-Gershwin) 3:14 500911-3
16. I've Got a Crush on You (Gershwin-Gershwin) 3:13 500911-4
17. But Not for Me (Gershwin-Gershwin) 3:12 500912-1
18. Soon (Gershwin-Gershwin) 2:44 500912-2
19. Someone To Watch Over Me (Gershwin-Gershwin) 3:13 500912-3
20. Maybe (Gershwin-Gershwin) 3:24 500912-4
21. Santa Claus Got Stuck in My Chimney (Hardy-Moore) 2:51 500926-1
22. Molasses, Molasses (Clinton) 3:03 500926-2
23. Little Small Town Girl (Loman-Rubens) 2:58 501220-1
24. I Still Feel the Same About You (Reid-Manning) 3:15 501220-2

CD: Classics (scheduled for release March 2001)

The Decca Years (1951)

LPD-19C THE CHRONOLOGICAL ELLA FITZGERALD/1951

1. Lonesome Gal (Brooks-Schumann) 2:47 510112-1
2. The Beanbag Song (DeLugg-DeLugg) 3:06 510112-2
3. The Chesapeake and Ohio (Sigman-Magidson) 3:01 510327-1
4. Little Man in a Flying Saucer 2:57 510327-2
5. Because of Rain (Roll-Cole-Harrington) 3:07 510327-3
6. The Hot Canary (Gilbert-Nero) 3:13 510327-4
7. Even as You and I (Johnson-Larkin) 3:26 510524-1
8. Do You Really Love Me? (Dant-Rinker) 3:08 510524-2
9. Love You Madly (Ellington) 3:10 510524-3
10. Mixed Emotions (Louchheim) 3:14 510626-1
11. Smooth Sailing (Fitzgerald-Cobb) 3:04 510626-2
12. Come On-a My House (Bagdasarian-Saroyan) 2:47 510626-3

13. It's My Own Darn Fault (George) 3:02   510718-1
14. I Don't Want to Take a Chance (Fitzgerald) 3:14   510718-2
15. There Never Was a Baby (Like My Baby) (Comden-Green-Styne) 2:46   510718-3
16. Give a Little, Get a Little (Love) (Comden-Green-Styne) 3:19   510718-4
17. Necessary Evil (Evans) 2:30   511123-1
18. Oops! (Mercer-Warren) 3:10   511123-2
19. Would You Like To Take a Walk? (Dixon-Rose-Warren) 3:15   511123-3
20. Who Walks In When I Walk Out? (Goodhart-Hoffman-Freed) 2:16   511123-4
21. Baby Doll (Mercer-Warren) 3:14   511226-1
22. What Does It Take? (Burke-Van Heusen) 2:57   511226-2
23. Lady Bug (Carr-Williams) 3:12   511226-3
24. Lazy Day (Raskin-Farnon) 2:48   511226-4

CD: Classics (scheduled for release March 2002)

The Decca Years (1952)

LPD-19D THE CHRONOLOGICAL ELLA FITZGERALD/1952

1. Air Mail Special (Fitzgerald-Goodman-Mundy-Christian) 3:00   520104-1
2. Rough Ridin' (Fitzgerald-Jones-Tennyson) 3:12   520104-2
3. A Guy Is a Guy (Brand) 2:52   520225-1
4. Nowhere Guy (Gordon-Myrow) 3:03   520225-2
5. Gee, Baby, But I'm Glad to Know You Love Me (Razaf-Redman) 3:04   520225-3
6. Goody Goody (Mercer-Malneck) 2:23   520225-4
7. Preview (Quinichette-Basie) 3:02   520626-1
8. Ding-Dong Boogie (Singleton-McRae) 2:38   520626-2
9. Mr. Paganini [You'll Have To Swing It], Part 1 (Coslow) 5:08   520626-3
10. Mr. Paganini [You'll Have To Swing It], Part 2 (Coslow)   520626-4
11. Angel Eyes (Brent-Dennis) 2:53   520626-5
12. Early Autumn (Mercer-Burns-Herman) 3:05   520626-6
13. Trying (Vaughn) 3:05   520811-1
14. The Greatest There Is (Fitzgerald-Ellington) 2:08   520811-2
15. My Bonnie (Gluckin) 2:45   520811-3
16. Ella's Contribution to the Blues (Fitzgerald-Jones) 2:25   520811-4
17. My Favorite Song (Magidson-Burke) 2:48   520919-1

18. Walking by the River Sour (Carlisle) 2:24   520819-2
19. I Can't Lie to Myself (Trace) 2:48   521130-1
20. Don't Wake Me Up (Gilbert-Wayne-Baer) 3:05   521130-2

CD: Classics (scheduled for release March 2003)

The Decca Years (1953-54)

LPD-19E THE CHRONOLOGICAL ELLA FITZGERALD, 1953–1954

1. Careless (Quadling-Howard-Jurgens) 2:44   530213-1
2. Blue Lou (Sampson-Mills) 2:45   530213-2
3. I Wondered What Kind of Guy You'd Be 3:02   530213-3
4. When the Hands of the Clock Pray at Midnight (Kurtz) 3:05   530611-1
5. Crying in the Chapel (Glenn) 2:49   530611-2
6. An Empty Ballroom (Clinton) 3:04   531223-1
7. If You Don't, I Know Who Will (Williams-Smith-Bryan) 3:10   531223-2
8. Melancholy Me (Thomas-Briggs) 2:50   531223-3
9. Moanin' Low (Dietz-Rainger) 2:34   531231-1
10. Taking a Chance on Love (Latouche-Fetter-Duke) 3:01   531231-2
11. Somebody Bad Stole de Weddin' Bell (Hilliard-Mann) 2:47   531223-4
12. I Wished on the Moon (Parker-Rainger) 3:08   540325-1
13. Baby (Huddleston-Colby) 2:44   540325-2
14. I Need (Care-Marcus) 2:40   540325-3
15. Who's Afraid? (Not I, Not I) (Lawrence-Tauber) 2:49   540325-4
16. I'm Glad There Is You (Madeira-Dorsey) 3:06   540329-1
17. Baby, What Else Could I Do? (Hirsch-Marks) 3:46   540329-2
18. What Is There to Say? (Harburg-Duke) 3:19   540329-3
19. Makin' Whoopee (Kahn-Donaldson) 3:03   540329-4
20. Until the Real Thing Comes Along (Cahn-Chaplin-Freeman-Holiner-Nichols) 3:32   540329-5
21. People Will Say We're in Love (Hammerstein-Rodgers) 3:08   540329-6
22. Please Be Kind (Cahn-Chaplin) 3:27   540330-1
23. Imagination (Burke-Van Heusen) 2:34   540330-2

CD: Classics (scheduled for release October 2004)

The Decca Years (1954–1955)

LPD-19f The Chronological Ella Fitzgerald, 1954–1955

1. My Heart Belongs to Daddy (Porter) 2:36   540330-3
2. You Leave Me Breathless (Freed-Hollander) 3:02 540330-4
3. Nice Work If You Can Get It (Gershwin-Gershwin) 2:37   540330-5
4. Star Dust (Parish-Carmichael) 3:58   540330-6
5. Lullaby of Birdland (Forster-Shearing) 2:46   540604-1
6. Later (Bradshaw-Glover) 2:28   540604-2
7. Thanks for the Memory (Robin-Rainger) 2:23 550401-1
8. It Might as Well Be Spring (Hammerstein-Rodgers) 2:35   550401-2
9. You'll Never Know (Gordon-Warren) 3:01   540401-3
10. I Can't Get Started (Gershwin-Duke) 2:59   540401-4
11. Between the Devil and the Deep Blue Sea (Koehler-Arlen) 2:10   550427-1
12. That Old Black Magic (Mercer-Arlen) 2:24 550427-2
13. Ol' Devil Moon (Harburg-Lane) 2:51   550427-3
14. Lover, Come Back to Me (Hammerstein-Romberg) 1:54   550427-4
15. Hard Hearted Hannah (Bigelow-Bates-Yellen-Ager) 2:57   550503-1
16. Pete Kelly's Blues (Cahn-Heindorf) 2:23   550503-2
17. Ella Hums the Blues (Fitzgerald-Heindorf) 5:09 550503-3
18. Soldier Boy (Williams-Jones) 3:06   550801-1
19. A Satisfied Mind (Hays-Rhodes) 2:29   550801-2
20. My One and Only Love (Mellin-Wood) 3:16 550805-1
21. The Impatient Years (Cahn-Van Heusen) 2:45 550805-2
22. But Not Like Mine (Welch) 2:55   550805-3
23. (Love Is) The Tender Trap (Cahn-Van Heusen) 2:59 550805-4

    CD: Classics (scheduled for release November 2005)

The Decca Years (1944–1949)

LPD-20 The Complete Jazz At The Philharmonic on Verve, 1944–1949

(Note: Tracks previously unissued are indicated by *)

Disc One
Trombone: J.J. Johnson; Tenor Saxophones: Illinois Jacquet, Jack McVea; Piano: Nat "King" Cole; Guitar: Les Paul; Bass: Johnny Miller; Drums: Lee Young. Recorded 2 July 1944, at Philharmonic Auditorium, Los Angeles (California)

1. Lester Leaps In (Lester Young) 9:09
2. Tea for Two (Youmans-Caesar) 12:37
3. Blues (first B-flat blues) (Etaoin-Jacquet) 10:34
4. Body and Soul (Green-Eyton-Heyman-Sour) 10:35

    Meade "Lux" Lewis (Piano). Recorded 2 July 1944, at Philharmonic Auditorium, Los Angeles (California)

5. Yancey Special (Medium Boogie) (Lewis) 3:09
6. Fast Boogie (à la Randini's Boogie) (Lewis) 1:52
7. DuPree Blues (Slow Boogie) (White-Harmon) 3:25
8. Honky Tonk Train Blues (Lewis) 2:24

    Trumpet: Shorty Sherock; Tenor Saxophones: Bumps Myers, Joe Thomas; Piano; Buddy Cole; Bass: Red Callender; Drums: Joe Marshall. Recorded 2 July 1944 at Philharmonic Auditorium, Los Angeles (California)

9. C Jam Blues (Ellington) 6:50

    Nat "King" Cole (Piano/Vocals), with Guitar: Les Paul; Bass: Johnny Miller; Drums: Lee Young. Recorded 2 July 1944 at Philharmonic Auditorium, Los Angeles (California)

10. Sweet Lorraine (Burwell-Parish) 3:14

    Trumpet: Shorty Sherock; Tenor Saxophones: Illinois Jacquet, Jack McVea; Piano: Nat "King" Cole; Basses: Red Callender, Johnny Miller; Drums: Lee Young; Vocals: Carolyn Richards (only on Track 11)

11. The Man I Love (Gershwin-Gershwin) 2:52
12. I've Found a New Baby (Palmer-Williams) 9:32

Disc Two
1. Rosetta (Hines-Woode) 6:40
2. Bugle Call Rag (Pettis-Myers-Schoebel) 4:42

    Tenor Saxophone: Illinois Jacquet; Piano: Nat "King" Cole; Bass: Red Callender; Drums: Lee Young. Recorded 30 July 1944, at Philharmonic Auditorium, Los Angeles (California)

3. One O'Clock Jump (Basie)* 2:44
4. Oh! Lady, Be Good! (Gershwin-Gershwin)* 3:04
5. Introduction by Al Jarvis, radio host 1:39

    Trumpets: Neal Hefti, Shorty Sherock; Tenor Saxophones: Corky Corcoran, Coleman Hawkins; Piano: Milt Raskin; Guitar: Dave Barbour; Bass: Charlie Mingus; Drums: Dave Coleman. Recorded 12 February 1945, at Philharmonic Auditorium, Los Angeles (California)

6. Stompin' at the Savoy (Sampson-Webb-Goodman)* 11:51
7. I've Found a New Baby (Palmer-Williams)* 7:55
8. Body and Soul (Green-Eyton-Heyman-Sour)* 4:09

    Billie Holiday (Vocals), with Trumpet: Howard McGhee; Trombone: possib. one; Alto Saxophone: Willie Smith; Tenor Saxophones: Wardell Gray, Illinois Jacquet, Charlie Ventura; Piano: prob. Mil Raskin; Guitar: prob. Dave Barbour; Bass: Charlie Mingus; Drums: Dave Coleman

9. Body and Soul (Green-Eyton-Heyman-Sour) 3:25

10. Strange Fruit (Allan-White-Holiday) 2:56

> Illinois Jacquet (Tenor Saxophone), with Trumpets: Neal Hefti, Shorty Sherock; Tenor Saxophones: Corky Corcoran and; or Charlie Ventura; Piano: Milt Raskin; Guitar: Dave Barbour; Bass: Charlie Mingus; Drums: Dave Coleman. Recorded 12 February 1945, at Philharmonic Auditorium, Los Angeles (California)

11. (I Don't Stand) A Ghost of a Chance (with You)* (Young-Crosby-Washington) 3:17

> Trumpets: Joe Guy, Howard McGhee; Alto Saxophone: Willie Smith; Tenor Saxophones: Illinois Jacquet, Charlie Ventura; Piano: Garland Finney; Guitar: Ulysses Livingston; Bass: Red Callender; Drums: Gene Krupa. Recorded 12 February 1945, at Philharmonic Auditorium, Los Angeles (California)

12. Oh! Lady, Be Good! (Gershwin-Gershwin) 11:57
13. How High the Moon (Lewis-Hamilton) 13:57
14. Announcement by Al Jarvis, radio host 0:24

DISC THREE

Slim Gaillard (Guitar, Vocals, Piano, Drums), with Bass, Piano, Vocals: Tiny "Bam" Brown. Recorded 12 February 1945, at Philharmonic Auditorium, Los Angeles (California)

1. Opera in Vout (Groove Juice Symphony) (various) 12:07

> Trumpets: Al Killian, Howard McGhee; Alto Saxophones: Charlie Parker, Willie Smith; Tenor Saxophone: Lester Young; Piano: Arnold Ross; Bass: Billy Hadnott; Drums: Lee Young. Recorded 28 January 1946, at Philharmonic Auditorium, Los Angeles (California)

2. Blues for Norman (Shrdlu) 8:39
3. Oh! Lady, Be Good! (Gershwin-Gershwin) 11:13
4. I Can't Get Started (Duke-Gershwin) 9:17
5. After You've Gone (Creamer-Layton) 7:35

> The Gene Krupa Trio. Tenor Saxophone: Charlie Ventura; Piano: Teddy Napoleon; Drums: Gene Krupa. Recorded 28 January 1946, at Philharmonic Auditorium, Los Angeles (California)

6. Stompin' at the Savoy (Samson-Webb-Goodman)* 6:59
7. Idaho (Stone) 6:29

> Trumpet: Dizzy Gillespie; Alto Saxophone: Willie Smith; Tenor Saxophones: Charlie Ventura, Lester Young; Piano: Mel Powell; Bass: Billy Hadnott; Drums: Lee Young. Recorded 28 January 1946, at Philharmonic Auditorium, Los Angeles (California)

8. Crazy Rhythm (Meyer-Kahn-Caesar) 8:41

DISC FOUR

Same, except add Trumpet: Al Killian

1. The Man I Love (Gershwin-Gershwin) 15:06
2. Sweet Georgia (Bernie-Casey-Pinkard) 9:35

> Meade "Lux" Lewis (Piano). Recorded 22 April 1946, at Embassy Auditorium, Los Angeles (California)

3. Blues de Lux (Lewis)* 3:31

4. Encore announcement by Norman Granz 0:23
5. Honky Tonk Blues (Lewis) 2:45

> Trumpet: Buck Clayton; Alto Saxophones: Charlie Parker, Willie Smith; Tenor Saxophones: Coleman Hawkins, Lester young; Piano; Kenny Kersey; Guitar: Irving Ashby; Bass: Billy Hadnott; Drums: Buddy Rich. Recorded 22 April 1946, at Embassy Auditorium, Los Angeles (California)

6. Announcement by Norman Granz 2:39
7. JATP Blues (Shrdlu) 11:00
8. I Got Rhythm (Gershwin-Gershwin) 12:58
9. I Surrender, Dear (Barris-Gordon) 10:27
10. I've Found a New Baby (Palmer-Williams) 8:13

DISC FIVE

Trumpets: Buck Clayton, Ray Linn; Alto Saxophone: Willie Smith; Tenor Saxophones: Corky Corcoran, Coleman Hawkins, Babe Russin, Young; Piano: Kenny Kersey; Guitar: prob. Irving Ashby; Bass: Billy Nadnott; Drums: Buddy Rich; Vocals: Lester Young. Recorded 22 April 1946, at Embassy Auditorium, Los Angeles

1. Bugle Call Rag (Pettis-Myers-Schoebel)*

> Trumpet: Buck Clayton; Tenor Saxophones: Coleman Hawkins, Illinois Jacquet, Lester Young; Piano: Kenny Kersey; Bass: Curly Russell; Drums: J.C. Heard. Recorded 27 May 1946, at Carnegie Hall, New York City

2. Philharmonic Blues (Carnegie Blues) 11:09
3. Oh! Lady, Be Good! (Gershwin-Gershwin) 10:46
4. I Can't Get Started (Duke-Gershwin) 9:04
5. Sweet Georgia Brown (Bernie-Casey-Pinkard) 7:47

> The Gene Krupa Trio. Tenor Saxophone: Charlie Ventura; Piano: Teddy Napoleon; Drums: Gene Krupa. Recorded 27 May 1946, at Carnegie Hall, New York City

6. The Man I Love (Gershwin-Gershwin) 9:09

> Trumpet: Buck Clayton; Tenor Saxophones: Coleman Hawkins, Lester Young; Piano: Kenny Kersey; Bass: Curly Russell; Drums: J.C. Heard. Recorded 27 May 1946, at Carnegie Hall, New York City

7. Slow Drag (Shrdlu) 9:24

> Billie Holiday, vocals, with Trumpet: Joe Guy; Alto Saxophone: Georgie Auld; Tenor Saxophones: Illinois Jacquet, Lester Young; Piano: Kenny Kersey; Guitar: prob. Tiny Grimes; Bass: Al McKibbon; Drums: J.C. Heard

8. The Man I Love (Gershwin-Gershwin) 3:05
9. Gee, Baby, Ain't I Good to You (Redman-Razaf) 2:21
10. All of Me (Simons-Marks) 2:01
11. Billie's Blues (I Love My Man) (Holiday) 3:08
12. Intermission commentary (Al Anderson) 4:34

DISC SIX

1. Opening announcement by Al Anderson, radio host 0:43

> Lester Young (Tenor Saxophone), with Trumpet: Joe Guy; Piano: Ken Kersey; Bass: Al McKibbon; Drums: J.C. Heard. Recorded 3 June 1946, at Carnegie Hall, New York City

2. Tea for Two (Youmans-Caesar) 7:42

3. Intermission announcement, radio hosts 2:11

> Coleman Hawkins (Tenor Saxophone), with Piano: Kenny Kersey; Bass: Al McKibbon; Drums: J.C. Heard. Recorded 3 June 1946, at Carnegie Hall, New York City

4. It's the Talk of the Town (Livingston-Neiburg-Symes)* 2:11

> Buck Clayton (Trumpet), with Piano: Kenny Kersey; Bass: Al McKibbon; Drums: J.C. Heard. Recorded 3 June 1946, at Carnegie Hall, New York City

5. My Honey's Lovin' Arms (Meyer-Ruby)* 3:07

> Kenny Kersey (Piano), with Bass: Al McKibbon; Drums: J.C. Heard. Recorded 3 June 1946, at Carnegie Hall, New York City

6. Boogie Woogie Cocktail (Kersey)* 3:32

> Lester Young (Tenor Saxophone), with Piano: Kenny Kersey; Bass: Rodney Richardson; Bass: Harold "Doc" West). Recorded 3 June 1946, at Carnegie Hall, New York City

7. D.B. Blues (Young)* 3:25

8. Saxobebop (Young)* 2:26

9. Lester Blows Again (Young)* 2:10

> Billie Holiday (Vocals), with Trumpet: Buck Clayton; Trombone: poss. one; Tenor Saxophones: Coleman Hawkins, Illinois Jacquet, Lester Young; Piano: Kenny Kersey; Guitar: John Collins; Bass: prob. Curly Russell; Drums: J.C. Heard. Recorded 3 June 1946, at Carnegie Hall, New York City

10. I Cried for You (Freed-Arnheim-Lyman) 2:18

11. Fine and Mellow (Holiday) 3:51

12. He's Funny That Way (Whiting-Moret) 3:17

> Trumpet: Dizzy Gillespie; Trombone: J.J. Johnson; Tenor Saxophones: Allen Eager-Illinois Jacquet; Piano: Kenny Kersey; Guitar: John Collins; Drums: J.C. Heard. Recorded 17 June 1946, at Carnegie Hall, New York City

13. Blues (second B-flat blues)*

> Trumpet: Buck Clayton; Trombone; Trummy Young; Tenor Saxophone: Lester Young; Piano: Kenny Kersey; Guitar: John Collins; Bass: Curley Russell or Rodney Richardson; Drums: J.C. Heard. Recorded 17 June 1946 at Carnegie Hall, New York City

14. Blues (Pres) 2:15

15. Just You, Just Me (Greer-Klages)* 2:18

16. I Got Rhythm (Gershwin-Gershwin) 2:14

> Slam Stewart (Bass), with Piano: Ken Kersey; Drums: J.C. Heard. Recorded 17 June 1946, at Carnegie Hall, New York City

17. My Blue Heaven (Donaldson-Whiting)* 2:18

18. Play, Fiddle, Play (Deutsch-Altman-Lawrence)* 3:24

> Illinois Jacquet (Tenor Saxophone), with Piano: Kenny Kersey; Guitar: John Collins; Bass: Rodney Richardson or Curly Russell; Drums: J.C. Heard. Recorded 17 June 1946, at Carnegie Hall, New York City

19. Flying Home (Goodman-Hampton) 3:37

> Billy Holiday (Vocals), with Trumpet: prob. Howard McGhee; Trombone: Trummy Young; Tenor Saxophone: prob. Illinois Jacquet; Piano: Kenny Kersey; Guitar: Barney Kessel; Bass: Charlie Drayton; Drums: Jackie Mills. Recorded 7 October 1946, at Shrine Auditorium, Los Anageles (California)

20. Trav'lin' Light (Mercer-Young-Mundy) 3:29

21. He's Funny That Way 2:53

> Trumpet: Buck Clayton; Trombone: Trummy Young; Alto Saxophone: Willie Smith; Tenor Saxophones: Coleman Hawkins, Flip Phillips; Piano: Kenny Kersey; Bass: Benny Fonville; Drums: Buddy Rich. Recorded 5 March 1947, at Syria Mosque, Pittsburgh (Pennsylvania)

22. How High the Moon (Lewis-Hamilton) 10:12

DISC SEVEN

> Trumpet: Buck Clayton; Trombone: Trummy Young; Alto Saxophone: Willie Smith; Tenor Saxophone: Flip Phillips; Piano: Kenny Kersey; Bass: Benny Fonville; Drums: Buddy Rich Recorded 5 March 1947, at Syria Mosque, Pittsburgh (Pennsylvania)

1. Bell Boy Blues

> Kenny Kersey (Piano), with Bass: Benny Fonville; Drums: Buddy Rich. Recorded 5 March 1947, prob. at Syria Mosque, Pittsburgh (Pennsylvania)

2. Boogie Woogie Cocktail (JATP Boogie) (Kersey) 3:06

3. Sweet Lorraine (Burwell-Parish) 2:28

> Trumpet: Roy Eldridge; Alto Saxophones: Pete Brown, Willie Smith; Tenor Saxophone: Flip Phillips; Guitar: Les Paul; Piano: Hank Jones; Bass: Benny Fonville; Drums: Alvin Stoller Recorded 24 May 1947, at Carnegie Hall, New York City

4. Blues (third B-flat blues)* 16:56

5. Announcement by Norman Granz 0:19

> Billie Holiday (Vocals), with Piano: Bobby Tucker. Recorded 24 May 1947, at Carnegie Hall, New York City

6. You'd Better Go Now (Graham-Reichner) 2:57

7. You're Driving Me Crazy (Donaldson) 1:32

8. There Is No Greater Love (Jones-Symes) 2:33

9. I Cover the Waterfront (Green-Heyman) 2:40

10. Announcement by Norman Granz 0:49

> Trumpet: Howard McGhee; Trombone; Bill Harris; Tenor Saxophones: Illinois Jacquet, Flip Phillips; Piano: Hank Jones; Bass: Ray Brown; Drums: Jo Jones. Recorded 27 September 1947, at Carnegie Hall, New York City

11. Perdido (Tizol) 16:12

12. Mordido (Shrdlu) 17:54

DISC EIGHT

1. I Surrender, Dear (Barris-Clifford) 10:30

2. Endido (Etaoin) 14:37

> Trumpet: Roy Eldridge; Trombone: Tommy Turk; Alto Saxophone: Charlie Parker; Tenor Saxophones: Flip Phillips, Lester Young; Piano: Hank Jones; Bass: Ray Brown; Drums:

Buddy Rich. Recorded 18 September 1949, at Carnegie Hall, New York City

3. Introduction by Norman Granz 0:19
4. The Opener (Shrdlu) 12:48
5. Lester Leaps In (Young) 12:16
6. Embraceable You (Gershwin-Gershwin) 10:35
7. The Closer (Etaoin) 10:43
8. Norman Granz introduction of Ella Fitzgerald 0:21

> Ella Fitzgerald (Vocals), with Piano: Hank Jones; Bass: Ray Brown; Drums: Buddy Rich Recorded 18 September 1949, at Carnegie Hall, New York City

9. Robbins' Nest (Jacquet-Thompson-Russell) 2:23 490918-1
10. A New Shade of Blue (Ackers-Farrow-Poll)* 2:53 490918-2

DISC NINE

1. Old Mother Hubbard (Tobias-Polla)* 2:56 490918-3
2. I'm Just a Lucky So-and-So (Ellington-David) 2:51 490918-4
3. Somebody Loves Me (Gershwin-DeSylva-MacDonald) 1:59 490918-5
4. Basin Street Blues (Williams) 3:09 490918-6

> Ella Fitzgerald (Vocals), with Trumpet: Roy Eldridge; Trombone: Tommy Turk; Alto Saxophone: Charlie Parker; Tenor Saxophones: Flip Phillips, Lester Young; Piano: Hank Jones; Bass: Ray Brown; Drums: Buddy Rich. Recorded 18 September 1949, at Carnegie Hall, New York City

5. Ow! (Gillespie) 0:30
6. Norman Granz announcement 0:09
7. Flying Home (Goodman-Hampton) 5:33 490918-7
8. Introduction by Norman Granz 0:47

> Oscar Peterson (Piano), with Bass: Ray Brown

9. Fine and Dandy (Swift-James) 3:50
10. I Only Have Eyes for You (Warren-Dubin) 7:09
11. Announcement by Norman Granz 0:35
12. Carnegie Blues (Peterson) 8:11

> Coleman Hawkins (Tenor Saxophone), with Piano: Hank Jones; Bass: Ray Brown; Drums: Buddy Rich Recorded 18 September 1949, at Carnegie Hall, New York City

13. Introduction by Norman Granz 0:56
14. Body and Soul (Green-Eyton-Heyman-Sour) 3:13
15. Rifftide (Hawkins) 4:25
16. The Big Head (Hawkins)* 4:27
17. Stuffy (Hawkins)* 6:27
18. Applause and chatter 0:56
19. Sophisticated Lady (Ellington)* 3:50
20. Introduction by Norman Granz 0:16

> Hank Jones (Piano), with Bass: Ray Brown; Drums: Buddy Rich. Recorded 18 September 1949, at Carnegie Hall, New York City

21. Ol' Man River (Kern-Hammerstein)* 4:57

22. Air Mail Special (Christian-Goodman-Mundy)* 4:42
23. Norman Granz introduction of Ella Fitzgerald 0:28

> Ella Fitzgerald (Vocals), with Piano: Hank Jones; Bass: Ray Brown; Drums: Buddy Rich Recorded 18 September 1949, at Carnegie Hall, New York City

24. Oh! Lady, Be Good! (Gershwin-Gershwin)* 2:51 490918-8
25. Black Coffee (Burke-Webster) 3:42 490918-9

DISC TEN

1. A-Tisket, A-Tasket (Fitzgerald-Feldman)* 2:26 490918-10
2. Norman Granz announcement 0:22

> Ella Fitzgerald (Vocals), with Trumpet: Roy Eldridge; Trombone: Tommy Turk; Alto Saxophone: Charlie Parker; Tenor Saxophones: Flip Phillips, Lester Young; Piano: Hank Jones; Bass: Ray Brown; Drums: Buddy Rich

3. How High the Moon (Lewis-Hamilton) 5:43 490918-11
4. Norman Granz announcement 0:31
5. Perdido (Tizol) 8:25 490918-12
6. Norman Granz announcement 0:11
7. Norman Granz introduction of Gene Krupa 0:53

> The Gene Krupa Trio. Tenor Saxophone: Charlie Ventura; Piano: Teddy Napoleon; Drums: Gene Krupa. Recorded March 1952

8. Stompin' at the Savoy (Sampson-Webb-Goodman) 7:40
9. Body and Soul (Green-Eyton-Heyman-Sour) 9:35
10. Dark Eyes 7:59

> Trombone: Bill Harris; Tenor Saxophone: Charlie Ventura; Piano: Ralph Burns; Guitar: Bill De Arango; Bass: Curly Russell; Drums: Dave Tough. Recorded 5 March 1947, at Carnegie Hall, New York City

11. Characteristically B.H. (Harris) 4:28

> Charlie Shavers (Trumpet), with Piano: Hank Jones; Bass: Curly Russell; Drums: Sid Catlett. Recorded 5 April 1947, at Carnegie Hall, New York City

12. Summertime (Gershwin-Gershwin) 5:03
13. Sid Flips His Lid (Jones) 7:39

> Trumpet: Charlie Shavers; Trombone: Bill Harris; Tenor Saxophone: Charlie Ventura; Piano: Ralph Burns; Guitar Bill De Arango; Bass: Curly Russell; Drums: Sid Catlett Recorded 5 April 1947, at Carnegie Hall, New York City

14. Medley: Lover, Come Back to Me (Romberg-Hammerstein); (I Don't Stand) A Ghost of a Chance (with You) (Young-Crosby-Washington) Just You, Just Me (Greer-Klages) 18:21

CD: Verve 314 523 893 (10 discs) (released October 1998). Playing times: Disc 1, 76:36; Disc 2, 79:00; Disc 3, 71:13; Disc 4, 76:47; Disc 5, 78:35; Disc 6, 77:51; Disc 7, 74:04; Disc 8, 77:40; Disc 9, 78:56; Disc 10, 79:21; Total playing time, 12:50:03

All concerts produced by **Norman Granz**. CD production supervised by **Michael Lang** and **Ben Young.** A 223-page softcover book with many photographs, reproductions of posters, and many other features, accompanies this set, containing: Track List/A Note on the Contents; An Introduction to JATP, by **John McDonough;** Interview with Norman Granz, by **Nat Hentoff;** Growing Up with JATP, by **Keith Shadwick;** Anatomy of a Jam, by **Bill Kirchner;** Biographies of the Musicians, by **Randy Hutton;** A History of JATP on Record, by **John Clement;** JATP Discography/Song Index/Personnel Index

The Decca Years (1950)

LPD-21 ELLA SINGS GERSHWIN/ ELLA FITZGERALD WITH ELLIS LARKINS AT THE PIANO

Pure Ella

1. Someone to Watch over Me (Gershwin-Gershwin) 3:13   500912-3
2. My One and Only (Gershwin-Gershwin) 3:13 500911-2
3. But Not for Me (Gershwin-Gershwin) 3:12 500912-1
4. Looking for a Boy (Gershwin-Gershwin) 3:06 500911-1
5. I've Got a Crush on You (Gershwin-Gershwin) 3:13 500911-4
6. How Long Has This Been Going On? (Gershwin-Gershwin) 3:14   500911-3
7. Maybe (Gershwin-Gershwin) 3:24   500912-4
8. Soon (Gershwin-Gershwin) 2:44   500912-2

LP: Decca DL 5300 (10") (Released 1951). Side One, Tracks 1–4 (12:56); Side Two, Tracks 5–8 (12:47). CD: **Pure Ella**, Tracks 1–8 (GRP Decca Jazz GRD-636) (Released February 1994). Total playing time: 25:43. Original sessions and LP produced by **Milt Gabler**; CD issue produced by **Orrin Keepnews**; The original LP liner notes are uncredited.

The Decca Years (1938–1951)

LPD-22 ELLA AND HER FELLAS

1. You Won't Be Satisfied (James-Stock)[1] 2:45   460118-1
2. That's the Way It Is (Whitney-Kramer)[2] 3:11 450226-2
3. Stone Cold Dead in de Market (Houdini)[3] 2:45 451008-1

4. I Gotta Have My Baby Back (Tilman)[4] 3:17   491107-2
5. Sentimental Journey (Green-Brown-Homer)[5] 3:16 470124-2
6. The Frim Fram Sauce (Ricardel-Evans)[1] 3:06 460118-2
7. (It's Only a) Paper Moon (Arlen-Rose-Harburg)[6] 2:32   450327-1
8. Dream a Little Dream of Me (Schwandt-André-Kahn)[1] 2:58   500825-1
9. Baby, It's Cold Outside (Loesser)[3] 2:37   490428-5
10. A-Tisket, A-Tasket (Fitzgerald-Alexander)[7] 2:35 380502-1
11. Would You Like to Take a Walk? (Warren-Dixon-Rose)[1] 3:10   511123-3
12. Don'tcha Go 'Way Mad (Mundy-Stillman)[8] 3:13 500202-2

[1] *with Louis Armstrong*
[2] *with The Ink Spots*
[3] *with Louis Jordan*
[4] *with The Mills Brothers*
[5] *with Eddie Heywood and His Orchestra*
[6] *with The Delta Rhythm Boys*
[7] *with Members of the Chick Webb Orchestra*
[8] *with Sy Oliver and His Orchestra*

LP: Decca DL 8477 (released 15 June 57). Side 1, Tracks 1–6 (18:45)/Side 2, Tracks 7–12 (17:30). Total playing time: 36:15. Produced by **Milt Gabler**/Liner notes by **Vic Bellerby**

The Decca Years (1946–1952)

LPD-23 ELLA FITZGERALD/ FOR SENTIMENTAL REASONS...

1. (I Love You) For Sentimental Reasons (Best-Watson) 3:10   460829-1
2. Guilty (Kahn-Akst-Whiting) 3:11   470124-1
3. It's Too Soon to Know (Chessler) 2:32   480820-1
4. Baby Doll (Mercer-Warren) 3:14   511226-1
5. Mixed Emotions (Louchheim) 3:14   510626-1
6. That Old Feeling (Brown-Fain) 2:25   471218-2
7. I'm Confessin' (That I Love You) (Dougherty-Reynolds-Neiburg) 3:21   441106-2
8. A Sunday Kind of Love (Belle-Prima-Leonard-Rhodes) 3:20   470319-1
9. There Never Was a Baby (Like My Baby) (Styne-Comden-Green) 2:47   510718-3
10. Walking by the River (Carlisle-Sour) 2:24   520811-3
11. Because of Rain (Poll-Cole-Harrington) 3:07 510327-3
12. Don't You Think I Ought to Know? (Johnson-Wettergreen) 3:06   470722-1

LP: Decca DL 8832 (released 7 February 1959). Side One, Tracks 1–6 (18:01)/Side Two, Tracks 7–12 (18:30). Total playing time: 36:31. Produced by **Milt Gabler**. Liner notes by **Ira Gitler**.

The Decca Years (1945–1953)

LPD-24 Ella Fitzgerald/ That's My Desire

1. There Never Was a Baby (Like My Baby) (Styne-Comden-Green) 2:46   510718-3
2. Dream a Little Longer (Kahn-Kahn) 2:58   490921-2
3. Walking by the River (Carlisle-Sour) 2:24   520811-3
4. (I Love You) For Sentimental Reasons (Best-Wilson) 3:08   460829-1
5. I Hadn't Anyone Till You (Noble) 2:57   490921-1
6. Happy Talk (Rodgers-Hammerstein) 2:25   490428-1
7. Because of Rain (Poll-Cole-Harrington) 3:07   510327-3
8. Mixed Emotions (Louchheim) 3:15   510626-1
9. I'm Gonna Wash That Man Right Outa My Hair (Hammerstein-Rodgers) 2:52   490428-2
10. Guilty (Kahn-akst-Whiting) 3:09   470124-1
11. Give a Little, Get a Little (Styne-Comden-Green) 3:16   510718-4
12. Careless (Quadling-Howard-Jurgens) 2:44   530213-1
13. A Sunday Kind of Love (Belle-Leonard-Rhodes-Prima) 3:18   470319-1
14. Foolish Tears (Carson) 2:56   490921-3
15. That's the Way It Is (Whitney-Kramer) 3:12   450226-2
16. Gee, but I'm Glad to Know (You Love Me) (Roberts-Allen) 3:04   520225-3
17. Crying (Chernis-Ross) 3:06   490720-1
18. That's My Desire (Kresa-Rhodes) 2:58   470319-2
19. In the Evening When the Sun Goes Down (Carr-Raye) 2:37   490920-1
20. The Hot Canary (Nero-Gilbert) 3:13   510327-4

CD: Blue Moon BMCD 3012 (released October 1994). Total playing time: 60:22. Produced by Blue Moon Producciones Discográficas, Barcelona, Spain. Liner notes by **Dom Messina**.

The Decca Years (1953)

LPD-25 Jazz At The Philharmonic in Tokyo/Live at the Nichigeki Theatre, 1953

Jazz At The Philharmonic All-Stars

1. Tokyo Blues (Eldridge-Carter-Phillips-Peterson-Ellis-Brown-Heard) 22:20
2. Cotton Tail (Ellington) 12:45
3. Ballad Medley: The Nearness of You (Carmichael-Washington) 2:15; Someone to Watch Over Me (Gershwin-Gershwin) 2:04; Flamingo (Grouya-Anderson) 2:26; I Surrender, Dear (Barris-Clifford) 2:08; Sweet and Lovely (Arnheim-Tobias-Lemare) 2:17; Star Dust (Carmichael-Parish) 2:10; Embraceable You (Gershwin-Gershwin) 2:35

The Oscar Peterson Trio

4. That Old Black Magic (Arlen-Mercer) 4:40
5. Tenderly (Gross-Lawrence) 4:54
6. Up (Eldridger-Carter-Phillips-Heard) 5:13
7. Sushi Blues (Peterson) 4:04
8. Alone Together (Schwartz-Dietz) 5:39
9. Swingin' Till the Girls Come Home (Pettiford) 6:34

The Gene Krupa Trio

10. Indiana (MacDonald-Hanley) 4:45
11. Cocktails for Two (Coslow-Johnston) 3:42
12. Don't Be That Way (Goodman-Sampson-Parish) 5:37
13. Stompin' at the Savoy (Goodman-Webb-Sampson-Razaf) 4:30

Ella Fitzgerald and Her Quartet

14. On the Sunny Side of the Street (McHugh-Fields) 1:55   531118-1
15. Body and Soul (Heyman-Sour-Eyton-Green) 4:10   531118-2
16. Why Don't You Do Right? (McCoy) 3:16   531118-3
17. Oh! Lady, Be Good! (Gershwin-Gershwin) 2:56   531118-4
18. I Got It Bad (and That Ain't Good) (Ellington-Webster) 3:12   531118-5
19. How High the Moon (Hamilton-Lewis) 3:10   531118-6
20. My Funny Valentine (Rodgers-Hart) 2:50   531118-7
21. Smooth Sailing (Cobb) 2:52   531118-8
22. The Frim Fram Sauce (Evans-Riciardello) 3:10   531118-9

Ella Fitzgerald with Jazz At The Philharmonic All-Stars

23. Perdido (Tizol-Lengsfelder-Drake) 6:15   531118-10

LP: Pablo Live 2620-104-2 (4 discs) (released August 1975). Disc 1, Tracks 1-2 (35:04)/Disc 2, Tracks 3–6 (31:05).

Disc 3, Tracks 7-13 (35:11/Disc 4, Tracks 14–23 (33:58). CD: Pablo Live PACD 2620-104-2 (2 discs) (released 1990). Disc 1, Tracks 1-6 (66:09)/Disc 2, Tracks 7–23 (69:09). Total playing time: 2:15:18. The concert and these recordings were produced by **Norman Granz.** Liner notes by **Alun Morgan.**

The Decca Years (1940–1953)

LPD-26 EARLY ELLA/GREAT BALLADS BY ELLA FITZGERALD

1. Mixed Emotions (Louchheim) 3:14   510626-1
2. It's Too Soon to Know (Chessler) 2:32   480820-1
3. Baby Doll (Mercer-Warren) 3:14   511226-1
4. Walking by the River (Carlisle-Sour) 2:24   520811-3
5. Melancholy Me (Thomas-Biggs) 2:50   531223-3
6. Someone Like You (Warren-Blane) 3:05   490114-3
7. I Hadn't Anyone Till You (Noble) 2:59   490921-1
8. Do You Really Love Me? (Rinker-Dant) 3:08   510524-2
9. So Long (Morgan-Harris-Melsher) 3:01   400925-2
10. Gee, But I'm Glad to Know That You Love Me (Roberts-Allen) 3:08   520225-3
11. Even As You and I (Johnson-Larkin) 3:26   510524-1
12. Crying (Chernis-Ross) 3:05   490720-1

    LP: Decca DL 4447 (mono)/Decca DL 74447 (stereo) (released 1962). Side One, Tracks 1-6 (17:44)/Side Two, Tracks 7–12 (19:12). Total playing time, 36:56. Produced by **Milt Gabler.** Liner notes by **Stanley Dance.**

The Decca Years (1949–1954)

LPD-27 MISS ELLA FITZGERALD AND MR. GORDON JENKINS INVITE YOU TO LISTEN AND RELAX

1. I Wished on the Moon (Parker-Rainger) 3:08   540325-1
2. Baby (Colby-Huddleston) 2:44   540325-2
3. I Hadn't Anyone Till You (Noble) 2:57   490921-1
4. A Man Wrote a Song (Franklin) 3:04   490921-4
5. Who's Afraid? (Not I, Not I) (Lawrence-Tauber) 2:49   540325-4
6. Happy Talk (Hammerstein-Rodgers) 2:26   490428-1
7. Black Coffee (Webster-Burke) 3:03   490428-3
8. Lover's Gold (Merrill-Nevins) 3:07   490428-4
9. I'm Gonna Wash That Man Right Outa My Hair (Hammerstein-Rodgers) 2:54   490428-2
10. Dream a Little Longer (Kahn-Kahn) 3:01   490921-2
11. I Need (Care-Marcus) 2:40   540325-3
12. Foolish Tears (Carson) 2:56   490921-3

    LP: Decca DL 8696 (released 28 April 1958). Side One, Tracks 1-6 (17:33)/Side Two, Tracks 7–12 (18:06). Vocalion 3797 (mono)/Vocalion 73797 (stereo)/Vocalion 73797E. All with titles, contents, and sequences as Decca LP. CD: MCA (Japan) MCVJ-19222 (released 1999). Total playing time, 35:39. (Contents, sequence and total playing time, same as above). Produced by **Milt Gabler.** The liner notes are uncredited.

The Decca Years (1949–1954)

LPD-28 ELLA FITZGERALD THE LAST DECCA YEARS, 1949–1954

1. In the Evening (When the Sun Goes Down) (Raye-Carr) 2:37   490920-1
2. Basin Street Blues (Williams) 3:06   490920-4
3. Solid as a Rock (Hilliard-Mann) 2:57   500306-1
4. I've Got the World on a String (Koehler-Arlen) 3:16   500306-2
5. Dream a Little Dream of Me (Kahn-Schwandt-Andrée) 3:04   500825-1
6. Can Anyone Explain? (Weiss-Benjamin) 3:10   500825-2
7. Because of Rain (Poll-Harrington-Cole) 3:09   510327-3
8. I Don't Want to Take a Chance (Fitzgerald) 3:14   510718-2
9. There Never Was a Baby Like My Baby (Comden-Green-Styne) 2:47   510718-3
10. Give a Little, Get a Little (Love) (Comden-Green-Styne) 3:19   510718-4
11. A Guy Is a Guy (Brand) 2:52   520225-1
12. Goody Goody (Mercer-Malneck) 2:23   520225-4
13. Mr. Paganini [You'll Have To Swing It] (Parts 1 & 2) (Coslow) 5:08   520626-3/4
14. Early Autumn (Mercer-Burns-Herman) 3:13   520626-6
15. Angel Eyes (Brent-Dennis) 2:56   520626-5
16. Preview (Quinichette) 3:02   520626-1
17. Careless (Quadling-Howard-Jurgens) 2:49   530213-1
18. Blue Lou (Sampson-Mills) 2:46   530213-2
19. Melancholy Me (Thomas-Briggs) 2:52   531223-3
20. Lullaby of Birdland (Forster-Shearing) 2:50   )   540604-1

    CD: GRP Decca Jazz GRD 668 (released March, 1999). Total playing time, 62:43. Original sessions produced by **Milt Gabler**. Reissue produced by **Orrin Keepnewws**. Liner notes by **Mark Edding**.

The Decca Years (1954)

LPD-29 ELLA FITZGERALD/ SONGS IN A MELLOW MOOD

Pure Ella

1. I'm Glad There Is You (Madeira-Dorsey) 3:06 540329-1
2. What Is There to Say? (Duke-Harburg) 3:19 540329-3
3. People Will Say We're in Love (Rodgers-Hammerstein) 3:08 540329-6
4. Please Be Kind (Cahn-Chaplin) 3:27 540330-1
5. Until the Real Thing Comes Along (Cahn-Chaplin-Freeman-Holiner-Nichols) 3:32 540329-5
6. Makin' Whoopee! (Donaldson-Kahn) 3:03 540329-4
7. Imagination (Van Heusen-Burke) 2:34 540330-2
8. Star Dust (Carmichael-Parish) 3:58 540330-6
9. My Heart Belongs to Daddy (Porter) 2:36 540330-3
10. You Leave Me Breathless (Hollander-Freed) 3:02 540330-4
11. (Baby,) What Else Can I Do? (Marks-Hirsch 3:46 540329-2
12. Nice Work If You Can Get It (Gershwin-Gershwin) 2:37 540330-5

LP: Decca DL 8068 (released 1954). Side One, Tracks 1-6 (19:14)/Side Two, Tracks 7-12 (18:50). CD: **Pure Ella**, Tracks 9-20 (GRP Decca Jazz GRD-636) (released February 1994).* Total playing time: 38:14. Produced by **Milt Gabler**. The original LP liner notes are uncredited. The reissue CD produced by **Orrin Keepnews**, with liner notes by **James Gavin**.

The Decca Years (1946–1954)

LPD-30 ELLA SINGS GERSHWIN (WITH AN ASSIST BY DUKE ELLINGTON AND JIMMY MCHUGH)

1. Someone to Watch over Me (Gershwin-Gershwin) 3:13 500912-3
2. My One and Only (Gershwin-Gershwin) 3:13 500911-2
3. But Not for Me (Gershwin-Gershwin) 3:12 500912-1
4. Looking for a Boy (Gershwin-Gershwin) 3:06 500911-1
5. Nice Work if You Can Get It (Gershwin-Gershwin) 2:37 540330-5
6. Oh! Lady, Be Good! (Gershwin-Gershwin) 3:13 470319-3
7. I've Got a Crush on You (Gershwin-Gershwin) 3:13 500911-4
8. How Long Has This Been Going On? (Gershwin-Gershwin) 3:14 500911-3
9. Maybe (Gershwin-Gershwin) 3:24 500912-4
10. Soon (Gershwin-Gershwin) 2:44 500912-2
11. I'm Just a Lucky So-and-So (David-Ellington) 2:46 460221-1
12. I Didn't Mean a Word I Said (Adamson-McHugh) 3:16 460221-2

LP: Decca DL4451 (mono)/Decca DL74451 (stereo) (released 12 August 1954). Side 1, Tracks 1-6 (18:59)/Side 2, Tracks 7–12 (19:02). Decca DL 8378 (stereo), same as above (released 12 November 1956). MCA 215E (stereo), same as above (released 1983). Total playing time: 38:01. Produced by **Milt Gabler**. Liner notes by **Tony Barton**.

The Decca Years (1949–1954)

LPD-31 JAZZ AT THE PHILHARMONIC/ THE ELLA FITZGERALD SET

1. A Foggy Day (in London Town) (Gershwin-Gershwin) 2:33 540917-1
2. Bill (Wodehouse-Kern) 2:48 530911-2
3. The Man That Got Away (Gershwin-Arlen) 4:30 540917-3
4. Hernando's Hideaway (Adler-Ross) 3:11 540917-4
5. Why Don't You Do Right? (McCoy) 3:07 530911-8
6. Later (Bradshaw-Glover) 2:22 540917-5
7. Robbins' Nest (Thompson-Jacquet) 2:27 490918-1
8. Black Coffee (Webster-Burke) 3:32 490918-9
9. I'm Just a Lucky So-and-So (David-Ellington) 2:42 490918-4
10. Somebody Loves Me (DeSylva-MacDonald-Gershwin) 1:47 490918-5
11. Basin Street Blues (Williams) 3:02 490918-6
12. Flying Home (Robin-Hampton-Goodman) 5:10 490918-7

LP: Verve 815 147 (released 1983). Side A, Tracks 1-6 (18:56)/Side B, Tracks 7-12 (19:05). Total Playing Time: (38:01). Jazz At The Philharmonic concerts and recordings produced under the personal supervision of **Norman Granz**. Liner notes by **Bob Porter**.

The Decca Years (1945-1955)

LPD-32 THE BEST OF ELLA, VOLUME II

1. It Might As Well Be Spring (Rodgers-Hammerstein) 2:35   550401-3
2. I Can't Get Started (Duke-Gershwin) 3:02 550401-4
3. Blue Lou (Sampson-Mills) 2:43   530213-2
4. Lullaby of Birdland (Shearing-Forster) 2:46 540604-1
5. Stone Cold Dead in de Market (Houdini) 2:40 451008-1
6. Goody Goody (Mercer-Malneck) 2:23   520225-4
7. You Turned the Tables on Me (Alter-Mitchell) 2:55 471223-2
8. That's My Desire (Kresa-Loveday) 2:59   470319-2
9. Guilty (Kahn-Akst-Whiting) 3:11   470124-1
10. That Old Feeling (Brown-Fain) 2:25   471218-2
11. A Kiss Goodnight (Slack-Victor-Herman) 3:06 450829-1
12. A Sunday Kind of Love (Belle-Prima-Leonard-Rhodes) 3:20   470319-1
13. Sentimental Journey (Green-Brown-Homer) 3:16 470124-2
14. There Never Was a Baby (Like My Baby) (Styne-Comden-Green) 2:47   510718-3
15. Careless (Quadling-Howard-Jurgens) 2:45 530213-1
16. Angel Eyes (Dennis-Brent) 2:53   520626-4
17. Cow Cow Boogie [Cuma-Ti-Yi-Yi-Ay] (Raye-De Paul-Carter) 3:03   431103-1
18. Taking a Chance on Love (Duke-Latouche-Fetter) 3:05   531231-2
19. You Don't Know What Love Is (Raye-De Paul) 3:26 411028-2
20. Baby Doll (Mercer-Warren) 3:14   511226-1

LP: MCA 2-4016 (2 discs) (mono); MCA2-4016E (stereo) (released 24 September 1973). Disc 1, Side 1, Tracks 1-5 (13:26)/Disc 1, Side 2, Tracks 6-10 (14:13). Disc 2, Side 1, Tracks 11-15 (15:34)/Disc 2, Side 2, Tracks 16–20 (16:01). Total playing time, 59:14. 8-Track Tape: MCA T2-4016 (2 tapes) Contents and sequence, same as LP issue. CT: MCAC 2-4016E (2 cassettes) Contents and sequence, same as LP issue. Original sessions produced by **Milt Gabler**

The Decca Years (1953–1955)

LPD-33 ELLA FITZGERALD/MEMORIES

1. Thanks for the Memory (Robin-Rainger) 2:23 550401-2

2. You'll Never Know (Warren-Gordon) 3:01 550401-1
3. Moanin' Low (Rainger-Dietz) 2:34   531231-1
4. Ol' Devil Moon (Lane-Harburg) 2:51   550427-2
5. Between the Devil and the Deep Blue Sea(Arlen-Koehler) 2:10   550427-4
6. Please Be Kind (Cahn-Chaplin) 3:27   540330-1
7. Makin' Whoopee! (Donaldson-Kahn) 2:56 540329-4
8. Star Dust (Carmichael-Parish) 3:48   540330-6
9. You Leave Me Breathless (Hollander-Freed) 2:55 540330-4
10. (Baby) What Else Can I Do? (Marks-Hirsch) 3:37 540329-2

LP: MCA 734E (stereo) (released 1973). Side 1, Tracks 1-5 (13:19)/Side 2, Tracks 6-10 (17:08). Total playing time: 30:27. Original sessions produced by **Milt Gabler.**

The Decca Years (1953-1955)

LPD-34 ELLA FITZGERALD/ SWEET AND HOT

1. Thanks for the Memory (Robin-Rainger) 2:23 550401-2
2. It Might as Well Be Spring (Rodgers-Hammerstein) 2:35   550401-3
3. You'll Never Know (Warren-Gordon) 3:01 550401-1
4. I Can't Get Started (Duke-Gershwin) 2:59 550401-4
5. Moanin' Low (Rainger-Dietz) 2:34   531231-1
6. Taking a Chance on Love (Duke-Latouche-Fetter) 3:01   531231-2
7. That Old Black Magic (Arlen-Mercer) 2:24 550427-1
8. Ol' Devil Moon (Lane-Harburg) 2:51   550427-2
9. Lover, Come Back to Me (Romberg-Hammerstein) 1:54   550427-3
10. Between the Devil and the Deep Blue Sea (Arlen-Koehler) 2:10   550427-4
11. Mr. Paganini [You'll Have To Swing It] (Coslow) 5:01   520626-2/3

LP: Decca DL 8155 (released 7 November 1955). Side 1, Tracks 1–6 (16:53)/Side 2, Tracks 7–11 (14:35). CD: MCA, Universal MCLD 19365 (**Lullabies of Birdland & Sweet and Hot**). Tracks 12-22 (released March 1998). Total playing time: 31:28. Produced by **Milt Gabler**. The original LP liner notes are uncredited.

The Decca Years (1939–1955)

LPD-35 ELLA FITZGERALD/
GOLDEN FAVORITES

1. Goody Goody (Mercer-Malneck) 2:23   520225-4
2. Stairway to the Stars (Parish-Malneck-Signorelli) 3:14   390629-2
3. Angel Eyes (Dennis-Brent) 2:53   520626-4
4. Ol' Devil Moon (Lane-Harburg) 2:51   550427-2
5. Takin' a Chance on Love (Duke-Latouche-Fetter) 3:05   531231-2
6. Cow Cow Boogie (Cuma-Ti-Yi-Yi-Ay) (Raye-De Paul-Carter) 3:03   431103-1
7. Lover, Come Back to Me (Hammerstein-Romberg) 1:54   550427-3
8. A Sunday Kind of Love (Belle-Prima-Leonard-Rhodes) 3:20   470319-1
9. A-Tisket, A-Tasket (Fitzgerald-Alexander) 2:35   380502-1
10. My Happiness (Peterson-Bergantine) 3:16   480430-1
11. Stone Cold Dead in de Market (Houdini) 2:40   451008-1
12. I Got It Bad (and That Ain't Good) (Webster-Ellington) 2:54   410731-4

LP: Decca DL 4129 (released 13 March 1961). Side One, Tracks 1–6 (17:54)/Side Two, Tracks 7–12 (17:04). Total playing time: 34:58. Original sessions produced by **Milt Gabler**. The liner notes are uncredited.

The Decca Years (1945-1955)

LPD-36 ELLA FITZGERALD/
LULLABIES OF BIRDLAND

1. Lullaby of Birdland (Shearing-Forster) 2:46   540604-1
2. Rough Ridin' (Fitzgerald-Jones) 3:10   520104-2
3. Angel Eyes (Dennis-Brent) 2:53   520626-4
4. Smooth Sailing (Cobb) 3:04   510626-2
5. Oh! Lady, Be Good! (Gershwin-Gershwin) 3:06   470319-3
6. Later (Bradshaw-Glover) 2:28   540604-2
7. Ella Hums the Blues (Fitzgerald-Heindorf) 5:05   550503-2
8. How High the Moon (Lewis-Hamilton) 3:14   471220-4
9. Basin Street Blues (Williams) 3:04   490920-4
10. Air Mail Special (Goodman-Mundy-Christian) 3:00   520104-1
11. Flying Home (Goodman-Hamilton-Robin) 2:27   451004-1

LP: Decca DL 8149 (Released 6 January 1956). Side 1, Tracks 1-6 (17:52)/Side 2, Tracks 7-11 (17:10). CD: MCA/Universal MCLD 19365 (**Lullabies of Birdland & Sweet and Hot**). Tracks 1-11 (released March 1998). Total playing time: 35:02. Produced by **Milt Gabler**. Liner notes by **Ken Barnes.**

The Decca Years (1945-1955)

LPD-37 ELLA FITZGERALD/
SMOOTH SAILING

1. Smooth Sailing (Cobb) 3:04   510626-2
2. Basin Street Blues (Williams) 3:04   490920-4
3. Preview (Quinichette) 3:02   520626-6
4. Oh! Lady, Be Good! (Gershwin-Gershwin) 3:06   470319-3
5. Rough Ridin' (Fitzgerald-Jones) 3:10   520104-2
6. How High the Moon (Lewis-Hamilton) 3:14   471220-4
7. Lullaby of Birdland (Shearing-Forster) 2:46   540604-1
8. Flying Home (Gooman-Hampton-Robin) 2:53   451004-1
9. Angel Eyes (Dennis Brent) 2:53   520626-4
10. Air Mail Special (Goodman-Mundy-Christian) 3:00   520104-1
11. Ella Hums the Blues (Heindorf) 5:05   550503-3
12. Later (Bradshaw-Glover) 2:28   540604-2

LP: Decca DL4887 (mono)/Decca DL74887 (stereo) (released 16 October 1967). Side One, Tracks 1–6 (19:05)/Side Two, Tracks 7–12 (19:30). Total playing time 38:35. Original sessions produced by **Milt Gabler**. Note: This album contains the same material as **Lullabies of Birdland** (Decca DL 8149), except that it has an additional track, "Preview."

The Decca Years (1955)

LPD-38 *PETE KELLY'S BLUES*/
PEGGY LEE AND ELLA FITZGERALD

Vocals by Peggy Lee

1. Oh, Didn't He Ramble (Handy) 2:14
2. Sugar (That Sugar Baby of Mine) (Pinkard-Mitchell-Alexander) 2:33
3. Somebody Loves Me (Gershwin-DeSylva-MacDonald) 3:25
4. I'm Gonna Meet My Sweetie Now (Davis-Greer) 2:13

5. I Never Knew (Kahn-Fiorito) 2:56

6. Bye, Bye, Blackbird (Dixon-Henderson) 3:37

7. What Can I Say After I Say I'm Sorry (Donaldson-Lyman) 2:07

Vocals by Ella Fitzgerald

8. Hard Hearted Hannah (Yellen-Ager-Bigelow-Bates) 2:57   550503-1

9. Ella Hums the Blues (Heindorf) 5:09   550503-3

Vocals by Peggy Lee

10. He Needs Me (Hamilton) 2:32

11. Sing a Rainbow (Hamilton) 2:43

Vocal by Ella Fitzgerald

12. Pete Kelly's Blues (Cahn-Heindorf) 2:23   550503-2

LP: Decca DL 8166 (released 25 July 1955). Side 1, Tracks 1–6 (17:27)/Side 2, Tracks 7-12 (18:19). Total playing time: 35:46. CD: MCA (Japan) MVCJ-19223 (released 1999). (Contents, sequence and total playing time, same as above). Produced by **Milt Gabler**. The author of the liner notes is uncredited. This album charted 17 September 1955/weeks, 10/peak #7.

The Decca Years (1947-1955)

LPD-39 ELLA FITZGERALD/ FIRST LADY OF SONG

1. My One and Only Love (Wood-Mellin) 3:16 550805-1

2. The Impatient Years (Van Heusen-Cahn) 2:45 550805-2

3. But Not Like Mine (Welch) 2:55   550805-3

4. I've Got the World on a String (Arlen-Koehler) 3:17 500306-2

5. An Empty Ballroom (Clinton) 3:04   531223-1

6. You Turned the Tables on Me (Alter-Mitchell) 2:55 471223-2

7. Ella's Contribution to the Blues (Fitzgerald-Jones) 2:25   520811-6

8. That's My Desire (Kresa-Loveday) 2:58   470319-2

9. A Satisfied Mind (Hayes-Rhodes) 2:29   550801-2

10. Careless (Quadling-Howard-Jurgens) 2:45 530213-1

11. Give a Little, Get a Little (Styne-Comden-Green) 3:16   510718-4

12. Blue Lou (Sampson-Mills) 2:43   530213-2

LP: Decca DL 8695 (released 1957). Side One, Track 1-6 (18:37)/Side Two, Tracks 7-12 (17:01). Total playing time: 35:38. CD: MCA (Japan) MCVJ-19221 (released 1999). (Contents, sequence and plaing time, same as above). Produced by **Milt Gabler**. Liner notes by **Burt Korall**.

The Decca Years (1938-1955)

LPD-40 THE BEST OF ELLA ...

1. A-Tisket, A-Tasket (Fitzgerald-Alexander) 2:35 380502-1

2. Undecided (Robin-Shavers) 3:13   390217-1

3. Stairway to the Stars (Signorelli-Malneck-Parish) 3:14   390629-2

4. Into Each Life Some Rain Must Fall (Roberts-Fisher) 3:05 440830-1

5. (It's Only a) Paper Moon (Harburg-Rose-Arlen) 2:32   450327-1

6. Flying Home (Robin-Hampton-Goodman) 2:27 451004-1

7. (I Love You) For Sentimental Reasons (Best-Watson) 3:10   460819-1

8. Oh! Lady, Be Good! (Gershwin-Gershwin) 3:13 470319-3

9. How High the Moon (Lewis-Hamilton) 3:15 471220-4

10. It's Too Soon To Know (Chessler) 2:32   480820-1

11. Basin Street Blues (Williams) 3:06   490920-4

12. I Hadn't Anyone Till You (Noble) 2:57   490921-1

13. I've Got the World on a String (Koehler-Arlen) 3:17 500306-2

14. Mixed Emotions (Louchheim) 3:14   510626-1

15. Smooth Sailing (Cobb) 3:04   510626-2

16. Mr. Paganini [You'll Have To Swing It], Pts. 1 and 2 (Coslow) 5:09   520626-2/3

17. Walking by the River (Carlisle-Sour) 2:24   520811-3

18. An Empty Ballroom (Clinton) 3:04   531223-1

19. I Wished on the Moon (Parker-Rainger) 3:08 540325-1

20. That Old Black Magic (Mercer-Arlen) 2:30 550427-1

21. Lover, Come Back to Me (Hammerstein-Romberg) 1:59   550427-3

22. My One and Only Love (Wood-Mellin) 3:18 550805-1

23. (Love Is) The Tender Trap (Cahn-Van Heusen) 2:59 550805-4

LP: Decca DL 8759 (2 discs) (released 11 August 1958). Side 1, Tracks 1-6 (17:31)/Side 2, Tracks 7-12 (18:38)/Side 3, Tracks 13-17 (17:28)/Side 4, Tracks 18-23 (17:23). Total playing time: 71:00. Decca DX-156 (mono)/Decca DXS-156 (stereo), same as above. MCA 4047E (stereo), same as above. 8-Track: MCA T2-4047 (mono) (2 tapes), same title, contents and sequence as LP releases. CT release: MCA MCAC2-4047E (stereo) (2 cassettes), same title, contents and sequence as LPs. Produced by **Milt Gabler**. Liner notes by **Nat Hentoff**.

The Verve Years (1956)

LPD-41 ELLA FITZGERALD SINGS THE COLE PORTER SONG BOOK

1. All Through the Night (Porter) 3:15   560208-4
2. Anything Goes (Porter) 3:21   560208-9
3. Miss Otis Regrets (She's Unable to Lunch Today) (Porter) 3:00   560207-6
4. Too Darn Hot (Porter) 3:47   560207-5
5. In the Still of the Night (Porter) 2:38   560209-2
6. I Get a Kick Out of You (Porter) 4:00   560209-6
7. Do I Love You? (Porter) 3:50   560207-9
8. (I'm) Always True to You in My Fashion (Porter) 2:48   560208-5
9. Let's Do It (Let's Fall in Love) (Porter) 3:32   560209-5*
10. Just One of Those Things (Porter) 3:30   560207-4
11. Ev'ry Time We Say Goodbye (Porter) 3:32   560207-10
12. All of You (Porter) 1:43   560209-3
13. Begin the Beguine (Porter) 3:37   560208-3
14. Get Out of Town (Porter) 3:22   560207-12
15. I Am in Love (Porter) 4:06   560207-11
16. From This Moment On (Porter) 3:17   560207-3
17. I Love Paris (Porter) 4:57   560207-8
18. You Do Something to Me (Porter) 2:21   560208-2
19. Ridin' High (Porter) 3:20   560207-1
20. Easy To Love (Porter) 3:24   560207-13
21. It's All Right with Me (Porter) 3:07   560207-2
22. Why Can't You Behave? (Porter) 5:04   560207-7
23. What Is This Thing Called Love? (Porter) 2:02   560208-8
24. You're the Top (Porter) 3:33   560208-6
25. Love for Sale (Porter) 5:52   560208-8
26. It's De-Lovely (Porter) 2:42   560209-3
27. Night and Day (Porter) 3:04   560327-1
28. Ace in the Hole (Porter) 1:58   560208-7
29. So in Love (Porter) 3:50   560209-1
30. I've Got You Under My Skin (Porter) 2:42   560209-7
31. I Concentrate on You (Porter) 3:11   560208-4
32. Don't Fence Me In (Porter) 3:19   560209-10
33. You're the Top (Porter)** 2:08   560327-3
34. I Concentrate on You (Porter)** 3:00   560327-4
35. Let's Do It (Let's Fall in Love) (Porter)** 5:25   560327-7*

*See 560327-6 in Discography

These tracks, previously unissued, are found in **The Complete Ella Fitzgerald Song Books (Verve 314 519 832-2) and in the Verve Master Edition release.

LP: Verve MG V-4001-2; MG V-4049/4050 (released July 1956). Disc 1, Side 1, Tracks 1-8 (27:14)/Side 2, Tracks, 9-16 (27:14). Disc 2, Side 1, Tracks 17-24 (28:23)/Side 2, Tracks, 25-32 (27:13). Total playing time: 1:49:54). Verve VE-2-2511, same contents and sequence as above. CD: Verve 821 989-2/990-2 (released 1985). Disc 1, Tracks 1-16 (53:46)/Disc 2, Tracks 1-16 (54:51) (1:48:37). Verve 314 519 832-2 (Discs One and Two) (See special entry, page 00). Disc 1, Tracks 1-16 (53:54)/Disc 2, Tracks 1-19 (69:16). Verve 314 519 833/834-2, same as above. Verve Master Edition 314 537 257, same as above (remastered). (released October 1997). Total playing time: 2:03:10. Produced under the personal supervision of **Norman Granz**. Recording Engineer: **Alan Emig**. Liner notes by **Norman Granz**. This album charted 28 July 1956/weeks, 15/peak, #1 (one week).

The Verve Years (1956)

LPD-42 METRONOME ALL STARS, 1956

The Metronome All Stars

1. Billie's Bounce

   Artists in order of appearance: One chorus by **Art Blakey** and **Charlie Mingus**; one chorus with those two joined by **Billy Taylor** and **Tal Farlow**; ensemble; then solos by **Zoot Sims**, **Eddie Bert**, **Serge Chaloff** (incidentally, see if you can tell at what point in his solo **Gerry Mulligan** walked into the studio), **Charlie Mingus**, Theodore C. Cohen, Tony Scott, Billy Taylor, Al Cohn, Tal Farlow, Lee Konitz, Art Blakey and **Thad Jones**.

Ella Fitzgerld with Count Basie and His Orchestra

2. April in Paris 4:46   560625-1

   ### *Ella Fitzgerald and Joe Williams* (duet) *with Count Basie and His Orchestra*

3. Every Day I Have the Blues 5:14   560625-3

   ### *Ella Fitzgerald and Joe Williams* (duet) *with Count Basie Small Band*

4. Party Blues 4:01   560625-4

   ### *Count Basie and His Orchestra*

5. Basie's Back in Town

   ### *George Wallington* (Piano Solo)

6. Lady Fair

   LP: Verve MG V-8030/Verve UM V-2510. Side 1: Track 1/Side 2, Tracks 2-6. Produced by **Norman Granz**. Liner notes by **Bill Coss**, Editor, *Metronome*. The royalties accruing from this record were divided between Local 802 (AFM) and a charity chosen by *Metronome*.

LPD-43 JAZZ AT THE HOLLYWOOD BOWL

Jazz At The Philharmonic All-Stars

1. Honeysuckle Rose (Razaf-Waller)
2. Medley: I Can't Get Started (Gershwin-Duke); If I Had You (Shapiro-Campbell-Connelly); I've Got the World on a String (Koehler-Arlen)
3. Jumpin' at the Woodside (Basie)

The Oscar Peterson Trio

4. 9:20 Special (Warren)
5. How About You? (Freed-Lane)

Art Tatum

6. Someone To Watch Over Me (Gershwin-Gershwin)
7. Begin the Beguine (Porter)
8. Willow, Weep for Me (Ronell)
9. Humoresque (Dvorak-Tatum)

Ella Fitzgerald and Her Quartet

10. Love for Sale (Porter) 4:15   560815-5
11. Just One of Those Things (Porter) 3:53   560815-6
12. Little Girl Blue (Rodgers-Hart) 3:46   560815-8
13. Too Close for Comfort (Bock-Holocener-Weiss) 2:52   560815-9
14. I Can't Give You Anything but Love (McHugh-Fields) 3:25   560815-10
15. Air Mail Special (Goodman-Mundy-Christian) 3:33   560815-11

Ella Fitzgerald with Louis Armstrong and His Orchestra

16. You Won't Be Satisfied (James-Stock) 4:23   560815-12
17. Undecided (Shavers-Robin) 3:42   560815-13

Entire Ensemble

18. When the Saints Go Marching In (Purvis-Black) 4:04   560815-14

LP: Verve MG V-8231-2 (2-LP set). Disc 1, Side 1, Tracks 1-2/Disc 1, Side 2, Tracks 3-5. Disc 2, Side 3, Tracks 9-12/Disc 2, Side 4, Tracks 13-18. CD: Tracks 16 and 17 on **The Complete Ella Fitzgerald and Louis Armstrong on Verve** (Verve Master Edition 314 537 284-2), Disc 2, Tracks, 15-16 (released October 1997). Produced under the personal supervision of **Norman Granz**. Liner notes by **Norman Granz**.

LPD-44 ELLA FITZGERALD AND LOUIS ARMSTRONG/ELLA AND LOUIS

1. Can't We Be Friends? (Swift-James) 3:45   560816-5
2. Isn't This a Lovely Day (Berlin) 6:14   560816-2
3. Moonlight in Vermont (Suessdorf-Blackburn) 3:40   560816-8
4. They Can't Take That Away from Me (Gershwin-Gershwin) 4:37   560816-1
5. Under a Blanket of Blue (Nieburg-Symes-Livingston) 4:16   560816-7
6. Tenderly (Gross-Lawrence) 5:06   560816-3
7. A Foggy Day (in London Town) (Gershwin-Gershwin) 4:30   560816-9
8. Stars Fell on Alabama (Parish-Perkins) 3:31   560816-4
9. Cheek to Cheek (Berlin) 5:51   560816-6
10. The Nearness of You (Carmichael-Washington) 5:40   560816-11
11. April in Paris (Harburg-Duke) 6:32   560816-10

LP: Verve MG V-4003, Verve 2V6S-8811 (Disc 1) (released October 1956). Side 1, Tracks 1-6 (28:03)/Side 2, Tracks 7-11 (26:29). Total playing time: 54:32. Verve VE-2507, same sequence and content (released 1983). CD: Verve 825 373-2 (54:18), same sequence and content (released 1985). **The Complete Ella Fitzgerald and Louis Armstrong on Verve** (Verve Master Edition 314 537 2842), Disc 1, Tracks 1-11 (released October 1997). Produced under the personal supervision of **Norman Granz.** Recording Engineer: **Val Valentin**. Liner notes by **Norman Granz**. This album charted 15 December 1956/weeks, 2, peak #12.

LPD-45 ELLA FITZGERALD SINGS THE RODGERS AND HART SONG BOOK

1. Have You Met Miss Jones? (Rodgers-Hart) 3:41   560830-4
2. You Took Advantage of Me (Rodgers-Hart) 3:27   560831-6
3. A Ship Without a Sail (Rodgers-Hart) 4:07   560830-3
4. To Keep My Love Alive (Rodgers-Hart) 3:34   560829-7
5. Dancing on the Ceiling (Rodgers-Hart) 4:06   560831-3
6. The Lady Is a Tramp (Rodgers-Hart) 3:21   560821-2
7. With a Song in My Heart (Rodgers-Hart) 2:44   560829-6

8. Manhattan (Rodgers-Hart) 2:48   560829-3
9. Johnny One-Note (Rodgers-Hart) 2:12   560828-4
10. I Wish I Were in Love Again (Rodgers-Hart) 2:36   560828-2
11. Spring Is Here (Rodgers-Hart) 3:38   560830-7
12. It Never Entered My Mind (Rodgers-Hart) 4:06   560830-5
13. This Can't Be Love (Rodgers-Hart) 2:54   560821-1
14. Thou Swell (Rodgers-Hart) 2:03   560829-2
15. My Romance (Rodgers-Hart) 3:42   560830-1
16. Where or When (Rodgers-Hart) 2:46   560831-4
17. Little Girl Blue (Rodgers-Hart) 3:53   560830-6
18. Give It Back to the Indians (Rodgers-Hart) 3:10   560828-5
19. Ten Cents a Dance (Rodgers-Hart) 4:06   560828-1
20. There's a Small Hotel (Rodgers-Hart) 2:48   560829-4
21. I Didn't Know What Time It Was (Rodgers-Hart) 3:46   560829-5
22. Ev'rything I've Got (Rodgers-Hart) 3:21   560904-15
23. I Could Write a Book (Rodgers-Hart) 3:38   560830-9
24. A Blue Room (Rodgers-Hart) 2:29   560831-2
25. My Funny Valentine (Rodgers-Hart) 3:52   560830-8
26. Bewitched (Bothered and Bewildered) (Rodgers-Hart) 7:01   560829-8
27. Mountain Greenery (Rodgers-Hart) 2:13   560828-3
28. Wait Till You See Her (Rodgers-Hart) 1:30   560829-9
29. Lover (Rodgers-Hart) 3:16   560821-5
30. Isn't It Romantic? (Rodgers-Hart) 3:00   560831-5
31. Here in My Arms (Rodgers-Hart) 1:52   560831-1
32. Blue Moon (Rodgers-Hart) 3:11   560829-1
33. My Heart Stood Still (Rodgers-Hart) 3:03   560830-2
34. I've Got Five Dollars (Rodgers-Hart) 2:39   560821-3
35. Lover (Rodgers-Hart) (monaural version) 3:16   560821-4

LP: Verve MG V-4002-2, Verve MG V6-4022/4023 (released October 1956). Disc 1, Side 1, Tracks 1-9 (26:09)/Side 2, Tracks 10-17 (30:36). Disc 2, Side 1, Tracks 18-25 (31:40)/Side 2, Tracks 26-34 (24:26). Total playing time: 1:52:51. Verve VE-2-2519 (released 1983), same titles and sequence as above. CT: Verve CT2-2519 (released 1983), same titles and sequence as above. CD: Verve 821 579-2 (Vol. 1), same titles and sequence as above (released 1985). Verve 821 580-2 (Vol. 2), same titles and sequence as above (released 1985). Verve 314 519 835-2 (Vol 1), Tracks 1-17 (56:45) (released 1993). Verve 314 519 836-2 (Vol. 2), Tracks 18-35 (59:21) (released 1993). Total playing time: 1:56:06. Verve 314 519 832-2 (Discs Three and Four) **The Complete Ella Fitzgerald Song Books**, same as 1993 re-issue (released October 1993). Verve Master Edi-

tion 314 537 258, same as above (remastered). (released October 1997). Produced under the personal supervision of **Norman Granz**. Recording Engineer: **Alan Emig**. The "liner notes" is a booklet containing an "Introduction," by **Richard Rodgers**; a "Foreword," by **Oscar Hammerstein II**;. an essay, "About Ella...," by music critic **William Simon**; and a note by producer **Norman Granz**. This album charted 16 March 1957/weeks, 4/peak, #11.

The Verve Years (1957)

LPD-46 JAZZ AT THE PHILHARMONIC, STOCKHOLM, 1957, FEATURING ELLA FITZGERALD

Jazz At The Philharmonic All-Stars

1. Norman Granz (Announcement) 1:02
2. Undecided (Shavers) 3:43
3. Embraceable You (Gershwin-Gershwin) 3:39
4. School Days (Cobb-Edwards) 3:40
5. Lester Leaps In (Young) 8:02
6. Moonlight in Vermont (Suessdorf-Blackburn) 4:20
7. Bugle Call Rag (Pettis-Meyers-Schoebel) 4:39

Ella Fitzgerald with The Ray Brown Quartet

8. Norman Granz (Announcement) 0:14
9. You Got Me Singing the Blues 2:22   570428-1
10. Angel Eyes (Brent-Dennis) 3:19   570428-2
11. Lullaby of Birdland (Shearing) 2:15   570428-3
12. Tenderly (Gross-Lawrence) 2:57   570428-4
13. Do Nothing Till You Hear from Me (Ellington-Russell) 3:50   570428-5
14. April in Paris (Harburg-Duke) 3:44   570428-6
15. I Can't Give You Anything but Love (McHugh-Fields) 3:49   570428-7
16. Love for Sale (Porter) 4:12   570429-1
17. It Don't Mean a Thing (Ellington-Mills) 7:55   570429-2
18. Norman Granz (Closing comments) 1:22

LP: Tax 3703 (released 1985). Side 1, Tracks 1-7 (36:57)/Side 2, Tracks 8-18 (29:51). Total playing time, 66:48. CD: Tax 3703-2 (released 1988)/Same contents and sequence as above. Produced by **Carl A. Hällström**/Engineered by **Olof Swembel**.

The Verve Years (1957)

LPD-47 ELLA FITZGERALD, BILLIE HOLIDAY AND CARMEN MCRAE AT NEWPORT

Ella Fitzgerald

1. This Can't Be Love (Rodgers-Hart) 1:44   570704-1
2. I Got It Bad (and That Ain't Good) (Ellington-Webster) 4:27   570704-2
3. Body and Soul (Heyman-Sour-Eyton-Green) 4:28   570704-3
4. Too Close for Comfort (Block-Holofcener-Weiss) 2:30   570704-4
5. Lullaby of Birdland (Shearing-Weiss) 2:23   570704-5
6. I've Got a Crush on You (Gershwin-Gershwin) 2:27   570704-6
7. I'm Gonna Sit Right Down and Write Myself a Letter (Young-Ahlert) 2:27   570704-7
8. April in Paris (Duke-Harburg) 4:02   570704-8
9. Air Mail Special (Christian-Goodman-Mundy) 4:20   570704-9
10. I Can't Give You Anything but Love 5:08   570704-10

Billie Holiday

11. Nice Work if You Can Get It (Gershwin-Gershwin) 2:39
12. Willow, Weep for Me (Ronell) 3:10
13. My Man (Willehetz-Charles-Pollack-Yvain) 3:32
14. Lover, Come Back to Me (Romberg-Hammerstein) 2:07
15. Lady Sings the Blues (Nichols-Holiday) 3:02
16. What a Little Moonlight Can Do (Woods) 3:15

Carmen McRae

17. I'll Remember April (DePaul-Johnston-Raye) 2:45
18. Body and Soul (Green-Heyman-Sour-Eyton) 3:34
19. Carmen McRae introduces "Skyliner" 0:18
20. Skyliner (Barnet) 2:14
21. Carmen McRae introduces band and "Midnight Sun" 1:04
22. Midnight Sun (Hampton-Burke-Mercer) 4:13
23. Our Love Is Here to Stay (Gershwin-Gershwin) 2:37
24. Perdido (Tizol-Drake-Lengsfelder) 2:48

    LP: Verve MG VS-6022 (Ella Fitzgerald & Billie Holiday at Newport). (Released October 1957). Side 1, Tracks 1-3, 7–10 (26:36)/Side 2, Tracks 11-16 (17:45). Total playing time, 44:21. Verve MG V-8234 (Billie Holiday and Ella Fitzgerald at Newport). Side 1, Tracks 11, 12, 14, 15, 13 (16:40)/Side 2, Tracks 1-3, 7–9 (21:28) Total playing time, 38:08. Verve MG V6-8825 (The Newport Years, Vol. 1, Ella Fitzgerald and Billie. Holiday). Side 1, Tracks 11–16 (17:45)/Side 2, Tracks 1-3, 7–10 (26:36). Total playing time, 44:21. CD: Verve 314 559 809 (Released March 2000). Tracks 1-24, as listed (Total playing time, 74:25). The tracks of each set appear in the sequence in which they were performed.

Note: Ella Fitzgerald tracks recorded at Freebody Park, Newport (Rhode. Island), on 4 July 1957. Tracks 4–6 previously unreleased. Billie Holiday tracks recorded (with Piano: Mel Waldron/Bass: Jo Benjamin/Drums: Jo Jones) at Freebody Park, Newport, 6 July 1957. (Miss Holiday's performances also appear in **The Complete Billie Holiday on Verve, 1945-1959**, 10-CD set, Verve 314 517 658.) Carmen McRae tracks recorded (with Piano: Junior Mance [17–19, 21]/Ray Bryant [tracks 20, 22, 23]/Carmen McRae [track 24]/Bass: Ike Isaacs/ Drums: Jimmy Cobb [tracks 17–19, 21, 24]/Specs Wright [tracks 20, 22, 23]) at Freebody Park, Newport, 5 July 1957. McRae tracks previously unreleased. Produced under the personal supervision of **Norman Granz.** Recording Engineer: **Edwin Outwater.** Liner notes for CD by **William Ruhlmann.** CD reissue supervised by Ben Young.

The Verve Years (1957)

LPD-48 ELLA FITZGERALD AND LOUIS ARMSTRONG/ELLA AND LOUIS AGAIN

1. Don't Be That Way (Goodman-Sampson-Parish) 4:57   570813-3
2. Makin' Whoopee (Kahn-Donaldson)** 3:55   (570731)
3. They All Laughed (Gershwin-Gershwin) 3:47   570723-5
4. Comes Love (Stept-Tobias-Brown)* 2:27   570723-9
5. Autumn in New York (Duke) 5:57   570723-3
6. Let's Do It (Let's Fall in Love) (Porter)** 8:41   (570731)
7. Stompin' at the Savoy (Sampson-Webb-Razaf-Goodman) 5:12   570723-7
8. I Won't Dance (Fields-McHugh) 4:45   570813-1
9. Gee, Baby, Ain't I Good to You (Redman-Razaf) 4:11   570723-6
10. Let's Call the Whole Thing Off (Gershwin-Gershwin) 4:12   570723-4
11. These Foolish Things (Marvell-Strachey-Link)* 7:37   570723-8
12. I've Got My Love To Keep Me Warm (Berlin) 3:09   570813-5
13. Willow, Weep for Me (Ronell)** 4:16   (570731)
14. I'm Putting All My Eggs in One Basket (Berlin) 3:25   570813-4
15. A Fine Romance (Kern-Fields) 3:51   570813-2
16. Ill Wind (Koehler-Arlen)* 3:41   570723-10
17. Our Love Is Here To Stay (Gershwin-Gershwin) 3:58   570723-1
18. I Get a Kick Out of You (Porter)** 4:15   (570731)
19. Learnin' the Blues (Silvers) 7:13   570723-2

* Ella only

** Louis only

    LP: Verve MG V-4006-2 (2 discs) (released October

1957). Disc 1: Side 1, Tracks 1-5 (21:24)/Side 2, Tracks 6-9 (22:59) (44:23). Disc 2: Side 3, Tracks 10-14 (23:00)/Side 4, Tracks 15-19 (23:19) (46:19). Mobile Fidelity AMOB 2248 (2 discs) (released February 1996), same as above. Total playing time, 1:50:42. CT: Verve 2V5JT-8811 (2 cassettes), contents same as above. CD: Verve 825 374-2 (released 1993). Tracks 1, 3, 5, 7, 8, 9, 10, 12, 14, 15, 17, 19 (the duet tracks). Total playing time: 55:03. Mobile Fidelity CMOB 651 (2 discs) (released February 1996). Disc 1, Tracks 1-9 (44:23)/Disc 2, Tracks 10-19 (46:19). Verve Master Edition 314 537 284-2 (3 discs), **The Complete Ella Fitzgerald and Louis Armstrong on Verve**, Disc 1, Tracks 12-16/Disc 2, Tracks 1–14 (released October 1997). Total playing time, 1:29:50. Original sessions produced under the personal supervision of **Norman Granz**. Recording Engineer: **Val Valentin**. Liner notes by **Norman Granz**.

The Verve Years (1957)

LPD-49 ELLA FITZGERALD AT THE OPERA HOUSE

1. It's All Right with Me (Porter) 2:31   570929-2
2. Don'tcha Go 'Way Mad (Mundy-Jacquet-Stillman) 2:42   570929-3
3. Bewitched, Bothered, and Bewildered (Rodgers-Hart) 3:01   570929-4
4. These Foolish Things (Strachey-Link-Marvell) 3:46 570929-5
5. Ill Wind (Arlen-Koehler) 2:45   570929-6
6. Goody Goody (Mercer-Malneck) 1:54   570929-7
7. Moonlight in Vermont (Suessdorf-Blackburn) 3:06 570929-8
8. Them There Eyes (Pinkard-Tauber-Tracey) 2:08 570929-9
9. Stompin' at the Savoy (Goodman-Sampson-Webb-Razaf) 6:12   570929-10
10. Oh! Lady, Be Good! (Gershwin-Gershwin) 4:04 570929-11
11. It's All Right with Me (Porter) 1:45   571009-1
12. Don'cha Go 'Way Mad (Mundy-Jacquet-Stillman) 2:32   571009-2
13. Bewitched, Bothered, and Bewildered (Rodgers-Hart) 3:22   571009-3
14. These Foolish Things (Strachey-Link-Marvell) 3:49 571009-4
15. Ill Wind (Arlen-Koehler) 2:54   571009-5
16. Goody Goody (Mercer-Malneck) 1:55   571009-6
17. Moonlight in Vermont (Suessdorf-Blackburn) 3:13 571009-7
18. Stompin' at the Savoy (Goodman-Sampson-Webb-Razaf) 7:15   571009-8
19. Oh! Lady, Be Good! (Gershwin-Gershwin) 4:24 571009-9

LP: Verve MG V-8264/Verve MG V6-6026 (released 1959). Side One, Tracks 1-5 (14:46)/Side Two, 6, 7, 9, 10 (16:02). Total playing time: 30:48. Note: The listing above is that of the CD release. The original LP issue contained 9 tracks, all recorded at the Chicago Civic Opera House, and including a version of "Oh! Lady, Be Good!" which does not appear on the CD, but omitting track 8 ("Them There Eyes"). The CD comprises the first eight tracks of the LP (as well as a bonus from this concert "Them There Eyes"), in addition to a concert recorded at the Shrine Auditorium in Los Angeles a week later. (See Recording Sessions for details.). CD release: Verve 831 269-2, Tracks 1-9, 11-19 (released 1990). Total playing time, 60:22. Original concerts and recordings produced by **Norman Granz**. Director of Engineering: **Val Valentin**. Prepared for CD, **Richard Seidel** and **Donald Elfman**, with liner notes by **Phil Schaap**.

The Decca Years/Verve Years (1947/1957)

LPD-50 ELLA FITZGERALD/ 18 TOP TRACKS/CD JAZZ

Jazz At The Philharmonic, Stockholm, Sweden, 28/29 August 1957 Ella Fitzgerald, with The Ray Brown Quartet

1. (You Got Me) Singin' the Blues (Endsley) 2:24 570428-1
2. Angel Eyes (Dennis-Brent) 3:20   570428-2
3. Lullaby of Birdland (Shearing) 2:15   570428-3
4. Tenderly (Gross-Lawrence) 3:11   570428-4
5. Do Nothin 'Till You Hear from Me (Ellington-Russell) 3:51   570428-5
6. April in Paris (Harburg-Duke) 4:17   570428-6
7. I Can't Give You Anything but Love (McHugh-Fields) 3:52   570428-7
8. Love For Sale (Porter) 4:06   570429-1
9. It Don't Mean a Thing (Ellington-Hodges)* 7:46 570429-2

*Roy Eldridge ,trumpet, and Stuff Smith, violin, also play on this track

Jazz At The Philharmonic, Shrine Auditorium, Los Angeles, 9 October 1957 Ella Fitzgerald, with Oscar Peterson and His Trio

10. Bewitched (Bothered and Bewildered) (Rodgers-Hart) 3:23   571009-3
11. These Foolish Things (Strachey-Link-Marvell) 3:51 571009-4

Ella Fitzgerald with the J.A.T.P. All Stars

12. Stompin' at the Savoy (Sampson-Webb) 6:32
    571009-8

*Jazz At The Philharmonic, Carnegie Hall,
29 September 1947 Ella Fitzgerald,
with Dizzy Gillespie and His Orchestra*

13. Almost Like Being in Love (Lerner-Loewe) 2:11
    470929-1
14. Stairway to the Stars (Malneck-Parish-Signorelli)
    4:15 470929-2
15. Lover Man (Ramirez-Davis-Sherman) 4:36
    470929-3
16. Flying Home (Hampton-Goodman) 2:25 470929-4
17. Oh! Lady, Be Good! (Gershwin-Gershwin) 3:34
    470929-5
18. How High the Moon (Hamilton-Lewis) 4:25
    470929-6

CD: Frequenz 044-006 (released 1994). Total playing time: 70:48. Original concerts and recordings produced by **Norman Granz**. Note: This rare compact disc was chosen to be included in this volume since, at the time of publication, it is believed to be only source of tracks 13-18 on CD.

The Verve Years (1956-1957)

LPD-51 ELLA FITZGERALD SINGS THE DUKE ELLINGTON SONG BOOK

1. Rockin' in Rhythm (Carney-Ellington-Mills) 5:18
   570626-5
2. Drop Me Off in Harlem (Ellington-Kenny-Kenny)
   3:49 570625-3
3. Day Dream (Strayhorn-Latouche) 3:58 570624-1
4. Caravan (Ellington-Tizol-Mills) 3:53 570627-3
5. Take the "A" Train (Strayhorn) 6:40 570624-2
6. I Ain't Got Nothin' But the Blues (Ellington-
   George) 4:41 570625-5
7. Clementine (Strayhorn) 2:39 570626-1
8. I Didn't Know About You (Ellington-Russell) 4:12
   570626-4
9. I'm Beginning to See the Light (Ellington-Hodges-
   James-George) 3:25 570626-3
10. Lost in Meditation (Ellington-Singer-Tizol) 3:25
    570625-4
11. Perdido (Tizol-Lengsfelder-Drake) 6:12 570627-12
12. Cotton Tail (Ellington) 3:24 560904-3
13. Do Nothin' Till You Hear from Me (Ellington-Rus-
    sell) 7:40 560904-5
14. Just A-Sittin' and A-Rockin' (Ellington-Strayhorn-
    Gaines) 3:32 560904-8

15. Solitude (Ellington-DeLange 2:06 560904-6
16. Rocks in My Bed (Ellington) 3:56 560904-2
17. Satin Doll (Ellington-Mercer) 3:28 560904-12
18. Sophisticated Lady (Ellington-Brown-Hardwicke-
    Parish) 5:19 560904-7
19. Just Squeeze Me (Ellington-Gaines) 4:15 560904-4
20. It Don't Mean a Thing (Ellington-Mills) 4:13
    560904-9
21. Azure (Ellington-Mills) 2:20 560904-13
22. I Let a Song Go Out of My Heart (Ellington-Nemo-
    Redmond) 4:09 560904-1
23. In A Sentimental Mood (Ellington-Kurtz) 2:45
    560904-14
24. Don't Get Around Much Anymore (Ellington-
    Hodges-Russell) 5:00 560904-11
25. Prelude to a Kiss (Ellington-Gordon) 5:27
    560904-10
26. Mood Indigo (Bigard-Ellington-Parish) 3:26
    571017-2
27. In a Mellow Tone (Ellington-Gabler) 5:09 571017-
    1
28. Love You Madly (Ellington) 4:39 571017-3
29. Lush Life (Strayhorn) 3:37 571017-4
30. Squatty Roo (Hodges-Fitzgerald) 3:39 571017-5
31. I'm Just a Lucky So-and-So 4:13 570626-2
32. All Too Soon (Ellington-Sigman) 4:22 570627-2
33. Everything But You (Ellington-James-George) 2:55
    570625-1
34. I Got It Bad (and That Ain't Good) (Ellington-Web-
    ster) 6:12 570625-2
35. Bli-Blip (Ellington-Kuller) 3:02 570627-4
36. Chelsea Bridge (Strayhorn) 3:23 570627-11
37. Portrait of Ella Fitzgerald: (Ellington-Strayhorn)
    16:16; First Movement: Royal Ancestry; Second
    Movement: All Heart; Third Movement: Beyond
    Category; Fourth Movement: Total Jazz
38. The E and D Blues (E for Ella, D for Duke) (Elling-
    ton-Sanders-Strayhorn) 4:50 570627-13
39. Chelsea Bridge (rehearsal) 4:03 570627-5
40. Chelsea Bridge (rehearsal) 3:37 570627-6
41. Chelsea Bridge (rehearsal) 3:59 570627-7
42. Chelsea Bridge (rehearsal) 3:20
43. Chelsea Bridge (rehearsal) 1:38
44. Chelsea Bridge (rehearsal) 1:20 570627-8
45. Chelsea Bridge (rehearsal) 5:35 570627-9
46. Chelsea Bridge (rehearsal) 3:39 570627-10
47. All Heart (rehearsal) 3:54
48. All Heart (rehearsal) 3:33
49. All Heart (rehearsal) 3:22
50. All Heart (rehearsal) 3:25

LP: Verve MG V-4008-2 (2 discs) **The Duke Ellington Song Book, Volume 1**. Disc 1, Side 1 (Tracks 2, 34, 4,

3, 9) (21:29). Disc 1, Side 2 (Tracks 5, 31, 32, 33, 35, 36) (24:50). Disc 2, Side 3 (Tracks 1, 6, 7, 8, 10, 11) (26:42). Disc 2, Side 4 (Tracks 37, 38) (21:08). Total playing time, 1:34:09.

Verve MG V-4009-2 (2 discs) **The Duke Ellington Song Book, Volume 2/The Small Group Sessions**. Disc 1, Side 1 (Tracks 18, 20, 13, 12, 21) (23:08). Disc 1, Side 2 (Tracks 15, 17, 22, 24, 16) (18:51). Disc 2, Side 1 (Tracks 25, 14, 19, 23) (16:08). Disc 2, Side 1 (Tracks 29, 30, 26, 27, 28) (20:32). Total playing time, 1:18:39.

Verve MG V-4010-2 (4 discs) **Ella Fitzgerald Sings the Complete Duke Ellington Song Book** (Same as above, in one package). (All the above were released in 1958). Verve VE-4-2540 (electronically enhanced for stereo), same contents. and sequence as above (released in 1983). CD: Verve 314 519 837/838/839-2 (3 discs) (released in 1985). Disc 1, Tracks 1-13 (59:48)/Disc 2, Tracks 14-28 (57:51). Disc 3, Tracks 29-38 (55:26)/Total playing time, 2:53:05.

Verve 314 519 832-2 **The Complete Ella Fitzgerald Song Books** (Discs 5 and 7 (same as first CD release, except included on Disc 7 are. Tracks 39 (rehearsal sessions) and 40 (alternative take). both. previously unreleased) (released 1993). Playing times: Disc 5, 59:48/Disc 6, 67:45/Disc 7, 59:26 (3:06:59). Verve 314 559 248 (released March 1999). Disc One, Tracks 1-18 (77:37)/Disc 2, Tracks 19-35 (69:23)/. Disc Three, Tracks 36-50 (65:24/Total playing time, 3:32:24.

Produced under the personal supervision of **Norman Granz**. Recording Engineer: **Val Valentin**. Liner notes by **Norman Granz** and **Leonard Feather**.

The Verve Years (1957)

LPD-52 ELLA FITZGERALD/ LIKE SOMEONE IN LOVE

1. There's a Lull in My Life (Gordon-Revel) 3:23 571015-1
2. More Than You Know (Youmans-Eliscu-Rose) 3:14 571015-3
3. What Will I Tell My Heart? (Tinturin-Lawrence) 3:27 571015-5
4. I Never Had a Chance (Berlin) 2:44 571015-10
5. Close Your Eyes (Petkere) 2:54 571015-8
6. We'll Be Together Again (Fischer-Laine) 3:18 571015-6
7. Then I'll Be Tired of You (Schwartz-Harburg) 3:10 571015-7
8. Like Someone in Love (Burke-Van Heusen) 3:07 571015-4
9. Midnight Sun (Hampton-Burke) 3:54   571015-11
10. I Thought About You (Mercer-Van Heusen) 2:51 571015-9
11. You're Blasé (Hamilton-Sievier) 3:55 571015-2
12. Night Wind (Rothberg-Pollack) 3:16 571028-2

13. What's New? (Haggart-Burke) 3:04   571028-7
14. Hurry Home (Meyer-Emmerick-Bernier) 4:37 571028-3
15. HowLongHasThisBeenGoingOn? (Gershwin-Gershwin) 5:48   571028-4
16. I'll Never Be the Same (Kahn-Malneck-Signorelli)* 4:23   571028-1
17. Lost in a Fog (Fields-McHugh)* 3:59   571028-5
18. Everything Happens to Me (Adair-Dennis)* 3:51 571028-6
19. So Rare (Sharpe-Herst)* 3:34   571028-8

*Tracks 16-19 not on the original LP; they are from **Ella Fitzgerald/Hello, Love** (Verve MG V-4034), which has not as yet been re-issued on compact disc.

LP: Verve MG V-4004 (mono), Verve MG VS-6000 (stereo) (released 1958) Side A, Tracks 1-8 (25:51)/Side B, Track 9-15 (27:51). Total playing time, 43:42. CD: Verve 314 511 524-2, Tracks 1-19 (released 1983). Total playing time, 69:41. Produced under the personal supervision of **Norman Granz**. Recording Engineer: **Val Valentin**. Liner notes by **Francis Davis**.

The Verve Years (1958)

LPD-53 ELLA FITZGERALD SINGS THE IRVING BERLIN SONG BOOK

1. Let's Face the Music and Dance (Berlin) 2:55 580318-7
2. You're Laughing at Me (Berlin) 3:14 580317-4
3. Let Yourself Go (Berlin) 2:16 580819-2
4. You Can Have Him (Berlin) 3:43 580314-2
5. Russian Lullaby (Berlin) 1:51 580317-5
6. Puttin' on the Ritz (Berlin) 2:14 580318-9
7. Get Thee Behind Me, Satan (Berlin) 3:45 580317-9
8. Alexander's Ragtime Band (Berlin) 2:40 580319-1
9. Top Hat, White Tie, and Tails (Berlin) 2:32 580319-3
10. How About Me? (Berlin) 3:14 580317-8
11. Cheek to Cheek (Berlin) 3:45 580318-3
12. I Used to Be Color Blind (Berlin) 2:30 580314-1
13. Lazy (Berlin) 2:36 580318-6
14. How Deep Is the Ocean? (Berlin) 3:08 580317-3
15. All by Myself (in the Morning) (Berlin) 2:26 580313-2
16. (You Forgot To) Remember (Berlin) 3:26 580318-10
17. Supper Time (Berlin) 3:15 580317-2
18. How's Chances? (Berlin) 2:45 580314-3
19. Heat Wave (Berlin) 2:22 580318-2
20. Isn't This a Lovely Day (To Be Caught in the Rain)? (Berlin) 3:25 580313-1

21. You Keep Coming Back Like a Song (Berlin) 3:32
    580317-1
22. Reaching for the Moon (Berlin) 2:15   580317-10
23. (Let's Go) Slumming on Park Avenue (Berlin) 2:21
    580313-3
24. The Song Is Ended (But the MelodyLingers On)
    (Berlin) 2:26   580318-4
25. I'm Putting All My Eggs in One Basket (Berlin) 2:57
    580313-4
26. Now It Can Be Told (Berlin) 3:09   580317-7
27. Always (Berlin) 3:05   580313-5
28. It's a Lovely Day Today (Berlin) 2:24   580318-8
29. Change Partners (Berlin) 3:14   580317-6
30. No Strings (I'm Fancy Free) (Berlin) 3:00   580314-4
31. I've Got My Love To Keep Me Warm (Berlin) 2:56
    580318-1
32. Blue Skies (Berlin) 3:44   580318-5

LP: Verve MGV-4019-2 (V-4030/V-4031) (mono) (2
discs) (released November 1958). Disc 1, Side 1: Tracks 1-8
(23:10)/Side 2: Tracks 9-16 (24:05). Disc 2, Side 3: Tracks
17-23 (20:23)/Side 4: Tracks 24-31 (23:24). Total playing
time, 1:31:02. Verve V6-4019-2 (V6-4030/V6-4031)
(stereo) (2 discs) (released 1961). Same contents and sequence as above. Verve 2683 027 (2 discs), same contents
and sequence as above, except. that Track 32 ("Blue Skies")
appears as Track 1 on Side 3. Disc 1, Side 1: Tracks 1-8
(23:10)/Side 2: Tracks 9-16 (24:05). Disc 2, Side 3: Tracks
17-24 (24:09)/Side 4: Tracks 25-31 (23:24). Verve 829
533-1 (829 534-1/829 535-1) (2 discs), same as Verve 2683
027. CT: Verve 829 533-4 (829 534-4/829 535-4) (2
discs), same as LP issue of. same number. CD: Verve 829
533-2 (829 534-2/829 535-2) (2 discs), same as Verve
2683 027. Disc 1, Tracks 1-16 (47:17)/Disc 2, Tracks 17-32
(47:53). Verve 314 519 832-2 (**The Complete Ella Fitzgerald Song Books**, Discs Eight and Nine), same as previous
CD issue, except that "Blue Skies". is at Disc Nine, Tracks
16) (released August 1993). Total playing times: 1:35:10.
Produced under the personal supervision of **Norman
Granz**. Recording Engineer: **Val Valentin**. Liner notes by
Nat Hentoff.

The Verve Years (1958)

LPD-54 ELLA IN ROME/
THE BIRTHDAY CONCERT

1. Introduction (in Italian) by Norman Granz 0:22
2. St. Louis Blues (Handy) 5:57   580424-1
3. These Foolish Things (Marvell-Strachey-Link) 3:28
   580425-14
4. Just Squeeze Me (Ellington-Gaines) 3:05   580425-17

5. Angel Eyes (Dennis-Brent) 3:37   580425-18
6. That Old Black Magic (Arlen-Mercer) 3:38
   580425-19
7. Just One of Those Things (Porter) 3:39   580425-
   20
8. I Loves You, Porgy (Gershwin-Heyward-Gershwin)
   4:56   580425-23
9. It's All Right with Me (Porter) 2:37   580425-24
10. I Can't Give You Anything but Love (Fields-
    McHugh) 3:26   580425-25
11. Introduction (in Italian) by Norman Granz 0:57
12. When You're Smiling (Fisher-Goodwin-Shay) 1:40
    580425-1
13. A Foggy Day (in London Town) (Gershwin-Gersh-
    win) 3:09   580425-2
14. Midnight Sun (Mercer-Burke) 3:40   580425-3
15. The Lady Is a Tramp (Rodgers-Hart) 2:46
    580425-4
16. Sophisticated Lady (Ellington-Parish-Mills) 3:58
    580425-7
17. Caravan (Ellington-Mills-Tizol) 2:43   580425-8
18. Stompin' at the Savoy (Goodman-Sampson-Webb-
    Razaf) 7:10   580425-27

LP: Verve 835 454 (released June 1988). Side 1, Tracks
1-7 (23:46)/Side 2, Tracks 8-10, 14, 17, 18 (24:43). Total
playing time, 48:29. CT: Verve 835 454-4, same contents
and sequence as LP issue (June 1988). CD: Verve 835 454-
2 (released October 1988). Tracks 1-18. Total playing time,
60:58. Concert produced by **Norman Granz**. Record produced and with liner notes by **Phil Schaap**.

The Verve Years (1958)

LPD-55 ELLA FITZGERALD/
ELLA SWINGS LIGHTLY

1. Little White Lies (Donaldson) 2:31   581123-11
2. You Hit the Spot (Revel-Gordon) 2:44   581122-1
3. What's Your Story, Morning Glory? (Williams-
   Lawrence-Webster) 2:38   581122-3
4. Just You, Just Me (Greer-Klages) 2:19   581122-4
5. As Long as I Live (Arlen-Koehler) 2:48   581123-2
6. Teardrops from My Eyes (Toombs) 3:45   581122-7
7. Gotta Be This or That (Skylar) 3:05   581123-4
8. Moonlight on the Ganges (Myers-Wallace) 2:22
   581123-6
9. My Kinda Love (Alter-Trent) 3:41   581122-5
10. Blues in the Night (Arlen-Mercer) 3:39   581122-2
11. If I Were a Bell (Loesser) 2:33   581122-6
12. You're an Old Smoothie (Brown-Whiting-DeSylva)
    2:45   581123-1

13. Little Jazz (Eldridge-Harding) 3:02   581123-9
14. You Brought a New Kind of Love to Me (Fain-Kahal-Norman) 2:18   581123-12
15. Knock Me a Kiss (Jackson-Razaf) 4:06   581123-3
16. 720 in the Books (Savitt-Watson-Adamson) 3:26   581123-5
17. Oh, What a Night for Love! (Hefti-Allen) (long version) 3:26   581123-7
18. Little Jazz (Eldridge-Harding) (alternative take) 3:01   581123-10
19. Dreams Are Made for Children (David-Livingston) 2:36   581123-13
20. Oh, What a Night for Love! (Hefti-Allen) (single version) 2:23   581123-8

LP: Verve MG V-4021 (mono)/Verve MG VS-6019 (stereo) (released April 1959). Side 1, Tracks 1-8 (22:32)/Side 2, Tracks 9-16 (25:17). Total playing time, 47:49. Verve MG V6-4021 (stereo), same as above (released 1961). CD: Verve 314 517 535-2 (Released November 1992). Tracks 1-20 (tracks 17-19, previously unissued). Total playing time, 59:24. Produced under the personal supervision of **Norman Granz**. Recording Engineer: **Val Valentin**. Liner notes by **James Gavin**.

The Verve Years (1957-1959)

LPD-56 ELLA FITZGERALD/HELLO, LOVE

1. You Go to My Head (Coots-Gillespie) 4:29   590325-1
2. Willow, Weep for Me (Ronell) 3:54   590325-2
3. I'm Through with Love (Malneck-Livingston-Kahn) 3:41   590325-5
4. Spring Will Be a Little Late this Year (Loesser) 3:13   590325-4
5. Everything Happens to Me (Adair-Dennis) 3:46   571028-6
6. Lost in a Fog (McHugh-Fields) 3:55   571028-5
7. I've Grown Accustomed to His Face (Lerner-Loewe) 2:59   590325-3
8. I'll Never Be the Same (Malneck-Signorelli-Kahn) 4:17   571028-1
9. So Rare (Herst-Sharpe) 3:30   571028-8
10. Tenderly (Lawrence-Gross) 3:03   570724-1
11. Stairway to the Stars (Malneck-Parish-Signorelli) 2:46   570724-3
12. Moonlight in Vermont (Suessdorf-Blackburn) 3:14   570724-2

LP: Verve MG V 4034 (mono)/Verve MG VS 6100 (released 1960). Side A, Tracks 1-6 (23:08)/Side B, Tracks 7-12 (19:49). Total playing time: 43:57. CD: MCA (Japan)

Polygram POCJ-2760 (released 1999). (Contents, sequence and playing time, same as above). Note: Tracks 5, 6, 8 and 9 are bonus tracks on the CD issue of **Like Someone in Love** (LPD-53). Produced under the personal supervision of **Norman Granz**. Director of Engineering: **Val Valentin**. There are no liner notes.

The Verve Years (1957-1959)

LPD-57 PORGY AND BESS/ELLA FITZGERALD AND LOUIS ARMSTRONG

1. Overture (Gershwin-Garcia) 10:52   (571014)
2. Summertime (Heyward-Gershwin) 4:59   570818-1
3. I Wants To Stay Here (Gershwin-Heyward-Gershwin) 4:38   570828-1
4. My Man's Gone Now (Heyward-Gershwin) 4:03   570828-2
5. I Got Plenty o' Nuttin' (Gershwin-Heyward-Gershwin) 3:52   570818-3
6. The Buzzard Song (Heyward-Gershwin) 2:58   570828-4
7. Bess, You Is My Woman Now (Gershwin-Heyward-Gershwin) 5:29   570818-2
8. It Ain't Necessarily So (Gershwin-Gershwin) 6:35   570818-4
9. What You Want Wid Bess? (Heyward-Gershwin) 1:59   570828-3
10. A Woman Is a Sometime Thing (Heyward-Gershwin)** 4:48   (570819)
11. Oh, Doctor Jesus (Heyward-Gershwin)* 2:00   570828-5
12. Medley: Here Comes de Honey Man (Heyward-Gershwn)* 3:29   570828-6; Crab Man (Heyward-Gershwin)** (570828); Oh, Dey's So Fresh an' Fine (Strawberry Woman) (Heyward-Gershwin)* 590325-9
13. There's a Boat Dat's Leavin' Soon for New York (Gershwin-Gershwin) 4:55   570819-1
14. Bess, Oh, Where's My Bess? (Gershwin-Gershwin)** 2:36   (570819)
15. Oh Lawd, I'm on My Way (Heyward-Gershwin)*** 2:58   (570819)

*Ella solo/**Louis solo/***Louis with choir/Others are duets

LP: Verve MG V-4011-2 (2 discs) (released December 1957). Disc 1: Side 1, Tracks 1-3 (20:34)/Side 2, Tracks 4-7 (16:29). Disc 2: Side 3, Tracks 8-11 (15:32)/Side 4, Tracks 12-15 (14:04). Total playing time, 66:39. Verve V-6040-2 (2 discs), same contents and sequence as above (1959). Verve VE2-2507 (2 discs), same contents and sequence as above (1976). -Track: Verve 8T2-2507 (2 tapes), same contents and sequence, asabove (1976). CT: Verve CT2-2507 (2 cassettes), same contents and sequence as above (1976). CD: Verve 827 475-2, same contents and sequence as above (released 1985). Verve Master Edition 314 537 284-2 (3 discs), **The Complete Ella Fitzgerald and Louis Armstrong on Verve**, Disc 3 (released October 1997). Produced under the personal supervision of **Norman Granz**. Recording Engineer: **Val Valentin**. Liner notes by **Norman Granz**.

The Verve Years (1958-1959)

LPD-58 ELLA FITZGERALD SINGS SWEET SONGS FOR SWINGERS

1. Sweet and Lovely (Arnheim-Tobias-Lemare) 3:06 581124-5
2. Let's Fall in Love (Koehler-Arlen) 2:59   581124-3
3. Makin' Whoopee (Kahn-Donaldson) 3:37   581124-8
4. That Old Feeling (Brown-Fain) 4:08   590711-3
5. I Remember You (Mercer-Schertzinger) 2:17 581124-4
6. Moonlight Serenade (Parish-Miller) 2:57   590711-5
7. Gone with the Wind (Magidson-Wrubel) 2:54 590711-2
8. Can't We Be Friends? (James-Swift) 3:15   581124-6
9. Out of This World (Mercer-Arlen) 4:23   581124-7
10. My Old Flame (Coslow-Johnston) 2:56   590711-1
11. East of the Sun (and West of the Moon) (Bowman) 3:38   581124-1
12. Lullaby of Broadway (Dubin-Warren) 2:21   581124-2

    LP: Verve MG V-4032 (mono)/MG V6 4032 (stereo) (released October 1959). Side One, Tracks 1-6 (19:29)/Side Two, Tracks 7-12 (19:52). Total playing time, 39:21. Produced under the personal supervision of **Norman Granz**. Recording Engineer: **Val Valentin**.

The Verve Years (1959)

LPD-59 ELLA FITZGERALD SINGS THE GEORGE AND IRA GERSHWIN SONG BOOK

1. Sam and Delilah (Gershwin-Gershwin) 3:16 590716-5
2. But Not for Me (Gershwin-Gershwin) 3:32 590108-3
3. My One and Only (Gershwin-Gershwin) 2:36 590326-1
4. Let's Call the Whole Thing Off (Gershwin-Gershwin) 4:26   590326-6
5. (I've Got) Beginner's Luck (Gershwin-Gershwin) 3:08   590105-10
6. Oh! Lady, Be Good! (Gershwin-Gershwin) 4:00 590108-7
7. Nice Work if You Can Get It (Gershwin-Gershwin) 3:32   590326-3
8. Things Are Looking Up (Gershwin-Gershwin) 3:03 590717-2
9. Just Another Rhumba (Gershwin-Gershwin) 5:35 590717-5
10. How Long Has This Been Going On? (Gershwin-Gershwin) 3:45   590105-6
11. 'S Wonderful (Gershwin-Gershwin) 3:28   590716-1
12. The Man I Love (Gershwin-Gershwin) 3:50 590105-7
13. That Certain Feeling (Gershwin-Gershwin) 3:02 590715-2
14. By Strauss (Gershwin-Gershwin) 2:30   590716-6
15. Someone to Watch Over Me (Gershwin-Gershwin) 4:32   590326-2
16. The Real American Folk song (Gershwin-Gershwin) 3:43   590718-6
17. Who Cares? (Gershwin-Gershwin) 3:05   590716-2
18. Looking for a Boy (Gershwin-Gershwin) 3:03 590326-7
19. They All Laughed (Gershwin-Gershwin) 3:03 590326-10
20. My Cousin in Milwaukee (Gershwin-Gershwin) 3:08   590717-1
21. Somebody from Somewhere (Gershwin-Gershwin) 3:06   590718-1
22. A Foggy Day (in London Town) (Gershwin-Gershwin) 3:31   590105-6
23. Clap Yo' Hands (Gershwin-Gershwin) 2:28 590107-3
24. For You, for Me, for Evermore (Gershwin-Gershwin) 3:23   590718-3
25. Stiff Upper Lip (Gershwin-Gershwin) 2:51 590717-3
26. Boy Wanted (Gershwin-Gershwin) 3:34   590715-4
27. Strike Up the Band (Gershwin-Gershwin) 2:34 590716-4
28. Soon (Gershwin-Gershwin) 2:20   590105-1
29. I've Got a Crush on You (Gershwin-Gershwin) 3:28 590108-2
30. Bidin' My Time (Gershwin-Gershwin) 2:40 590105-8
31. Aren't You Kinda Glad We Did? (Gershwin-Gershwin) 3:28   590718-4
32. Of Thee I Sing (Baby) (Gershwin-Gershwin) 3:07 590318-2
33. "The Half of It, Dearie" Blues (Gershwin-Gershwin) 3:46   590715-5

34. I Was Doing All Right (Gershwin-Gershwin) 3:26 590318-3

35. He Loves and She Loves (Gershwin-Gershwin) 2:46 590105-9

36. Love Is Sweeping the Country (Gershwin-Gershwin) 3:24 590718-2

37. Treat Me Rough (Gershwin-Gershwin) 3:54 590716-3

38. Our Love Is Here To Stay (Gershwin-Gershwin) 3:53 590105-3

39. Slap That Bass (Gershwin-Gershwin) 3:21 590107-2

40. Isn't It a Pity? (Gershwin-Gershwin) 3:24 590718-5

41. Shall We Dance (Gershwin-Gershwin) 3:07 590715-1

42. Love Walked In (Gershwin-Gershwin) 3:51 590326-4

43. You've Got What Gets Me (Gershwin-Gershwin) 2:13 590107-5

44. They Can't Take That Away from Me (Gershwin-Gershwin) 3:08 590105-5

45. Embraceable You (Gershwin-Gershwin) 4:51 590108-1

46. I Can't Be Bothered Now (Gershwin-Gershwin) 2:48 590318-1

47. Boy! What Love Has Done to Me! (Gershwin-Gershwin) 3:47 590715-3

48. Fascinating Rhythm (Gershwin-Gershwin) 3:23 590318-5

49. Funny Face (Gershwin-Gershwin) 3:23 590318-4

50. The Lorelei (Gershwin-Gershwin) 3:20 590715-6

51. Oh, So Nice (Gershwin-Gershwin) 3:40 590717-4

52. Let's Kiss and Make Up (Gershwin-Gershwin) 3:50 590326-9

53. I Got Rhythm (Gershwin-Gershwin) 3:06 590105-2

54. Somebody Loves Me (Gershwin-DeSylva-MacDonald) 2:36 590107-1

55. Cheerful Little Earful (Warren-Gershwin-Rose) 2:06 590107-4

56. Oh! Lady, Be Good! (Gershwin-Gershwin) (alternative take) 4:08 590108-4

57. But Not for Me (Gershwin-Gershwin) (45 rpm take)* 2:04 590326-5

58. Ambulatory Suite (George Gershwin) 7:10 (590820); a. Promenade (Walking the Dog); b. March of the Swiss Soldiers; c. Fidgety Feet

59. The Preludes (George Gershwin) 6:30 (590820); a. Prelude I; b. Prelude II; c. Prelude III

60. The Lorelei (alternative take) 3:00 590326-8

61. Our Love Is Here to Stay (partial alternative take, edited) 3:51 590105-4

62. Oh! Lady, Be Good (alternative take) 3:56 590108-5

63. Oh! Lady, Be Good (alternative take) 4:12 590108-6

64. But Not for Me (monaural mix) 3:32 590108-3

65. Fascinating Rhythm (monaural mix) 3:21 590318-5

66. They All Laughed (monaural mix) 3:02 590326-10

67. The Man I Love (monaural mix) 3:50 590105-7

68. Nice Work If You Can Get It (edited monaural mix) 3:32 590326-3

69. Clap Yo' Hands (monaural mix) 2:29 590107-3

70. Let's Call the Whole Thing Off (monaural mix) 4:26 590326-6

71. I Was Doing All Right (monaural mix) 3:25 590318-3

72. He Loves and She Loves (monaural mix) 2:46 590105-9

73. (I've Got) Beginner's Luck (monaural mix) 3:07 590105-10

*Includes very brief conversation, Fitzgerald-Riddle, re "Oh! Lady, Be Good"

LP: Verve MG V-4029-5 (Verve MG V-4024/25/26/27/28) (mono) (December 1959). Verve MG VS-6082-5 (Verve MG VS-6077/78/79/80/81) (stereo) (December 1959). Disc 1: Side 1, Tracks 1-5 (16:58)/Side 2, 6-10 (19:55). Disc 2: Side 3, Tracks 11-15 (17:22)/Side 4, Tracks 16-21 (19:08). Disc 3: Side 5, Tracks 22-27 (18:21)/Side 6, Tracks 28-32 (15:03). Disc 4: Side 7, Tracks 33-37 (17:16)/Side 8, Tracks 38-43 (19:49). Disc 5: Side 9, Tracks 44-48 (17:57)/Side 10, Tracks 49-53 (17:19). BonusDisc (Verve MG V-100) (10"): Side 1, Track 58 (7:10)/Side 2,. Track 59 (6:30). Total playing time, 3:12:48.

Verve MG V-4029-5 was initially issued in a "Complete Deluxe Set," enclosed. in a walnut box that contained not only the five 12" LP discs and. the bonus 10" LP disc, but also a special edition hard-cover book, **The Gershwins/Words Upon Music**, by Lawrence D. Stewart and five Bernard. Buffet lithographs drawn especially for these albums and suitable. for framing.

Verve MG V-6082-5 was initially released in the same manner, except. that instead of a 10" LP disc, it contained a 7" EP version (MG VS-100).

Verve V6-4029-5 (Verve V6-4024/25/26/27/28), without bonuses in cardboard box (released 1961).

Verve VE2-2525 (2 discs) (stereo) (released 1978). Disc 1: Side 1, Tracks 2, 4, 6, 7, 8, 11, 12 (25:51). Disc 1: Side 2, Tracks 13, 14, 15, 17, 19, 20, 22, 23 (25:19). Disc 2: Side 3, Tracks 28, 29, 30, 32, 33, 38, 40 (22:38). Disc 2: Side 4, Tracks 41, 43, 44, 45, 46, 48, 50, 53 (25:56). Total playing time, 1:39:44.

Verve 2615063 (stereo), same contents and sequence as Verve V6-4029-5,. with 44-page booklet (released 1978).

8-Track: Verve 8T2-2525 (2 tapes), same contents as Verve VE2-2525 LP. (released 1978).

CT: Verve CT2-2525 (2 cassettes), same contents as Verve VE2-2525 LP. (released 1985).

CD: Verve 825 024-2 (3 discs), with 44-page booklet (released 1985). Disc 1, Tracks 1-17 (55:21)/Disc 2, Tracks 18-35 (60:50)/Disc 3,. Tracks 36-53 (60:43). Total playing time, 2:56:53.

Verve 314 519 832-2 (**The Complete Ella Fitzgerald Song Books**, Discs. Ten, Eleven, and Twelve) (released August 1993). Disc Ten, Tracks 58, 59, 1-17 (75:48). Disc Eleven, Tracks 18-35 (56:37). Disc Twelve, Tracks 36-57 (73:49). (Note: Tracks 58 and 59 are issued here for the first time on CD;. tracks 54 and 55 originally appeared on LP, **Ella Fitzgerald/Get Happy!**. (Verve MG V-4036); track 56 is previously unissued; track 57, originally. a 7" 45 issue (Verve 10180), also appears on Verve VE2-2525. Total playing time, 3:26:14.

Verve Master Edition 314 539 759-2 (4 discs) (released June 1998). Disc 1: Tracks 58, 59, 1-16 (72:37)/Disc 2: Tracks 17-37 (66:05). Disc 3: Tracks 38-53 (55:56)/Disc 4: Tracks 54,55,57,56.62-73(60:16). Total playing time, 4:14:54.

Conceived and produced by **Norman Granz**/Recording Engineer: **Val Valentin**. Enclosed in the package is a book, **The Gershwins/Words Upon Music**, by Lawrence D. Stewart.

The Verve Years (1957-1959)

LPD-60 ELLA FITZGERALD/GET HAPPY!

1. Somebody Loves Me (DeSylva-Macdonald-Gershwin) 2:33   590107-1
2. Cheerful Little Earful (Gershwin-Rose-Warren) 2:50 590107-4
3. You Make Me Feel So Young (Gordon-Myrow) 2:17 590711-6
4. Beat Me, Daddy, Eight to the Bar (Raye-Prince-Sheehy) 2:28   590903-3
5. Like Young (Webster-Previn) 2:57   590903-1
6. Cool Breeze (Dameron-Eckstine-Gillespie) 1:55 590903-2
7. Moonlight Becomes You (Burke-Van Heusen) 3:03 590711-4
8. Blue Skies (Berlin) 3:40   580318-5
9. You Turned the Tables on Me (Mitchell-Alter) 2:31 570724-6
10. The Gypsy in My Soul (Jaffe-Boland) 2:40 570724-7
11. Goody-Goody (Mercer-Malneck) 2:27   570724-8
12. St. Louis Blues (Handy) 3:50   570724-9
13. A-Tisket, A-Tasket (Fitzgerald-Feldman) 2:20 570724-5
14. Swingin' Shepard Blues (Kossman-Jacobson-Roberts) 2:50   580319-6

LP: Verve MG V-4036 (mono)/Verve MG VS-6102 (stereo) (Released 1961). Side 1, Tracks 1-6 (15:15)/Side 2, Tracks 7-12 (18:26). Total playing time, 33:41.

CD: Verve 523 321-2 (Released October 1998). Tracks 1-14/Total playing time: 38:42.

Produced under the personal supervision of **Norman Granz**. Liner notes by Benny Green, **The Observer**, London.

*Note: Tracks 1 and 2 appear as bonus tracks on the CD release of **Ella Swings Brightly with Nelson** (LPD-68), q.v. Track 13 appeared originally as a 45rpm single (backed with "Goody Goody" from the same session), and was subsequently included in the LP album **Verve's Choice/The Best of Ella Fitzgerald** (LPD-73), q.v., and again in the 3-CD collection **Ella Fitzgerald/First Lady of Song** (LPD-86), q.v. Track 14, previously unreleased, is an alternative take of the master which appears also on the same 3-CD collection (q.v.).*

The Verve Years (1956-1960)

LPD-61 ELLA IN BERLIN: MACK THE KNIFE THE COMPLETE ELLA IN BERLIN: MACK THE KNIFE

1. Setting up stage; tuning up; Granz and Fitzgerald talking 0:20
2. That Old Black Magic (Mercer-Arlen) 3:51 600213-1
3. Our Love Is Here To Stay (Gershwin-Gershwin) 3:19   600213-2
4. Gone with the Wind (Magidson-Wrubel) 2:25 600213-3
5. Misty (Garner-Burke) 2:38   600213-4
6. Applause and fanfare interlude 0:19
7. The Lady Is a Tramp (Rodgers-Hart) 2:40   600213-5
8. Fanfare and announcement 0:28
9. The Man I Love (Gershwin-Gershwin) 3:42 600213-6
10. Love for Sale (Porter)* 2:57   560815-1
11. Just One of Those Things (Porter)* 3:53   560815-2
12. Summertime (Heyward-Gershwin) 3:02   600213-7
13. Too Darn Hot (Porter) 3:17   600213-8
14. Applause and fanfare interlude 0:24
15. The Lorelei (Gershwin-Gershwin) 3:27   600213-9
16. Mack The Knife (Weill-Brecht-Blitzstein) 4:39 600213-10
17. Fanfare and announcement
18. How High the Moon (Lewis-Hamilton) 6:58 600213-11
19. Applause and closing fanfare 1:06

*These two tracks were not recorded in Berlin, but were from a concert performance at the Hollywood Bowl on Wednesday, 15 August 1956.

LP: Verve MG V-4041 (mono) (**Ella in Berlin/Mack The Knife**) (released 1960). Side 1, Tracks 4, 5, 7, 9, 12 (14:27)/Side 2, Tracks 13, 15, 16, 18 (18:21). Total playing time, 32:48.

Verve MG VS-6163 (stereo), same contents and sequence as above. CT: Verve 825 670-4 (released 1985). CD: Verve 825 670-2 (**Mack The Knife/Ella in Berlin**) (released 1985). Same contents and sequence as above. Verve 314 519 564-2 (**Mack The Knife/The Complete Ella in Berlin**). Tracks 1-19 (released 1993).

Original concerts and records produced by **Norman Granz**. **Mack The Knife/The Complete Ella in Berlin** produced by **Phil Schaap**. Liner notes by **Norman Granz**. This album charted 12 December 1960/weeks, 20/peak, #11.

The Verve Years (1960)

LPD-62 ELLA FITZGERALD SINGS SONGS FROM *LET NO MAN WRITE MY EPITAPH*

The Intimate Ella

1. Black Coffee (Webster-Burke) 3:27   600414-3
2. Angel Eyes (Dennis-Brent) 3:27   600414-2
3. I Cried for You (Arnheim-Lyman-Freed) 3:26   600414-5
4. I Can't Give You Anything but Love (McHugh-Fields) 3:28   600419-2
5. Then You've Never Been Blue (Fiorito-Lewis-Young) 3:10   600419-4
6. I Hadn't Anyone Till You (Noble) 2:49   600414-4
7. My Melancholy Baby (Burnett-Norton) 2:57   600414-1
8. Misty (Garner-Burke) 2:51   600414-6
9. September Song (Anderson-Weill) 3:40   600419-5
10. One for My Baby (and One More for the Road) (Mercer-Arlen) 4:17   600419-7
11. Who's Sorry Now? (Snyder-Kalmar-Ruby) 3:26   600419-1
12. I'm Getting Sentimental Over You (Bassman-Washington) 2:36   600419-3
13. Reach for Tomorrow (McHugh-Washington) 2:24   600419-6

LP: Verve MG V-4043 (**Ella Fitzgerald Sings Songs from *Let No Man Write My Epitaph***) (released 1960). Side 1, Tracks 1-6 (19:49)/Side 2, Tracks 7-13 (22:11). Total playing time: 42:00.

CT: Verve 839 838-4 (***The Intimate Ella***), same contents as above (released 1990). CD: Verve 839 838-2 (***The Intimate Ella***), same contents as above (released 1989 in The Netherlands, 1990 in the U.S.). Produced under the personal supervision of **Norman Granz**. Original liner notes by **Norman Granz**. Liner notes for CD reissue by **Imme Schade van Westrum**.

The Verve Years

LPD-63 ELLA WISHES YOU A SWINGING CHRISTMAS

1. Jingle Bells (Pierpont-DeVol) 2:23   600715-2
2. Santa Claus Is Coming to Town (Gillespie-Coots) 2:19   600715-1
3. Have Yourself a Merry Little Christmas (Martin-Blane) 2:58   600716-5
4. What Are You Doing New Year's Eve? (Loesser) 3:32   600716-3
5. Sleigh Ride (Parish-Anderson) 2:55   600805-2
6. The Christmas Song (Tormé-Wells) 2:58   600805-3
7. "Good Morning" Blues (Basie-Durham-Rushing) 3:17   600805-1
8. Let It Snow! Let It Snow! Let It Snow! (Styne-Cahn) 3:44   600716-2
9. Winter Wonderland (Smith-Bernard) 2:16   600716-1
10. Rudolph, the Red-Nosed Reindeer (Marks) 2:55   600715-6
11. Frosty, the Snow Man (Nelson-Rollins) 2:12   600715-3
12. White Christmas (Berlin) 3:00   600805-4

LP: Verve MG V-4042/Verve VE1-2539 (released 1960). Side 1, Tracks 1-6 (17:05)/Side 2, Tracks 7-12 (17:24). Total playing time, 34:29. CT: Verve 827-150-4, same contents and sequence as above (released 1988). CD: Verve 827-150-2, same contents and sequence as above (released 1988). Recorded under the personal supervision of **Norman Granz**. Recording Engineer: **Val Valentin**. The author of the liner notes is uncredited. Prepared for compact disc by **Richard Seidel** and **Seth Rothstein**.

The Verve Years (1960-1961)

LPD-64 ELLA FITZGERALD SINGS THE HAROLD ARLEN SONG BOOK

1. Blues in the Night (Arlen-Koehler) 7:11   610114-2

2. Let's Fall in Love (Arlen-Koehler) 4:01   610116-2
3. Stormy Weather (Arlen-Koehler) 5:13   610114-4
4. Between the Devil and the Deep Blue Sea (Arlen-Koehler) 2:22   610116-1
5. My Shining Hour (Arlen-Mercer) 3:59   610115-1
6. Hooray for Love (Arlen-Robin) 2:42   600801-1
7. This Time the Dream's on Me (Arlen-Mercer) 4:35 610115-4
8. That Old Black Magic (Arlen-Mercer) 4:08 610114-1
9. I've Got the World on a String (Arlen-Koehler) 4:50 600801-8
10. Let's Take a Walk Around the Block (Arlen-Gershwin-Harburg) 3:59   600802-5
11. Ill Wind (Arlen-Koehler) 3:51   610115-2
12. Ac-Cent-Tchu-Ate the Positive (Arlen-Mercer) 3:38 600801-6
13. When the Sun Comes Out (Arlen-Koehler) 5:06 600801-2
14. Come Rain or Come Shine (Arlen-Mercer) 3:21 610116-5
15. As Long As I Live (Arlen-Koehler) 3:45   600801-3
16. Happiness Is (Just) a Thing Called Joe (Arlen-Harburg) 3:28   610116-3
17. (It's Only a) Paper Moon (Arlen-Harburg-Rose) 3:34   600801-4
18. The Man That Got Away Gershwin) 5:18   600801-5
19. One for My Baby (and One More for the Road) (Arlen-Mercer) 3:55   610114-5
20. It Was Written in the Stars (Arlen-Robin) 5:08 610115-5
21. Get Happy! (Arlen-Koehler) 3:29   600802-1
22. I Gotta Right To Sing the Blues (Arlen-Koehler) 5:10   610114-3
23. Out of This World (Arlen-Mercer) 2:42   610116-4
24. Over the Rainbow (Arlen-Harburg) 4:16   610115-3
25. Ding-Dong! The Witch Is Dead (Arlen-Harburg) 3:16   600802-4
26. Sing, My Heart (Arlen-Koehler) 2:45   600802-2
27. Let's Take a Walk Around the Block (Arlen-Gershwin-Harburg)* 3:58   600802-6
28. Sing, My Heart (Arlen-Koehler)* 2:32   600802-3

LP: Verve MG V-4046-2 (MG V-4057/58) (mono) (2 discs) (released May 1961). Verve V6-4047-2 (V6-4057/58) (2 discs). Disc 1: Side 1, Tracks 1-6 (25:33)/Side 2, Tracks 7-12 (25:06). Disc 2: Side 1, Tracks 13-18 (24:37)/Side 2, Tracks 19-24 (24:45). Total playing time: 1:40:01.

Verve 817 526-1 (2 discs) 817 527-1, Vol. 1/817 528-1, Vol. 2 (1984). Disc 1: Side 1, Tracks 1-6 (25:33)/Side 2, Tracks 7-12, 26 (27:52). Disc 2: Side 1, Tracks 13-18 (24:37)/Side 2, Tracks 19-25 (28:02). Total playing time: 1:46:02.

CT: Verve 817 526-4 (2 cassettes), same contents and sequence as above (1984). CD: Verve 817 527-2 (Vol. 1)/817 528-2 (Vol. 2), same contents and sequence. as the 1984 LP releases (released 1988).

Verve 314 519 832-2 (**The Complete Ella Fitzgerald Song Books**, Discs. Thirteen and Fourteen) (released 1993). Disc Thirteen, Tracks, 1-12 (51:18)/Disc Fourteen, Tracks 13-28*(65:52). Total playing time: 1:57:10.

*Tracks 27 and 28 previously unreleased.

Produced under the personal supervision of **Norman Granz**. Director of Engineering: **Val Valentin**. Liner notes, "About Ella Fitzgerald…," by Benny Green; "About Harold Arlen…," by **Edward Jablonski**.

The Verve Years (1961)

LPD-65 ELLA RETURNS TO BERLIN

1. Introductions and announcements 1:20
2. Give Me the Simple Life (Ruby-Bloom) 2:03 610211-1
3. Take the "A" Train (Strayhorn) 3:46   610211-2
4. (I'd Like to Get You on a) Slow Boat to China (Loesser) 2:21   610211-3
5. Medley: a. Why Was I Born? (Kern-Hammerstein)/ 5:37   610211-4; b. Can't Help Lovin' Dat Man (Kern-Hammerstein)/c. People Will Say We're in Love (Rodgers-Hammerstein)
6. Introduction 0:11
7. You're Driving Me Crazy (Donaldson) 3:24   610211-5
8. Rock It for Me (Werner-Werner) 3:24   610211-6
9. Witchcraft (Coleman-Leigh) 2:55   610211-7
10. Anything Goes (Porter) 2:34   610211-8
11. Cheek to Cheek (Berlin) 3:44   610211-9
12. Misty (Burke-Garner) 2:57   610211-10
13. Caravan (Ellington-Parish-Mills) 2:02   610211-11
14. Mr. Paganini (You'll Have To Swing It) (Coslow) 4:45   610211-12
15. Mack the Knife (Weill-Brecht-Blitzstein) 3:30 610211-13
16. Fanfare for Ella 0:22
17. 'Round Midnight (Monk-Williams-Hanighen) 3:31 610211-14
18. Joe Williams' Blues (Fitzgerald) 5:27   610211-15
19. Fanfare for Ella 0:53
20. This Can't Be Love (Rodgers-Hart) 4:30   610211-16
21. Closing announcements by Norman Granz 0:54

LP: Verve 837 758-1 (released October 1991). Side 1: Tracks 1-10 (27:35)/Side 2: Tracks 11-21) (32:36). Total playing time: 60:11. CT: Verve 837-758-4 (released October

1991), same as above. CD: Verve 837-758-2 (released October 1991), same as above. DCC: Verve 837-758-5 (released 1994), same as above. Total playing times (CT, CD, DCC): 60:11. Original concert produced by **Norman Granz**/Release conceived by **Richard Seidel**. Liner notes by **Michael Bourne**.

The Verve Years (1961)

LPD-66 ELLA IN HOLLYWOOD WITH THE LOU LEVY QUARTET

1. This Could Be the Start of Something Big (Allen) 2:23   610516-5
2. I've Got the World on a String (Koehler-Arlen) 3:47 610514-5
3. You're Driving Me Crazy (Donaldson) 3:20 610516-3
4. Just in Time (Comden-Green-Styne) 1:55   610514-1
5. It Might as Well Be Spring (Hammerstein II-Rodgers) 3:00   610519-4
6. Take the "A" Train (Strayhorn) 9:27   610521-4
7. Stairway to the Stars (Parish-Malneck-Signorelli) 3:47   610521-2
8. Mr. Paganini (You'll Have To Swing It) (Coslow) 4:27   610512-1
9. Satin Doll (Strayhorn-Mercer-Ellington) 2:51 610517-2
10. Blue Moon (Rodgers-Hart) 3:20   610516-4
11. Baby, Won't You Please Come Home (Williams-Warfield) 3:48   610516-6
12. Air Mail Special (Goodman-Mundy-Chrisian) 5:42 610517-4

LP: MG V-4052 (mono)/MG VS-4052 (stereo) (released October 1961). Side 1, Tracks 1-6 (24:07)/Side 2, Tracks 7-12 (24:30). Total playing time: 48:37. CD: Verve POCJ-2647 (released only in Japan; limited marketing elsewhere). Produced under the personal supervision of **Norman Granz**. Liner notes by Paul Gris.

Note: Of the many tracks recorded at The Crescendo during this ten-day gig, only one other has surfaced on a recording. "A-Tisket, A-Tasket" may be found on the CD/Cassette releases, Compact/Walkman Jazz (Verve 831 367-2/4). This album was charted 6 January 1962/weeks, 1/peak, #35.

The Verve Years (1961)

LPD-67 ELLA FITZGERALD/CLAP HANDS! HERE COMES CHARLIE!

1 A Night in Tunisia (Gillespie-Paparelli-Hendricks) 4:06   610624-4

2. You're My Thrill (Gorney-Clare) 3:35   610622-5
3. My Reverie (Debussy-Clinton) 3:16   610623-3
4. Stella by Starlight (Young-Washington) 3:17 610622-1
5. 'Round Midnight (Hanighen-Williams-Monk) 3:28 610623-2
6. The Jersey Bounce (Feyne-Bradshaw-Johnson-Plater-Wright) 3:33   610622-4
7. Signing Off (Campbell-Travers-Hassan-Virtue) 3:45 610624-2
8. Cry Me a River (Hamilton) 4:13   610624-1
9. This Year's Kisses (Berlin) 2:14   610622-2
10. Good Morning, Heartache (Drake-Fisher-Higginbotham) 4:17   610622-6
11. (I Was) Born to Be Blue (Tormé-Wells) 2:42 610623-1
12. Clap Hands! Here Comes Charlie! (Rose MacDonald-Meyer) 2:41   610624-3
13. Spring Can Really Hang You Up the Most (Wolf-Landesman) 6:13   610622-3
14. The Music Goes 'Round and 'Round (Riley-Farley-Hodgson) 2:27   610624-5
15. The One I Love Belongs to Somebody Else (Jones-Kahn)* 2:12   610123-6
16. I Got a Guy (Sunshine)* 3:43   610123-7
17. This Could Be the Start of Something Big (Allen)* 2:43   610123-9

LP: Verve MG V-4053 (mono)/V6-4053 (stereo) (Released December 1961). Side 1, Tracks 1-7 (25:06)/Side 2, Tracks 8-14 (24:54). Total playing time: 50:00. CT release: Verve 835 646-4 (Tracks 1-17) (Released 1989). CD release: Verve 835 646-2 (Tracks 1-17) (Released 1989). Total playing time: 59:30. *Tracks 15-17 previously unissued. Produced under the personal supervision of **Norman Granz**. Director of Engineering: **Val Valentin**. Liner notes by **Benny Green**.

The Verve Years (1959/1961)

LPD-68 ELLA* SWINGS BRIGHTLY WITH NELSON*

Fitzgerald-Riddle

1. When Your Lover Has Gone (Swan) 3:00   611114-6
2. Don't Be That Way (Goodman-Parish-Sampson) 3:47   611227-1
3. Love Me or Leave Me (Donaldson-Kahn) 2:49 611115-5
4. I Hear Music (Lane-Loesser) 2:19   611114-5
5. What Am I Here For? (Ellington-Laine) 2:43 611114-1

6. I'm Gonna Go Fishin' (Ellington-Lee) 3:00
611227-3

7. I Won't Dance (Fields-McHugh) 3:30   611227-2

8. I Only Have Eyes for You (Warren-Dubin) 2:37
611114-3

9. The Gentleman Is a Dope (Rodgers-Hammerstein)
3:58   611115-2

10. Mean to Me (Ahlert-Turk) 2:55   611113-2

11. Alone Together (Schwartz-Dietz) 2:45   611114-2

12. Pick Yourself Up (Kern-Fields) 2:06   611115-1

13. Call Me Darling (Fryberg-Marbet-Reisfeld-Dick)*
2:34   611115-3

14. Somebody Loves Me (Gershwin-DeSylva-Macdonald)* 2:33   590107-1

15. Cheerful Little Earful (Warren-Gershwin-Rose)*
2:06   590107-4

LP: Verve MG V-4054 (mono)/V6-4054 (stereo) (Released March 1962). Side One, Tracks 1-6 (17:47)/Side Two,
Tracks 7-12 (18:00). Total playing time, 35:47. CD: Verve
314 519 347-2 (Released July 1993). Tracks 1-15. Total playing time, 43:27. Note: *Track 13 originally issued on 7"
45rpm single, Verve 10248. Tracks 14 and 15 originally issued on **Ella Fitzgerald/Get Happy!**,. Verve MG V/V6
4036, q.v. Produced under the personal supervision of **Norman Granz**. Original recordings engineered by **Val
Valentin**. Liner notes by **Benny Green**. CD re-issue supervised by **Michael Lang**.

The Verve Years (1962)

LPD-69 ELLA FITZGERALD/ RHYTHM IS MY BUSINESS

1. Rough Ridin' (Fitzgerald-Jones-Tennyson) 2:50
620131-5

2. Broadway (Woods-McRae-Bird) 2:43   620130-2

3. You Can Depend on Me (Carpenter-Dunlap-Hines)
3:32   620130-4

4. Runnin' Wild (Grey-Wood-Gibbs) 2:41   620131-4

5. Show Me the Way to Go Out of This World (Clark-
Dennis) 2:44   620131-2

6. I'll Always Be in Love with You (Ruby-Green-Stept)
2:48   620129-1

7. Hallelujah! I Love Him So (Charles) 2:30   620130-5

8. I Can't Face the Music (Without Singing the Blues)
(Koehler-Bloom) 5:01   620130-3

9. No Moon at All (Evans-Mann) 2:36   620131-3

10. Laughing on the Outside (Crying on the Inside)
(Raleigh-Wayne) 4:51   620131-1

11. After You've Gone (Creamer-Layton) 4:08   620130-1

12. Taking a Chance on Love (Latouche-Fetter-Duke)
2:35   620231-6

13. If I Could Be with You (Creamer-Johnson) 2:39
620130-6

LP: Verve MG V-4056 (mono)/V6-4056 (stereo) (released September 1962). Side One, Tracks 1-6 (17:33)/Side
Two, Tracks 7-11 (19:21). Total playing time, 36:54. CD:
Verve 314 559 513-2 (released January 1999). Tracks 1—
13/Total playing time, 42:27. Produced under the personal
supervision of **Norman Granz**. Engineers: **Ray Hall-Clair
Crepps**/Director of Recording: **Val Valentin**. Liner notes
by **Benny Green**. CD re-issue: Produced by **Richard Seidel**/Supervised by **Bryan Koniarz** and **Jerry Rappa-
port**/Researched and restored by **Ben Young**.

The Verve Years (1961-1962)

LPD-70 ELLA SWINGS GENTLY WITH NELSON

1. Sweet and Slow (Warren-Dubin) 3:15   620410-5

2. Georgia on My Mind (Carmichael-Gorrell) 3:29
611113-3

3. I Can't Get Started (Duke-Gershwin) 3:33   611113-4

4. Street of Dream (Young-Lewis) 3:12   620409-3

5. Imagination (Van Heusen-Burke) 3:47   620410-2

6. The Very Thought of You (Noble) 2:46   620410-4

7. It's a Blue World (Forrest-Wright) 2:44   620409-1

8. Darn That Dream (Van Heusen-De Lange) 2:31
611113-1

9. He's Funny That Way (Moret-Whiting) 3:14
620409-2

10. I Wished on the Moon (Parker-Rainger) 2:44
620410-1

11. It's a Pity to Say Goodnight (Reid) 2:34   611114-4

12. My One and Only Love (Mellin-Wood) 3:12
620410-3

13. Body and Soul (Green-Eyton-Heyman-Sour) 3:44
620409-4

14. Call Me Darling (Freiberg-Marbet-Reisfeld-Dick)*
3:41   611115-4

15. All of Me (Marks-Simons)* 3:22   611115-6

LP: Verve MG V-4055 (mono)/MG V6-4055 (stereo)
(released November 1962). Side One, Tracks 1-6
(19:57)/Side Two, Tracks 7-13 (21:27). Total playing time:
41:24. CD: Verve 314 519 348-2 (Tracks 1-15) (48:17) (released July 1993). *Note: Track 14 is previously unreleased.
Track 15 originally issued on LP **All-Star Festival: A
United Nations. Unique Record To Aid the World's
Refugees**, the only Ella Fitzgerald track thereon. Produced
under the personal supervision of **Norman Granz**. Director of Engineering: **Val Valentin**. Liner notes by **Benny
Green**. Compact disc reissue supervised by **Michael Lang**.

The Verve Years (1962)

LPD-71 ELLA SINGS BROADWAY

1. Hernando's Hideaway (Adler-Ross) (from **Pajama Game**) 3:15   621002-4
2. If I Were a Bell (Loesser) (from **Guys and Dolls**) 2:21   621004-2
3. Warm All Over (Loesser) (from **Guys and Dolls**) 2:45   621003-4
4. Almost Like Being in Love (Lerner-Loewe) (from **Brigadoon**) 3:00   621004-1
5. Dites-Moi (Rodgers-Hammerstein) (from **South Pacific**) 2:28   621003-3
6. I Could Have Danced All Night (Lerner-Loewe) (from **My Fair Lady**) 2:20   621002-1
7. Show Me (Lerner-Loewe) (from **My Fair Lady**) 2:22   621004-3
8. No Other Love (Rodgers-Hammerstein) (from **Me and Juliet**) 2:20   621003-2
9. Steam Heat (Adler-Ross) (from **Pajama Game**) 3:35   621001-3
10. Whatever Lola Wants (Lola Gets) (Adler-Ross) (from **Damn Yankees**) 3:10   621002-2
11. Guy and Dolls (Loesser) (from **Guys and Dolls**) 2:43   621002-3
12. Somebody Somewhere (Loesser) (from **Guys and Dolls**) 3:11   621003-1

LP: Verve V-4059 (mono)/V6-4059 (stereo) (released 1963). Side A, Tracks 1-6 (16:26)/Side B, Tracks 7-12 (17:46). Total playing time: 34:12. Produced under the personal supervision of **Norman Granz**. Director of Engineering: **Val Valentin**. Liner notes by **Benny Green**.

The Verve Years (1963)

LPD-72 ELLA FITZGERALD SINGS THE JEROME KERN SONG BOOK

1. Let's Begin (Kern-Harbach) 2:56   630107-3
2. A Fine Romance (Kern-Fields) 3:36   630105-2
3. All the Things You Are (Kern-Hammerstein) 3:15   630107-5
4. I'll Be Hard to Handle (Kern-Dougall) 3:47   630105-3
5. You Couldn't Be Cuter (Kern-Fields) 3:13   630107-1
6. She Didn't Say "Yes" (Kern 3:20   630107-2
7. I'm Old Fashioned (Kern-Mercer) 3:27   630105-1
8. Remind Me (Kern-Fields) 3:50   630107-4
9. The Way You Look Tonight (Kern-Fields) 4:28   630106-1
10. Yesterdays (Kern-Harbach) 2:51   630106-3

11. Can't Help Lovin' Dat Man (Kern-Hammerstein) 3:54   630106-2
12. Why Was I Born? (Kern-Hammerstein) 3:44   630106-4

LP: Verve MG V-4060 (mono)/MG V6-4060 (stereo) (released September 1964). Side One, Tracks 1-6 (00:00)/Side 2, Tracks 7-12 (00:00). Total playing time: 00:00. Verve 825 669-1 (stereo), same contents and sequence (released November 1985). CT: Verve 825 669-4 (stereo), same contents and sequence (released November 1985). CD: Verve 825 669-2 (stereo), same contents and sequence (released 1986). Verve 314 519 832-2 (stereo) (**The Complete Ella Fitzgerald Song Books**, Disc Fifteen), same contents and sequence (released August 1993). Produced under the personal supervision of **Norman Granz**. Director of Engineering: **Val Valentin**. Liner notes by **Benny Green**.

The Verve Years (1957-1963)

LPD-73 VERVE'S CHOICE!/ THE BEST OF ELLA FITZGERALD

1. Mack the Knife (Brecht-Blitzstein-Weill) 5:07   600213-10
2. A Beautiful Friendship (Styne-Kahn) 2:32   560327-2
3. Mr. Paganini (You'll Have To Swing It) (Coslow) 4:27   610512-1
4. Lorelei (Gershwin-Gershin) 3:27   600213-9
5. Goody Goody (Mercer-Malneck) 2:27   571009-6
6. Desafinado (Slightly Out of Tune) (Jobim-Mendonà-Hendricks-Cavanagh) 2:11   621001-1
7. Bill Bailey, Won't You Please Come Home (Cannon) 3:24   620629-23
8. Shiny Stockings (Fitzgerald-Foster) 3:30   630716-1
9. A-Tisket, A-Tasket (Fitzgerald-Alexander) 2:20   570724-5
10. How High the Moon (Hamilton-Lewis 7:56   600213-11

LP: Verve V-4063 (mono)/Verve V6-4063 (stereo). Side One, Tracks 1-5 (18:20)/Side Two, Tracks 6-10 (19:41). Total playing time, 38:01. Produced under the personal supervision of **Norman Granz.** Director of Engineering: **Val Valentin**. Liner notes by **Jack Maher**.

The Verve Years (1963)

LPD-74 ELLA AND BASIE!/ ON THE SUNNY SIDE OF THE STREET

1. Honeysuckle Rose (Waller-Razaf) 2:39   630715-5

2. 'Deed I Do (Rose-Hirsch) 2:40   630715-2

3. Into Each Life Some Rain Must Fall (Roberts-Fisher) 3:20   630716-8

4. Them There Eyes (Tracey-Tauber-Pinkard) 5:04 630716-1

5. Dream a Little Dream of Me (Schwandt-Andree-Kahn) 4:02   630716-2

6. Tea for Two (Youmans-Caesar) 3:10   630716-9

7. Satin Doll (Mercer-Ellington) 3:13   630715-4

8. I'm Beginning to See the Light (James-Ellington-Rodgers-George) 3:55   630715-1

9. Shiny Stockings (Foster-Fitzgerald) 3:30   630716-3

10. My Last Affair (Johnson) 3:12   630716-4

11. Ain't Misbehavin' (Waller-Brooks-Razaf) 3:09 630716-7

12. On the Sunny Side of the Street (McHugh-Fields) 3:00   630715-3

13. My Last Affair (alternative take) 3:17   630716-5

14. My Last Affair (alternative take) 3:22   630716-6

15. Robbins' Nest (Thompson-Jacquet)—breakdown 1:11 630716-10

16. Robbins' Nest (Thompson-Jacquet)—take 5 3:24 630716-11

17. Robbins' Nest (Thompson-Jacquet)—take 6 3:01 630716-12

18. Robbins' Nest (Thompson-Jacquet)—take 13 2:57 630716-13

LP: Verve MG V-4061 (mono)/MG V6-4061 (stereo) (released October 1963). Side One, Tracks 1-6 (21:25)/Side 2, Tracks 7-12 (21:20). Total playing time, 42:45. Verve 2304 049 (stereo), same contents and sequence (released 1984). CT: Verve 3113 108 (stereo), same contents and sequence (released 1984). CD: Verve 821 576-2 (stereo), same contents and sequence (released 1986). Verve Master Edition 314 539 059-2, Tracks 1-18 (remastered) (released October 1997) (Total playing time, 61:00). Produced under the personal supervision of, and with liner notes by, **Norman Gtanz**.

The Verve Years (1963)

LPD-75 ELLA FITZGERALD: THESE ARE THE BLUES

1. Jail House Blues (Smith-Williams) 3:25   631028-4

2. In the Evening (When the Sun Goes Down) (Carr) 4:27   631029-4

3. See See Rider (Rainey) 2:39   631028-2

4. You Don't Know My Mind (Liston-Gray-Williams) 4:49   631029-1

5. Trouble in Mind (Jones) 3:31   631028-3

6. How Long, How Long, Blues (Carr) 3:57   631028-1

7. Cherry Red (Johnson-Turner) 4:09   631028-6

8. Down Hearted Blues (Hunter-Austin) 3:08 631029-2

9. St. Louis Blues (Handy) 6:28   631029-3

10. Heah Me Talkin' to Ya (Armstrong) 3:01   631028-5

LP: Verve MG V-4062 (mono)/MG V6-4062 (stereo) (released February 1964). Side One, Tracks 1-5 (19:03)/Side Two, Tracks 6-10 (20:55). Total playing time: 38:58. CD: Verve829536-2 (stereo), same contents and sequence (released December 1986). Total playing time: 42:11. Recorded under the personal supervision of, and liner notes by, **Norman Granz**.

The Verve Years (1964)

LPD-76 ELLA FITZGERALD/ HELLO, DOLLY!

1. Hello, Dolly! (Herman) 2:15   640407-2

2. People (Merrill-Styne) 3:43   640407-3

3. Can't Buy Me Love(Lennon-McCartney) 2:36 640407-1

4. The Sweetest Sounds (Rodgers) 2:06   640407-4

5. Miss Otis Regrets (Porter) 3:56   640304-6

6. My Man (Mon Homme) (Charles-Willemetz-Pollack-Yvain) 3:56   640304-3

7. How High the Moon (Hamilton-Lewis) 3:57 640303-2

8. Volare (Nel Blu, Di Pinto Di Blu) (Modugno-Migliacci-Parish) 2:38   640304-7

9. The Thrill Is Gone (Brown-Henderson) 3:19 640304-4

10. Memories of You (Blake-Razaf) 2:43   640303-4

11. Lullaby of the Leaves (Petkere-Young) 2:55 640304-1

12. Pete Kelly's Blues (Cahn-Heindorf) 3:56   640303-3

LP: Verve MG V-4064 (mono)/Verve V6-4064 (stereo) (released August 1964). Side One, Tracks 1-6 (18:47)/Side Two, Tracks 7-12 (19:43). Total playing time: 38:30. Produced under the personal supervision of **Norman Granz**. Director of Engineering: **Val Valentin**. Liner notes by **Leonard Feather**.

The Verve Years (1957-1964)

LPD-77 THE BEST OF ELLA FITZGERALD

1. I Won't Dance (Harbach-Hammerstein II) 3:27 611227-2

2. Gone with the Wind (Magidson-Wrubel) 2:55
   600213-3
3. See See Rider (Rainey) 2:40   631028-2
4. The Thrill Is Gone (Brown Henderson) 3:19
   640304-4
5. Show Me (Lerner-Loewe) 2:22   621004-3
6. Honeysuckle Rose (Waller-Razaf) 2:29   630716-8
7. When Your Lover Has Gone (Swan) 3:00   611114-6
8. Sweet and Slow (Dubin-Warren) 3:11   620410-5
9. People (Merrill-Styne) 3:43   640407-3
10. Broadway (Woods-McKay-Bird) 2:43   620130-2
11. Don't Be That Way (Goodman-Sampson-Parish)
    3:45   570813-3

LP: Verve V-8720 (mono)/V6-8720 (stereo) (released December 1967). Side One, Tracks 1-6 (17:27/Side Two, Tracks 7-11 (16:34). Total playing time, 34:01. 8-Track: Verve 8140-8720M, same contents and sequence (released 1971). Original sessions produced under the personal supervision of **Norman Granz**. Director of Engineering, **Val Valentin**.

The Verve Years (1964)

LPD-78 ELLA AT JUAN-LES PINS

1. Day In, Day Out (Mercer-Bloom) 2:48   640728-3
2. Just A-Sitting' and A-Rockin' (Gaines-Strayhorn-Ellington) 4:03   640728-2
3. The Lady Is a Tramp (Rodgers-Hart) 4:20
   640728-9
4. Summertime (Heyward-Gershwin) 2:36   640728-10
5. St. Louis Blues (Handy) 6:09   640728-13
6. Honeysuckle Rose (Razaf-Waller) 4:33   640728-16
7. Goody-Goody (Mercer-Malneck) 2:39   640729-15
8. The Boy from Ipanema (De Moraes-Gimbel-Jobim)
   3:12   640729-16
9. They Can't Take That Away from Me (Gershwin-Gershwin) 2:32   640729-17
10. You'd Be So Nice to Come Home To (Porter) 2:46
    640729-20
11. Somewhere in the Night (Raksin-May) 1:40
    640729-18
12. I've Got You Under My Skin (Porter) 3:00
    640729-21
13. The Cricket Song (Fitzgerald, et al.) 1:53   640729-25
14. How High the Moon (Hamilton-Lewis) 3:51
    640729-26
15. Cutie Pants (Allen) 1:35   640728-11

LP: Verve V-4065 (mono)/Verve VS-4065 (stereo) (released February 1965). Side One, Tracks 1-6 (24:44)/Side Two, Tracks 9-14 (15:57). Total playing time, 40:41. Verve

(French) 3716 (released November 1964). Side One, Tracks 1-6 (24:44)/Side Two, Tracks 7-15 (22:32). Total playing time, 47:16. Concert produced under the personal supervision of **Norman Granz**. Recording made by the technical services of the RTF during the Fifth Festival of Jazz of Antibes. Director of Engineering, **Val Valentin**. Liner notes by **Norman Granz**.

The Verve Years (1964)

LPD-79 ELLA FITZGERALD IN CONCERT/ JUAN-LES-PINS, JULY 29, 1964

1. Hello, Dolly! (Herman) 2:20   640729-1
2. Day In — Day Out (Mercer-Bloom) 2:40   640729-2
3. Just A-Sittin' and A-Rockin' (Gaines-Strayhorn-Ellington) 4:00   640729-3
4. I Love Being Here with You 3:25   640729-4
5. People (Merrill-Styne) 4:00   640729-5
6. Someone to Watch Over Me (Gershwin-Gershwin)
   3:50   640729-6
7. Can't Buy Me Love (Lennon-McCartney) 2:50
   640729-7
8. Them There Eyes (Pinkard-Tracey-Tauber) 2:45
   640729-8
9. The Lady Is a Tramp (Rodgers-Hart) 4:35
   640729-9
10. Summertime (Heyward-Gershwin) 3:10   640729-10
11. Cutie Pants (Allen) 1:35   640729-11
12. I'm Putting All My Eggs in One Basket (Berlin) 2:45
    640729-12
13. St. Louis Blues (Handy) 7:00   640729-13
14. Perdido (Lengsfelder-Drake-Tizol) 8:20   640729-14

CD: The "Jazz" Collection JCD 01 (50:75) (released in 1994). Total playing time, 53:15. Produced by Editoriale Pantheon, Rome (Italy). Note: The producers were negligent in annotating this disc: titles are mis-named, and lyricists/composers are mis-credited. Corrections are made here. However, it is nice to have this album, since it supplements quite nicely Miss Fitzgerald's performance at the fifth annual Festival Mondial du Jazz Antibes-Juan-les Pins of the previous day, which is released by Verve (see LPD 78).

The Verve Years (1964)

LPD-80 ELLA FITZGERALD SINGS THE JOHNNY MERCER SONG BOOK

1. Too Marvelous for Words (Mercer-Whiting) 2:31
   641021-1

2. Early Autumn (Mercer-Burns-Herman) 3:51 641019-5

3. Day In — Day Out (Mercer-Bloom) 2:49   641020-1

4. Laura (Mercer-Raksin) 3:43   641021-2

5. This Time the Dream's on Me (Mercer-Arlen) 2:54 641020-2

6. Skylark (Mercer-Carmichael) 3:12   641020-3

7. Single-O (Mercer-Kahn) 3:19   641020-4

8. Something's Gotta Give (Mercer) 2:33   641021-3

9. Trav'lin' Light (Mercer-Mundy-Young) 3:47 641019-1

10. Midnight Sun (Mercer-Burke-Hampton) 4:55 641020-5

11. Dream (When You're Feeling Blue) (Mercer) 2:58 641019-6

12. I Remember You (Mercer-Schertzinger) 3:38 641021-4

13. When a Woman Loves a Man (Mercer-Jenkins-Hanighen) 3:51   641021-5

LP: Verve V-4067 (mono)/Verve V6-4067 (stereo) (released August 1965). Side One, Tracks 1-7 (22:36)/Side Two, Tracks 8-13 (21:59). Total playing time, 44:35. Verve 823 247-1 (mono), same contents and sequence (released November 1985). CT: Verve 823 247-4 (mono), same contents and sequence (released November 1985). CD: Verve 823 247-2 (mono), same contents and sequence (released 1986). Verve 314 519 832-2 (**The Complete Ella Fitzgerald Song Books**, Disc Sixteen). (stereo), same contents and sequence (released November 1993). Verve Master Edition 314 539 057-2, same contents and sequence (released. October 1997). Total playing time: 44:35. Produced under the personal supervision of **Norman Granz**. Director of Engineering: **Val Valentin**. Liner notes by **Benny Green**.

The Verve Years (1956-1964)

The Complete Ella Fitzgerald Song Books

Disc One Ella Fitzgerald Sings the Cole Porter Song Book (Vol. 1) 53:54

Disc Two Ella Fitzgerald Sings the Cole Porter Song Book (Vol. 2) 69:16

Disc Three Ella Fitzgerald Sings the Rodgers and Hart Song Book (Vol.1) 56:45

Disc Four Ella Fitzgerald Sings the Rodgers and Hart Song Book (Vol.2) 59:21

Disc Five Ella Fitzgerald Sings the Duke Ellington Song Book (Vol. 1) 59:48

Disc Six Ella Fitzgerald Sings the Duke Ellington Song Book (Vol. 2) 67:45

Disc Seven Ella Fitzgerald Sings the Duke Ellington Song Book (Vol. 3) 59:26

Disc Eight Ella Fitzgerald Sings the Irving Berlin Song Book (Vol. 1) 47:17

Disc Nine Ella Fitzgerald Sings the Irving Berlin Song Book (Vol. 2) 47:53

Disc Ten Ella Fitzgerald Sings the George and Ira Gershwin Song Book (Vol.1) 75:48

Disc Eleven Ella Fitzgerald Sings the George and Ira Gershwin Song Book (Vol.2) 56:37

Disc Twelve Ella Fitzgerald Sings the George and Ira Gershwin Song Book (Vol.3) 73:49

Disc Thirteen Ella Fitzgerald Sings the Harold Arlen Song Book (Vol. 1) 51:18

Disc Fourteen Ella Fitzgerald Sings the Harold Arlen Song Book (Vol. 2) 65:52

Disc Fifteen Ella Fitzgerald Sings the Jerome Kern Song Book 43:02

Disc Sixteen Ella Fitzgerald Sings the Johnny Mercer Song Book 44:35

CD: Verve 314 519 832-2 (released 2 November 1993). Total playing time (16-CD set), 15:32:26. Original sessions produced under the personal supervision of **Norman Granz**. Discs One–Four engineered by **Alan Emig**. Discs Five–Sixteen engineered by **Val Valentin**.

The Complete Ella Fitzgerald Song Books produced by **Michael Lang**. This boxed set of 16 CDs won the National Academy of Recording Arts and Sciences "Grammy" Award as the Best Historical Album for Mr. Lang, his second, having won the previous year (1994) for his production of **The Complete Billie Holiday on Verve, 1945-1959**.

The "liner notes" for this set is in the form of a 5" x 5", 120-page hard-bound book, which contains not only the complete table of contents of each of the discs, with discography, but also two outstanding essays: "Of Porter, Rodgers and Hart, Ellington, Berlin, the Gershwins, Arlen, Kern, and Mercer...." by **Benny Green**, which is dated July 1993; and "The History of the Songbooks," by **John McDonough**, dated August 1993. Credits and an alphabetical list of song are also included, as well as rare photographs and outstanding original art work directed and designed by **Chris Thompson**.

The Verve Years (1965)

LPD-81 Ella in Hamburg '65

1. Walk Right In (Darling-Svance) 3:35   650326-1

2. That Old Black Magic (Arlen-Mercer) 4:15 650326-2

3. Body and Soul (Green-Heyman-Sour-Eyton) 4:38 650326-3

4. Here's That Rainy Day (Burke-Van Heusen) 3:23
650326-4
5. And the Angels Sing (Elman-Mercer) 3:40
650326-5
6. A Hard Day's Night (Lennon-McCartney) 3:03
650326-12
7. Ellington Medley: 6:19   650326-6; a. Do Nothin'
Till You Hear from Me (Ellington-Russell); b. Mood
Indigo (Bigard-Mills-Ellington); c. It Don't Mean a
Thing (Ellington-Mills)
8. The Boy from Ipanema (Jobim-deMoraes-Gimbel)
2:54   650326-11
9. Don't Rain on My Parade (Styne-Merrill) 3:01
650326-7
10. Angel Eyes (Dennis-Brent) 3:26   650326-8
11. Smooth Sailing (Cobb) 3:49   650326-9
12. Old McDonald Had a Farm (Bergman-Keith-
Spence) 2:05   650326-10

LP: Verve V-4069 (mono)/V6-4069 (stereo) (released
1965). Side One, Track 1-6 (22:49)/Side Two, Tracks 6-12
(21:49). Total playing time, 44:38. CD: Verve POCJ 2649
(released only in Japan; limited marketing elsewhere).
Recorded under the personal supervision of **Norman
Granz**. Director of Engineering: **Val Valentin**. Liner notes
by **Jack Maher**.

The Verve Years

LPD-82 ELLA AT DUKE'S PLACE/
ELLA FITZGERALD AND DUKE ELLINGTON

1. Something to Live For (Strayhorn-Ellington) 3:33
651019-3
2. A Flower Is a Lovesome Thing (Strayhorn-Ellington)
4:58   651019-4
3. Passion Flower (Strayhorn-Ellington-Raskin) 4:36
651020-2
4. I Like the Sunrise (Ellington) 3:24   651019-1
5. Azure (Ellington) 6:50   651018-4
6. Imagine My Frustration (Wilson-Strayhorn-
Ellingon) 4:47   651017-2
7. Duke's Place (Bigard-Thiele-Roberts-Katz) 4:08
651018-3
8. The Brown Skinned Gal in the Calico Gown (Webster-Ellington) 5:02   651020-4
9. What Am I Here For? (Ellington-Laine) 5:30
651018-1
10. Cotton Tail (Ellington) 3:40   651019-2

LP: Verve MG V-4070/Verve V6-4070 (released February 1966). Side A, Tracks 1-5 (23:33)/Side B, Tracks 6-
10 (23:19). Total playing time, 46:52.

8-Track: Verve8140-4070M, same contents and sequence (released 1971). CD: Verve 314 529 700, same contents and sequence (released February 1996). Total playing
time: 46:46.

Produced under the personal supervision of **Norman
Granz**. Director of Engineering, **Val Valentin**. Liner notes
by **Leonard Feather**.

The Verve Years (1966)

LPD-83 ELLA FITZGERALD/
DUKE ELLINGTON/
THE STOCKHOLM CONCERT, 1966

1. Imagine My Frustration (Wilson-Strayhorn-Elling-
ton) 5:12   660208-1
2. Duke's Place (Thiele-Roberts-Katz-Ellington) 4:43
660208-2
3. Satin Doll (Mercer-Strayhorn-Ellington) 2:46
660208-3
4. Something to Live For (Strayhorn-Ellington) 4:25
660208-4
5. Wives and Lovers (David-Bacharach) 2:09
660208-5
6. Só Danò Samba (Jobim-De Moraes) 3:35   660208-6
7. Let's Do It (Porter) 4:48   660208-7
8. Lover Man (Davis-Ramirez-Sherman) 4:50
660208-8
9. Cotton Tail (Ellington) 4:59   660208-9
10. How High the Moon (Hamilton-Lewis) 8:08
660208-10
11. Mr. Paganini (Coslow) 4:04   660208-11

LP: Pablo Live 2308-242 (released 1984). Side 1,
Tracks 1-4 (17:11)/Side 2, Tracks 5-9 (20:26). Total playing time: 37:37.

CT: Pablo Live 52308-242, same contents and sequence (released 1987). CD: Pablo Live PACD 2308-242-
2, same contents and sequence (released 1987). Pablo PACD
002 (**Ella Fitzgerald/The Pablo CD Collection**), Disc 1.
Jazz World JWD 102.213 (released July 1996). Tracks 1-11
(Total playing time: 49:46) (Note: As can be seen, this
1996 release contains two additional tracks never before
released.).

Produced by **Norman Granz**. Recorded in performance at The Circus, Stockholm (Sweden). (*Note: The
Pablo Live release indicates that the concert on the LP and
CD discs was recorded at Konserthut on Sunday evening, 7
February 1966. Whereas, W.R. Timner, in his* **Ellingtonia**,
*4th Edition, confirms that the LP and CD recordings were
from the Monday evening concert at The Circus.*)

The Verve Years (1966)

LPD-84 ELLA FITZGERALD/WHISPER NOT

1. Sweet Georgia Brown (Casey-Pinkard) 3:31
   660720-1
2. Whisper Not (Feather-Golson) 3:00   660720-2
3. I Said "No" (Loesser-Styne) 4:00   660720-3
4. Thanks for the Memory (Robin-Rainger) 4:00
   660720-4
5. Spring Can Really Hang You Up the Most (Landesman-Wolf) 3:45   660720-5
6. Ol' MacDonald (Bergman-Keith-Spence) 2:15
   660720-6
7. Time After Time (Cahn-Styne) 4:21   660720-7
8. You've Changed (Cary-Fisher) 3:18   660720-8
9. I've Got Your Number (Leigh-Coleman) 3:09
   660720-9
10. Lover Man (Davis-Ramirez-Sherman) 4:21
    660720-10
11. Wives and Lovers (David-Bacharach) 2:20
    660720-11
12. Matchmaker, Matchmaker (Harnick-Ross) 2:46
    660720-12

LP: Verve V-4071 (mono)/Verve V6-4071 (stereo) (re-
leased November 1966). Side 1, Tracks 1-6 (20:41)/Side 2,
Tracks 7-12 (20:25). Total playing time: 41:06. Verve
UMV-2668, same contents and sequence (released 1981).
CT: Verve UCV-2668, same contents and sequence (re-
leased 1981). Produced under the personal supervision of
Norman Granz. Recording Engineer: **Val Valentin**. Liner
notes by **Leonard Feather**.

The Verve Years (1966)

LPD-85 ELLA AND DUKE
AT THE CÔTE D'AZUR

Duke Ellington and His Orchestra

1. Diminuendo in Blue/Blow by Blow (Ellington) 8:06
2. Caravan (Tizol-Ellington)* 6:06
3. Rose of the Rio Grande (Gorman-Warren-Leslie)
   2:51
4. Tutti for Cootie (Hamilton-Ellinton)* 6:24
5. Skin Deep (Bellson)* 10:49
6. Passion Flower (Strayhorn)* 4:51
7. Things Ain't What They Used To Be (M. Ellington)*
   3:02
8. Wings and Things (Hodges)* 10:27
9. The Star-Crossed Lovers (Ellington-Strayhorn)*
   4:20

10. Such Sweet Thunder (Ellington-Strayhorn)* 3:24
11. Madness in Great Ones (Strayhorn-Ellington)* 5:23
12. Kinda Dukish (Ellington)/Rockin' in Rhythm (Car-
    ney/Ellington)* 5:07
13. Things Ain't What They Used to Be (M. Ellington)*
    2:35
14. Main Stem (Ellington)* 3:53
15. Medley: Black and Tan Fantasy (Ellington-
    Miley)/Creole Love Call (Ellington)/The Mooche
    (All by Ellington)* 8:55
16. West Indian Pancake (Ellington) 4:45
17. The Matador (El Viti) (Wilson) 4:01
18. The Opener (Ellington)* 3:01
19. La Plus Belle Africaine (Ellington)* 11:50
20. Azure (Mills-Ellington)* 7:44
21. Duke Ellington Introduces Ella Fitzgerald* 1:05

Ella Fitzgerald and The Jimmy Jones Trio
with Duke Ellington and His Orchestra

22. Let's Do It (Porter)* 4:08   660727-8
23. Satin Doll (Mercer-Strayhorn)* 3:16   660727-9
24. Cotton Tail (Ellington)* 7:07   660727-10

Duke Ellington and His Orchestra

25. Take the "A" Train (Strayhorn)* 5:47
26. Take the "A" Train (Strayhorn)* 0:55
27. Such Sweet Thunder (Strayhorn-Ellington)* 3:06
28. Half the Fun (Strayhorn-Ellington)* 4:24
29. Madness in Great Ones (Strayhorn-Ellington)* 5:26
30. The Star-Crossed Lovers (Strayhorn-Ellington)* 4:21
31. I Got It Bad (and That Ain't Good) (Webster-Elling-
    ton)* 2:18
32. Things Ain't What They Used to Be (M. Ellington)*
    2:28
33. Wings and Things (Hodges)* 8:26
34. Kinda Dukish (Ellington)/Rockin' in Rhythm
    (Carney-Ellington)* 5:10
35. Chelsea Bridge (Strayhorn)* 4:18
36. Skin Deep (Bellson) 12:12
37. Sophisticated Lady (Ellington)* 4:13
38. Jam with Sam (Ellington)* 3:19
39. Things Ain't What They Used to Be (M. Ellington)
    2:18
40. Soul Call (Bellson-Bellson) 2:41
41. West Indian Pancake (Ellington)* 4:37
42. The Matador (El Viti) (Wilson)* 1:19
43. The Opener (Ellington)* 3:08
44. La Plus Belle Africaine (Ellington) 13:23
45. Take the "A" Train (Strayhorn)* 4:54
46. Trombonio-Bustoso-Issimo (Anderson) 4:21
47. Such Sweet Thunder (Strayhorn-Ellington)* 3:11
48. Half the Fun (Strayhorn-Ellington)* 4:15
49. Madness in Great Ones (Strayhorn-Ellington)* 4:44
50. The Star-Crossed Lovers (Strayhorn-Ellington)* 4:20

51. Prelude to a Kiss (Ellington)* 4:26
52. Things Ain't What They Used to Be (M. Ellington)* 2:47
53. The Old Circus Train Turn-Around Blues (Ellington) 11:29

Ella Fitzgerald and The Jimmy Jones Trio with Duke Ellington and His Orchestra

54. Who? (Harbach-Hammerstein-Kern)/Thou Swell (Rodgers-Hart)* 1:39   660728-1
55. Satin Doll (Mercer-Strayhorn-Ellington)* 2:42 660728-2
56. Wives and Lovers (David-Bacharach)* 2:22 660728-3
57. Something To Live For (Strayhorn)* 4:13   660728-4
58. Let's Do It (Porter)* 4:06   660728-5

Ella Fitzgerald with The Jimmy Jones Trio

59. The More I See You (Gordon-Warren) 3:57 660728-7
60. You Go to My Head (Coots-Gillespie)/Goin' Out of My Head (Randazzo-Weinstein) 3:01   660728-8
61. Só Danò Samba (Jazz Samba) (Jobim-deMoraes-Gimbel) 5:49   660728-9
62. Lullaby of Birdland (Weiss-Shearing) 2:53 660728-10
63. How Long Has This Been Going On?(Gershwin-Gershwin) 3:07   660728-11

Ella Fitzgerald and The Jimmy Jones Trio with Duke Ellington and His Orchestra

64. Mack the Knife (Brecht-Blitzstein-Weill) 5:01 660728-12

Duke Ellington and His Orchestra

65. Medley: Black and Tan Fantasy (Miley-Ellington)/Creole Love Song (Ellington)/The Mooche (Ellington)* 9:42
66. Soul Call (Bellson-Bellson)* 4:33
67. West Indian Pancake (Ellington)* 4:43
68. The Matador (El Viti) (Ellington)* 4:09
69. La Plus Belle Africaine (Ellington)* 12:30
70. Such Sweet Thunder (Strayhorn-Ellington)* 3:12
71. Half the Fun (Strayhorn-Ellington)* 4:20
72. Madness in Great Ones (Strayhorn-Ellington)* 5:00
73. The Star-Crossed Lovers (Strayhorn-Ellington)* 4:08
74. Wings and Things (Hodges)* 3:22
75. Things Ain't What They Used to Be (M. Ellington)* 1:58

Ella Fitzgerald and The Jimmy Jones Trio with Duke Ellington and His Orchestra

76. Who? (Harbach-Hammerstein-Kern)/Thou Swell (Rodgers-Hart)* 2:00   660729-1

77. Satin Doll (Mercer-Strayhorn-Ellington)* 2:42 660729-2
78. Wives and Lovers (David-Bacharach)* 2:29 660729-3
79. Something To Live For (Strayhorn)* 3:23   660729-4
80. Let's Do It (Porter)* 3:26   660729-5
81. Sweet Georgia Brown (Pinkard-Casey-Bernie)* 3:36   660729-6
82. You Go to My Head (Coots Gillespie)/Goin' Out of My Head (Randazzo-Weinstein)* 3:34   660729-7
83. Só Danò Samba (Jazz Samba) (Jobim-deMoraes-Gimbel)* 6:07   660729-8
84. Lullaby of Birdland (Weiss-Shearing)* 3:06 660729-9
85. Moment of Truth (Satterwhite-Scott)* 2:14 660729-10
86. Misty (Burke-Garner) 3:26   660729-11
87. Mack The Knife (Brecht-Blitzstein-Weill)* 5:36 660729-12
88. Cotton Tail (Ellington)* 7:13   660729-13

Duke Ellington and His Orchestra

89. The Trip (High Passage) (Ellington) 4:44
90. Jive Jam (Ellington) 9:34
91. All Too Soon (Ellington) 7:18
92. The Old Circus Train Turn-Around Blues (Ellington)* 7:18

Ella Fitzgerald with Duke Ellington and His Orchestra

93. It Don't Mean a Thing (Ellington) 7:14   660729-14

Ella Fitzgerald with Duke Ellington Sextet

94. Just Squeeze Me (Gaines-Ellington) 4:27   660729-15

Duke Ellington and His Orchestra/Rehearsal

95. The Old Circus Train Turn-Around Blues (Ellington)* 1:09
96. The Old Circus Turn-Around Blues (Ellington)* 1:31
97. The Old Circus Turn-Around Blues (Ellington)* 1:50
98. The Old Circus Turn-Around Blues (Ellington)* 1:11
99. The Old Circus Turn-Around Blues (Ellington)* 2:40
100. The Old Circus Turn-Around Blues (Ellington)* 3:38
101. The Old Circus Turn-Around Blues (Ellington)* 2:00
102. Blue Fuse No. 2 (Ellington)* 1:39
103. Blue Fuse No. 2 (Ellington)* 0:44
104. Blue Fuse No. 1 (Ellington)* 0:37
105. Blue Fuse No. 1 (Ellington)* 0:51
106. Blue Fuse No. 1 (Ellington)* 2:57
107. The Shepherd (Ellington)* 3:33

108. The Old Circus Turn-Around Blues (Ellington)*
4:44
109. The Old Circus Turn-Around Blues (Ellington)*
8:07

Duke Ellington, solo piano

110. Tingling Is a Happiness (Ellington)* 4:00

*Previously unreleased tracks

    LP: Verve MG V-4072-2 (mono) (2 discs)/V6-4072-2 (stereo) (2 discs) (released February 1967). Disc One, Side One, Tracks 64, 53, 62 (20:19). Disc Two, Side Two, Tracks 46, 60, 63, 1 (17:42). Disc Two, Side Three, Tracks 93, 91, 86 (18:03). Disc One, Side Four, Tracks 61, 3, 59, 17, 94 (21:15). Total playing time, 1:17:19.

    CD: Verve 314 539 030 (2 discs) (released November 1997). Disc 1, Tracks 64, 53, 62, 46, 60, 63, 1, 90 (45:40). Disc 2, Tracks 94, 91, 86, 61, 3, 59, 17, 94, 89, 39 (46:28). Total playing time, 1:32:08.

    Verve 314 539 033-2 (8 discs) (released September 1998). Disc One: Tracks 1–13 (73:25)/Disc Two: Tracks 14–25 (65:32). Disc Three: Tracks 26–39 (62:54)/Disc Four: Tracks 40–52 (58:06). Disc Five: Tracks 53–64 (50:19)/Disc Six: Tracks 65–80 (71:37). Disc Seven: Tracks 81–94 (71:27)/Disc Eight: Tracks 95–110 (40:11). Total playing time, 8:13:31.

    Concert produced under the personal supervision of **Norman Granz**. Director of Engineering: **Val Valentin**. Liner notes by **Norman Granz**. CD releases supervised by **Michael** and **Ben Young**

The Verve Years (1949–1966)

LPD-86 Ella Fitzgerald/
First Lady of Song

1. Perdido (Drake-Lengsfelder-Tizol) 8:29   490918-12
2. Lullaby of Birdland (Shearing-Weiss)* 2:18
540917-2
3. Too Young for the Blues (Meyer-Jones)* 3:13
560125-3
4. Too Darn Hot (Porter) 3:46   560207-5
5. Miss Otis Regrets (Porter) 3:03   560207-6
6. April in Paris (Duke-Harburg) 4:40   560625-1
7. Undecided (Shavers-Robin) 3:38   560815-8
8. Can't We Be Friends? (Swift-James) 3:45   560816-5
9. Bewitched, Bothered and Bewildered (Rodgers-Hart)
7:01   560829-8
10. Just A-Sittin' and A-Rockin' (Ellington-Strayhorn-Gaines) 3:30   560904-8
11. I'm Just a Lucky So-and-So (Ellington-David) 4:12
570626-2

12. Air Mail Special (Christian-Goodman-Mundy) 4:14
570704-11
13. A-Tisket, A-Tasket (Fitzgerald-Feldman) 2:20
570724-5
14. Baby, Don't You Go 'Way Mad (Jacquet-Mundy-Stillman)* 2:34   570724-10
15. Angel Eyes (Brent-Dennis)* 3:20   570724-11
16. I Won't Dance (Fields-McHugh) 4:45   570813-1
17. Summertime (Gershwin-Heyward) 4:58   570818-1
18. Oh! Lady, Be Good! (Gershwin-Gershwin) 4:24
571009-9
19. More Than You Know (Youmans-Eliscu-Rose) 3:44
571015-3
20. Lush Life (Strayhorn) 3:37   571017-4
21. Blue Skies (Berlin) 3:43   580318-5
22. Swingin' Shepherd Blues (Kossman-Jacobson-Roberts) 2:39   580319-5
23. These Foolish Things (Link-Strachey-Marvell) 3:28
580425-14
24. Trav'lin' Light (Mercer-Mundy-Young) 3:10
580701-2
25. You're an Old Smoothie (Brown-Whiting-DeSylva)*
2:45   581122-8
26. Makin' Whoopee (Donaldson-Kahn) 3:41   581124-8
27. How Long Has This Been Going On?(Gershwin-Gershwin) 3:44   590105-6
28. Detour Ahead (Carter-Ellis-Frigo)* 3:17   590325-8
29. Mack The Knife (Weill-Brecht-Blitzstein) 5:13
600213-10
30. How High the Moon (Lewis-Hamilton) 8:09
600213-11
31. Black Coffee (Burke-Webster) 3:27   600414-3
32. Let It Snow! Let It Snow! Let It Snow! (Styne-Cahn)
3:44   600716-2
33. Get Happy! (Arlen-Koehler) 3:30   600802-1
34. Heart and Soul (Carmichael-Loesser)* 3:34
610115-6
35. Mr. Paganini (You'll Have To Swing It) (Coslow)
4:03   610512-1
36. A Night in Tunisia (Gillespie-Paparelli) 4:06
610624-4
37. I Can't Get Started (Duke-Gershwin) 3:29   611113-4
38. Don't Be That Way (Goodman-Parish-Sampson)
3:45   611227-1
39. After You've Gone (Creamer-Layton) 4:08   620130-1
40. Hernando's Hideaway (Allen-Ross) 3:15   621002-4
41. A Fine Romance (Kern-Fields) 3:35   630105-2
42. 'Deed I Do (Rose-Hirsch) 2:40   630715-2
43. Heah Me Talkin' to You (Armstrong) 3:01   631028-5
44. Can't Buy Me Love (Lennon-McCartney) 2:36
640407-1
45. Day In — Day Out (Bloom-Mercer) 2:55   640728-3
46. Something's Gotta Give (Mercer) 2:30   641021-3

47. Here's That Rainy Day (Van Heusen-Burke) 3:20
650316-4
48. (I've Got) Something to Live For (Ellington-Strayhorn) 3:34   651019-3
49. You've Changed (Fisher-Carey) 3:17   660720-8
50. Jazz Samba (Jobim-de Moraes) 5:45   660728-9
51. It Don't Mean a Thing (If It Ain't Got That Swing) (Ellington-Mills) 7:11   660729-14

*Previously unissued tracks

CD: Verve 314 517 898-2 (3 discs in hard-bound booklet) (released April 1993). Disc 1, Tracks 1-16 (65:44). Disc 2, Tracks 17-34 (68:54). Disc 3, Tracks 35-51 (64:24). Total playing time: 3:19:02.

Original sessions produced under the personal supervision of **Norman Granz**. Original sessions' Director of Engineering: **Val Valentin**.

The hard-cover book in which these discs are presented contains a track list with complete discographical details; an excellent essay, "Ella by Starlight," by **Gene Lees**, adapted from an essay he wrote for the January 1992 issue of *Jazzletter*, a monthly newsletter on all styles and eras of jazz which he publishes; a scholarly analysis of the tracks and their times, by **Geoffrey Mark Fidelman**, adapted from the text of his book, *First Lady of Song: Ella Fitzgerald for the Record* (New York: Carol Publishing Co., 1994); and a very useful alphabetical track index.

The Verve Years (1966)

LPD-87 DUKE ELLINGTON AND ELLA FITZGERALD/LIVE AT THE GREEK THEATRE, LOS ANGELES

Duke Ellington and His Orchestra

1. Take the "A" Train (Strayhorn) 1:01
2. Take the "A" Train (Strayhorn) 4:49
3. Soul Call (Bellson) 2:28
4. In a Sentimental Mood (Ellington-Kurtz-Mills) 2:43
5. Prowling Cat (Anderson) 3:11
6. La Plus Belle Africaine (Ellington) 12:25
7. Old Circus Train (Ellington) 7:35

Ella Fitzgerald with Duke Ellington and His Orchestra

8. Sweet Georgia Brown (Bernie-Pinkard-Casey) 3:43
660923-1

Ella Fitzgerald with The Jimmy Jones Trio

9. Star Dust (Carmichael-Parish) 5:22   660914-2
10. Só Danò Samba (Jobim-deMoraes) 6:12   660923-3
11. How Long Has This Been Going On? (Gershwin-Gershwin) 2:25   660923-4

Ella Fitzgerald with The Jimmy Jones Trio and Duke Ellington and His Orchestra

12. St. Louis Blues (Handy) 5:05   660923-5

Ella Fitzgerald with The Jimmy Jones Trio

13. Misty (Garner-Burke) 2:52   660923-6

Ella Fitzgerald and The Jimmy Jones Trio with Duke Ellington and His Orchestra

14. Mack The Knife (Weill-Brecht-Blitzstein) 4:42
660923-7

Billy Briggs with Rhythm Accompaniment

15. Dancer's Blues (Tap routine)

Ella Fitzgerald with Duke Ellington and His Orchestra

16. Cotton Tail (Ellington) 4:45   660923-8

Ella Fitzgerald with The Jimmy Jones Trio

17. Things Ain't What They Used to Be (M. Ellington) 0:45   660923-9

CD: Status DSTS 1013 (released July 1995). Total playing time, 73:48. Original concert produced by **Norman Granz**/This CD produced by **Dave Kay**. With liner notes by **Alun Morgan**.

The Two Years with Capitol Records (1967)

LPD-88 ELLA FITZGERALD'S BRIGHTEN THE CORNER!

1. Abide with Me (Lyte-Monk) 3:24   670200-4
2. Just a Closer Walk with Thee (Morris) 5:00
670200-8
3. The Old Rugged Cross (Bennard) 3:50   670200-10
4. Brighten the Corner (Where You Are) (Ogden-Gabriel) 2:33   670200-6
5. I Need Thee Every Hour (Hawks-Lowry) 3:38
670200-12
6. In the Garden (Miles) 3:14   670200-5
7. (God Be With You) Till We Meet Again (Rankin-Tomer) 1:19   670200-3
8. God Will Take Care of You (Martin-Martin) 3:29
670200-1
9. The Church in the Wildwood (Pitts) 3:00
670200-14
10. Throw Out the Lifeline (Ufford) 3:12   670200-9
11. I Shall Not Be Moved (Ackley) 2:40   670200-7
12. Let the Lower Lights Be Burning (Bliss) 2:46
670200-13
13. What a Friend We Have in Jesus (Scriven-Converse) 4:02   670200-2

14. Rock of Ages, Cleft for Me (Toplady-Hastings) 1:58
    670200-11

    LP: Capitol T 2685 (mono)/Capitol ST 2685 (stereo) (released March 1967). Side One, Tracks 1-7 (23:16)/Side Two, Tracks 8-14 (21:25). Total playing time: 44:41. Capitol SM-11793 (stereo) (released 1978). CD Capitol C21Y 95151 (released 0000) (44:43). Produced by **Dave Dexter, Jr.**/Engineer: **John Kraus**.

The Verve Years (1967)

LPD-89 THE GREATEST JAZZ CONCERT IN THE WORLD

The Oscar Peterson Trio

1. Smedley (Oscar Peterson) 4:16
2. Some Day My Prince Will Come (Churchill-Morey) 4:59
3. Daytrain (Peterson) 5:53

Jam Session

4. Now's the Time (Parker) 8:26
5. The Ballad Medley: Memories of You (Blake-Razaf)/ 2:22
6. Misty (Garner-Burke)/ 2:45
7. I Can't Get Started (Gershwin-Duke) 2:26
8. Wee (Best) 9:49

Coleman Hawkins with The Oscar Peterson Trio

9. Moonglow (Hudson-De Lange-Mills) 3:29
10. Sweet Georgia Brown (Bernie-Pinkard-Casey) 4:28

Jam Session

11. C Jam Blues (Ellington) 6:12
12. Woman, You Must Be Crazy (Walker) 9:08
13. Stormy Monday (Walker) 6:40

The Duke Ellington Orchestra

14. Swamp Goo (Ellington) 4:54
15. Gurdle Hurdle (Ellington) 2:51
16. The Shepherd (Ellington) 6:33
17. Rue Bleue (Ellington) 2:44
18. Salomé (Fol) 3:34
19. A Chromatic Love Affair (Ellington) 3:58
20. Mount Harrissa (Ellington) 6:39
21. Blood Count (Manuscript) (Strayhorn) 3:50
22. Rockin' in Rhythm (Ellington-Mills-Carney) 3:40
23. Very Tenor (Ellington) 7:51
24. Onions (Wild Onions) (Ellington) 1:50
25. Take the "A" Train (Strayhorn) 5:12
26. Satin Doll (Ellington-Strayhorn-Mercer) 4:50
27. Tootie for Cootie (Ellington-Hamilton) 6:13
28. Up Jump (Ellington) 2:56

29. Prelude to a Kiss (Gordon-Mills-Ellington) 4:32
30. Medley: Mood Indigo (Ellington-Mills-Bigard) 3:41; I Got It Bad (Ellington-Webster) 2:23
31. Things Ain't What They Used to Be (Ellington-Persons) 4:25

Ella Fitzgerald and The Jimmy Jones Trio with The Duke Ellington Orchestra

32. Don't Be That Way (Goodman-Sampson-Parish) 4:03   670326-1
33. You've Changed (Carey-Fisher) 4:07   670326-2
34. Let's Do It (Porter) 4:22   670326-3
35. On the Sunny Side of the Street (McHugh-Fields) 2:03   670326-4

Ella Fitzgerald with The Jimmy Jones Trio

36. (It's Only a) Paper Moon (Rose-Harburg-Arlen) 2:27   670326-5
37. Day Dream (Ellington-Latouche-Strayhorn) 4:42 670326-6
38. If I Could Be with You (Johnson-Creamer) 3:17 670326-7
39. BetweentheDevilandtheDeepBlueSea(Koehler-Arlen) 3:39   670326-8

Ella Fitzgerald and The Jimmy Jones Trio with The Duke Ellington Orchestra

40. Cotton Tail (Ellington) 5:10   670326-9

    LP: Pablo 2660 109 (4 discs) (stereo) (released 1975). CD release: Pablo 3-PACD 2625 742 (3 discs) (released 1989). Disc 1, Tracks 1-13 (76:01). Disc 2, Tracks 14-25 (60:27). Disc 3, Tracks 26-40 (66:25). Total playing time, 3:22:53. Concerts produced by **Norman Granz**. Director of Engineering: **Val Valentin**.

The Two Years with Capitol Records (1967)

LPD-90 ELLA FITZGERALD'S CHRISTMAS

1. O Holy Night (Cappeau de Roquemaure-Dwight-Adam) 1:48   670718-6
2. It Came Upon the Midnight Clear (Willis-Sears) 3:20   670718-3
3. Hark! The Herald Angels Sing (Wesley-Mendelssohn) 1:49   670717-2
4. Away in a Manger (Murray) 2:13   670718-2
5. Joy to the World (Watts-Handel) 1:40   670718-5
6. The First Noël (Sandys) 1:50   670718-9
7. Silent Night (Gruber-Mohr) 2:50   670717-1
8. O Come, All Ye Faithful (Reading-Oakeley) 2:45 670718-7
9. Sleep, My Little Jesus (Gannett-Geibel) 2:16 670718-4

10. Angels We Have Heard on High (Unknown ancients) 1:45   670717-3
11. O Little Town of Bethlehem (Brooks-Redner) 2:10   670718-1
12. We Three Kings of Orient Are (Hopkins) 2:08   670717-4
13. God Rest Ye Merry, Gentlemen (Unknown ancients) 1:25   670718-8

LP: Capitol ST-2805 (stereo) (released 2 October 1967). Side One, Tracks 1-7 (14:30)/Side Two, Tracks 8-13 (13:33). Total playing time, 28:03. CT: Capitol C41C-94452, contents and sequence same as above. (released November 1988). CD: Capitol C21K-94452, contents and sequence same as above. (released November 1988). Capitol CDP 594452, contents and sequence same as above. (released October 1990). Produced by **Dave Dexter, Jr.**/Engineer: **John Kraus.**

The Two Years with Capitol Records (1967)

LPD-91 ELLA FITZGERALD/MISTY BLUE

1. Misty Blue (Montgomery) 2:26   671221-4
2. Walking in the Sunshine (Miller) 2:26   671220-4
3. It's Only Love (Cochran) 3:00   671221-1
4. Evil on Your Mind (Howard) 2:15   671222-1
5. I Taught Him Everything He Knows (Dee-Kent) 2:42   671220-1
6. Don't Let That Doorknob Hit You (McAlpin) 2:24   671222-2
7. Turn the World Around (the Other Way) (Peters) 2:41   671220-3
8. The Chokin' Kind (Howard) 1:59   671221-3
9. Born To Lose (Daffan) 3:13   671221-2
10. This Gun Don't Care (Lee) 2:44   671222-3
11. Don't Touch Me (Cochran) 2:52   671220-2

LP: Capitol ST 2888 (stereo) (released 1968). Side One, Tracks 1-6 (15:38)/Side Two, Tracks 7-11 (13:54). Total playing time: 29:32. Pickwick SPC-3259 (stereo) (released 1975) Same as Capitol release. CD: Capitol C21Y-95152, contents and sequence, same as above. (released February 1991). Capitol CDP 7 95152-2, contents and sequence, same as above. (released 1993). Produced by **Dave Dexter, Jr.**

The Two Years with Capitol Records (1968)

LPD-92 30 BY ELLA

1. Medley No. 1: My Mother's Eyes (Gilbert-Baer); Try a Little Tenderness (Woods-Campbell-Connelly); I Got It Bad (and That Ain't Good) (instrumental) (Ellington-Webster); Everything I Have Is Yours (Lane-Adamson); I Never Knew (I Could Love Anybody) (Pitts-Egan-Marsh-Whitman); Goodnight, My Love (Gordon-Revel) 12:22   680529-2
2. Medley No. 2: Four or Five Times (Gay-Hellman); Maybe (Flynn-Madden); Taking a Chance on Love (instrumental) (Duke-Latouche-Fetter); Elmer's Tune (Albrecht-Gallop-Jurgens); At Sundown (Donaldson); It's a Wonderful World (Savitt-Watson-Adamson) 6:20   680603-3
3. Medley No. 3: On Green Dolphin Street (Kaper-Washington); How Am I To Know? (King-Parker); Just Friends (instrumental) (Klenner-Lewis); I Cried for You (Arnheim-Lyman-Freed); Seems Like Old times (Lombardo-Loeb); You Stepped Out of a Dream (Brown-Kahn) 7:07   680528-2
4. Medley No. 4: If I Give My Heart to You (Crane-Jacobs-Brewster); Once in a While (Edwards-Green); Ebb Tide (instrumental) (Maxwell-Sigman); The Lamp Is Low (DeRose-Shefter-Parish); Where Are You? (McHugh-Adamson); Thinking of You (Donaldson) 11:09   680529-1
5. Medley No. 5: Candy (Kramer-Gordon-Whitney); All I Do Is Dream of You (Brown-Freed); Spring Is Here (instrumental) (Rodgers-Hart); 720 in the Books (Savitt-Watson-Adamson); It Happened in Monterrey (Wayne-Rose); What Can I Say After I Say I'm Sorry? (Donaldson-Lyman) 6:43   680603-1
6. Medley No. 6: No Regrets (Tobias-Ingram); I've Got a Feelin' You're Foolin' (Brown-Freed); Don't Blame Me (instrumental) (McHugh-Fields); Deep Purple (DeRose-Parish); Rain (Ford); You're a Sweetheart (McHugh-Adamson) 9:48   680528-1
7. Hawaiian War Chant (Freed-Noble-Leleiohaku) 2:18   680603-2

*Timings are correct as given here, not as they appear in the liner notes of the discs.

LP: Capitol ST 2960 (stereo) (released October 1968). Side 1, Tracks 1-3 (26:05)/Side 2, Tracks 4-6 (27:36). Total playing time: 53:41. Capitol SN 16276, contents and sequence, tracks 1-6 (released 1983). CT: Capitol 4N 16276, contents and sequence, tracks 1-6 (released 1983). CD: Capitol C21Y-48333, contents and sequence, tracks 1-6 (released 1988). Capitol CDP 7 48333-2, contents and sequence, tracks 1-6 (released 1993). Capitol Jazz 20090, contents and sequence as listed, with track 7 a bonus track on this Blue Note Records release. Total playing time, 55:56(released June 1999). Produced by **Dave Dexter, Jr.**/Recording Engineer: **Rex Updegraft.** Liner notes by **Dave Dexter, Jr.** Blue Note Records 20-bit remastered reissue produced by **Michael Cuscuna.**

Ella on the Road/In San Francisco (1968)

LPD-93 ELLA FITZGERALD/ SUNSHINE OF YOUR LOVE

1. Hey, Jude (Lennon-McCartney) 3:49　690200-1
2. Sunshine of Your Love (Bruce-Brown-Clapton) 3:18 690200-2
3. The Girl's in Love with You (Bacharach-David) 4:25 690200-3
4. Watch What Happens (Legrand-Gimbel) 3:56 690200-4
5. Alright, Okay, You Win (Wyche-Watts) 3:45 690200-5
6. Give Me the Simple Life (Ruby-Bloom) 2:00 690200-6
7. Useless Landscape (Jobim-Gilbert) 5:07　690200-7
8. Ol' Devil Moon (Harburg-Lane) 4:17　690200-8
9. Don'cha Go 'Way Mad (Munday-Jacquet-Stillmn) 3:33　690200-9
10. A House Is Not a Home (Bacharach-David) 4:10 690200-10
11. Trouble Is a Man (Wilder) 4:10　690200-11
12. Love You Madly (Ellington) 3:03　690200-12

LP: **Sunshine of Your Love** (MPS 15.250) (released 1970). Side 1, Tracks 1-6 (22:00)/Side 2, Tracks 7-12 (25:00). Total playing time, 47:00. **Sunshine of Your Love** (Prestige PR 7685 (mono)/PRST 7685 (stereo). **Watch What Happens** (BASF 20712), same contents and sequence as above. **Love You Madly** (Pausa 7130), same contents and sequence as above. CD: **Sunshine of Your Love** (Verve 314 533 102-2), same contents and sequence. as above (released 1996). Total playing time, 45:55. Cabaret performances produced under the personal supervision of **Norman Granz**. Recording Engineer: **Wally Heider**. Liner notes by **Norman Granz**.

Ella on the Road/In London (1969)

LPD-94 ELLA FITZGERALD/ELLA

1. Get Ready (Robinson) 2:33　690530-1
2. The Hunter Gets Captured by the Game (Robinson) 3:00　690530-2
3. Yellow Man (Newman) 2:18　690526-3
4. I'll Never Fall in Love Again (Bacharach-David) 2:50　690526-1
5. Got to Get You into My Life (Lennon-McCartney) 3:06　690528-3
6. I Wonder Why (Newman) 3:09　650529-1
7. Ooo, Baby, Baby (Robinson-Moore) 2:40　690530-3
8. Savoy Truffle (Harrison) 2:46　690528-2

9. Open Your Window (Nilsson) 2:32　690526-2
10. Knock on Wood (Floyd-Cropper) 3:58　690528-1

LP: Reprise S-6354 (released November 1969). Side One, Tracks 1-5 (13:49)/Side 2, Tracks 6-10 (15:06). Total playing time, 28:55. 8-Track: Reprise M 86354, same contents and sequence (released 1971). CT: Reprise M 56354, same contents and sequence (released 1971). CD: Reprise 9 20623-2 (Album combines this release, **Ella**, with **Things Ain't What They Used to Be (And You Better Believe It)**, Reprise S-6432. [q.v.] on a single CD, released in 1989.). Produced by **Richard Perry**/Engineered by **Gene Shiveley**.

Ella on the Road/in Budapest (1970)

LPD-95 ELLA FITZGERALD IN BUDAPEST

1. Crazy Rhythm (Ceasar-Meyer-Kahn) 3:16 700520-1
2. Medley: a. This Guy's in Love with You (Bacharach-David)/b. I'm Gonna Sit Right Down and Write Myself a Letter (Young-Ahlert) 4:57　700520-2
3. Open Your Window (Nilsson) 4:16　700520-3
4. Satin Doll (Mercer-Ellington-Strayhorn) 2:39 700520-4
5. Spinning Wheel (Thomas) 3:41　700520-5
6. As Time Goes By (Hupfeld) 3:27　700520-6
7. You'd Better Love Me (Martin-Gray) 2:01　700520-7
8. I'll Never Fall in Love Again (Bacharach-David) 2:44 700520-9
9. Hello, Young Lovers (Rodgers-Hammerstein) 4:05 700520-9
10. Medley: a. I Concentrate on You (Porter)/b. You Go to My Head (Coots-Gillespie) 5:12　700520-10
11. The Girl from Ipanema (Jobim-de Moraes-Gimbel) 6:33　700520-11
12. Cabaret (Kander-Ebb) 3:18　700520-12
13. Dancing in the Dark (Schwartz-Dietz) 3:12 700520-13
14. Raindrops Keep Falling on My Head (Bacharach-David) 5:33　700520-14
15. The Lady Is a Tramp (Rodgers-Hart) 3:01 700520-15
16. Summertime (Heyward-Gershwin) 2:56　700520-16
17. Mr. Paganini (Coslow) 4:11　700520-17
18. Mack the Knife (Weill-Brecht-Blitzstein) 7:40 700520-18
19. People (Merrill-Styne) 3:22　700520-19

CD: Pablo PACD 5308 (released May 1999). Total playing time, 78:16. Concert produced by **Norman Granz**/CD produced by **Eric Miller**. Liner notes by **Joe Goldberg**.

Ella on the Road/In Burbank at Warner Bros. (1970)

LPD-96 ELLA FITZGERALD/THINGS AIN'T WHAT THEY USED TO BE (AND YOU BETTER BELIEVE IT)

1. Sunny (Hebb) 5:17   700105-2
2. Mas Que Nada (Deane) 3:48   700106-2
3. A Man and a Woman (Un Homme et une Femme) (Barouh-Keller-Lai) 3:15   700105-3
4. Days of Wine and Roses (Mercer-Mancini) 2:20   701221-3
5. Black Coffee (Webster-Burke) 4:26   700104-4
6. Tuxedo Junction (Feyne-Hawkins-Johnson-Dash) 3:15   700104-3
7. I Heard It Through the Grapevine (Whitfield-Strong) 3:44   701222-1
8. Don't Dream of Anybody but Me (Hefti-Howard) 4:06   701221-2
9. Things Ain't What They Used to Be (Parson-Ellington) 3:10   701222-2
10. Willow, Weep for Me (Ronell) 4:40   700104-1
11. Manteca (Fuller-Gonzales-Gillespie) 2:31   701106-1
12. Just When We're Falling in Love (Russell-Thompson-Jacquet) 2:29   701221-1

LP: Reprise S-6432 (released 1971). Side One, Tracks 1-6 (22:46)/Side Two, Tracks 7-12 (21:05). Total playing time: 43:51. 8-Track: Reprise M8-6432, same contents and sequence (released 1971). CT: Reprise M5-6432, same contents and sequence (released1971). CD: Reprise 9 26023-2 (CD combines **Ella I**Reprise S-6354I with this album. and is titled **Ella/Things Ain't What They Used to Be (And You Better Believe It)**. Released December 1989. Total playing time: 72:30. Produced under the personal supervision of **Norman Granz.**

Ella on the Road/In Nice (1971)

LPD-97 ELLA À NICE

1. Night and Day (Porter) 6:43   710721-1
2. The Many Faces of Cole Porter: Get Out of Town/Easy to Love/You Do Something to Me (Porter) 5:22   710721-2
3. The Ballad Medley: Body and Soul (Green-Heyman-Eyton-Sour)/The Man I Love (Gershwin-Gershwin)/I Wants to Stay Here (Gershwin-Heyward-Gershwin) 4:42   710721-3
4. The Bossa Nova Scene: The Girl from Ipanema (Jobim-deMoraes-Gimbel)/How High the Moon (Lewis-Hamilton)/O Nossa Amor (Carnival Samba) (Jobim-deMoraes)/Cielito Lindo/Madalena (Lins-Martins)/Agua De Beber (Water To Drink) (Jobim-deMoraes-Gimbel) 5:35   710721-4
5. Summertime (Gershwin-Heyward) 2:36   710721-5
6. They Can't Take That Away from Me (Gershwin-Gershwin) 4:14   710721-6
7. Aspects of Duke: Mood Indigo (Ellington-Bigard-Mills)/Do Nothin' Till You Hear from Me (Ellington-Russell)/It Don't Mean a Thing (if It Ain't Got That Swing) (Ellington-Mills) 7:16   710721-7
8. Something (Harrison) 3:33   710721-8
9. St. Louis Blues (Handy) 2:59   710721-9
10. Close to You (David-Bacharach) 2:45   710721-10
11. Put a Little Love in Your Heart (DeShannon-Holiday-Meyers) 4:29   710721-11

LP: Pablo 2308 234 (released 1983). Side One, Tracks 1-5 (25:48)/Side Two, Tracks 6-11 (25:36). Total playing time, 51:24. CD: Original Jazz Classics OJCCD-442-2 (released 1990). Total playing time, 51:50. Concert produced under the personal supervision of **Norman Granz.** Liner notes in French by **Alain Tercinet**; English translation by **Terri Hinte.**

Ella on the Road/In Santa Monica (California)

LPD-98 JAZZ AT THE SANTA MONICA CIVIC '72

Ella Fitzgerald/Count Basie/Oscar Peterson/Stan Getz/Roy Eldridge/Eddie "Lockjaw" Davis/Ray Brown/Harry Edison/Al Grey/Tommy Flanagan/Ed Thigpen/Keeter Betts

Count Basie and His Orchestra

1. Norman Granz: Introduction 1:00
2. Basie Power (Wilkins) 2:45
3. The Spirit Is Willing (Nestico) 4:05
4. The Meetin' (Nelson) 4:25
5. Blues in Hoss's Flat (Basie-Foster) 4:30
6. Good Time Blues (Wilkins) 5:10

Jazz At The Philharmonic All-Stars

7. In a Mellow Tone (Ellington) 17:12
8. Loose Walk (Stitt-Richards) 10:43
   Ballad Medley:
9. Makin' Whoopee (Donaldson-Kahn) 2:52
10. If I Had You (Shapiro-Campbell-Connelly) 3:19
11. She's Funny That Way (Whiting-Moret) 2:55
12. Blue and Sentimental (Basie-Livingston-David) 1:54
13. I Surrender, Dear (Barris-Clifford) 3:07
14. 5400 North (Eldridge) 12:46

Oscar Peterson/The Ray Brown Duo

15. You Are My Sunshine (Davis-Mitchell) 9:11

Ella Fitzgerald and The Tommy Flanagan Trio with The Count Basie Orchestra

16. L.O.V.E. (Kaempfert-Gabler) 2:22   720602-1
17. Begin the Beguine (Porter) 4:12   720602-2
18. Indian Summer (Herbert-Dubin) 4:24   720602-3
19. You've Got a Friend (King) 4:58   720602-4
20. What's Going On? (Cleveland-Benson-Gaye) 3:59   720602-5

Ella Fitzgerald with The Tommy Flanagan Trio

21. Night and Day (Porter) 5:10   720602-6
22. Spring Can Really Hang You Up the Most(Wolf-Landesman) 4:05   720602-7
23. Little White Lies (Donaldson) 3:15   720602-8
24. Madalena (Lins-Martins) 3:28   720602-9

Ella Fitzgerald and The Tommy Flanagan Trio with The Count Basie Orchestra

25. Shiny Stockings (Foster) 3:30   720602-10
26. Cole Porter Medley: Too Darn Hot(Porter)/It's All Right with Me (Porter) 3:07   720602-11
27. Street Beater (**Sanford and Son** Theme) (Jones-Fitzgerald) 2:38   720602-12
28. I Can't Stop Loving You (Gibson) 5:20   720602-13

FINALE: Ella Fitzgerald, Count Basie, and the Jazz At The Philharmonic All-Stars

29. C Jam Blues (Ellington) 10:34   720602-14

LP: Pablo 2625 701 (3 discs) (released 1972). Disc 1, Side 1, Tracks 1-5 (17:05)/Side 2, Tracks 6-7 (22:17). Disc 2, Side 3, Tracks 8-13 (23:30)/Side 4, Tracks 14-15 (22:02). Disc 3, Side 5, Tracks 16-21 (25:30)/Side 6, Tracks 22-29 (36:22). Total playing time: 2:26:46. CD: Pablo 2625-701-2 (3 discs) (released 1989). Disc 1, Tracks 1-7 (41:21)/Disc 2, Tracks 8-15 (48:45). Disc 3, Tracks 16-29 (65:43)/Total playing time: 2:34:49. Concert produced under the personal supervision of **Norman Granz**. Recording Engineer: **Val Valentin**. Liner notes by **Norman Granz**.

One for Atlantic Recording (1972)

LPD-99 ELLA LOVES COLE

New Interpretations by Ella Fitzgerald of the Great Cole Porter Songs

1. I Get a Kick Out of You (Porter) 4:18   720612-1
2. Down in the Depths (on the Ninetieth Floor) (Porter) 3:37   720612-2
3. At Long Last Love (Porter) 2:29   720612-3
4. I've Got You Under My Skin (Porter) 3:13   720612-4
5. So Near and Yet So Far (Porter) 2:16   720612-5
6. All of You (Porter) 2:15   720612-6
7. Without Love (Porter) 2:46   720612-7

8. My Heart Belongs to Daddy (Porter) 2:28   720612-8
9. Love for Sale (Porter) 4:28   720612-9
10. Just One of Those Things (Porter) 3:48   720612-10
11. I Concentrate on You (Porter) 4:00   720612-11
12. Anything Goes (Porter) 2:46   720612-12
13. C'est Magnifique (Porter) 2:27   720612-13

LP: Atlantic SD 1631 (stereo) (released 1973). Side One, Tracks 1-6 (18:33)/Side Two, Tracks 7-13 (23:08). Total playing time, 41:41. 8-Track: Atlantic TP-1631, same contents and sequence (released 1973). CT: Atlantic CS-1631, same contents and sequence (released 1973). *NOTE: This album was reissued by Pablo in 1978 with two additional tracks with the title **Dream Dancing**, q.v..*

Produced under the personal supervision of, and with liner notes, by **Norman Granz**. Recording Engineer: **Val Valentin**. Liner notes by **Norman Granz**.

Ella on the Road/Newport Jazz Festival, Carnegie Hall, New York (1973)

LPD-100 ELLA FITZGERALD/ NEWPORT JAZZ FESTIVAL/LIVE AT CARNEGIE HALL, JULY 5, 1973

Ella Fitzgerald with The Chick Webb Orchestra, Eddie Barefield, Leader

1. Opening Announcement by Eddie Barefield/Let's Get Together (Webb) (instr) 1:04
2. Stompin' at the Savoy (Webb-Razaf-Goodman-Sampson) (instr) 3:46
3. A-Tisket, A-Tasket (Alexander-Fitzgerald) 3:16   730705-1
4. Indian Summer (Dubin-Herbert) 5:08   730705-2
5. Smooth Sailing (Cobb) 3:38   730705-3
6. Eddie Barefield Original (Barefield) (instr) 3:30
7. Band Introductions/Let's Get Together (Webb) 2:01
8. Announcement by George Wein 1:04

Ella Fitzgerald with Ellis Larkins

9. You Turned the Tables on Me (Mitchell-Alter) 5:01   730705-4
10. Nice Work if You Can Get It (Gershwin-Gershwin) 2:57   730705-5
11. I've Got a Crush on You (Gershwin-Gershwin) 2:48   730705-6
12. Introduction of Jazz at Carnegie All-Stars by George Wein 1:46
13. Somebody Loves Me (instr) 9:19
14. Medley: I Can't Get Started (Gershwin-Duke) (instr) 2:24; The Young Man with a Horn (Anthony) (instr)

3:33; 'Round Midnight; (Hanighen-Williams-Monk) (instr) 3:06

15. Star Dust (Parish-Carmichael) (instr) 3:58
16. Avalon (Jolson-DeSylva-Rose) (instr) 13:10
17. C Jam Blues (Roberts-Katz-Thiele-Ellington) (instr) 12:33

Ella Fitzgerald with The Tommy Flanagan Quartet

18. Introductions of Ella Fitzgerald by George Wein and Carmen McRae 2:26
19. I've Gotta Be Me (Marks) 3:04   730705-7
20. Down in the Depths(Porter) 4:55   730705-8
21. Good Morning, Heartache (Higginbotham-Fisher-Drake) 5:42   730705-9
22. What's Going On? (Gaye-Benson-Cleveland) 4:17 730705-10
23. Miss Otis Regrets(Porter) 4:55   730705-11

Ella Fitzgerald with Joe Pass, Guitar

24. Don't Worry 'Bout Me (Koehler-Bloom) 3:10 730705-12
25. These Foolish Things (Marvell-Link-Strachey) 3:28 730705-13

Ella Fitzgerald with The Tommy Flanagan Quartet

26. Any Old Blues (Fitzgerald) 4:44   730705-14
27. Taking a Chance on Love (Duke-Latouche) 2:09 730705-15
28. I'm in the Mood for Love (McHugh-Fields) 1:19 730705-16
29. Lemon Drop (Wallington) 4:49   730705-17
30. A-Tisket, A-Tasket (excerpt) (Alexander-Fitzgerald) 2:13   730705-18
31. Some of These Days (Brooks) 6:29   730705-19
32. People (Merrill-Styne) 4:45   730705-20
33. A-Tisket, A-Tasket (excerpt) (Alexander-Fitzgerald) 0:42   730705-21

LP: Columbia KG/PG 32557 (2 discs) (released 1973). Disc 1, Side One, Tracks 19, 21, 23–26 (22:14)/Side Two, 3–5,9–11 (19:14). Disc 2, Side Three, Tracks 14, 15, 17 (24:13)/Side Four, 27–29, 31, 32 (15:34). CD: CBS 466547-2 (Vol. 1)/CBS 466548-2 (Vol. 2) (Released 1989). Vol. 1, same as Disc 1, LP release (41:28). Vol. 2, same as Disc 2, LP release (39:47). Total playing time, 1:21:15. Legacy/Columbia C2K 66809 (2 discs) (Released July 1995). Disc 1, Tracks 1-16 (71:31)/Disc 2, Tracks 17-33 (70:41). Total playing time, 2:22:11.

Carnegie Hall concert produced by **Norman Granz**. Recording produced by **John Hammond** and **Teo Macero**. Concert and Editing Engineer: **Stan Tonkel**. Liner notes by **Irving Townsend**. Legacy/Columbia liner notes by **Chris Albertson**.

The Pablo Years (1973)

LPD-101 TAKE LOVE EASY/ ELLA FITZGERALD • JOE PASS

1. Take Love Easy (Ellington-Latouche) 4:32 730828-1
2. Once I Loved (Gilbert-Jobim-DeMoraes) 2:15 730828-2
3. Don't Be That Way (Goodman-Sampson-Parish) 4:38   730828-3
4. You're Blasé (Sievier-Hamilton) 3:34   730828-4
5. Lush Life (Strayhorn) 3:29   730828-5
6. A Foggy Day (in London Town) (Gershwin-Gershwin) 6:05   730828-6
7. Gee, Baby, Ain't I Good to You (Redman-Razaf) 4:00   730828-7
8. You Go to My Head (Gillespie-Coots) 5:40 730828-8
9. I Want to Talk About You (Eckstine) 3:25 730828-9

LP: Pablo 2310 702 (released May 1974). Side One, Tracks 1-5 (19:00)/Side Two, Tracks 6-9 (19:00). Total playing time, 38:00. 8-Track: Pablo S10711, same contents and sequence (released May 1974). CT: Pablo K10702, same contents and sequence (released May 1974). CD: Pablo PACD 2310 702-2, same contents and sequnce (released 1987). Pablo PACD 002 (**Ella Fitzgerald/The Pablo CD Collection**), Disc 2. JVC XRCD-0031-2 ("extended resolution"), same contents and sequence. (released 1997).

Produced under the personal supervision of **Norman Granz**. Recording Engineer: **Rafael Valentin**. Liner notes by **Benny Green**.

The Pablo Years (1974)

LPD-102 "FINE AND MELLOW"/ ELLA FITZGERALD JAMS

1. Fine and Mellow (Holiday) 6:05   740108-1
2. I'm Just a Lucky So-and-So (Ellington) 6:35 740108-7
3. A Ghost of a Chance (Young-Crosby-Washington) 5:01   740108-2
4. Rockin' in Rhythm (Ellington) 6:00   740108-9
5. I'm in the Mood for Love (Fields-McHugh) 3:15 740108-8
6. 'Round Midnight (Williams-Monk-Hanighen) 4:37 740108-3
7. I Can't Give You Anything but Love (Fields-McHugh) 4:10   740108-7

8. The Man I Love (Gershwin-Gershwin) 6:45
   740108-6
9. Polka Dots and Moonbeams (Burke-Van Heusen)
   5"03 740108-4

LP: Pablo 2310 829 (released November 1979). Side
One, Tracks 1-4 (23:45)/Side Two, Tracks 5-9 (23:57).
Total playing time, 47:42. CT: Pablo 52310 829, same contents and sequence (released 1988). CD: Pablo PACD 2310
829-2, same contents and sequence (released 1988). Pablo
PACD 002 (**Ella Fitzgerald/The Pablo CD Collection**),
Disc 10. Produced under the personal supervision of **Norman Granz**. Recording Engineer: **Ed Greene**. Liner notes
by **Leonard Feather**.

The Pablo Years (1974)

LPD-103 ELLA IN LONDON

1. Sweet Georgia Brown (Bernie-Pinkard-Casey) 3:15
   740411-1
2. They Can't Take That Away from Me (Gershwin-
   Gershwin) 5:11   740411-2
3. Ev'ry Time We Say Goodbye (Porter) 2:57   740411-3
4. The Man I Love (Gershwin-Gershwin) 8:10
   740411-4
5. It Don't Mean a Thing (Ellington-Mills) 7:25
   740411-5
6. You've Got a Friend (King) 6:45   740411-6
7. Lemon Drop (Wallington) 3:50   740411-7
8. The Very Thought of You (Noble) 4:12   740411-8
9. Happy Blues (Fitzgerald) 6:00   740411-9

LP: Pablo 2310 711 (released February 1975). Side
One, Tracks 1-4 (19:48)/Side Two, Tracks 5-9 (28:32).
Total playing time, 48:10. CD: Pablo PACD 2310 711, same
contents and sequence (released 1988). Pablo PACD 002
(**Ella Fitzgerald/The Pablo CD Collection**), Disc 3. Pro-
duced under the personal supervision of **Norman Granz**.
Liner notes by **Benny Green**.

The Pablo Years (1975)

LPD-104 ELLA AND OSCAR

1. Mean to Me (Turk-Ahlert) 3:25   750519-1
2. How Long Has This Been Going On? (Gershwin-
   Gershwin) 4:48   750519-2
3. When Your Lover Has Gone (Swan) 4:54   750519-3
4. More Than You Know (Youmans-Rose-Eliscu) 4:32
   750519-4
5. There's a Lull in My Life (Revel-Gordon) 4:55
   750519-5

6. Midnight Sun (Mercer-Burke-Hampton) 3:37
   750519-6
7. I Hear Music (Lane-Loesser) 5:06   750519-7
8. Street of Dreams (Young-Lewis) 4:03   750519-8
9. April in Paris (Harburg-Duke) 8:35   750519-9

LP: Pablo 2310 759 (released 1976). Side One, Tracks
1-5 (22:54)/Side Two, Tracks 6-9 (21:36). Total playing
time: 44:30. 8-Track: Pablo S10759, same contents and sequence (released 1976). CT release: Pablo K10759, same
contents and sequence (released 1976). CD release: Pablo
2310759-2, same contents and sequence (released1987).
Pablo PACD 002 (**Ella Fitzgerald/The Pablo CD Collection**), Disc 5.

Produced under the personal supervision of **Norman
Granz**. Liner notes by **Benny Green**.

The Pablo Years (1975)

LPD-105 MONTREUX JAZZ FESTIVAL, 1975/ELLA

1. Caravan (Ellington-Tizol-Mills) 2:20   750717-1
2. Satin Doll (Ellington-Strayhorn-Mercer) 2:37
   750717-2
3. Teach Me Tonight (DePaul-Cahn) 4:27   750717-3
4. Wave (Jobim) 5:02   750717-4
5. It's All Right with Me (Porter) 2:49   750717-5
6. Let's Do It (Porter) 5:29   750717-6
7. How High the Moon (Lewis-Hamilton) 6:20
   750717-8
8. The Girl from Ipanema (Jobim-de Moraes-Gimbel)
   6:49   750717-9
9. 'Tain't Nobody's Biz-Ness (if I Do) (Grainger-
   Robins) 5:42   750717-10

LP: Pablo 2310 751 (released December 1975). Side
One, Tracks 1-6 (20:00)/Side Two, Tracks 7-9 (39:00).
Total playing time: 59:00. 8-Track: Pablo S10751, same
contents, and sequence (released 1988). CT: Pablo K10751,
same contents and sequence (released 1988). CD: Pablo
PACD 2310 751-2, same contents and sequence (released
1988). Pablo PACD 002 (**Ella Fitzgerald/The Pablo CD
Collection**), Disc 4.

Produced under the personal supervision of **Norman
Granz**. Liner notes by **Benny Green**.

The Pablo Years (1976)

LPD-106 FITZGERALD AND PASS ... AGAIN

1. I Ain't Got Nothin' but the Blues (Ellington-George-
   Fotin) 4:04   760130-2

2. 'Tis Autumn (Nemo) 5:05   760129-3
3. My Old Flame (Johnston-Coslow) 4:49   760208-1
4. That Old Feeling (Brown-Fain) 2:45   760208-2
5. Rain (Ford) 2:22   760208-3
6. I Didn't Know About You (Russell-Ellington) 4:41 760129-1
7. You Took Advantage of Me (Rodgers-Hart) 3:35 760130-3
8. I've Got the World on a String (Koehler-Arlen) 4:07 760130-4
9. All Too Soon (Ellington-Sigman) 4:24   760130-1
10. The One I Love (Belongs to Somebody Else) (Kahn-Jones) 4:02   760129-4
11. Solitude (Ellington DeLange-Mills) 3:43   760208-4
12. Nature Boy (Ahbez) 2:24   760129-5
13. Tennessee Waltz (Stewart-King) 3:48   760130-5
14. One Note Samba (Jobim-Mendonà-Hendricks) 5:00   760129-2

LP: Pablo 2310 772 (released 1976). Side One, Tracks 1-7 (24:00)/Side Two, Tracks 8-14 (25:00). Total playing time: 49:00. 8-Track: PabloS10772, same contents and sequence (released 1976). CT: Pablo K10772, same contents and sequence (released 1976). CD: Pablo 2310 772-2, same contents and sequence (released 1988). Produced under the personal supervision of **Norman Granz**. Liner notes by **Benny Green**.

The Pablo Years (1977)

LPD-107 ELLA FITZGERALD WITH THE TOMMY FLANAGAN TRIO/MONTREUX '77

1. Too Close for Comfort (Bock-Holofcener-Weiss) 3:27   770714-1
2. I Ain't Got Nothing but theBlues (Ellington-George) 4:07   770714-2
3. My Man (Mon Homme) (Yvain-Willemetz-Charles) 3:48   770714-3
4. Come Rain or Come Shine (Mercer-Arlen) 2:30 770714-4
5. Day by Day (Cahn-Stordahl-Weston) 1:46 770714-5
6. Ordinary Fool (Williams) 3:20   770714-6
7. One Note Samba (Jobim-Mendonà-Hendricks) 6:26 770714-7
8. I Let a Song Go Out of My Heart (Ellington-Nemo-Mills-Redmond) 4:31   770714-8
9. Billie's Bounce (Parker) 4:49   770714-9
10. You Are the Sunshine of My Life (Wonder) 3:53 770714-10

LP: Pablo Live 2308 206 (released 1977). Fantasy Original Jazz Classics OJC 376 (released October 1989). Side One, Tracks 1-6 (21:02)/Side Two, Tracks 7-10 (21:11). Total playing time, 42:13. 8-Track: Pablo S08206, same contents and sequence (released 1977). CT: Pablo K08206, same contents and sequence (released 1977). Fantasy OJC 5376 same contents and sequence (released October 1989). CD: Fantasy OJCCD-376-2, same contents and sequence(released October 1989). Produced under the personal supervision of **Norman Granz**. Recording Engineer: **Val Valentin**. Liner notes by **Norman Granz**.

The Pablo Years (1978)

LPD-108 DREAM DANCING/ELLA FITZGERALD & COLE PORTER

1. Dream Dancing (Porter) 3:59   780213-1
2. I've Got You Under My Skin (Porter) 3:14   720612-4
3. I Concentrate on You (Porter) 4:01   720612-11
4. My Heart Belongs to Daddy (Porter) 2:30   720612-8
5. Love for Sale (Porter) 4:32   720612-9
6. So Near and Yet So Far (Porter) 2:17   720612-5
7. Down in the Depths (on the Ninetieth Floor) (Porter)3:36   720612-2
8. After You — Who? (Porter) 3:11   780213-2
9. Just One of Those Things (Porter) 3:43   720612-10
10. I Get a Kick Out of You (Porter) 4:18   720612-1
11. All of You (Porter) 2:14   720612-6
12. Anything Goes (Porter) 2:48   720612-12
13. At Long Last Love (Porter) 2:23   720612-3
14. C'est Magnifique (Porter) 2:28   720612-13
15. Without Love (Porter) 2:46   720612-7

LP: Pablo 2310 814 (released 1978). Side One, Tracks 1-7 (24:39)/Side Two, Tracks 8-15 (24:36). Total playing time: 49:15. CT: Pablo K10814, same contents and sequence (released 1978). CD: Pablo PACD 2310 814-2, same contents and sequence (released 1988). Pablo PACD 002 (**Ella Fitzgerald/The Pablo CD Collection**), Disc 9. Produced under the personal supervision of, and with liner notes by, **Norman Granz**. Recording Engineer: **Val Valentin**.

The Pablo Years (1978)

LPD-109 LADY TIME/ELLA

1. I'm Walkin' (Domino-Bartolomew) 5:34   780620-5
2. All or Nothing at All (Lawrence-Altman) 6:31 780619-3
3. I Never Had a Chance (Irving Berlin) 4:05 780619-1

4. I Cried for You (Arnheim-Lyman-Freed) 3:17
   780620-7
5. What Will I Tell My Heart (Tinturim-Lawrence-
   Gordon) 1:58   780620-4
6. Since I Fell for You (Johnson) 4:26   780619-4
7. And the Angels Sing (Mercer-Elman) 3:07
   780620-6
8. I'm Confessin' (Dougherty-Reynolds-Neiburg) 2:50
   780619-2
9. Mack the Knife (Weill-Brecht) 2:57   780620-2
10. That's My Desire (Kresa-Loveday) 3:02   780620-1
11. I'm in the Mood for Love (McHugh-Fields) 4:36
    780620-3

LP: Pablo 2310 825 (released 1978). Side One, Tracks 1-5 (21:45)/Side Two, Tracks 6-11 (21:23). Total playing time: 43:05. CT: Pablo K10825, same contents and sequence (released 1978). CD: Pablo PACD 2310 825-2, same contents and sequence (released 1988). Produced under the personal supervision of **Norman Granz**. Recording Engineer: **Val Valentin**. Liner notes by **Norman Granz**.

The Pablo Years (1979)

LPD-110 "A CLASSY PAIR"/ELLA FITZGERALD SINGS/COUNT BASIE PLAYS

1. The Organ Grinder's Swing (Parish-Hudson) 5:53
   790216-5
2. Just A-Sittin' and A-Rockin' (Gaines-Strayhorn-
   Ellington) 4:43   790215-1
3. My Kind of Trouble Is You (Vandervoort-Carter)
   4:37   790216-1
4. Ain't Misbehavin' (Razaf-Waller-Brooks) 4:01
   790215-5
5. Some Other Spring (Herzog-Kitchings)* 3:45
   790712-3
6. Teach Me Tonight (Cahn-DePaul) 3:17   790216-3
7. I'm Getting Sentimental Over You (Washington-
   Bassman) 2:53   790215-2
8. Don't Worry 'Bout Me (Koehler-Bloom) 3:31
   790216-2
9. Honeysuckle Rose (Razaf-Waller) 6:09   790216-4
10. Sweet Lorraine (Parish-Burwell) 4:25   790215-3
11. Please Don't Talk About Me When I'm Gone (Clare-
    Stept)*2:26   790712-1

*These two tracks were recorded at Jazz Montreux/11th Montreux International Festival, of which the balance of Ella's released performances may be found on **A Perfect Match/Ella and Basie** (LPD-111) and **Digital III at Montreux** (LPD-112).

LP: Pablo 2312 132 (released 1982). Side One, Tracks 9, 3, 6, 1 (19:34)/Side Two, Tracks 8, 7, 4, 2, 10 (19:11). Total

playing time: 38:45. Musical Heritage Society MHS7342, same contents and sequence (released 1986). CT: Pablo K12132, same contents and sequence (released 1982). CD: Pablo PACD 2312 132-2, same contents and sequence (released 1987). Pablo PACD 002 (**Ella Fitzgerald/The Pablo CD Collection**), Disc 6. Tracks in sequence as listed above. Total playing time: 46:29.

Produced under the personal supervision of **Norman Granz**. Recording Engineer: **Val Valentin**. Liner notes by **Leonard Feather**.

The Pablo Years (1979)

LPD-111 A PERFECT MATCH/ ELLA AND BASIE

1. Please Don't Talk About Me When I'm Gone (Clare-
   Stept) 1:40   790712-1
2. Sweet Georgia Brown (Bernie-Casey-Pinkard) 2:44
   790712-2
3. Some Other Spring (Herzog-Kitchings) 3:58
   790712-3
4. Make Me Rainbows (Bergman-Bergman-Williams)
   3:02   790712-4
5. After You've Gone (Creamer-Layton) 3:23   790712-5
6. 'Round Midnight (Hanighen-Williams-Monk) 3:40
   790712-6
7. Fine and Mellow (Holiday) 2:25   790712-7
8. You've Changed (Carey-Fischer) 3:10   790712-11
9. Honeysuckle Rose (Waller-Razaf) 2:58   790712-12
10. St. Louis Blues (Handy) 4:49   790712-13
11. Basella (Basie-Fitzgerald) 9:20   790712-14

LP: Pablo Today/Digital 2312 110 (released 1980). Side One, Track 1-7 (21:22)/Side Two, Tracks 8-11 (20:32). Total playing time: 41:54. CT: Pablo K12 110, same contents and sequence (released 1980). CD: Pablo PACD 2312 110-2, same contents and sequence (released 1987). Produced under the personal supervision of **Norman Granz**. Recording Engineer: **Dave Richards**. There are no liner notes.

The Pablo Years (1979)

LPD-112 JOE PASS/ELLA FITZGERALD/ COUNT BASIE/DIGITAL III AT MONTREUX

Count Basie and His Orchestra

1. I Can't Get Started (Gershwin-Duke) 3:39
2. Good Mileage (Wilson) 7:00

Ella Fitzgerald with Count Basie and His Orchestra

3. A Ghost of a Chance (Crosby-Washington-Young) 3:19   790712-8
4. Flying Home (Hampton-Goodman-Robin) 7:52 790712-9

Joe Pass, Guitar

5. I Cover the Waterfront (Heyman-Green) 3:34
6. Li'l Darlin' (Hefti) 4:30

Joe Pass, Guitar, and Niels-Henning Ørsted Pederson, Bass

7. In Your Own Sweet Way (Brubeck) 6:51
8. Oleo (Rollins) 4:10

LP: Pablo Live 2308 223 (released 1980). Side One, Tracks 1-4 (21:49)/Side Two, Tracks 5-8 (19:05). Total playing time: 40:57. CD: Pablo Live PACD 2308 223-2, same contents and sequence (released 1988). Produced under the personal supervision of, and with liner notes by, **Norman Granz**. Recording Engineer: **Dave Richards**.

The Pablo Years (1980)

LPD-113 ELLA ABRAÇA JOBIM/ ELLA FITZGERALD SINGS THE ANTONIO CARLOS JOBIM SONG BOOK

1. Dreamer (Vivo Sonhando) (Jobim-Lees) 4:53 800917-1
2. This Love I've Found (Só Tinha de Ser Com Vôce) (Jobim-Oliveira) 5:15   800923-1
3. The Girl from Ipanema (Garôta de Ipanema) (Jobim-de Moraes) 3:47   810318-1
4. Somewhere in the Hills (Favela) (Jobim-de Moraes-Gimbel) 3:56   810319-1
5. Photograph (Fotografia) (Jobim-Gilbert) 3:44 800919-5
6. Wave (Jobim) 5:19   800917-2
7. Triste (Jobim) 4:04   800919-6
8. Quiet Nights of Quiet Stars (Corcovado) (Jobim-Lees) 5:38   800918-2
9. Water to Drink (Agua de Beber) (Jobim-de Moraes-Gimbel) 2:40   800918-1
10. Bonita (Jobim-Lees-Gilbert) 2:49   800918-3
11. Off Key (Desafinado) (Jobim-Mendonà-Lees) 3:38 810318-2
12. He's a Carioca (Ele é Carioca) (Jobim-Gilbert-de Moraes) 5:10   810318-3
13. Dindi (Jobim-Oliveira-Gilbert) 6:35   800919-1
14. How Insensitive (Insensatez) (Jobim-deMoraes-Gimbel) 2:59   800919-2

15. One Note Samba (Samba de Uma Nota Só) (Jobim-Mendonà) 3:48   800919-4
16. A Felicidade (Jobim-de Moraes) 2:17   800917-3
17. Useless Landscape (Inútil Paisagem) (Jobim-Oliveira-Gilbert) 7:59   800919-3
18. Don't Ever Go Away (Por Causa de Vôce) (Jobim-Gilbert-Duran) 2:45   810320-2
19. Song of the Jet (Samba do Aviao) (Jobim-Lees) 3:39 810320-1

LP: Pablo Today 2630 201 (2 discs) (released 1981). Disc One, Side One, Tracks 4-3-13-11-9 (20:43). Disc One, Side Two, Tracks 1-8-10-15-18 (20:01). Disc Two, Side Three, Tracks 7-14-12-2-16 (19:53). Disc Two, Side Four, Tracks 6-19-5-17 (20:47). Total playing time, 1:21:24. CT: Pablo Today 2630201 (2cassettes), same contents and sequence (released 1981). CD: Pablo PACD 2630, sequence as listed, except that due to lack of space on the single CD release, tracks 18 and 19 were omitted (released 1991). Total playing time, 75:11. Produced under the personal supervision of, and with liner notes by, **Norman Granz**. Recording Engineers: **Humberto Gatica, Paul Aronoff, Allen Sides**.

The Pablo Years (1982)

LPD-114 ELLA FITZGERALD/ THE BEST IS YET TO COME

1. Don't Be That Way (Goodman-Sampson-Parish) 3:58   820204-1
2. God Bless the Child (Holiday-Herzog) 4:42 820204-2
3. I Wonder Where Our Love Has Gone (Johnson) 3:48   820205-1
4. You're Driving Me Crazy (Donaldson) 3:23 820204-3
5. Any Old Time (Shaw) 4:19   820204-4
6. Good-Bye (Jenkins) 3:58   820205-2
7. Autumn in New York (Duke) 3:24   820205-3
8. The Best Is Yet To Come (Coleman-Leigh) 5:19 820204-5
9. Deep Purple (Parish-DeRose) 3:57   820205-4
10. Somewhere in the Night (Raskin-May) 2:58 820205-5

LP: Pablo Today 2312 138 (released 1982). Side One, Tracks 1-5 (20:10)/Side Two, Tracks 6-10 (19:36). Total playing time: 39:46. CT: Pablo Today K12 138, same contents and sequence (released 1982). Pablo 52312 138, same contents and sequence (released 1988). CD: Pablo PACD 2312 138, same contents and sequence (released 1988). Pablo PACD 002 (**Ella Fitzgerald/The Pablo CD Collection**),

Disc 7. Original Jazz Classics OJCCD 889 (Released March 1996). Produced under the personal supervision of **Norman Granz**. Recording Engineer: **Allen Sides**. Liner notes by **Leonard Feather**.

The Pablo Years (1983)

LPD-115 "Speak Love"/ Ella Fitzgerald/Joe Pass

1. Speak Low (Weill-Nash) 4:11   830321-1
2. Comes Love (Brown-Tobias-Stept) 3:00   830322-9
3. There's No You (Adair-Hopper) 4:38   830322-4
4. I May Be Wrong (But I Think You're Wonderful) (Ruskin-Sullivan) 5:06   830322-8
5. At Last (Gordon-Warren) 4:18   830321-3
6. The Thrill Is Gone (Medley) (Brown-Henderson) 4:12   830322-10
7. Gone with the Wind (Magidson-Wrubel) 3:52   830321-6
8. Blue and Sentimental (Basie-Livingston-David) 3:02   830322-1
9. Girl Talk (Hefti-Troup) 4:09   830321-2
10. Georgia on My Mind (Carmichael-Gorrell) 6:05   830322-5

LP: Pablo D2310 888 (released 1983). Side One, Tracks 1-5 (21:33) /Side Two, Tracks 6-10, (21:40). Total playing time: 43:13. CT: Pablo 52310 888, same contents and sequence (released 1987). CD: Pablo PACD2310 888-2, same contents and sequence (released1987). Produced under the personal supervision of **Norman Granz**. Recording Engineers: **Dennis Sands** and **Arne Frager**. Liner notes by **Norman Granz**.

The Pablo Years (1983)

LPD-116 Nice Work If You Can Get It/ Ella Fitzgerald and André Previn Do Gershwin

1. A Foggy Day (in London Town) (Gershwin-Gershwin) 3:58   830523-1
2. Nice Work If You Can Get It (Gershwin-Gershwin) 5:23   830523-2
3. But Not for Me (Gershwin-Gershwin) 3:58   830523-8
4. Let's Call the Whole Thing Off (Gershwin-Gershwin) 2:54   830523-5
5. How Long Has This Been Going On?(Gershwin-Gershwin) 4:58   830523-9

6. Who Cares? (Gershwin-Gershwin) 4:39   830523-4
7. Medley: I've Got a Crush on You (Gershwin-Gershwin)/Someone To Watch Over Me (Gershwin-Gershwin)/Embraceable You (Gershwin-Gershwin) 7:23   830523-3
8. They Can't Take That Away from Me(Gershwin-Gershwin) 3:36   830523-7

LP: Pablo Today D2312 140 (released 1983). Side One, Tracks 1-4 (18:34)/Side Two, Tracks 5-8 (19:53). Total playing time, 38:27. CT: Pablo Today D52312140, same contents and sequence (released 1987). CD: Pablo Today D2312140-2, same contents and sequence (released 1987). Pablo PACD 002 (**Ella Fitzgerald/The Pablo CD Collection**), Disc 8. Produced under the personal supervision **Norman Granz**. Recording Engineer: **Bob Simpson**. Liner notes by **Benny Green**.

The Pablo Years (1983)

LPD-117 "Return to Happiness"/ Jazz At The Philharmonic Yoyogi National Stadium, Tokyo, 1983

The J.A.T.P. All-Stars

1. Sunday (Kroeger-Miller-Cohen-Styne) 10:21
2. Undecided (Shavers-Robbins) 10:32

Al Grey

3. I Can't Get Started (Gershwin-Duke) 2:39
4. God Bless the Child (Holiday-Herzog) 3:08

Harry "Sweets" Edison

5. Ain't Misbehavin' (Razaf-Waller-Brooks) 3:07
6. Memories of You (Razaf-Blake) 2:53

Zoot Sims

7. Emily (Mandel-Mercer) 1:52
8. These Foolish Things (Strachey-Marvell-Link) 2:27

J.J. Johnson

9. Misty (Garner-Burke) 3:06
10. What's New? (Haggart-Burke) 2:56

Eddie "Lockjaw" Davis

11. Don't Blame Me (McHugh-Fields) 2:31
12. But Beautiful (Van Heusen-Burke) 2:26

Clark Terry

13. My Romance (Rodgers-Hart) 2:40
14. When Lights Are Low (Carter-Williams) 3:11

J.A.T.P. All-Stars

15. Spotlite (Hawkins) 9:10

Oscar Peterson/Joe Pass/
Niels-Henning Ørsted Pedersen/Martin Drew

16. Peace (Peterson) 7:26
17. My Shining Hour (Gold) 4:27
18. Mississauga Rattler (Peterson) 5:59
19. Alice in Wonderland (Fain-Hilliard) 7:03

The Oscar Peterson Four

20. City Lights (Peterson) 6:24
21. Blues (Peterson) 3:56

Ella Fitzgerald with Paul Smith,
Keeter Betts, Bobby Durham

22. Manteca (Fuller-Gillespie) 2:25   831000-1
23. Willow, Weep for Me (Ronell) 5:16   831000-2
24. All of Me (Simons-Marks) 3:38   831000-3
25. Blue Moon (Rodgers-Hart) 3:56   831000-4
26. Night and Day (Porter) 3:37   831000-5
27. They Can't Take That Away from Me (Gershwin-Gershwin) 3:35   831000-6
28. Medley: The Man I Love (Gershwin-Gershwin)/Body and Soul (Green-Heyman-Eyton-Sour) 5:33   831000-7
29. 'Round Midnight (Williams-Monk-Hanighen) 3:52   831000-8

Ella Fitzgerald with The J.A.T.P. All-Stars

30. Flying Home (Hampton-Goodman) 8:31 831000-9

LP: Pablo Live 2620 117 (3 discs) (released 1987). Disc One, Side One, Tracks 1-2 (20:58)/Side Two, Tracks 3-9 (19:42). Disc Two, Side Three, Tracks 10-15 (23:39)/Side Four, Tracks 16-19 (25:10). Disc Three, Side Five, Tracks 20-25 (26:01)/Side Six, 26-30 (25:28). Total playing time, 2:20:58. CT: Pablo Live 52620117 (3 cassettes), same contents and sequence (released 1987). CD: Pablo Live PACD 2620 117-2 (2 discs):. Disc One, Tracks 1-16 (72:30). Disc Two, Tracks 17-30 (73:16). Total playing time, 2:15:46. Produced under the personal supervision of **Norman Granz**. Liner notes by **Benny Green**.

The Verve/Pablo Years

LPD-118 ELLA/THE CONCERT YEARS

Jazz At The Philharmonic in Tokyo/
Live at the Nichigeki Theatre, 1953

1. On the Sunny Side of the Street (McHugh-Fields) 1:58   531118-1
2. Body and Soul (Heyman-Sour-Eyton-Green) 4:07 531118-2
3. Why Don't You Do Right? (McCoy) 3:19   531118-3
4. Oh! Lady, Be Good! (Gershwin-Gershwin) 2:56 531118-4

5. I Got It Bad (And That Ain't Good) (Ellington-Webster) 3:35   531118-5
6. How High the Moon (Hamilton-Lewis) 3:10 531118-6
7. My Funny Valentine (Rodgers-Hart) 2:50   531118-7
8. Smooth Sailing (Cobb) 2:52   531118-8
9. The Frim Fram Sauce (Evans-Ricardel) 3:10 531118-9
10. Perdido (Tizol-Lengsfelder-Drake) 6:14   531118-10

Ella Fitzgerald/Duke Ellington/
The Stockholm Concert, 1966

11. Imagine My Frustration (Ellington-Strayhorn-Wilson) 4:42   660208-4
12. Duke's Place (Fitzgerald-Ellington-Katz-Roberts-Thiele) 4:32   660208-5
13. Satin Doll (Ellington-Strayhorn-Mercer) 2:44 660208-6
14. Something To Live For (Strayhorn-Ellington) 4:21 660208-7
15. Só Danò Samba (Jobim-deMoraes) 3:25   660208-9

The Greatest Jazz Concert in the World

16. Don't Be That Way (Goodman-Sampson-Parish) 4:03   670326-1
17. You've Changed (Carey-Fischer) 4:07   670326-2
18. Let's Do It (Porter) 4:22   670326-3
19. On the Sunny Side of the Street (McHugh-Fields) 2:03   670326-4
20. Cotton Tail (Ellington) 5:10   670326-9

Ella à Nice

21. Night and Day (Porter) 6:48   710721-1
22. The Many Faces of Cole Porter: Get Out of Town/Easy To Love/You Do Something to Me 5:24 710721-2
23. The Ballad Medley: Body and Soul (Heyman-Sour-Eyton-Green)/ The Man I Love (Gershwin-Gershwin)/ I Loves You, Porgy (Heyward-Gershwin-Gershwin) 4:44   710721-3
24. The Bossa Nova Scene: The Girl from Ipanema (Jobim-deMoraes-Gimbel)/ Fly Me to the Moon (Howard)/ O Nossa Amor (Carnival Samba) (Jobim-deMoraes)/ Cielito Lindo (Mendoza y Cortez-Fernandez-Yradier-Wilson)/ Madalena (Lins-deSouza)/ Agua de Beber (Jobim-deMoraes-Gimbel) 5:37   710721-4
25. They Can't Take That Away from Me (Gershwin-Gershwin) 4:14   710721-6
26. St. Louis Blues (Handy) 3:01   710721-9

Jazz at the Santa Monic Civic '72

27. L.O.V.E. (Kaempfert-Gabler) 2:22   720602-1
28. Begin the Beguine (Porter) 4:12   720602-2
29. Indian Summer (Dubin-Herbert) 4:24   720602-3

30. You've Got a Friend (King) 5:02   720602-4
31. Spring Can Really Hang You Up the Most (Wolf-Landesman) 3:57   720602-7
32. Madalena (Lins-deSouza) 3:28   720602-9
33. Shiny Stockings (Fitzgerald-Foster) 3:30   720602-10
34. I Can't Stop Loving You (Gibson) 5:20   720602-13
35. C-Jam Blues (Ellington) 10:50   720602-14

Ella in London

36. Sweet Georgia Brown (Bernie-Pinkard) 3:15   740411-1
37. They Can't Take That Away from Me (Gershwin-Gershwin) 4:41   740411-2
38. Ev'ry Time We Say Goodbye (Porter) 2:52   740411-3
39. The Man I Love (Gershwin-Gershwin) 8:22   740411-4
40. It Don't Mean a Thing (If It Ain't Got That Swing) (Ellington-Mills) 7:21   740411-5
41. Lemon Drop (Wallington) 3:47   740411-7
42. The Very Thought of You (Noble) 4:14   740411-8
43. Happy Blues (Fitzgerald) 5:56   740411-9

Montreux Jazz Festival, 1975/Ella

44. Caravan (Ellington-Tizol-Mills) 2:19   750717-2
45. Satin Doll (Mercer-Ellington-Strayhorn) 2:37   750717-3
46. Teach Me Tonight (DePaul-Kahn) 4:27   750717-4
47. Wave (Jobim) 5:01   750717-5
48. It's All Right with Me (Porter) 2:48   750717-6
49. How High the Moon (Hamilton-Lewis) 7:18   750717-8
50. T'Ain't Nobody's Bizz-Ness (If I Do) (Grainger-Robbins) 5:42   750717-10

Ella Fitzgerald with The Tommy Flanagan Trio/Montreux '77

51. Too Close for Comfort (Bock-Holofcener-Weiss) 3:25   770714-1
52. I Ain't Got Nothin' but the Blues (Ellington-George) 4:06   770714-2
53. Day by Day (Cahn-Stordahl-Weston) 1:46   770714-5
54. Ordinary Fool (Williams) 3:15   770714-6
55. Billie's Bounce (Parker) 4:44   770714-9

A Perfect Match/Ella and Basie

56. Please Don't Talk About Me When I'm Gone (Clare-Stept) 1:46   790712-1
57. Make Me Rainbows (Bergman-Bergman-Williams) 3:12   790712-4
58. After You've Gone (Creamer-Layton) 3:34   790712-5
59. 'Round Midnight (Monk-Williams-Hanighen) 4:21   790712-6
60. You've Changed (Carey-Fischer) 3:04   790712-11
61. Basella (Basie-Fitzgerald) 10:00   790712-14

"Return to Happiness"/Jazz at the Philharmonic Yoyogi National Stadium, 1983

62. Manteca (Fuller-Gillespie) 2:30   831000-1
63. Willow Weep for Me (Ronell) 5:17   831000-2
64. All of Me (Simons-Marks) 3:34   831000-3
65. Blue Moon (Rodgers-Hart) 3:58   831000-4
66. Night and Day (Porter) 3:37   831000-5
67. Flying Home (Hampton-Goodman-Robin) 8:38   831000-9
   CD: Pablo 4CD-4414 (4 discs) (released 1994). Disc One: Tracks 1-20 (77:41). Disc Two: Tracks 21-35 (77:10). Disc Three: Tracks 36-50 (75:24). Disc Four: Tracks 51-67 (77:25). Total playing time, 5:7:40. Original concert performances produced by **Norman Granz.** This compilation produced by **Eric Miller.** Liner notes by **Benny Green.**

The Pablo Years (1986)

LPD-119 ELLA FITZGERALD AND JOE PASS/"EASY LIVING"

1. My Ship (Gershwin-Weill) 4:26   860228-1
2. Don't Be That Way (Goodman-Sampson-Parish) 3:00   860228-4
3. My Man (Mon Homme) (Yvain-Willemetz-Charles-Pollac) 3:28   860228-5
4. Don't Worry 'Bout Me (Bloom-Koehler) 2:46   860228-6
5. Days of Wine and Roses (Mancini-Mercer) 3:04   860228-7
6. Easy Living (Robin-Rainger) 4:14   860228-8
7. A Ghost of a Chance (Crosby-Washington-Young) 6:02   860228-9
8. Love for Sale (Porter) 4:38   860228-11
9. Moonlight in Vermont (Suessdorf-Blackburn) 4:20   860228-10
10. On Green Dolphin Street (Washington-Kaper) 3:25   860228-2
11. Why Don't You Do Right? (McCoy-Melrose) 2:56   860228-3
12. By Myself (Dietz-Schwartz) 3:26   860228-12
13. I Want a Little Girl (Henry-Hyde) 2:46   860228-13
14. I'm Making Believe (Monaco-Gordon) 2:38   860228-14
15. On A Slow Boat to China (Loesser) 5:05   860228-15
   LP: Pablo 2310 921 (released 1986). Side One, Tracks 1-7 (27:30)/Side Two, Tracks 8-15 (29:49). Total playing time: 57:19. CT: Pablo 52310 921, same contents and sequence (released 1987). CD: Pablo PACD 2310 921-2, same contents and sequence (released 1987). Produced under the personal supervision of **Norman Granz.** Recording Engineer: **Dennis Sands.** Liner notes by **Benny Green.**

The Pablo Years (1989)

LPD-120 ELLA FITZGERALD/ ALL THAT JAZZ

1. Dream a Little Dream of Me (Kahn-Schwandt-Andre) 4:58   890316-1
2. My Last Affair (Johnson) 4:33   890320-1
3. Baby, Don't You Quit Now (Rowles-Mercer) 5:06   890320-2
4. Oh, Look at Me Now (DeVries-Buskin) 5:09   890316-2
5. The Jersey Bounce (Johnson-Brashaw-Plater-Feyne) 3:42   890320-3
6. When Your Lover Has Gone (Swan) 4:58   890316-3
7. That Old Devil Called Love (Roberts-Fisher) 4:47   890315-1
8. All That Jazz (Stillman-Carter) 4:02   890322-1
9. Just When We're Falling in Love (Russell-Thompson-Jacquet) 5:22   890315-2
10. Good Morning, Heartache (Fischer-Drake-Higginbotham) 5:27   890316-4
11. Little Jazz (Eldridge-Harding) 5:35   890315-3
12. The Nearness of You (Carmichael-Washington) 7:08   890322-2

LP: Pablo 2310 938 (released 1990). Side One, Tracks 1-5 (23:28)/Side Two, Tracks 6-10 (24:36). Total playing time: 48:04. CT: Pablo 52310 938, same contents and sequence (released 1990). CD: Pablo PACD 2310 938-2 (Tracks 1-12) (released 1990). Total playing time, 61:15. Produced under the personal supervision of **Norman Granz**. Recording Engineer: **Angel Balestier**. Liner notes by **Norman Granz**.

VII. The "B" Collection: Contents

This collection comprises LPs and CDs that contain one or more recordings not found in albums in **The "A" Collection**, as well as those "unofficial" concert albums which have not yet been released by GRP, Verve, or Pablo/Original Jazz Classics. Tracks previously released only on the 78rpm format appear in bold type immediately following the title of the album — except for the concert albums, all tracks of which (with a few exceptions) have not been released previously.

LPD-121 Ella Fitzgerald/The Complete Recordings **1935–1939** Affinity AFS-1020-3 (England) 3-CD set Disc 3, Track 6. **If You Only Knew** (Take A) (2:51) (380503-10)

This set of three discs duplicates exactly **The Chronological Ella Fitzgerald** Classics series, **1935–1937** (LPD-7), **1937–1938** (LPD-9), **1938–1939** (LPD-10), and the first three tracks of **1939** (LPD-12), except that it also contains "Wake Up and Live" (on Disc 2, track 3) which appears only on **The Chronological Chick Webb and His Orchestra, 1935–1938** (LPD-8), and Take A of "If You Only Knew" (as above), which is not to the editor's knowledge, included in any other collection or compilation.

Released 1991. Disc One, Tracks 1–25 (72:36)/Disc Two, Tracks 26–50 (78:19)/Disc Three, 51–75 (75:50)/ Total playing time, 3:46:45/Produced by Charly Records, Limited, London

LPD-122 Ella Fitzgerald/"The First Lady of Song" MCA 510.184/185 (France) 2-LP set
Disc 1, Track 10. **Sugar** (2:53) (500306-3)
Disc 2, Track 6. **Robbins' Nest** (2:28) (471223-4)
Disc 2, Track 11. **Petootie Pie** (2:37) (451015-1)
Disc 2, Track 15. **The Greatest There Is** (2:08) (520811-2)

DISC 1   1. Betcha Nickel (390629-1)/2. Cow-Cow Boogie (431103-1)/3. Into Each Life Some Rain Must Fall (440830-1)/4. Big Boy Blue (370114-3)/5. You Turned the Tables on Me (471223-2)/6. M-I-S-S-I-S-S-I-P-P-I(500509-1)/7. (It's Only a) Paper Moon (450327-1)/8. (I Love You) For Sentimental Reasons (460819-1)/9. Blue Lou (530213-2)/10. Sugar Foot Rag (500306-3)/11. Goody Goody (520225-4)/12. In the Evening (When the Sun Goes Down) (490920-1)/13. Don'tcha Go 'Way Mad (500202-2)/14. Solid as a Rock (500306-1)/15. Early Autumn (520626-5)/16. Mr. Paganini (You'll Have To Swing It) (520626-2/3)

DISC 2   1. Sentimental Journey (470124-2)/2. Guilty (470124-1)/3. I'm Just a Lucky So-and-So (460221-1)/4. My Heart Belongs to Daddy (540330-3)/5. Imagination (540330-2)/6. Robbins' Nest (471223-4)/7. Pete Kelly's Blues (550503-2)/8. Hard-Hearted Hannah (550503-1)/9. That Old Black Magic (550427-1)/10. Lover, Come Back to Me (550427-3)/11. Petootie Pie (451015-1)/12. Baby, It's Cold Outside (490428-5)/13. Between the Devil and the Deep Blue Sea (550427-4)/14. Ol' Devil Moon (550427-2)/15. The Greatest There Is (520811-2)/16. Ella's Contribution to the Blues (520811-6)

Disc 1, Side A, Tracks 1-8 (23:26)/Side B, Tracks 9-16 (25:19)/Disc 2, Side A, Tracks 17-24 (22:50)/Side B, Tracks 25-32 (19:21)/Total playing time, 1:26:56

There are twelve Decca singles that have never appeared in long-play albums or on compact discs issued in the U.S., but which do appear in a set of six European LPs, entitled **ELLA**. The albums, unique with their contents of 16 tracks each, were issued in Germany and The Netherlands, and had some distribution in the United Kingdom, although it appears that any distribution was very limited. Now virtually impossible to find, the collector will still be interested. Contents of the first three albums are not known to the editor, although all tracks included therein (1935-1941) have been issued on CD. The contents of Volumes 4, 5, and 6, are given herewith:

**Ella, Volume 1, 1935–1939, with Chick Webb
 & His Orchestra**
　　MCA Coral 6.21818 (PCO 7332) (Germany) (LP)
Ella, Volume 2, 1936–1939, and Her Savoy Eight
　　MCA Coral 6.21819 (PCO 7333) (Germany) (LP)
Ella, Volume 3, 1939–1941, and Her Famous Orchestra
　　MCA Coral 6.21820 (PCO 7334) (Germany) (LP)

**LPD-123 Ella, Volume 4, 1937–1952, and the Vocal
 Groups** MCA Coral 6.22065 (PCO7665) (Germany) (LP)

Side 2, Track 2. **I've Got a Feelin' I'm Fallin'** (2:33)
 (471223-1)
Side 2, Track 5. **I Don't Want the World** (2:11)
 (500509-2)
Side 2, Track 7. **The Bean Bag Song** (3:06) (510112-2)

　　SIDE 1　1. Big Boy Blue (370114-3)/2. Dedicated to You (370203-1)/3. Mama, Come Home (420410-2)/4. (I Put) A Four-Leaf Clover in Your Pocket (420731-2)/5. Into Each Life Some Rain Must Fall (440830-1)/6. I'm Beginning To See the Light (450226-1)/7. (It's Only) A Paper Moon (450327-1)/8. It's a Pity To Say Goodnight (460819-2)

　　SIDE 2　1. And Her Tears Flowed Like Wine (441106-1)/2. I've Got a Feeling I'm Falling (471223-1)/3. You Turned the Tables on Me (471223-2)/4. M-I-S-S-I-S-S-I-P-P-I(500509-1)/5. I Don't Want the World (500509-2)/6. I Still Feel the Same About You (501220-2)/7. The Bean Bag Song (510112-2)/8. Air Mail Special (520104-1) Total playing time, 45:32.

LPD-124 Ella, Volume 5, 1941–1955 MCA Coral
 6.22178 (PCO 7666) (Germany) (LP)

Side 2, Track 2. **I Cried and Cried and Cried** (2:53)
 (471223-3)

　　SIDE 1 1. Jim (411006-1)/2. This Love of Mine (411006-2)/3. Somebody Nobody Loves (411028-1)/4. Who Are You? (411105-1)/5. Make Love to Me (411105-3)/6. He's My Guy (420731-3)/7. My Baby Likes to Re-Bop (471220-1)/8. No Sense (471220-2)

　　SIDE 2 1. How High the Moon (471220-4)/2. I Cried and Cried and Cried (471223-3)/3. Robbins' Nest (471223-4)/4. Petootie Pie (451015-1)/5. Don't Cry, Cry-Baby (490428-6)/6. Ain't Nobody's Business But My Own (500815-1)/7. Preview (520626-6)/8. Hard Hearted Hannah (550503-1). Total playing time, 48:01

LPD-125 Ella, Volume 6, 1949-1954 MCA Coral
 6.22179 (PCO 7667) (Germany) (LP)

Side 1, Track 2. **Talk Fast, My Heart, Talk Fast** (490920-2)
Side 1, Track 3. **I'm Waitin' for the Junk Man** (490920-3)
Side 1, Track 6. **The Chesapeake and Ohio** (510327-1)
Side 1, Track 7. **Little Man in a Flying Saucer** (510327-2)
Side 2, Track 2. **Nowhere Guy** (520225-2
Side 2, Track 4. **Ding-Dong Boogie** (520626-1)
Side 2, Track 6. **I Wondered What Kind of Guy You'd
 Be** (530213-3)
Side 2, Track 7. **If You Don't, I Know Who Will**
 (531223-2)

　　SIDE 1 1. In the Evening (When the Sun Goes Down) (490920-1)/2. Talk Fast, My Heart, Talk Fast (490920-2)/3. I'm Waiting for the Junk Man (490920-3)/4, Solid as a Rock (500306-1)/5. Sugarfoot Rag (500306-3)/6. The Chesapeake and Ohio (510327-1)/7. Little Man in a Flying Saucer (510327-2)/8. The Hot Canary (510327-4)

　　SIDE 2 1. I Don't Want To Take a Chance (510718-2)/2. Nowhere Guy (520225-2)/3. Goody Goody (520225-4)/4. Ding-Dong Boogie (520626-1)/5. Early Autumn (520626-5)/6. I Wondered What Kind of a Guy You'd Be (530213-3)/7. If You Don't, I Know Who Will (531223-2)/8. Lullaby of Birdland (540604-1)

LPD-126 Louis Armstrong/"Because of You" Ambassador CLA 1918 (CD)

15. **Necessary Evil** (2:30) (511123-1)
16. **Oops!** (3:10) (511123-2)

　　All performances by Louis Armstrong): 1. La Vie en Rose/2. C'est Si Bon/3. Life Is So Peculiar (duet with Louis Jordan)/4. You Rascal You (duet with Louis Jordan)/5. Dream a Little Dream of Me (duet with Ella Fitzgerald)/6. Can Anyone Explain? (duet with Ella Fitzgerald)/7. You're Just in Love (duet with Velma Middleton)/8. If (duet with Velma Middleton)/9. Big Butter and Egg Man (duet with Velma Middleton)/10. Gone Fishin' (duet with Bing Crosby)/11. A Kiss To Build a Dream On/12. I Get Ideas/13. Because of You/14. Cold, Cold Heart/15. Necessary Evil (duet with Ella Fitzgerald)/16. Oops! (duet with Ella Fitzgerald)/17. Would You Like To Take a Walk? (duet with Ella Fitzgerald)/18. Who Walks In When I Walk Out? (duet with Ella Fitzgerald)/19. I Laughed at Love/20. Takes Two To Tango/21. Your Cheating Heart/22. Congratulations to Someone/23. Sittin' in the Sun (2:59)/24. Dummy Song.

Released 1994. Ambassador Records is a non-profit label dedicated to Louis Armstrong and his music. Total playing time, 71:01.

LPD-127 Gene Krupa and Buddy Rich/The Drum Battle at JATP Verve 314 559 810 (CD)

Track 7. **Perdido** (5:01) (520913-1)

1. Introduction by Norman Granz/2. Idaho/3. Sophisticated Lady/4. Flying Home/5. Drum Boogie/6. The Drum Battle/7. Perdido (vocal by Ella Fitzgerald) JATP concerts produced by **Norman Granz**.
Released May 1999. Total playing time, 35:45
(Originally LP issue: **Jazz At The Philharmonic, Vol. 15** (Clef MG, Vol. 15), a 3-LP set, with all released tracks of the JATP concert on this date. This portion of the concert reissued as **The Drum Battle at JATP** (Verve MGV8369).

LPD-128 Sinatra/The Soundtrack Sessions Bravura BRCD 7106 (CD)

15. **Necessity** (duet with Ella Fitzgerald) (3:00) (541120-1)

All performances by Frank Sinatra **MEET DANNY WILSON** (1951): 1. When You're Smiling/2. How Deep Is the Ocean/3. You're a Sweetheart/4. She's Funny That Way/5. A Good Man Is Hard To Find (duet with Shelley Winters)/6. Lonesome Man Blues/7. That Old Black Magic/ 8. I've Got a Crush on You (with The Ebonaires)/9. I've Got a Crush on You (alternative take not used in film) (with The Ebonaires)/10. All of Me
FINIAN'S RAINBOW (1954) (Never released): 11. If This Isn't Love (with Ella Logan and Chorus)/12. Ad-Lib Blues (with Louis Armstrong)/13. Necessity/ 14. Ol' Devil Moon (with Ella Logan)/15. Necessity (with Ella Fitzgerald)/16. That Great Come and Get It Day
CAROUSEL (1955): 17. If I Loved You (with Shirley Jones)
THE MAN WITH THE GOLDEN ARM (1955): 18. The Man with the Golden Arm (not used in film)
THE JOKER IS WILD (1956): 19. At Sundown/20. All the Way/21. If I Could Be with You/22. I Cried for You
ADVISE AND CONSENT (1961): 23. The Loser's Song
Total playing time, 60:29

LPD-129 Here Come the Girls Verve MG V-2036 (LP)

Track 5 **It's Only a Man** (3:22) (560125-5)
Track 14 **The Silent Treatment** (2:48) (560821-6)

The contents of the album, title/performer: 1. A Beautiful Friendship (Ella Fitzgerald) (560327-2)/2. The Getaway and the Chase (Anita O'Day)/3. Mind If I Make Love to You (Jane Powell)/4. We Got To Live, Got To Grow Up (Toni Harper)/5. It's Only a Man (Ella Fitzgerald) (560125-5)/6. Honeysuckle Rose (Anita O'Day)/7. Tired (Pearl Bailey)/8. True Love (Jane Powell)/9.Too Young for the Blues (Ella Fitzgerald) (560125-4)/10. Love Is a Wonderful Thing (Toni Harper)/11. Go Back Where You Stayed Last Night (Pearl Bailey)/12. You're the Top (Anita O'Day)/13. I Telephoned, I Telegraphed (Toni Harper)/14. The Silent Treatment (Ella Fitzgerald) (560821-6) Side 1, Tracks 1-7 (20:22)/Side 2, Tracks 8-14 (19:14)/Total playing time, 39:36. Produced under the personal supervision of **Norman Granz**

LPD-130 One O'Clock Jump/Ella Fitzgerald-Count Basie-Joe Williams Verve 314 559 806 (CD)

Track 1. **Too Close for Comfort** (560625-2)

1. Too Close for Comfort (vocal by Ella Fitzgerald)/2. Smack Dab in the Middle/3. Amazing Love/4. Only Forever/5. Don't Worry 'Bout Me/6. Stop, Pretty Baby, Stop/7. One O'Clock Jump/8. Jamboree/9. I Don't Like You No More/10. From Coast to Coast/11. Too Close for Comfort (instr)/12. One O'clock Jump (EP version)/13. One O'-Clock Jump (alternative take).
Released June 1999.
(Tracks 1-10 originally issued on LP (same title), Verve MGV 8288).

LPD-131 The Essential American Singers Verve 314 517 176 (CT/CD)

Track 1. **Your Red Wagon** (2:54) (580701-1)

The contents of the album (title/performer): 1. Your Red Wagon (Ella Fitzgerald)/2. Sweet Lorraine (Louis Armstrong)/3. All My Life (Ernestine Anderson)/4. I Worry 'Bout You (Arthur Prysock)/5. Memories of You (Shirley Horn)/6. Sweet Slumber (Jimmy Witherspoon)/7. A Fine Romance (Ella Fitzgerald and Louis Armstrong)/8. I Apologize (Billy Eckstine)/9. Make Yourself Comfortable (Sarah Vaughan)/10. This Love of Mine (Al Hibbler)/11. What a Diff'rence a Day Makes (Dinah Washington)/12. I Ain't Got Nothing' but the Blues (Joe Williams)/13. Please Don't Talk About Me When I'm Gone (Billie Holiday)/14. Passing Strangers (Billy Eckstine and Sarah Vaughan)
Released 1992. Total playing time, 53:06

LPD-132 Have Yourself a Jazzy Little Christmas Verve 840 501 (CT/CD)

Track 4. **The Secret of Christmas** (2:45) (590902-5)*
Track 10. **White Christmas** (3:44) (600716-4)**

The contents of the album, title/performer(s): 1. A Child Is Born (Oscar Peterson)/2. Medley: Carol of the Bells/Melodies for the Day/O Sanctissimo (The Swingle Singers)/3. Jingle Bells (Jimmy Smith)/4. The Secret of

Christmas* (Ella Fitzgerald)/5. We Free Kings (Roland Kirk)/6. Christmas Eve (Billy Eckstine)/7. I've Got My Love To Keep Me Warm (Billie Holiday)/8. Ole Santa (Dinah Washington)/9. Santa Claus Is Coming to Town (Bill Evans)/10. White Christmas** (Ella Fitzgerald)/11. O Little Town of Bethlehem (Rosetta Thorpe)/12. The Christmas Song (Mel Tormé)/13. God Rest Ye Merry, Gentlemen (Jimmy Smith)/14. Silent Night (Dinah Washington)/15. Have Yourself a Merry Little Christmas (Ella Fitzgerald)

*Previously released only on 45rpm single (Verve 10186).
**Previously unreleased.*

Released 1989. Total playing time, 48:50

LPD-133 Compact Jazz/Walkman Jazz/Ella Fitzgerald (CD/CT Verve 831 367)

Track 6. **A-Tisket, A-Tasket** (1:53) (610512-8)

The contents of the album (all titles performed by Ella Fitzgerald): 1. Mack The Knife (600213-10)/2. Desafinado (621001-1)/3. Mr. Paganini (You'll Have To Swing It) (610512-1)/4. I Can't Get Started (611113-4)/5. A Night in Tunisia (610624-4)/6. A-Tisket, A-Tasket (610512-8)/7. Shiny Stockings (630716-1)/8. Smooth Sailing (650326-11)/9. Goody Goody (570724-8)/10. Rough Ridin' (620131-5)/11. The Boy from Ipanema (650326-13)/Sweet Georgia Brown (660720-1)/13. Duke's Place (651000-10)/14. Misty (600414-6)/15. Somebody Loves Me (590107-1)/16. How High the Moon (600213-11)

Released 1987. Total playing time, 58:48

LPD-134 Verve Elite Edition Collector's Disc Verve 314 547 265 (CD)

Track 11, **Duke's Place** (651018-2)

The contents of the album (title/performers): 1. Let's Fall in Love (Louis Armstrong, trumpet, vocal; Oscar Peterson, piano; Herb Ellis, guitar; Ray Brown, bass; Louis Bellson, drums)/2. Dancing in the Dark (Bill Evans, piano; Gary Peacock, bass; Paul Motian, drums)/3. La Rosita (Coleman Hawkins, tenor saxophone; Ben Webster, tenor saxophone; Oscar Peterson, piano; Herb Ellis, guitar; Ray Brown, bass; Alvin Stoller, drums)/4. Shine On, Harvest Moon (Coleman Hawkins, tenor saxophone; Ben Webster, tenor saxophone; Oscar Peterson, piano; Herb Ellis, guitar; Ray Brown, bass; Alvin Stoller, drums)/5. Memories for the Count (Harry "Sweets" Edison, trumpet; Buck Clayton, trumpet; Jimmy Forrest, tenor saxophone; Jimmy Jones, piano; Freddie Green, guitar; Joe Benjamin, bass; Charlie Persip, drums)/6. The Moon Is Low (Roy Eldridge, trumpet; Benny Carter, alto saxophone; Bruce McDonald, piano; John Simmons, bass; Alvin Stoller, drums)/7. Close Your Eyes (Oscar Peterson, piano; Ray Brown, bass; Ed Thigpen, drums)/8. Playboy Peterson (Oscar Peterson,

piano; Ray Brown, bass; Ed thigpen, drums)/9. The Prayer, a Jazz Hymn (aka Hymn to Freedom) (Oscar Peterson, piano; Ray Brown, bass; Ed Thigpen, drums)/10. Squatty Roo (Johnny Hodges, alto saxophone; Dizzy Gillespie, trumpet; Junior Mance, piano; Les Spann, guitar; Sam Jones, bass; Lex Humphries, drums)/11. Duke's Place (Ella Fitzgerald, vocal, with Duke Ellington and His Orchestra—Trumpets: Cat Anderson-Mercer Ellington-Herbie Jones-Cootie Williams/Trombones: Lawrence Brown-Buster Cooper/Bass Trombone: Chuck Connors/Clarinets: Harry Carney-Jimmy Hamilton-Russell Procope/Bass Clarinet: Harry Carney/Tenor Saxophones: Jimmy Hamilton-Paul Gonsalves/Alto Saxophones: Johnny Hodges-Russell Procope/Baritone Saxophone: Harry Carney/Piano: Duke Ellington/Bass: John Lamb/Drums: Louis Bellson/Arrangement: Duke Ellington)/12. With the Wind and the Rain in Your Hair (Tal Farlow, guitar; Barry Galbraith, guitar; Oscar Pettiford, bass; Joe Morello, drums)/13 Broadway (Jimmy Smith, organ; Kenny Burrell, guitar; Ron Carter or Ben Tucker, bass; Grady Tate, drums)/14. Let's Fall in Love (Louis Armstrong, trumpet, vocal; Oscar Peterson, piano; Herb Ellis, guitar; Ray Brown, bass; Louie Bellson, drums).

Released August 1999.

LPD-135 Route 66/Capitol Sings Coast to Coast Capitol D103060 (CD)

Track 20. **Hawaiian War Chant** (2:17) (680603-2)

The contents of the album (title/performer): 1. Moonlight in Vermont (Margaret Whiting)/2. Old Cape Cod (Susan Barrett)/3. Broadway (Dakota Staton)/4. Autumn in New York (Jo Stafford)/5. When It's Sleepy Time Down South (Dean Martin)/6. Carolina in the Morning (Judy Garland)/7. Georgia on My Mind (The Four Knights)/8. Basin Street Blues (Peggy Lee)/9. Mississippi Mud (Dinah Shore)/10. Chattanooga Choo Choo (Ray Anthony and His Orchestra)/11. (Back Home Again in) Indiana (Kay Starr)/12. Route 66 (King Cole Trio)/13. Chicago (Tony Bennett)/14. You Came a Long Way from St. Louis (June Christy)/15. When It's Springtime in the Rockies (Gordon Macrae)/16. I Lost My Sugar in Salt Lake City (Peggy Lee)/17. I Lost My Heart in San Francisco (Nancy Wilson)/18. San Fernando Valley (Johnny Mercer)/19. Avalon (The Pied Pipers)/20. Hawaiian War Chant (Ella Fitzgerald)

Released 1994. Total playing time, 52:22

LPD-136 The Big Bands' Greatest Vocalists/Ella Fitzgerald with Skitch Henderson and His Orchestra Joyce 6045 (LP)

Track 3, **It's Up to Me and You** (2:44) (680510-1)

The contents of the album, all songs by Ella Fitzgerald; interviewer is Skitch Henderson. 1. Pick Yourself Up

(611115-1)/Misty Blue (671221-4)/It's Up to Me and You (680510-1) 2. The Sweetest Sounds (640407-4)/Volare (640304-7)/I Taught Him Everything He Knows (671220-1) 3. You Couldn't Be Cuter (630107-1)/All the Things You Are (630107-5)/Turn the World Around the Other Way (671220-3) 4.Duke's Place (651017-6)/Evil on Your Mind (671222-1)/Born To Lose (671221-2

Side One, Track 1 (12:56), Track 2 (11:42)/Side Two, Track 3 (11:26)/Track 4 (11:54). Total playing time, 47:58

This album is mis-titled; it contains no tracks with Ella accompanied by the Skitch Henderson Orchestra. Instead, it is a group of four commercial radio spots broadcast in May 1968 for the National Guard, entitled **Guard Session**: Mr. Henderson serves as host, interviews Ella briefly before each song, and then plays a previously released Ella recording. Fortunately, two tracks previously issued only on 45rpm singles were used. "It's Up to Me and You" was previously released on Capitol 2212, backed with "Brighten the Corner," from her Capitol album of the same title. An edited "Duke's Place" from the album **Ella at Duke's Place** was previously released on Verve 10408, backed with "The Shadow of Your Smile," both recorded with Duke Ellington and His Orchestra.

LPD-137 The Montreux Collection/Highlights of the Montreux Jazz Festival 1975 Pablo 2625-707 (2-LP set)

Disc 1, Side B, Track 3. **The Man I Love** (6:07) (750717-1)

The contents of the album (title/performers): Disc 1, Side A, 1. Collection Blues (Count Basie, piano; Johnny Griffin, tenor saxophone; Milt Jackson, vibraphone; Roy Eldridge, trumpet; Niels Pederson, bass; Louis Bellson, drums) (12:04)/2. Sunday (Benny Carter, alto saxophone; Roy Eldridge, trumpet; Clark Terry, trumpet; Zoot Sims, tenor saxophone; Joe Pass, guitar; Tommy Flanagan, piano; Keter Betts, bass; Bobby Durham, drums) (9:25)/Disc 1, Side B, 1. Alison (Joe Pass, guitar) (4:23)/2. Slow Death (Milt Jackson's Big 4: Milt Jackson, vibraphone; Oscar Peterson, piano; Niels Pederson, bass; Mickey Roker, drums) (6:41)/3. The Man I Love (Ella Fitzgerald, vocal; Tommy Flanagan, piano; Keter Betts, bass; Bobby Durham, drums) (6:07)/Disc 2, Side C, l. Woodyn' You (Oscar Peterson's Big 6: Oscar Peterson, piano; Milt Jackson, vibraphone; Joe Pass, guitar; Toots Thielemans, harmonica; Niels Pedersen, bass; Louis Bellson, drums) (9:30)/2. Lullaby of the Leaves (The Trumpet Kings: Dizzy Gillespie, trumpet; Roy Eldridge, trumpet; Clark Terry, trumpet; Oscar Peterson, piano; Niels Pedersen, bass; Louis Bellson, Drums) (11:19)/Disc 2, Side D, 1. Cubana Chant (Oscar Peterson, piano) (5:10)/2. I'll Remember April (Dizzy: Dizzy Gillespie, trumpet; Johnny Griffin, tenor saxophone; Eddie

"Lockjaw" Davis, tenor Saxophone; Milt Jackson, vibraphone; Tommmy Flanagan, piano; Niels Pederson, bass; Mickey Roker, drums) (15:49). Total playing time, 82:30.

In 1999, this album was released on a single compact disc (Pablo 5306). The contents are the same with the exception that the order of play has been changed, and, for reasons of space, one track, "Lullaby of the Leaves," (on LP, Disc 2, Side C, Track 2) has been omitted. The contents thus are: 1. Cubano Chant 2. Sunday 3. Collection Blues 4. Slow Death 5. Alison 6. Woody 'n You 7. I'll Remember April 8. The Man I Love

Total playing time, 71:11

LPD-138 Back on the Block (LP/CT/CD QWest/Warner Bros. 26020)

Track 6 **Wee B. Doinit** (3:34) (890000-1)
Track 8 **Jazz Corner of the World** (2:53) (890000-2)
Track 9 **Birdland** (5:34) (890000-3)

The contents of the album (performers on each track too numerous to list here): 1. Prologue (2 Q's Rap)/2. Back on the Block/3. I Don't Go for That/4. I'll Be Good for You/5. The Verb To Be/6. Wee B. Dooinit/7. The Places You Find Love/8. Jazz Corner of the World/9. Birdland/10. Setembro (Brazilian Wedding Song)/11. One Man Woman/12. Tomorrow (A Better You, Better Me)/13. Prelude to The Garden/14. The Secret Garden (Sweet Seduction Suite)

Produced by **Quincy Jones**. Total playing time, 57:54

Ella and Al Jarreau team up for "A Funky Feelin'," and Ella, Sarah Vaughan, and Bobby McFerrin perform some scat solos in the "Repeat Chorus" on "Wee B. Doinit" (Track 6). Ella is introduced and scats on "Jazz Corner of the World" (Track 8). Ella and Sarah are also featured on "Birdland" (Track 9). Ella's performances specifically for this recording are, in the editor's view, suspect. Since her voice on any track is virtually indistinguishable, there is the possibility that her voice tracks (or portions thereof) from concert and/or studio performances were used. Attempts by the editor to confirm specific recording sessions for this album have elicited no response from QWest, Warner Bros. or Quincy Jones.

LPD-139 The Setting Sun (a.k.a. Sunset), Japanese film soundtrack, 1992 RCA Japan VICP 8084 (CD)

Track 1. **The Setting Sun** (5:45) (920100-1)

The contents of the album are unknown to the editor, although it is known that Ella Fitzgerald sings the title song under the opening credits, following which is the very beautiful score composed by Maurice Jarre with an orchestra conducted by Billy May. The recordings were made at Warner Bros. studio in January, 1992.

Following are out-of-print, difficult-to-find albums of European origin featuring various Ella Fitzgerald concerts, and are included here for the serious devotee.

LPD-140 Ella Fitzgerald/Só Danço Samba (CD, Jazz Birdies of Paradise)

Ella Fitzgerald with The Duke Ellington Orchestra, Brussells, 22 February 1966/Ella Fitzgerald with The Jimmy Jones Trio 1. Satin Doll (660222-1)/2. Wives and Lovers (660222-2)/3. Something to Live For (660222-3)/4. Let's Do It (660222-4)/5. Sweet Georgia Brown (660222-5)/6. Midnight Sun (660222-6)/7. How High the Moon (660222-7)/8. I'm Just a Lucky So-and-So (660222-8)/9. Só Danço Samba (660222-9)/10. Mack The Knife (660222-10)

Ella Fitzgerald at the Newport Jazz Festival, Newport, 1957* 11. Too Close for Comfort (570704-6)/12. Just One of Those Things (570704-7)13. Lullaby of Birdland (570704-8)/14. Tenderly (570704-9)/15. I Can't Give You Anything but Love (570704-10)/16. Air Mail Special (570704-11)

*Having listened to the Newport Jazz Festival tracks very carefully, Ben Young, producer at Verve Records, is convinced that not all of these tracks came from this concert. It is quite possible that he is correct; for it is common practice among some compact disc producers to "manufacture" a concert, given the program, from various sources, and then pass it on to the public as the real thing. That may be the case here; however, this disc is included for the enjoyment of those who will accept it for whatever it is (or is not).

LPD-141 Duke Ellington/Live in Europe/Guest Star: Ella Fitzgerald Musica Jazz MJCD 1099 (CD)

Duke Ellington and His Orchestra 1. Theme: Take the "A" Train/2. Johnny Come Lately/3. Swamp God/4. Up Jump/5. The Shepherd/6. Take the "A" Train/7. Chromatic Love Affair/8. Rue Bleu/9. Wild Onions/10. Mara Gold/11. Beautiful Woman Walks Well

Ella Fitzgerald and The Jimmy Jones Trio with Duke Ellington and His Orchestra 12. On the Sunny Side of the Street (670128-1)/13. You've Changed (670128-2)/14. Mack The Knife (670128-3)/15. Cotton Tail (670128-4) Released May 1994. Total playing time, 66:35

LPD-142 Duke and Ella in Concert, Milan, 30 January 1966 Jazz-Blues-Soul JBS 93B2b (CD)

Duke Ellington and His Orchestra 1. Theme: Take the "A" Train/2. Medley: Black and Tan Fantasy/Creole Love Call/The Mooche/3. Soul Call/4. Chelsea Bridge/5. El Viti/6. The Opener/7. Sophisticated Lady/8. Take the "A" Train/9. Passion Flower/10. Things Ain't What They Used To Be/11. Wings and Things/12. Jam with Sam

Ella Fitzgerald with The Jimmy Jones Trio 13. Introduction by Norman Granz/ 14. How High the Moon (660130-1)/15. Lover Man (660130-2)/16. Mack the Knife (660130-3)

Ella Fitzgerald with The Jimmy Jones Trio and the Duke Ellington Orchestra 17. Cotton Tail (660130-4) Released 1995. Total playing time, 66:18

LPD-143 Ella Fitzgerald with The Tommy Flanagan Trio Laserlight 17 109 (CD)

Ella Fitzgerald with The Tommy Flanagan Trio 1. I Won't Dance (690729-1)/2. That Old Black Magic (690729-2)/3. Medley: It Happened in Monterey/No Regrets/It's a Wonderful World (690729-3)/4. Cabaret (690729-4)/5. Love You Madly (690729-5)/6. A Man and a Woman (Un Homme et une Femme) (690729-6)/7. Alright, Okay, You Win (690729-7)/8. People (690729-8)/9. I Concentrate on You (690729-9)/10. Mr. Paganini (You'll Have To Swing It) (690729-10)

Ella Fitzgerald with the Lou Levy Trio 11. I'm Beginning To See the Light (580701-3)/12. My Heart Belongs to Daddy (580701-4)/13. Just One of Those Things (580701-5)/14. I Can't Give You Anything But Love (580701-6) Released 1997. Total playing time, 48:29 (not 54:37, as stated on CD) The first ten tracks of this disc were released in Europe in 1996 by LRC Ltd. (CDC-9076), with the title **Jazz Ladies/Ella Fitzgerald**.

Tracks 11-14 were recorded in performance at the Cannes Jazz Festival on 1 July 1958. (See Part I. **The Recording Sessions,** for other releases of this concert.)

LPD-144 Ella Fitzgerald/The Lady Is a Tramp Jazz Door 1268 (CD)

Ella Fitzgerald with The Lou Levy Quartet, 21 February 1961 1. Too Close for Comfort (610221-1)/2. A Foggy Day (in London Town) (610221-2)/3. Cole Porter Medley: Get Out of Town/Easy To Love (610221-3)/4. You're Driving Me Crazy (610221-4)/5. Cheek to Cheek (610221-5)/6. Caravan (610221-6)/7. Oh! Lady, Be Good! (610221-7)/8. 'Round Midnight (610221-8)/9. The Lady Is a Tramp (610221-9)/10. Mr. Paganini (You'll Have To Swing It) (610221-10)

Ella Fitzerald with The Tommy Flanagan Trio, 18 May 1971 11. Lullaby of Birdland (710518-1)/12. Duke Ellington Medley: Mood Indigo/It Don't Mean a Thing (710519-2)/13. Days of Wine and Roses (710518-3)/14. Something (710518-4)/15. Summertime (710518-5)/16. Mack The Knife (710518-6)/17. Hello, Dolly! (710518-7)/18. Put a Little Love in Your Heart (710518-8)/19. How High the Moon (710518-9)

Released 1994. Playing times: 1961 concert, 39:53/1971 concert, 34:47.

Total playing time, 74:40

LPD-145 Count Basie Orchestra/Live from Tilburg Holland, 1971/Featuring Ella Fitzgerald & Live from La Cabaret Casino, Paradise Island, Nassau, Bahamas, 1969 Jazz Band EBCD 2121-2 (CD)

Live from Tilburg, Holland, 7 May 1971 1. St. Louis Blues (710507-1)/2. Willow, Weep for Me (710507-2)/3. Close to You (710507-3)/4. Mas Que Nada (710507-4)/5. Things Ain't What They Used To Be (710507-5)/6. They Can't Take That Away from Me (710507-6)/7. Li'l Darling (710507-7)/8. Manteca (710507-8)/9. C Jam Blues (710507-9)

Live from La Cabaret Casino, Paradise Island, Nassau, Bahamas, 12 February 1969 (No Ella Fitzgerald vocals) 10. Introduction/11. Splanky/12. Hittin' Twelve/13. One Mint Julep/14. Bye, Bye, Blackbird/15. Good Time Blues/16. April in Paris/17. Basie/18. Li'l Darlin'/19. Cute/20. One O'Clock Jump

Released December 1994. Playing times: Tilburg session, 33:47/Nassau session, 37:11. Total playing time, 70:57

LPD-146 Ella Fitzgerald in Edinburgh (CT only)

1. From This Moment On (810726-1)/2. Satin Doll (810726-2)/3. Ain't Misbehavin' (810726-3)/4. Manhattan (810726-4)/5. It's All Right with Me (810726-5)/6. Oh! Lady, Be Good! (810726-6)/7. Let's Do It (810726-7)/8. Blue Moon (810726-8)/9. People (810726-9)/10. St. Louis Blues (810726-10)/11. Hard Hearted Hannah (810726-11)/12. Meditation (Meditaao) (810726-12)

Not officially released, but taped by many fans from BBC and National Public Radio broadcasts; thus, it is included in this volume. The author has corresponded with BBC Scotland, and has been informed that sale to the public is not permitted.

This concert, produced by **Norman Granz**, took place at Edinburgh Playhouse Theatre on Sunday, 26 July 1981. Miss Fitzgerald was accompanied by a 60-piece BBC Concert Orchestra, and by her own trio, pianist Jimmy Rowles, bassist Keter Betts, and drummer Bobby Durham.

VIII. Radio and Television Collection: Contents

The albums listed in this collection are compilations from radio and television broadcasts. There are two kinds of "transcriptions" with which we are concerned: First, a "radio (or television) transcription" is one which is recorded from a "live" radio or television broadcast. This is common practice: almost all broadcasts are recorded, and for many reasons, not the least of which is that it provides a record for posterity. Second, a "commercial transcription," as it is generally known, was usually recorded in a studio in the same manner as a commercially released record. These recordings, however, were not for public sale, but were leased by radio stations for broadcasting. Many of the songs recorded at these sessions — in fact, most of them — were also recorded for commercial sale, but these sessions were intended to introduce new songs and songwriters to the public using radio advertisers as the catalyst.

At one time, the demand was so great for these "commercial transcriptions" that bands, under contract to the record companies, were known to circumvent the provisions of their contracts with record companies by recording under assumed names and pocketing a nice recording fee. Ever hear of Chuck Warner and His Orchestra, featuring Evelyn Fields? Yes, they were Chick and Ella. Naturally, when a commercially transcribed song gained popularity, it was recorded, and everyone came out ahead.

Many of these transcriptions, of both kinds, have been issued on both LP and CD. The following albums are the important ones. There are many of these collections now in release, particularly with the advent of the CD, purporting to be recordings of "live" radio or television broadcasts, but are often compilations from several broadcasts. We have not listed those. The discs listed here are verifiably from the broadcasts identified or collections of "commercial transcriptions."

LPD-147 Bronzeville Stomp/ Chick Webb in the 1930's

1. Liza (Gershwin-Gershwin-Kahn) (instr) 2:45 380503-7
2. Big John Special (Henderson) (instr) 3:34 360219-1
3. You Hit the Spot (Gordon-Revel) (vEF) 2:24 360219-2
4. Stompin' at the Savoy (Razaf-Goodman-Sampson-Webb (instr) 2:58 360219-3

5. Don't Be That Way (Parish-Sampson) (instr) 2:24 360219-4
6. Shine (Mack-Brown-Dabney) (vEF) 3:05 360219-5
7. Go Harlem (Razaf-Johnson) (instr) 2:10 360219-6
8. The Darktown Strutter's Ball (Brooks) (vEF) 1:37 360219-7
9. Keepin' Out of Mischief Now (Razaf-Waller) (instr) 2:14 360219-8
10. Nit Wit Serenade (Hudson-Webb) (instr) 2:45 360219-9

11. King Porter Stomp (Morton) (instr) 3:14   360219-10
12. If Dreams Come True (Sampson-Goodman-Mills)
    (instr) 2:34   360219-11
13. Rhythm and Romance (Johnson-Whiting-Schwartz)
    (vEF) 2:20   360219-12
14. Bronzeville Stomp (instr) 371210-1
15. She's Tall, She's Tan, She's Terrific (Davis-Coots
    [vEF]) 371210-2
16. Honeysuckle Rose (Razaf-Waller) (vEF) 371210-3

LP: Jazz Archives JA 33 (released 1976). Side One, Tracks 1-8/Side Two, Tracks 9-16. Track 1 is a commercial recording. Tracks 2—13 are World Broadcasting Systems commercial transcriptions. Tracks 14—16 are WNEW "live" radio transcriptions broadcast from the Savoy. Ballroom, 10 December 1937.

LPD-148 THE SATURDAY NIGHT SWING CLUB IS ON THE AIR

Bunny Berigan

1. Introduction/I Can't Get Started (Gershwin-Duke)
   0:45   380702
2. Alexander's Ragtime Band (Berlin) 2:20   380702
3. Beale Street Blues (Handy) 2:53   380702
4. Hold Tight (Kent-Robinson-Ware-Brandon-
   Spottswood) 1:56   390121
5. Ol' Man Mose (Armstrong-Randolph) 2:23
   390128

Bobby Hackett and His Jazz Band

6. At the Jazz Band Ball (Edwards-LaRocca-Spargo-
   Shields) 3:08   380625

Tommy Dorsey and His Orchestra

7. Swing That Music (Dorsey) 3:25   380423

Jack Teagarden with The Paul Whiteman Swing Sing and The Modernaires

8. The Dixieland Band (Mercer-Hanighen) 2:25
   380625

Duke Ellington and His Orchestra

9. Swing Session Medley (Ellington) 5:08   370508

Fats Waller and J.P. Johnson

10. I Found a New Baby (Palmer-Williams) 2:18
    380702
11. Hold My Hand (Yellen-Caesar-Henderson) 1:12
    380702

Jimmie Lunceford and His Orchestra

12. Cheatin' on Me (Yellen-Pollack) 2:40   390128
13. 'Tain't What Cha Do (It's the Way That You Do It)
    (Oliver-Young) 3:22   390128
14. Well, All Right Then (Lunceford) 1:21   390611

Ella Fitzgerald with Chick Webb and His Orchestra

15. (I've Been) Saving Myself for You (Cahn-Chaplin)
    5:00   380813-1
16. I Let a Tear Fall in the River (David-Livingston-
    Webb) 3:18   390121-1

LP: Fanfare Records LP 17-117 (released 1978). Side 1, Tracks 1-9 (24:23), Side 2, Tracks 10-16 (20:11). Total playing time: 44:34. Liner notes by Robert Inman.

LPD-149 CHICK WEBB & HIS ORCHESTRA/ELLA FITZGERALD-THE INK SPOTS

1. Have a Good Night, Folks! (Webb) (vBand Members) 1:10   370208-1
2. Open 'Em Up, Chick! (Sampson) (instr) 3:02
   370208-2
3. Swing, Mr. Charlie, Swing! (vThe Ink Spots) 1:57
   370208-3
4. Vote for Mr. Rhythm (Robin-Rainger) (vEF) 2:37
   370208-4
5. Wanton Rhythm Man (instr) 2:11   370208-5
6. Big Boy Blue (Tinturin-Lawrence-Howell) (vEF)
   2:33   370208-6
7. A Blue Room (Hart-Rodgers) (instr) 2:18   390210-1
8. Deep in a Dream of You (DeLange-Van Heusen)
   (vEF) 4:08   390210-2
9. One O'clock Jump (Basie) (instr) 3:12   390210-3
10. That Was My Heart (Johnson-Webb) (vEF) 3:28
    390210-4
11. Who's To Blame? (vThe Ink Spots) 3:00
12. Into Each Life Some Rain Must Fall (Roberts-Fisher)
    (vThe Ink Spots) 1:50
13. On the Sunny Side of the Street (Fields-McHugh)
    (vThe Ink Spots) 1:50
14. You Are Happiness (vThe Ink Spots) 4:11
15. When You're Smiling (Fisher-Goodwin-Shay) (vThe
    Ink Spots) 2:34
16. If I Didn't Care (Lawrence) (vThe Ink Spots) 4:23
17. Medley: Into Each Life Some Rain Must Fall
    (Roberts-Fisher)
18. To Each His Own (Livingston-Evans)
19. It's No Secret
20. If I Didn't Care (Lawrence) (vThe Ink Spots) 1:58
21. September Song (Anderson-Weill) (vThe Ink Spots)
    2:44

LP: Twinkgost Rogo CWIS 37. Side One, Tracks 1–10 (26:36)/Side Two, Tracks 11–21 (22:30). Total playing time: 49:06. Tracks 1–6 are radio transcriptions broadcast from WJZ, Radio City Music. Hall, 8 February 1937. Tracks 7–10 are radio transcriptions broadcast from The Blue Room, Lincoln. Hotel, New York City, on 10 February 1939. Tracks

11–21 are The Ink Spots radio transcriptions from various radio broadcasts. No information is given on the jacket nor on the record, other than "Original broadcasts courtesy of Gorgo. Edited, Printed, Mastered, Railhead Georgia."

LPD-150 THE KING OF THE DRUMS/ CHICK WEBB AND HIS SAVOY BALLROOM ORCHESTRA

Chick Webb and His Rhythm Makers
(all instrumentals)

1. Crazy Rhythm (Caesar-Mayer-Kahn) 2:20   390109-5
2. Sugar Foot Stomp (Melrose-Oliver) 3:26   390109-6
3. Grand Terrace Rhythm (Cahn-Chaplin) 3:39   390109-7
4. By Heck (Gilbert-Henry) 3:10   390109-8
5. Blue Skies (Berlin) 2:06   390109-9
6. Dinah (Lewis-Young-Akst) 3:00   390109-10
7. Who Ya Hunchin'? (Fitzgerald-Webb) 3:29   390109-11
8. Liza (All the Clouds'll Roll Away) (Gershwin-Gershwin-Kahn) 2:27   390109-12
9. Tea for Two (Caesar-Youmans) 2:12   390109-1
10. How Am I to Know? (Parker-King) 2:25   390109-2
11. One O'Clock Jump (Basie) 3:41   390109-3
12. A Blue Room (Hart-Rodgers) 2:31   390109-4

Chick Webb and His Orchestra

13. Let's Get Together (Sampson) 0:39   390504-1
14. Poor Little Rich Girl (Coward) 3:31   390504-2
15. A New Moon and an Old Serenade (Silver-Coslow-Block) (vEF) 3:55   390504-3
16. Break 'Em Down (Sampson) 4:17   390504-4
17. If I Didn't Care (Lawrence) (vEF) 4:30   390504-5
18. The Stars and Stripes Forever (Souza) 3:07   390504-6
19. I Never Knew Heaven Could Speak (Gordon-Revel) (vEF) 3:43   390504-7
20. My Wild Irish Rose (Olcott) 2:44   390504-8
21. Chew, Chew, Chew (Your Bubblegum) (vEF) (Fitzgerald-Ram-Vance-Webb) 3:00   390504-9
22. Let's Get Together (Sampson) 0:19   390504-10

CD: Tax CD 3706-2 (released 1989). Tracks 1—12 are commercial transcriptions recorded at Radio City. Music Hall, New York, 9 January 1939. Tracks 13 — 22 are "live" radio transcriptions broadcast from Southland. Café, Boston, 4 May 1939. Total playing time: 65:01. Original source materal: **Ken Crawford**. Reissue produced by **Carl A. Hällström**, Stockholm, Sweden.

LPD-151 ELLA FITZGERALD/ON THE AIR/ THE COMPLETE 1940 BROADCASTS

Disc 1, Ella Fitzgerald and Her Famous Orchestra

1. A-Tisket, A-Tasket (Opening Theme) (Fitzgerald-Feldman) (vEF) 0:33   400122-1
2. Traffic Jam (McRae-Shaw) (instr) 2:41   400122-2
3. A Lover Is Blue (Young-Mundy-Carpenter) (vEF) 3:37   400122-3
4. Dodging the Dean (Clinton) (instr) 2:53   400122-4
5. 'Tain't What You Do (Oliver-Young) (vEF) 2:55   400122-5
6. I'm Confessin' (Dougherty-Reynolds-Young) (instr) 4:03   400122-6
7. Blue Lou (Sampson-Mills) (instr) 3:17   400122-7
8. What's the Matter with Me? (Shand-Lewis) (vEF) 3:59   400122-8
9. I Want the Waiter (Werner-Werner) (vEF) 3:11   400122-9
10. Let's Get Together (Closing Theme) (Sampson) (instr) 2:41   400122-10
11. A-Tisket, A-Tasket (Opening Theme) (Fitzgerald-Feldman) (vEF) 0:37   400125-1
12. Limehouse Blues (Braham-Furber) (instr) 3:35   400125-2
13. This Changing World (Suesse-Adamson) (vEF) 3:14   400125-3
14. Oh! Johnny! Oh! Johnny! Oh! (Olman-Rose) (vEF) 4:10   400125-4
15. Diga Diga Doo (McHugh-Fields) (instr) 2:36   400125-5
16. Thank Your Stars (Silver-Kent-Adamson) (vEF) 3:43   400125-6
17. Take It from the Top (McRae) (instr) 4:11   400125-7
18. Vagabond Dreams (Carmichael-Lawrence) (vEF) 2:24   400125-8
19. Breakin' Down (Sampson) (instr) 4:24   400125-9
20. Let's Get Together (Sampson) (Closing Theme) (instr) 0:47   400125-10

Disc 2, Ella Fitzgerald and Her Famous Orchestra

1. A-Tisket, A-Tasket (Opening Theme) (Fitzgerald-Feldman) (vEF) 0:36   400226-1
2. Royal Garden Blues (Williams-Williams) (instr) 3:19   400226-2
3. Sing Song Swing (Carmichael-Adams) (vEF) 2:57   400226-3
4. Sugar Blues (Williams-Fletcher) (vEF) 3:15   400226-4
5. Make Believe (Kern-Hammerstein) (instr) 3:14   400226-5
6. Sweet Sue (Young-Harris) (instr) 2:34   400226-6
7. It's a Blue World (Forrest-Wright) (vEF) 4:01   400226-7
8. Is There Somebody Else? (Mysels-Robertson-Cogane) (vEF) 2:46   400226-8
9. One Moment, Please (Vance) (instr) 5:38   400226-9
10. I've Got to Be a Rug Cutter (Ellington) (instr) 2:08   400226-10
11. A-Tisket, A-Tasket (Opening Theme) (Fitzgerald-Feldman) (vEF) 0:30   400304-1

12. I Got Rhythm (Gershwin-Gershwin) (instr) 3:43
    400304-2
13. One Cigarette for Two (Metzger-Dougherty-Ryan)
    (vEF) 4:25   400304-3
14. Chewing Gum (Fitzgerald-Ram-Webb) (vEF) 3:29
    400304-4
15. Lover, Come Back to Me (Romberg-Hammerstein)
    (instr) 3:11   400304-5
16. Who Ya Hunchin? (Fitzgerald-Webb) (instr) 3:52
    400304-6
17. The Starlit Hour (Parish-Rose) (vEF) 3:21   400304-7
18. Sing Song Swing (Carmichael-Adams) (vEF) 2:55
    400304-8
19. Goin' and Gettin' It (Vance) (instr) 3:53   400304-9
20. Let's Get Together (Closing Theme) (Sampson)
    (instr) 1:11   400304-10

CD: Masters of Jazz MJCD 137/138 (Released 1997).
Playing times: CD 1, 59:40/CD 2, 61:05 (2:00:45). Produced by **Christian Bonnet** and **Alain Tercinet**. Liner notes by **Alain Tercinet**.

LPD-152 ELLA FITZGERALD/
ROYAL ROOST SESSIONS

(All tracks with Ella Fitzgerald vocals)

1. Ool-Ya-Koo (Gillespie-Fuller) 2:58   481127-1
2. Love that Boy (DePaul-Raye) 2:30   481127-2
3. Mr. Paganini (You'll Have To Swing It) (Coslow)
   3:27   481127-3
4. It's Too Soon to Know (Chessler) 1:51   481127-4
5. I Never Knew (Fiorito-Kahn) 3:14   481127-5
6. How High the Moon (Lewis-Hamilton) 7:20
   481127-6
7. Heat Wave (Berlin) 2:10   481204-1
8. Old Mother Hubbard (Tobias-Polla) 1:56   481204-2
9. Bop Goes the Weasel (Owen-Bentley) 2:18   481204-3
10. Ool-Ya-Koo (Gillespie-Fuller) 2:23   481204-4
11. Flying Home (Goodman-Hampton) 4:14   481204-5
12. Old Mother Hubbard (Tobias-Polla) 1:52   490415-1
13. Mr. Paganini (You'll Have To Swing It) (Coslow)
    4:17   490415-2
14. There's a Small Hotel (Hart-Rodgers) 3:33   490415-3
15. How High the Moon (Lewis-Hamilton) 3:35
    490415-4
16. Robbins' Nest (Thompson-Jacquet) 2:23   490423-1
17. As You Desire Me (Wrubel) 2:41   490423-2
18. Thou Swell (Hart-Rodgers) 1:56   490423-3
19. Flyin' Home (Goodman-Hampton) 4:31   490423-4
20. Someone Like You (Warren-Blane) 1:27   490430-1
21. Again (Newman-Cochran) 2:54   490430-2
22. In a Mellow Tone (In a Mellotone) (Ellington) 2:15
    490430-3
23. Lemon Drop (Wallington) 1:48   490430-4

CD: Cool 'n' Blue CD-112 (released 1993). Total playing time, 68:23. The author of the liner notes is uncredited.

LPD-153 ELLA FITZGERALD AND
BING CROSBY/MY HAPPINESS

1. Stay with the Happy People** (Styne-Hilliard) 2:03
   500503-1
2. I Hadn't Anyone Till You (Noble) 3:02   500503-2
3. A Dreamer's Holiday** (Gannon-Wayne) 2:50
   491109-1
4. My Happiness (Bergantine-Peterson) 3:05   491109-2
5. Basin Street Blues** (Williams) 2:53   501129-1
6. Can Anyone Explain? (Benjamin-Weiss) 2:32
   501129-2
7. Five Foot Two, Eyes of Blue* (Henderson-Lewis-
   Young) 1:58   501129-3
8. Silver Bells** (Livingston-Evans) 2:08   501129-4
9. Medley: a. Trying (Vaughan); b. My Favorite Song
   (Gold-Charlap); c. Between the Devil and the Deep
   Blue Sea (Koehler-Arlen) 5:31   521218-1
10. I Can Dream, Can't I?* (Fain-Kahal) 1:42   491109-3
11. Rudolph, The Red-Nosed Reindeer** (Marks) 2:28
    521218-2
12. Someone to Watch Over Me (Gershwin-Gershwin)
    3:50   531227-1
13. White Christmas** (Berlin) 3:26   531213-1
14. A Marshmallow World** (DeRose-Sigman) 2:54
    501129-5
15. Moanin' Low (Rainger-Dietz) 4:28   531213-2
16. That's A-Plenty** (Pollack) 2:21   540214-1
17. Taking a Chance on Love (Duke-Latouche-Fetter)
    3:07   540214-2
18. 'Way Back Home*** (Lewis-Waring) 3:11   491109-4
19. Medley: a. I Hadn't Anyone Till You (Noble); b. I
    You Ever Should Leave (Cahn-Chaplin); c. I Can't
    Give You Anything but Love (Fields-McHugh) 4:57
    530101-1
20. Istanbul (Simon-Kennedy) (trumpet solo, Ziggy
    Elman)** 2:45   531227-2
21. Looking for a Boy (Gershwin-Gershwin) 3:19
    531227-3
22. Chicago Style** (Burke-Van Heusen) 3:09   530101-2
23. Everything I Have Is Yours* (Adamson-Lane) 2:12
    491123-1
24. Undecided (Shavers-Robin) 2:10   511128-1
25. Memphis Blues**** (Mercer-Handy) 2:52   501129-6

Unstarred selections, Ella Fitzgerald, solo/*Bing Crosby, solo/**Ella Fitzgerald and Bing Crosby, duet/***Ella Fitzgerald, Bing Crosby, and The Mills Brothers/****Ella Fitzgerald, Bing Crosby, and The Firehouse Five + Two). All titles with John Scott Trotter's Orchestra, except 18 and 25.

CD: Parrot PARCD 002 (released 1992). Total playing time, 75:52. Produced by **Cindy Hacker** and **Dave Bennett**. Research, compilation, and liner notes by **Geoff Milne**.

LPD-154 U.S. ALL-STARS IN BERLIN

1. Jam Session No. 1 (instr) 15:04   550200-1
2. Jam Session No. 2 (instr) 13:54   550200-2
3. Willow, Weep for Me (Ronell) (instr) 2:17   550200-3
4. I Don't Know Why (Turk-Ahlert) (instr) 2:24   550200-4
5. Imagination (Burke-Van Heusen) (instr) 2:32   550200-5
6. My Old Flame (Coslow-Johnston) (instr) 2:38   550200-6
7. Mop Mop (instr) 10:05   550200-7
8. Easy Does It (Oliver-Young) (instr) 5:37   550200-8
9. Seven Come Eleven (instr) 5:53   550200-9
10. Billie's Bounce (Parker) (instr) 5:44   550200-10
11. Papa Loves Mambo (Reichner-Hoffman-Manning) (vEF) 2:52   550200-11
12. Perdido (Lengsfelder-Drake-Tizol) (vEF) 2:26   550200-12

CD: Jazz Band JBCD 2113 (released 1993). Total playing time: 71:26. Produced by Flyright Record and Distribution Co., Ltd., Bexhill-on-Sea, East Sussex, U.K. These sessions are radio transcriptions recorded at the Armed Forces Radio Network, Berlin, Germany, in February 1955.

The U.S.A. All-Stars

Trumpets: Dizzy Gillespie, Roy Eldridge; Trombone: Bill Harris; Tenor Saxophone: Flip Phillips; Piano: Oscar Peterson; Guitar: Herb Ellis; Bass: Ray Brown; Drums: Louis Bellson; Vocalist: Ella Fitzgerald

Tracks 1 and 2, the jam sessions, are the work of all the All-Stars, except. Ella Fitzgerald. Track 3, "Willow, Weep for Me," features Roy Eldridge. Track 4, "I Don't Know Why," features Flip Phillips. Track 5, "Imagination," features Bill Harris. Track 6, "My Old Flame," features Dizzy Gillespie. Track 7, "Mop Mop," features Louis Bellson. Tracks 8 and 9, "Easy Does It" and "Seven Come Eleven," are by The Oscar. Peterson Trio (Oscar Peterson, Ray Brown, and Herb Ellis). Track 10, "Billie's Bounce," is by The Buddy de Franco Quintet. Track 11, "Papa Loves Mambo," is by Ella Fitzgerald, with Don Abney at piano. Track 12, "Perdido," features Ella Fitzgerald with the All-Star Band.

LPD-155 ONE NIGHT STAND WITH STAN KENTON AND MUSIC '55

Featuring Ella Fitzgerald/Plus Hoagy Carmichael & The Tigertown 5

1. Theme and Introduction (instr)
2. How High the Moon (Lewis-Hamilton) (vEF) 550802-1
3. Someone To Watch Over Me (Gershwin-Gershwin) (vEF)   550802-2
4. Collaboration (Kenton) (instr)
5. Hong Kong Blues (Carmichael) (vHoagy Carmichael)
6. Muskrat Ramble (Gilbert-Ory) (Tigertown 5)
7. That's A-Plenty (Pollack) (Tigertown 5)
8. Medley (vHoagy Carmichael): a. Rockin' Chair (Carmichael); b. Georgia on My Mind (Gorrell-Carmichael); c. Ol' Buttermilk Sky (Brooks-Carmichael
9. The Nearness of You (Washington-Carmicael) (instr)
10. Skylark (Mercer-Carmichael) (vEF)   550802-3
11. Star Dust (Parish-Carmichael) (vEF-Hoagy Carmichael, duet)   550802-4
12. Theme and Sign Off (instr)
13. Theme and Introduction (instr)
14. Southern Scandal (Carmichael) (instr)
15. Easy to Love (Porter) (instr)
16. Bags (Kenton) (instr)
17. Adios (Woods-Madriguera) (instr)
18. Theme and Sign Off (instr)

LP: Joyce 1130. Side One, Tracks 1-8 (00:00)/Side Two, Tracks 9-18 (00:00). Total playing time, 00:00. Tracks 1-12, CBS Network radio broacast, 2 August 1955. Tracks 13-18, Broadcast, The Hollywood Palladium, January 1953.

LPD-156 SWING INTO SPRING THE CLASSIC NBC TELEVISION BROADCAST OF APRIL 9, 1958

1. Let's Dance/Benny Goodman Band; Swing Into Spring/Benny Goodman Band; Ridin' High/Ella Fitzgerald with Benny Goodman Band
2. Sometimes I'm Happy/Benny Goodman Band; Don't Be That Way/Benny Goodman Quintet; Rachel's Dream/Benny Goodman Quintet
3. Blue Champagne/Ray Eberle with Benny Goodman Band; Let's Get Away from It All/Jo Stafford with Benny Goodman Band; King Porter Stomp/Benny Goodman Band, featuring Harry James
4. Medley: Benny Goodman Quintet, featuring Harry James; I Got a Right to Sing the Blues/Ella Fitzgerald; Limehouse Blues-How Come You Do Me Like You Do/Jo Stafford; Poor Butterfly-Hard Hearted Hannah/Ella Fitzgerald; I Got It Bad (and That Ain't Good)/Jo Stafford; St. Louis Blues/Ella Fitzgerald and Jo Stafford
5. Spring Rhapsody/Benny Goodman Band with Ralph Burns and His Orchestra
6. Blue Skies/The McGuire Sisters with Benny Goodman Band; Gotta Be This or That/Benny Goodman Band, plus Red Norvo and Teddy Wilson, with vocals

by Benny Goodman, Ella Fitzgerald, Jo Stafford, and The McGuire Sisters; Goodbye/Benny Goodman Band; Swing Into Spring/Benny Goodman Band

LP: Sandy Hook Release No. 57 (released 1981). Side A, Tracks 1-3 (33:10)/Side B, Tracks 4-6 (19:02). CD: Sandy Hook CDSH 2057 (released 1991). Total playing time: 42:12. This program was telecast "live" on "The Texaco Star Theatre" on 9 April 1958 on NBC-TV.

LPD-157 SWING INTO SPRING THE CLASSIC CBS TELEVISION BROADCAST OF 10 APRIL 1959

1. Let's Dance/Benny Goodman Band signature theme; 'S Wonderful/Ella Fitzgerald with Benny Goodman Band; Things Are Swingin'/Peggy Lee with Benny Goodman Band and Quintet
2. Three Faces of Spring:/Ralph Burns Orchestra; Concertino for Clarinet/Benny Goodman, clarinet; Bach Goes to Town/Ralph Burns Orchestra; Swing Low, Sweet Clarinet/Benny Goodman, clarinet, and chorus
3. Ah! Men! Ah! Women! Medley:/André Previn, piano; Ah! Men! Ah! Women!/Benny Goodman, Ella Fitzgerald, Peggy Lee; I Must Have That Man/Ella Fitzgerald with Benny Goodman Quartet; Sweet Georgia Brown/vocal by Benny Goodman; I'm Just Wild About Harry/Peggy Lee; Sweet Lorraine/vocal by Benny Goodman; The Gentleman Is a Dope/Ella Fitzgerald; When a Woman Loves a Man/Peggy Lee; The Glory of Love/vocals by Goodman, Fitzgerald and Lee
4. Air Mail Special/Benny Goodman Quintet
5. Why Don't You Do Right?/Peggy Lee with Benny Goodman Band
6. Mountain Greenery/Ella Fitzgerald with Benny Goodman Band
7. Junior Prom Medley:/Benny Goodman Band; String of Pearls/instr; Goody Goody/with The Hi-Lo's; You Turned the Tables on Me/Donna Musgrove and The Hi-Lo's; One O'Clock Jump/instr
8. Swing Into Spring/Ella Fitzgerald, Peggy Lee, The Hi-Lo's, chorus; Goodbye/Benny Goodman Band closing theme

LP: A & R 2000/20001 (each side of LP was numbered consecutively) (released in April 1959 in limited quantities to executives, musicians, and cast members). Side 1 (A&R 2000), Tracks 1-3/Side 2 (A&R 2001), Tracks 4-8. Note: This program was broadcast on "The Texaco Star Theatre" on 10 April 1959, on CBS-TV.

LPD-158 FRANK SINATRA/ THE TELEVISION YEARS

1. The Lonesome Road (Shilkret-Austin) 3:41

2. All the Way (Kahn-Small-Van Heusen) 3:42
3. This Can't Be Love (Hart-Rodgers) 1:23
4. Bewitched, Bothered and Bewildered (Hart-Rodgers) 3:18
5. Night and Day (Porter) 2:28
6. The House I Live In (Robinson-Allan) 4:15
7. I've Got the World on a String (Koehler-Arlen) 2:08
8. It's All Right with Me (Porter) 3:25
9. Just One of Those Things (Porter) 2:54
10. Tell Her You Love Her (Ward-Watkins) 1:55
11. I'm an Old Cowhand 1:49
12. Medley (Duet with Ella Fitzgerald)*; Moonlight in Vermont (Suessdorf-Blackburn)/I May Be Wrong (Ruskin-Sullivan)/Party Blues (Basie-Fitzgerald-Williams) 5:40   580509-4
13. I'm Gonna Sit Right Down and Write Myself a Letter (Ahlert-Young) 1:53
14. Last Night When We Were Young (Harburg-Arlen) 3:05
15. How Are Ya Fixed for Love? (Van Heusen-Cahn) 2:18
16. Can't We Be Friends? (Swift-Warburg) (Duet with Ella Fitzgerald)** 3:06   591213-4
17. My Heart Stood Still (Hart-Rodgers) 1:56
18. My Kind of Town (Van Heusen-Cahn) 3:39
19. The September of My Years (Van Heusen-Cahn) 3:06
20. At Long Last Love (Porter) 2:25
21. Fly Me to the Moon (Howard) 2:45
22. Please Be Kind (Chaplin-Cahn) 2:45
23. The Gal That Got Away (Gershwin-Arlen) 3:55
24. Everybody Has the Right to Be Wrong (Van Heusen-Cahn) 2:48
25. Too Marvelous for Words (Mercer-Whiting) 2:05

*This medley telecast on **The Frank Sinatra Show**, ABC Television Studios, Los Angeles, 9 May 1958. See Part I, The Recording Sessions, for other performances not yet released.

This track telecast on **An Afternoon with Frank Sinatra, ABC Television Studios, Los Angeles, 13 December 1959. See Part I, The Recording Sessions, for other performances not yet released.

CD: Bravura BRCD 105. Total playing time, 72:23.

LPD-159 FRANK & DAN'S PARTY BY THE BAY

1. Opening Theme 2:58
2. Welcome by Joey Bishop 1:32
3. Rowan and Martin 5:21

Ella Fitzgerald

4. Something's Gotta Give (Mercer) 3:20   660907-1
5. Body and Soul (Heyman-Sour-Green-Eyton) 3:01 660907-2

6. Too Marvelous for Words (Mercer-Whiting) 2:40
   660907-3
7. Joey Rats on Dean and Frank 2:36

Dean Martin

8. Bourbon from Heaven (Parody of "Pennies from Heaven" by Johnston-Burke) 2:25
9. Hello, Governor! (Parody of "Hello, Dolly!" by Herman-David) 1:21
10. Dino's Monologue 1:54
11. Everybody Loves Somebody (Taylor-Lane) 3:07
12. Volare (Migliacci-Parish-Modugno) 1:02
13. On an Evening in Roma 1:42
14. The Leader Arrives! 0:45

Frank Sinatra

15. I've Got the World on a String (Koehler-Arlen) 2:11
16. Fly Me to the Moon (Howard) 1:59
17. The Shadow of Your Smile (Mandel-Webster) 3:01
18. I've Got You Under My Skin (Porter) 3:27
19. It Was a Very Good Year (Drake) 4:24
20. You Make Me Feel So Young (Myrow-Gordon) 3:38
21. Show Closes 2:38

CD: BMD 2260 (Private Circulation Only). This disc is taken from a television broadcast from Civic Auditorium, San Francisco, California, of a campaign fundraiser for the re-election of Governor Pat Brown, Wednesday evening, 7 September 1966. He lost the election to Ronald Reagan.

LPD-160 ELLA FITZGERALD LIVE FROM THE CAVE SUPPER CLUB, VANCOUVER, B.C., CANADA 19 MAY 1968

1. I'm Beginning to See the Light (George-Hodges-James-Ellington) 6:16 680519-1
2. Medley: a. Blue Skies (Berlin)/b. On a Clear Day (Lerner-Lane)/c. A Foggy Day (in London Town) (Gershwin-Gershwin) 4:20 680519-2
3. Girl Talk (Hefti-Troup) 3:21 680519-3
4. Sweet Georgia Brown (Casey-Pinkard) 3:32 680519-4
5. Introduction of Trio by Ella 2:07
6. Gone with the Wind (Magidson-Wrubel) 5:10 680519-5
7. Sunny (Hebb) 2:53 680519-6
8. Goin' Out of My Head (Randazzo-Weinstein) 7:21 680519-7
9. For Once in My Life (Miller-Murden) 3:47 680519-8
10. One Note Samba (Mendonà-Jobim) 4:27 680519-9
11. Satin Doll (Mercer-Ellington) 2:42 680519-10

12. I Can't Stop Loving You (Gibson) 6:44 680519-11
13. Just One of Those Things (Porter) 2:36 680519-12
14. Closing 0:43

CD: Jazz Band EBCD 2144 (released March 1999). Total playing time, 56:07. Produced by Flyright Records, Bexhill-on-Sea, East Sussex, U.K. Master Tape engineered by Ed Burke. Liner notes by Doug Campbell.

LPD-161 ELLA FITZGERALD ON THE AIR VOLUME 3/1944–1947

1. A-Tisket, A-Tasket (Fitzgerald-Feldman) 2:49
   440501-1
2. Do Nothing' Till You Hear from Me (Ellington-Russell) 2:34 440501-2
3. Is You Is, Or Is You Ain't My Baby (Jordan-Austin) 3:05 441000-1
4. St. Louis Blues (Handy) 4:17 441000-2
5. A-Tisket, A-Tasket (Fitzgerald-Feldman) 2:33
   450228-1
6. That's Rich (Oliver) 3:22 451012-1
7. I'll Always Be in Love with You (Stept-Ruby-Green) 4:27 451012-2
8. I'll See You in My Dreams (Jones-Kahn) 4:06
   451012-4
9. The Honeydripper (Liggins) 3:43 460121-1
10. Guilty (Whiting-Akst-Kahn) 3:12 470222-1
11. Blue Skies (Budella) (Berlin) 4:05 470301-1
12. Across the Alley from the Alamo (Greene) 2:25
    470806-1
13. Oh! Lady, Be Good! (Gershwin-Gershwin) 3:40
    470806-2
14. It's Almost Like Being in Love (Loewe-Lerner) 2:14
    470929-1
15. Stairway to the Stars (Malneck-Signorelli-Parish) 4:19 470929-2
16. Lover Man (Ramirez-Davis-Sherman) 4:41 470929-3
17. Flying Home (Hampton-Goodman) 2:17 470929-4
18. Oh! Lady, Be Good! (Gershwin-Gershwin) 3:47
    470929-5
19. How High the Moon (Lewis-Hamilton) 5:48
    470929-6

CD: Masters of Jazz MJCD 169 (released February 2000) Total playing time, 67:57. Produced by **Christian Bonnet** and **Alain Tercinet**. Transfers and mastering: **Christophe Hénault**, Art & Son Studio. Album notes: **Alain Tercinet**/English translation: **Patricia and Jean-François Kresser**. For the first two volumes of this series, see LPD-151.

LPD-162 ELLA FITZGERALD IN THE GROOVE

1. A-Tisket, A-Tasket (Opening Theme) (Fitzgerald-Feldman) 0:26 390815-1

2. Oh Boy! I'm in the Groove (Fitzgerald) 2:23
   390921-1
3. Day In — Day Out (Mercer-Bloom) 2:07   390826-1
4. (I Always Dream of) Billy (Goodwin-Kendis-Paley)
   2:30 390826-2
5. Please Tell Me the Truth (Fitzgerald-Sampson) 3:05
   390815-2
6. Sing Song Swing (Cook-Garrett) 2:45   400000-1
7. The Starlit Hour (Parish-DeRose) 3:42   400000-2
8. Yodelin' Jive (Prince-Raye) 2:47   400000-3
9. Baby, What Else Can I Do? (Hirsch-Marks) 3:41
   390921-2
10. My Wubba Dolly (Werner-Werner) 3:14   391214-1
11. My Prayer (Boulanger-Kennedy) 4:02   391214-2
12. Betcha Nickel (Fitzgerald-Webb) 2:41   390716-1
13. To You (Davis-Dorsey-Shapiro) 3:17   390824-1
14. (Hep! Hep!) The Jumpin' Jive (Calloway-Palmer-
    Froeba) 2:30 390824-2
15. Careless (Quadling-Howard-Jurgens) 3:52
    400000-4
16. Well All Right (Faye-Howell-Raye) 2:31   390921-3
17. Stairway to the Stars (Malneck-Parish-Signorelli)
    3:13 390815-3
18. That's All, Brother (David-Livingston-Hager) 2:52
    390716-2
19. The Lamp is Low (Ravel-DeRose-Parish-Shefter)
    3:25 390720-1
20. Little White Lies (Donaldson) 2:40   390720-3
21. St. Louis Blues (Handy) 4:45   390720-3

CD: Buddha Records 74465 99702 2 (released 18 April 2000) Total playing time, 62:34. Produced by Rob Santos, Glenn Korman, and Vince Giordano. Master Transfers, Vince Giordano and Ron Olson. Audio Restoration and CD Mastering, Doug Pomeroy. Album notes, Will Friedwald.

✄

There are several companies both here and abroad that specialize in the release of cassettes containing old radio programs. Among the most notable is one called Radio Yesteryear. They have released a number of old radio programs featuring Ella Fitzgerald recordings; however, most of the programs feature commercial recordings, although it would seem from listening to them that the recordings were "live." A good example is the "Let's Go Nightclubbing" radio programs. The announcer introduces the featured singer, they talk about her new record releases and about her current appearance at a certain nightclub, and then we hear a vocal with orchestra. This is all done at the radio station where there is no orchestra, and the vocal we hear is one of the singer's newest commercial recordings. Here are some of the current offering of Radio Yesteryear featuring Ella Fitzgerald:

Let's Go Nightclubbing   28 February 1945   CT 12741
Let's Go Nightclubbing   21 January 1946   CT 12742
WOR Twenty-Fifth Anniversary Broadcast   22 February
    1947   CT 1690
A Salute to Bing Crosby   CT 3748
Ella Fitzgerald at Basin Street   CT 20382
Frank Sinatra/A Man and His Music + Ella + Jobim
    CT 34924
The Timex All-Star Swing Festival/NBC Television   29
    November 1972   CT 11545
All Star Swing Festival (Television)   19 March 1977
    CT 20629
Just Call Me Maestro/PBS Television   15 July 1979
    CT 21546
Jazz Alive!/National Public Radio   12 August 1983
    CT 28215

LPD-163 THE ENCHANTING ELLA FITZGERALD LIVE AT BIRDLAND 1950–1952

1. Old Mother Hubbard (Ellington-Wallace) 1:44
   501230-1
2. These Foolish Things (Marvell-Strachey-Link) 3:30
   501230-2
3. In a Mellow Tone (Gabler-Ellington) 2:06
   501230-3
4. Flying Home (Goodman-Hampton-Robin) 2:48
   501230-4
5. Back in Your Own Back Yard (Jolson-Dreyer-Rose)
   1:32 501230-5
6. Jumping with Symphony Syd (Lester Young) 1:55
   501230-6
7. How High the Moon (Lewis-Hamilton) 3:53
   501230-7
8. Show Me the Way to Get Out of This World
   (Clark-Dennis) 2:43   520607-1
9. Angel Eyes (Brent-Dennis) 4:19   520607-2
10. Walkin' My Baby Back Home (Turk-Ahlert) 3:09
    520607-3
11. Goody Goody (Mercer-Malneck) 2:38   520607-4
12. Air Mail Special (Hampton) 2:29   520607-5
13. How High the Moon (Lewis-Hamilton) 4:43
    520607-6
14. (Its Only a) Paper Moon (Harburg-Rose-Arlen) 2:41
    520816-1
15. Be Anything (But Be Mine) (Gordon) 2:54
    520816-2
16. Preview (Quinichette) 2:47   520816-3
17. You're Driving Me Crazy (Donaldson) 3:45
    520816-4
18. Lemon Drop (Wallington) 2:08   520816-5

19. The Frim Fram Sauce (Ricardel-Evans) 3:56
    520816-6
20. Imagination (Burke-Van Heusen) 3:00   510519-2
21. How Long Has This Been Going On? (Gershwin-Gershwin) 4:20   510519-5
22. Someone to Watch Over Me (Gershwin-Gershwin)
    3:13   510519-7
23. Jumping with Symphony Syd (Young) 2:53
    510519-8
24. I Can't Get Started (with You) (Gershwin-Duke)
    3:43   540000-1
25. Later (Bradshaw-Glover) 2:44   550803-1
26. That Old Black Magic (Mercer-Arlen) 2:04
    550803-2

CD: Baldwin Street Music BJH 309 (released June 2000). Total playing time: 78:00.

IX. The Ella Collections: Contents

The albums listed here have not been assigned LPD numbers and, therefore, are not noted in the detail of the discography since all selections on these discs have previously appeared on other LPs or CDs that are detailed in the discography. However, the Discographer Reference Number (DRN) is given for each selection to simplify identification.

There are probably as many as a hundred compact disc collections of Ella's recordings, many of which are produced in Europe where copyright laws are less restrictive concerning reissue of recordings. These are imported to the U.S. by the tens of thousands and are available in almost any record store. For the most part, they are of inferior quality to those produced by the U.S. companies in whose vaults repose the original discs or tapes, which offer us, on occasion, digitally remastered transfers. In fact, except for a relatively few sessions, these masters are held by GRP (the Decca masters), Polygram (the Verve masters), and Fantasy (the Pablo masters), all of which occasionally reissue a collection of Ella's songs. Here, then, are the important Ella collections.

THE DECCA YEARS

ELLA: The Legendary Decca Recordings (GRP GRD 4-648), the 4-CD set has been reissued as single compact discs as follows: **The Best of Ella Fitzgerald** (GRP Decca Jazz GRD 659) is the same as Disc 1; **Ella and Friends** (GRP Decca Jazz GRD 663) is the same as Disc 2; **Pure Ella** (GRP Decca Jazz GRD 636) is the same as Disc 3. It is assumed that Disc 4 will eventually be released as a single CD.

Ella Fitzgerald with Chick Webb/Swingsation (GRP GRD-9921)*

1. Sing Me a Swing Song (and Let Me Dance) (360602-2) 2. Blue Minor (inst) (340706-1) 3. When I Get Low, I Get High (360407-5) 4. A Little Bit Later On (360602-3) 5. Don't Be That Way (inst) (341119-2) 6. Vote for Mr. Rhythm (361029-5) 7. The Organ Grinder's Swing (361118-2) 8. Blue Lou (341119-4) 9. Oh, Yes, Take Another Guess (370114-1) 10. I Want To Be Happy (371217-1) 11. Clap Hands! Here Comes Charlie (inst) (370324-5 12. A-Tisket, A-Tasket (380502-1) 13. I'm Just a Jitterbug (380502-3) 14. Harlem Congo (inst) 371101-5) 15. Wacky Dust (380817-1) 16. Undecided 390217-1) 17. 'Tain't What

You Do (It's the Way That Cha Do It) (390217-2) 18. Liza (380503-7) (inst)

*All tracks with vocals by Ella Fitzgerald, except instrumentals.

Priceless Jazz Collection/Ella Fitzgerald (GRP GRD-9870)

1. A-Tisket, A-Tasket (380502-1) 2. Goody Goody (520225-4) 3. Someone to Watch Over Me (500912-3) 4. Making' Whoopee (540329-4) 5. Flying Home (451004-1) 6. Nice Work If You Can Get It (540330-5) 7. How High the Moon (471220-4) 8. But Not for Me (500912-1 9. Mr. Paganini (520626-2/3) 10. Oh! Lady, Be Good! (470319-3) 11. My Heart Belongs to Daddy (540330-3) 12. Lullaby of Birdland (540604-1) 13. It Might As Well Be Spring (550401-3) 14. Stairway to the Stars (390629-2) 15. Ol' Devil Moon (550427-1) 16. Lover, Come Back to Me (550427-2)

Priceless Jazz Collection/More Ella Fitzgterald (GRP GRD-9916)

1. Between the Devil and the Deep Blue Sea (550427-3) 2. Angel Eyes (520626-4) 3. Hard Hearted Hannah (550503-1) 4. My One and Only (500911-2) 5. I've Got the World on a String (500306-2) 6. Baby, It's Cold Outside

(490428-5) 7. Basin Street Blues (490920-4) 8. Air Mail Special (520104-1) 9. I Gotta Have My Baby Back (491107-2) 10. Looking for a Boy (500911-1) 11. Black Coffee (490428-3) 12. A Sunday Kind of Love (470319-1) 13. Soon (500912-2) 14. Thanks for the Memory (550401-2) 15. That Old Black Magic (550427-4) 16. Star Dust (540330-6) 17. Undecided (390217-1)

THE VERVE YEARS

The Best of Ella and Louis (Verve 314 537 909)

1. Let's Call the Whole Thing Off (570723-4) 2. Our Love Is Here To Say (570723-1) 3. The Nearness of You (560816-11) 4. Stars Fell on Alabama (560816-4) 5. Gee, Baby, Ain't I Good to You? (570723-6) 6. They Can't Take That Away from Me (560816-1) 7. Autumn in New York (570723-3) 8. Summertime (570818-1) 9. Tenderly (560816-3) 10. Stompin' at the Savoy (570723-7) 11. Under a Blanket of Blue (560816-7) 12. I Wants To Stay Here (570828-1) 13. I've Got My Love To Keep Me Warm (570813-5) 14. There's a Boat Dat's Leavin' Soon for New York (570819-1) 15. You Won't Be Satisfied (Until You Break My Heart) (560815-7)

The Best of Ella Fitzgerald: First Lady of Song (Verve 314 523 382)

1. Too Young for the Blues (560125-3) 2. Can't We Be Friends? (duet with Louis Armstrong) (560816-5) 3. Be-witched, Bothered and Bewildered (560829-8) 4. Just A-Sittin' and A-Rockin' (560904-8) 5. I'm Just a Lucky So-and-So (570626-2) 6. Baby, Don'tcha Go 'Way Mad (570724-10) 7. Angel Eyes (570724-11) 8. I Won't Dance (570813-1) 9. Lush Life (5710-17-4) 10. Blue Skies (580318-5) 11. The Swingin' Shepherd Blues (580319-5) 12. You're an Old Smoothie (581122-11) 13. Detour Ahead (590325-8) 14. Don't Be That Way (611227-1) 15. A Fine Romance (630105-2) 16. 'Deed I Do (630715-2)

The Best of the Song Books (Verve 314 519 804)

1. Something's Gotta Give (641020-6) 2. Our Love Is Here to Stay (590105-3) 3. Bewitched (Bothered and Be-wildered) (560829-8) 4. I've Got My Love To Keep Me Warm (580318-1) 5. The Lady Is a Tramp (560821-2) 6. I Got It Bad (and That Ain't Good) (6:13) (570625-2) 7. Miss Otis Regrets (560207-11) 8. 'S Wonderful (590716-1) 9. Between the Devil and the Deep Blue Sea (610116-1) 10. Love for Sale (560208-8) 11. They Can't Take That Away from Me (590105-4) 12. Midnight Sun (641021-1) 13. Hooray for Love (600801-1) 14. Why Was I Born? (630106-4) 15. Cotton Tail (560904-3) 16. Ev'ry Time We Say Goodbye (560207-4)

The Best of the Song Books: The Ballads (Verve 314 521 867)

1. Oh! Lady, Be Good! (590108-7) 2. I'm Old Fash-ioned (630105-1) 3. Laura (641021-2) 4. Day Dream (570624-1) 5. Easy To Love (560207-13) 6. It Was Writ-ten in the Stars (610115-5) 7. How Long Has This Been Going On? (590105-5) 8. Let's Begin (630107-3) 9. Now It Can Be Told (580317-7) 10. There's a Small Hotel (560829-4) 11. Do Nothing Till You Hear from Me (560904-5) 12. Ill Wind (610115-2) 13. You're Laughing at Me (580317-4) 14. A Ship Without a Sail (560830-3) 15. Trav'lin' Light (641019-1) 16. This Time the Dream's on Me (610115-4)

Love Songs: The Best of the Verve Song Books (Verve 831 762)

1. From This Moment On (560207-3) 2. Solitude (560904-6) 3. Love You Madly (571017-3) 4. All the Things You Are (630107-5) 5. I Concentrate on You (560209-4) 6. Out of This World (610116-6) 7. How About Me? (580317-8) 8. I'm Beginning to See the Light (570626-3) 9. The Man I Love (570105-7) 10. I Remember You (641021-4) 11. I Let a Song Go Out of My Heart (560904-1) 12. Always (580313-5) 13. Just One of Those Things (560207-4) 14. Prelude to a Kiss (560904-10) 15. All Too Soon (570627-2) 16. Lover (560821-5)

The three albums immediately above are packaged as a set, **The Best of the Song Books Collection/Ella Fitzgerald** (Verve 3 33247)

Compact Jazz/Ella Fitzgerald Live (Verve 833 294) (CD)

1. Oh! Lady, Be Good! (570929-11) 2. Summertime (600213-7) 3. Honeysuckle Rose (640728-16) 4. Body and Soul (570704-3) 5. Just Squeeze Me (660729-15) 6. These Foolish Things (571009-4) 7. Stompin' at the Savoy (571009-8) 8. Baby, Won't You Please Come Home (610516-6) 9. You'd Be So Nice to Come Home To (640729-18) 10. The More I See You (660728-7) 11. I've Got a Crush on You (570704-5) 12. I Can't Give You Any-thing But Love (560815-5) 13. The Man I Love (600213-6) 14. Take the "A" Train (610521-4)

*Note: **Compact Jazz/Ella Fitzgerald** (Verve 831 367), having a track not previously released, appears as LPD-133 in Section II, of this Part.*

Compact Jazz/Ella Fitzgerald and Louis Armstrong (Verve 835 313)

1. They Can't Take That Away from Me (560816-1) 2. Gee, Baby! Ain't I Good to You (570723-6) 3. I Won't Dance (570813-1) 4. It Ain't Necessarily So (570818-4) 5. A Fine Romance (570813-2) 6. Stompin' at the Savoy (570723-7) 7. A Foggy Day (in London Town) (560816-9) 8. Don't Be That Way (570813-3) 9. Summertime (570818-1) 10. Cheek to Cheek (560816-6) 11. Can't We Be Friends (560816-5) 12. Let's Call the Whole Thing Off (570723-4)

Compact Jazz/Ella Fitzgerald and Duke Ellington (Verve 314 517 953)

1. Take the "A" Train (570624-2) 2. Caravan (570627-3) 3. I Got It Bad (and That Ain't Good) (570625-2) 4. I'm Beginning to See the Light (570626-3) 5. I Didn't Know About You (570626-4) 6. I Ain't Got Nothin' but the Blues (570625-2) 7. Everything but You (570625-1) 8. (I've Got) Something to Live For (651017-3) 9. Duke's Place (651017-6) 10. Passion Flower (651020-2) 11. Cotton Tail (660729-13) 12. Mack the Knife (660728-12) 13. It Don't Mean a Thing (If It Ain't Got That Swing) (660729-14)

Day Dream: Best of the Duke Ellington Song Book (Verve 314 527 223)

1. Take the "A" Train (570624-2) 2. Day-Dream (570624-1) 3. Everything But You (570625-1) 4. Azure (560904-13) 5. Solitude (560904-6) 6. The E and D Blues (E for Ella, D for Duke) (570627-9) 7. Bli-Blip (570627-7) 8. It Don't Mean a Thing (If It Ain't Got That Swing) (560904-9) 9. I Ain't Got Nothin' But the Blues (570625-5) 10. I Got It Bad (and That Ain't Good) (570625-2) 11. Just Squeeze Me (560904-4) 12. Cotton Tail (560904-3) 13. Squatty Roo (571017-5) 14. Rocks in My Bed (560904-2) 15. Rockin' in Rhythm (570626-5) 16. Mood Indigo (571017-6) 17. All Too Soon (570627-3)

Ella Fitzgerald/Verve Jazz Masters 6 (Verve 314 519 822)

1. I Hear Music (611114-5) 2. I Ain't Got Nothin' but the Blues (570625-5) 3. Ev'rything I've Got (Belongs to You) (560904-15) 4. I Loves You, Porgy (570828-1) 5. Mack the Knife (600213-10) 6. I'm Putting All My Eggs in One Basket (570813-4) 7. The Man That Got Away (600801-5) 8. Just You, Just Me (581122-4) 9. I've Got the World on a String (600801-8) 10. A-Tisket, A-Tasket (570724-5) 11. These Foolish Things (570723-8) 12. Heat Wave (580318-2) 13. I Never Had a Chance (571015-10) 14. How High the Moon (600213-11) 15. In the Evening (When the Sun Goes Down) (631029-4) 16. Signing Off (610623-5)

Ella Fitzgerald & Louis Armstrong/Verve Jazz Masters 24 (Verve 314 521 851)

1. I've Got My Love to Keep Me Warm (570813-5) 2. Isn't This a Lovely Day (To Be Caught in the Rain) (560816-2) 3. Learnin' the Blues (570723-2) 4. I Got Plenty o' Nuttin' (570818-3) 5. Moonlight in Vermont (560816-7) 6. Under a Blanket of Blue (560816-6) 7. I'm Putting All My Eggs in One Basket (570813-4) 8. Our Love Is Here to Stay (570723-1) 9. April in Paris (560816-9) 10. Tenderly (560816-3) 11. Bess, You Is My Woman Now (570818-2) 12. They All Laughed (570723-5)

The Essential Ella Fitzgerald/The Great Songs (Verve 314 517 170)

1. Oh! Lady, Be Good! (slow version) (590108-7) 2. Oh! Lady, Be Good! (scat version) (571009-9) 3. There's a Lull in My Life (571015-1) 4. Little Jazz (581123-6) 5. Drop Me Off in Harlem (570625-3) 6. Angel Eyes (600414-2) 7. Ding! Dong! The Witch Is Dead (600802-4) 8. A-Tisket, A-Tasket (610512-8) 9. Summertime (duet with Louis Armstrong) (570818-1) 10. Into Each Life Some Rain Must Fall (630716-8) 11. Spring Can Really Hang You Up the Most (610622-3) 12. Pick Yourself Up (611115-1) 13. Cool Breeze (590903-2) 14. Imagine My Frustration (651017-3) 15. Mack The Knife (600213-10) 16. Dream (641021-2)

For the Love of Ella Fitzgerald, Disc 1/Monuments of Swing (Verve 841765)

1. A-Tisket, A-Tasket (610512-8) 2. Oh! Lady, Be Good! (571009-9) 3. Stompin' at the Savoy (571009-8) 4. How High the Moon (600213-11) 5. Mr. Paganini (You'll Have To Swing It) (610512-1) 6. Sweet Georgia Brown (660720-1) 7. Mack the Knife (600213-10) 8. Caravan (580425-8) 9. A Night in Tunisia (610624-4) 10. Rockin' in Rhythm (570626-5) 11. Honeysuckle Rose (630715-5) 12. I Got Rhythm (590105-2) 13. A Fine Romance (570813-2) 14. On the Sunny Side of the Street (630715-3) 15. Party Blues (560625-5) 16. Cotton Tail (560904-3)

For the Love of Ella Fitzgerald, Disc 2/Ballads & Blues (Verve 841-765)

1. Misty (600213-4) 2. Sophisticated Lady (560904-7) 3. Midnight Sun (641020-5) 4. Solitude (560904-6) 5. How Long, How Long Blues (631028-1) 6. I Loves You, Porgy (580425-23) 7. Summertime (600213-7) 8. Mood Indigo (571017-2) 9. Laura (641021-2) 10. Stormy Weather (610114-4) 11. Autumn in New York (570723-3) 12. These Foolish Things (571009-4) 13. I Can't Get Started (611113-4) 14. See See Rider (631028-2) 15. I Love Paris (560207-8) 16. Blues in the Night (610114-2)

Jazz 'Round Midnight/Ella Fitzgerald (Verve 314 511 035)

1. The Man I Love (590105-8) 2. Reaching for the Moon (580317-10) 3. Blue Moon (560829-1) 4. Moonlight Becomes You (590711-4) 5. Our Love Is Here to Say (590105-3) 6. With a Song in My Heart (560829-6) 7. How Deep Is the Ocean (580317-3) 8. September Song (600419-5) 9. Good Morning, Heartache (610622-6) 10. 'Round Midnight (610623-2) 11. I Got It Bad (and That Ain't Good) (570625-2) 12. One for My Baby (600419-7) 13. Cry Me a River (610624-1) 14. Do Nothin' Till You Hear from Me (560904-5)

Jazz 'Round Midnight Again/Ella Fitzgerald (Verve 314 527 032)

1. A Flower Is a Lovesome Thing (651019-3) 2. Easy To Love (560207-13) 3. Embraceable You (590108-7) 4. Midnight Sun (641020-5) 5. Misty (600414-6) 6. I Get a Kick Out of You (590209-6) 7. You've Changed (660720-8) 8. Now It Can Be Told (580317-7) 9. The Man That Got Away (600801-5) 10. Ill Wind (610115-2) 11. The Way You Look Tonight (630106-1) 12. I Didn't Know About You (570626-4) 13. Bewitched (Bothered and Bewildered) (560829-8) 14. Early Autumn (641019-5) 15. My Shining Hour (610115-1) 16. It Might As Well Be Spring (610519-4)

Jazz 'Round Midnight/Ella Fitzgerald and Louis Armstrong

(Verve 314 557 352) 1. Can't We Be Friends (560816-5) 2. I Got Plenty o' Nuttin' (570818-3) 3. They All Laughed (570723-5) 4. I've Got My Love to Keep Me Warm (570813-5) 5. Summertime (570818-1) 6. Comes Love (570723-9) 7. Under a Blanket of Blue (560816-7) 8. I Won't Dance (570813-1) 9. Don't Be That Way (570813-3) 10. Bess, You Is My Woman Now (570819-5) 11. I'm Putting All My Eggs in One Basket (570813-4) 12. April in Paris (560816-10) 13. Our Love Is Here To Stay (570723-1) 14. Stars Fell on Alabama (560816-4)

The Jazz Sides/Ella Fitzgerald/Jazz Masters 46 (Verve 314 527 655)

1. Let's Do It (560209-5) 2. Caravan (570627-3) 3. They Can't Take That Away from Me (560816-1) 4. Ev'rything I've Got Belongs to You (560904-15) 5. In a Mellow Tone (571017-1) 6. One for My Baby (600419-7) 7. You Hit the Spot (581122-1) 8. Born to Be Blue (610623-1) 9. Them There Eyes (630716-1) 10. Knock Me a Kiss (581123-1) 11. The Jersey Bounce (600622-4) 12. Black Coffee (600414-3) 13. Heah Me Talkin' to Ya (631028-5) 14. (It's Only a) Paper Moon (600801-4) 15. Passion Flower (651020-2) 16. The Music Goes 'Round and 'Round (610623-8)

Oh! Lady, Be Good! Best of the Gershwin Song Book

(Verve 314 529 581)

1. Fascinating Rhythm (590318-5) 2. 'S Wonderful (590716-1) 3. Someone to Watch Over Me (590326-2) 4. He Loves and She Loves (590105-10) 5. Oh! Lady, Be Good! (590108-7) 6. A Foggy Day (in London Town) (590105-7) 7. How Long Has This Been Going On? (590105-6) 8. Let's Call the Whole Thing Off (590326-6) 9. But Not for Me (590108-3) 10. My One and Only (590326-1) 11. I've Got a Crush on You (590108-2) 12. Nice Work If You Can Get It (590326-3) 13. The Man I Love (590105-8) 14. Funny Face (590318-4) 15. Embraceable You (590108-1) 16. They Can't Take That Away from Me (590105-5) 17. I Got Rhythm (590105-2)

Our Love Is Here to Stay/Ella Fitzgerald and Louis Armstrong Sing Gershwin (Verve 314 539 679)

1. I Got Plenty o' Nuttin' (570818-3) 2. He Loves and She Loves (590105-10) 3. A Woman Is a Sometime Thing (570819-2) 4. They Can't Take That Away from Me (560816-1) 5. Let's Call the Whole Thing Off (570723-4) 6. Strike Up the Band (590716-4) 7. Things Are Looking Up (590717-2) 8. They All Laughed (590326-10) 9. A Foggy Day (in London Town) (560816-9) 10. How Long Has This Been Going On? (570723) 11. Summertime (570818-1) 12. Our Love Is Here to Stay (570723-1) 13. There's a Boat Dat's Leavin' Soon for New York (570819-1) 14. 'S Wonderful (590716-1) 15. I Was Doing All Right (571014) 16. Oh! Lady, Be Good! (571009-9)

Pure Ella (Verve 314 539 206)

1. Mack The Knife (600213-10) 2. Blue Skies (580318-5) 3. A-Tisket, A-Tasket (610512-8) 4. They Can't Take That Away from Me (560816-1) 5. Misty (600414-6) 6. Mr. Paganini (You'll Have To Swing It) (610512-1) 7. Tea for Two (630716-9) 8. Our Love Is Here to Stay (590105-3) 9. Night and Day (560327-1) 10. My Funny Valentine (560830-8) 11. The Boy from Ipanema (650327-13) 12. Too Marvelous for Words (641021-1) 13. Take the "A" Train (570624-2) 14. Summertime (570818-1) 15. How High the Moon (600213-11) 16. All the Things You Are (630107-5) 17. Over the Rainbow (610115-3) 18. Oh! Lady, Be Good! (570929-11)

Note: Do not confuse this album with the GRP Decca Jazz (GRD-636) album of the same title. See LPD-20 and LPD-27.

Quiet Now/Ella's Moods (Verve 314 559 736)

1. Prelude to a Kiss (560904-10) 2. Detour Ahead (590325-8) 3. Let's Do It (560209-5) 4. I Cried for You (600414-5) 5. I Concentrate on You (560208-4) 6. Spring Can Really Hang You Up the Most (610622-3) 7. Black Coffee (600414-3) 8. Cry Me a River (610624-1) 9. Bewitched, Bothered and Bewildered (560829-8) 10. How Deep Is the Ocean (580317-3) 11. Dream a Little Dream of Me (630716-2) 12. Lush Life (571017-4)

The Silver Collection/The Song Books (Verve 823 445)

1. Oh! Lady, Be Good! (590108-7) 2. My Funny Valentine (560830-8) 3. Fascinatin' Rhythm (590318-5) 4. Puttin' on the Ritz (580318-9) 5. Skylark (641020-3) 6. Can't Help Lovin' Dat Man (630106-2) 7. Manhattan (560829-3) 8. (It's Only a) Paper Moon (600801-4) 9. All the Things You Are (630107-5) 10. Laura (641021-2) 11. Come Rain or Come Shine (610116-5) 12. Over the Rainbow (610115-3) 13. This Time the Dream's on Me (610115-4) 14. Alexander's Ragtime Band (580319-1) 15. Nice Work If You Can Get It (590326-3) 16. The Lady Is a Tramp (560821-2) 17. Yesterdays (630106-3) 18. Cheek to Cheek (580318-3) 19. Have You Met Miss Jones? (560830-4)

Ultimate Ella Fitzgerald (Selected by Joe Williams)

(Verve 314 539 054)

1. A-Tisket, A-Tasket (610512-8) 2. Oh! Lady, Be Good! (590108-7) 3. Lullaby of Birdland (540917-2) 4. Angel Eyes (600414-2) 5. Imagine My Frustration (651017-2) 6. Midnight Sun (641020-5) 7. Mack The Knife (600213-10) 8. Bess, You Is My Woman Now (570818-2) 9. How High the Moon (600213-11) 10. All Too Soon (570627-2) 11. Blue Skies (580318-5) 12. Mr. Paganini (610512-1) 13. There's a Lull in My Life (571015-1) 14. Robbins' Nest (490918-1) 15. Lush Life (571017-4) 16. Too Close for Comfort (560625-2)

A Special Decca Jazz-Verve Collaboration/Ella Fitzgerald: Something to Live For (Verve 314 547 800)

(2-CD Set)

1. A-Tisket, A-Tasket (380502-1) 2. You Showed Me

the Way (370324-4) 3. Stairway to the Stars (390502-2) 4. How High the Moon (471220-4) 5. Perdido (490918-12) 6. Can Anyone Explain? (duet with Louis Armstrong) (500825-2) 7. Ella's Contribution to the Blues (520811-4) 8. But Not for Me (500912-1) 9. Thanks for the Memory (550401-1) 10. Ridin' High (560207-1) 11. Ev'ry Time We Say Goodbye (560207-10) 12. Angel Eyes (570724-11) 13. Goody Goody (570724-8) 14. Oh! Lady, Be Good! (571009-9) 15. The Lady Is a Tramp (560821-2) 16. Body and Soul (570704-3) 17. Airmail Special (570704-11) 18. Midnight Sun (571015-11) 19. Summertime (600213-7) 20. Mack the Knife (600213-10) 21. Misty (600414-6) 22. The Man I love (590105-8) 23. Mr. Paganini (You'll Have To Swing It) (610512-1) 24. 'Round Midnight (610623-2) 25. Bill Bailey, Won't You Please Come Home (620629-23)* 26. Yesterdays (630106-3) 27. Lover Man (660720-10)* 28. Duke's Place (651018-3) 29. Sweet Georgia Brown (660729-6) 30. Something to Live For (660729-4)

*All tracks included in this set have appeared previously on compact disc, except tracks 25 and 27. The former appears on the LP album, **Verve's Choice!/The Best of Ella Fitzgerald** (cf. LPD-73), and the latter on the LP album, **Whisper Not** (cf. LPD-84). Refer to PART ONE: THE RECORDING SESSIONS/A DISCOGRAPHY for details.

This special compilation was released in November 1999 as a companion to the **Thirteen WNET/New York** television station **American Masters** series production, **Ella Fitzgerald: Something to Live For.** The 90-minute special was premiered on Wednesday, 5 November 1999, at the Auditorium Saint-Germain-des Près in Paris, subsequently airing on France inter television on 21 and 28 November.

The program was broadcast in the U.S. on public television stations throughout the nation, first in Chicago (WTTW) on 27 November, and then through December at some thirty other stations. It is expected that this program will be made available on VHS video tape and on DVD video disc in 2000.

THE PABLO YEARS

The Best of Ella Fitzgerald (LP: Pablo PBM 001/CD: Pablo PACD-2405-421)

1. Dreamer (Vivo Sonhando) (800917-1) 2. You're Blasé (730828-4) 3. Fine and Mellow (740108-1) 4. Honeysuckle Rose (790215-1) 5. I Wonder Where Our Love Has Gone (820204-3)* 6. Street of Dreams (750519-8) 7. I'm Walkin' (780619-1) 8. This Love That I've Found (Só Tinha de Ser Com Você) (800917-2) 9. I'm Getting Sentimental Over You (790215-6) 10. Any Old Time (820204-5)* 11. How Long Has This Been Going On? (750519-2) 12. Since I Fell for You (780619-6)* 13. Don't Be That Way (820204-1) 14. You Go to My Head (730828-8)*

*On Compact Disc only

Bluella: Ella Fitzgerald Sings the Blues (Pablo PACD 2310-960)

1. Smooth Sailing (531118-8) 2. Duke's Place (660208-5) .3. St. Louis Blues (710721-9) 4. C-Jam Blues (720602-14) 5. Fine and Mellow (740108-1) 6. Happy Blues (740411-6) 7. Billie's Bounce (770714-9) 8. I'm Walkin' (780619-1) 9. Fine and Mellow (790712-7) 10. St. Louis Blues (790712-13) 11. Basella (790712-14)

Ella's Records: An Alphabetical Listing

The artist designation "Ella Fitzgerald" appears on the face of almost all albums. In this index, the name is omitted unless it is a part of the title of the album. Albums in **ELLA'S RECORDS/IV** (The Ella Collections) are not assigned LPD numbers; they, therefore, are indexed here simply as "IV." *Indicates album is on LP only; all others are on CD.

The Early Years/Part 1 (1935–1938) (GRP Decca Jazz GRD-2-618) LPD-1

The Early Years/Part 2 (1939–1941) (GRP Decca Jazz GRD-2-623) LPD-2

"Easy Living"/Ella Fitzgerald and Joe Pass (Pablo PACD 2310 921) LPD-119

18 Top Tracks/CD Jazz/Ella Fitzgerald (Frequenz 044-006) LPD-50

Ella (Reprise 9 20623) LPD-94

Ella/The Concert Years (Pablo 4CD-4414) LPD-118

Ella à Nica (Original Jazz Classics OJCCD 442) LPD-97

Ella Abraça Jobim/The Antonio Carlos Jobim Song Book (Pablo PACD 2630 201) LPD-113

Ella and Basie!/On the Sunny Side of the Street (Verve 314 539 059) LPD-74

Ella and Basie/A Perfect Match (Pablo Today 2312 110) LPD-111

Ella and Friends (GRP Decca Jazz GRD 663) IV

Ella and Her Fellas (Decca DL 8832)* LPD-22

Ella and Louis/Ella Fitzgerald and Louis Armstrong (Verve 314 537 2842) LPD-44

Ella and Louis Again/Ella Fitzgerald and Louis Armstrong (Verve 314 537 284) LPD-48

Ella and Oscar (Pablo PACD 2310 759) LPD-104

Ella and Pass … Again (Pablo PACD 2310 772) LPD-106

Ella at Duke's Place (Verve 314 529 700) LPD-82

Ella at Juan-les Pins(Verve MG V-4065) LPD-78

Ella at the Opera House (Verve 821 269) LPD-49

Ella Fitzgerald/Verve Jazz Masters 6 (Verve 314 519 822) IV

Ella Fitzgerald and André Previn Do Gershwin/Nice Work If You Can Get It (Pablo 2312 140) LPD-116

Ella Fitzgerald and Bing Crosby/My Happiness (Parrot PARCD 002) LPD-153

Ella Fitzgerald and Cole Porter/Dream Dancing (Pablo PACD 2310 814) LPD-108

Ella Fitzgerald and Joe Pass/"Easy Living" (Pablo PACD 2310 921) LPD-119

Ella Fitzgerald and Joe Pass/"Speak Love" (Pablo PACD 2310 888) LPD-115

Ella Fitzgerald and Louis Armstrong/Ella and Louis (Verve 314 527 2842) LPD-44

Ella Fitzgerald and Louis Armstrong/Ella and Louis Again (Verve 314 537 284) LPD-48

Ella Fitzgerald and Louis Armstrong/Verve Jazz Masters 24 (Verve 314 521 851) IV

Ella Fitzgerald and Louis Armstrong Sing Gershwin/Our Love Is Here to Stay (Verve 314 539 679) IV

Ella Fitzgerald — Count Basie — Joe Williams/One O'-Clock Jump (Verve 314 559 806) LPD-130

Ella Fitzgerald/Duke Ellington/The Stockholm Concert, 1966 (Jazz World JWD 102.213) LPD-83

Ella Fitzgerald in Budapest (Pablo PACD 5308) LPD-95

Ella Fitzgerald in Concert with Roy Eldridge and the

Tommy Flanagan Trio (The Jazz Collection JCD 01) LPD-79

Ella Fitzgerald in Edinburgh (CT only/no number) LPD-146

Ella Fitzgerald/In the Groove (Buddha Records 74465 99702 0) LPD-162

Ella Fitzgerald Jams/Fine and Mellow (Pablo PACD 2310 829) LPD-102

Ella Fitzgerald on the Air/The Complete 1940 Broadcasts (Masters of Jazz MJCD 137/138) LPD-151

Ella Fitzgerald on the Air, Volume 3/1944–1947 (Masters of Jazz MJCD 169) LPD-161

Ella Fitzgerald Sings/Count Basie Plays/"A Classy Pair" (Pablo Today PACD 2310 132) LPD-110

Ella Fitzgerald Sings Songs from *Let No Man Write My Epitaph*/The Intimate Ella (Verve 839 838) LPD-62

Ella Fitzgerald Sings Sweet Songs for Swingers (Verve MG V-4032)* LPD-58

Ella Fitzgerald Sings the Blues/Bluella (Pablo PACD 2310 960) IV

Ella Fitzgerald Sings the Cole Porter Song Book (Verve 314 537 257) LPD-41

Ella Fitzgerald Sings the Duke Ellington Song Book (Verve 314 559 248) LPD-51

Ella Fitzgerald Sings the George and Ira Gershwin Song Book (Verve 314 539 759) LPD-59

Ella Fitzgerald Sings the Harold Arlen Song Book (Verve 314 519 845) LPD-64

Ella Fitzgerald Sings the Irving Berlin Song Book (Verve 314 519 841) LPD-53

Ella Fitzgerald Sings the Jerome Kern Song Book (Verve 314 519 841) LPD-53

Ella Fitzgerald Sings the Jerome Kern Song Book (Verve 825 669) LPD-72

Ella Fitzgerald Sings the Johnny Mercer Song Book (Verve 314 539 057) LPD-80

Ella Fitzgerald Sings the Rodgers and Hart Song Book (Verve 314 537 258) LPD-45

Ella Fitzgerald with Chick Webb/Swingsation (GRP Decca Jazz GRD 9921) IV

Ella Fitzgerald with Skitch Henderson and His Orchestra/The Big Bands' Greatest Vocalists (Joyce 6045)* LPD-136

Ella Fitzgerald with The Tommy Flanagan Trio (Laswerlight 17 109) LPD-143

Ella Fitzgerald with The Tommy Flanagan Trio/Montreux '77 (Fantasy OJCCD 376) LPD-107

Ella Fitzgerald's Christmas (Capitol CDP 7 94452) LPD-90

Ella in Hamburg (Verve POCJ 2649) LPD-81

Ella in Hollywood with The Lou Levy Quartet (Verve POCJ-2647) LPD-66

Live at Birdland, 1950–1952, The Enchanting Ella Fitzgerald (Baldwin Street Music BJH 309)   LPD-162

Live at the Greek Theatre, Los Angeles/Duke Ellington and Ella Fitzgerald (Status 1013)   LPD-87

Live from The Cave Supper Club, Vancouver, B.C. (Jazz Band EBCD 2144)

Louis Armstrong/"Because of You" (Ambassador CLA 1918)   LPD-126

Love Songs: The Best of the Verve Song Books (Verve 831 762) IV

Lullabies of Birdland (MCA Universal MCLD 19365)   LPD-36

Mack the Knife/The Complete Ella in Berlin (Verve 314 519 564)   LPD-61

Memories (MCA 734)*   LPD-33

Metronome All-Stars, 1956 (Verve MG V-8030)*   LPD-42

Miss Ella Fitzgerald and Mr. Gordon Jenkins Invite You to Listen and Relax (Decca DL 8696)*   LPD-27

Misty Blue (Capitol CDP 7 95152)   LPD-91

The Montreux Collection (Pablo PACD 5306)   LPD-137

Montreux Jazz Festival, 1975/Ella (Fantasy OJCCD 789)   LPD-105

Montreux '77/Ella Fitzgerald with The Tommy Flanagan Trio (Fantasy OJCCD 376)   LPD-107

My Happiness/Ella Fitzgerald and Bing Crosby (Parrot PARCD 002)   LPD-153

Newport, Ella Fitzgerald and Billie Holiday at (Verve 314 559 809)   LPD-47

Newport Jazz Festival/Live at Carnegie Hall, 5 July 1973 (Legacy/Columbia C2K 66809)   LPD-100

Nice Work If You Can Get It/Ella Fitzgerald and André Previn Do Gershwin (Pablo 2312 140)   LPD-116

Oh! Lady, Be Good!/Best of the Gershwin Song Book (Verve 314 529 581) IV

On the Air, Volume 3/1944–1947 (Masters of Jazz MJCD 169)   LPD-161

On the Sunny Side of the Street/Ella and Basie! (Verve 314 539 059)   LPD-74

One Night Stand with Stan Kenton and Music '55 (Joycde 1130)*   LPD-155

One O'Clock Jump/Ella Fitzgerald — Count Basie — Joe Williams (Verve 314 559 806)   LPD-130

Our Love Is Here to Stay/Ella Fitzgerald and Louis Armstrong Sing Gershwin (Verve 314 539 679) IV

A Perfect Match/Ella and Basie (Pablo Today PACD 2312 110)   LPD-111

Pete Kelly's Blues/Peggy Lee and Ella Fitzgerald (Decca DL 8166)*   LPD-38

Porgy and Bess/Ella Fitzgerald and Louis Armstrong (Verve 314 537 284)   LPD-57

Priceless Jazz Collection/Ella Fitzgerald (GRP GRD 9870) IV

Priceless Jazz Collection/More Ella Fitzgerald (GRP GRD 9916) IV

Pure Ella (GRP Decca Jazz GRD 636) IV

Pure Ella/Ella Sings Gershwin (GRP Decca Jazz GRD 636)   LPD-21

Pure Ella (Verve 314 539 206) IV

Quiet Now/Ella's Moods (Verve 314 559 736) IV

Return to Happiness/Jazz At The Philharmonic/Yoyogi National Stadium, Tokyo, 1983 (Pablo PACD 2620 117)   LPD-117

Rhythm Is My Business (Verve 314 559 513)   LPD-69

Rodgers and Hart Song Book, Ella Fitzgerald Sings the (Verve 314 537 258)   LPD-45

Route 66/Capitol Sings Coast to Coast (Capitol D103060)   LPD-135

Royal Roost Sessions with The Ray Brown Trio and Quintet (Cool N' Blue 9117)   LPD-152

The Saturday Night Swing Club Is on the Air (Fanfare 17-117)*   LPD-148

The Setting Sun (Film Soundtrack) (RCA Japan VICP 8084)   LPD-139

75th Birthday Anniversary Celebration (GRP Decca Jazz GRD-2-619)   LPD-3

The Silver Collection/The Song Books (Verve 823 445) IV

Sinatra/The Soundtrack Sessions (Bravura BRCD 7106)   LPD-128

Sinatra: The Television Years (Bravura BRCD 105)   LPD-158

Smooth Sailing (Decca DL 4887)*   LPD-37

Só Danço Samba (Jazz Birdies of Paradise)   LPD-140

The Song Books/The Silver Collection (Verve 823 445) IV

Songs in a Mellow Mood/Pure Ella (GRP Decca Jazz GRD-636)   LPD-29

The Soundtrack Sessions/Sinatra (Bravura BRCD 7106)   LPD-128

Souvenir Album (Decca DL 5084)*   LPD-15

"Speak Love"/Ella Fitzgerald and Joe Pass (Pablo PACD 2310 888)   LPD-115

Stairway to the Stars (Decca DL 4446)*   LPD-16

The Stockholm Concert, 1966/Ella Fitzgerald/Duke Ellington (Jazz World JWD 102.213)   LPD-83

Sunshine of Your Love (Verve 314 533 102)   LPD-93

Sweet and Hot (MCA/Universal MCLD 19365)   LPD-34

Sweet Songs for Swingers, Ella Fitzgerald Sings (Verve MG V-4032)*   LPD-58

Swing Into Spring/The Classic NBC Broadcast of April 9, 1958 (Sandy Hook 2057)   LPD-156

Swing Into Spring/The Classic CBS Broadcast of April 10, 1959 (A&R 2000/2001)*   LPD-157

Take Love Easy (Pablo PACD 2310 702)   LPD-101

That's My Desire (Blue Moon BMCD 3012) LPD-24

These Are the Blues (Verve 829 536) LPD-75

Things Ain't What They Used to Be (and You Better Believe It) (Reprise 9 26023) LPD-96

30 by Ella (Capitol CDP 7 48333) LPD-93

Ultimate Ella Fitzgerald (Selected by Joe Williams) (Verve 314 539 054) IV

U.S. All Stars in Berlin, February 1955 (Jazz Band EBCD 2113) LPD-154

Verve Elite Edition Collector's Disc (Verve 314 547 265) LPD-134

Verve Jazz Masters 6/Ella Fitzgerald (Verve 314 519 822) IV

Verve Jazz Masters 24/Ella Fitzgerald and Louis Armstrong (Verve 314 521 851) IV

Verve Jazz Masters 46/The Jazz Sides/Ella Fitzgerald (Verve 314 527 655) IV

Verve's Choice: The Best of Ella Fitzgerald (Verve MG V-4063)* LPD-73

The War Years (1941–1947) (GRP Decca Jazz GRD-2-628) LPD-4

Whisper Not (Verve V-4071)* LPD-84

Part Three

The Songs Ella Sings

Annotated Song Index

Here, listed alphabetically, are the songs that Ella sings, all 1117 of them, a unique panorama of American popular music in the 20th century. The list comprises more titles than have ever been recorded by another singer. For this there are several reasons: First, Ella had a longer recording career than has any other singer, from 12 June 1935 until the spring of 1991, almost fifty-six years. Second, her manager, Norman Granz, recorded, or had others record, a great many of her concert performances, not a few of which were released on records. Third, Ella liked to experiment, recording the material of the day, sometimes not necessarily suited to her voice or personality, although as one pundit remarked, "Ella could sing a telephone book and make it sound good." She worked very hard at expanding her repertoire, listened to many other singers on radio and television, and when she found a song she liked, she wanted to record it. Also, in her years at Decca, she was assigned material according to her popularity. The more popular her recordings, the more songs she was required to record, and for a while, she was the most popular singer in America. Perceiving that her talent was being wasted on material of little consequence, Norman Granz eventually bought out her contract with Decca, and founded the Verve label especially for the purpose of presenting her in a new persona, both as a performer on records and as a performer on the concert stage.

This index lists the songs in her repertoire, their copyright dates, the lyricists and composers, and short notes about their origins and performance histories.

The index is cross-indexed with **Part One: The Recording Sessions — A Discography**, giving the Discographer Reference Number (DRN), so that it becomes a simple matter to find a certain performance in the discography, as well as determining when and where she sang each song. The DRN is printed in bold text for those songs that have been released on record, and in standard text for those that are as yet unreleased. The index does not pretend to list all of Ella's performances, for there are many, many concert performances that have never been considered for release, but were recorded nevertheless as an archival source.

There are 2279 known recorded performances listed, and these may well be supplemented by half that many more undocumented in the vaults, although it is doubtful that few, if any, new titles will be discovered.

The titles have been carefully researched, and sometimes the title given in this index is not the same as it appears on an album or on a record, although alternative titles are also indexed. Information about the songs comes from many sources, some more reliable than others. If readers discover errors or misinformation, please write to the author of this volume in care of the publisher, whose address is given on the publication page in the front of the book, and any corrections or additional information will be given to those who request it.

A Felicidade (1959)

Lyrics and music by Vinícius de Moraes, Andre Salvet and Antonio Carlos Jobim

Written especially for the award-winning 1959 Brazilian film *Orfeu Negro (Black Orpheus)*. First titled "Adieu, Tristesse," the song acquired the present title with de Moraes's lyrics.   621001-4, **800917-3**

Abide with Me (1861)

Lyrics by Henry Francis Lyte, music by William Henry Monk

There are two conflicting traditions about the origin of this famous hymn. The first — and the rather more plausible one — is that Rev. Lyte, an Anglican clergyman, wrote the poem in 1820 after attending the deathbed of a friend who, as he lay dying, implored him ceaselessly, "Abide with me." The other story is that Rev. Lyte wrote the poem a little more than two months before his own death. The music was composed by the Rev. Dr. Monk for the first edition of *Hymns, Ancient and Modern* (1861), of which he was the first musical editor. According to Dr. Monk's widow, the tune, first called "Eventide," was composed in 1847 as she and her husband watched a sunset.   **670200-4**

**Ac-Cent-Tchu-Ate the Positive
[Mister In-Between]** (1944)

Lyrics by Johnny Mercer, music by Harold Arlen

The title came about, according to one story, from a newspaper clipping sent to Mercer by a friend who quoted the Harlem revivalist preacher, Father Divine, using the phrase. Introduced by Bing Crosby and Sonny Tufts in the 1944 Paramount film *Here Come the WAVES*. Best-selling records by Bing Crosby and The Andrews Sisters (Decca), and Johnny Mercer (Capitol). Four times No. 1, during its 13 weeks on "Your Hit Parade" (1944). Nominated for an Academy Award, Best Original Song, 1945.

600801-6, 610520-9

Ace in the Hole (1941)

Lyrics and music by Cole Porter

Introduced by Mary Jane Walsh, Sunny O'Dea, Nanette Fabray, and ensemble in the 1941 musical play *Let's Face It*. Sung by Betty Hutton in the 1943 Paramount film adaptation. (This song is not to be confused with the piano-bar sing-along song of the same title by George E. Mitchell and James E. Dempsey (1926), and recorded so memorably by Johnny Mercer and Bobby Darin in their Capitol album *Two of a Kind*.)   **560208-7**

Across the Alley from the Alamo (1947)

Lyrics and music by Joe Green

Introduced by The Mills Brothers (Decca). Sometimes confused with the 1922 hit, "On the Alamo," by Gus Kahn and Isham Jones.

470806-1, 580810-5, 610512-4, 610519-22

Adeste Fideles *see* **O Come, All Ye Faithful**.

(What Can I Say) After I Say I'm Sorry? (1926)

Lyrics and music by Abe Lyman and Walter Donaldson

Introduced by Abe Lyman and His Orchestra. Sung with great success by torch-singer Ruth Etting. Sung by Peggy Lee in the 1955 Warner Bros. film *Pete Kelly's Blues*.
391012-2, 680603-1f

After You— Who? (1932)

Lyrics and music by Cole Porter.

Introduced by Fred Astaire in the 1933 musical play *The Gay Divorce*. Mr. Astaire repeated his performance in the 1934 RKO film adaptation, *The Gay Divorcée*.

780213-2

After You've Gone (1918)

Lyrics by Henry Creamer, music by Turner Layton

The song became a hit with Al Jolson's performance at the Winter Garden (New York), and with Sophie

Tucker's use in her vaudeville act. Louis Armstrong scored his first major success with this song (Okeh). Performed by Larry Parks (dubbed by Al Jolson) on the soundtrack of the 1949 Columbia film *Jolson Sings Again*. Featured in the 1975 theatre revue *Me and Bessie*.

620130-1, 790712-5

Again (1948)

Lyrics by Dorcas Cochran, music by Lionel Newman

Introduced by Ida Lupino in the 1949 20th Century-Fox film *Roadhouse*. Vic Damone revived it in 1954 with a best selling disc (Mercury).   **490430-2**

Água de Beber [Water to Drink] (1965)

Portuguese lyrics Vinícius de Moraes, English lyrics by Norman Gimbel, music by Antonio Carlos Jobim

Introduced by Antonio Carlos Jobim. Sensational recording by Ella Fitzgerald in *Ella Abraça Jobim/The Antonio Carlos Jobim Song Book* (Pablo). **710721-4f, 800918-1**

Ah! Men! Ah! Women! (1959)

Special material by Maurice Zolotow, Ralph Burns and Benny Goodman

Introduced by Benny Goodman, Ella Fitzgerald and Peggy Lee, accompanied by André Previn at the piano during the telecast of the CBS Television Special *Swing into Spring*, on 10 April 1959, at CBS Television Studios, New York (CBS Network).   **590410-3**

Ain't Misbehavin' (1929)

Lyrics by Andy Razaf, music by Thomas "Fats" Waller and Harry Brooks

Introduced by Margaret Simms, Paul Bass, and Russel Wooding's Hallelujah Singers in the 1929 all-Black musical revue *Hot Chocolate*. Louis Armstrong's 1929 Okeh recording has become a jazz classic. In 1941 Dmitri Shostokovich "lifted" the music for the first movement of his *Symphony No. 7* ("Leningrad"). Interpolated in the 1978 muscial revue *Ain't Misbehavin'*.

630716-7, 630000-22, 790215-5, 810726-3

Ain't Nobody's Business (but My Own) (1936)

Lyrics and music by Irving Taylor

Introduced by Bessie Smith in performance and on one of her last recordings (Columbia). (Not to be confused with the more widely recorded "'Tain't Nobody's Biz-Ness If I Do," q.v.)   **500815-1**

Air Mail Special (1941)

Scat lyrics by Ella Fitzgerald, music by Benny Goodman, Jimmy Mundy, and Charlie Christian

Hit instrumental introduced by Benny Goodman and

His Orchestra (Columbia), after an earlier version by the Benny Goodman Sextet titled "Good Enough To Keep" (Okeh). Ella first recorded this in 1952, and it has since become a popular part of her concert repertoire.

520104-1, 520607-5, 560121-3, 560202-19, **560815-11, 570704-9, 610517-4**

Alexander's Ragtime Band (1911)

Lyrics and music by Irving Berlin

Introduced by performers in Columbia burlesque vaudeville shows, but nobody paid much attention to it. Recorded in 1911 by Arthur Collins, and by Byron Harland and Billy Murray. But it was diva Emma Carus's singing it in her vaudeville act in Chicago that gave Berlin his first big hit. Accusations that one of the lines in the lyric was warmongering led Berlin in 1965 to change "so natural that you want to go to war" to "so natural that you want to hear some more." **580319-1**

All By Myself (1921)

Lyrics and music by Irving Berlin

Introduced by Charles King in vaudeville at the Palace Theatre, New York. One of Berlin's most successful ballads up to that time, it sold more than a million copies of sheet music, 1,250,000 phonograph records, and 150,000 piano rolls. First recorded by Ted Lewis (Columbia). Revived by Bing Crosby in the 1946 MGM film *Blue Skies*. **580313-2**

All I Do Is Dream of You (1934)

Lyrics by Arthur Fred, music by Nacio Herb Brown

Introduced by Gene Raymond in the 1934 MGM film *Sadie McKee*. Revived by Debbie Reynolds in the 1952 MGM film *Singin' in the Rain*. **680603-1b**

All I Need Is You (1942)

Lyrics by Mitchell Parish, music by Peter DeRose and Benny Davis

Introduced by Dinah Shore (Bluebird). **420410-1**

All My Life (1936)

Lyrics by Sidney D. Mitchell, music by Sammy H. Stept

Introduced by Phil Regan in the 1936 Republic film *Laughing Irish Eyes*, and revived in the 1942 Republic film *Johnny Doughboy*. **360317-2**

All of Me (1931)

Lyrics by Seymour Simons, music by Gerald Marks

Introduced by Belle Baker in the 1932 Fox film *Careless Lady*. Revived by Frank Sinatra in the 1952 Universal film *Meet Danny Wilson*; Sinatra subsequently had one of his best sellers when he recorded it for Capitol.

611115-6, 620629-6, 620629-16, 620630-21, **831000-3**

All of You (1954)

Lyrics and music by Cole Porter

Introduced by Don Ameche in the 1955 musical play *Silk Stockings*. Sung and danced by Fred Astaire and Cyd Charisse (dubbed by Carole Richards) in the 1957 MGM film adaptation. **560209-9, 720612-6**

All or Nothing at All (1940)

Lyrics by Jack Lawrence, music by Arthur Altman

Introduced by Harry James and His Music Makers, with vocal by Frank Sinatra. This Columbia recording did only moderately well in 1940 when it was released, but with Sinatra's meteoric rise to fame in 1943, the record was revived to sell more than a million discs. **780619-3**

All Over Nothing at All (1937)

Lyrics and music by Peter Tinturin and Jack Lawrence

Introduced by Ella Fitzgerald and Her Savoy Eight (Decca). **370524-1**

All That Jazz (1975)

Lyrics by Fred Ebb, music by John Kander

Introduced by Chita Rivera and company in the 1975 musical revue *Chicago*. **890322-1**

All the Livelong Day (and the Long, Long Night) (1964)

Lyrics by Ira Gershwin, music by George Gershwin

Introduced by Ray Walston in the 1964 United Artists film *Kiss Me, Stupid*. In 1964, Ira Gershwin revised lines 9-11, refrain 2, especially for Ella's recording in *Ella Fitzgerald Sings the George and Ira Gershwin Song Book*. The original: "Believe me when this man says:/You're the Why and Wherefore/I am here to care for." The revision: "No doubt my lifelong plan says:/You're the Why and Wherefore/I was born to care for." This is one of many Gershwin melodies used posthumously to which lyrics were written by Ira Gershwin, a number of which have been recorded by Miss Fitzgerald. **641019-2**

All the Things You Are (1939)

Lyrics by Oscar Hammerstein II, music by Jerome Kern

Introduced by Herman Sherman, Frances Mercer, Hollace Shaw, and Ralph Stuart in the 1939 musical play *Very Warm for May*. Sung by Ginny Simms in the 1944 MGM film adaptation *Broadway Rhythm*, the only song from the Broadway show to be used in the film. Two consecutive weeks as No. 1 of its eleven weeks on "Your Hit Parade" (1939). **630107-5**

All Through the Night (1934)

Lyrics and music by Cole Porter

Introduced by Bettina Hall and William Gaxton in the

1934 musical play *Anything Goes*. Bing Crosby sang it in both the 1936 and the 1956 Paramount film adaptations.
560208-4

All Too Soon (1940)

Lyrics by Carl Sigman, music by Duke Ellington

Introduced by Duke Ellington and His Orchestra (Victor).   **570627-2, 660729-1, 760130-1**

(It's) Almost Like Being in Love (1947)

Lyrics by Alan Jay Lerner, music by Frederick Loewe

Introduced by David Brooks and Marion Bell in the 1947 musical play *Brigadoon*. Sung by Gene Kelly in the 1954 MGM film adaptation.   **470929-1, 621004-1**

Alone Together (1932)

Lyrics by Howard Dietz, music by Arthur Schwartz

Introduced by Jean Sargent and danced by Clifton Webb and Tamara Geva in the 1932 musical play *Flying Colors*. First recorded by Leo Reisman and His Orchestra.   **611114-2**

Alright, Okay, You Win (1955)

Lyrics and music by Sid Wyche and Mamie Watts

Introduced by Count Basie and His Orchestra, vocal by Joe Williams (Crest).   **690200-5, 690729-7**

Always (1925)

Lyrics and music by Irving Berlin

Introduced by Gladys Clark and Henry Gergman in vaudeville. One story avers that this is one of several ballads written under the stimulus of Berlin's romance with Ellin Mackay whom he married in 1926, and to whom he presented all rights to the song as a wedding gift.
580313-5

Always True to You in My Fashion (1948)

Lyrics and music by Cole Porter

Introduced by Lisa Kirk in the 1948 musical play *Kiss Me, Kate!* Ann Miller and Tommy Rall performed it in the 1953 MGM film adaptation. The title is taken from Ernest Dowson's poem, "Cynara": "I have been faithful to thee, Cynara! in my fashion." (Johnny Mercer also consulted Dowson for "Days of Wine and Roses," q.v.)   **560208-5**

Am I Blue? (1929)

Lyrics by Grant Clark, music by Harry Akst

Introduced by Ethel Waters in the 1929 Warner Bros. film *On with the Show,* the first all-color, all-talking, all-singing musical film, and on a recording for Columbia.
610513-3, 610518-15, 610520-27a

Amor Em Paz *see* Once I Loved

And Her Tears Flowed Like Wine (1944)

Lyrics by Joe Greene, music by Stan Kenton and Charles Lawrence

Introduced with a hit Capitol record by Stan Kenton and His Orchestra, vocal by Anita O'Day.   **441106-1**

And the Angels Sing (1939)

Lyrics by Johnny Mercer, music by Ziggy Elman

Originally written as an instrumental, "Frälich in Swing," and recorded by Ziggy Elman and His Orchestra (Bluebird). Mercer wrote lyrics and the song became a hit with a recording by Benny Goodman and His Orchestra, vocal by Martha Tilton and trumpet solo by Elman (Victor). During twelve successive weeks on "Your Hit Parade" (1939), four weeks as No. 1.
560121-1, 560202-14, **650326-5, 780620-7**

Angel Eyes (1953)

Lyrics by Earl Brent, music by Matt Dennis

Introduced by Matt Dennis in the 1953 Allied Artists film *Jennifer*. Memorable recording by Frank Sinatra (Capitol).

520607-2, 520626-5, 530911-5, 560815-7,
570428-2, 570724-11, 580425-9, **580425-18**,
580509-2, **600414-2**, 620630-17, **650326-8**

Angels We Have Heard on High (Ancient)

Lyrics are traditional Latin; music, an old French tune

There is a tradition that Pope Telesphorus (A.D. 125-136?) ordained that all should sing this hymn on Christmas: "On the birth of the Lord, masses should be said at night … and the angelic hymn — that is, 'Gloria in Excelsis Deo'— should be said before the sacrifice." Others say that the custom did not originate until the Third Century at the very earliest. The music is that of an old French carol whose authorship is lost in the mists of time. **670717-3**

Any Old Blues (1973)

Lyrics and music by Ella Fitzgerald

Introduced by Ella in her concert appearances. First recorded at the Jazz At The Philharmonic 1973 concert at Carnegie Hall, and issued on Columbia Jazz Masterpieces series (Legacy/Columbia C2K 66809) *Ella Fitzgerald/Newport Jazz Festival/Live at Carnegie Hall, July 5, 1973.*
730705-14

Any Old Time (1938)

Lyrics and music by Artie Shaw

Introduced by Billie Holiday with Artie Shaw and His Orchestra (Bluebird).   **820204-4**

Anything Goes (1934)

Lyrics and music by Cole Porter

Introduced by Ethel Merman and The Foursome (Marsall Smith, Ray Johnson, Del Porter and Dwight Snyder) in the 1934 musical play *Anything Goes*. Sung by Miss Merman in the 1936 Paramount film adaptation, and by Mitzi Gaynor in the 1956 Paramount film adaptation. **560208-9, 610211-8,** 610518-4, 610520-21, **720612-12**

April in Paris (1932)

Lyrics by E.Y. "Yip" Harburg, music by Vernon Duke

Introduced by Evelyn Hoey in the 1932 revue *Walk a Little Faster*, where it attracted little attention. The song first became successful in intimate bôites of New York's East Side. Marian Chase, a society chanteuse, recorded it for Liberty, and it was this recording that was largely responsible for establishing its permanent popularity. **560625-1, 560816-10, 570428-6, 570704-8,** 580509-1, **750519-9**

Aren't You Kinda Glad We Did? (1946)

Lyrics by Ira Gershwin, music by George Gershwin

Introduced by Dick Haymes and Betty Grable in the 1947 20th Century-Fox film *The Shocking Miss Pilgrim*. Written in the early 1930s, the song never found the right spot in a Gershwin show, but Ira Gershwin liked the tune and while working on the film (with a posthumous score by George Gershwin), he adapted a new set of lyrics, "changing it from an epithalamium of the Depression to a mid-Victorian colloquy." **590718-4**

As Long As I Live (1934)

Lyrics by Ted Koehler, music by Harold Arlen

Introduced by Lena Horne and Avon Long in the revue *Cotton Club Parade*. First recorded by Harold Arlen for Victor, coupled with his "Ill Wind" from the same revue. **581123-2, 600801-3**

As Time Goes By (1931)

Lyrics and music by Herman Hupfeld

Introduced by Frances Williams in the 1931 musical revue *Everybody's Welcome*. Revived by Dooley Wilson in the 1942 Warner Bros. film *Casablanca*. **700520-6**

As You Desire Me (1932)

Lyrics and music by Allie Wrubel

A promotional song introduced by Russ Columbo to publicize the 1932 MGM film of the same title. **490423-2**

At Last (1942)

Lyrics by Mack Gordon, music by Harry Warren

Introduced by Glenn Miller and His Orchestra in the 1942 20th Century-Fox film *Sun Valley Serenade*, vocals by Lynn Bari (dubbed by Pat Friday) and Ray Eberle. Miller repeated his performance in the 1942 20th Century-Fox film *Orchestra Wives*. **830321-3**

At Long Last Love (1938)

Lyrics and music by Cole Porter

Introduced by Clifton Webb in the 1938 musical play *You Never Know*. **720612-3**

At Sundown (1927)

Lyrics and music by Walter Donaldson

Introduced by Cliff "Ukelele Ike" Edwards at the Palace Theatre in New York, with more than two million records by various artists selling during its first year. **680603-3e**

A-Tisket, A-Tasket (1938)

Lyrics and music by Ella Fitzgerald and Al Feldman (Van Alexander)

Introduced by Ella Fitzgerald and Chick Webb and His Orchestra in performance at Levaggi's nitery in Boston in April 1938, where they were broadcasting on the nightly radio. On 2 May 1938 they recorded it at Decca Recording Company studios in New York. The song went on the charts at #10 on 18 June 1938, and hit #1 two weeks later, remaining on the hit parade for a total of 19 weeks. This was Ella's first big success, and it made her a star; by November the same year, she was voted the most popular female vocalist in America. The song was revived in 1942, when she performed it in her first movie role, a maid in the Universal film *Ride 'Em, Cowboy,* an Abbott and Costello starrer that assured a wide audience. It had sold more than a million records by 1950. The song was proposed by Ella, and she and Al Feldman worked on a rewrite of the lyrics which Ella remembered as a poem from her childhood. Ella, with the reworking of the lyric and the success of the song, was proudly admitted to ASCAP in 1939. **380502-1, 390815-1, 391200-1, 400122-1, 400125-1, 400226-1, 400304-1, 400325-1, 440410-1, 450228-1, 490918-10,** 560202-17, **570724-5, 610512-8,** 610513-9, 610518-21, 61-0520-2, 610519-23, 630000-18, 640800-18, **730705-1, 730705-18, 730705-21**

Autumn in New York (1934)

Lyrics and music by Vernon Duke

Introduced by J. Harold Murray in the finale of the 1935 revue *Thumbs Up!* Like Duke's "April in Paris," this song had to wait a number of years before achieving recognition, which came chiefly through a recording by Louella Hogan. **570723-3, 820205-3**

Away in a Manger (Luther's Cradle Hymn) (Ancient)

Lyrics by an unknown author; music, probably, by James R. Murray

This hymn was for many years attributed to Martin Luther. Investigations by Richard Hill in the 1940s proved that Luther had nothing to do with the carol. In an amusing article, "Not So Far Away in the Manger," Mr. Hill finally traced the first appearance of the two verses to *A Little Children's Book for Schools and Families*, published in 1885 under the auspices of the Evangelical Lutheran Church in North America. Here, the verses were unattributed and set to an obscure hymn, "St. Kilda," by J.E. Clark. The third stanza was added later, and even its authorship is uncertain. In 1887, James R. Murray, the American harmonizer, in *Dainty Songs for Little Lads and Lasses*, called the poem "Luther's Cradle Hymn" (composed by Martin Luther for his children and still sung by German mothers to their little ones). This was complete fabrication. The source of the tune is still unknown, but it was likely composed by a member of the German Lutheran colony of Pennsylvania. Certain authorities attribute it to Carl Müller.) **670718-2**

Azure (1937)

Lyrics by Irving Mills, music by Duke Ellington

Introduced with a very successful recording by Duke Ellington and His Orchestra (Master), and has become a standard in his repertoire. **560904-13, 651018-4, 660727-1**

B-flat Blues (Music '55) (1955)

Scat lyrics by Ella Fitzgerald, music by N. Etaoin*

Originally a Jazz At The Philharmonic instrumental standard, Ella adds her touch to a composition that is the result of the combined talents of the J.A.T.P. All-Stars who performed it. There are at least three recorded versions.

*"Etaoin" is a typesetter's placeholder, used when a word in a manuscript is indecipherable, and is replaced when the proper word is found. Used by some music publishers to indicate multiple composers. **550913-1**

Babalu [Ba-Ba-Lu] (1939)

English lyrics by Bob Russell, Spanish lyrics and music by Margarita Lecuona.

Introduced by Xavier Cugat and His Orchestra, who also performed it in the 1944 MGM film *Two Girls and a Sailor*. Its chief success was due to Miguelito Valdés, with whom it was identified and who sang it in the 1945 RKO film *Pan-Americana*. The song later became something of a trademark for Desi Arnaz. **530911-7**

Baby (1954)

Lyrics by Floyd Huddleston, music by Robert Colby

Introduced by Ella Fitzgerald with Gordon Jenkins and His Orchestra on a successful Decca recording, and then became a part of their album *Ella Fitzgerald and Gordon Jenkins Invite You To Listen and Relax.* **540325-2**

Baby, Bye-Bye (1964)

Lyrics and music by John Delafose

Introduced by John Delafose and The Eunice Playboys on a Rounder record. This may be Ella's only foray into Cajun music, and it seems a shame that that this track has never been released. **660914-9**

Baby Doll (1951)

Lyrics by Johnny Mercer, music by Harry Warren

Introduced by Fred Astaire and Vera-Ellen (dubbed by Anita Ellis) in the 1952 MGM film *The Belle of New York*. **511126-1**

Baby, Don't You Quit Now (1989)

Lyrics by Johnny Mercer, music by Jimmy Rowles

Mr. Rowles was Ella's accompanist on piano, and part of her trio, on many concert engagements. She liked the tune, and prevailed upon Johnny Mercer to write a lyric, which he obligingly wrote especially for her. **890320-2**

Baby, It's Cold Outside (1948)

Lyrics and music by Frank Loesser

Never intending it for public consumption, Loesser wrote this song for performances at private gatherings; however, he interpolated it in his score for the 1949 MGM film *Neptune's Daughter*, where it was introduced by Esther Williams and Ricardo Montalban (and repeated as a comedy reprise by Red Skelton and Betty Garrett). Eight weeks on "Your Hit Parade" in 1949. Won an Academy Award for Best Original Song, 1949. **490428-5**

Baby, What Else Can I Do? (1939)

Lyrics by Walter Hirsch, music by Gerald Marks

Introduced by Ella Fitzgerald and Her Famous Orchestra, vocal by Ella Fitzgerald.

390921-2, 391012-3, 540329-2

Baby, Won't You Please Come Home? (1919)

Lyrics by Charles Warfield, music by Clarence Williams

Introduced with great success in night clubs by Eva Taylor with Clarence Williams at the piano. Revived in 1932 by The Mills Brothers (Brunswick). Jimmy Lunceford's recording (Columbia) has become a jazz classic.

400215-1, 610516-6, 610520-27c, 610520-28

Baby, Won't You Say You Love Me? (1950)

Lyrics by Mack Gordon, music by Joseph Myrow

Introduced by Betty Grable in the 1950 20th Century-Fox film *Wabash Avenue.* **500202-1**

Back in Your Own Back Yard (1928)

Lyrics and music by Al Jolson, Billy Rose, and Dave Dreyer

Introduced by Al Jolson in vaudeville performances with different lyrics, entitled "It's Nobody's Fault but Mine." With new lyrics (1928), introduced by Paul Ash and His Orchestra. Sung by Al Jolson (dubbed for Larry Parks) in the 1949 Columbia Pictures film *Jolson Sings Again* **501230-5**

Basella (1979)

Scat lyrics by Ella Fitzgerald, music by Duke Ellington

This is Ella's special material, using Ellington's "C-Jam Blues" and her own special lyrics and scat as a tribute to Count Basie, with whom she recorded it. **790712-14**

Basin Street Blues (1928)

Lyrics and music by Spencer Williams

Introduced by Louis Armstrong and His Orchestra. A very succesful Columbia recording was made in 1931 by a group calling itself The Charleston Chasers; among the personnel were Benny Goodman (leader and clarinet), Glenn Miller (arranger and trombone), Gene Krupa (drums), and Jack Teagarden (vocals and trombone). **490918-6, 490920-4, 501129-1**, 521015-1

Be Anything (but Be Mine) (1952)

Lyrics and music by Irving Gordon

Introduced by Eddy Howard on a best-selling Mercury record in 1952. **520816-2**

Beale Street Blues (Beale Street) (1916)

Lyrics and music by W.C. Handy

Introduced by Prince's Orchestra. First ecorded in 1927 by Alberta Hunter. Danny Thomas's song, "Bring Back Our Beale Street Blues," was written when Beale Street in Memphis, Tennessee, was renamed Beale Avenue. **560208-1**

The Beanbag Song (1951)

Lyrics by Martin DeLugg, music by Anne Renfer DeLugg

Introduced with a successful recording by Ella Fitzgerald (Decca). **510112-2**

Beat Me, Daddy, Eight to the Bar (1940)

Lyrics and music by Don Raye, Hughie Prince and Eleanor Sheehy

Introduced by Will Bradley and His Orchestra, vocal by Ray McKinley (Columbia). **590903-3**

A Beautiful Friendship (1956)

Lyrics by Stanley Styne, music by Donald Kahn

Introduced by Ella Fitzgerald on a Verve recording. (Lyricist Stanley Styne is son of composer Jule Styne; composer Donald Kahn is the son of lyricist Gus Kahn.) **560327-2, 560815-2**

Be-Bop Boogie [Boppin' Boogie]/[Re-Bop Boogie] (1946)

Scat lyrics by Ella Fitzgerald, music by Benny Carter

Introduced by Benny Carter and His Orchestra (Deluxe). **481204-4**

Because of Rain (1951)

Lyrics and music by Ruth Roll, Nat "King" Cole, and Bill Harrington

Introduced by Nat "King" Cole on a Capitol recording. **510327-3**

Begin the Beguine (1935)

Lyrics and music by Cole Porter

Introduced by June Knight in the 1935 musical play *Jubilee.* It made little impression at the time, **except**: Artie Shaw in 1936 was contracted by RCA Victor to record for the Bluebird label. He was advised to make a swing version of "Indian Love Call" (Jeanette MacDonald and Nelson Eddy were very big in 1936) but consented only on the condition that he be permitted to record the then little known "Begin the Beguine" on the flip side. "I just happened to like it," he explained later, "so I insisted on recording it at the first session in spite of the recording manager who thought it was a complete waste of time." Shaw's recording sold two million records, becoming one of the largest-sellinng instrumentals by an American band in recording history. In 1963, the song was selected by ASCAP as one of sixteen numbers in its All-Time Hit Parade during the first half-century of its existence. **560208-3, 720602-2**

(I've Got) Beginner's Luck (1936)

Lyrics by Ira Gershwin, music by George Gershwin

Introduced by Fred Astaire in the 1937 RKO film *Shall We Dance*, and popularized by Mr. Astaire on a Brunswick recording. **590105-11**

Bei Mir Bist du Schoen (1933)

Yiddish lyrics by Jacob Jacobs, English lyrics (1937) by Sammy Cahn and Saul Chaplinn, music by Sholom Secunda

Introduced by Aaron Lebedoff in the 1933 Yiddish musical play *I Would If I Could*, with the title "Bei Mir Bistu Schön." The new version was Sammy Cahn's first big song hit, popularized in a Decca recording by The Andrews Sisters. Two weeks in the #1 spot of its 9-week tenure in 1938 on "Your Hit Parade." **371221-1**

Benny's Coming Home on Saturday (1945)

Lyrics and music by Allan Roberts and Doris Fisher

Introduced by Ella Fitzgerald on a Decca recording.
450829-2

Bernie's Tune (1953)

Lyrics and music by Bernie Miller, Mike Stoller and Jerry Lieber

Introduced as an instrumental by the Gerry Mulligan Quartet (Pacific Jazz). 560202-9

Bess, You Is My Woman (1935)

Lyrics by DuBose Heyward and Ira Gershwin, music by George Gershwin

Introduced by Todd Duncan (as Porgy) and Anne Wiggins Brown (as Bess) in Act II, Scene 1, of the 1935 folk opera *Porgy and Bess*. Sung by Sidney Poitier (dubbed by Robert McFerrin) and Dorothy Dandridge (dubbed by Adele Addison) in the 1959 Columbia film adaptation.
570818-2

The Best Is Yet to Come (1959)

Lyrics by Carolyn Leigh, music by Cy Coleman

Introduced and popularized by Tony Bennett (Columbia). **820204-5**

Betcha Nickel (1939)

Lyrics and music by Ella Fitzgerald and Chick Webb

Introduced by Ella Fitzgerald and Her Famous Orchestra (Decca). **390629-1, 390716-1**, 390818-5

Between the Devil and the Deep Blue Sea (1930)

Lyrics by Ted Koehler, music by Harold Arlen

Introduced by Bill Robinson and Aida Ward in the 1931 Cotton Club revue *Rhythmania*.
521218-1c, 550427-41 610116-1, 670326-8

Bewitched, Bothered, and Bewildered (1940)

Lyrics by Lorenz Hart, music by Richard Rodgers

Introduced by Vivienne Segal in the 1940 musical play *Pal Joey*. Sung by Rita Hayworth (dubbed by Jo Ann Greer) and reprised by Frank Sinatra in the 1957 Columbia film adaptation. In 1950, it reached the top spot on "Your Hit Parade," where it remained for five weeks of the total of sixteen weeks on the program.
560829-8, 570929-4, 571009-3,
580810-9, 620629-17, 620630-29

Bidin' My Time (1930)

Lyrics by Ira Gershwin, music by George Gershwin

Introduced by The Foursome (Marshall Smith, Ray Johnson, Del Porter and Dwight Snyder) in the 1930 musical play *Girl Crazy*. Sung by Judy Garland and The King's Men in the 1943 MGM film adaptation. **590105-9**

Big Boy Blue (1937)

Lyrics and music by Peter Tinturin, Jack Lawrence, and Dan Howell

Introduced and popularized by Ella Fitzgerald with Chick Webb and His Orchestra on a Decca recording.
370114-3, 370208-6

Bill (1937)

Lyrics by P.G. Wodehouse, music by Jerome Kern

Introduced by Helen Morgan in the 1927 musical play *Show Boat*. Sung by Miss Morgan in both the 1929 and the 1936 Universal film adaptations. Sung by Ava Gardner (dubbed by Annette Warren) in the 1951 MGM film adaptation, although Miss Gardner's voice is on the MGM soundtrack recording. **530911-2**

Bill Bailey, Won't You Please Come Home? (1902)

Lyrics and music by Hughie Cannon

Introduced by John Queen, a minstrel, in *Town Topics*, a show produced in Newburgh, New York. Bill Bailey was a member of the vaudeville team, Bailey and Cowan, and a friend of Cannon, a song-and-dance man. It became an early ragtime classic, achieving such popularity that a deluge of Bill Bailey songs flooded the market ("I Wonder Why Bill Bailey Don't Come Home," "Since Bill Bailey Came Back Home," etc.). It remained a favorite of top-flight entertainers for generations.
620629-4, **620629-23**, 620630-19, 620630-20,
630000-11, 630000-16, 640800-11, 640800-16, 790712-10

Billie's Bounce (1945)

Scat lyrics by Ella Fitzgerald, music by Charlie Parker

Introduced as an instrumental by Charlie Parker with Dizzy Gillespie; Miles Davis; Curley Russell; and Max Roach. One of many instrumentals which Ella uses with scat routines. **770714-9**

(I Always Dream of) Billy (1911)

Lyrics by Joe Goodwin, music by James Kendis and Herman Paley

Introduced in vaudeville. Revived in 1939 by Ella Fitzgerald (Decca). **390818-2, 390826-2**

Birdland (1989)

Lyrics and music by Joe Zawinul

This is a track on Quincy Jones's 1989 album "Back on the Block," in which Ella, along with Miles Davis, James Moody, George Benson, Sarah Vaughan, Dizzy Gillespie and the song's composer all participate. Jones refers to Ella in his liner notes as "our most distinguished Grande Dame Ella Fitzgerald (past seven decades and still knocking us out)." **890000-2**

The Birth of the Blues (1926)

Lyrics by B.G. DeSylva and Lew Brown, music by Ray Henderson

Introduced by Harry Richman in the 1926 revue *George White's Scandals,* and popularized by him on a Vocalion record. 530911-4

Black Coffee (1948)

Lyrics by Paul Francis Webster, music by Sonny Burke

Introduced by Sarah Vaughan on a Musicraft recording. A memorable recording by Peggy Lee in her album *Black Coffee* (Capitol).
490428-3, 490918-9, 600414-3, 700104-4

Bli-Blip (1941)

Lyrics by Sid Kuller and Duke Ellington, music by Duke Ellington

Introduced by Marie Bryant and Paul White in the 1941 musical revue *Jump for Joy* which premiered at the Mayan Theatre in Los Angeles in May, 1941. **570627-4**

Blue and Sentimental (1938)

Lyrics by Jerry Livingston and Mack David, music by William "Count" Basie

Introduced and popularized as an instrumental by Count Basie and His Orchestra. Lyrics were added in 1947.
610520-27b, 830322-1

Blue Lou (1933)

Lyrics and music by Edgar M. Sampson and Irving Mills

Introduced by Benny Carter and His Orchestra (Okeh), and popularized by Chick Webb and His Orchestra, with vocal by Ella Fitzgerald (Decca, 1940).
391200-9, 400122-7, 400325-9, 530213-2

Blue Moon (1934)

Lyrics by Lorenz Hart, music by Richard Rodgers

First called "The Prayer," the song was intended for an MGM film starring Jean Harlow. Discarded, it was rewritten as "The Bad in Every Woman," and sung by Shirley Ross in the 1934 MGM film *Manhattan Melodrama.* Subjected to a third revision, it was published as an independent number, and achieved the largest sheet-music sale of any Rodgers and Hart song up to that time.
560829-1, 610513-7, **610516-4,** 610518-10, 610520-6, **810726-8, 831000-4**

A Blue Room (1926)

Lyrics by Lorenz Hart, music by Richard Rodgers

Introduced by Eva Puck and Sammy White in the 1926 musical play *The Girl Friend.* First recordings by The Revelers, Sam Lanin and His Orchestra, and The Melody Sheiks. **560831-2**

Blue Skies (1926)

Lyrics and music by Irving Berlin

Upon Belle Baker's insistence that he supply her with a song for the Rodgers and Hart show *Betsy,* Berlin wrote "Blue Skies" for her. While revues featured interpolated numbers, it was rare that a book show in the 1920s would include one. This was especially true of Rodgers and Hart shows, which by contract prohibited anyone from interpolating songs into their scores. Berlin would not have contributed his number for any reason except the request of the show's star. Much to Rodgers's and Hart's annoyance, Berlin's song was the only hit to come from that show. It was also the only time they allowed a song to be interpolated in one of their shows (and, in this case, very much against their wills). First recorded by Ben Selvin and His Orchestra. **580318-5, 680518-2a**

Blues in the Night (1941)

Lyrics by Johnny Mercer, music by Harold Arlen

Introduced by William Gillespie in the 1941 Warner Bros. film *Blues in the Night.* Mercer and Arlen set out to write this song for a scene in the film (then called *Hot Nocturne*) not only to fit the setting, but also the performer — a scene in jail in which a black man in a cell is singing the blues. The finished song and its performance by Gillespie proved so effective that the producers decided to change the title of the film to that of the Mercer-Arlen song. Nominated for an Academy Award, Best Original Song, 1941. Jerome Kern felt so strongly that this song deserved the award (which that year had gone to Kern himself and Oscar Hammerstein II for "The Last Time I Saw Paris") that he went to work to get the Academy by-laws changed. After 1941, therefore, only songs written specifically for the screen were eligible — a ruling that would have eliminated "The Last Time I Saw Paris" from Academy competition in 1941.
581122-2, 610114-2, 640729-22

Body and Soul (1930)

Lyrics by Edward Heyman, Robert Sour and Frank Eyton; music by Johnny Green

Green wrote the song for Gertrude Lawrence, who introduced it on a BBC broadcast in England — he was her accompanist at the time. The broadcast was heard by Bert Ambrose, then one of London's most popular bandleaders, who played it and made it a hit. Max Gordon, a producer, secured the American rights for his 1930 revue *Three's a Crowd*, in which it was sung by Libby Holman and danced by Clifton Webb and Tamara Geva.

500900-11, **531118-2,** 570704-3,**620409-4, 650326-3, 660907-2, 710721-3a,** 810726-16b, **831000-7b**

Bonita (1965)

Lyrics by Ray Gilbert and Gene Lees, music by Antonio Carlos Jobim

Introduced by Antonio Carlos Jobim in performance and on several recordings.   **800918-3**

Bop Goes the Weasel (1948)

Scat lyrics by Ella Fitzgerald, music by Reginald Owen and Jack Bentley

Introduced by Ella Fitzgerald with the Ray Brown Quintet at the Royal Roost night club in 1948. **481204-3**

Boppin' Boogie *see Be-Bop Boogie.*

(I Was) Born to Be Blue (1947)

Lyrics and music by Robert Wells and Mel Tormé

Introduced by Mel Tormé on a Musicraft recording.   **610623-1**

Born to Lose (1943)

Lyrics and music by Frankie Brown

Introduced and popularized by Ted Daffan. Recorded by many "country" singers. A memorable recording is that of Ray Charles (ABC).   **671221-2**

The Boy from Ipanema (Namorado de Ipanema) *see* The Girl from Ipanema

The Boy Next Door (1944)

Lyrics by Ralph Blane, music by Hugh Martin

Introduced by Judy Garland in the 1944 MGM film *Meet Me in St. Louis*. Miss Garland also had a best-selling Decca recording.   500900-6

Boy Wanted (1921)

Lyrics by Ira Gershwin, music by George Gershwin

Introduced by "The Girls from the Glowworm," led by Lorna Sanderson, Virginia Clark, Mary Woodyatt, and Mae Carmen, in the 1921 musical play *A Dangerous Maid*. With a revised lyric by Ira Gershwin and Desmond Carter, introduced by Heather Thatcher and ensemble in the 1924 musical play, *Primrose*. For the recording production of *Ella Fitzgerald Sings the George and Ira Gershwin Song Book* (1959), Ira Gershwin again revised the lyrics for refrains 1 and 2, although the verses remain the same.   **590715-4**

Boy! What Love Has Done to Me (1930)

Lyrics by Ira Gershwin, music by George Gershwin

Introduced by Ethel Merman in the 1930 musical play *Girl Crazy*. Listed in the pre-Broadway and opening-night New York programs as "Look What Love Has Done to Me."   **590715-3**

Breakin' It Up [Breakin' 'Em Down] [Breakin' Down] (1937)

Music by Edgar M. Sampson

Introduced by Chick Webb and His Orchestra in club and dance-hall performances as a successful instrumental, although no studio recording was ever made by his orchestra.   **391200-4, 400125-9, 400325-4**

Brighten the Corner Where You Are (1913)

Lyrics by Ina Duly Ogden, music by Charles H. Gabriel

The lyric is the creation of a woman whose circumstances — her mother's illness, chiefly — thwarted her carefully planned career as a Chatauqua lecturer. She composed the poem as a balm for herself, to reconcile herself to the petty details of daily domestic duties. Mr. Gabriel, her friend, saw the possibilities of the words and set them to music. Homer Rodeheaver's voice did the rest; Mr. Rodeheaver traveled widely with many evangelists, serving from 1909-1931 as music director for Billy Sunday.   **670200-6**

Broadway (1940)

Lyrics and music by Henry Woode, Theodore McRae, and Bill Bird

Introduced and successfully recorded by Count Basie and His Orchestra.

620130-2, 620629-13

The Brown-Skinned Gal in a Calico Gown (1941)

Lyrics by Paul Francis Webster, music by Duke Ellington

Introduced by Dorothy Dandridge, Herb Jeffries, and The Calico Girls (Artie Brandon, Lucille Battle, Avanelle Harris, Doris Ake, Myrtle Fortune, and Suzette Johnson) in the 1941 musical revue *Jump for Joy*, which premiered at the Mayan Theatre in Los Angeles in May, 1941.

651020-3, **651020-4**

Budella (1947)

Scat lyrics by Ella Fitzgerald and Buddy Rich, conventional lyrics and music by Irving Berlin

The music is that of Irving Berlin's "Blue Skies"; the vocal, scat. First performed on the "WNEW Saturday Night Swing Show," broadcast from NBC Radio studios in New York, and recorded for issue on V-Disc for the Armed Forces Network.   **470301-1**

But Not for Me (1930)

Lyrics by Ira Gershwin, music by George Gershwin

Introduced by Ginger Rogers and reprised in a comedy sketch by Willie Howard in the 1930 musical play *Girl Crazy*. Sung by Judy Garland in the 1943 MGM film adaptation; and by Connie Francis and Harve Presnell in the 1965 MGM film adaptation *When the Boys Meet the Girls*. Interpolated as a recurrent instrumental theme in the 1958 Paramount film *But Not for Me*, in which Ella Fitzgerald sang the title song under the opening credits, a performance for which, in 1959, she received the Grammy (NARAS) Award for the Verve recording as Best Female Solo Vocal Performance.

500912-1, 590108-3, 590326-5,
610518-17, 830523-8

But Not Like Mine (1955)

Lyrics and music by Kenneth Howard Welch

Introduced by Ella Fitzgerald with Toots Camarata and his orchestra and chorus on a Decca recording.

550805-3

The Buzzard Song (1935)

Lyrics by DuBose Heyward, music by George Gershwin

Introduced by Todd Duncan as Porgy in the 1935 folk opera *Porgy and Bess*, in pre-Broadway try-outs. Because of the length of the opera, it was cut before reaching its Broadway performances. Nor was it used in the 1959 Columbia film adaptation. It is, however, found in the wonderful Houston Grand Opera recording of the complete score (RCA ARL3-2109 (LP); RCA RCD3-2109 (CD)). And, of course, Ella does it in the glorious *Ella Fitzgerald and Louis Armstrong/Porgy and Bess* (Verve).   **570828-4**

By Myself (1937)

Lyrics by Howard Dietz, music by Arthur Schwartz

Introduced by Jack Buchanan in the 1937 musical play *Between the Devil*. Memorably performed by Fred Astaire in the 1953 MGM film *The Band Wagon*, and also by Judy Garland in the 1963 Barbican/United Artists film *I Could Go On Singing*.   **860228-12**

By Strauss (1936)

Lyrics by Ira Gershwin, music by George Gershwin

Introduced by Gracie Barrie and Robert Shafter, then danced by Mitzi Mayfair, in the 1936 revue *The Show Is On*. Sung by Gene Kelly, Oscar Levant, and Georges Guétary (with a lyric revision of the first six lines of the verse by Ira Gershwin) in the 1951 MGM film *An American in Paris*.

590716-6

C.C. Rider *see* **See See Rider**

C Jam Blues (1942)

Scat by Ella Fitzgerald, music by Duke Ellington and Barney Bigard

Introduced and popularized by Duke Ellington and His Orchestra as an instrumental (Victor), and performed by them in the 1944 Columbia film *Jam Session*.

710507-8, 720602-14

Cabaret (1966)

Lyrics by Fred Ebb, music by John Kander

Introduced by Jill Haworth in the 1966 musical play *Cabaret*. Sung by Liza Minelli in the 1972 ABC film adaptation.

690729-4, 700520-12

Cabin in the Sky (1940)

Lyrics by John Latouche, music by Vernon Duke

Introduced by Ethel Waters and Dooley Wilson in the 1940 musical play *Cabin in the Sky*. Sung by Ethel Waters and Eddie "Rochester" Anderson in the 1943 MGM film adaptation.   **401108-2**

Call Me Darling (German: Sag' mir Darling) (1931)

English lyrics by Dorothy Dick, German lyrics and music by Bert Reisfeld, Mart Fryberg, and Rolf Marbet

Introduced and popularized in the U.S. by Russ Columbo (Victor).   **611115-3, 611115-4**

Can Anyone Explain? (No! No! No!) (1950)

Lyrics and music by Bennie Benjamin and George Weiss

Introduced and popularized by The Ames Brothers (Coral).   **500825-2, 501129-2**

Candy (1944)

Lyrics by Mack David, music by Joan Whitney and Alex Kramer

Popularized by Johnny Mercer, Jo Stafford and The Pied Pipers (Capitol).   **610518-6, 680603-1a**

Can't Buy Me Love (1964)

Lyrics and music by John Lennon and Paul McCartney

Introduced by The Beatles in the 1964 Gaumont-British film *A Hard Day's Night*. Best-selling record by The Beatles (Capitol). Winner of the Ivor Novello Award, Best Song, 1964.   **640407-1, 640728-7, 640729-7**

Can't Help Lovin' Dat Man (1927)

Lyrics by Oscar Hammerstein II, music by Jerome Kern

Introduced by Helen Morgan, Norma Terris, Howard Marsh, Aunt Jemima (Tess Gardella), and Allen Campbell in the 1927 musical play *Show Boat*. Though the song was played in a fast tempo in the show to set the mood for an effective dance, it became popular as a torch song, a tradition initiated by Helen Morgan in night clubs. Sung by Helen Morgan in the 1929 Universal film adaptation, by Irene Dunne in the 1936 Universal film adaptation, by Ava Gardner (dubbed by Annette Warren) in the 1951 MGM film adaptation — but Ava Gardner herself is heard on the MGM soundtrack record release.

410731-6, 610211-4b, 630106-2,
630000-14, 640800-14

Can't We Be Friends? (1929)

Lyrics by Paul James (pseudonym for James Warburg), music by Kay Swift

Introduced by Libby Holman in the 1929 revue *The Little Show* (first edition).

560816-5, 581124-6, 591213-4

Caravan (1937)

Lyrics by Irving Mills, music by Duke Ellington and Juan Tizol

Introduced by Duke Ellington and His Orchestra (Victor).

570627-3, 580425-8, 580425-22,
610211-11, 610221-6, 610513-6,
610516-10, 610519-17, **750717-1**

Careless (1939)

Lyrics and music by Lew Quadling, Eddy Howard, and Dick Jurgens

Introduced by Dick Jurgens and His Orchestra, vocal by Eddy Howard. The song was submitted to the Irving Berlin publishing company by the writers who were, respectively, the arranger, the vocalist, and the leader of a popular band. Berlin heard Dave Dreyer, his company manager, going over the melody at the piano. Liking the tune, but not the lyric or the title, they foresaw a problem: If they rejected the song, they felt that Jurgens, who had a lot of air time with his band, would not play any future songs published by the Berlin company. Berlin took the song home, and, overnight, wrote a new lyric with the new title, "Careless." His company published the song, though Berlin received neither credit nor royalty as a writer. It became a huge success, thanks to the recordings by Jurgens (Vocalion).   **400000-4, 530213-1**

Carnival Samba see O Nosso Amor

C'est Magnifique (1953)

Lyrics and music by Cole Porter

Introduced by Lilo and Peter Cookson in the 1953 musical play *Can-Can.* Sung by Frank Sinatra and Shirley MacLaine in the 1960 20th Century-Fox film adaptation.
620629-21, 620630-4, 620630-11, **720612-13**

Change Partners (1938)

Lyrics and music by Irving Berlin

Introduced by Fred Astaire and Ginger Rogers in the 1938 RKO film *Carefree.* Nominated for an Academy Award, Best Original Song, 1938.   **5803176**

Cheek to Cheek (1935)

Lyrics and music by Irving Berlin

Introduced by Fred Astaire and danced by Astaire and Ginger Rogers in the 1935 RKO film *Top Hat.* Nominated for an Academy Award, Best Original Song, 1935. Bears a slight resemblance to Chopin's Polonaise in A-flat.

560816-6, 580318-3, 610211-9, 610221-5,
630000-1, 630000-13, 640800-1, 640800-13

Cheerful Little Earful (1930)

Lyrics by Ira Gershwin and Billy Rose, music by Harry Warren

Introduced by Hannah Williams and Jerry Norris in the 1930 revue *Sweet and Low.* The song brought Hannah Williams featured billing in the show and a certain measure of temporary stage fame before her marriage to boxer Jack Dempsey.   **590107-4**

Chelsea Bridge (1941)

Scat lyrics by Ella Fitzgerald, music by Billy Strayhorn

Introduced and popularized by Duke Ellington and His Orchestra (Victor). This beautiful instrumental was composed, Strayhorn said, with a painting by James McNeill Whistler in mind (Whistler painted many scenes of the rivers and bridges of London, although never specifically Chelsea Bridge).

570627-5, 570627-6, 570627-7, 570627-8,
570627-9, 570627-10, 570627-11

Cherry Red (1934)

Lyrics and music by Pete Johnson and Joe Turner

Introduced by Pete Johnson and Joe Turner in Kansas City, and then recorded by them for Vocalion in 1941.
631028-6

The Chesapeake and Ohio (1951)

Lyrics and music by Carl Sigman and Herbert Magidson

Introduced by Ella Fitzgerald with Sy Oliver and his orchestra on a Decca recording.   **510327-1**

Chew, Chew, Chew (Your Bubble Gum) (1939)

Lyrics and music by Ella Fitzgerald, Buck Ram, Dick Vance, and Chick Webb

Introduced and popularized by Ella Fitzgerald with Chick Webb and His Orchestra (Decca).

390302-6, 390504-9

Chewin' Gum (1940)

Lyrics and music by Ella Fitzgerald, Buck Ram, and Chick Webb

Another "gum" song — this one did not make it to a studio recording, although it was featured in radio broadcasts after Chick's death in 1939.   **400304-4**

Chicago Style (1953)

Lyrics by Johnny Burke, music by James Van Heusen

Introduced by Bing Crosby and Bob Hope in the 1953 Paramount film *The Road to Bali*.   **530101-2**

The Chokin' Kind (1967)

Lyrics and music by Harlan Howard

Introduced and popularized by Waylon Jennings (Victor). Revived in 1969 by Joe Simon.   **671221-3**

Christmas Island (1946)

Lyrics and music by Lyle L. Moraine

Introduced by The Andrews Sisters with Guy Lombardo and His Royal Canadians (Decca).   600715-5

The Christmas Song (1945)

Lyrics and music by Robert Wells and Mel Tormé

Tormé: "One excessively hot afternoon, I drove out to Bob's house in Toluca Lake (California) for a work session. The San Fernand Valley, always ten degrees warmer than the rest of the town, blistered in the July sun … I opened the front door and walked in … I called for Bob. No answer. I walked over to the piano. A writing pad rested on the music board. Written in pencil on the open page were four lines of verse: 'Chestnuts roasting on an open fire/Jack Frost nipping at your nose/Yuletide carols being sung by a choir/And folks dressed up like Eskimos.' When Bob finally appeared, I asked him about the little poem … 'It was so hot today,' he said, 'I thought I'd write something to cool myself off. All I could think of was Christmas and cold weather.' 'You know,' I said, 'this might make a song.' We sat down together at the piano, and improbable as it may sound, 'The Christmas Song' was completed about forty-five minutes later. Excitedly, we called Carlos Gastel (Nat "King" Cole's manager), sped into Hollywood, played it for him, then for Johnny Burke, then for Nat Cole, who fell in love with the tune. It took a full year for Nat to get into a studio to record it, but the record finally came out in the late fall of 1946; and the rest could be called our financial pleasure. A humorous footnote: When Nat initially recorded 'The Christmas Song' he sang the last line of the bridge: "To see if **reindeers** really know/How to fly.' After the first pressings were released we pointed out the grammatical error. Nat, a true gentleman and a dogged perfectionist, stewed over the mistake, and sure enough, at the end of another recording session of his, with the same-sized orchestra at hand, he re-recorded our song, properly singing **reindeer**. The second version is virtually identical to the first, but those early first pressings have become collectors' items." Almost every balladeer in the business has recorded this song, but Nat "King" Cole's versions remain the standards.   **590903-4,** 600715-7, **600805-3**

The Church in the Wildwood (1865)

Lyrics and music by William Savage Pitts

Nashua, Iowa, is on U.S. Highway 218, forty miles southeast of Mason City and 31 miles north of Cedar Falls, Iowa. Here, Iowa State Highway 346 leads eastward a mile or so to the hamlet of Bradford and the site of The Little Brown Church in the Vale, a Congregational church immortalized by the familiar hymn. Built in the 1850s, the church serves a congregation of some hundred families. Hundreds of couples travel many miles each year to be married in "The Church in the Wildwood."   **670200-14**

Cielito Lindo (1919)

Spanish lyrics and music by Quirino Mendoza y Cortez, and adapted by Carlo Fernandez and Sebastian Yradier; English lyrics by Neil C. Wilson, 1923.

Very popular traditional Mexican love song.   **710721-4d**

Clap Hands! Here Comes Charlie! (1925)

Lyrics by Billy Rose and Ballard Macdonald, music by Joseph Meyer

Introduced in vaudeville by Salt and Pepper. Van and Schenck also helped to popularize it. First recording by Johnny Marvin. The Goofus Five made a hit recording for Okeh. Revived in the 1930s by Chick Webb and His Orchestra, and in the 1940s it became the theme song of Charlie Barnet and His Orchestra. In the original title of this song, "Charlie" was spelled "Charley," and this is the way it was first copyrighted, but during the 1930s, the former became the preferred spelling of persons of this name, and, consequently, the title of the song changed.   **610624-3**, 620630-10

Clap Yo' Hands [Clap-a Yo' Hands] (1926)

Lyrics by Ira Gershwin, music by George Gershwin

Introduced and danced by Harlan Dixon, Betty Compton, Paulette Winston, Constance Carpenter, Janette Gilmore and ensemble in the 1926 musical play *Oh, Kay!*   **590107-3**

Clementine (1942)

Lyrics by Stanley Clayton, Ruth Roberts, and Bill Katz, music by Billy Strayhorn

Introduced by Duke Ellington and His Orchestra. A

definitive reading is on the RCA recording **The Blanton-Webster Band**, featuring Ellington and his orchestra. Later vocal versions of this song give its title as "Baby Clementine," and credit a fourth lyricist, Bob Thiele, the record producer.   **570626-1**

Close to You (1943)

Lyrics by Al Hoffman and Jerry Livingston, music by Carl G. Lampl

Introduced and popularized by Frank Sinatra on a Columbia recording.   **710507-3, 710721-10**

Close Your Eyes (1932)

Lyrics and music by Bernice Petkere

Introduced and popularized by Ruth Etting.

571015-8

Come On-a My House (1949)

Lyrics and music by Ross Bagdasarian and William Saroyan

Written by playwright Saroyan and his cousin Bagdasarian while on an automobile trip across New Mexico in 1949. Interpolated in the Saroyan short play *Son*, in 1950. First recorded by Kay Armen. Mitch Miller convinced a reluctant Rosemary Clooney to record it in 1951 (Columbia); it became her first major recording success, selling over a million records.   **510626-3**

Come Rain or Come Shine (1946)

Lyrics by Johnny Mercer, music by Harold Arlen

Introduced by Ruby Hill and Harold Nicholas in the 1946 musical play *St. Louis Woman*.
580810-26, **610116-5**, 610518-3, 610520-13, **770714-4**

Comes Love (1939)

Lyrics by Charles Tobias and Lew Brown, music by Sam Stept

Introduced by Phil Silvers and Judy Canova and danced by Dixie Dunbar in the 1939 musical play *Yokel Boy*. Sung by Joan Davis in the 1942 Republic film adaptation.   **570723-9, 830322-9**

Confessin' see I'm Confessin' (that I Love You)

Coochi-Coochi-Coo (1939)

Lyrics and music by Kay and Sue Werner

Introduced by Chick Webb and His Orchestra, vocal by Ella Fitzgerald (Decca).   **390421-7**

Cool Breeze (1958)

Lyrics and music by Billy Eckstine, Dizzy Gillespie, and Tad Dameron

Introduced by Billy Eckstine on an RCA Victor recording. Decca covered it with this recording by Ella.   **590903-2**

Corcovado see Quiet Nights of Quiet Stars

Cotton Tail (1940)

Scat lyrics by Ella Fitzgerald, music by Duke Ellington

Introduced and popularized by Duke Ellington and His Orchestra as an instrumental. This is one of many instrumentals for which Ella has devised vocal scat and lyrics.
560904-3, 651019-2, 660130-4, 660208-14, 66072710. 660728-13, **66072913,** 660914-11, **660923-8, 670128-4, 670326-9, 670430-6**

Cow Cow Boogie (1941)

Lyrics by Don Raye, music by Gene DePaul and Benny Carter

Written for the 1941 Bud Abbott-Lou Costello Universal film *Ride 'Em, Cowboy*, in which it was delightfully performed as a production number by Ella Fitzgerald, but the sequence was deleted before the film was released. It was successfully recorded by Ella Mae Morse with Freddie Slack and His Orchestra (Capitol), the first big hit for the newly formed record company; and then performed by Morse and Slack in the 1943 RKO film *Reveille with Beverly*.
431103-1

Crazy Rhythm (1928)

Lyrics by Irving Caesar, music by Joseph Meyer and Roger Wolfe Kahn

Introduced by Ben Bernie, Peggy Chamberlain, and June O'Dea in the 1928 musical play *Here's How*. Immortalized in dance by Patrice Wymore in the 1950 Warner Bros. film version of *No, No, Nanette*, entitled *Tea for Two*.
700520-1

The Cricket Song (1964)

Scat lyrics by Ella Fitzgerald, music ad lib impromptu by the musicians of her trio

The Antibes-Juan-les Pins Jazz Festivals were always held in an open air park setting in the lovely Pinède Gould between the two cities. The crickets were in full song the evening of 28 July 1964, during Ella's set at the festival. During their shrillest, Ella bowed to them with an impromptu scat with her musicians, which, being recorded, was released on her album *Ella at Juan-les Pins*, as "The Cricket Song."   **640729-25**

Cry Me a River (1953)

Lyrics and music by Arthur Hamilton

Popularized in 1955 by Julie London (Liberty), her first successful release.   560121-5, **610624-1**

(I'm Gonna Hurry You Out of My Mind and) Cry You Out of My Heart (1945)

Lyrics and music by Johnny Lange, Richard Loring and Hy Heath

Introduced by Ella Fitzgerald on this Decca recording.
450327-3, **450328-1**

Cryin' Mood (1937)

Lyrics by Andy Razaf, music by Chick Webb

Introduced by Chick Webb and His Orchestra, vocal by Ella Fitzgerald (Decca). **370324-7**

Cryin' My Heart Out for You (1936)

Lyrics by J.C. Johnson, music by Claude D. Hopkins

Introduced by Chick Webb and His Orchestra, vocal by Ella Fitzgerald (Decca). **360407-3**

Crying (1949)

Lyrics by Barney Ross, music by Sir Jay Chernis

Introduced by Ella Fitzgerald with Sonny Burke and his orchestra on a Decca recording. **490720-1**

Crying in the Chapel (1953)

Lyrics and music by Artie Glenn

Introduced by Darrell Glenn, the composer's son, and popularized by The Orioles (Jubilee). **530611-2**

Cutie Pants (1963)

Lyrics and music by Steve Allen and Ray Brown

Introduced on a television program by Steve Allen with guest Ray Brown. **640728-11, 640729-11**

Dancing in the Dark (1931)

Lyrics by Howard Dietz, music by Arthur Schwartz

Introduced by John Barker, to a dance by Tillie Losch, in the 1931 musical revue *The Band Wagon*. Danced by Fred Astaire and Cyd Charisse in the 1953 MGM film version. Artie Shaw and His Orchestra had a best-seller record (RCA Victor) in 1941. **700520-13**

Dancing on the Ceiling (1930)

Lyrics by Lorenz Hart, music by Richard Rodgers

Originally written for the 1930 Ziegfeld production *Simple Simon*, but dropped before the New York opening. Introduced in London by Jessie Matthews and Sonnie Hale in the 1930 musical play *Ever Green*. Matthews and Hale repeated their performance in the 1935 Gaumont-British film adaptation. **560831-3**

The Darktown Strutters' Ball (1917)

Lyrics and music by Shelton Brooks

Introduced in vaudeville by the team of Benny Fields, Jack Salisbury and soon-to-be-songwriter Benny Davis. It was given to the Original Dixie Land Jazz Band to record at their first session for Columbia on 30 January 1917. One of the sixteen songs selected by ASCAP in 1963 for its All-Time Hit Parade during its first half-century of existence. **360219-7, 361119-2**

Darn That Dream (1939)

Lyrics by Eddie DeLange, music by James Van Heusen

Introduced by Benny Goodman and His Orchestra, Maxine Sullivan, Louis Armstrong, Bill Bailey, The Dandridge Sisters, The Rhythmettes, and The Deep River Boys in the 1939 musical play *Swingin' the Dream*. (The musical was based on Shakespeare's *A Midsummer Night's Dream*, but despite its outstanding cast, ran for only 13 performances.) **611113-1**

Day by Day (1945)

Lyrics by Sammy Cahn, music by Axel Stordahl and Paul Weston

Introduced by Jo Stafford, with Paul Weston and His Orchestra. **770714-5**

Day Dream (1941)

Lyrics by John Latouche, music by Billy Strayhorn

Introduced by Duke Ellington and His Orchestra (Bluebird). **570624-1, 670326-6**

Day In — Day Out (1939)

Lyrics by Johnny Mercer, music by Rube Bloom

Introduced by Bob Crosby and The Bobcats, vocal by Helen Ward. Achieved #1 on "Your Hit Parade for ten weeks. **390826-1, 640728-3, 640729-2, 641020-1**

Days of Wine and Roses (1962)

Lyrics by Johnny Mercer, music by Henry Mancini

Introduced by Andy Williams who sang it under the titles of the 1962 Warner Bros. film *Days of Wine and Roses*. Won the Academy Award as Best Original Song, 1962. The Henry Mancini recording received the Grammy Award for Best Record, 1963. The title derives from a poem by Ernest Christopher Dawson (1867–1900), "Vitae summa brevis spem nos vetat incohare longam" ("The short span of life forbids us to encourage prolonged hope" [Horace]): "They are not long, the weeping and the laughter,/Love and desire and hate:/I think they have no portion in us after/We pass the gate.//They are not long, the days of wine and roses:/Out of a misty dream/Our path emerges for a while, then closes/Within a dream." This is not first time Mr. Dawson was consulted for an idea for a popular song. Cf. "Always True to You in My Fashion," by Cole Porter.
701221-3, 710518-3, 860228-7

Dedicated to You (1936)

Lyrics by Sammy Cahn, music by Saul Chaplin and Hy Zaret

Introduced by Pha Terrel with Andy Kirk and His Twelve Clouds of Joy.   **370203-1**

'Deed I Do (1926)

Lyrics by Walter Hirsch, music by Fred Rose

Introduced and popularized by Ben Bernie and His Orchestra.   **630715-2**

Deedle-De-Dum (1940)

Music and lyrics by Ella Fitzgerald

Introduced on a Decca recording by Ella Fitzgerald and Her Famous Orchestra, vocals by Ella Fitzgerald.

400509-1

Deep in a Dream (1938)

Lyrics by Eddie DeLange, music by Jimmy Van Heusen

Introduced and first popularized by Russ Morgan and His Orchestra. Featured on "Your Hit Parade" for fourteen weeks.   **390210-2**

Deep in the Heart of the South (1937)

Lyrics and music by Peter Tinturin and Jack Lawrence

Introduced by Ella Fitzgerald and Her Savoy Eight (Decca).   **370524-5**

Deep Purple (1934/1939)

Lyrics by Mitchell Parish, music by Peter DeRose

The music originated in 1934 as a piano solo composition, part of the tone poem, "Three Shades of Blue." A year later Domenico Savino arranged "Deep Purple" for orchestra; its success, however, came only after Mitchell Parish provided it with lyrics in 1939. Babe Ruth, the great baseball star, loved the song so dearly that on each of his birthdays during the last decade of his life, he had Peter DeRose sing it for him.

610516-2, 630000-2, 640800-2, **680528-1d, 820205-4**

Desafinado [Slightly Out of Tune]/[Off Key] (1958)

Portuguese lyrics by Newton Mendonça, English lyrics ("Slightly Out of Tune") by Jon Hendricks and Jessie Cavanaugh (pseudonym of Harry S. Richmond), English lyrics (Off Key) by Gene Lees; music by Antonio Carlos Jobim

Introduced in Brazil in 1958 by Antonio Carlos Jobim. The best-selling instrumental by Stan Getz and Charlie Byrd became the winner of the Grammy Award (NARAS), Best Jazz Performance, 1962. English lyrics by Jon Hendricks and Jessie Cavanaugh added in 1962, a vocal version of which was introduced by Pat Thomas (MGM). Another English lyric by Gene Lees is entitled, "Off Key." The Hendricks-Cavanaugh version was recorded by Ella in 1962; the Lees version was recorded by Ella on her *Ella Abraça Jobim/Ella Fitzgerald Sings the Antonio Carlos Jobim Song Book* album.   **621001-1, 810318-2**

Detour Ahead (1948)

Lyrics and music by Herb Ellis, Lou Carter, and John Frigo

Introduced by The Soft Winds, a vocal quartet.

590325-8

Devoting My Time to You (1936)

Lyrics and music by Chick Webb and Sandy Williams

Introduced by Chick Webb and His Orchestra, vocal by Ella Fitzgerald (Decca).   **360602-5**

Did You Mean It? (1927)

Lyrics by Sid Silvers and Abe Lyman, music by Phil Baker

Introduced by Marion Harris (Victor); and popularized by Abe Lyman and His Orchestra.   **361105-3**

Diga Diga Doo (1928)

Lyrics by Dorothy Fields, music by Jimmy McHugh

Introduced by Adelaide Hall (in her Broadway debut) in the all-Black revue *Lew Leslie's Blackbirds of 1928*.

391200-2, 400125-5, 400325-2

Dindi (1965)

Portuguese lyrics by Aloysio de Oliveira, English lyrics by Ray Gilbert, music by Antonio Carlos Jobim

Introduced and popularized by Antonio Carlos Jobim and His Orchestra. A memorable recording by Ella Fitzgerald on her Pablo album *Ella Abraça Jobim/Ella Fitzgerald Sings the Antonio Carlos Jobim Song Book* (1983).

800919-1

Ding-Dong Boogie (1952)

Lyrics and music by Charlie Singleton and Ted McRae

Introduced by Ella Fitzgerald on this Decca recording.

520626-2

Ding-Dong! The Witch Is Dead (1939)

Lyrics by E.Y. "Yip" Harburg, music by Harold Arlen

Introduced by Judy Garland, Billie Burke (dubbed by Lorraine Bridges), and The Singing Midgets (The Munchkins) (electronically re-recorded voices) in the 1939 MGM film *The Wizard of Oz*.   **600802-4**

The Dipsy Doodle (1937)

Lyrics and music by Larry Clinton

Introduced by Larry Clinton and His Orchestra.

371217-3

Dites-Moi (1949)

Lyrics by Oscar Hammerstein II, music by Richard Rodgers

Introduced by Michael DeLeon and Barbara Luna in the 1949 musical play *South Pacific*. Performed by Mitzi

Gaynor and children in the 1958 Magna Theatre Corporation film adaptation. **621003-3**

Dixie [Dixie's Land] (1859)

Lyrics and music by Daniel Decatur Emmett

Introduced by The Bryant Minstrels (of which Emmett was a member) at Mechanics Hall, New York, 4 April 1859. By 1861, it was the most popular song in the nation. During the Civil war, it was adopted as a "national anthem" by The Confederate States of America. After Appomatox, Lincoln remarked that since the North had conquered the South, "Dixie" was part of the spoils of war. As testimony to his enthusiasm for the song, he requested the band outside The White House to play it for him. **531118-11b**

Do I Love You? (1939)

Lyrics and music by Cole Porter

Introduced by Ethel Merman and Ronald Graham in the 1939 musical play *DuBarry Was a Lady.* Sung by Gene Kelly in the 1943 MGM film adaptation. **560207-9**

Do Nothin' Till You Hear from Me (1943)

Lyrics by Bob Russell, music by Duke Ellington

Adapted from the 1940 instrumental composition by Ellington "Concerto for Cootie." Introduced by Duke Ellington and His Orchestra. **440410-2, 440501-2, 560904-5, 570428-5, 650326-6b, 710721-7b**

Do You Really Love Me? (1952)

Lyrics and music by Charles G. Dant and Al Rinker

Introduced by Tony Martin. Covered with this Decca record by Ella Fitzgerald. **510524-2**

Dodging the Dean (1940)

Lyrics and music by Larry Clinton

Introduced by Larry Clinton and His Orchestra. Popularized by Ella Fitzgerald and Her Famous Orchestra, vocal by Ella Fitzgerald (Decca). **400122-4**

Don'cha Go 'Way Mad (1950)

Lyrics by Al Stillman, music by Jimmy Mundy and Illinois Jacquet

Adapted from the Illinois Jacquet instrumental composition "Black Velvet." Best-selling record by Ella Fitzgerald (Decca). **500202-2, 570724-10, 570929-3, 571009-2, 690200-9**

Don't Be That Way (1934/1938)

Lyrics by Mitchell Parish, music by Edgard Sampson

Introduced by Chick Webb and His Orchestra as an instrumental in 1934. With lyrics added in 1938, popularized by Benny Goodman and His Orchestra. **570813-3, 611227-1, 670326-1, 671113-2e, 730828-3, 820204-1, 860228-4**

Don't Cry, Cry-Baby (1943)

Lyrics and music by Stella Unger, Saul Bernie, and James P. Johnson

First recordings by Erksine Hawkins and His Orchestra (Bluebird), and Lucky Millinder and His Orchestra (Decca). **490428-6**

Don't Cry, Joe (1949)

Lyrics and music by Joe Marsala

Introduced by Gordon Jenkins and His Orchestra and Chorus, vocal by Betty Brewer (Decca). **500900-1, 671113-1b**

Don't Dream of Anybody but Me (1969)

Lyrics by Bart Howard, music by Neal Hefti

The music is that of Neal Hefti's "Li'l Darlin'," (q.v.) an instrumental that was first recorded by Count Basie and His Orchestra. In 1969, lyrics were added. **701221-2**

Don't Ever Go Away [Por Causa de Vôce] (1965)

Portuguese lyrics by Dolores Duran, English lyrics by Ray Gilbert, music by Antonio Carlos Jobim

Introduced by Antonio Carlos Jobim and His Orchestra. Outstanding recording by Ella Fitzgerald in her Pablo album *Ella Abraça Jobim/Ella Fitzgerald Sings the Antonio Carlos Jobim Song Book* (1981). **810320-2**

Don't Fence Me In (1944)

Lyrics and music by Cole Porter

Based on a poem by Robert Fletcher, the song was written for the 1934-35 Warner Bros. film *Adios, Argentina,* that was never produced. Introduced by Roy Rogers in the 1946 Warner Bros. film *Hollywood Canteen,* and sung again by Rogers in the 1945 Republic film *Don't Fence Me In.* Sixteen weeks on "Your Hit Parade" in 1944, eight as # 1. **560209-10**

Don't Get Around Much Any More (1940/1942)

Lyrics by Bob Russell, music by Duke Ellington

Introduced by Duke Ellington and His Orchestra, vocal by Al Hibbler (Columbia). Adapted from the 1940 Ellington composition "Never No Lament," recorded by Ellington in 1940. **560904-11**

Don't Let That Doorknob Hit You (1967)

Lyrics and music by Vic McAlpin

Introduced by Vic McAlpin. Ella covered the recording with this version for her *Misty Blue* album.

671222-2

Don't Rain on My Parade (1964)

Lyrics by Bob Merrill, music by Jule Styne

Introduced by Barbra Streisand in the 1964 musical play *Funny Girl*. Streisand repeated her performance in the 1968 Columbia film adaptation.

650326-7, 650626-4

Don't Touch Me (1966)

Lyrics and music by Hank Cochran

Introduced by Jeannie Seely (Monument).

671220-2

Don't Wake Me Up (1925)

Lyrics by L. Wolfe Gilbert, music by Mabel Wayne and Abel Baer

Featured and recorded by Vincent Lopez and His Orchestra (Okeh), and by Howard Lanin and His Orchestra (Victor).

521130-2

Don't Worry 'Bout Me (1939)

Lyrics by Ted Koehler, music by Rube Bloom

Introduced by Cab Calloway in the 1939 musical revue *Cotton Club Parade*.

390421-1, 730705-12, 790216-2, 860228-6

Don't You Think I Ought to Know? (1947)

Lyrics and music by William Johnson and Melvin R. Wettergreen

Introduced by Ella Fitzgerald with Bob Haggart and His Orchestra on this recording for Decca.

470722-1

Down Hearted Blues (1923)

Lyrics by Alberta Hunter, music by Lovie Austin

Introduced by Alberta Hunter. This was Bessie Smith's first Columbia blues recording, which took place on 16 February 1923, and sold 780,000 copies in six months.

631029-2

Down in the Depths (on the Ninetieth Floor) (1936)

Lyrics and music by Cole Porter

Introduced by Ethel Merman in the 1936 musical play *Red, Hot and Blue*. Porter wrote the song during the Boston try-out, and it was in the show two days later. Merman recorded it, coupled with "It's De-Lovely" from the same show (Liberty Music Shops).

720612-2, 730705-8

Dream (1944)

Lyrics and music by Johnny Mercer

Introduced by Johnny Mercer as the closing theme of his CBS Chesterfield radio program in 1945. Subsequently popularized by The Pied Pipers (Capitol).

641019-5

Dream a Little Dream of Me (1931)

Lyrics by Gus Kahn, music by Wilbur Schwandt and Fabian André.

Introduced and recorded by Wayne King and His Orchestra (Victor). Popularized by Kate Smith, who featured it on her first CBS radio program on 1 May 1931.

500825-1, 630716-2, 640203-4, 890316-1

Dream a Little Longer (1950)

Lyrics by Gus Kahn, music by Grace LeBoy Kahn (his wife)

Introduced by Tex Beneke and the Glenn Miller Orchestra (Victor).

490921-2

Dream Dancing (1941)

Lyrics and music by Cole Porter

Introduced (danced) by Fred Astaire and Rita Hayworth in the 1941 Columbia film *You'll Never Get Rich*.

780213-1

Dreamer [Vivo Sonhando (I Live Dreaming)] (196)

English lyrics by Gene Lees, Portuguese lyrics and music by Antonio Carlos Jobim

Introduced by Antonio Carlos Jobim on a Verve recording. Outstanding recording by Ella Fitzgerald in her Pablo album *Ella Abraça Jobim/Ella Fitzgerald Sings the Antonio Carlos Jobim Song Book*, 1981.

800917-1

A Dreamer's Holiday (1949)

Lyrics by Kim Gannon, music by Mabel Wayne

Popular recordings by Perry Como (Victor); Buddy Clark (Columbia); and the orchestras of Gordon Jenkins (Decca), and Ray Anthony (Capitol).

491109-1

Dreams Are Made for Children (1958)

Lyrics by Mack David, music by Jerry Livingston

Introduced by Ella Fitzgerald on this Verve recording.

581123-13

**Drop Me Off in Harlem
(Drop Me Off at Harlem)** (1933)

Lyrics by Nick Kenny, music by Duke Ellington

Introduced by Duke Ellington and His Orchestra (Brunswick), and later popularized by Ellington on a Columbia recording.

570625-3

Duke's Place (1942/1958)

Lyrics by Ruth Roberts, Bill Katz, and Robert Thiele (1958); music by Duke Ellington (1942)

Based on Ellington's composition "C Jam Blues." Vocal version also introduced by Ellington.

650326-1, 651018-2, 651018-3, 660208-5, 660207-2

The E and D Blues (E for Ella, D for Duke) (1957)

Scat lyrics by Ella Fitzgerald, music by Duke Ellington, Billy Strayhorn, and John Sanders

Introduced by Ella Fitzgerald with Duke Ellington and His Orchestra (Verve). **570627-13**

Early Autumn (1948/1952)

Lyrics by Johnny Mercer, music by Ralph Burns and Woody Herman

Adapted from a segment of a 1946 orchestral composition "Summer Sequence" by Ralph Burns. Recorded as an instrumental in 1948 by Woody Herman and The Woodchoppers with the present title. Lyrics added by Johnny Mercer in 1952, and introduced by Mercer (Capitol).

520626-6, 641019-4

East of the Sun and West of the Moon (1935)

Lyrics and music by Brooks Bowman

Introduced in the 1935 Princeton University Triangle Club production *Stags at Bay*. Bowman, a senior, was offered a contract to compose songs for movies after graduation. En route to California, he was killed in an auto accident. **581124-1**

Easy Living (1937)

Lyrics by Leo Robin, music by Ralph Rainger

Introduced in the 1937 Paramount film *Easy Living*. Associated with Billie Holiday, who recorded it twice; first, with Teddy Wilson's combo (Brunswick), and later with her own orchestra (Decca). **860228-8**

Easy to Love (1936)

Lyrics and music by Cole Porter

Originally written for William Gaxton in the 1934 musical play *Anything Goes*, the song was dropped because Gaxton did not have the vocal range required. Porter reworked the lyric and it was introduced by James Stewart, danced by Eleanor Powell, and reprised by Frances Langford in the 1936 MGM film *Born To Dance*.

560207-13, 610221-3b, 710721-2b

Ele é Carioca see **He's a Carioca**

Ella (1938)

Lyrics and music by Chick Webb and Bob Ellsworth

Introduced by Chick Webb and His Orchestra, with a vocal duet of Ella Fitzgerald and Taft Jordan (Decca). **380609-4**

Ella Hums the Blues (1955)

Scat by Ella Fitzgerald, music by Ray Heindorf

Introduced by Ella Fitzgerald in the 1955 Warner Bros. film *Pete Kelly's Blues*. **550503-3, 550724-2**

Ella's Blues (1963)

Scat lyrics and music by Ella Fitzgerald

Introduced in performance in Tokyo, and planned for the album *Ella in Nippon*, which, although planned in every detail, was never released. **640800-12, 640800-20**

Ella's Contribution to the Blues (1952)

Scat lyrics by Ella Fitzgerald, music by Hank Jones

Introduced by Ella Fitzgerald with Leroy Kirkland and His Orchestra, with Hank Jones at piano (Decca).

520811-4

Ella's Twist (1962)

Scat lyrics and music by Ella Fitzgerald, based on Cole Porter's "Too Darn Hot"

Created by Ella Fitzgerald during a concert at The Crescendo night club, Los Angeles, when she stopped her introduction of Cole Porter's "Too Darn Hot," because the music being played upstairs for dancing was distracting her. They were playing a twist, very big at the time, so Ella devised her own version of the twist in tempo to the distraction, and her trio obligingly followed. The title is discographer Phil Schaap's, who titled it after listening to the tape of the concert. 620630-27

Elmer's Tune (1941)

Lyrics and music by Elmer Albrecht, Sammy Gallop, and Dick Jurgens

Introduced by Dick Jurgens and His Orchestra. Bestselling record by Glenn Miller and His Orchestra, vocal by Ray Eberle and The Modernaires. **680603-3d**

Embraceable You (1930)

Lyrics by Ira Gershwin, music by George Gershwin

Introduced and reprised by Ginger Rogers and Allen Kearns in the 1930 musical play *Girl Crazy*. The song was originally written for the unproduced musical play *Ming Toy*. Sung by Eddie Quillan and Dixie Lee in the 1932 film adaptation; and by Harve Presnell in the 1965 MGM film adaptation *When the Boys Meet the Girls*.

590108-1, 830523-3c

An Empty Ballroom (1953)

Lyrics and music by Larry Clinton

Introduced by Larry Clinton and His Orchestra.

531223-1

Even As You and I (1950)

Lyrics by Ted Johnson, music by Joe Larkin

Introduced by pianist Joe Larkin. This is believed to be the first recording of this lovely song. **510524-1**

Every Day I Have the Blues (1950)

Lyrics and music by Peter Chatman

Introduced by Lowell Fulson under its original title, "Nobody Loves Me" (Swing Time). Under the present title, best-selling recording in 1952 by Joe Williams with Count Basie and His Orchestra (Clef). **560625-4**

Everybody Step (1921)

Lyrics and music by Irving Berlin

Introduced by The Brox Sisters in the first edition of the 1921 *The Music Box Revue of 1921.* First recorded by Paul Whiteman and His Orchestra (Victor), then by Ted Lewis and His Orchestra (Columbia). **380609-3**

Everyone's Wrong But Me (1937)

Lyrics by Sammy Cahn, music by Saul Chaplin

Introduced in the musical revue *The New Grand Terrace Revue* and first recorded by Chick Webb and His Orchestra, vocal by Ella Fitzgerald (Decca). **370524-4**

Everything but You (1945)

Lyrics by Don George, music by Duke Ellington and Harry James

Introduced, featured, and recorded by Duke Ellington and His Orchestra, vocal by Joya Sherrill (Victor).

570625-1

Everything Happens to Me (1941)

Lyrics by Tom Adair, music by Matt Dennis

Introduced by Tommy Dorsey and His Orchestra, vocal by Frank Sinatra (Victor). **571028-6**

Everything I Have Is Yours (1933)

Lyrics by Harold Adamson, music by Burton Lane

Introduced by Joan Crawford and Art Jarrett in the 1933 MGM film *Dancing Lady.*

491123-1, 680529-2d

Evil on Your Mind (1966)

Lyrics and music by Harlan Howard

Introduced by Jan Howard (Decca). **671222-1**

Ev'ry Time We Say Goodbye (1944)

Lyrics and music by Cole Porter

Introduced by Nan Wynn and Jere McMahon in the 1944 revue *The Seven Lively Arts.*

560207-10, 740411-3

Ev'rything I've Got (Belongs to You) (1942)

Lyrics by Lorenz Hart, music by Richard Rodgers

Introduced by Ray Bolger and Benay Venuta in the 1942 musical play *By Jupiter.* **560904-15**

Exactly Like You (1930)

Lyrics by Dorothy Fields, music by Jimmy McHugh

Introduced by Gertrude Lawrence and Harry Richman in the 1930 revue *Lew Leslie's International Revue.*
580810-25, 610521-6, 620629-18,
620630-3, 620630-13, 620630-15

Fairy Tales (1949)

Lyrics and music by William J. Reitz

Introduced and popularized by Owen Bradley and His Orchestra as an instrumental (Coral). Introduced with lyrics by Ella Fitzgerald (Decca). **491107-1**

Fascinating Rhythm (1924)

Lyrics by Ira Gershwin, music by George Gershwin

Introduced by Fred Astaire and Cliff "Ukelele Ike" Edwards in the 1924 musical play *Lady, Be Good!* Sung by Connie Russell and danced by Eleanor Powell and The Berry Brothers in the 1941 MGM film adaptation.

590318-5

Favela *see* **Somewhere in the Hills**

Fine and Mellow (1940)

Lyrics and music by Billie Holiday

Introduced, featured and recorded by Billie Holiday (Commodore). **740108-1, 790712-7**

A Fine Romance (1936)

Lyrics by Dorothy Fields, music by Jerome Kern

Introduced by Fred Astaire and Ginger Rogers in the 1936 RKO film *Swing Time.*
560202-6, **570813-2, 630105-2**

The First Noël [The First Nowell] (1833)

Lyrics by William Sandys, music is ancient French or English

The tune is undoubtedly very old. It was first published with lyrics by William Sandys in the 1833 edition of *Christmas Carols, Ancient and Modern.* 670721-1

The Five O'Clock Whistle (1940)

Lyrics and music by Josef Myrow, Kim Gannon, and Gene Irwin

Introduced on radio, recorded and popularized by Glenn Miller and His Orchestra, vocal by Marion Hutton (Bluebird). **400925-1**

A Flower Is a Lovesome Thing (1941)

Lyrics and music by William Thomas (Billy) Strayhorn

Introduced as an instrumental by Duke Ellington and His Orchestra, and also recorded by Johnny Hodges (Sunrise), with the title "Passion." Lyrics added for Ella Fitzgerald for inclusion in the Fitzgerald-Ellington album *Ella at Duke's Place* (Verve) in 1965. The title was inspired by Thomas Edward Brown's poem "My Garden" that contains the line, "A Garden is a lovesome thing, God wot!" **6510019-4**

Fly Me to the Moon (1954)

Lyrics and music by Bart Howard

Introduced in cabaret by Mabel Mercer. First recording by Felicia Saunders under the title "In Other Words" (Columbia). **640800-5, 710721-4b**

Flyin' Home (1939)

Lyrics by Sid Robin, music by Lionel Hampton and Benny Goodman

Introduced by The Benny Goodman Sextet, featuring Lionel Hampton (Columbia).
451004-1, 451004-2, 470929-4, 481204-10, 490211-4, **490423-4, 490918-7, 501230-4, 790712-9, 831000-9**

A Foggy Day (in London Town) (1937)

Lyrics by Ira Gershwin, music by George Gershwin

Introduced by Fred Astaire in the 1937 RKO film *A Damsel in Distress* and recorded by him (Brunswick).
540917-1, 560816-9, 580425-2, 580425-13, **590105-7, 611021-2, 650518-2c, 730828-6, 830523-1**

Foolish Tears (1948)

Lyrics and music by Jenny Lou Carson

Best-selling records by Tex Williams (Capitol), Al Morgan (London), Spade Cooley (Victor), and Axel Stordahl and His Orchestra (Columbia). **490921-3**

Fools Rush In (1940)

Lyrics by Johnny Mercer, music by Rube Bloom

Based on a Bloom composition "Shangri-La." With Mercer's lyrics added, it became a top hit record with many recordings. 560121-7a

For Once in My Life (1965)

Lyrics by Ronald Miller, music by Orlando Murden

This song did not do well until Tony Bennett recorded it for Columbia in 1967, when it became a runaway best-seller. Also recorded with success by Stevie Wonder in 1968 (Tamla). **6805188**

(I Love You) For Sentimental Reasons (1945)

Lyrics by Ivory "Deke" Watson, music by William Best

Introduced by The Ink Spots (of which Watson was a member) (Decca). **460819-1**

For You, For Me, For Evermore (1946)

Lyrics by Ira Gershwin, music by George Gershwin

Introduced by Dick Haymes and Betty Grable in the 1947 20th Century–Fox film *The Shocking Miss Pilgrim*. George Gershwin wrote the melody some time in 1936 or early 1937, then put it aside. Found after his death in a batch of manscripts, it, among others, was adapted into a nine-song score for the film by Ira Gershwin and Kay Swift. **590718-3**

Fotographia *see* **Photograph**

(I Put) A Four-Leaf Clover in Your Pocket (1942)

Lyrics and music by John Jacob Loeb and Benny Davis

Introduced on this Decca recording by Ella Fitzgerald. **420731-2**

Four or Five Times (1927)

Lyrics by Marco H. Hellman, music by Byron Gay

Introduced by Jimmie Noone and His Apex Club Orchestra (Vocalion). First hit record by King Oliver and His Jazz Band, vocal by Andy Pendleton and Willie Jackson (Brunswick). **680603-3a**

Franklin D. Roosevelt Jones (1938)

Lyrics and music by Harold Rome

Introduced by Rex Ingram and ensemble in the 1938 revue *Sing Out the News*. First recorded by Chick Webb and His Orchestra, vocal by Ella Fitzgerald (Decca). **381006-1**

The Frim Fram Sauce (1946)

Lyrics and music by Joe Ricardel and Redd Evans

Introduced and popularized by Louis Armstrong and Ella Fitzgerald (Decca). **460118-2, 520816-6, 531118-9**

From This Moment On (1950)

Lyrics and music by Cole Porter

Introduced by Priscilla Gillette and William Eythe in the 1950 musical play *Out of This World* during its out-of-town try-outs; it was dropped from the show before it reached New York. Adapted as a ballet sequence and sung by Ann Miller, Tommy Rall, Bobby Van, Bob Fosse, and Carol Haney in the 1953 MGM film *Kiss Me, Kate!*
560207-3, 810726-1

Frosty, the Snow Man (1950)

Lyrics and music by Steve Nelson and Jack Rollins

Introduced by Gene Autry as a follow-up to "Rudolph, the Red-Nosed Reindeer" with grand and enduring success (Columbia). **600715-3**

Funny Face (1927)

Lyrics by Ira Gershwin, music by George Gershwin

Introduced by Fred and Adele Astaire in the 1927 musical play *Funny Face*. Sung by Fred Astaire in the 1957 Paramount film adaptation. **590318-4**

Gee, Baby, Ain't I Good to You (1929)

Lyrics by Don Redman and Andy Razaf, music by Don Redman

Introduced by McKinney's Cotton Pickers.
570723-6, 730828-7

Gee, But I'm Glad to Know (That You Love Me) (1952)

Lyrics and music by Robert Allen and Allan Roberts

Introduced by Ella Fitzgerald on this Decca recording
.520225-3

The Gentleman Is a Dope (1947)

Lyrics by Oscar Hammerstein II, music by Richard Rodgers

Introduced by Lisa Kirk in the 1947 musical play *Allegro*. **480601-2, 590410-5d, 611115-2**

Georgia on My Mind (1930)

Lyrics by Stuart Gorrell, music by Hoagy Carmichael

Introduced and popularized by Hoagy Carmichnael (Decca). Revived in 1960 by Ray Charles, whose ABC-Paramount recording won two Grammy (NARAS) Awards in 1960 for Best Male Vocal Recording, and for Best Popular Single Performance of the Year. In 1978, Willie Nelson's recording (Columbia) won the Grammy Award (NARAS), Best Male Country Vocal Performance. Incidentally, the lyricist Stuart Gorrell is the same gentleman who was present that evening at the University of Indiana when Hoagy Carmichael composed "Star Dust," and it was he who christened the composition, although he did not write the lyrics; that honor went to Mitchell Parish a few years later. (Cf. "Star Dust".)
611113-3, 830322-5

Get Happy! (1930)

Lyrics by Ted Koehler, music by Harold Arlen

This was Harold Arlen's first hit. While working as an orchestrator for Vincent Youmans's musical play *Great Day!* he substituted as rehearsal pianist one day. Growing bored, he began repeating the standard two-bar vamp used to set the tempo of a musical number. He began to vary and improvise on the strain, and the tune of "Get Happy!" evolved. It was brought to the attention of Koehler, who wrote a lyric and succeeded in getting it into the 1930 revue *The 9:15 Revue* where it was introduced by Ruth Etting. Miss Etting recorded it, as did Nat Shilkret and His Orchestra. Revived by Judy Garland when she performed it in the 1950 MGM film *Summer Stock* considered by many to be the quintessential Garland performance — and, incidentally, her last on an MGM soundstage. **600802-1**

Get Out of Town (1930)

Lyrics and music by Cole Porter

Introduced by Tamara (Geva) in the 1938 musical play *Leave It to Me*. **560207-12, 610221-3a, 710721-2a**

Get Ready (1966)

Lyrics and music by William "Smokey" Robinson
Introduced by The Temptations (Gordy). **690530-1**

Get Thee Behind Me, Satan (1935)

Lyrics and music by Irving Berlin

Originally introduced by Ginger Rogers in the 1935 RKO film *Top Hat* but the sequence was deleted from the film before its release. Reintroduced by Harriet Hilliard in the 1936 RKO film *Follow the Fleet*. Hilliard also recorded it with husband Ozzie Nelson's Orchestra (Brunswick). **580317-9**

(I Don't Stand) A Ghost of a Chance (with You) (1932)

Lyrics by Bing Crosby and Ned Washington, music by Victor Young

Introduced by Bing Crosby (Brunswick).
740108-2, 790712-8, 860228-9

The Girl from Ipanema (Garôta de Ipanema) (1962)

Portuguese lyrics by Vinícius de Moraes, English lyrics by Norman Gimbel; music by Antonio Carlos Jobim

Introduced by Jobim on recording in Brazil, where it was also recorded by The Tamba Trio, and by singer Pery Ribeiro. Also recorded with Gil Gilberto doing the Portuguese lyrics with Astrud singing in English. Introduced and popularized in the U.S. by Astrud Gilberto and The Stan Getz Quartet at the Café au Go Go in New York. The definitive recording is that of Jobim and the Gilbertos for Verve records. Jobim's televised debut at Carnegie Hall further popularized the song. The Gilberto-Getz recording was awarded the Grammy (NARAS) Award, Record of the Year, 1964.

**640729-16, 650326-11, 700520-11,
710721-4a, 750717-9, 810318-1**

Girl Talk (1964)

Lyrics and music by Neal Hefti and Bobby Troup

Introduced by Neal Hefti and His Orchestra. Recorded also by Bobby Troup.

680518-3, 830321-6

Give a Little, Get a Little (Love) (1951)

Lyrics by Betty Comden and Adolph Green, music by Jule Styne

Introduced by Dolores Gray in the 1951 revue *Two on the Aisle.* **510718-4**

Give It Back to the Indians (1939)

Lyrics by Lorenz Hart, music by Richard Rodgers

Introduced by Mary Jane Walsh and danced by Hal LeRoy and Students (including Van Johnson) in the 1939 musical play *Too Many Girls.* Sung by Lucille Ball in the 1940 RKO film adaptation. ("It" refers to Manhattan, and it is said Rodgers and Hart wrote it as a counterfoil to their earlier hit of that name.) **560828-5**

Give Me the Simple Life (1945)

Lyrics by Harry Ruby, music by Rube Bloom

Introduced by John Payne and June Haver in the 1946 20th Century–Fox film *Wake Up and Dream.* Used for the 1977 Campbell's Soup commercial promotion campaign and titled "Give Me the Campbell Life."

610211-1, 610513-13, 610518-13,
610519-16, **690200-6**

Glad to Be Unhappy (1936)

Lyrics by Lorenz Hart, music by Richard Rodgers

Introduced by Doris Carson and David Morris in the 1936 musical play *On Your Toes.* 560121-7b, 560202-11

The Glory of Love (1936)

Lyrics and music by Billy Hill

Introduced, featured, and recorded by Rudy Vallée and His Orchestra (Melotone). **590410-5f**

God Be with You Till We Meet Again *see God Will Take Care of You*
Till We Meet Again

God Bless the Child (1941)

Lyrics and music by Arthur Herzog, Jr., and Billie Holiday
Introduced and popularized by Billie Holiday. Sung by

Diana Ross in the 1972 Paramount film *Lady Sings the Blues;* and interpolated in the 1976 revue *Bubblin' Brown Sugar.*

820204-2

God Rest Ye Merry, Gentlemen (18th century)

Lyric, traditional 18th-century English; music, traditional 18th-century London

This famous carol is not so old as to date back to Merrie England, the very epitome of which many think it to be. In its existence of two and a half centuries, it has become one of our most popular carols. Its perfect balance of joy and humility places it securely in the realm of high poetry. William Sandys included it in the text of his 1833 collection *Christmas Carols, Ancient and Modern.* The melody is probably much older than the poem. Sir John Stainer wrote the harmonization. **670719-4**

God Will Take Care of You (1905)

Lyrics by Civilla D. Martin, music by W.S. Martin

This hymn immediately became a standard on its publication by Rev. and Mrs. W.S. Martin, especially so in Methodist churches. **670200-3**

Goin' and Gettin' It (1940)

Lyrics by Luther Frank, music by Dick Vance

Introduced by Ella Fitzgerald and Her Famous Orchestra as an instrumental. Performed on her radio programs, but never recorded in a studio. **400304-9**

Goin' Out of My Head (1964)

Lyrics and music by Teddy Randazzo and Bobby Weinstein

Best-selling record by Little Anthony and The Imperials (DCP). The Lettermen revived it in 1968 with a Top 10 medley version with "Can't Take My Eyes Off of You."

**660727-2b, 660728-8b, 660729-7b,
671113-1d, 680518-7b**

Gone with the Wind (1937)

Lyrics by Herb Magidson, music by Allie Wrubel

The title of Margaret Mitchell's 1936 best-seller inspired many songwriters, no doubt with the hope that their efforts would be included in the much publicized forthcoming movie, the filming of which had begun the same year with great fanfare. However, this seems to be the only surviver, but it could have stood on its own in any case. Introduced and popularized by Horace Heidt and His Orchestra.

560202-8, **590711-2, 600213-3,**
610519-3, **680518-5, 830321-6**

Good Morning Blues (1938)

Lyrics and music by William "Count" Basie, Ed Durham, and James Rushing.

Introduced and recorded by Count Basie and His Orchestra, vocal by Jimmy (James) Rushing. Also a hit for Huddie "Leadbelly" Ledbetter (Asch).   **600805-1**

Good Morning, Heartache (1946)

Lyrics and music by Irene Higginbotham, Ervin Drake, and Dan Fisher

Introduced and recorded by Billie Holiday with Artie Shaw and His Orchestra (Decca).
          610622-6, 620630-9, **730705-9, 890316-4**

Good-Bye (1935)

Lyrics and music by Gordon Jenkins

Closing theme of Benny Goodman and His Orchestra.   **820205-2**

Goodnight, My Love (1936)

Lyrics by Mack Gordon, music by Harry Revel

Introduced by Shirley Temple and reprised by Alice Faye in the 1936 20th Century-Fox film *Stowaway*.
          361105-1, 680529-2f

Goody Goody (1936)

Lyrics by Johnny Mercer, music by Matty Malneck

Best-selling records by the orchestras of Benny Goodman, vocal by Helen Ward (Victor); Freddy Martin; and Bob Crosby.
          520225-4, 520607-4, **570724-8**, 570929-7,
          571009-6, 640203-5, **640729-15**

Got to Get You into My Life (1966)

Lyrics and music by John Lennon and Paul McCartney

Introduced by The Beatles in their album *Revolver* (Capitol).   **690528-3**

Gotta Be This or That (1945)

Lyrics and music by Sunny Skylar

Introduced by Benny Goodman and His Orchestra, vocal by Benny Goodman (Victor).
          580409-3. 581123-4

Gotta Pebble in My Shoe (1938)

Lyrics by Charles Tobias, music by Van Alexander (Al Feldman)

Introduced by Chick Webb and His Orchestra, vocal by Ella Fitzgerald (Decca).   **380817-2**

The Greatest There Is (1952)

Lyrics by Ella Fitzgerald, music by Mercer Ellington

Introduced by Ella Fitzgerald with Leroy Kirkland and His Orchestra (Decca).   **520811-2**

Guilty (1931)

Lyrics by Gus Kahn, music by Harry Akst and Richard A. Whiting

Introduced, recorded and popularized by Ruth Etting, for whom the song was written.   470124-1, 470222-1

Gulf Coast Blues (1923)

Lyrics and music by Clarence Williams

Introduced by Monette Moore (Paramount). Best-selling records by Bessie Smith, accompanied by Clarence Williams at the piano (coupled with Smith's first recording, "Down Hearted Blues").   **400509-3**

A Guy Is a Guy (1951)

Lyrics and music by Oscar Brand

Adapted from the 1719 English broadside ballad, "I Went to the Alehouse (A Knave Is a Knave)," of which a World War II version was called "A Gob Is a Slob." New version introduced by Doris Day, with Paul Weston's Orchestra, on a best-selling Columbia record.   **520225-1**

Guys and Dolls (1950)

Lyrics and music by Frank Loesser

Introduced by Stubby Kaye and Johnny Silver in the 1950 musical play *Guys and Dolls*. Sung by Frank Sinatra, Stubby Kaye, and Johnny Silver in the 1955 MGM film adaptation.   **621002-3**

The Gypsy in My Soul (1937)

Lyrics by Moe Jaffe, music by Clay Boland

Introduced in the 1937 University of Pennsylvania Mask and Wig Club revue *Fifty-Fifty*.   **570724-7**

"The Half of It, Dearie" Blues (1924)

Lyrics by Ira Gershwin, music by George Gershwin

Introduced by Fred Astaire and Kathleen Martyn in the 1924 musical play *Lady, Be Good!*   **590715-5**

Hallelujah! (1927)

Lyrics by Leo Robin and Clifford Grey, music by Vincent Youmans

Introduced by Stella Mayhew and chorus in the 1927 musical play *Hit the Deck!* Sung by Marguerite Padula in the 1930 RKO film adaptation; and by Tony Martin, Vic Damone, and Russ Tamblyn in the 1955 MGM film adaptation. Youmans wrote the music in 1917 while serving in the Navy in World War I. He showed it to the bandmaster at Great Lakes Naval Training Station where he was serving. The bandmaster liked it so well that it soon became a favorite with Navy bands, and he encouraged Youmans to consider songwriting as a career. It was often featured by John Philip Sousa and his band in their programs.
          371102-1, 371102-2, **371217-5**

Hallelujah, I Love Him So (1956)

Lyrics and music by Ray Charles

Introduced by Ray Charles (Atlantic); it became a best-selling record for Peggy Lee (Capitol).
620130-5, 620629-2, 620630-14, 640800-8, 640800-19

Hands Off the Man [The Flim Flam Man] (1967)

Lyrics and music by Laura Nyro

Introduced by Laura Nyro in her album *More Than a New Discovery* (Verve)
700124-2

Happiness Is (Just) a Thing Called Joe (1942)

Lyrics by E.Y. "Yip" Harburg, music by Harold Arlen

Introduced by Ethel Waters in the 1943 MGM film *Cabin in the Sky*, for which the song was especially written for the film adaptation of the 1940 musical play. Nominated for an Academy Award (AMPAS), Best Original Song, 1943.
610116-3, 610519-5

Happy Birthday (to You) (1893)

Lyrics by Patty Smith Hill, music by Mildred J. Hill

Introduced by the Hills locally in Louisville, Kentucky. The unauthorized use of the song in the 1933 Irving Berlin musical revue *As Thousands Cheer* took the Hills to court, resulting in a decision that still requires royalties to be paid to their estate.
610520-11

Happy Blues (1974)

Lyrics and music by Ella Fitzgerald

Introduced by Ella Fitzgerald in concert, and on her Pablo album *Ella in London*, 1974.
740411-6

Happy Talk (1949)

Lyrics by Oscar Hammerstein II, music by Richard Rodgers

Introduced by Juanita Hall in the 1949 musical play *South Pacific*. Performed by Juanita Hall (dubbed by Muriel Smith\Sung by Muriel Smith) in the 1958 20th Century-Fox film adaptation.
490428-1

A Hard Day's Night (1964)

Lyrics and music by John Lennon and Paul McCartney

Introduced by the Beatles in the 1964 United Artists film *A Hard Day's Night*. The title comes from Beatle Ringo Starr's comment, referring to an all-night recording session of some of the songs for the film. Winner of the Ivor Novello Award for Best Song, 1964. The Beatles' recording won the Grammy Award (NARAS) for Best Performance by a Vocal Group, 1964.
650326-12, 660208-3b

Hard Hearted Hannah (The Vamp of Savannah) (1929)

Lyrics by Bob Bigelow, Charles Bates, and Jack Yellen, music by Milton Ager

Introduced by Frances Williams in the 1929 musical play *Innocent Eyes*. Memorably performed by Ella Fitzgerald in the 1955 Warner Bros. film *Pete Kelly's Blues*, after which it was successfully revived on record by Ella (Decca).
550503-1, 550724-1, 580409-2e, 620629-12, **810726-11**

Hark! The Herald Angels Sing (1855)

Lyrics by Charles Wesley, George Whitefield, et al.; music by Felix Mendelssohn-Bartoldy

Charles Wesley intended his hymn to deal with the Incarnation, rather than with Christmas, thus, his opening lines "Hark! How all the welkin rings,/Glory to the King of Kings." George Whitefield, a personal friend and associate, altered the lines to include the Herald Angels. Welsey's stanzas were four lines long, and were probably originally sung to a simple hymn tune. Over a hundred years after the text was written, William Cummings, organist of Waltham Abbey (England) rearranged the words into ten-line stanzas, and set them to an adaptation of the second chorus of "Festgesang am die Künstler," a cantata for male chorus and brass Herr Mendelssohn had written in 1846 to celebrate the 400th anniversary of the invention of printing with movable type!
670717-2

Have Mercy! (1939)

Lyrics by Buck Ram, music by Buck Ram and Chick Webb

Introduced and popularized by Ella Fitzgerald with Chick Webb and His Orchestra (Decca).
390421-5, 480525-1, 700104-2

Have You Met Miss Jones? (1937)

Lyrics by Lorenz Hart, music by Richard Rodgers

Introduced by Joy Hodges and Austin Marshall in the 1937 musical play *I'd Rather Be Right*.
560830-4

Have Yourself a Merry Little Christmas (1944)

Lyrics by Ralph Blane, music by Hugh Martin

Introduced by Judy Garland in the 1944 MGM film *Meet Me in St. Louis* in a poignant scene in which she sang it to an unhappy Margaret O'Brien. Now a Christmas standard recorded by almost every singer, choir and chorus who have a Christmas album.
600716-5

Hawaiian War Chant (1936)

Lyrics by Ralph Freed, music by Prince William Pitt Leleiohaku, and adapted by Johnny Noble

Introduced by Johnny Noble and His Orchestra.
680603-2

He Loves and She Loves (1927)

Lyrics by Ira Gershwin, music by George Gershwin

Introduced by Adele Astaire and Allen Kearns in the 1927 musical play *Funny Face*. Sung by Fred Astaire and danced by Astaire and Audrey Hepburn in the 1957 Paramount film adaptation.   **590105-10**, 591213-3

He's/She's a Carioca [Ele/Ela é Carioca] (1965)

Portuguese lyrics by Vinícius de Moraes, English lyrics by Ray Gilbert, music by Antonio Carlos Jobim.

Introduced in performance and on Brazilian records by Antonio Carlos Jobim.   **810318-3**

He's/She's Funny That Way (I Got A Man/Woman Crazy for Me) (1928)

Lyrics by Richard A. Whiting, music by Neil Moret

Introduced by Gene Austin (Victor). This was a rare case of composer Whiting writing a lyrics to someone else's melody.   **620409-2**

He's My Guy (1942)

Lyrics and music by Don Raye and Gene DePaul

Introduced by Harry James and His Orchestra, vocal by Helen Forrest (Columbia).   **420731-3**

He's My Kind of Boy

Research has revealed neither the authors nor the origins of this song, and since none of Ella's recorded performances has been released, there are no performance notes to consult.   620629-14, 620630-1, 620630-22

He's Tall, He's Tan, He's Terrific *see* She's Tall, She's Tan, She's Terrific

Heah Me Talkin' to Ya (1928)

Lyrics and music by Gertrude "Ma" Rainey

Introduced and first recording by Ma Rainey (Paramount). Most famous versions by Louis Armstrong on several recordings.   **631028-5**

Hear My Heart (1957)

Lyrics and music by Albert "Buddy" Lester

It is believed that Ella's recording of this song in 1957 for Verve was the first recording.   **570114-1**

Heart and Soul (1938)

Lyrics by Frank Loesser, music by Hoagy Carmichael

Introduced by Larry Clinton and His Orchestra in a 1938 film short *A Song Is Born*.   **610115-6**

Heart of Mine (1938)

Lyrics and music by Chick Webb and Edward Heyman

Introduced by Chick Webb and His Orchestra, vocal by Ella Fitzgerald (Decca).   **380502-2**

Heat Wave (1933)

Lyrics and music by Irving Berlin

Introduced by Ethel Merman and danced by Letitia Ide and José Limon in the 1933 revue *As Thousands Cheer*.   **481204-1**, 580318-2

Hello, Dolly! (1963)

Lyrics and music by Jerry Herman

Introduced by Carol Channing and David Hartmann and chorus in the 1964 musical play *Hello, Dolly!* Received the Grammy Award (NARAS), Best Song of the Year, 1964; and the same award to Louis Armstrong as Best Male Performance of the Year for his Kapp recording.   **640407-2**, 640728-1, **640729-1**, 710518-7

Hello, Ma! I Done It Again (1941)

Lyrics by Leo Robin, music by Ralph Rainger

At the time of Ella's recording of this song, Robin and Rainger were among the most prolific of film musical songwriters; however, research has failed to reveal the origins of this song. It is believed that it was written but not used in a film. Ella was noted to pursue the latest in popular songs to record, and this may be a case where hers was the first the first and only recording.   **410108-2**

Hello, Young Lovers (1951)

Lyrics by Oscar Hammerstein II, music by Richard Rodgers

Introduced by Gertrude Lawrence in the 1951 musical play *The King and I*. Sung by Deborah Kerr (dubbed by Marni Nixon) in the 1956 20th Century–Fox film version.   **700520-9**

(Hep! Hep!) The Jumpin' Jive *see* The Jumpin' Jive

Here Come de Honey Man (1935)

Lyrics by DuBose Heyward, music by George Gershwin

Introduced by Todd Duncan (as Porgy) and members of the chorus in the 1935 folk opera *Porgy and Bess.*   **570828-6**

Here in My Arms (1925)

Lyrics by Lorenz Hart, music by Richard Rodgers

Introduced by Helen Forde and Charles Purcell in the 1925 musical play *Dearest Enemy*.   560831-1

Here's That Rainy Day (1953)

Lyrics by Johnny Burke, music by James Van Heusen

Introduced by John Raitt in the 1953 musical play *Carnival in Flanders*.   **650326-4**

Hernando's Hideaway (1954)

Lyrics and music by Richard Adler and Jerry Ross

Introduced by John Raitt and Carol Haney in the 1954 musical play *The Pajama Game*. They reprised their performances in the 1957 Warner Bros. film adaptation

.**540917-4, 621002-4**

Hey, Jude (1968)

Lyrics and music by John Lennon and Paul McCartney

Introduced by The Beatles (Apple). Winner of the Ivor Novello Award for Best Song, 1968-69. Interpolated in the 1980 revue *Beatlemania*.   **690200-1**

Hey, There! (1954)

Lyrics and music by Richard Adler and Jerry Ross

Introduced by John Raitt in the 1954 musical play *The Pajama Game*. Sung by Doris Day and John Raitt in the 1957 Columbia film adaptation.   540918-2

Holiday in Harlem (1937)

Lyrics by E. Reed, music by Chick Webb

Introduced by Chick Webb and His Orchestra, vocal by Ella Fitzgerald (Decca).   **371027-4**

The Honeydripper (1945)

Lyrics and music by Joe Liggins

Introduced by Joe Liggins in 1945, with a best-selling record for Exclusive Records. Ella never recorded this in a studio, but, fortunately, we have a recording from a radio broadcast.   **460121-1**

Honeysuckle Rose (1929)

Lyrics by Andy Razaf, music by Thomas "Fats" Waller

Introduced as a dance number in the 1929 revue *Load of Coal* at Connie's Inn, New York. First radio performance by Paul Whiteman and His Orchestra.
371210-3, 630715-5, 640728-16,
790216-4, 790712-12

Hooray for Love (1948)

Lyrics by Leo Robin, music by Harold Arlen

Introduced by Tony Martin in the 1948 Universal film *Casbah*.   **600801-1**

The Hot Canary (1948)

Lyrics by Ray Gilbert (1949), music by Paul Nero

A jazz adaptation of "Le Canari" by Paul Yakim ("Poliakin"). Best-selling instrumental by Paul Weston and His Orchestra, with Nero as solo violinist.   **510327-4**

Hotta Chocolata (1956)

Lyrics by Milton Drake, music by Vic Mizzy

Introduced by Ella Fitzgerald, with Russ Garcia and His Orchestra (Verve).   **570114-2**

A House Is Not a Home (1964)

Lyrics by Hal David, music by Burt Bacharach

Title song of the 1964 Embassy film of the same title. Introduced and popularized by Dionne Warwick.
690200-10

How About Me? (1928)

Lyrics and music by Irving Berlin

Popularized by Fred Waring and His Pennsylvanians.
580317-8

How Am I to Know? (1929)

Lyrics by Dorothy Parker, music by Jack King

Introduced by Russ Columbo in the 1930 MGM film *Dynamite*.   **680528-2b**

How Deep Is the Ocean (1932)

Lyrics and music by Irving Berlin

Popularized by the recording of Bing Crosby (Decca).
580317-3

How High the Moon (1940)

Lyrics by Nancy Hamilton, music by Morgan Lewis

Introduced by Frances Comstock and Alfred Drake and danced by Tommy Wonder, Eunice Healey, William Archibald and Nadine Gae in the 1940 revue *Two for the Show*. First recorded by Larry Clinton and His Orchestra, vocal by Terry Allen (Victor). Outstanding scat performances by Ella Fitzgerald on tours, in concert, and on recordings — identified with Ella the world over.
470929-6, 471220-3, 471220-4, 471220-5,
481127-6, 481204-6, 490415-4, 490918-11,
501230-7, 520607-6, 531118-6, 550802-1,
560202-7, 580810-24, **590809-1, 600213-11,**
610513-21, **640303-2, 640729-26, 660130-1,**
660222-7, 660208-3a, **66020812, 670430-1,**
710518-9, 750717-8

How Insensitive (Insensatez [Foolishness]) (1963)

Portuguese lyrics by Vinícius de Moraes, English lyrics by Norman Gimbel, music by Antonio Carlos Jobim

Introduced by Antonio Carlos Jobim in performances and on Brazilian records. Memorably performed by Ella Fitzgerald on her 1981 Pablo album *Ella Abraça Jobim/Ella Fitzgerald Sings the Antonio Carlos Jobim Song Book*.
800919-2

How Long Has This Been Going On? (1927)

Lyrics by Ira Gershwin, music by George Gershwin

Introduced by Adele Astaire and Stanley Ridges in the out-of-town try-outs of the musical play *Funny Face* but replaced for the New York opening by "He Loves and She Loves." With a slightly revised lyric, reintroduced by Bobbe Arnst in the 1928 musical play *Rosalie*. Sung by Audrey Hepburn in the 1957 Parmount film adaptation.

500911-3, **510519-5**, 570724-4, 571015-12, **571028-4**, 580810-4, **590105-5**, 620629-20, **660727-3**, **660923-4**,750919-2, 830523-9

How Long, How Long Blues (1929)

Lyrics and music by Leroy Carr

Introduced by Leroy Carr, who recorded it in numbered versions five times in two years (Vocalion).

631028-1

How's Chances? (1933)

Lyrics and music by Irving Berlin

Introduced by Marilyn Miller and Clifton Webb in the 1933 revue *As Thousands Cheer*.   **580314-3**

The Huckle-Buck (1948)

Lyrics by Roy Alfred, music by Andy Gibson

Introduced by Paul Williams and His Orchestra as an instrumental (Savoy). Vocal version introduced by Frank Sinatra in 1949 (Columbia).   500900-10

The Hunter Gets Captured by the Game (1966)

Lyrics and music by William "Smokey" Robinson

Introduced by Smokey Robinson. Popular recording by The Marvelettes (Tamla).   **690530-2**

Hurry Home (1938)

Lyrics and music by Joseph Meyer, Buddy Bernier, and Bob Emmerich

Introduced by Thelma Carpenter (Majestic).

571028-3

I Ain't Got Nothin' But the Blues (1944)

Lyrics by Don George, music by Duke Ellington

Introduced by Duke Ellington and His Orchestra, vocal by Al Hibbler (Victor).

570625-5, 760130-2, 770714-2

I Am in Love (1953)

Lyrics and music by Cole Porter

Introduced by Peter Cookson in the 1953 musical play *Can-Can*. Sung by Louis Jourdan in the 1960 20th Century-Fox film adaptation.   **560207-11**

I Can't Be Bothered Now (1937)

Lyrics by Ira Gershwin, music by George Gershwin

Introduced by Fred Astaire in the 1937 RKO film *Damsel in Distress*.   **590318-1**

I Can't Believe That You're in Love with Me (1926)

Lyrics by Clarence Gaskill, music by Jimmy McHugh

Introduced by Aida Ward at the Cotton Club in Harlem, New York. Sung by Winnie Lightner in the 1927 revue *Gay Paree*.   **410731-1**

I Can't Face the Music (Without Singing the Blues) (1938)

Lyrics by Ted Koehler, music by Rube Bloom

Introduced by Mildred Bailey with Red Norvo's Orchestra (Vocalion).   **620130-3**

I Can't Get Started (with You) (1935)

Lyrics by Ira Gershwin, music by Vernon Duke

Introduced by Bob Hope and Eve Arden and ensemble in the revue *Ziegfeld Follies of 1936*.

540000-1, **550401-4**, 610519-15, **611113-4**

I Can't Give You Anything but Love (1927)

Lyrics by Dorothy Fields, music by Jimmy McHugh

Introduced by Aida Ward and Willard McLean in the 1928 revue *Lew Leslie's Blackbirds of 1928*. Originally written for Patsy Kelly to perform in the 1927 revue *Harry Delmar's Revels* but was dropped.

530101-1c, 560202-15, **560815-10**, **570428-7**, 570704-10, **580425-25**, 5908004, 600419-2, 740108-3

I Can't Go On Without You (1949)

Lyrics and music by Henry Glover and Sally Mix

Best-selling record by Ella Fitzgerald (Decca).

480820-2

I Can't Lie to Myself (1952)

Lyrics and music by Albert J. Trace

Introduced by Ella Fitzgerald on this Decca recording.   **521130-1**

I Can't Stop Loving You (1938)

Lyrics and music by Chuck Jones and Chick Webb

Introduced by Chick Webb and His Orchestra, vocal by Ella Fitzgerald (Decca).   **380817-3**

I Can't Stop Loving You (1958)

Lyrics and music by Don Gibson

Introduced by Don Gibson (Victor). Ray Charles's

version (ABC-Paramount) won a Grammy Award (NARAS) as Rhythm and Blues Song of the Year, 1962. **680518-11, 720602-13**

I Concentrate on You (1939)

Lyrics and music by Cole Porter

Introduced by Douglas McPhail and danced by Fred Astaire and Eleanor Powell in the 1939 MGM film *Broadway Melody of 1940*.

560209-4, 560327-4, 690729-9, 700520-10a, 720612-11

I Could Have Danced All Night (1956)

Lyrics by Alan Jay Lerner, music by Frederick Loewe

Introduced by Julie Andrews in the 1956 musical play *My Fair Lady*. Performed by Audrey Hepburn (dubbed by Marnie Nixon) in the 1964 Warner Bros. film adaptation. **560815-3, 621002-1**

I Could Write a Book (1940)

Lyrics by Lorenz Hart, music by Richard Rodgers

Introduced by Gene Kelly and Leila Ernst in the 1940 musical play *Pal Joey*. Sung by Frank Sinatra in the 1957 Columbia film adaptation. **560830-9**

I Couldn't Stay Away (1948)

Lyrics and music by Ben Raleigh and Bernie Wayne

Introduced by Ella Fitzgerald on this Decca recording. **490114-1**

I Cover the Waterfront (1933)

Lyrics by Edward Heyman, music by John W. Green

Written to exploit the 1933 United Artists film of the same title. The film was released before the song was written, but after being introduced by Ben Bernie and His Orchestra, the song became such a hit that the film was recalled briefly in order to re-score the music to include the melody. **481204-5**

I Cried and Cried and Cried (1947)

Lyrics and music by Lee Kuhn

Research has revealed no other recording of this song, and it may be assumed that Ella's is the only recording. **471223-3**

I Cried for You (1933)

Lyrics and music by Arthur Freed, Gus Arnheim, and Abe Lyman

This was the first big hit for each of the writers. Arnheim was playing piano in Lyman's orchestra at the time. Introduced by Abe Lyman and His Orchestra. **600414-5, 680528-2d, 780620-7**

I Didn't Know About You (1942/1944)

Lyrics by Bob Russell, music by Duke Ellington

Adapted from a 1942 Ellington composition, "Sentimental Lady," recorded by Ellington in 1942. Vocal version introduced by Duke Ellington and His Orchestra, vocal by Joya Sherrill, in 1944 (Victor). **570626-4, 760129-1**

I Didn't Know What Time It Was (1939)

Lyrics by Lorenz Hart, music by Richard Rodgers

Introduced by Marcy Westcott and Richard Kollmar in the 1939 musical play *Too Many Girls*. Sung by Lucille Ball (dubbed by Trudi Erwin), Eddie Bracken, Hal LeRoy and Desi Arnaz in the 1940 RKO film adaptation. **560829-5**

I Didn't Mean a Word I Said (1946)

Lyrics by Harold Adamson, music by Jimmy McHugh

Introduced by Dick Haymes in the 1946 20th Century–Fox film *Do You Love Me?* **460221-2**

I Don't Know Why (I Love You Like I Do) (1931)

Lyrics by Roy Turk, music by Fred E. Ahlert

Introduced, featured and recorded by Russ Columbo (Vocalion). **691023-1**

I Don't Stand a Ghost of a Chance with You *see* A Ghost of a Chance

I Don't Want the World (1950)

Lyrics and music by Hy Heath and Johnny Lange

Introduced by Ella Fitzgerald on this Decca recording. **500509-2**

I Don't Want to Take a Chance (1951)

Lyrics and music by Ella Fitzgerald

Introduced by Ella Fitzgerald on this Decca recording. **510718-2**

I Fell in Love with a Dream (1940)

Lyrics and music by Ella Fitzgerald, ? Skye, and ? Goldsmith

Introduced by Ella Fitzgerald and Her Famous Orchestra, vocal by Ella Fitzgerald (Decca). **400509-4**

I Found a New Baby (1926)

Lyrics and music by Jack Palmer and Spencer Williams

Introduced by The Chicago Rhythm Kings (Brunswick). **610513-1, 610516-1, 610520-25**

I Found My Yellow Basket (1938)

Lyrics and music by Ella Fitzgerald and Van Alexander (Al Feldman)

Introduced by Ella Fitzgerald with Chick Webb and His Orchestra (Decca). A "sequel" to the enormously successful "A-Tisket, A-Tasket." Ella often sang the two songs in medley; and although this song was moderately popular, it never reached the success of its forebear.

381006-4

I Get a Kick Out of You (1934)

Lyrics and music by Cole Porter

Introduced by Ethel Merman and William Gaxton in the 1934 musical play *Anything Goes.* Sung by Miss Merman and Bing Crosby in the 1936 Paramount film adaptation; and by Jeanmaire, who also danced it, in the 1956 Paramount film adaptation. **560209-6, 720612-1**

I Got a Guy (1937)

Lyrics and music by Marion Sunshine

Introduced by Chick Webb and His Orchestra, vocal by Ella Fitzgerald (Decca).

371027-2, 490211-2, **610123-7**, 610123-8

I Got a Man Crazy for Me see He's Funny That Way

I Got It Bad (and That Ain't Good) (1941)

Lyrics by Paul Francis Webster, music by Duke Ellington

Introduced by Ivie Anderson in the 1941 revue *Jump for Joy*, and popularized by Ellington and His Orchestra, vocal by Anderson (Victor), considered in some jazz circles as Miss Anderson's finest recorded performance.

410731-4, 531118-5, 570625-2, 570704-2

I Got Plenty o' Nuttin' (1935)

Lyrics by Ira Gershwin and DuBose Heyward, music by George Gershwin

Introduced by Todd Duncan as Porgy in Act II, Scene 1, of the 1935 folk opera *Porgy and Bess.* Performed by Sidney Poitier (dubbed by Robert "Bobby" McFerrin) in the 1959 Samuel Goldwyn film adaptation. The Verve recording of *Porgy and Bess* with Ella Fitzgerald and Louis Armstrong is counted by many to be the best non-operatic rendition recorded. It is certainly unique, and contains material not in the original production. **570818-3**

I Got Rhythm (1930)

Lyrics by Ira Gershwin, music by George Gershwin

Introduced by Ethel Merman and The Foursome (Marshall Smith, Ray Johnson, Del Porter and Dwight Snyder) in the 1930 musical play *Girl Crazy.* Sung by Judy Garland in the 1943 MGM film adaptation; used as a production number in the 1965 MGM film adaptation *When the Boys Meet the Girls.* Used as a theme for Gershwin's concert work, "Variations on I Got Rhythm," for piano and

orchestra, introduced by Charles Previn conducting the Leo Reisman Orchestra, with the composer at the piano.

400304-2, 590105-2

I Got the Spring Fever Blues (1936)

Lyrics and music by Kay Werner and Sue Werner

Introduced by Chick Webb and His Orchestra, vocal by Ella Fitzgerald (Decca). **361029-4**

I Gotta Have My Baby Back (1949)

Lyrics and music by Floyd Tillman

Introduced by Floyd Tillman (Columbia).

491107-2

I Gotta Right to Sing the Blues (1932)

Lyrics by Ted Koehler, music by Harold Arlen

Introduced by Lillian Shade in the 1932 revue *Earl Carroll's Vanities, 10th Edition.* **580409-2a, 610114-3**

I Had to Find Out for Myself (1956)

Lyrics by Max Lief, music by Manning Sherwin

Introduced by Ella Fitzgerald on this Verve recording which was never released, a great shame since it is a lovely song, beautifully performed. **560327-5, 560327-6**

I Had to Live and Learn (1939)

Lyrics and music by Johnson, May, and Chick Webb

Introduced by Chick Webb and His Orchestra, with Ella as vocalist, on this Decca recording, one of the last of his compositions to be recorded during his lifetime.

390302-2

I Hadn't Anyone Till You (1938)

Lyrics and music by Ray Noble

Introduced by Ray Noble and His Orchestra, vocal by Tony Martin (Brunswick).

490430-5, 490921-1, 500503-2, 501008-2, 530101-1a, 600414-4

I Hear Music (1940)

Lyrics by Frank Loesser, music by Burton Lane

Introduced by Peter Lind Hayes, Eddie Quillan, Frank Jenks, and Robert Paige in the 1941 Paramount film *Dancing on a Dime.* **611114-5, 750519-7**

I Heard It Through the Grapevine (1966)

Lyrics and music by Norman Whitfield and Barrett Strong

Introduced by Gladys Knight and the Pips (Soul).

701222-1

I Let a Song Go Out of My Heart (1938)

Lyrics by Henry Nemo, John Redmond, and Irving Mills; music by Duke Ellington

Introduced as an instrumental by Duke Ellington and His Orchestra. Vocal version introduced by Mildred Bailey, with Red Norvo and His Orchestra.

560904-1, 770714-8

I Let a Tear Fall in the River (1938)

Lyrics by Mack David, music by Jerry Livingston and Chick Webb

Introduced by Chick Webb and His Orchestra, vocal by Ella Fitzgerald (Decca). **380818-4, 390121-1**

I Like the Sunrise (1947)

Lyrics and music by Duke Ellington

From Ellington's "Liberian Suite." Introduced by Duke Ellington and His Orchestra, vocal by Al Hibbler at Carnegie Hall, New York, in 1947. **651019-1**

I Love Being Here with You (1963)

Lyrics and music by Peggy Lee and William Schluger

Introduced by Ernestine Anderson.
640203-6, 640728-4, **640729-4**, 640800-4

I Love Each Move You Make (1938)

Lyrics and music by Grumble and Chick Webb

Introduced by Chick Webb and His Orchestra, vocal by Ella Fitzgerald (Decca). **381006-2**

I Love Paris (1953)

Lyrics and music by Cole Porter

Introduced by Lilo in the 1953 musical play *Can-Can*. Sung by Frank Sinatra and Maurice Chevalier in the 1960 20th Century–Fox film adaptation. Porter was inspired to write this song by the stunning sets designed by Jo Meilzner depicting Paris roof-tops during the stage production. **560207-8**

I Love You for Sentimental Reasons *see*
For Sentimental Reasons.

I Loves You, Porgy *see* *I Wants To Stay Here*

I May Be Wrong (But I Think You're Wonderful) (1929)

Lyrics by Harry Ruskin, music by Henry Sullivan

Introduced by Jimmy Savo and Trixie Friganza in the 1929 revue *Murray Anderson's Almanac*.

580509-4b, 830322-8

I Must Have That Man (1928)

Lyrics by Dorothy Fields, music by Jimmy McHugh

Introduced by Adelaide Hall in the 1928 revue *Lew Leslie's Blackbirds of 1928*. **410731-2, 590410-4**

I Need (1954)

Lyrics and music by Ralph Care and Sol Marcus

Introduced by Ella Fitzgerald on this Decca recording. **540325-3**

I Need Thee Every Hour (1872)

Lyrics by Annie Sherwood Hawks, music by Robert Lowry

When Mrs. Hawks wrote the hymn, it was at once set to music by Rev. Lowry, minister of the Hanson Street Baptist Church, Brooklyn, which she attended. Perhaps he, rather than the author, provided the magic touch—both lyrics and music of "Where Is My Wandering Boy Tonight?" a major hit in its day, came from his pen. **670200-12**

I Never Had a Chance (1934)

Lyrics and music by Irving Berlin

Introduced and recorded by Isham Jones and His Orchestra (Decca). **571015-10, 780619-1**

I Never Knew (I Could Love Anybody) (1920)

Lyrics and music by Tom Pitts, Raymond B. Egan, and Roy Marsh

Recorded and popularized by Paul Whiteman and His Orchestra (Victor). **481127-5, 680529-2e**

I Never Knew Heaven Could Speak (1939)

Lyrics by Mack Gordon, music by Harry Revel

Introduced by Alice Faye in the 20th Century–Fox film *Rose of Washington Square*. **390504-7**

I Only Have Eyes for You (1934)

Lyrics by Al Dubin, music by Harry Warren

Introduced by Dick Powell in the 1934 First National film *Dames*. **611114-3**

I Put a Four-Leaf Clover in Your Pocket *see*
A Four-Leaf Clover in Your Pocket

I Remember You (1942)

Lyrics by Johnny Mercer, music by Victor Schertzinger

Introduced by Dorothy Lamour and Bob Eberly, with Jimmy Dorsey and His Orchestra, in the 1942 Paramount film *The Fleet's In*. **581124-4, 641021-4**

I Said No (1941)

Lyrics by Frank Loesser, music by Jule Styne

Introduced by Betty Jane Rhodes in the 1942 Paramount film *Sweater Girl*, and on a Decca recording.
641022-2, **660720-3**

I Shall Not Be Moved (1908)

Lyrics and music by Alfred H. Ackley

This hymn was a favorite of the great singer-evangelist, Homer A. Rodeheaver, who toured to every corner of the U.S. with Billy Sunday, from 1909-1931, serving as his musical director. **670200-7**

I Still Feel the Same About You (1950)

Lyrics and music by Don Reid and Dick Manning

Best-selling records in 1951 by Georgia Gibbs, with The Owen Bradley Sextet (Coral); and The Three Suns with The Sons of the Pioneers (Victor). **501220-2**

I Taught Her/Him Everything She/He Knows

Lyrics by Sylvia Dee, music by Arthur Kent

Ella chose this Dee-Kent classic for her album *Misty Blue* for Capitol in 1967. **671220-1**

I Thought About You (1939)

Lyrics by Johnny Mercer, music by Jimmy Van Heusen

Introduced by Benny Goodman and His Orchestra, vocal by Mildred Bailey. **571015-9**

I Used to Be Color Blind (1938)

Lyrics and music by Irving Berlin

Introduced by Fred Astaire and Ginger Rogers in the 1938 RKO film *Carefree*. **580314-1**

I Wanna Be a Rug-Cutter
[I've Gotta Be a Rug Cutter] (1937)

Lyrics and music by Duke Ellington

Introduced and recorded by Duke Ellington and His Orchestra (Victor). **400226-10**

I Want a Little Girl (1930)

Lyrics by Billy Moll, music by Murray Mencher

Introduced by McKinney's Cotton Pickers (Vocalion). **860228-13**

I Want the Waiter (with the Water) (1939)

Lyrics and music by Kay Werner and Sue Werner

Introduced by Ella Fitzgerald and Her Famous Orchestra, vocal by Ella (Decca).
390629-3, 391200-8, 400122-9, 400325-8

I Want to Be Happy (1924)

Lyrics by Irving Caesar, music by Vincent Youmans

Introduced by Charles Winninger, Louis Groody and ensemble in the 1924 musical play *No, No, Nanette!* Sung by Bernice Claire and ensemble in the 1930 First National film adaptation. Sung by Anna Neagle in the 1940 RKO film adaptation.
371102-3, 371102-4, **371217-1, 371217-2**

I Want to Learn About Love (1947)

Lyrics and music by Lester Lee and Allan Roberts

Introduced by Ella Fitzgerald on this Decca recording. **471218-1**

I Want to Talk About You (1972)

Lyrics and music by Billy Eckstine

Introduced and popularized by Billy Eckstine. **730828-9**

I Wants to Stay Here (1935)

Lyrics by DuBose Heyward and Ira Gershwin, music by George Gershwin

This is the correct (and original) title of the song more commonly known now as "I Loves You, Porgy." Ella has recorded the song under both titles. Introduced by Anne Brown as Bess and Todd Duncan as Porgy in the 1935 folk opera *Porgy and Bess*. Performed by Dorothy Dandridge (dubbed by Adele Addison) in the 1959 Warner Bros. film adaptation. **570828-1, 580425-23, 710721-3c**

I Was Born to Be Blue *see* **Born to Be Blue**

I Was Doing All Right (1937)

Lyrics by Ira Gershwin, music by George Gershwin

Introduced by Ella Logan in the 1937 United Artists film *The Goldwyn Follies of 1938*. This was one of George Gershwin's last songs; he was working on the film score when he died. **380125-2, 590318-3**

I Wish I Were in Love Again (1937)

Lyrics by Lorenz Hart, music by Richard Rodgers

Introduced by Grace McDonald and Rolly Pickert in the 1937 musical play *Babes in Arms*. The song was not used in the Garland-Rooney MGM film adaptation of the play. **560828-2**

I Wished on the Moon (1936)

Lyrics by Dorothy Parker, music by Ralph Rainger

Introduced by Bing Crosby in the 1936 Paramount film *The Big Broadcast of 1936*. **540325-1, 620410-1**

I Wonder What Kind of a Guy You'd Be

Lyrics and music by (unknown)

Research on this title reveals no information whatever, not even its authors. It was released as a single, and appeared on the German issue LP *Ella, Volume 6* (See LPD-125) **530213-3**

I Wonder Where Our Love Has Gone (1958)

Lyrics and music by Woodrow "Buddy" Johnson

Introduced on a recording by Lou Rawls.

820205-1

I Wonder Why (1968)

Lyrics and music by Randy Newman

Introduced on a recording by Randy Newman.

690529-1

I Won't Dance (1935)

Lyrics by Dorothy Fields, music by Jimmy McHugh

Introduced by Fred Astaire in the 1935 RKO film *Roberta*. Sung and danced by Marge and Gower Champion in the 1952 MGM film adaptation *Lovely to Look At.* (Strange the egos of song-writers: Fields and McHugh had to share credits with Otto Harbach, Oscar Hammerstein II, and Jerome Kern, who were under contract for the score of the film, and whose names appear on most published versions of the song, and, of course, whose estates share the royalties.) **570813-1, 611227-2, 690729-1**

If Anything Happened to You (1939)

Lyrics and music by Jimmy Van Heusen

Introduced by Ella Fitzgerald and Her Savoy Eight, vocal by Ella Fitzgerald (Decca). **390421-2**

If Dreams Come True (1937)

Lyrics by Irving Mills, music by Edgar Sampson and Benny Goodman

Introduced by Chick Webb and His Orchestra, vocal by Ella Fitzgerald (Decca). **371217-4**

If I Could Be with You (1930)

Lyrics by Henry Creamer, music by James P. Johnson

Introduced by, and became the theme song of McKinney's Cotton Pickers (Victor). **620130-6, 670326-7**

If I Didn't Care (1939)

Lyrics and music by Jack Lawrence

Introduced by Chick Webb and His Orchestra, vocal by Ella Fitzgerald on a radio broadcast. Popularized by The Ink Spots on a Decca recording that became their biggest hit up to that time. They also performed it in the 1941 20th Century–Fox film *The Great American Broadcast.* **390504-5**

If I Give My Heart to You (1954)

Lyrics and music by Jimmie Crane, Al Jacobs, and Jimmy Brewster

Introduced by Denise Lor (Major). **680529-1a**

If I Were a Bell (1950)

Lyrics and music by Frank Loesser

Introduced by Isabel Bigley in the 1950 musical play *Guys and Dolls*. Performed by Jean Simmons in the 1955 MGM film adaptation. **581122-6, 621004-2**

If It Weren't for You (1939)

Lyrics and music by Vic Mizzy and Irving Taylor

Introduced by Ella Fitzgerald and Her Famous Orchestra, with Ella doing the vocals. **400215-2**

If That's What You're Thinking (You're Wrong) (1939)

Lyrics and music by Jack Lawrence

Introduced by Chick Webb and His Orchestra, vocals by Ella Fitzgerald. This recording was made at Webb's last studio recording session. **390421-3**

If You Can't Sing It, You'll Have To Swing It *see* Mr. Paganini

If You Don't, I Know Who Will (1923)

Lyrics and music by Clarence Williams, Chris Smith, and Tim Bryan

Introduced by Bessie Smith, this song became identified with her and she sang it often during personal appearances. **531223-2**

If You Ever Change Your Mind (1939)

Lyrics and music by Grady Watts, Maurice Sigler, and Bud Green

Introduced by Glen Gray and The Casa Loma Orchestra. **390421-4**

If You Ever Should Leave (1937)

Lyrics by Sammy Cahn, music by Saul Chaplin

Introduced in the 1937 musical revue *The New Grand Terrace Revue,* and first recorded by Ella Fitzgerald and Her Savoy Eight, vocal by Ella Fitzgerald (Decca). 370524-2, **370524-3, 530101-1b**

If You Never Come to Me *see* Useless Landscape

If You Only Knew (1938)

Lyrics and music by Charlie Beals and Chick Webb

Introduced by Ella Fitzgerald and Her Savoy Eight, vocal by Ella Fitzgerald (Decca).

380503-10, 380503-11

I'll Always Be in Love with You (1928)

Lyrics and music by Bud Green, Herman Ruby, and Sam H. Stept

Introduced in the 1928 FBO film *Stepping High*. Sung by Morton Downey in the 1929 RKO film *Syncopation*.

451012-2, 620129-1

I'll Be Hard to Handle (1933)

Lyrics by Bernard Dougall, music by Jerome Kern

Introduced by Lyda Roberti in the 1933 musical play *Roberta*. Sung by Ginger Rogers (with new lyrics by Dougall) and danced by Fred Astaire and Rogers in the 1935 film adaptation. Sung (with new lyrics by Dorothy Fields) and danced by Ann Miller in the 1952 MGM film adaptation *Lovely to Look At*. Ella's recorded version is that with the lyrics by Fields.   **630105-3**

I'll Chase the Blues Away (1935)

Lyrics by Ken Harrison, music by Edgar Sampson

Introduced by Chick Webb and His Orchestra, with vocal by Ella Fitzgerald in her first recording on 12 June 1935. This version was not released in the U.S. at the time, and the song was re-recorded in October 1935 for U.S. release. Now, with the advent of reissues of all Ella's recordings and of the CD with enhancing technology, it is interesting to note how much more confident Ella sounds in October as compared with the shy, almost retiring performance just four months previously.

350612-1, 351012-3

I'll Never Be Free (1950)

Lyrics and music by Bennie Benjamin and George Weiss

Best-selling record by both Kay Starr and Tennessee Ernie Ford (whose first successful record it was) (Capitol).   **500815-2**

I'll Never Be the Same (1932)

Lyrics by Gus Kahn, music by Matty Malneck and Frank Signorelli

First recorded as an instrumental in 1931 by Joe Venuti and Eddie Lang under its original title, "Little Buttercup." With the addition of the lyrics, introduced by Mildred Bailey, with Paul Whiteman and His Orchestra.   **571028-1**

I'll Never Fall in Love Again (1964)

Lyrics by Hal David, music by Burt Bacharach

Introduced by Jill O'Hara and Jerry Orbach in the 1968 musical play *Promises, Promises*.

690526-1, 700520-8

I'll Remember April (1942)

Lyrics by Don Raye and Patricia Johnston, music by Gene DePaul

Introduced by Dick Foran in the 1942 Universal film *Ride 'Em, Cowboy* (in which Ella made her film debut).

500900-4

I'll See You in My Dreams (1924)

Lyrics by Gus Kahn, music by Isham Jones

Introduced and popularized by Isham Jones and His Orchestra. Jones's wife gave him a baby grand piano for his thirtieth birthday anniversary on 31 January 1924, and *within an hour*, so the story goes, he had composed the music for "I'll See You in My Dreams," "The One I Love Belongs to Somebody Else," "Spain," and "It Had to Be You," all of which became hits. Such a burst of creativity remains unparalleled, as each is now a part of the standard American popular song repertoire.

451012-3, **451012-4**, 640304-2

Ill Wind (1934)

Lyrics by Ted Koehler, music by Harold Arlen

Introduced by Adelaide Hall in the 1934 revue *Cotton Club Parade*.

570723-10, 570929-6, 571009-5, 610115-2

I'm a Poached Egg (Without Toast) (1964)

Lyrics by Ira Gershwin, music by George Gershwin

Introduced by Cliff Osmond and Ray Walston in the 1964 United Artists film *Kiss Me, Stupid*. The music is from the vast cache of unused tunes left by George Gershwin on his death in 1937, of which Ira Gershwin has used many over the years, writing lyrics for use in various films. Refrain 3 was especially written by Ira Gershwin for Ella in this recording.   **641019-3**

I'm Beginning to See the Light (1944)

Lyrics and music by Don George, Johnny Hodges, Harry James, and Duke Ellington

Introduced by Harry James and His Orchestra, vocal by Kitty Kallen. Remained 11 weeks on "Your Hit Parade," two, as #1.

450226-1, 570626-3, 590800-1, 630715-1, 630716-2, 640203-2, 680518-1

I'm Confessin' (that I Love You) (1930)

Lyrics by Al J. Neiburg, music by Doc Dougherty and Ellis Reynolds

Popularized by Rudy Vallée. First recorded by Louis Armstrong (Okeh). Became a standard in the repertoire of many dance orchestras and singers, with innumerable recordings with varying degrees of popularity.

391200-10, 400122-6, 400325-10, 441106-2, 481204-8, 780620-8

I'm Fallin' in Love (1964)

Lyrics and music by Barney Kessel

Introduced by Ella Fitzgerald on this Verve recording.

641023-2

I'm Getting Mighty Lonesome for You (1942)

Lyrics and music by Buck Ram

Introduced by Ella Fitzgerald on this Decca recording. **420311-1**

I'm Getting Sentimental Over You (1932)

Lyrics by Ned Washington, music by George Bassman

Introduced and first recorded by The Dorsey Brothers Orchestra (Brunswick). When the brothers parted, Tommy adopted this as his theme song. **600419-3, 790215-2**

I'm Glad There Is You (1941)

Lyrics by Paul Madeira, music by Jimmy Dorsey

Introduced by Jimmy Dorsey and His Orchestra, vocal by Bob Eberly. **540329-1**, 580810-3, 610512-5

I'm Gonna Go Fishin' (1959)

Lyrics by Peggy Lee, music by Duke Ellington

Introduced and recorded by Peggy Lee (Capitol). The music is an extension and adaptation of a theme from Ellington's score for the 1959 Columbia film *Anatomy of a Murder*. **611227-3**

I'm Gonna Sit Right Down and Write Myself a Letter (1935)

Lyrics by Joe Young, music by Fred Ahlert

Introduced by Fats Waller. Memorable recording by Frank Sinatra. **570704-7, 700520-2b**

I'm Gonna Wash That Man Right Outa My Hair (1949)

Lyrics by Oscar Hammerstein II, music by Richard Rodgers

Introduced by Mary Martin in the 1949 musical play *South Pacific*. Sung by Mitzi Gaynor in the 1958 20th Century-Fox film adaptation. **490428-2**

I'm in the Mood for Love (1935)

Lyrics by Dorothy Fields, music by Jimmy McHugh

Introduced by Frances Langford in the 1935 Paramount film *Every Night at Eight*. **730705-16, 740108-5, 780620-3**

I'm Just a Jitterbug (1938)

Lyrics by Mack David, music by Jerry Livingston

Introduced by Chick Webb and His Orchestra, vocal by Ella Fitzgerald (Decca). **380502-3**

I'm Just a Lucky So-and-So (1945)

Lyrics by Mack David, music by Duke Ellington

Introduced by Duke Ellington and His Orchestra, vocal by Al Hibbler (Victor).

460221-1, 490918-4, 570624-3, 570626-2, 660130-5, **660222-8, 660914-2, 740108-7**

I'm Making Believe (1944)

Lyrics by Mack Gordon, music by James V. Monaco

Introduced by Benny Goodman and His Orchestra in the 1944 20th Century–Fox film *Sweet and Low-Down*. Nominated for an Academy Award (AMPAS), Best Original Song, 1944. Best-selling record by Ella Fitzgerald with The Ink Spots (Decca). **440830-2, 860228-14**

I'm Not Complainin' (1938)

Lyrics by Ira Gershwin, music by Vernon Duke

Written for and intended for use in the 1938 United Artists film *The Goldwyn Follies of 1938,* but not used. Vernon Duke assumed the duties of composer for the score of the film on the death of George Gershwin, who died during the filming. **390818-4**

I'm Old Fashioned (1942)

Lyrics by Johnny Mercer, music by Jerome Kern

Introduced by Fred Astaire and Rita Hayworth (dubbed by Nan Wynn), with Xavier Cugat and His Orchestra, in the 1942 Columbia film *You Were Never Lovelier*. **630105-1**

I'm Putting All My Eggs in One Basket (1936)

Lyrics and music by Irving Berlin

Introduced by Fred Astaire and danced by Astaire and Ginger Rogers in the 1936 RKO film *Follow the Fleet*. **570813-4, 580313-4**, 640728-12, **640729-12**

I'm the Lonesomest Gal in Town (1912)

Lyrics by Lew Brown, music by Albert von Tilzer

A hit ballad of the 1910s. Revived in the 1940s by Kay Starr, whose Capitol recording helped establish her as a star. **401108-3**

I'm Thrilled (1941)

Lyrics by Sylvia Dee, music by Sidney Lippman

Introduced by Glenn Miller and His Orchestra, vocal by Ray Eberle (Bluebird). Miller included the complete score of this song as arranged by Jerry Gray in his book on arranging *Glenn Miller's Method for Orchestra Arranging* (Mutual Music Society, New York, 1943), as an example of writing for a popular orchestra and singer. **411105-2**

I'm Through with Love (1931)

Lyrics by Gus Kahn, music by Matty Malneck and Fud Livingston

Introduced by Mildred Bailey. **590325-5**

I'm Up a Tree (1939)

Lyrics by Al Stillman, music by Charles L. Cooke and Chick Webb

Introduced by Chick Webb and His Orchestra, vocal by Ella Fitzgerald (Decca).   **390302-5**

I'm Waitin' for the Junk Man (1949)

Lyrics and music by (unknown)

Ella recorded this song in September, 1949, and research does not reveal any other recording, nor does it reveal the author(s).   **490920-3**

I'm Walkin' (1957)

Lyrics and music by Antoine "Fats" Domino and Dave Bartholemew

Introduced by "Fats" Domino (Imperial). Featured by Ricky Nelson in his singing debut in the *Ozzie and Harriet* television series in April 1957; his recording for Verve sold more than a million copies, his first song hit.

780620-5

I'm Wearing a New Shade of Blue *see* **A New Shade of Blue**

Imagination (1940)

Lyrics by Johnny Burke, music by Jimmy Van Heusen

Introduced by Fred Waring and His Pennsylvanians.
400215-4, 501008-1, 510519-2,
540330-2, 610513-10, **620410-2**

Imagine My Frustration (1965)

Lyrics by Billy Strayhorn and Duke Ellington, music by Billy Strayhorn, Duke Ellington, and Gerald Wilson

Originally an instrumental by Gerald Wilson, entitled "When I'm Feeling Kinda Blue," credited to Jo Villasenor, Wilson's wife. Wilson performed the song with his orchestra and recorded it prior to introducing it to Ellington. The retitled version was introduced by Duke Ellington and His Orchestra at the 1965 Monterrey Jazz Festival, and featured alto saxophonist Johnny Hodges. The vocal version was introduced on the Ella Fitzgerald-Duke Ellington Verve album *Ella at Duke's Place*.
651017-1, **651017-2,** 651017-3, **660207-1,** 660728-14

The Impatient Years (1955)

Lyrics by Sammy Cahn, music by Jimmy Van Heusen
Introduced by Frank Sinatra in the 1955 television musical production of Thorton Wilder's *Our Town*.

550805-2

In a Mellow Tone (In a Melotone) (1940)

Lyrics by Milt Gabler, music by Duke Ellington

Originally introduced by Duke Ellington and His Orchestra as an instrumental. Vocal version recorded by Ella Fitzgerald (Decca), and by The Mills Brothers (Decca).
490430-3, 501230-3, 560202-4, **571017-1**

In a Sentimental Mood (1935)

Lyrics by Manny Kurtz and Irving Mills, music by Duke Ellington

Introduced and recorded by Duke Ellington and His Orchestra (Brunswick).   **560904-14**

In My Dreams (1948)

Lyrics and music by Jimmy Shearer
Introduced and featured by Vaughan Monroe and His Orchestra, with The Moon Maids (Victor).   **481110-2**

In the Evening (When the Sun Goes Down) (1935)

Lyrics and music by Leroy Carr

Introduced on a recording by Leroy Carr.
490920-1, 631029-4

In the Garden (1912)

Lyrics and music by C. Austin Miles

"I seemed to be standing at the entrance to a garden, looking down a gently winding path shaded by olive branches," wrote Rev. Miles of the remarkable experience — almost a trance — that produced this hymn. "A woman in white walked slowly into the shadows. It was Mary. As she came to the tomb, she bent over to look in, and leaning her head upon her arm, she wept. Turning herself, she saw Jesus standing beside her; so did I. I knew it was He...." Miles awakened from his vision at that moment, profoundly moved, inspiration vibrant within him. "I wrote as quickly as the words could be formed, the poem exactly as it has since appeared. That same evening I wrote the music." It was a March day in 1912.   **670200-5**

In the Mood (1938)

Lyrics by Andy Razaf, music by Joe Garland

Based on the 1937 Joe Garland-Wingy Manone instrumental "Tar Paper Stomp," the new version was introduced by Edgar Hayes and His Orchestra (Decca). The Glenn Miller and His Orchestra 1939 recording became an enormous success, and the song remains associated with him and his orchestra. The Miller orchestra performed it in the 1941 20th Century–Fox film *Sun Valley Serenade*, and it was performed by the orchestra in the 1954 Universal film *The Glenn Miller Story*.   700105-1

In the Still of the Night (1937)

Lyrics and music by Cole Porter

Introduced by Nelson Eddy in the 1937 MGM film *Rosalie*.   **560209-2**

In the Wee Small Hours (of the Morning) (1955)

Lyrics by Bob Hilliard, music by David Mann

Introduced and recorded by Frank Sinatra (Capitol), who chose the title for one of his most successful albums. Revived in 1994 by Melissa Manchester, who included the seldom-heard verse, in a memorable recording.

580810-11, 580810-33, 610513-19,
610516-11, 610518-19, 610520-32

Indian Summer (1919/1939)

Lyrics by Al Dubin, music by Victor Herbert

Introduced as a piano solo by Victor Herbert in 1919. With lyrics added in 1939, the song was popularized by the orchestras of Tommy Dorsey, vocal by Jack Leonard (Victor); and Glenn Miller, vocal by Ray Eberle (Bluebird).

720602-3, 730705-2

Insensatez *see* How Insensitive

Into Each Life Some Rain Must Fall (1944)

Lyrics and music by Allan Roberts and Doris Fisher

Introduced by Ella Fitzgerald and The Ink Spots (Decca).

440830-1, 630716-8

Is There Somebody Else? (1940)

Lyrics and music by Dick Robertson, Nelson Cogane, and Sammy Mysels

Introduced by Ella Fitzgerald and Her Famous Orchestra, vocal by Ella Fitzgerald (Decca).

400126-1, 400226-8

Is You Is, or Is You Ain't (Ma' Baby)? (1943)

Lyrics and music by Billy Austin and Louis Jordan

Introduced by Louis Jordan in the 1944 MGM film *Follow the Boys*.

441000-1

Isn't It a Pity? (1932)

Lyrics by Ira Gershwin, music by George Gershwin

Introduced by Jack Buchanan (during the pre-Broadway try-outs), and on Broadway by George Givot and Josephine Huston in the 1933 musical play *Pardon My English*, George Gershwin's last Broadway show.

590718-5

Isn't It Romantic? (1932)

Lyrics by Lorenz Hart, music by Richard Rodgers

Introduced by Maurice Chevalier, Jeanette MacDonald, Bert Roach, Rolf Sedan, and Tyler Brook in the 1932 Paramount film *Love Me Tonight*.

560831-5

Isn't This a Lovely Day (To Be Caught in the Rain)? (1935)

Lyrics and music by Irving Berlin

Introduced by Fred Astaire in the 1935 RKO film *Top Hat*. Popular recording by Fred Astaire (Brunswick).

560816-2, 580313-1

Instanbul (1953)

Lyrics by Jimmy Kennedy, music by Nat Simon

Introduced in a popular recording by The Four Lads (Columbia).

531227-2

It Ain't Necessarily So (1935)

Lyrics by DuBose Heyward and Ira Gershwin, music by George Gershwin

Introduced by John W. Bubbles (as Sportin' Life) in Act II, Scene II, of the 1935 folk opera *Porgy and Bess*. Performed by Sammy Davis, Jr., in the 1959 Warner Bros. film adaptation.

570818-4

It All Depends on You (1925)

Lyrics by B.G. DeSylva and Lew Brown, music by Ray Henderson

Introduced by Al Jolson in the 1925 musical play *Big Boy*. Jolson also sang it in the 1928 Warner Bros. film *The Singing Fool*.

560202-1

It Came Upon the Midnight Clear (1850)

Lyrics by Edmund H. Sears, music by Richard S. Willis

The poem, written by Rev. Sears, a Harvard-trained Unitarian clergyman, was first published in *The Christian Register* magazine in 1850. Mr. Willis had another hymn, "See Israel's Gentle Shepherd Stand," in mind when he wrote the music associated with this carol, but its pairing with these words formed a close union. Mr. Willis, whose father was founder of *The Youth's Companion* magazine, graduated from Yale, and later studied music in Europe with Felix Mendelssohn, among others. Mendelssohn, he boasted, had revised some of his compositions.

670718-3

It Don't Mean a Thing (If It Ain't Got That Swing) (1932)

Lyrics by Irving Mills, music by Duke Ellington

Introduced by Duke Ellington and His Orchestra, vocal by Ivie Anderson (Victor). This song might well be the first to use the word "swing" in context with the form of music to become popular in the late 1930s.

560904-9, 570429-2, 650326-6c, 660729-14,
710518-2b, 710721-7c, 740411-5

It Had to Be You (1924)

Lyrics by Gus Kahn, music by Isham Jones

Introduced by Isham Jones and His Orchestra with phenomenal success, and recorded by virtually every singer and orchestra in America.   620629-15, 620630-12

It Happened in Monterey (1930)

Lyrics by Billy Rose, music by Mabel Wayne

Introduced by John Boles and Jeanette Loff in the 1930 Universal film *The King of Jazz*.

680603-1e, 690729-3a

It Might As Well Be Spring (1945)

Lyrics by Oscar Hammerstein II, music by Richard Rodgers

Introduced by Jeanne Crain (dubbed by Luanne Hogan) in the 1945 20th Century–Fox film *State Fair*. Winner of the Academy Award (AMPAS) for Best Original Song, 1945. Sung by Pamela Tiffin (dubbed by Anita Gordon) in the 1962 20th Century–Fox remake of the film.   550401-2, 610519-4, 620629-7

It Never Entered My Mind (1940)

Lyrics by Lorenz Hart, music by Richard Rodgers

Introduced by Shirley Ross in the 1940 RKO film *Higher and Higher*.   560830-5

It Was Written in the Stars (1948)

Lyrics by Leo Robin, music by Harold Arlen

Introduced by Tony Martin in the 1948 Universal film *Casbah*. Revived by Ella Fitzgerald in *Ella Fitzgerald Sings the Harold Arlen Song Book,* in 1961. She told Arlen that this was her favorite Arlen Song.   610115-5

It's a Blue World (1939)

Lyrics and music by Robert Wright and Chet Forrest

Introduced by Tony Martin in the 1939 Columbia film *Music in My Heart*. Nominated for an Academy Award (AMPAS) for Best Original Song, 1940.

400226-7, 620409-1

It's a Good Day (1947)

Lyrics and music by Peggy Lee and Dave Barbour

Introduced and popularized by Peggy Lee (Capitol), with whom the song has long been associated.

590325-7

It's a Lovely Day Today (1950)

Lyrics and music by Irving Berlin

Introduced by Galina Talva and Russell Nype in the 1950 musical play *Call Me Madam*. Sung by Donald O'-Connor and Vera-Ellen (dubbed by Carole Richards) in the 1953 20th Century–Fox film adaptation.   580318-8

It's a Pity to Say Goodnight (1945)

Lyrics and music by Billy Reid

Introduced and popularized by Ella Fitzgerald with The Delta Rhythm Boys (Decca).   460829-2, 611114-4

It's a Wonderful World (1940)

Lyrics by Harold Adamson, music by Jan Savitt and Leo Watson

Introduced and recorded by Jan Savitt and His Orchestra, vocal by Bon Bon (Decca). Louis Armstrong's more recent recordings are all classics.

680603-3f, 690729-3c

It's All Right with Me (1953)

Lyrics and music by Cole Porter

Introduced by Peter Cookson in the 1953 musical play *Can-Can*. Sung by Frank Sinatra and Louis Jourdan in the 1960 20th Century–Fox film adaptation.

560207-2, 570929-1, 570929-2,
571009-1, 580425-24, 610513-5,
610514-6, 720602-11b, 750717-5, 810726-5

It's Almost Like Being in Love see **Almost Like Being in Love**

It's D'Lovely [It's De-Lovely] (1936)

Lyrics and music by Cole Porter

Introduced by Ethel Merman and Bop Hope in the 1936 musical play *Red, Hot and Blue*.

560209-3, 610519-6

It's Foxy (1938)

Lyrics and music by Joe Bishop and Chick Webb

Introduced by Chick Webb and His Orchestra, vocal by Ella Fitzgerald (Decca).   381006-3

It's My Own Darn Fault (1951)

Lyrics and music by Don George

Introduced by Ella Fitzgerald on this Decca recording.

510718-1

It's My Turn Now (1937)

Lyrics by Sammy Cahn, music by Saul Chaplin

Introduced by Chick Webb and His Orchestra, vocal by Ella Fitzgerald (Decca).   371221-2

It's Only a Man (1951)

Lyrics by Paul Francis Webster, music by Hal Horne

Introduced by Ella Fitzgerald on this Verve recording.

560125-5

(It's Only) a Paper Moon see A Paper Moon

It's Only Love (1966)

Lyrics and music by Hank Cochran

Introduced and popularized by Jeannie Seely (Monument). **671221-1**

It's Too Soon to Know (1947)

Lyrics and music by Deborah Chessler

Best-selling record in 1948 by The Orioles (Natural). **480820-1**, **481127-4**

It's Up to Me and You (1968)

Lyrics and music by Ella Fitzgerald

Introduced by Ella Fitzgerald in a Vancouver, B.C., concert and later recorded, this is Ella's tribute to Dr. Martin Luther King, Jr. **680510-1**

It's Wonderful (1938)

Lyrics by Mitchell Parish, music by Robert Wells and Smith

Introduced and recorded by Ella Fitzgerald and Her Savoy Eight, vocal by Ella Fitzgerald (Decca). **380125-1**

(I've Been) Saving Myself for You see Saving Myself for You

I've Got a Crush on You (1928)

Lyrics by Ira Gershwin, music by George Gershwin

Introduced by Clifton Webb and Mary May in the 1928 musical play *Treasure Girl*. Sung and danced by Gordon Smith and Doris Carson in the 1930 musical play *Strike Up the Band*. Lee Wiley first recorded and popularized it as a sentimental ballad — it had formerly been performed only in quick tempo.
500911-4, 560202-20, **570704-6**, **590108-2**, 610513-4, 610518-23, 610520-5. 620629-19, **730705-6**, 790712-15, **830523-3a**

I've Got a Feeling I'm Falling (1929)

Lyrics by Billy Rose, music by Harry Link and Thomas "Fats" Waller

Introduced by "Fats" Waller. Sung by Helen Morgan in the 1929 Paramount film *Applause*. **471223-1**

I've Got a Feelin' You're Foolin' (1935)

Lyrics by Arthur Freed, music by Nacio Herb Brown

Introduced by Robert Taylor and June Knight, and reprised by Frances Langford, in the 1936 MGM film *Broadway Melody of 1936*. **680528-1b**

I've Got Beginner's Luck see Beginner's Luck

I've Got Five Dollars (1931)

Lyrics by Lorenz Hart, music by Richard Rodgers

Introduced by Jack Whiting and Harriet Lake (Ann Sothern) in the 1931 musical play *America's Sweetheart*. **560821-3**

I've Got My Love to Keep Me Warm (1937)

Lyrics and music by Irving Berlin

Introduced by Dick Powell, Alice Faye, and E.E. Clive in the 1937 20th Century–Fox film *On the Avenue*. **570813-5**, **580318-1**

I've Got the World on a String (1932)

Lyrics by Ted Koehler, music by Harold Arlen

Introduced by Aida Ward in the 1932 revue *Cotton Club Parade*.
500306-2, **600801-8**, **610514-5**, **760130-4**

I've Got You Under My Skin (1936)

Lyrics and music by Cole Porter

Introduced by Virginia Bruce in the 1936 MGM film *Born to Dance*. Nominated for an Academy Award (AMPAS), Best Original Song, 1936.
560209-7, 640800-7, **640729-21**, 720612-4

I've Got Your Number (1962)

Lyrics by Carolyn Leigh, music by Cy Coleman

Introduced by Swen Swenson in the 1962 musical play *Little Me*. 641022-4, **660720-9**

I've Gotta Be a Rug-Cutter see I Wanna Be a Rug-Cutter

I've Gotta Be Me (1967)

Lyrics and music by Walter Marks

Introduced by Steve Lawrence in the 1968 musical play *Golden Rainbow*. **730705-7**

I've Grown Accustomed to His (Her) Face (1956)

Lyrics by Alan Jay Lerner, music by Frederick Loewe

Introduced by Rex Harrison in the 1956 musical play *My Fair Lady*, in which it was the closing number. Mr. Harrison reprised his performance in the 1964 Warner Bros. film adaptation. **590325-3**, **641019-2**

Jail House Blues (1923)

Lyrics and music by Bessie Smith and Clarence Williams

Introduced and first recorded by Bessie Smith with Clarence Williams at the piano (Columbia). Virginia Liston also recorded with with Williams at piano (Okeh). **631028-4**

Jazz Corner of the World (1989)

Lyrics and music by Kool Moe Dee, Big Daddy Kane, and Quincy Jones

More than a hundred artists queued up to appear in the 1989 Quincy Jones recording extravaganza *Back on the Block.* This track is a rap number to which Ella contributed, along with how many others would be only a guess.

890000-3

Jazz Samba see Só Danço Samba

The Jersey Bounce (1941)

Lyrics by Buddy Feyne and Robert B. Wright (1946), music by Bobby Plater, Tiny Bradshaw, Edward Johnson, and Robert B. Wright

Introduced by Tiny Bradshaw and His Orchestra as an instrumental in 1941. Lyrics added in 1946. Interpolated in the 1956 Universal film *The Benny Goodman Story.*

610622-4, 890320-3

Jim (1941)

Lyrics by Nelson Shawn, music by Caesar Petrillo and Edward Ross

Introduced and recorded by Dinah Shore (Bluebird).

411006-1

Jingle Bells [The One-Horse Open Sleigh] (1857)

Lyrics and music by James S. Pierpont

Pierpont wrote this song for a local Sunday School entertainment in Boston. A perennial Christmas favorite, the 1943 Decca record by Bing Crosby and The Andrews Sisters sold more than a million copies.   **600715-2**

Joe Williams' Blues (1956)

Lyrics and music by Ella Fitzgerald

Introduced and recorded by Ella Fitzgerald, and used in many of her personal appearances.

560121-2, 560202-5, **610211-15**, 610513-12, 610516-13, 610518-11, 610518-24, 610520-7, 610629-3

Johnny One-Note (1937)

Lyrics by Lorenz Hart, music by Richard Rodgers

Introduced by Wynn Murray and chorus, and danced by Mitzi Green and Duke McHale in the 1937 musical play *Babes in Arms.* Sung by Judy Garland in the 1948 MGM film *Words and Music.* The song was not used in the 1941 MGM film adaptation of the play.   **560828-4**

Joy to the World (1719)

Lyrics by Isaac Watts, music by George Frederick Handel

The text is from Isaac Watts's *Psalms of David Imitated in the Language of the New Testament,* published in 1719. It is an adaptation of Psalm 98, which includes the lines, "Make a joyful noise unto the Lord, all the earth." The melody is a Handelian cento—a clever mosaic from *The Messiah.* Most of it echoes the chorus, "Lift up your heads"; at the fourth line it turns to "Comfort Ye," the first tenor aria of the oratorio. The melody, as it stands in this carol, has been credited to various composers, among them Lowell Mason, but its origin has never been determined.

670719-1

Jubilee Swing (1940)

Music by Teddy MacRae

Instrumental introduced by Ella Fitzgerald and Her Famous Orchestra on radio broadcasts in 1940. Never recorded in studio by the orchestra, but there exists recordings taken from her broadcasts.   **400320-3**

(Hep! Hep!) The Jumpin' Jive (1939)

Lyrics and music by Cab Calloway, Jack Palmer, and Frank Froeba

Introduced by Cab Calloway and His Orchestra. In performance, this number was the quintessential Calloway, the dancing, "jiving" performer in white tails. His recording was a great success.   **390824-2**

Jumping with Symphony Syd (1948)

Scat lyrics by Ella Fitzgerald, music by Lester Young

Tenor-saxophonist Lester Young's tribute to Sydney Torrin, co-owner and host of the night club, Bridland. Many performances were broadcast from Birdland in the late 1940s and early 1950s, and Syd always requested that performers close their broadcasts with this tune.

501230-6, 510519-8

Just a Closer Walk with Thee (1912)

Lyrics and music by Kenneth Morris

The stately tempo and chromatic melody of this "folk hymn" has made it a natural choice for the funeral marches that jazz bands used to create so picturesquely when they were hired for such occasions around the turn of the century, especially in New Orleans. Performed in the 1967 Warner Bros. film *Cool Hand Luke,* which sparked a popular revival.   **670200-8**

Just a Simple Melody (1937)

Lyrics by Sammy Cahn, music by Saul Chaplin

Introduced by Chick Webb and His Orchestra, vocal by Ella Fitzgerald (Decca).   371027-1

Just A-Sittin' and A-Rockin' [Just A-Settin' and A-Rockin'] (1941)

Lyrics by Lee Gaines, music by William Thomas (Billy) Strayhorn

Introduced by Duke Ellington and His Orchestra, vocal by Ivie Anderson (Victor), as "Just A-Settin' and A-Rockin'." **560904-8**, **640728-2**, **640729-3**, **790215-1**

Just Another Samba (1937)

Lyrics by Ira Gershwin, music by George Gershwin

Written for Ella Logan to perform in the 1938 United Artists film *The Goldwyn Follies of 1938*, but it was not used. First recorded in 1959 by Ella Fitzgerald for *Ella Fitzgerald Sings the George and Ira Gershwin Song Book*. **590717-5**

Just Friends (1931)

Lyrics by Samuel M. Lewis, music by John Klenner

Introduced by Russ Colombo on radio and with a Vocalion recording. Also popular were performances and a recording by Red McKenzie and His Orchestra. **6805282c**

Just in Time (1956)

Lyrics by Betty Comden and Adolph Green, music by Jule Styne

Introduced by Sidney Chaplin and Judy Holliday in the 1956 musical play *Bells Are Ringing*. Sung by Dean Martin in the 1960 MGM film adaptation. Mr. Styne has said that this is one of his two favorite creations, the other being "Never-Never Land." **610514-1**

Just One of Those Things (1935)

Lyrics and music by Cole Porter

Introduced by June Knight and Charles Walters in the 1935 musical play *Jubilee*.
560207-4, **560815-6**, **580425-20**, **590800-3**, **680618-12**, **720612-10**

Just Squeeze Me (1940/1946)

Lyrics by Lee Gaines, music by Duke Ellington

Adapted from the Ellington instrumental, "Subtle Slough," which he recorded in 1940 with a small unit led by Rex Stewart. Introduced with lyrics in 1946 by Ellington and His Orchestra, vocal by Ray Nance.
560904-4, 580425-5, **580425-17**, 610513-16, 610519-10, **660729-15**

Just When We're Falling in Love (1947/1951)

Lyrics by Bob Russell, music by Sir Charles Thompson and Illinois Jacquet

The jazz instrumental version, "Robbins' Nest," was introduced by Illinois Jacquet, and dedicated to disc jockey Fred Robbins, those program, "Robbins' Nest" was a great favorite with jazz aficionados. The vocal version was introduced by Les Brown and His Band of Renown, vocal by Lucy Ann Polk (Decca).
701221-1, **890315-2**

Just You, Just Me (1929)

Lyrics by Raymond Klages, music by Jesse Greer

Introduced by Marion Davies and Lawrence Gray in the 1929 MGM film *Marianne*. **581122-4**, 591213-2

Keep Cool, Fool (1941)

Lyrics and music by Joseph Myrow and Doc Rhythm

Introduced by Ella Fitzgerald and Her Famous Orchestra, vocal by Ella Fitzgerald, on radio and a recording (Decca). **410331-1**

A Kiss Goodnight (1945)

Lyrics and music by Freddie Slack, Floyd Victor, and Reba Nell Herman

Introduced by Freddie Slack and His Orchestra, vocal by Liza Morrow (Capitol). **450829-1**

Knock Me a Kiss (1942)

Lyrics and music by Mike Jackson, special lyrics by Andy Razaf

Best-selling record by Louis Jordan and His Tympany Five (Decca). **581123-3**

Knock on Wood (1966)

Lyrics and music by Eddie Floyd and Steve Cropper

Introduced by Eddie Floyd (Stax). **690528-1**

Lady Bug (1951)

Lyrics by Elizabeth Carr, music by Joe Williams

Introduced by Joe Williams in personal appearances, and later recorded with Count Basie and His Orchestra. **511126-3**

The Lady Is a Tramp (1937)

Lyrics by Lorenz Hart, music by Richard Rodgers

Introduced by Mitzi Green in the 1937 musical play *Babes in Arms*. Sung by June Preisser in the 1939 MGM film adaptation.
560821-2, **580425-4**, 580425-16, 580810-7, 580810-17, **600213-5**, 610221-9, 610519-7, 610520-14, 620629-8, 620203-12, **640728-9**, **640729-9**, 671113-3, 700520-15

The Lady's in Love with You (1939)

Lyrics by Frank Loesser, music by Burton Lane

Introduced by Shirley Ross and Bob Hope, with Gene Krupa and His Orchestra, in the 1939 Paramount film *Some Like It Hot*. 610518-1

The Lamp Is Low (1939)

Lyrics by Mitchell Parish, music by Peter DeRose and Bert Schefter

Introduced by Larry Clinton and His Orchestra. The melody is based on a theme from Maurice Ravel's "Pavane for a Dead Infanta" (1899).   **390720-1, 680529-1d**

Later (1953)

Lyrics and music by Tiny Bradshaw and Joe Glover

Introduced by Tiny Bradshaw and His Orchestra in a recording.   **540604-2, 540917-5, 550803-1**

Laughing on the Outside (Crying on the Inside) (1946)

Lyrics by Ben Raleigh, music by Bernie Wayne

Introduced by Sammy Kaye and His Orchestra, vocal by Billy Williams (Victor).   **620131-1**

Laura (1945)

Lyrics by Johnny Mercer, music by David Raksin

The music is from David Raksin's score for the 1944 20th Century–Fox film *Laura*. Lyrics were added several months after the release of the film, by which time the melody had become popular. Introduced on radio by Johnny Johnston, who recorded it for Capitol. Woody Herman's 1945 Columbia recording sold over a million records.   **500900-2, 641021-2**

Lazy (1924)

Lyrics and music by Irving Berlin

Introduced by The Brox Sisters and by Blossom Seeley in vaudeville.   **580318-6**

Lazy Day (1951)

Lyrics and music by Milton W. Raskin and Robert Farnon

Introduced by Tony Bennett, and covered by Ella on this recording.   **511126-4**

Learnin' the Blues (1955)

Lyrics and music by Dolores Vicki Silvers

Introduced and recorded by Frank Sinatra (Capitol).   **570723-2**

Lemon Drop (1948)

Scat by Ella Fitzgerald, music by George Wallington

A jazz instrumental, introduced by Chubby Jackson and His Jazz Five.   **490430-4, 510519-4, 520816-5, 730705-17, 740411-8**

Let It Snow! Let It Snow! Let It Snow! (1945)

Lyrics by Sammy Cahn, music by Jule Styne

Introduced by Vaughan Monroe and His Orchestra, vocal by Vaughan Monroe (Victor).   **600716-2**

Let the Lower Lights Be Burning (1905)

Lyrics and music by Philip Bliss

Bliss was well on his way to challenging Ira D. Sankey as the foremost gospel singer of the era when he lost his wife in a railroad wreck in 1876. The inspiration for the hymn, related Bliss, came from a sermon by Dwight L. Moody, who told of a shipwreck which occurred because, though the big top light of the lighthouse was burning, the lower lights along the shore were out. Moody drew this moral: "The Master will take care of the great light; let us keep the lower lights burning." Much impressed, Bliss sang his version of Moody's moral at the next service.   **670200-13**

Let Yourself Go (1936)

Lyrics and music by Irving Berlin

Introduced by Fred Astaire in the 1936 RKO film *Follow the Fleet*.   **580319-2**

Let's Begin (1933)

Lyrics by Otto Harbach, music by Jerome Kern

Introduced by George Murphy and reprised by Ray Middleton, Bob Hope and Tamara (Geva) in the 1933 musical play *Roberta*. Sung by Fred Astaire in the 1935 RKO film adaptation; and by Marge and Gower Chapion in the 1952 MGM film adaptation *Lovely to Look At*.   **630107-3**

Let's Call the Whole Thing Off (1936)

Lyrics by Ira Gershwin, music by George Gershwin

Introduced by Fred Astaire and Ginger Rogers in the 1937 RKO film *Shall We Dance*, which they followed with a dance routine on roller skates.   **570723-4, 590326-6, 830523-5**

Let's Do It (1928)

Lyrics and music by Cole Porter

Introduced by Irene Bordoni and Arthur Margetson in the 1928 musical play *Paris*. Sung by Jessie Matthews and Sonnie Hale in the 1929 London revue *Wake Up and Dream*. Adapted for a Rheingold beer television and radio commercial.   **560209-5, 560327-7, 660208-10, 660222-4, 660727-8, 660728-5, 660729-5, 660914-7, 670326-3, 750717-6, 810726-7**

Let's Face the Music and Dance (1936)

Lyrics and music by Irving Berlin

Introduced by Fred Astaire and Ginger Rogers in the 1936 RKO film *Follow the Fleet*. During the rehearsal of the dance routine that followed the song, Rogers wore an extremely heavy beaded gown. Each time she did a quick turn, Astaire tried to avoid being hit by the heavy sleeve.

During the filming, the sleeve actually did strike Astaire in the mouth and eye, and though made groggy by the blow which somehow eluded the camera, he continued dancing without losing a step; the take was perfect.   **580318-7**

Let's Fall in Love (1933)

Lyrics by Ted Koehler, music by Harold Arlen

Introduced by Art Jarrett and reprised by Ann Sothern in the 1934 Columbia film *Let's Fall in Love*.
                 581124-3, **610116-2**, 810726-15

Let's Get Together (1934)

Music by Chick Webb

Introduced by Chick Webb and His Orchestra as its theme song.
                 400122-10, **400125-10**, **400304-10**

Let's Go Slumming on Park Avenue see *Slumming on Park Avenue*

Let's Kiss and Make Up (1927)

Lyrics by Ira Gershwin, music by George Gershwin

Introduced by Fred and Adele Astaire in the 1927 musical play *Funny Face*. Developed from an earlier unused song called, "Come, Come, Come Closer." Sung by Fred Astaire in the 1957 Paramount film adaptation.
                 590326-9

Let's Take a Walk Around the Block (1934)

Lyrics by Ira Gershwin and E.Y. "Yip" Harburg, music by Harold Arlen

Introduced by Dixie Dunbar and Earl Oxford in the musical revue *Life Begins at 8:40*.   **600802-5**, **600802-6**

Like Someone in Love (1944)

Lyrics by Johnny Burke, music by Jimmy Van Heusen

Introduced by Dinah Shore in the 1945 International film *Belle of the Yukon*.   **571015-4**

Like Young (1958)

Lyrics by Paul Francis Webster, music by André Previn

Introduced as an instrumental by André Previn on piano with David Rose and His Orchestra (MGM). First vocal recording by Ann Henry (Dynasty).   **590903-1**

Li'l Darlin' (1960)

Scat lyrics by Ella Fitzgerald, music by Neal Hefti

Jazz standard introduced and recorded by Count Basie and His Orchestra (Roulette). This is one of the many instrumentals to which Ella has her own brand of scat lyrics,

but, unlike many others, this song also has legitimate lyrics: Cf. "Don't Dream of Anyone but Me."
                 610516-9, **710507-7**

Limehouse Blues (1922)

Lyrics by Douglas Furber, music by Philip Braham

Introduced by Teddie Gerard in the 1922 London revue *A to Z*. Introduced in the U.S. by Gertrude Lawrence, Robert Hobbs, and Fred Leslie in the revue *André Charlot's Revue of 1924*.   **391200-7**, **400125-2**, **400325-7**

Lindy Hoppers' Delight (1939)

Music by Eddie Barefield and Teddy McRae

Instrumental introduced by Ella Fitzgerald and Her Famous Orchestra (Decca).   **391012-5**

A Little Bit Later On (1936)

Lyrics by Al J. Neiberg, music by Jerry Levinson (before he became Jerry Livingston)

Introduced by Chick Webb and His Orchestra, vocal by Ella Fitzgerald (Decca).   **360602-3**

Little Boy (1956)

Lyrics by Alan and Marilyn Bergman, music by Henry Mancini (?)

Ella recorded this song at Zardi's nightclub in Los Angeles on the evening of 2 February 1956, and since her recording has never been issued, it is not certain that this is the Bergman-Mancini composition; however, a fan who was at the performance identifies it tentatively.
                 560202-16

Little Girl Blue (1935)

Lyrics by Lorenz Hart, music by Richard Rodgers

Introduced by Gloria Grafton in the 1935 musical play *Jumbo*. Sung by Doris Day in the 1962 MGM film adaptation *Billy Rose's Jumbo*.
                 560815-8, **560830-6**, 610518-7,
                 610519-18, 610520-20, 620629-9

Little Jazz (1957)

Scat lyrics by Ella Fitzgerald, music by Roy Eldridge and Buster Harding

Introduced by Artie Shaw and His Orchestra, featuring Roy Eldridge, as an instrumental. Also recorded by Roy Eldridge later with his small group.
                 581123-9, **581123-10**, **890315-3**

Little Man in a Flying Saucer (1951)

Research has revealed no author/composer of this song. It is assumed that this is the only recording.
                 510327-2

Little Small Town Girl (1945)

Lyrics by Jules Loman, music by Hugo Rubens

Introduced by The Delta Rhythm Boys on a Decca recording.   **501220-1**

Little White Lies (1930)

Lyrics and music by Walter Donaldson

Written for, introduced, and recorded by Guy Lombardo and His Royal Canadians.

390421-6, 390720-2, 581123-11,
610520-7, 720602-8

Lola's Theme *see* **Watch What Happens**

Lonely Is (1967)

Lyrics and music by Clinton Ballard, Jr., and Hal Hackaday

Introduced on this recording by Ella, this song was chosen for Side 2 of the 45rpm release of her recording of the title song for the 1968 MGM film "A Place for Lovers," q.v.   **671021-2**

Lonesome Gal (1951)

Lyrics by Jack Brooks, music by Walter Schumann

Ella's may be the only recording of this song.

510112-1

Looking for a Boy (1925)

Lyrics by Ira Gershwin, music by George Gershwin

Introduced by Queenie Smith in the 1925 musical play *Tip Toes*. Miss Smith sang the song downstage while the set was being changed behind the drop curtain.

500911-1, 531227-3, 590326-7

The Lorelei (1932)

Lyrics by Ira Gershwin, music by George Gershwin

Introduced by Lyda Roberti in out-of-town try-outs, and on Broadway by Carl Randall and Barbara Newberry in the 1933 musical play *Pardon My English*.

590326-8, 590715-6, 600213-9, 610519-21

Lost in a Fog (1934)

Lyrics by Dorothy Fields, music by Jimmy McHugh

The music was written as a theme for The Dorsey Brothers' Orchestra, and was introduced during the band's debut at Ben Marden's Riviera Cafe in New Jersey, with Jimmy McHugh doing the vocal. The orchestra then recorded it with their regular singer, Bob Crosby (Decca).

571028-5

Lost in Meditation (1938)

Lyrics by Irving Mills, music by Duke Ellington, Juan Tizol, and Lou Singer

Introduced by Duke Ellington and His Orchestra.

570625-4

Lotus Blossom (1946)

Scat lyrics by Ella Fitzgerald, music by William Thomas (Billy) Strayhorn

Introduced by Johnny Hodges and His Orchestra, with the title, "Charlotte Russe." Retitled and introduced by Duke Ellington and His Orchestra.

Louisville, K-Y (1940)

Lyrics and music by Sonny Skylar

Introduced by Sonny Skylar and His Orchestra, and covered by Ella Fitzgerald and Her Famous Orchestra with this recording.   **400925-3, 400925-4**

L-O-V-E (1964)

Lyrics and music by Milt Gabler and Bert Kaempfert

Introduced by Bert Kaempfert and His Orchestra. Best-selling recording by Nat "King" Cole (Capitol), one of his last.   **720602-1**

Love and Kisses (1927)

Lyrics by Sid Silvers, music by Phil Baker

Introduced by Paul Whiteman and His Orchestra (Victor). This was Ella Fitzgerald's first released recording, made on 12 June 1935, accompanied by Chick Webb and His Orchestra (Decca).   **350612-4**

Love for Sale (1930)

Lyrics and music by Cole Porter

Introduced by Kathryn Crawford and The Three Girl Friends (June Shafer, Ida Peterson, and Stella Friend) in the 1930 musical play *The New Yorkers*. Long banned from radio broadcasts because of its suggestive lyrics, the song became a hit, however, with a recording by Fred Waring and His Pennsylvanians, with vocals by the original Three Girl Friends (Victor).

560208-8, 560815-5, 570429-1,
610521-1, 720612-9, 860228-11

Love Is Sweeping the Country (1931)

Lyrics by Ira Gershwin, music by George Gershwin

Introduced by George Murphy, June O'Dea, and ensemble in the 1931 musical play *Of Thee I Sing*. This was the music for the interlude (patter); it was originally composed for the unproduced *Ming Toy*.   **590718-2**

Love Is the Tender Trap *see* **The Tender Trap**

Love Is the Thing (So They Say) (1933)

Lyrics by Ned Washington, music by Victor Young

Introduced and recorded by Ethel Waters (Brunswick).   **370324-8**

Love Marches On (1937)

Lyrics and music by John Loeb and Charles Tobias

Introduced by the trio Ella Fitzgerald-Louis Jordan-Charles Linton on this recording with Chick Webb and his Orchestra. This is Webb's first attempt at vocal trio work on record, and he tried it the next day with "There's Frost on the Moon" (q.v.). Ella was recording with The Mills Brothers at the time, and one may assume that Webb wanted to save the credit for members of his own band rather than sharing it with outsiders. **370114-2**

Love Me or Leave Me (1928)

Lyrics by Gus Kahn, music by Walter Donaldson

Introduced by Ruth Etting in the 1928 musical play *Whoopee!* Miss Etting sang it again in the 1930 musical play *Simple Simon.* 580810-21, **611115-5**

Love That Boy (1948)

Lyrics by Don Raye, music by Gene DePaul

Introduced by Gail Robbins and Cully Richards in the 1948 RKO film *Race Street.* **481127-2**

Love Walked In (1937)

Lyrics by Ira Gershwin, music by George Gershwin

Introduced by Kenny Baker in the 1938 United Artists film *The Goldwyn Follies of 1938.* **590326-4**

Love You Madly (1951)

Lyrics and music by Duke Ellington

Introduced by Duke Ellington and His Orchestra (Victor), this became a popular number in his concert repertoire.
510524-3, 530911-6, **571017-3, 690200-12, 690728-5**

Love, You're Just a Laugh (1936)

Lyrics by Nat Gardner and Sammy Cahn, music by Saul Chaplin

Introduced by Chick Webb and His Orchestra, vocal by Ella Fitzgerald (Decca).
360407-1, 360407-2, **360602-4**

Lover (1932)

Lyrics by Lorenz Hart, music by Richard Rodgers

Introduced by Jeanette MacDonald in the 1932 Paramount film *Love Me Tonight.*
560821-4, 560821-5, 580810-13

Lover, Come Back to Me (1928)

Lyrics by Oscar Hammerstein II, music by Sigmund Romberg

Introduced by Evelyn Herbert in the 1928 operetta

The New Moon. Sung by Lawrence Tibbett and reprised by Grace Moore in the 1930 MGM film adaptation *New Moon* (the article was dropped for the movie title). Sung by Jeanette MacDonald in the 1940 MGM film adaptation.
400304-5, **510519-6,** 530911-3, **550427-4,** 610512-2, 610520-15

A Lover Is Blue (1939)

Lyrics and music by James Oliver "Trummy" Young, James R. "Jimmy" Mundy, and Charles Carpenter.

Introduced by Tommy Dorsey and His Orchestra, vocal by Jack Leonard (Victor). **400122-3**

Lover Man (1942)

Lyrics and music by Jimmy Davis, Roger "Ram" Ramirez, and Jimmy Sherman

Introduced by and identified with Billie Holiday, who recorded it with Toots Camarata's Orchestra (Decca).
470929-3, 490211-5, 650625-4, **660130-2, 660208-11, 660720-10, 670430-2**

Lover's Gold (1949)

Lyrics by Bob Merrill, music by Morty Nevins

Introduced by The Three Suns (of which Nevins was a member). **490428-4**

Lucky

Lyrics and music by Benny Goodman, Jack Palmer, and Edgar M. Sampson

Ella recorded this title at the time of her making her album *Things Ain't What They Used to Be (and You Better Believe It),* but it was never released, and since there are several other songs with this title, its origin is uncertain, although it is thought to be the Goodman-Palmer-Sampson composition. 700124-1

Lullaby of Birdland (1952)

Lyrics by B.Y. Forster, music by George Shearing

Shearing has said that once, while he was playing the Gus Kahn-Walter Donaldson standard, "Love Me or Leave Me," he improvised a jazz chorus for the number, the melody of which became this standard. The title comes from the New York jazz club, Birdland. Introduced and recorded by Shearing (MGM). A memorable Decca album of the mid-1950s contains tens versions of the number by various artists, and became a best-seller.
540604-1, 540917-2, **560121-6,** 560202-12, **570428-3,** 570704-5, 610513-8, 610518-16, 610519-9, 610520-10, 660727-7, **660728-10,** 660729-9, 710518-1

Lullaby of Broadway (1935)

Lyrics by Al Dubin, music by Harry Warren

Introduced by Winifred Shaw and Dick Powell in the 1935 Warner Bros. film *Gold Diggers of 1935*. The spectacular Busby Berkeley production number was one of the longest filmed, lasting almost fifteen minutes on the released film. Winner of the Academy Award (AMPAS), Best Original Song, 1935. **581124-2**

Lullaby of the Leaves (1932)

Lyrics by Joe Young, music by Bernice Petkere

Introduced by Freddie Berrens and His Orchestra on radio. First recorded by Ben Selvin and His Orchestra. **640304-1**

Lush Life (1938)

Lyrics and music by Billy Strayhorn

Introduced by Billy Strayhorn on piano, with Duke Ellington and His Orchestra. First recorded by Nat "King" Cole in 1949 (Capitol). 570627-1, **571017-4**, **730828-5**

Mack The Knife (Moritat) (1938)

German lyrics by Bertolt Brecht, English lyrics by Mark Blitzstein, music by Kurt Weill

Introduced by Kurt Gerron in the operetta *Dreigroschenoper (Three-Penny Opera)*, in Berlin in 1928. English-language version introduced by 1952 in a concert performance at Brandeis University, New York. Introduced by Scott Merrill in the English-language off-Broadway production in 1954. First recorded in the U.S. by Lotte Lenya in German. Ella Fitzgerald's 1960 concert performance in Berlin created a sensation; recorded in performance by Verve, the number won a Grammy Award (NARAS) and the Best Female Vocal Performance, and the album (on first release, an abbreviated version of the concert) won the Grammy for the best jazz album of the year, and is now looked upon by jazz aficionados as a classic.
600213-10, **620211-13**, 610513-11, 610513-20, 610516-12, 610518-9, 610518-22, 610520-4, 610521-5, 620629-5, 640800-21, 640203-15, 640728-15, 640729-24, **660130-3**, **660222-10**, **660728-12**,**660729-12**, 660914-10,**660923-7**, **670128-3**, 670430-5, 700520-18, 710518-6, **780620-2**

MacPherson Is Rehearsin' (To Swing) (1938)

Lyrics and music by Marion Sunshine

Introduced by Chick Webb and His Orchestra, vocal by Ella Fitzgerald (Decca). **380609-2**

Madalena (1968)

Lyrics by Vítor Martins, music by Ivan Lins

Introduced by the composer at the 1968 Universitário Festival which was televised, and gained him instant fame. **710721-4e**, **720602-9**

Make Believe (1927)

Lyrics by Oscar Hammerstein II, music by Jerome Kern

Introduced by Howard Marsh and Norma Terris in the 1927 musical play *Show Boat*. Sung by Irene Dunne and Allan Jones in the 1936 Universal film adaptation, and by Kathryn Grayson and Howard Keel in the 1951 MGM film adaptation. **400226-5**, **400304-9**

Make Love to Me (1941)

Lyrics by Kim Gannon, music by Paul Mann and Stephen Weiss

Introduced by Ella Fitzgerald on this recording. **411105-3**

Make Me Rainbows (1967)

Lyrics by Alan and Marilyn Bergman, music by John Williams

Introduced by Dick Van Dyke in the 1967 United Artists film *Fitzwilly*. **790712-4**

Makin' Whoopee (1928)

Lyrics by Gus Kahn, music by Walter Donaldson

Introduced by Eddie Cantor in the 1928 musical play *Whoopee!* Sung by Mr. Cantor in the 1930 Paramount film adaptation, and, dubbing for Keefe Brasselle, in the 1954 Warner Bros. film *The Eddie Cantor Story*. *The Oxford Dictionary* and *English Words* (by John Moore) credit this song title for the popular phrase, "makin' whoopee." Actually, the phrase was coined several years earlier by Walter Winchell in his column in the New York *The Daily Mirror* newspaper. **540329-4**, **581124-8**

Mama, Come Home (1942)

Lyrics by Edgar M. Battle and Kim Gannon, music by Josef Myrow

Introduced by Ella Fitzgerald with The Four Keys on this Decca recording. **420410-2**

A Man and a Woman [Une Homme et Une Femme] (1966)

French lyrics by Pierre Barouh, English lyrics by Jerry Keller, music by Francis Lai

Introduced as a recurring theme in the 1966 Allied Artists film *A Man and a Woman*. Introduced on records by Francis Lai and His Orchestra (United Artists). **690729-6**, **700105-3**

The Man I Love (1924)

Lyrics by Ira Gershwin, music by George Gershwin

Originally written for Adele Astaire for the opening scene in the 1924 musical play *Lady, Be Good!*, it was dropped. Then unsuccessfully tried out in the 1927 musical play *Strike Up the Band!*, and for Marilyn Miller in the

1928 musical play *Rosalie*. By the time the second version in *Strike Up the Band!* was staged, the song was too famous to be used. It was, therefore, never heard on the Broadway stage. The song was originally introduced by Eva Gauthier in a concert at Derby, Connecticut, with George Gershwin at the piano. Lady Louis Mountbatten arranged for the Berkeley Square Orchestra to introduce it in London — it became a hit with jazz orchestras. From London the song went on to conquer Paris, and only then did it return to the U.S. to become a hit.

590105-8, 600213-6, 710721-3b, 740108-6, 740411-4, 750717-7, 831000-7a

The Man That Got Away (1954)

Lyrics by Ira Gershwin, music by Harold Arlen

Introduced by Judy Garland in the 1954 Warner Bros. film *A Star Is Born*. Of her rendition *Time* magazine said: "Her big dark voice sobs, sighs, sulks, and socks it out like a cross between Tara's harp and the late Bessie Smith." Nominated for an Academy Award (AMPAS), Best Original Song, 1954. **540917-3, 600801-5**

A Man Wrote a Song (1949)

Lyrics and music by Dave Franklin

Introduced by Ella Fitzgerald on this Decca recording. **490921-4**

Manhattan (1925)

Lyrics by Lorenz Hart, music by Richard Rodgers

Introduced by Sterling Holloway and June Cochrane in the 1925 revue *The Garrick Gaieties*. **560829-3, 810726-4**

Manteca (1948)

Scat lyrics by Ella Fitzgerald, music by John Birks "Dizzy" Gillespie and Gil Fuller

Introduced by Dizzy Gillespie and His Orchestra (Victor). Vocal version introduced by Ella Fitzgerald. **700106-1, 701106-1, 710507-8, 831000-1**

A Marshmallow World (1950)

Lyrics by Carl Sigman, music by Peter DeRose

This Christmas song was introduced and recorded by Bing Crosby (Decca). Featured in a duet with Ella Fitzgerald on his Christmas radio show in 1950. **501129-4**

Mas, Que Nada [Oh, Come On] (1963)

English lyrics by Loryn Deane, Portuguese lyrics and music by Jorge Ben

Introduced by Jorge Ben, his first big hit, in performance and on a Brazilian recording. Popularized in the U.S. by Sérgio Mendez and Brazil '66, with Lani Hall and Karen Philip singing in Portuguese. **700106-2, 701106-2, 710507-4**

Matchmaker, Matchmaker (1964)

Lyrics by Sheldon Harnick, music by Jerry Ross

Introduced by Joanna Merlin, Julia Migenes, and Tanya Everett in the 1964 musical play *Fiddler on the Roof*. Sung by Rosalind Harris, Neva Small, Elaine Edwards, Candy Bonstein, and Michele Marsh in the 1971 United Artists film adaptation. 650626-2, **660720-12**

Maybe (1926)

Lyrics by Ira Gershwin, music by George Gershwin

Introduced by Gertrude Lawrence and Oscar Shaw in the 1926 musical play *Oh, Kay!* **500912-4**

Maybe (1935)

Lyrics and music by Allan Flynn and Frank Madden

Popular big-band number of the mid–1930s and early 1940s. **680603-3b**

Mean to Me (1929)

Lyrics by Roy Turk, music by Fred E. Ahlert

Introduced by, and a favorite in the repertoire of, Ruth Etting, who also recorded it (Columbia). **611113-2, 750519-1**

Meditation [Meditção] (1962)

Portuguese lyrics by Newton Mendonça, English lyrics by Norman Gimbel, music by Antonio Carlos Jobim.

Introduced by Antonio Carlos Jobim in Brazil in performance and on Brazilian recordings. Introduced in the U.S. as an instrumental by jazz guitarist Charlie Byrd (Riverside). First English-lyric vocal version by Pat Boone (Dot). Popular recording by Claudine Longet (A&M). **810726-12**

Melancholy Baby see My Melancholy Baby

Melancholy Me (1954)

Lyrics and music by Joe Thomas and Howard Biggs

Popular recordings by Eddy Howard (Mercury), and The Smith Brothers ("X"). **531223-3**

Melancholy Serenade (1953)

Scat lyrics by Ella Fitzgerald, music by Jackie Gleason

Introduced as an instrumental theme on the telvision series *The Jackie Gleason Show*. **641022-7**

Melinda, the Mousie (1941)

Lyrics by Kim Gannon, music by Josef Myrow and Gene Irwin

Introduced by Ella Fitzgerald and Her Famous Orchestra, vocal by Ella Fitzgerald (Decca). **410731-5**

Memories of You (1930)

Lyrics by Andy Razaf, music by Eubie Blake

Introduced by Minto Cato in the 1930 revue *Lew Leslie's Blackbirds of 1930*. First recorded by Ethel Waters (Okeh).   **640303-4**

Memphis Blues (1913)

Lyrics by George A. Norton, music by W.C. Handy

This is Handy's first published song. He wrote it in 1912, titled "Mr. Crump," as an instrumental to help elect Edward H. Crump as mayor of Memphis. Recorded by virtually every jazz artist up to the 1930s.   **501129-5, 5111128-2**

Midnight Sun (1947/1954)

Lyrics by Johnny Mercer, music by Lionel Hampton and Sonny Burke

Introduced as an instrumental by Lionel Hampton and His Orchestra (Decca). With lyrics added, vocal version introduced by Ella Fitzgerald in 1954 (Decca).   **571015-11, 580425-3, 580425-15, 641020-5, 660222-6, 750519-6**

Miss Otis Regrets (1954)

Lyrics and music by Cole Porter

Written by Porter for the private delectation of friends. When he played it one evening, Monty Wooley proceeded to borrow a morning coat and silver tray and impersonated a butler while delivering the lines to Porter's accompaniment. Introduced by Donald Byng, at the London Paladium, in the revue *Hi, Diddle, Diddle*. Mr. Wooley reprised his performance in the 1946 Warner Bros. film *Night and Day*.   **560207-6, 640304-6, 730705-11**

M-I-S-S-I-S-S-I-P-P-I (1916)

Lyrics by Bert Hanlon and Benny Ryan, music by Harry Tierney

Written for and introduced by Frances White in the 1916 Ziegfeld revue *Midnight Follies*.   **500509-1**

Mr. Paganini (You'll Have To Swing It) (1936)

Lyrics and music by Sam Coslow

Introduced by Martha Raye in the 1936 Paramount film *Rhythm on the Range*. This song has been titled "(If You Can't Sing It) You'll Have To Swing It" on several recordings. The original copyright title is "Mr. Paganini," according to Sam Coslow himself in his autobiography *Cocktails for Two: The Life and Lyrics of the Giant Songwriter, Sam Coslow*.

361029-1, 361029-2, 481127-3, 490415-2, 520626-3/4, 610211-12, 610221-10, 610405-2, 610511-1, 610512-1, 610513-14, 610514-7, 610517-1, 610519-11, 610520-23, 610521-3, 610825-1, 660208-13, 690729-10, 700520-17

Misty (1954)

Lyrics by Johnny Burke, music by Erroll Garner

Introduced by The Errol Garner Trio as an instrumental in 1954 (Mercury). In 1956 Garner recorded it with Mitch Miller and His Orchestra (Columbia). The same year, lyrics were added, and the vocal version recorded by Johnny Mathis (Columbia).

600213-4, 600414-6, 610211-10, 620629-1, 640800-9, 660727-5, 660729-11, 660923-6

Misty Blue (1967)

Lyrics and music by Bob Montgomery

Introduced by Ella Fitzgerald on her album of the same title.   **671221-4**

Mixed Emotions (1951)

Lyrics and music by Stuart F. Louchheim

Introduced by Ella Fitzgerald on this Decca recording.   **510626-1**

Moanin' Low (1929)

Lyrics by Howard Dietz, music by Ralph Rainger

Introduced by Libby Holman and danced by Clifton Webb in the 1929 revue *The Little Show*.   **531213-2, 531231-1**

Molasses, Molasses (1950)

Lyrics and music by Larry Clinton

Introduced and recorded by Larry Clinton and His Orchestra.   **500926-2**

The Moment of Truth (1965)

Lyrics by Collen Gray "Tex" Satterwhite, music by Frank Scott

Introduced on a recording by Tony Bennett.   **660719-10, 660914-2**

Mood Indigo (1931)

Lyrics by Mitchell Parish and Irving Mills, music by Albany "Barney" Bigard and Duke Ellington

Originally an instrumental, this was first recorded in 1930 by Duke Ellington and His Orchestra with the title, "Dreamy Blues." With lyrics and a change of title, it became one of Ellington's first outstanding popular song hits (Victor and Decca).   **571017-2, 650326-6a, 710518-2a, 710721-7a**

Moon Ray (1939)

Lyrics and music by Artie Shaw, Paul Madison, and Arthur L. Quenzer

Introduced and recorded by Artie Shaw and His Orchestra, vocal by Helen Forrest (Bluebird).   **391012-6**

Moonlight Becomes You (1942)

Lyrics by Johnny Burke, music by James Van Heusen

Introduced by Bing Crosby in the 1942 Paramount film *The Road to Morocco*.   **590711-4**

Moonlight in Vermont (1944)

Lyrics by John Blackburn, music by Karl Suessdorf

Title from, but not used in, the 1944 Universal film of the same name. Introduced as an instrumental by Billy Butterfield and His Orchestra. Popular recording by Margaret Whiting (Capitol), with whom it became identified.
          **560816-8, 570724-2, 570929-8,
          571009-7, 580509-4a, 860228-10**

Moonlight on the Ganges (1926)

Lyrics by Chester Wallace, music by Sherman Myers

Introduced and recorded by Paul Whiteman and His Orchestra.   **581123-6**

Moonlight Serenade (1939)

Lyrics by Mitchell Parish, music by Glenn Miller

Probably the most popular original theme song of the big band era, the song was introduced as an instrumental by Glenn Miller and His Orchestra (Bluebird). Miller composed "Moonlight Serenade" while studying composition with Joseph Schillinger, and playing trombone with Ray Noble's orchestra. Edward Heyman wrote the original lyric, titled, "Now I Lay Me Down to Weep." When Miller formed his own band and decided to adopt it as his theme song, he felt that the title was too negative and asked Parish to write a new lyric.   **590711-5**

The More I See You (1945)

Lyrics by Mack Gordon, music by Harry Warren

Introduced by Dick Haymes in the 1945 20th Century–Fox film *Billy Rose's Diamond Horseshoe*.
          660727-6, 660728-7

More Than You Know (1929)

Lyrics by Billy Rose and Edward Eliscu, music by Vincent Youmans

Introduced by Mayo Methot in the 1929 musical play *Great Day!*   **571015-3, 750519-4**

Mountain Greenery (1926)

Lyrics by Lorenz Hart, music by Richard Rodgers

Introduced by Bobbie Perkins and Sterling Holloway in the 1926 revue *The Garrick Gaieties*.
          560828-3, 590410-2

The Muffin Man (1941)

Lyrics and music by Ella Fitzgerald

Introduced by Ella Fitzgerald and Her Famous Orchestra, vocal by Ella Fitzgerald (Decca).   **410108-5**

The Music Goes 'Round and 'Round (1935)

Lyrics by "Red" Hodgson, music by Edward Farley and Michael Riley

A nonsense song about a French horn (with origins in "If You Want to Know Who We Are," from Gilbert and Sullivan's *The Mikado*). Introduced and made popular by the Riley-Farley Band in broadcasts from The Onyx Club, New York. Recorded by Farley and Riley for the then newly organized Decca Recording Company in America — this release was the first to show them a profit.   **610624-5**

My Baby Likes to Be-Bop (1947)

Lyrics and music by Walter Bishop

Introduced by Ella Fitzgerald on this Decca recording.
          471220-1, 480601-1

My Bonnie (1951)

Lyrics and music by Lewis Gluckin

Introduced by Les Elgart and His Orchestra.
          520811-3

My Cousin in Milwaukee (1932)

Lyrics by Ira Gershwin, music by George Gershwin

Introduced by Lyda Roberti in the 1933 musical play *Pardon My English*.   **590717-1**

My Echo, My Shadow, and Me see We Three

My Favorite Song (1944)

Lyrics by Herb Magidson, music by Joe Burke

Introduced by Ella Fitzgerald on this Decca recording.
          520919-1, 521218-1b

My Funny Valentine (1937)

Lyrics by Lorenz Hart, music by Richard Rodgers

Introduced by Mitzi Green in the 1937 musical play *Babes in Arms*. Not used in the 1939 MGM film adaptation with Rooney and Garland.
          531118-7, 560830-8, 580810-34

My Happiness (1948)

Lyrics by Betty Peterson, music by Borney Bergantine

Popular recordings in 1948 by Jon and Sondra Steele, and by The Pied Pipers with Paul Weston and His Orchestra (Capitol).   **480430-1, 491109-2**

My Heart and I Decided

Lyrics and music by Walter Donaldson

The Al Jolson Song Book, 1942   **420731-1**

My Heart Belongs to Daddy (1938)

Lyrics and music by Cole Porter

Introduced by Mary Martin in her sensational Broadway debut in the 1938 musical play *Leave It to Me.*

390217-5, **540330-3**, 560202-18,
580810-16, 590800-2, 610520-15,
620629-11, 620630-23, **720612-8**

My Heart Stood Still (1927)

Lyrics by Lorenz Hart, music by Richard Rodgers

Originally written for the Charles B. Cochran revue in London *One Dam Thing After Another*, where it was introduced by Jessie Matthews and Richard Dolman, the song was introduced in New York by William Gaxton and Constance Carpenter in the 1927 musical play *A Connecticut Yankee.* Interpolated in the 1931 Fox film adaptation. The song is said to have been inspired when Messrs. Rodgers and Hart, narrowly avoiding a collision in a Paris taxi, overheard one of the ladies in their party remark, "My heart stood still."   **560830-2**

My Kind of Trouble Is You (1955)

Lyrics by Paul Vandervoort II, music by Benny Carter

Introduced by Benny Carter and His Orchestra, vocal by Helen Carr.   **790216-1**

My Kinda Love (1929)

Lyrics by Jo Trent, music by Louis Alter

Interpolated in the 1928 musical revue *Americana*, after the New York opening.   **581122-5**

My Last Affair (1936)

Lyrics and music by Haven Johnson

Introduced by Billie Haywood in the musical revue *New Faces of 1936.*

361118-1, 630717-5, 630716-5, 630716-6,
640800-23, 640203-3, **890320-1**

My Last Goodbye (1939)

Lyrics and music by Eddy Howard

Introduced and recorded by Dick Jurgens and His Orchestra, vocal by Eddy Howard.   **390818-1**

My Man (Mon Homme) (1921)

French lyrics by Albert Willehetz and Jacques Charles, English lyrics by Channing Pollack, music by Maurice Yvain

Introduced by Mistinguette in Paris in the 1921 revue

Paris Qui Jazz. The French version was introduced in the U.S. by Irene Bordoni. The American version was intended for Mistinguette's American debut in *The Ziegfeld Follies of 1921*, but, upon her arrival, Ziegfeld lost interest in her and dropped her from the production; Fannie Brice was selected to do the number instead. Miss Brice also sang the song in her talking-picture debut in the 1929 Warner Bros. film *My Man.*   **410331-3**, **640304-3**, **770714-3**, **860228-5**

My Man's Gone Now (1935)

Lyrics by DuBose Heyward, music by George Gershwin

Introduced by Ruby Elzy in the 1935 folk opera *Porgy and Bess.* In the 1959 Columbia film adaptation, the song was performed by Ruth Attaway (dubbed by Inez Matthews).   **570828-2**

My Melancholy Baby (1912)

Lyrics by George A. Norton, music by Ernie Burnett

Introduced and popularized in performances in night clubs and vaudeville, particularly by Walter van Brunt, and by Gene Austin, who revived it in 1928.

360317-1, **600414-1**

My Mother's Eyes (1928)

Lyrics by L. Wolfe Gilbert, music by Abel Baer

Introduced by George Jessel in vaudeville; he also sang it in his first film starring role, in the 1929 Tiffany-Stahl film *Lucky Boy.* It was his trademark throughout his long career.   **680529-2a**

My Old Flame (1934)

Lyrics by Sam Coslow, music by Arthur Johnston

Introduced by Mae West, with Duke Ellington and His Orchestra, in the 1934 Paramount film *Belle of the Nineties.*   500900-7, **590711-1**, 760208-1

My One and Only (1927)

Lyrics by Ira Gershwin, music by George Gershwin

Introduced by Fred Astaire, Gertrude MacDonald, Betty Compson and ensemble in the musical play *Funny Face.*   **500911-2**, **590326-1**, **620410-3**

My One and Only Love (1953)

Lyrics by Robert Mellin, music by Guy Wood

New lyrics in 1953 gave new life to a 1927 song, "Music from Beyond the Moon." The new version was introduced by Frank Sinatra (Capitol). The melody is based on Anton Rubenstein's "Romance."   **550805-1**

My Own Best Friend (1975)

Lyrics by Fred Ebb, music by John Kander

Introduced by Gwen Verdon and Chita Rivera in the

1975 musical revue *Chicago*. The ladies may be heard in the New York original cast recording (Arista). **741018-2**

My Prayer (1939)

Lyrics and musical adaptation by James Kennedy, music by Georges Boulanger

Jimmy Kennedy adapted Boulanger's violin piece, "Avant de Mourir," to a lovely song for popular British singing star Vera Lynn. Due, perhaps, to the imminence World War II, the song became an enormous hit. Introduced in the U.S. by Sammy Kaye and His Orchestra. Revived with a best-selling Mercury recording by The Platters in 1956. **391214-2**

My Reverie (1938)

Lyrics and music by Larry Clinton

Introduced and recorded by Larry Clinton and His Orchestra, vocal by Bea Wain, this song was responsible for his first major success as a bandleader. The melody is adapted from "Reverie," by Claude Debussy. Clinton and his publisher were under the erroneous impression that the original work was in the public domain. After the record's success, which was phenomenal, the Debussy estate sued for copyright infringement and was awarded royalties of over $60,000, an amount, as it happened, that exceeded Debussy's lifetime earnings from all his music! **610623-3**

My Romance (1935)

Lyrics by Lorenz Hart, music by Richard Rodgers

Introduced by Donald Novis and Gloria Grafton in the 1935 musical revue *Jumbo*. Sung by Doris Day in the 1962 MGM film adaptation *Billy Rose's Jumbo*. **560830-1**

My Shining Hour (1943)

Lyrics by Johnny Mercer, music by Harold Arlen

Introduced by Joan Leslie and Fred Astaire in the 1943 RKO Radio film *The Sky's the Limit*, which also provided a production dance number for the stars. In his autobiography, Astaire confesses that while the picture was being produced, no one suspected that the song would be a hit, but several months after the film's release, it became the number one song of the day. Nominated for an Academy Award (AMPAS), Best Original Song, 1943. **610115-1**

My Ship (1941)

Lyrics by Ira Gershwin, music by George Gershwin

Introduced by Gertrude Lawrence in the 1941 musical play *Lady in the Dark*. Popular recordings by Gertrude Lawrence (Victor), and by Danny Kaye (who was also in the show) (Columbia). Other than a few melodic bars, the song was not used in the 1944 Paramount film adaptation. **860228-1**

My Wubby Dolly (1939)

Lyrics and music by Kay and Sue Werner

Introduced by Ella Fitzgerald and Her Famous Orchestra, vocal by Ella Fitzgerald (Decca). **391012-4, 391214-1**

Nature Boy (1946)

Lyrics and music by Eden Ahbez

Introduced on a recording by Nat "King" Cole (Capitol), which sold a million records during the first month of its release. Ahbez left the manuscript for his song at the stage door of a California theatre where Cole was appearing. Impressed by its haunting originality, Cole recorded it. Ten weeks on "Your Hit Parade" in 1948, six of which it held the #1 spot. **760208-1**

The Nearness of You

Lyrics by Ned Washington, music by Hoagy Carmichael

Introduced by Gladys Swarthout in the 1938 Paramount film *Romance in the Dark*. **560816-11, 890322-2**

Necessary Evil (1950)

Lyrics and music by Redd Evans.

Introduced on a recording by Redd Evans. Ella's duet with Louis Armstrong on this Decca recording is one of their most memorable. **511123-1**

Necessity (1946)

Lyrics by E.Y. "Yip" Harburg, music by Burton Lane

Introduced by Dolores Martin in the 1947 musical play *Finian's Rainbow*. Ella Fitzgerald recorded it in a duet with Frank Sinatra for the soundtrack of a planned 1955 animated feature film adaptation, but the film was never produced. Sung by Brenda Arnau in the 1968 Warner Bros. film adaptation. **541120-1**

Nel Blu, Dipinto di Blu *see* Volare

A New Moon and an Old Serenade (1939)

Lyrics and music by Abner Silver, Sam Coslow, and Martin Block

Featured and recorded by Charlie Barnet and His Orchestra (Bluebird), and by Cab Calloway an His Orchestra (Vocalion). **390504-3**

(I'm Wearing) A New Shade of Blue (1948)

Lyrics by Ruth Poll, music by Andy Ackers and Johnny Farrow

Introduced in a successful recording by Billy Eckstine (MGM). **490720-2, 490918-2**

Nice Work If You Can Get It (1937)

Lyrics by Ira Gershwin, music by George Gershwin

Introduced by Fred Astaire and a trio (Jan Duggan, Mary Dea, and Pearl Amatore) in the 1937 RKO Radio film *A Damsel in Distress*.

540330-5, 580810-2, **590326-3**, 610519-14, **730705-5, 830523-2**

Night and Day (1932)

Lyrics and music by Cole Porter

Introduced by Fred Astaire and Clair Luce in the 1932 musical play *The Gay Divorce*. Sung by Mr. Astaire and danced by him with Ginger Rogers in the 1934 film adaptation *The Gay Divorcée* (the title was changed for the film in deference to the feelings of those who objected that a divorce can never be a gay affair). One of the sixteen songs selected by ASCAP in 1963 for its All-Time Hit Parade during the first half-century of its existence.

500900-8, **560327-1, 710721-1, 720602-6, 831000-5**

A Night in Tunisia (1944)

Lyrics by Jon Hendricks, music by John Birks "Dizzy" Gillespie and Frank Paparelli

Introduced, but never recorded, by Earl Hines and His Orchestra as an instrumental. First recording by Boyd Raeburn and His Orchestra in 1945.   **610524-4**

Night Wind (1935)

Lyrics by Bob Rothberg, music by Dave Pollock

A favorite of jazz artists, with many popular recordings, notably by the orchestras of Benny Goodman, vocal by Helen Ward (Columbia); The Dorsey Brothers, vocal by Bob Crosby (Decca); Taft Jordan (Mellotone); Fats Waller (Victor) Cozy Cole (Guild); and Billy Taylor's Big Eight — the bass player, not the pianist (Key).   **571028-2**

No Moon at All (1948)

Lyrics by Redd Evans, music by David Mann

Popular recordings by The King Cole Trio in 1949; with a best-selling record by The Ames Brothers with Les Brown and His Orchestra (Columbia).   **620131-3**

No Nothing (1941)

Lyrics and music by Ben Ryan and Mann Kurtz, music by Lou Handman

Introduced on this Decca recording by Ella Fitzgerald and Her Famous Orchestra.   **410331-2**

No Other Love (1953)

Lyrics by Oscar Hammerstein II, music by Richard Rodgers

Introduced by Bill Hayes and Isabel Bigley in the 1953 musical play *Me and Juliet*. The melody is from a tango in the section entitled, "Beneath the Southern Cross," from Rodgers's score for *Victory at Sea*, a 1952–53 television documentary.   **621003-2**

No Regrets (1936)

Lyrics by Harry Tobias, music by Roy Ingraham

Introduced and featured by Billie Holiday (Vocalion).   **680528-1a, 690729-3b**

No Sense (1947)

Lyrics by Ella Fitzgerald, music by Ray Brown

Introduced by Ella Fitzgerald on this Decca recording.   **471220-2**

No Strings (I'm Fancy Free) (1935)

Lyrics and music by Irving Berlin

Introduced by Fred Astaire in the 1935 RKO film *Top Hat*.   **580314-4**

Now It Can Be Told (1938)

Lyrics and music by Irving Berlin

Introduced by Don Ameche and reprised by Alice Faye in the 1938 20th Century–Fox film *Alexander's Ragtime Band*. Nominated for an Academy Award (AMPAS), Best Original Song, 1938.   **580317-7**

Nowhere Guy (1952)

Lyrics Mack Gordon, music by Josef Myrow

Introduced by Ella Fitzgerald on this Decca recording.   **520225-2**

O Come, All Ye Faithful [Adeste Fideles] (1750)

Lyrics and music by John Francis Wade

Only recently have the historical facts about this hymn become known, and we have Dom John Stephan of Buckfast Abbey (England) to thank for them. By diligent research in old manuscripts, he discovered that both the Latin words and music were written by John Francis Wade, an Englishman who spent his life copying and teaching music in Douai, France, where there was a large colony of English Catholics centered around the famous college there. The English translation was made by Rev. Francis Oakeley in 1841, while he was rector of All Saints Church of England in London. His opening lines read: "Ye faithful, approach ye,/Joyfully triumphant…." The familiar words "O come, all ye faithful,/Joyful and triumphant…;" first appeared in a revision printed in 1852.   **670719-3**

O Holy Night (Cantique de Noël) (1847)

Lyrics by Placide Cappeau de Roquemaure, English translation by John Sullivan Dwight, music by Adolph Adam

Adolphe Adam gained fame as a composer of ballets. Today, he is chiefly remembered for one ballet *Giselle,* and this carol. The translator, John S. Dwight, was a co-founder of the Harvard music Society. Placide Cappeau wrote the lyrics to the French carol in Paris in 1847, and it was immediately set to music by Adam. It became an immediate success and has remained a favorite carol of the French. The English versions (there were two by Mr. Dwight) were first published in London in 1855.

670719-2

O Little Town of Bethlehem (1868)

Lyrics by Phillip Brooks, music by Lewis H. Redner

Phillip Brooks was one of the truly great preachers America has produced. In December, 1865, he visited the Holy Land, and on the day before Christmas, he rode horseback from Jerusalem to Bethlehem. Three years later, back at Holy Trinity Church in Philadelphia, and wanting to write a Christmas carol for the children of his congregation, he recalled his first glimpse of Bethlehem resting peacefully under the night sky of winter. He wrote the lyrics and then asked his church organist and Sunday School superintendent, Lewis H. Redner, to write some music for the poem. All during Christmas week Redner, struggled to write an appropriate tune, but inspiration had eluded him when he retired to his bed on Christmas Eve. During the night he awoke with an "angel strain" sounding in his ears. He jotted the melody down immediately, and wrote the harmony for it early the next morning. He always referred to the tune as his "gift from Heaven." **600715-4b, 670718-1**

O Morro No Tem Vez *see* Somewhere in the Hills

O Nosso Amor [Carnival Samba] (1959)

Lyrics by Vinícius de Moraes, music by Antonio Carlos Jobim

Introduced in *Orfeo Negro (Black Orpheus),* a 1959 Brazilian film which won the Grand Prize, Cannes Film Festival, and the Academy Award (AMPAS), Best Foreign Film, 1959. **710721-4c**

Of Thee I Sing (1931)

Lyrics by Ira Gershwin, music by George Gershwin

Introduced by William Gaxton, Lois Moran, and ensemble in the 1931 musical play *Of Thee I Sing!*

590318-2

Off-Key *see* Desafinado

Oh Boy! I'm in the Groove (1939)

Lyrics and music by Ella Fitzgerald

Introduced by Ella Fitzgerald during her performances at the Savoy Ballroom, New York, in 1939. Never recorded by Decca, the song was, however, recorded by WNEW-AM

during broadcasts of Ella Fitzgerald and Her Famous Orchestra. **390921-1**

Oh, Dey's So Fresh an' Fine [Strawberry Woman] (1935)

Lyrics by DuBose Heyward, music by George Gershwin

A street cry in Act II, Scene 3, of the 1935 folk opera *Porgy and Bess,* sung by members of the chorus.

570828-7

Oh, Doctor Jesus (1935)

Lyrics by DuBose Heyward, music by George Gershwin

Introduced by a member of the chorus in Act II, Scene 4, of the 1935 folk opera *Porgy and Bess.* **570828-5**

Oh! Johnny! Oh! Johnny! Oh! (1916)

Lyrics by Ed Rose, music by Abe Olman

Written during World War I, the lyric read, "Oh! Johnny! Oh! Johnny! How you can fight!..." The song received no attention at all until the lyric was changed to "How you can love!..." Introduced by Henry Lewis in the 1917 musical play *Follow Me!*

391200-5, 400125-4, 400325-5

Oh! Lady, Be Good! (1924)

Lyrics by Ira Gershwin, music by George Gershwin

Introduced by Walter Catlett and the ladies of the ensemble in the 1924 musical play *Lady, Be Good!* Sung by Ann Sothern, Robert Young, and Red Skelton in the 1941 MGM film adaptation. "Oh! Lady, Be Good!" became one of the most successful of Ella's scat routines, and it was demanded by audiences everywhere she appeared on the concert stage.

470319-3, 470806-2, 470929-5, 480525-2,
490415-5, **490918-8, 531118-4,** 560815-4,
570929-11, 571009-9, 590108-4, 590108-5,
590108-6, 590108-7, 610221-7, 610520-12,
810726-6, 810726-16c

Oh! Look at Me Now! (1941)

Lyrics by John DeVries, music by Joe Bushkin

Introduced and first recorded by Tommy Dorsey and His Orchestra, vocals by Frank Sinatra and Connie Haines (RCA Victor). **890316-2**

Oh, So Nice! (1928)

Lyrics by Ira Gershwin, music by George Gershwin

Introduced by Gertrude Lawrence and Paul Frawley in the 1928 musical play *Treasure Girl,* but was dropped soon after the New York opening. This is a waltz *not* in three-quarter time! "My number...is an effort to get the effect of a Viennese waltz in fox-trot time," explained George Gershwin. **590717-4**

Oh, What a Night for Love!

Lyrics and music by Neal Hefti and Steve Allen

Introduced by Neal Hefti and His Orchestra. Also, successfully recorded by Mel Tormé.

581123-7, 581123-8

Oh, Yes, Take Another Guess (1936)

Lyrics by Charles Newman and Al Sherman, music by Murray Mencher

Introduced by Chick Webb and His Orchestra, vocal by Ella Fitzgerald. Ella also recorded it with Benny Goodman and His Orchestra (Victor).   **361105-2, 370114-1**

Ol' Devil Moon (1946)

Lyrics by E.Y. "Yip" Harburg, music by Burton Lane

Introduced by Ella Logan and Donald Richards in the 1947 musical play *Finian's Rainbow*. In 1955, Ella Logan and Frank Sinatra recorded the song for the planned animated feature film adaptation of the play, but the film was never produced. Sung by Petula Clark and Don Francks in the 1968 Warner Bros. film adaptation.

550427-3, 690200-8

Ol' MacDonald (1960)

Lyric and music adapted by Ella Fitzgerald (1964)

The words of the original song may well have derived from a song by Thomas D'Urfey (1653-1723), no music for which exists. The music may have derived from the music of "Littoria! Littoria!" copyrighted 19 August 1959, as "Students' Song No. 8," as sung by the students of Yale College." The first printing of the familiar music and lyrics was in October 1917, in *Tommy's Tunes*, collected by F.T. Nettlingham, and published (curiously) by Erskine MacDonald (London). On page 84, the title is given as "Ohio," and it is "Old MacDougal" who has the farm. New lyrics, a clever parody, by Alan and Marilyn Bergman with music arranged by Lew Spence, was introduced and recorded by Frank Sinatra (Capitol) in 1960, who populated the farm with more shapely "chicks." Ella's version, however, sticks more to the traditional, complete with quack-quacks, oink-oinks, and chick-chicks, branding her version as her own.

641022-1, **650326-10, 660720-6**

Ol' Man Mose (1938)

Lyrics and music by Louis Armstrong and Zilner Trenton Randolph

Introduced, featured, and recorded by Louis Armstrong and His Orchestra.   **620630-18**

Old Mother Hubbard (1948)

Lyrics by Babe Wallace, music by Ray Ellington

The original poem is by Sarah Catherine Martin (1768–1826), daughter of Sir Henry Martin, and an early love of Prince William Henry (later King William IV). In 1804, at age 36, she was visiting her future brother-in-law, John Pollexfen Bastard, M.P., of Kitley, Devon. As he tried to write a letter he was distracted by her chattering, and cavalierly suggested that she "run away and write one of your stupid little rhymes." She did, and the result was "The Comic Adventures of Old Mother Hubbard and Her Dog." Of course, Wallace and Ellington have somewhat changed the character of the original piece, and Ella gives it a unique interpretation.

481204-2, 490114-2, 490211-3, **490415-1,**
490918-3, **501230-1,** 510519-3

The Old Rugged Cross (1913)

Lyrics and music by George Bennard

Here is the genesis of this hymn related by the author-composer himself, a guitar-playing evangelical preacher: "I was praying for a full understanding of the Cross and its plan in Christianity. I read and studied and prayed. I saw Christ and the Cross inseparably. The Christ and the Cross became more than a symbol…. It was like seeing John 3:16 leave the printed page, take form, and act out the meaning of Redemptionm. While watching the scene in my mind's eye, the theme of the song came to me, and with it the melody; but only the words of the theme, 'The old rugged Cross,' came. An inner voice seemed to say, 'Wait!'" The Rev. Bennard was "holding evangelistic meetings in Michigan" when this first revelation came. Apparently the spirit did not move him elsewhere, for he had to "wait" until he returned to Michigan. Here "the floodgates were loosed," and the song was finished. It was widely publicized by Homer E. Rodeheaver, the popular evangelist, singer, and trombonist.   **670200-10**

On a Clear Day (You Can See Forever) (1966)

Lyrics by Alan J. Lerner, music by Burton Land

Introduced by John Cullum in the 1966 muscal play *On a Clear Day You Can See Forever*. Sung by Yves Montand and reprised by Barbra Streisand in the 1970 Paramount film version.

On A Slow Boat to China (1948)

Lyrics and music by Frank Loesser

Independently published, this song became one of the leading hits of 1948–49. Introduced by Benny Goodman and His Orchestra, vocal by Al Hendrickson (Capitol).

610123-1, **610211-3,** 610516-7,
610518-14, 610520-26, **860228-15**

On Green Dolphin Street (1947)

Lyrics by Ned Washington, music by Bronislaw Kaper

This music is an adaptation of the Kaper theme from

the 1947 MGM film *Green Dolphin Street*. With lyrics, it was introduced by Jimmy Dorsey and His Orchestra, vocal by Bill Lawrence (MGM). **680528-2a, 860228-2**

On the Street of Dreams see ***Street of Dreams***

On the Sunny Side of the Street (1930)

Lyrics by Dorothy Fields, music by Jimmy McHugh

Introduced by Harry Richman and Gertrude Lawrence in the 1930 musical revue *Lew Leslie's International Revue*. The definitive recording is the 1945 Tommy Dorsey and His Orchestra rendition with The Pied Pipers (Victor), the arrangement for which, by Sy Oliver, is considered by many to be the finest arrangement for a popular song ever devised.

531118-1, 580810-14, 610513-2, 610520-18, 620629-10, 620629-22, 620630-5, **630715-3, 670128-1, 670326-4**

Once I Loved [*Amor Em Paz*] [*Love in Peace*] (1965)

Portuguese lyrics by Vinícius de Moraes, English lyrics by Ray Gilbert, music by Antonio Carlos Jobim

Introduced by Antonio Carlos Jobim on a Verve recording. Memorable recording by Frank Sinatra. **730828-2**

Once in a While (1937)

Lyrics by Bud Green, music by Michael Edwards

Introduced by Tommy Dorsey and His Orchestra, vocal by Jack Leonard (Victor). This song was the last recorded by Bing Crosby, cut three days before he died of a heart attack on a golf course in Spain on 14 October 1977. **680529-1b**

Once Is Enough for Me (1939)

Lyrics and music by Ella Fitzgerald and Chick Webb

Introduced and recorded by Ella Fitzgerald and Her Savoy Eight (Decca). **390302-1**

Once It Was All Right, Now... (1968)

Lyrics and music by Laura Nyro

Introduced and recorded by Laura Nyro. 700123-1

Once Too Often (1944)

Lyrics by Mack Gordon, music by James V. Monaco

Introduced by Betty Grable, singing and dancing with Hermes Pan, with Charlie Spivak and His Orchestra in the 1944 20th Century–Fox film *Pin-Up Girl*. **440321-2**

One Cigarette for Two (1938)

Lyrics and music by Rios Metzger, Dan Dougherty and Ben Ryan

Introduced by Freddy Martin and His Orchestra, vocal by Eddie Stone (Bluebird). **400304-3**

One for My Baby (and One More for the Road) (1943)

Lyrics by Johnny Mercer, music by Harold Arlen

Introduced by Fred Astaire in the 1943 RKO film *The Sky's the Limit*. Astaire regarded this as "one of the best pieces of material written especially for me." The song was also one of Arlen's favorites among his own creations. The quintessential performances, however, are those of Frank Sinatra in his two Reprise recordings, with Bill Miller at the piano solo, and again with Miller and orchestra.

600419-7, 610114-5, 610519-19

The One-Horse Open Sleigh see ***Jingle Bells***

The One I Love Belongs to Somebody Else (1924)

Lyrics by Gus Kahn, music by Isham Jones

Introduced by Isham Jones and His Orchsetra. Jones's wife gave him a baby grand piano for his 30th birthday on 31 January 1924, and *within an hour*, so the story goes, he had composed the music for "I'll See You in My Dreams," "The One I Love Belongs to Somebody Else," "Spain," and "It Had to Be You." Such a burst of creativity remains unparalleled, as each is now a part of the standard American song repertoire. **410108-4, 610123-6, 760129-4**

One Moment, Please (1940)

Music by Dick Vance

This instrumental was introduced by Ella Fitzgerald and Her Famous Orchestra in a 1940 broadcast, with the composer as first trumpet in the band. **400226-8**

One Note Samba [*Samba de Uma Nota Só*] (1961)

Portuguese lyrics by Newton Mendonça, English lyrics by Antonio Carlos Jobim, and a second version of lyrics by Jon Hendricks, music by Antonio Carlos Jobim

Introduced in the U.S. by João Gilberto (Capitol). First recording of the Hendricks version by Pat Thomas (Verve). English-language version with Jobim lyrics introduced by Jobim with Herbie Mann (Atlantic). Ella recorded both lyrics, the 1976 recording with the the Hendricks lyrics, the 1977 and 1980 recordings are with the Jobim lyrics.

680518-9, 760208-14, 770714-7, 800919-14

One O'Clock Jump (1937)

Scat by Ella Fitzgerald, music by Count Basie

Instrumental introduced and recorded by Count Basie and His Orchestra, with trumpet solo by Harry James (Vocalion). 530911-9

One Side of Me (1939)

Lyrics and music by Marion Sunshine

Introduced and recorded by Chick Webb and His Orchestra, vocal by Ella Fitzgerald (Decca). **390217-4**

Oo-Bop-Sh'Bam (1946)

Scat lyrics by Ella Fitzgerald, music by Walter G. Fuller, Jay Roberts, and John Birks "Dizzy" Gillespie.

Bop instrumental introduced by Dizzy Gillespie and His Orchestra (Musicraft). **580810-29**

Ool-Ya-Koo (Royal Roost Bop Boogie) (1948)

Scat lyrics by Ella Fitzgerald, music by Walter G. Fuller and John Birks "Dizzy" Gillespie

Introduced by Dizzie Gillespie and His Orchestra. Ella Fitzgerald's vocal versions in her appearances at The Royal Roost, New York, are outstanding. **481127-1, 481204-9,** 490211-6

Ooo, Baby, Baby (1965)

Lyrics and music by William "Smokey" Robinson and Warren Moore

Introduced by "Smokey" Robinson. **690530-3**

Oops! (1952)

Lyrics by Johnny Mercer, music by Harry Warren

Introduced by Fred Astaire and Vera-Ellen (dubbed by Anita Ellis) in the 1952 MGM film *The Belle of New York*. **511123-2**

Open Your Window (1968)

Lyrics and music by Harry Nilsson

Introduced by Harry Nilsson on an RCA recording. **690526-2, 700520-3**

Ordinary Fool (1975)

Lyrics and music by Paul Williams

Introduced on a recording by The Carpenters. **770714-6**

The Organ Grinder's Swing (1936)

Lyrics by Mitchell Parish, music by Will Hudson

Introduced and recorded by The Hudson-DeLange Orchestra (Brunswick). **361118-2, 790216-6**

Our Love Is Here to Stay (1938)

Lyrics by Ira Gershwin, music by George Gershwin and Vernon Duke

This is the last piece of music written by George Gershwin before his death in 1937. Since the song was left unfinished, it was completed by Vernon Duke. Duke recalls: "All that could be found ... was a twenty-bar incomplete lead sheet; fortunately, Oscar Levant remembered the harmonies from George's frequent piano performances of the song, and I was able faithfully to reconstruct it." Introduced by Kenny Baker in the 1938 Goldwyn-United Artists film *The Goldwyn Follies of 1938*. The *original* title of this song is "Our Love Is Here to Stay." Ira Gershwin, among others, including discographers and musicologists, consistently refer to it as "Love Is Here to Stay," which does not convey the true sense of the song, nor of the scene where it was first sung in the film. **570723-1, 590105-3, 590105-4, 600213-2,** 610518-2

Out of Nowhere (1931)

Lyrics by Edward Heyman, music by Johnny Green

Introduced by Guy Lombardo and His Royal Canadians. This was Bing Crosby's first hit recording as a solo vocalist (Decca). **390629-5**

Out of This World (1945)

Lyrics by Johnny Mercer, music by Harold Arlen

Introduced by Eddie Bracken (dubbed by Bing Crosby) in the 1945 Paramount film *Out of This World*. This film has no connection with the 1950 Cole Porter musical play of the same title. **581124-7, 610116-6**

Over the Rainbow (1959)

Lyrics by E.Y. "Yip" Harburg, music by Harold Arlen

Introduced by Judy Garland in the 1939 MGM film *The Wizard of Oz*. During the production, and, indeed, after the preview release, there was not much enthusiasm for the song at MGM. On three separate occasions there were attempts to delete the song from the film, but each time, the producer, Arthur Freed, stormed into the front offices and insisted that it be restored. Awarded the Academy Award (AMPAS), Best Original Song, 1939. Eternally associated with Judy Garland, the song was the most requested during her long career on the concert stage, *but*, did she ever record the verse? Indeed, did she ever sing it? Ella Fitzgerald's recording of the complete lyrics in *Ella Fitzgerald Sings the Harold Arlen Song Book* will be a revelation to those who have never heard it — it gives the song a new dimension. One of the sixteen songs selected by ASCAP in 1963 for its All-Time Hit Parade during the first half-century of its existence. **610115-3**

Pack Up Your Sins and Go to the Devil (1922)

Lyrics and music by Irving Berlin

Introduced by The McCarthy Sisters in the revue *Music Box Revue of 1922*. **380609-1**

Papa Loves Mambo (1954)

Lyrics and music by S. Bickley Reichner, Al Hoffman, and Dick Manning

Introduced on a recording by Perry Como. **550210-1**

(It's Only a) Paper Moon (1932)

Lyrics by E.Y. "Yip" Harburg and Billy Rose, music by Harold Arlen

Introduced by Claire Carlton in the 1932 play *The Great Magoo*. At the time, the song was called "If You Believe in Me," and it served as a recurring theme throughout the play, which ran only eleven performances. With a new title, it was "introduced" again by June Knight and Buddy Rogers in the 1933 Paramount film *Take a Chance*. **450327-1, 450327-2, 460121-1, 520816-1, 600801-4, 670326-5**

Party Blues (1956)

Lyrics and music by William "Count" Basie, Ella Fitzgerald, and Joseph Goreed Williams

Introduced by Ella Fitzgerald and Joe Williams, with Count Basie and His Orchestra, on a Verve recording. **560625-5, 580509-4c**

Passion Flower (1944)

Lyrics by Milton Raskin, music by Billy Strayhorn

Introduced as an instrumental by Duke Ellington and His Orchestra for Johnny Hodges. Vocal version first performed by Ella Fitzgerald with the Ellington Orchestra on their 1965 album *Ella at Duke's Place*. 650120-1, **651020-2**

Peas and Rice (1950)

Lyrics and music by Nelson Larkin

Introduced by Ella Fitzgerald on this Decca recording. **500306-4**

Pennies from Heaven (1936)

Lyrics by Johnny Burke, music by Arthur Johnston

Introduced by Bing Crosby in the 1936 Paramount film *Pennies from Heaven*, and further popularized by his recording (Decca). Nominated for an Academy Award (AMPAS), Best Original Song, 1936. Thirteen weeks on "Your Hit Parade" in 1936, four in the #1 position. 590325-6

People (1964)

Lyrics by Bob Merrill, music by Jule Styne

Introduced by Barbra Streisand in the 1964 musical play *Funny Girl*. Miss Streisand's Capitol recording received the Grammy Award for Best Femals Vocal Performance, 1964; and Best Accompaniment Arrangement (by Peter Matz), 1964. Sung by Barbra Streisand in the 1968 Columbia film adaptation. **640407-3**, 640728-5, **640729-5, 690729-8**, 70052019, 730705-20, 810726-9

People Will Say We're in Love (1943)

Lyrics by Oscar Hammerstein II, music by Richard Rodgers

Introduced by Alfred Drake and Joan Roberts in the 1943 musical play *Oklahoma!* Sung by Gordon MacRae and Shirley Jones in the 1955 Magna Theatre film adaptation. **540329-6, 610211-4c**

Perdido (1942)

Lyrics by H.J. Lengsfelder and Ervin Drake, music by Juan Tizol

Introduced as an instrumental by Duke Ellington and His Orchestra (Victor). Best-known jazz version performed by Flip Phillips and Illinois Jacquet at *Jazz At The Philharmonic* concerts and recordings (Norgan/Verve) in the late 1940s. Lyrics added in 1944. **490918-12, 520913-1, 531118-10,** 540917-6, **550210-2, 570627-12,** 580810-6, 580810-32, 610520-30, 620630-16, 640800-24, 640203-14, 640728-14, **640729-14**

Pete Kelly's Blues (1955)

Lyrics by Sammy Cahn, music by Ray Heindorf

Introduced by Ella Fitzgerald in the 1955 Warner Bros. film *Pete Kelly's Blues*, and popularized by her Decca recording. **550503-2, 550724-3, 640303-3**

Petootie Pie (Peetootie Pie) (1944)

Lyrics by Raymond Leveen, music by Frank Paparelli and Lorenzo Pack

Introduced by Louis Jordan and His Tympany Five, and subsequently recorded with Ella in a memorable recording for Decca. **451008-2, 451015-1**

Photograph (Fotografia) (1978)

Lyrics by Ray Gilbert, music by Antonio Carlos Jobim

Introduced by Jobim and recorded in 1978 for his album with orchestra conducted by Nelson Riddle *The Wonderful World of Antonio Carlos Jobim*. **800919-5**

Pick Yourself Up (1936)

Lyrics by Dorothy Fields, music by Jerome Kern

Introduced by Fred Astaire and Ginger Rogers in the 1936 RKO film *Swing Time*. A great favorite with jazz musicians. **611115-1**

A Place for Lovers (1967)

Lyrics by Norman Gimbel, music by Manuel de Sica

Introduced by Ella Fitzgerald singing the song under the titles of the 1968 MGM film of the same name, starring Faye Dunaway and Marcello Mastroianni. The film (*Amanti*, in Italy; *Le Temps des Amants*, in France) was popular though not a critical success, and the recording was issued only on a 45rpm record in the U.S. "Lonely Is" (q.v.) is on the reverse side.   **671021-1**

Please Be Kind (1938)

Lyrics by Sammy Cahn, music by Saul Chaplin

Introduced by Red Norvo and His Orchestra, vocal by Mildred Bailey (Brunswick).   **540330-1**

Please Don't Talk About Me When I'm Gone (1930)

Lyrics by Sidney Clare, music by Sam H. Stept

Introduced by Bea Palmer in vaudeville, and on radio by Kate Smith, who featured it in her first CBS broadcast on 1 May 1931.   **790712-1**

Please Tell Me the Truth (1939)

Lyrics and music by Ella Fitzgerald and Edgar Sampson

Introduced by Ella Fitzgerald and Her Famous Orchestra, vocal by Ella Fitzgerald (Decca).   **390815-2, 390818-3**

Polka Dots and Moonbeams (1940)

Lyrics by Johnny Burke, music by James Van Heusen

Introduced and recorded by Tommy Dorsey and His Orchestra, vocal by Frank Sinatra (Victor).   **740108-4**

Poor Butterfly (1916)

Lyrics by John Golden, music by Raymond Hubbell

Introduced by Heru Onuki (a Chinese-American *not* Japanese) in the 1916 revue *The Big Show*. First recording by Edna Brown (Victor); and then by the Joseph C. Smith Orchestra (Victor); and the Victor Military Band. Sold several million copies of sheet music and more than a million records, the biggest hit of its time.   **580409-2d**

Porgy and Bess Medley (1935)

Lyrics by Ira Gershwin and DuBose Heyward, music by George Gershwin

Especially devised medley from the 1935 folk opera *Porgy and Bess*, used by Miss Fitzgerald at her performance at Mr. Kelly's, Chicago, in August, 1958.   580810-23

Prelude to a Kiss (1938)

Lyrics by Irving Gordon and Irving Mills, music by Duke Ellington

Introduced and recorded by Duke Ellington and His Orchestra (Brunswick).   **560904-10**

Preview (1952)

Lyrics and music by Paul Quinichette and William "Count" Basie

Introduced by Count Basie and His Orchestra.   **520626-1, 520816-3**

Private Jam Session (1963)

At the conclusion of the second and last recording session for the Verve album *These Are the Blues*, Ella and the boys, Roy Eldridge, Wild Bill Davis, Herb Ellis, Ray Brown, and Gus Johnson settled down to their own private jam session. The session was recorded, but, unfortunately, has never been issued. Perhaps, someday, Ella's fans will prevail.   **631029-5**

Put a Little Love in Your Heart (1969)

Lyrics and music by Jimmy Holiday, Randy Myers, and Jackie DeShannon

Introduced and recorded by Jackie DeShannon (Imperial).   **710518-8, 710721-11**

Put Your Dreams Away (1942)

Lyrics by Ruth Lowe, music by Stephan Weiss and Paul Mann

Introduced by Frank Sinatra and used as the signature theme of his radio programs. Best-selling Columbia record by Sinatra with Axel Stordahl's Orchestra in 1945.   **580509-4d**

Puttin' on the Ritz (1929)

Lyrics and music by Irving Berlin

Introduced by Harry Richman in the 1930 United Artists film *Putting' on the Ritz*. Performed by Clark Gable and "his girls" in the 1939 MGM film *Idiot's Delight*. The girls were Virginia Grey, Lorraine Krueger, Paula Stone, Virginia Dale, Joan Marsh, and Bernadene Hayes. With new lyrics by Berlin, it was reintroduced by Fred Astaire in the 1946 MGM film *Blue Skies*. Miss Fitzgerald's version is that written for Fred Astaire.   **580318-9**

Quiet Nights of Quiet Stars [Corcovado] (1962)

English lyrics by Gene Lees, Portuguese lyrics and music by Antonio Carlos Jobim

Introduced by The Stan Getz Quintet, with Antonio Carlos Jobim at piano, and vocals by João and Astrid Gilberto on a Verve recording. First recording with English lyrics by Tony Bennett (Columbia).   **800919-2**

Rain (1927)

Lyrics and music by Eugene Ford, Carey Morgan, and Arthur Swanstrom

Introduced by Rudy Vallée in a performance in which he first used a megaphone that became something of a trademark in his early career before the general use of microphones.   **680528-1e, 760208-3**

Raindrops Keep Fallin' on My Head (1969)

Lyrics by Hal David, music by Burt Bacharach

Introduced by the voice of B.J. Thomas in the 1969

20th Century–Fox film *Butch Cassidy and the Sundance Kid.* Won the Academy Award for Best Song, 1969. Best-selling record (Scepter) by B.J. Thomas, 1969–1970.

700520-14

Reach for Tomorrow (1960)

Lyrics by Ned Washington, music by Jimmy McHugh

Introduced by Ella Fitzgerald in the 1960 Warner Bros. film *Let No Man Write My Epitaph.*   **600419-6**

Reaching for the Moon (1931)

Lyrics and music by Irving Berlin

Introduced by Bing Crosby in the 1931 United Artists film *Reaching for the Moon*, but the vocal was deleted before release, although the melody was retained as background on the soundtrack. Mr. Crosby then recorded it (Columbia).   **580317-10**

The Real American Folk Song (Is a Rag) (1918)

Lyrics by Ira Gershwin, music by George Gershwin

This is the first song on which the Gershwin brothers collaborated. Introduced by Nora Bayes in the 1918 musical play *Ladies First*. In 1958, it was published for the first time, and soon afterward recorded for the first time — by Ella Fitzgerald in her *Ella Fitzgerald Sings the George and Ira Gershwin Song Book* (Verve, 1959).   **590718-6**

Remember (1925)

Lyrics and music by Irving Berlin

One of Mr. Berlin's autobiographic love songs, originally titled "You Forgot To Remember," said to have been inspired by his courtship with Ellin Mackay. First recorded by Isham Jones and His Orchestra.   **580318-10**

Remind Me (1940)

Lyrics by Dorothy Fields, music by Jerome Kern

Introduced by Peggy Moran in the 1940 Universal film *One Night in the Tropics*. Kern and Fields wrote the song some years earlier for an unproduced film, but this was its first use. Mabel Mercer featured it in supper clubs and later recorded it (Atlantic); it then began to receive recognition by other singers and musicians, and there are many recordings.   **630107-4**

Rhythm and Romance (1935)

Lyrics by George Whiting and Nat Schwartz, music by J.C. Johnson

Introduced and recorded by Chick Webb and His Orchestra, vocal by Ella Fitzgerald (at her first recording session) (Decca).   **351012-1, 360219-12**

Ridin' High (1930)

Lyrics and music by Cole Porter

Introduced by Ethel Merman in the 1936 musical play *Red, Hot and Blue!* Sung by Betty Hutton in the 1949 Paramount film adaptation.   **560207-1, 580409-1**

Robbins' Nest (1947)

Scat by Ella Fitzgerald, music by Sir Charles Thompson and Illinois Jacquet

Introduced and recorded as a jazz instrumental by Illinois Jacquet and His Orchestra (Apollo), and dedicated to the New York disc jockey Fred Robbins. Lyrics added in 1951 and the piece retitled "Just When We're Falling in Love," q.v.

471223-4, 490211-1, **490423-1, 490918-1, 630716-10, 630716-11, 630716-12, 630716-13**

Rock It for Me (1937)

Lyrics and music by Kay Werner and Sue Werner

Introduced by Chick Webb and His Orchestra, vocal by Ella Fitzgerald. First recorded by Teddy Grace (Decca); one authority claims that this recording was withheld until Webb had made it a hit at the Savoy Ballroom and recorded it (Decca).   **371101-3, 610211-6,** 610514-2

Rock of Ages (1831)

Lyrics by Augustus Montague Toplady, music by Thomas Hastings

This poem first appeared in *The Gospel* magazine for March, 1776, of which Toplady was the editor. Under the heading, "A Living and Dying Prayer for the Holiest Believer in the World," it concluded with a curious statistical essay on sin. Calculating one sin per second, Toplady (graciously omitting the extra days of leap years) reckoned that at eighty years, each of us is "chargeable" with 2,522,880,000 infractions of God's laws. Hastings composed the music long after Mr. Toplady's death.   **670200-11**

Rockin' in Rhythm (1930)

Scat by Ella Fitzgerald, music by Duke Ellington, Irving Mills, and Harry Carney

Introduced and recorded by Duke Ellington and His Orchestra as an instrumental (Brunswick). The vocal version was introduced by Ella Fitzgerald with the Ellington Orchestra on her *Ella Fitzgerald Sings the Duke Ellington Song Book, Volume II* (Verve, 1957). The original title was "Rockin' Rhythm."   **570626-5, 740108-9**

Rocks in My Bed (1941)

Lyrics and music by Duke Ellington

Introduced and recorded by Duke Ellington and His Orchestra, vocal by Ivie Anderson (Victor).   **560904-2**

Rough Ridin' (1952)

Lyrics and music by Ella Fitzgerald, Henry Jones, and Bill Tennyson

Introduced by Ella Fitzgerald, with Ray Brown and His Trio (Decca). **520104-2, 620131-5**

'Round Midnight ['Round About Midnight] (1944)

Lyrics by Bernie Hanighen, music by Charles Melvin "Cootie" Williams and Thelonius Monk

Introduced bgy Cootie Williams and His Orchestra (Majestic).
610123-5, **610211-14, 610221-8**, 610512-6, 610513-15, **610623-2, 740108-8, 790712-6, 831000-8**

Roxie (1975)

Lyrics by Fred Ebb, music by John Kander

Introduced by Gwen Verdon and male chorus in the 1975 musical revue *Chicago*. The New York original cast of the show may be heard on the Arista recording.
741018-1

Royal Garden Blues (1919)

Lyrics and music by Spencer Williams and Clarence Williams

Introduced and recorded by The Original Dixieland Jazz Band, vocal by Al Bernard (Victor). **400226-2**

Royal Roost Bop Boogie *see* **Ool-Ya-Koo**

Rudolph, the Red Nosed Reindeer (1949)

Lyrics and music by Johnny Marks

Introduced by Gene Autry at Madison Square Garden in 1949, and recorded by Mr. Autry with The Pinafores (Columbia)—the record has sold more than 100 million copies, second only to the best-selling record of all time, Bing Crosby's "White Christmas," which has sold more than 200 million copies. Recorded by almost everyone in the music business with a Christmas album, with more than 500 different recordings. ASCAP selected this song in 1963 as one of sixteen in its All-Time Hit Parade during the first half-century of its existence. **521218-2, 600715-6**

Run, Joe, Run (1949)

Lyrics and music by Walt Merrick, Joe Willoughby, and Louis Jordan

Introduced by Louis Jordan and His Tympany Five (Decca). 500900-5

Runnin' Wild! (1922)

Lyrics by Joe Gray and Leo Wood, music by A. Harrington Gibbs

Hit song popularized in vaudeville by Art Hickman and His Orchestra. **620131-4**

Russian Lullaby (1927)

Lyrics and music by Irving Berlin

The recordings of this song by Franklyn Baur and His Orchestra (Victor) who introduced it, organist Jesse Crawford (Victor), and the orchestras of Roger Wolfe Kahn and Ernie Golden (Brunswick), and the many vaudeville and radio performances made this another hit for Berlin.
580317-5

'S Wonderful (1927)

Lyrics by Ira Gershwin, music by George Gershwin

Introduced by Allen Kearns and Adele Astaire in the 1927 musical play *Funny Face*. Sung by Fred Astaire and Audrey Hepburn in the 1957 Paramount film adaptation.
560121-4, 560202-10, 580810-28, **590410-1a, 590410-1c, 590410-6, 590716-1**, 610513-18, 610514-3, 610517-3, 610518-12, 610519-13, 640800-6, 810726-14

St. Louis Blues (1914)

Lyrics and music by W.C. Handy

Mr. Handy wrote this song to capitalize on the success of his 1913 hit, "The Memphis Blues," which he had sold outright for $50 and which had made a fortune for its publisher, Theron A. Bennett Co., New York. Mr. Handy formed his own company with Henry Place in Memphis for the express purpose of publishing the song. It failed, until he moved the venture to New York. Sophie Tucker heard it, became interested, and introduced it successfully in her vaudeville act. Victor released an instrumental recording that did so well that others followed. In time, "St. Louis Blues" has become one of the most popular songs ever written.

390720-3, 441000-2, 570724-9, 580409-2g, 580424-1, 580425-10, 580425-26, 580810-12, 580810-22, 610405-1, 610514-4, **631029-3, 640728-13, 640729-13, 660923-5, 670430-4, 710507-1, 710721-9, 790712-13, 810726-10**

Salty Lips (1956)

Lyrics and music by William "Count" Basie, Joe Williams, and Ella Fitzgerald

This song was recorded by Ella and Joe at the 1956 session with the Count Basie Orchestra that produced, in part, the famous *One O'Clock Jump* album, with the Metronome All Stars. The recording was rejected for some cause, and has never been rerecorded. 560625-3

Sam and Delilah (1930)

Lyrics by Ira Gershwin, music by George Gershwin

Introduced by Ethel Merman — her opening number in her Broadway debut — in the 1930 musical play *Girl Crazy*. Not used in the 1932 RKO film adaptation. Sung by Judy Garland in the 1943 MGM film adaptation.

590716-5

Samba de Avião *see* *Song of the Jet*

Samba de Uma Nota Só *see* *One Note Samba*

"Sanford and Son" Theme *see* *Street Beater*

Santa Claus Got Stuck in My Chimney (1950)

Lyrics and music by Bill Hardy and Billy Moore, Jr.

Introduced by Ella Fitzgerald on this Decca recording.

500926-1

Santa Claus Is Comin' to Town (1934)

Lyrics by Haven Gillespie, music by J. Fred Coots

Written in 1932, the song was turned down by many leading publishers who considered it uncommercial because it was a "kiddie number." Mr. Coots, who was then writing special material for Eddie Cantor's radio show, offered it to Mr. Cantor, who was not interested. But Mrs. Cantor, Ida, influenced him into using it in one of his weekly programs. It was introduced by Eddie Cantor on his show the week before Thanksgiving, 1934. It became an instantaneous hit with Ethel Shutta's performance with George Olsen's Orchestra.   **600715-1**

Satin Doll (1958)

Lyrics by Johnny Mercer, music by Billy Strayhorn and Duke Ellington

Introduced by Duke Ellington and His Orchestra as an instrumental in 1953. With lyrics added in 1958, it became a part of nearly every singer's repertoire.

560904-12, 610517-2, 630715-4, 660208-6, 660222-1, 660727-9, 660728-2, 660729-2, 660914-4, 680518-10, 700520-4, 750717-2, **810726-2**

A Satisfied Mind (1955)

Lyrics and music by J.H. "Red" Hays and Jack Rhodes

Popular recordings by Red and Betty Foley (Decca); Jean Shepard (Capitol); and Porter Wagoner (Victor). Revived in 1966 by Bobby Hibb (Philips).   **550801-2**

(I've Been) Saving Myself for You (1938)

Lyrics by Sammy Cahn, music by Saul Chaplin

Introduced in the 5th Edition of *The Grand Terrace Review*, and first recorded by Benny Goodman and His Orchestra (Victor).   380503-8, **380503-9**, 380813-1

Savoy Truffle (1969)

Lyrics and music by George Harrison

Introduced and recorded by The Beatles.

690528-2

Scat Song (1967)

Devised and performed by Ella Fitzgerald and Frank Sinatra in a duet on his television show which aired on 13 November 1967.   **671113-2d**

The Secret of Christmas (1959)

Lyrics by Sammy Cahn, music by James Van Heusen

Introduced by Bing Crosby in the 1959 Paramount film *Say One for Me*.   **590903-5**

See See Rider (C.C. Rider) (1925)

Lyrics and music by Gertrude "Ma" Rainey

Adapted from a traditional blues song. Introduced by "Ma" Rainey in clubs and on a recording (Paramount).   **631028-2**

Seems Like Old Times (1946)

Lyrics and music by Carmen Lombardo and John Jacob Loeb

Introduced by Guy Lombardo and His Royal Canadians, vocal by Carmen Lombardo (Decca). Theme of "The Arthur Godfrey Show" on radio.   **680528-2e**

Sentimental Journey (1944)

Lyrics by Bud Green, music by Les Brown and Ben Homer

Introduced and recorded by Les Brown and His Band of Renown, vocal by Doris Day. This was the first major success for the orchestra, and for Miss Day. Les Brown adopted it as the theme song for his orchestra. Sixteen weeks on "Your Hit Parade" with five in the #1 position.

470124-2

September Song (1938)

Lyrics by Maxwell Anderson, music by Kurt Weill

Introduced by Walter Huston in the 1938 musical play *Knickerbocker Holiday*. Huston made a classic recording the same year (Brunswick). Sung by Charles Coburn in the 1944 United Artists film adaptation. One of the sixteen songs selected by ASCAP in 1963 for its All-Time Hit Parade during the first half-century of its existence.

600419-5

The Setting Sun (1991)

Lyrics by (author unknown), music by Maurice Jarre

Introduced by Ella Fitzgerald under the titles of the 1992 Japanese film *The Setting Sun*. Billy May conducted the orchestra for Ella's contribution. This was her last officially released song. The irony of the title is too obvious, but let it be known that the sun will never set on the songs of Ella Fitzgerald.   **920100-1**

720 in the Books (1939)

Lyrics by Harold Adamson, music by Jan Savitt and Johnny Watson

Introduced and recorded by Jan Savitt and His Orchestra, for their biggest instrumental hit.

581123-5, 680603-1d

The Shadow of Your Smile (1965)

Lyrics by Paul Francis Webster, music by Johnny Mandel

Introduced by a chorus under the final credits of the 1965 Columbia film *The Sandpiper*. Popular recording by Tony Bennett (Columbia). Received the Academy Award (AMPAS), Best Original Song, 1965. Awarded the Grammy Award (NARAS) as Song of the Year, 1965 (Songwriter's Award); and for the score of the film for the Best Original Score from a Motion Picture or Television Show (Composer's Award).   **650326-2, 660406-1**

Shake Down the Stars (1940)

Lyrics by Eddie DeLange, music by James Van Heusen

Introduced and recorded by Glenn Miller and His Orchestra (Bluebird).   **400509-2**

Shall We Dance (1937)

Lyrics by Ira Gershwin, music by George Gershwin

Introduced by Fred Astaire in the 1937 RKO film *Shall We Dance*. The song was written to replace "Wake Up, Brother, and Dance" when "Shall We Dance" was chosen for the title of the film. The title is correct as shown, no question mark.   **590715-1**

She Didn't Say "Yes" (1931)

Lyrics by Otto Harbach, music by Jerome Kern

Introduced by Bettina Hall in the 1931 musical play *The Cat and the Fiddle*. Sung by Jeanette MacDonald in the 1934 MGM film adaptation.   **630107-2**

She's Just a Quiet Girl (1964)

Lyrics by Paul Vance, music by Riziero Ortolani.

Introduced on an A&M recording by Herb Alpert and His Tijuana Brass.   **650706-1**

She's Tall, She's Tan, She's Terrific (1937)

Lyrics by Benny Davis, music by J. Fred Coots

Introduced in the 1937 revue *The Cotton Club Parade (3rd Edition)*.   **3712102**

Shine (1924)

Lyrics by Cecil Mack (pseudonym of Richard C. McPherson) and Lew Brown, music by Fred Dabney

Featured in vaudeville and recorded by Van and Schenck (Columbia). Revived in 1936 by Chick Webb and His Orchestra, vocal by Ella Fitzgerald (Decca). This is the song which began Frank Sinatra's career, when, as a member of The Hoboken Four, he sang it on Major Bowes's Amateur Hour, winning the competition.

360219-5, 361119-1

Shiny Stockings (1963)

Lyrics by Jon Hendricks, music by Frank Foster and Ella Fitzgerald

Introduced by Ella Fitzgerald with Count Basie and His Orchestra in concerts and on a Verve recording. Frank Foster was a tenor saxophonist with the Basie orchestra.   **630716-3, 640800-15, 640203-11, 640729-19, 720602-10**

A Ship Without a Sail (1929)

Lyrics by Lorenz Hart, music by Richard Rodgers

Introduced by Jack Whiting in the 1929 musical play *Heads Up!* Sung by Charles "Buddy" Rogers in the 1930 Paramount film adaptation.   **560830-3**

Show Me (1951)

Lyrics by Alan Jay Lerner, music by Frederick Loewe

Introduced by Julie Andrews in the 1956 musical play *My Fair Lady*. Sung by Audrey Hepburn (dubbed by Marnie Nixon) and Jeremy Brett in the 1964 Warner Bros. film adaptation.   **621004-3**

Show Me the Way to Get Out of This World (1950)

Lyrics by Les Clark, music by Matt Dennis

Introduced by Matt Dennis in night clubs.

510519-1, 520607-2, 620131-2

Signing Off (1960)

Lyrics and music Leonard Feather and Jessyca Russell

Introduced by Sarah Vaughan, and also successfully recorded by George Shearing.   **610624-2**

Silent Night (1818)

Lyrics by Josef Mohr, music by Franz Gruber

On Christmas Eve, 1818, the organ in St. Nikola's Church in Oberndorf, Austria, broke down. This left the organist Franz Gruber in a critical position, for all the numbers planned for that evening's services relied on organ accompaniment. This statement by Gruber explains what happened. He wrote it in his own hand: "It was on the 24th of December of the year 1818 that the incumbent assistant priest, Father Josef Mohr of St. Nikola's Church in Oberndorf, handed over a poem to the organist of that church, Franz Gruber, who at the same time was also a school teacher in Arnsdorf, with the request to write an accompanying melody for two solo voices, chorus, with guitar accompaniment. The latter, in accordance with the appropriate request of this holy man who was himself a musician, handed over his simple composition and it was performed that Christmas Eve to general approval." (Note: Please read Paul Gallico's wonderful little book *The Story of "Silent Night": The Birth of the Universal Christmas Hymn* (Crown Publishers, New York, 1967). Better still, if possible, read it to your children, or, indeed, any children, on Christmas Eve. **670717-1**

The Silent Treatment (1956)

Lyrics by Stanley Styne, music by Donald Kahn

Introduced by Ella Fitzgerald on a Verve recording. (Lyricist Stanley Styne is the son of composer Jule Styne, composer Donald Kahn is the son of lyricist Gus Kahn.) **560821-6**

Silver Bells (1950)

Lyrics and music by Ray Evans and Jay Livingston

Introduced in the 1950 Columbia film *The Lemon Drop Kid,* it has now become a Christmas holiday standard. **501129-3**

Since I Fell for You (1948)

Lyrics and music by Buddy Johnson

Popular recordings by Paul Gayten and His Trio, vocal by Annie Lauri (Deluxe); Mel Tormé, with George Shearing (Capitol); Laura Lee (Hot Wax); and Charlie Rich (Epic). Revived in 1963 by Lenny Welch (Cadence). **780619-4**

Sing Me a Swing Song and Let Me Dance (1936)

Lyrics by Stanley Adams, music by Hoagy Carmichael

Introduced by Benny Goodman and His Orchestra (Victor). Covered by Chick Webb and His Orchestra, vocal by Ella Fitzgerald (Decca). **360602-2**

Sing, My Heart (1939)

Lyrics by Ted Koehler, music by Harold Arlen

Introduced by Irene Dunne in the 1939 RKO Radio film *Love Affair.* **600802-2, 600802-3**

Sing Song Swing (1940)

Lyrics and music by Charles L. Cooke

Introduced on this recording by Ella Fitzgerald and Her Famous Orchestra, the song became a mild hit. **400000-1, 400215-3, 400226-3, 400304-8**

(You Got Me) Singin' the Blues (1931)

Lyrics by Dorothy Fields, music by Jimmy McHugh

Introduced in the play with music *Singin' the Blues* in 1931. **570428-1**

Single-O (1964)

Lyrics by Johnny Mercer, music by Donald Kahn

Introduced by Ella Fitzgerald on this recording; in fact the song was actually copyrighted on 26 October 1964, six days after Ella recorded it. As far as can be determined, no other recording of this song exists, except that which Mr. Mercer himself made on a demonstration recording, which was never publicly released. Mr. Donald Kahn, the composer, is the son of Gus Kahn, the esteemed lyricist. **641020-4**

Skylark (1942)

Lyrics by Johnny Mercer, music by Hoagy Carmichael

Introduced by Johnny Mercer on radio. **550802-3, 641020-3**

Slap That Bass (1936)

Lyrics by Ira Gershwin, music by George Gershwin

Introduced by Fred Astaire and Dudley Dickerson in the 1937 RKO film *Shall We Dance.* **590107-2**

Sleep, My Little Jesus (1882)

Lyrics by William C. Gannett, music by Adam Geibel

Rev. Gannett was a Unitarian minister in Rochester, New York. An industrious writer, he may well be best remembered by this simple little lullaby. The effective setting comes from the pen of the blind musician, Adam Geibel, who came to the United States from Germany at the age of seven. An organist, choirmaster, composer and publisher, he made a respected name for himself in the musical life of Philadelphia. Originally titled "Mary's Manger-Song." **670718-4**

Sleigh Ride (1948)

Lyrics by Mitchell Parish, music by Leroy Anderson

One of Mr. Anderson's many wonderful musical vignettes, this was originally an instrumental, and was introduced by the Boston "Pops" Orchestra in 1948. Lyrics were added in 1950, and it has become a perennial holiday classic. **600805-2**

Slightly Out of Tune see Desafinado

(When It's) Slumber Time Along the Swanee (1939)

Lyrics and music by Peter Tinturin and Tony Sacco

Introduced on this recording by Chick Webb and His Orchestra, vocals by Ella Fitzgerald. **390302-4**

(Let's Go) Slumming on Park Avenue (1937)

Lyrics and music by Irving Berlin

Introduced by Alice Faye and The Ritz Brothers in the 1937 20th Century-Fox film *On the Avenue*.

580313-3

Smoke Gets in Your Eyes (1933)

Lyrics by Otto Harbach, music by Jerome Kern

Introduced by Tamara (Tamara Geva) in the 1933 musical play *Roberta*. Sung by Irene Dunne and danced by Fred Astaire in the 1935 RKO-Radio film version. Sung by Kathryn Grayson in the 1952 MGM film version *Lovely to Look At*. The best selling record by The Platters (Mercury) in 1958–1959.

660208-30

Smooth Sailing (1950)

Scat lyrics by Ella Fitzgerald, music by Arnett Cobb

Best-selling Decca record in 1951 by Ella Fitzgerald.

510626-2, 531118-8, 650326-9, 730705-3

Só Danço Samba (Jazz Samba) (I Only Dance the Samba) (1962)

Lyrics and music by Antonio Carlos Jobim and Vinícius de Moraes

Introduced in 1962 in the Brazilian-Italian-French film *Copacabana Palace* when the film opened in Europe. In 1968, the film was shown in the U.S. with the title *Girl Game*, the song became a standard among jazz musicians and Norman Gimbel penned English lyrics, "Jazz Samba."

660207-6, 660208-2, **660208-9, 660222-9**, 660727-2, **660728-9, 660729-8, 660923-3, 670430-3**

So in Love (1948)

Lyrics and music by Cole Porter

Introduced by Patricia Morison, and reprised by Alfred Drake, in the 1948 musical play *Kiss Me, Kate!* Sung by Kathryn Grayson and Howard Keel in the 1953 MGM film adaptation.

560209-1

So Long (1940)

Lyrics and music by Russ Morgan, Remus Harris, and Irving Melsher

Introduced and recorded by Russ Morgan and His Orchestra, who also adopted it as his signature theme.

400925-2

So Near and Yet So Far (1941)

Lyrics and music by Cole Porter

Introduced by Fred Astaire in the 1941 Columbia film *You'll Never Get Rich*.

720612-5

So Rare (1937)

Lyrics by Jack Sharpe, music by Jerry Herst

Introduced and recorded by Jimmy Dorsey and His Orchestra (Decca), and adopted as his closing theme. On "Your Hit Parade" for eleven weeks in 1937.

571028-8

Só Tinha de Ser Com Vôce *see* **This Love That I've Found**

Soldier Boy (1955)

Lyrics and music by Theodore Williams, Jr., and David Jones

Introduced and recorded by The Four Fellows (Glory).

550801-1

Solid As a Rock (1949)

Lyrics by Bob Hilliard, music by Dave Mann

Introduced by The Deep River Boys.

500306-1

Solitude (1933)

Lyrics by Eddie DeLange and Irving Mills, music by Duke Ellington

This was Ellington's first successful song, first in a recording in 1933 (Victor) and then in 1934 (Brunswick). In 1934, it received an ASCAP award of $2500 as The Best Song of the Year.

560904-6, 760208-4

Some of These Days (1910)

Lyrics and music by Shelton Brooks

Introduced by Sophie Tucker at White City Park, Chicago, in 1910. It became her theme song, and her autobiography is titled *Some of These Days*. The melody was played on an organ at Sophie Tucker's funeral on 11 February 1966.

730705-19

Some Other Spring (1939)

Lyrics by Arthur Herzog, Jr., music by Irene Kitchings

Introduced and recorded by Billie Holiday (Vocalion).

790712-3

Somebody Bad Stole de Weddin' Bell (1953)

Lyrics by Bob Hilliard, music by Dave Mann

Introduced and featured in a Copacabana (New York) night club show.

531223-4

Somebody from Somewhere (1931)

Lyrics by Ira Gershwin, music by George Gershwin

Introduced by Janet Gaynor in the 1931 Fox film *Delicious*.

590718-1

Somebody Loves Me (1924)

Lyrics by Buddy DeSylva and Ballard MacDonald, music by George Gershwin

Introduced by Winnie Lightner and Tom Patricola in the 1924 revue *George White's Scandals of 1924*. Blossom Seeley made it popular with her vaudeville performances. First recorded by Marion Harris and His Orchestra (Brunswick).   **490918-5, 590107-1**

Somebody Nobody Loves (1941)

Lyrics and music by Seymour Miller

Introduced, featured, and recorded by Dinah Shore (Bluebird).   **411028-1**

Somebody Somewhere (1956)

Lyrics and music by Frank Loesser

Introduced by Jo Sullivan in the 1956 musical play *The Most Happy Fella*.   **621003-1**

Someone Like You (1949)

Lyrics by Ralph Blane, music by Harry Warren

Introduced by Doris Day in the 1949 Warner Bros. film *My Dream Is Yours*.   **490114-3, 490430-1**

Someone to Watch Over Me (1926)

Lyrics by Ira Gershwin, music by George Gershwin

Introduced by Gertrude Lawrence in her first appearance in an American musical in the 1926 musical play *Oh, Kay!*

500912-3, 510519-7, 531227-1, 550802-2, 590326-2, 640728-6, **640729-6, 830523-3b**

Something (1969)

Lyrics and music by George Harrison

Introduced and recorded by The Beatles. Won the Ivor Novello Award for Best Song, 1970–1971.
710518-4, 710721-8

Something to Live For (1939)

Lyrics and music by Billy Strayhorn

Introduced by Duke Ellington and His Orchestra.
651019-3, 660208-7, 660222-3, 660728-4, 660729-4, 660914-6

Something's Gotta Give (1955)

Lyrics and music by Johnny Mercer

Introduced by Fred Astaire in the 1955 RKO film *Daddy Long-Legs*. Nominated for an Academy Award (AMPAS) Best Original Song, 1955. Provided the title for, and planned that it be sung by Marilyn Monroe, in her last film, only a few scenes of which were completed before her death in 1962.   **641021-3, 660907-1**

Somewhere in the Hills [Favela] [O Morro No Tem Vez] (1963)

Portuguese lyrics by Vinícius de Moraes, English lyrics by Ray Gilbert, music by Antonio Carlos Jobim

Introduced by Antonio Carlos Jobim in performance and on a Brazilian recording.   **810319-1**

Somewhere in the Night (1962)

Lyrics by Milton Raskin, music by Billy May

The music is the theme from the television series *Naked City*. Lyrics added in 1962, and vocal version introduced by Teri Thornton (Dauntless).
640729-20, 820205-5

The Song Is Ended (1927)

Lyrics and music by Irving Berlin

Introduced by "Whispering Jack" Smith in the musical play *Will o' the Whispers*.   **580318-4**

The Song Is You (1932)

Lyrics by Oscar Hammerstein II, music by Jerome Kern

Introduced by Tullio Carminati and Natalie Hall in the 1932 musical play *Music in the Air*. Sung by John Boles in the 1934 Fox film adaptation.   **6711132a**

Song of the Jet [Samba do Avião) (1962)

English lyrics by Gene Lees, Portuguese lyrics and music by Antonio Carlos Jobim

Introduced in the 1962 Brazilian-French-Italian film *Copacabana Palace* when it opened in Europe. The film was released in the U.S. with the title *Girl Game* in 1968, popularizing the song here. First recording with English lyrics by Tony Bennett (Columbia).   **810320-1**

Soon (1927)

Lyrics by Ira Gershwin, music by George Gershwin

Introduced by Margaret Schilling and Jerry Goff in the 1930 musical play *Strike Up the Band!* Not used in the Garland-Rooney 1940 MGM film adaptation.
500912-2, 590105-1

Sophisticated Lady (1933)

Lyrics by Mitchell Parish and Irving Mills, music by Duke Ellington

Introduced by Duke Ellington and His Orchestra in 1933 as an instrumental. When lyrics were added the following year, it became one of Ellington's most popular songs.   **560904-7, 580425-7**, 580425-21

Speak Low (1943)

Lyrics by Ogden Nash, music by Kurt Weill

Introduced by Mary Martin (in her first Broadway starring role) and reprised by Kenny Baker in the 1943 musical play *One Touch of Venus*. Sung by Dick Haymes and Ava Gardner (dubbed by Eileen Wilson) in the 1948 Universal film adaptation.   **830321-1**

Spinning Wheel (1968)
Lyrics and music by David Clayton Thomas

Best-selling 1969 record by Blood, Sweat and Tears (Columbia).   **700520-5**

S'posin' (1929)
Lyrics by Andy Razaf, music by Paul Denniker

Introduced and recorded by Rudy Vallée and His Connecticut Yankees.   **530911-1**

Spring Can Really Hang You Up the Most (1955)
Lyrics by Fran Landesman, music by Tommy Wolf

Introduced in the original 1955 St. Louis production of the musical play *The Nervous Set*.

610123-3, **610622-3**, 641022-6, **660720-5, 720602-7**

Spring Is Here (1938)
Lyrics by Lorenz Hart, music by Richard Rodgers

Introduced by Vivienne Segal and Dennis King in the 1938 musical play *I Married an Angel*. Sung by Jeanette MacDonald and Nelson Eddy in the 1942 MGM film adaptation.   **560830-7**

Spring Will Be a Little Late This Year (1944)
Lyrics and music by Frank Loesser

Introduced by Deanna Durbin in the 1944 Universal film *Christmas Holiday*.   **590325-4**

Squatty-Roo
Scat by Ella Fitzgerald, music by Johnny Hodges

Introduced by Johnny Hodges and His Orchestra as an instrumental (Victor). Popular recording by Duke Ellington and His Orchestra. The vocal version was introduced by Ella Fitzgerald in her album *Ella Fitzgerald Sings the Duke Ellington Song Book, Volume II* (Verve).
571017-5

Stairway to the Stars (1935)
Lyrics by Mitchell Parish, music by Matty Malneck and Frank Signorelli

The melody is from Malneck's tone poem "Park Avenue Fantasy," recorded in 1935 (Columbia). Lyrics added in 1939. On "Your Hit Parade" for twelve weeks in 1939, one week in the #1 spot.

390629-2, 390815-3, 470929-2, 570724-3, 610521-2

Star Dust (1927)
Lyrics by Mitchell Parish, music by Hoagy Carmichael

Carmichael was on a visit to his alma mater, the University of Indiana, in 1927, when, one evening, he sat on the so-called "spooning wall," recalling a girl he had once loved and lost. There the melody occurred to him, and he went over to the University "Book Nook," which had a piano, and wrote the melody. Stu Gorrell, a former schoolmate, baptised the composition "Star Dust," because, he said, "it sounded like dust from stars drifting down through the summer sky." Carmichael later remarked, "I had no idea what the title meant, but I thought it was gorgeous." The piece was introduced by Don Redman and His Orchestra as an instrumental in 1929, in which year it was also recorded by Isham Jones and His Orchestra, and Emile Seidel and His Orchestra with the composer at the piano. Parish wrote the lyrics in 1929, and the song was introduced in a Cotton Club revue in Harlem the same year. The rest is history: It has been recorded more than 700 times with at least 50 different arrangements for every possible instrument or combination of instruments; the lyric has been translated into forty languages. It may be the only song recorded on both sides of the same 78-rpm record in two different performances, Tommy Dorsey and His Orchestra on one side, and Benny Goodman and His Orchestra on the other. Also, probably the only song the verse of which has been recorded as a lone entity (Sinatra, for Reprise). Selected by ASCAP in 1963 for its All-Time Hit parade during the first half-century of its existence.

540330-6, 550802-4, 580810-27, **660914-1, 660923-2**

Star Dust Bossa Nova (1962)

See above. This is Ella's special version.   **621001-2**

The Starlit Hour (1939)
Lyrics by Mitchell Parish, music by Peter DeRose

Introduced in the 1940 revue *Earl Carroll's Vanities*.
400000-2, 400126-3, 400304-7

Stars Fell on Alabama (1934)
Lyrics by Mitchell Parish, music by Frank Perkins

Introduced, recorded, and identified with Jack Teagarden and His Orchestra, with two recordings featuring his vocal and trombone solos (Brunswick and Capitol).
560816-4

Stay There, Stay There (1956)
Lyrics by Stanley Styne, music by Donald Kahn

Introduced on this recording by Ella, who in January 1956, just prior to recording the Cole Porter song book, recorded a handful of tunes that were released on 45rpm singles. Unfortunately, the 45rpm record remains the only source of this lovely tune. **560125-1**

Stay with the Happy People (1950)

Lyrics by Bob Hilliard, music by Jule Styne

Introduced by Lina Romay in the 1950 revue *Mike Todd's Peep Show.* **500503-1**

Steam Heat (1954)

Lyrics and music by Richard Adler and Jerry Ross

Introduced by Carol Haney, Buzz Miller and Pat Gennaro in the 1954 musical play *The Pajama Game.* The song was written for the revue *John Murray's Almanac,* of the previous year, but was not used. Carol Haney, Buzz Miller and Kenneth Leroy performed the song in the 1957 Warner Bros. film adaptation. **621001-3**

Stella by Starlight (1944)

Lyrics by Ned Washington, music by Victor Young

Introduced as theme music in the 1944 Paramount film *The Uninvited.* Mr. Young wrote the "Serenade" for the lovely Gail Russell in her film debut in the role of Stella Meredith. Lyrics were added the same year.

610123-10, **610622-1**

Stiff Upper Lip (1937)

Lyrics by Ira Gershwin, music by George Gershwin

Introduced by Gracie Allen in the 1937 RKO film *Damsel in Distress.* **590717-3**

Stompin' at the Savoy (1936)

Lyrics by Andy Razaf, music by Benny Goodman, Edgar Sampson, and Chick Webb

Introduced by recorded by Chick Webb and His Orchestra as an instrumental (Columbia). Vocal version introduced in 1938 by Ella Fitzgerald with the Webb Orchestra.

570723-7, 570929-10, 571009-8, 580424-2, 580425-11, **580425-27,** 610519-12, **671113-2c**

Stone Cold Dead in de Market (1946)

Lyrics and music by Wilmoth Houdini

Introduced and recorded by Wilmoth Houdini, the Calypso singer. Best-selling recording by Ella Fitzgerald with Louis Jordan and His Tympany Five (Decca). **451008-1**

Stormy Weather (1933)

Lyrics by Ted Koehler, music by Harold Arlen

Introduced by Harold Arlen on a recording with Leo Reisman's Orchestra. At the time, Koehler and Arlen were writing songs for the Cotton Club revues. The song was written for Cab Calloway, but since Calloway was not appearing that year, the song was offered to Ethel Waters, whom they had induced to appear in the 1933 *Cotton Club Parade.* But the recording was already a hit; nevertheless, it became Miss Waters's song — she sang it under a lamppost against a log-cabin backdrop, a midnight blue spot pointing a finger at her. "Singing 'Stormy Weather' proved to be a turning point in my life," she wrote in her autobiography. "I sang it from the depths of my private hell in which I was being crushed and suffocated." Lena Horne performed the song in the 1943 20th Century–Fox film *Stormy Weather,* in an exquisite and memorable production number that culminated with Katherine Dunham and her dancers. From the day the movie opened in New York "Stormy Weather" has belonged to Lena Horne, her most requested song in night club and concert appearances.

610114-4

Street Beater ("Sanford and Son" Theme) (1972)

Lyrics by Ella Fitzgerald, music by Quincy Jones

Introduced by Ella Fitzgerald in her set at th 1972 concert *Jazz at the Santa Monica Civic Auditorium.* The concert was recorded and released on the Pablo label.

72060212

(On the) Street of Dreams (1932)

Lyrics by Samuel M. Lewis, music by Victor Young

Introduced, featured, and recorded by Morton Downey (Perfect). **620409-3, 750519-8**

Strictly from Dixie (1938)

Lyrics and music by James Cavanaugh, Chick Webb, and Harry Brooks

Introduced by Ella Fitzgerald and Her Savoy Eight (Decca). **380818-1**

Strike Up the Band! (1927)

Lyrics by Ira Gershwin, music by George Gershwin

Introduced by Max Hoffman, Jr., in the 1927 pre-Broadway try-outs of the 1927 musical play *Strike Up the Band!* That show never opened on Broadway. But, with revisions, the show did open in 1930, when the song was introduced again by Jim Townsend, Jerry Goff and ensemble. Busby Berkeley staged a rousing finale using the number in the 1940 MGM film adaptation.

590716-4

Sugar Blues (1919)

Lyrics by Lucy Fletcher, music by Clarence Williams

Introduced and recorded by Leona Williams and Her Dixie Land Band (Columbia). Revived in 1936 by Clyde McCoy (Decca), when he adopted it as his theme song, and his distinctive trombone solo will always identify the piece with him.   **400126-2, 400226-4**

Sugar Pie (1939)

Lyrics and music by Charlie Beal and Chick Webb

Introduced by Chick Webb and His Orchestra, vocal by Ella Fitzgerald (Decca).   **390302-3**

Sugarfoot Rag (1950)

Lyrics by George Vaughn, music by Hank Garland

Introduced by Red Foley, featuring a guitar solo by Garland.   **500306-3**

Summertime (1935)

Lyrics by DuBose Heyward, music by George Gershwin

Introduced by Abbie Mitchell in the opening scene of the 1935 folk opera *Porgy and Bess*. First popular recording by Billie Holiday (Vocalion). Sung by Dorothy Dandridge (dubbed by Loulie Jean Norman) in the 1959 Columbia film adaptation.

570818-1, 580810-10, **600213-7, 640728-10, 640729-10, 700520-16, 710518-5, 710721-5,** 810726-13

The Sun Forgot to Shine This Morning (1956)

Lyrics by William D. Carey, music by Gene Howard

Although Ella introduced this song on one of her first recordings for Verve, it later became a big hit for Dinah Washington.   **560125-2**

Sunday (1926)

Lyrics and music by Ned Miller, Chester Conn, Jule Styne, and Bennie Kreuger

Introduced by The Williams Sisters at the Rendezvous Café (nightclub) in Chicago. This was Jule Styne's first hit.   **481204-7**

A Sunday Kind of Love (1946)

Lyrics and music by Barbara Belle, Louis Prima, Anita Leonard, and Stan Rhodes

Introduced by Claude Thornhill and His Orchestra, vocal by Fran Warren (Columbia).   **470319-1**

Sunny (1965)

Lyrics and music by Bobby Hebb

Introduced and recorded on a best-selling record in 1966 by Bobby Hebb (Philips).   **680518-6, 700105-2**

Sunshine of Your Love (1968)

Lyrics and music by Jack Bruce, Peter Brown, and Eric Clapton

Introduced and recorded by Eric Clapton.   **690200-2**

Supper Time (1933)

Lyrics and music by Irving Berlin

Introduced by Ethel Waters in the 1933 musical play *As Thousands Cheer*, in which it was a show-stopper.   **580317-2**

Sweet and Lovely (1931)

Lyrics and music by Gus Arnheim, Harry Tobias, and Jules Lemare

Introduced by Gus Arnheim and His Orchestra at the Coconut Grove (Los Angeles), and recorded by him (Victor).   **581124-5**

Sweet and Slow (1935)

Lyrics by Al Dubin, music by Harry Warren

This is one of the few Dubin-Warren songs that was not introduced in a movie. This was the year in which they did the songs for *Go into Your Dance* (with Jolson) *Broadway Gondolier* (with Dick Powell), and *Gold Diggers of 1935*, among others. Fats Waller made this a bigger hit than most of their movie songs that year.   **620410-5**

Sweet Georgia Brown (1925)

Lyrics by Kenneth Casey, music by Maceo Pinkard

Introduced, featured, and recorded by Ben Bernie and His Orchestra. Popular recordings by Isham Jones and His Orchestra, and by Ethel Waters.

650626-3, 660208-1, **660222-5, 660720-1,** 660728-6, **660729-6,** 660914-8, **660923-1, 680518-4,** 740411-1, 790712-2

Sweet Lorraine (1928)

Lyrics by Mitchell Parish, music by Clifford Burwell

Introduced and recorded by Rudy Vallée and His Orchestra (the composer was playing piano in the orchestra at the time). This is the song that transformed Nat "King" Cole from an instrumentalist into a singer: He was appearing with The King Cole Trio, an instrumental ensemble, at The Swanee Inn (nightclub, Los Angeles) in 1937, when an inebriated patron insisted he sing "Sweet Lorraine." He finally complied, although he had never sung publicly. He proved so successful that from that time he continued doing vocals with the group. He revived the song in the 1950s.   **790215-3**

Sweet Sue, Just You (1928)

Lyrics by Will J. Harris, music by Victor Young

Written for and dedicated to Sue Carol (later, Mrs. Alan Ladd), a star of films at the time. Her protrait and the dedication appear on the cover of the sheet music, which is believed by some to be the first time that this had been done.   **400226-5**

The Sweetest Sound (1962)

Lyrics and music by Richard Rodgers

Introduced by Richard Kiley and Diahann Carroll in the 1962 musical play *No Strings*.   **640407-4**

Sweethearts on Parade (1928)

Lyrics by Charles Newman, music by Carmen Lombardo

Introduced, featured, and recorded by Guy Lombardo and His Royal Canadians (Columbia); in three weeks it had become a nationwide hit. Gave its title to and featured in the 1930 Columbia film *Sweethearts on Parade*.

531118-11a

Swing Into Spring (1958)

Special arrangement by Ralph Burns of the Gershwins' "'S Wonderful," written for NBC's television special *Swing Into Spring*, broadcast live from New York on 9 April 1958. The production was so successful that the idea was repeated by CBS, in a televison special of the same title broadcast from New York on 10 April 1959. Ella participated in both productions.   **590410-6**

The Swingin' Shepherd Blues (1958)

Lyrics by Rhoda Roberts and Kenny Jacobson, music by Moe Koffman

Introduced by recorded by Moe Koffman and His Orchestra in his Canadian jazz album *Cool and Hot Sax* (Jubilee).   **580319-5, 580319-6**

Swinging on the Reservation (1936)

Lyrics and music by Wayman Carver and Chick Webb

Introduced by Chick Webb and His Orchestra, vocal by Ella Fitzgerald (Decca).   **361029-3**

'Tain't Nobody's Biz-Ness (If I Do) (1922)

Lyrics and music by Porter Grainger and Everett Robbins

Performed, featured, and recorded by Bessie Smith (Columbia). This was the first song recorded by Thomas "Fats" Waller (Victor).   **750717-10**

'Tain't What You Do (It's the Way That 'Cha Do It) (1939)

Lyrics and music by Sy Oliver and James "Trummy" Young

Introduced by Jimmie Lunceford and His Orchestra. **390217-2, 391200-3, 400122-5, 400325-3**

Take It from the Top (1940)

Music by Teddy McRae

Instrumental introduced by Ella Fitzgerald and Her Famous Orchestra at the Savoy Ballroom, and recorded by the orchestra (Decca).   **400125-7, 400320-1**

Take Love Easy (1947)

Lyrics by John Latouche, music by Duke Ellington

Introduced by Bernice Parks in the 1947 musical play *Beggar's Holiday*.   **730828-1**

Take the "A" Train (1941)

Lyrics and music by Billy Strayhorn

Introduced by Duke Ellington and His Orchestra (Victor), and performed by the Ellington Orchestra in the 1943 Columbia film *Reveille with Beverly*. The song served for a time as the Ellington Orchestra signature theme. The song refers to the New York City Eighth Avenue subway express to Harlem, and its composition came about on Strayhorn's first trip to New York to meet with Ellington. To make an impression on Ellington, Strayhorn composed the song from the directions the bandleader had given him to get to Harlem by subway. Strayhorn explains: "'"A" Train' was born without any effort — it was like writing a letter to a friend. It was composed in 1939, though it wasn't used right away. I put together all the ideas I had in my head and perfected them, then I sat down before the piano and I wrote the tune in a really short time. This is the way I like to work. All my most meaningful pieces were born like that."

570624-2, 610211-2, 610512-7, 610516-8, 610518-18, 610520-22, **610521-4**, 640800-17

Taking a Chance on Love (1940)

Lyrics by John Latouche and Ted Fetter, music by Vernon Duke

Introduced by Ethel Waters, and reprised by Miss Waters and Dooley Wilson in the 1940 musical play *Cabin in the Sky*. The song was added three days before the Broadway opening. Duke and Fetter had written an earlier version, titled "Fooling Around with Love." Latouche altered it to fit the character and the scene. Miss Waters and Eddie "Rochester" Anderson sang it in the 1943 MGM film adaptation, following which the song spent seventeen weeks on "Your Hit Parade."

401108-1, 531231-2, 540214-2, 620131-6, 620630-8, 730705-15

Talk Fast, My Heart, Talk Fast (1949)

Lyrics by Don Raye, music by Gene DePaul

Since the Raye-DePaul team wrote a great many songs for movies, it seems odd that research does not reveal that this was one of their film songs. However, Ella's record makes up for any negligence.   **490920-2**

Tea Dance (1940)

Music by Dick Vance

Instrumental introduced by Ella Fitzgerald and Her Famous Orchestra (Decca).   **400320-2**

Tea for Two (1924)

Lyrics by Irving Caesar, music by Vincent Youmans

Introduced by Louise Groody, John Barker, and chorus in the 1925 musical play *No, No, Nanette!* Sung by Bernice Claire in the 1930 First National film adeaptation, by Anna Neagle in the 1940 RKO film adaptation, and by Gordon MacRae and Doris Day in the 1950 Warner Bros. film adaptation *Tea for Two*. Sung by Susan Watson, Roger Rathburn, and chorus in the 1971 Broadway revival.
630716-9

Tea Leaves (1948)

Lyrics and music by Morty Berk, Frank Capano, and Max C. Freedman

Introduced by Ella Fitzgerald and The Song Spinners (Decca).
480429-1

Teach Me How to Cry (1958)

Lyrics and music by Phil J. Tuminello

This is one of the two singles Ella recorded right at the end of her sessions with Paul Weston doing the Irving Berlin Song Book.
580319-4

Teach Me Tonight (1953)

Lyrics by Sammy Cahn, music by Gene DePaul

Introduced by Janet Brace with Jack Pleis's Orchestra (Decca).
620630-2, 620630-7, 620630-25,
750717-3, 790216-3

Teardrops from My Eyes (1950)

Lyrics and music by Rudolph Toombs

Popular recordings in 1950 and 1959 by Ruth Brown (Atlantic).
581122-7

Ten Cents a Dance (1930)

Lyrics by Lorenz Hart, music by Richard Rodgers

Introduced by Ruth Etting in the 1930 musical play *Simple Simon*. Sung by Doris Day in a memorable performance in the 1955 MGM film *Love Me or Leave Me*.
560828-1, 640203-7

(Love Is) The Tender Trap (1955)

Lyrics by Sammy Cahn, music by James Van Heusen

Introduced by Frank Sinatra, singing it under the titles of the 1955 MGM film *The Tender Trap*. Popular recording by Sinatra (Capitol). Nominated for an Academy Award (AMPAS), Best Original Song, 1955.
550805-4, 560202-13

Tenderly (1945)

Music by Jack Lawrence, music by Walter Gross

Introduced by Clark Dennis on a recording (Capitol). Revived in 1952 with a hit record by Rosemary Clooney (Columbia).
560202-2, **560816-3, 570428-4, 570724-1**

Tennessee Waltz (1947)

Lyrics and music by Redd Stewart and Pee Wee King

Introduced by Redd Stewart with Pee Wee King and His Orchestra in 1947 on a Louisville, Kentucky, radio station. First recording by The Short Brothers in 1948 (Decca), followed by a recording by Redd Stewart with Pee Wee King and His Orchestra. First popular recording by Erskine Hawkins and His Orchestra in 1949. Best selling record by Patti Page in 1950, selling more than three million copies in one year. On "Your Hit Parade" for fifteen weeks (1950), one in the #1 spot. In 1965, the State of Tennessee adopted this song as its Official State Song.
760130-5

Thank Your Stars (1940)

Lyrics and music by Abner Silver, Walter Kent, and Harold Adamson

Introduced by Ella Fitzgerald and Her Famous Orchestra on this Decca recording.
400125-6

Thanks for the Memory (1937)

Lyrics by Leo Robin, music by Ralph Rainger

Introduced by Bob Hope (in his screen debut) and Shirley Ross in the 1937 Paramount film *The Big Broadcast of 1938*. The tremendous success of the song led Paramount to star Mr. Hope and Miss Ross in a new film in 1938, appropriately titled *Thanks for the Memory*. Awarded the Academy Award (AMPAS), Best Original Song, 1938.
550401-1, 641022-5, **660720-4**

That Certain Feeling (1925)

Lyrics by Ira Gershwin, music by George Gershwin

Introduced by Allen Kearns and Queenie Smith in the 1925 musical play *Tip Toes*.
590715-2

That Old Black Magic (1942)

Lyrics by Johnny Mercer, music by Harold Arlen

Introduced by Johnny Johnston and danced by Vera Zorina in a production number in the 1942 Paramount film *Star-Spangled Rhythm*. Louis Prima and Keely Smith sang it in the 1958 Columbia film *Senior Prom*. Their Dot recording in 1958 won the Grammy Award (NARAS), Best Performance by a Vocal Group, 1958. Nominated for an Academy Award (AMPAS), Best Original Song, 1943.
540918-1, **550427-2, 550803-2**,
580425-6, **580425-19, 600213-1**,
610114-1, 610519-8, **650326-2, 690729-2**

That Old Devil Called Love (1947)

Lyrics and music by Doris Fisher and Allan Roberts

Ella recorded this lovely ballad in her album with Joe Pass; originally made famous by Billie Holiday.

890315-1

That Old Feeling (1937)

Lyrics by Lew Brown, music by Sammy Fain

Introduced by Virginia Verrill in the 1937 United Artists film *Vogues of 1938*. Nominated for an Academy Award (AMPAS), Best Original Song, 1937.

471218-2, 590711-3, 760208-2

That Ringo Beat (1964)

Lyrics and music by Ella Fitzgerald

Introduced by Ella Fitzgerald on a 1964 Verve single.

641023-1

That Was My Heart (1939)

Lyrics and music by Jimmy Johnson and Chick Webb

Introduced by Chick Webb and His Orchestra, vocal by Ella Fitzgerald (Decca). This was Chick Webb's last recording. **390210-4, 390421-8**

That's A-Plenty (1954)

Lyrics and music by Lew Pollack and Nick Ariondo

Ella recorded this song in a duet with Bing Crosby on a General Electric Show; Bobby Hackett had a success with an instrumental version. **540214-1**

That's All, Brother (1939)

Lyrics and music by Jerry Livingstone and Mack David

Ella chose this Livingstone-David number to record in her first session after the death of Chick Webb. Research does not reveal another recording.

390629-4, 390716-2

That's My Desire (1931)

Lyrics by Carroll Loveday, music by Helmy Kress

Introduced on radio by Lanny Ross in 1931, the song went virually unnoticed until it was revived in 1947 by Frankie Laine in his night-club act. A Mercury Records executive heard him sing it in a Los Angeles night spot, had him record it, and the record sold a million and a half records the first year, elevating Mr. Laine to recording stardom and establishing Mercury Records as an important label. **470319-2, 780620-1**

That's Rich (1945)

Scat lyrics by Ella Fitzgerald and Buddy Rich, music by Sy Oliver

Ella Fitzgerald and Her V-Disc Jumpers were recording a V-Disc session in October 1945. She and the drummer, Buddy Rich, devised this scat routine and recorded it for the Armed Forces Network. The music was kindly donated by Sy Oliver. **451012-1**

That's The Way It Is (1945)

Lyrics and music by Joan Whitney and Alex Kramer

Introduced by Ella Fitzgerald and The Ink Spots on this Decca recording. **450226-2**

Them There Eyes (1930)

Lyrics and music by Maceo Pinkard, William Tracey, and Doris Tauber

Introduced and recorded by Gus Arnheim and His Orchestra. Diana Ross sang it in the 1972 Paramount film *Lady Sings the Blues*.

570929-9, 630716-1, 640203-10, 640728-8, **640729-8**, 810726-16a

Then I'll Be Tired of You (1934)

Lyrics by E.Y. "Yip" Harburg, music by Arthur Schwartz

Introduced by Isham Jones and His Orchestra, vocal by Joe Martin (Decca). **571015-7**

Then You've Never Been Blue (1929)

Lyrics by Sam Lewis and Joe Young, music by Ted Fiorito

Introduced by Ted Fiorito and His Orchestra (Columbia). **600419-4**

There Are Such Things (1942)

Lyrics by Abel Baer and Stanley Adams, music by George W. Meyer

This was the last hit song for each of the three writers … but what a hit! Introduced and recorded by Tommy Dorsey and His Orchestra, vocal by Frank Sinatra and The Pied Pipers, whose Victor recording sold more than a million copies in 1942. On "Your Hit Parade" for eighteen weeks, one in the #1 spot. **640304-5**

There! I've Said It Again (1941)

Lyrics and music by Redd Evans and Dave Mann

Introduced and recorded by Benny Carter and His Orchestra (Bluebird). Revived in 1945 when Redd Evans took the song to Vaughn Monroe, a still young and unknown Boston bandleader, who recorded it with himself and The Norton Sisters doing the vocals. The 3 million record sale that followed established Mr. Monroe as a recording star. **640303-1**

There Never Was a Baby Like My Baby (1951)

Lyrics by Betty Comden and Adolph Green, music by Jule Styne

Introduced by Bert Lahr and Dolores Gray in the 1951 musical revue *Two on the Aisle*.   **510718-3**

There's a Boat Dat's Leavin' Soon for New York (1935)

Lyrics by Ira Gershwin, music by George Gershwin

Introduced by John W. Bubbles (as Sportin' Life) in the 1935 folk opera *Porgy and Bess*. Sung by Sammy Davis, Jr., in the 1959 Columbia film adaptation.   **570819-1**

There's a Lull in My Life (1937)

Lyrics by Mack Gordon, music by Harry Revel

Introduced by Alice Faye in the 1937 20th Century–Fox film *Wake Up and Live*.
571015-1, 591213-1, **750519-5**

There's a Small Hotel (1936)

Lyrics by Lorenz Hart, music by Richard Rodgers

Originally written for the 1935 musical play *Jumbo*, it was dropped before the New York opening. Introduced by Ray Bolger and Doris Carson in the 1936 musical play *On Your Toes*. Interpolated instrumentally in the 1939 Warner Bros. film adaptation. Betty Garrett sang it in the 1948 MGM film *Words and Music*, and Frank Sinatra sang it in the 1957 Columbia film *Pal Joey*.   **490415-3, 560829-4**

There's Frost on the Moon (1937)

Lyrics by Joe Young, music by Fred E. Ahlert

Featured and recorded by Tommy Dorsey and His Orchestra, vocal by Edythe Wright (Victor).   **370115-1**

There's No You (1944)

Lyrics by Tom Adair, music by Hal Hopper

Introduced by recorded by Jo Stafford (Capitol).
830322-4

These Boots Are Made for Walkin' (1965)

Lyrics and music by Lee Hazelwood

Introduced and recorded by Nancy Sinatra (Reprise), whose recording sold more than a million records, her first success.   **660914-5**

These Foolish Things (Remind Me of You) (1935)

Lyrics by Holt Marvel (Erich Maschwitz), music by Jack Strachey and Harry Link

Introduced by Madge Elliott and Cyril Ritchard in the 1935 London revue *Spread It Abroad*. Thirteen weeks on "Your Hit Parade," one in the #1 spot.
**501230-2, 570723-8, 570929-5,
571009-4, 580425-14, 730705-13**

They All Laughed (1937)

Lyrics by Ira Gershwin, music by George Gershwin

Introduced by Fred Astaire and Ginger Rogers in the 1937 RKO film *Shall We Dance*. Ira Gershwin took the title from a correspondence school advertisement of the 1930s with the heading: "They all laughed when I sat down to play the piano."   **570723-5, 590326-10**

They Can't Take That Away from Me (1937)

Lyrics by Ira Gershwin, music by George Gershwin

Introduced by Fred Astaire in the 1937 RKO film *Shall We Dance*. This is the only song by the Gershwins to be nominated for an Academy Award.
**560816-1, 590105-5, 640729-17, 671113-2b,
710507-6, 710721-6, 740411-2, 830523-7, 831000-6**

They Pass by Singin' (1935)

Lyrics by DuBose Heyward, music by George Gershwin

Introduced by Todd Duncan (as Porgy) in Act I of the 1935 folk opera *Porgy and Bess*. Not used in the Goldwyn Films film adaptation. This track was cut by Louis and Ella during their recording of *Porgy and Bess*, but has not as yet been issued.   **570819-4**

Things Ain't What They Used to Be (and You Better Believe It) (1943/1953)

Lyrics by Ted Parsons, music by Mercer Ellington and Duke Ellington

Introduced by Duke Ellington and His Orchestra as an instrumental entitled "Time's A-Wastin'." First recorded by Johnny Hodges and His Orchestra (Bluebird). Used as the Ellington Orchestra's theme song during a part of the 1940s. Lyrics were written in 1953 by Mr. Persons.
660923-9, 701222-2, 710507-5

Things Are Looking Up (1937)

Lyrics by Ira Gershwin, music by George Gershwin

Introduced by Fred Astaire, and danced by Mr. Astaire and Joan Fontaine in the 1937 RKO film *A Damsel in Distress*.   **590717-2**

Thinking of You (1927)

Lyrics by Bert Kalmar, music by Harry Ruby

Introduced by Oscar Shaw and Mary Eaton in the 1927 musical play *The Five O'Clock Girl*. Kay Kyser recorded it, and it became his orchestra's theme song. Performed by Fred Astaire and Vera-Ellen in the 1950 MGM film *Three Little Words*.   **680529-1f**

This Can't Be Love (1938)

Lyrics by Lorenz Hart, music by Richard Rodgers

Introduced by Marcy Westcott and Eddie Albert in the 1938 musical play *The Boys from Syracuse*. Rosemary Lane sang it in the 1940 Universal film adaptation. Cyd Charisse and Dee Turnell performed it in the 1948 MGM film *Words and Music*, and Doris Day sang it in the 1962 MGM film *Billy Rose's Jumbo*.

560815-1, 560821-1, 570704-1, 610211-16

This Changing World (1940)

Lyrics by Harold Adamson, music by Dana Suesse

Introduced by Ella Fitzgerald and Her Famous Orchestra, vocal by Ella Fitzgerald (Decca). **400125-3**

This Could Be the Start of Something (Big) (1956)

Lyrics and music by Steve Allen

Introduced by Les Brown and His Orchestra on the Steve Allen Sunday Night Show (television). The song became Allen's theme.

610123-9, 610513-17, **610516-5,** 610518-5, 610519-1, 610519-20, 610520-8, 610520-24

This Girl's/Guy's in Love with You (1968)

Lyrics by Hal David, music by Bert Bacharach

Introduced by Bert Bacharach in personal appearances. Popular recording by Herb Alpert and The Tijuana Brass (A&M), and by singer Dionne Warwick (Scepter). **690200-3, 700520-2a**

This Gun Don't Care (1966)

Lyrics and music by Larry Lee

Larry Lee had a hit with his composition, and Ella covered him with a recording on her *Misty Blue* album for Capitol. **671222-3**

This Love of Mine (1941)

Lyrics by Frank Sinatra, music by Sol Parker and Henry Sanicola

Introduced and recorded by Tommy Dorsey and His Orchestra, vocal by Frank Sinatra (Victor). Interpolated in the 1957 Universal film *Spring Reunion*. **411006-2**

This Love That I've Found
[Só Tinha que Ser Com Você] (1978)

Lyrics by Louis Oliveira, music by Antonio Carlos Jobim

Introduced by Antonio Carlos Jobim on a Verve recording. Ella gives it her special treatment on her *Alla Abraça Jobim* album. **800923-1**

This Time It's Real (1938)

Lyrics and music by Buddy Bernier and Bob Emmerich

Introduced by Ella Fitzgerald and Her Savoy Eight on this Decca record. **380503-1**

This Time the Dream's on Me (1941)

Lyrics by Johnny Mercer, music by Harold Arlen

Introduced by Priscilla Lane with Jimmie Lunceford and His Orchestra in the 1941 Warner Bros. film *Blues in the Night*. 600801-7, **610115-4,** 641020-2

This Year's Kisses (1937)

Lyrics and music by Irving Berlin

Introduced by Alice Faye and Dick Powell in the 1937 20th Century–Fox film *On the Avenue*. Popular recording by Alice Faye (Brunswick). 610123-4, **610622-2**

Thou Swell (1927)

Lyrics by Lorenz Hart, music by Richard Rodgers

Introduced by William Gaxton and Constance Collier in the 1927 musical play *A Connecticut Yankee*. Performed by June Allyson and The Blackburn Twins in the 1948 MGM film *Words and Music*. (Note: *A Connecticut Yankee*, a 1931 Fox film, and the 1949 Paramount film *A Connecticut Yankee in King Arthur's Court* are not related to the Rodgers and Hart musical.)

490423-3, 560829-2, 660728-1b, 660729-1b

Three Little Words (1930)

Lyrics by Bert Kalmar, music by Harry Ruby

Introduced by Bing Crosby and The Rhythm Boys with Duke Ellington and His Orchestra in the 1930 film *Check and Double Check*. Fred Astaire and Red Skelton sang it in the 1950 MGM film *Three Little Words*. **410108-1**

The Thrill Is Gone (1931)

Lyrics by Lew Brown, music by Ray Henderson

Introduced by Everett Marshall and Ross McLean, and danced by Dorothy and Harry Dixon, in the 1931 revue *George White's Scandals of 1931*. This, and other hits songs from the musical revue, were recorded by Bing Crosby and The Boswell Sisters on two sides of a 12" 78-rpm Brunswick, one of the earliest attempts to record the score of a musical show on records. Performed by Dan Dailey, Ernest Borgnine, and Gordon MacRae in the 1956 20th Century–Fox film *The Best Things in Life Are Free*.

640304-4, 830322-10

Throw Out the Lifeline (1890)

Lyrics and music by Edward S. Ufford

Rev. Ufford wrote this hymn at a time when the country was becoming aware of the Pentecostal movement taking place in religious circles. The song became an immedite "hit" with many congregations. **670200-9**

(God Be with You) Till We Meet Again

Lyrics by Jeremiah E. Rankin, music by William G. Tomer

Rev. Dr. Rankin, one of the great preachers of the 19th century, was inspired to write this hymn when he read the dictionary definition of *good-bye*: "A condensation of 'God be with you.'" He needed a theme for a hymn to dismiss his congregation after the Christmas service. He had two organists meddling with his verses before they reached final form. William Tomer was the first, and the musical fabric is chiefly his.   **670200-3**

Time After Time (1947)

Lyrics by Sammy Cahn, music by Jule Styne

Introduced by Frank Sinatra in the 1947 MGM film *It Happened in Brooklyn*.   650625-1, **660720-7**

Time Alone Will Tell (1944)

Lyrics by Mack Gordon, music by James V. Monaco

Introduced by Charlie Spivak and His Orchestra in the 1944 20th Century–Fox film *Pin-Up Girl*.   **440321-1**

Timer (1967)

Lyrics and music by Laura Nyro

Introduced in 1968 by Laura Nyro in her album *Eli and the Thirteenth Confession* (Columbia).   700124-3

'Tis Autumn (1941)

Lyrics and music by Henry Nemo

Introduced by Woody Herman and The Woodchoppers, vocal by Herman and Carolyn Grey.   **760129-3**

To Keep My Love Alive (1943)

Lyrics by Lorenz Hart, music by Richard Rodgers

Written for and introduced by Vivienne Segal for the 1943 revival of the musical play *A Connecticut Yankee*.   **560829-7**

To Make a Mistake Is Human (1948)

Lyrics and music by Jimmy Shirl and Ervin M. Drake

Introduced by Ella Fitzgerald on this Decca recording.   **481110-1**

Too Close for Comfort (1956)

Lyrics by Larry Holofcener and George Weiss, music by Jerry Bock

Introduced by Sammy Davis, Jr., in the 1956 musical play *Mr. Wonderful*.
560625-2, 560815-9, 570704-6, 580810-18, **610221-1**, 610520-16, 620630-24, 630000-3, 640729-23, **770714-1**

Too Darn Hot (1948)

Lyrics and music by Cole Porter

Introduced by Lorenzo Fuller, Eddie Sledge, and Fred Davis in the 1948 musical play *Kiss Me, Kate!* Sung and danced by Ann Miller in the 1953 MGM film adaptation.

560207-5, 600213-8, 620630-26, 620630-28, **720602-11a**

Too Marvelous for Words (1937)

Lyrics by Johnny Mercer, music by Richard Whiting

Introduced by Wini Shaw and Ross Alexander (dubbed by James Newill), then reprised by Ruby Keeler, who danced it with Lee Dixon on a giant typewriter, in the 1937 Warner Bros. film *Ready, Willing and Able*. This is the song with which Richard Whiting's daughter, Margaret, began her successful career as a singer on the Johnny Mercer NBC radio program in 1940.   641021-1, **660907-3**

Too Young for the Blues (1956)

Lyrics and music by Biff Jones and Chuck Meyer

This was one of four songs that Ella recorded during her first month with Verve Records, during the planning stages of her first Song Book (Cole Porter). The four sides were issued on both 78rpm and 45rpm records, and also later included in the LP album *Here Come the Girls*, which featured Ella, Pearl Bailey, Toni Harper, Anita O'Day, and Jane Powell, all new signees to the Verve label.

560125-3, 560125-4

Top Hat, White Tie and Tails (1935)

Lyrics and music by Irving Berlin

Introduced by Fred Astaire in a lavish production number in the 1935 RKO film *Top Hat*.   **580319-3**

To You (1939)

Music and lyrics by Benny Davis, Tommy Dorsey, and Ted Shapiro

Introduced with a RCA Victor Bluebird recording by Tommy Dorsey and His Orchestra. Glenn Miller and His Orchestra also provided a record, but despite its auspicious launching, it was never a big success. Listen to Ella's version here (Decca never had her record it in a studio), and see if you can judge why the song is long forgotten.

390824-1

Traffic Jam (1939)

Music by Artie Shaw and Teddy McRae

Introduced by Artie Shaw and His Orchestra as an instrumental in the 1939 MGM film *Dancing Co-Ed*.
391200-6, 400122-2, 400325-6

Trav'lin' Light (1943)

Lyrics by Johnny Mercer, music by Jimmy Mundy and James "Trummy" Young

Introduced by Charlie Spivak and His Orchestra. Popular recording by Paul Whiteman and His Orchestra, vocal by Billie Holiday (using the pseudonym, Lady Day).
580701-2, 641019-1

Treat Me Rough (1930)

Lyrics by Ira Gershwin, music by George Gershwin

Introduced by William Kent and ensemble in the 1930 musical play *Girl Crazy*. Sung by Mickey Rooney and June Allyson in the 1943 film adaptation. Ira Gershwin revised the lyrics of the verse especially for Ella Fitzgerald's recording of *Ella Fitzgerald Sings the George and Ira Gershwin Song Book* (Verve, 1959). The new lyric is: When I was born, they found a silver spoon in my mouth,/and so I always had the best of care./When winter came up North, of course, they motored me South/Where I was princess in our villa there./Tutors and headwaiters fawned on me;/Life was just a bore until it dawned on me/the cushy sheltered way of life was really no fun!/From now on some manhandling must be done. **590716-3**

Triste (Sad) (1967)

Lyrics and music by Antonio Carlos Jobim

Introduced by Antonio Carlos Jobim on a Verve recording. **800919-6**

Trouble in Mind (1926)

Lyrics and music by Richard M. Jones

Introduced and recorded by Richard Jones and His Orchestra (Bluebird). **631028-3**

Trouble Is a Man (1944)

Lyrics and music by Alec Wilder

Introduced by Mabel Mercer in her night club appearances. **690200-11**

Try a Little Bit (1969)

Lyrics and music by John Benson Sebastian

Tnis song was recorded by Ella and the Gerald Wilson Orchestra during the time of their assembling her *Things Ain't What They Used to Be (and You Better Believe It)* album, but was issued only on a 45rpm record and not included in the album. It is a rarity for collectors of Ella. **691023-2**

Try a Little Tenderness (1932)

Lyrics and music by Harry Woods, Jimmy Campbell, and Reg Connelly

First published in England (Campbell and Connelly were writer-publishers). Introduced in the U.S. by Ruth Etting (Melotone). **680529-2b**

Trying (1952)

Lyrics and music by Billy Vaughn

Popular recordings by The Hilltoppers (Dot), and Johnny Desmond (Coral). **520811-1, 521218-1a**

Turn the World Around (the Other Way) (1967)

Lyrics and music by Ben Peters

Introduced and recorded by Eddy Arnold (Victor). **671220-3**

Tuxedo Junction (1939)

Lyrics by Buddy Feyne, music by Erskine Hawkins, William Johnson, and Julian Dash

Introduced at the Savoy Ballroom (New York) and recorded by Erskine Hawkins and His Orchestra (Bluebird). Popular recording by Glenn Miller and His orchestra — it became the band's biggest hit (Bluebird). Performed by The Glenn Miller Orchestra in the 1953 Universal film *The Glenn Miller Story*. Tuxedo Junction is a railroad junction in Alabama. **700104-3**

Undecided (1939)

Lyrics by Sid Robin, music by Charlie Shavers

Introduced and first recorded by John Kirby and "The Biggest Little Band in the Land," featuring Charlie Shavers on trumpet (Decca).

390217-1, 511128-1, 560815-13

Under a Blanket of Blue (1933)

Lyrics by Marty Symes and A. J. Nieburg, music by Jerry Levinson (before he became Jerry Livingston)

Introduced, featured, and recorded by Glen Gray and The Casa Loma Orchestra, vocal by Kenny Sargent. **560816-7**

Under the Spell of the Blues (1936)

Lyrics by Ken Harrison, music by Edgar Sampson

Introduced by Chick Webb and His Orchestra, vocal by Ella Fitzgerald (Decca). **360407-4**

Until the Real Thing Comes Along (1936)

Lyrics and music by Sammy Cahn, Saul Chaplin, L.E. Freeman, Mann Holiner, and Alberta Nichols

Introduced by Andy Kirk and His Twelve Clouds of Joy, vocal by Pha Terrell. This song became Andy Kirk's signature theme. This is a revision of the 1931 "Till the Real Thing Comes Along" (lyrics by Sammy Cahn and Mann Holiner, music by Alberta Nichols), which was introduced by Ethel Waters and reprised by The Berry Brothers in the 1931 revue *Rhapsody in Black*. **540329-5**

Untitled Instrumental (1940)

This instrumental was recorded by Ella Fitzgerald and Her Famous Orchestra and has been released on Gilles Pétard's Classics series, but the composer remains a mystery, and it is probable that it was never given a title and never intended for release. This gives rise to the theory that it was probably composed by a member of the her orchestra at the time; Dick Vance, Taft Jordan and Ted McRae, all composers, were members at this time.   **400320-4**

Useless Landscape [Inútil Paisagem]
[If You Never Come to Me] (1965)
Portuguese lyrics by Aloysio de Oliveira, English lyrics by Ray Gilbert, music by Antonio Carlos Jobim

Introduced by Antonio Carlos Jobim on a Verve recording.   **690200-7, 800919-3**

Vagabond Dreams (1939)
Lyrics by Jack Lawrence, music by Hoagy Carmichael

Introduced by Hoagy Carmichael on radio and with a recording.   **400125-8**

The Very Thought of You (1934)
Lyrics and music by Ray Nobl

Introduced and recorded by Ray Noble and His Orchestra (Victor), and adopted by Noble as his signature theme.   **620410-4, 740411-9**

Vivo Sonhando *see* **Dreamer**

Volare [Nel Blu, Dipinto di Blu] (1958)
Italian lyrics by Domenico Modugno and Francesco Migliacci, English lyrics by Mitchell Parish, music by Domenico Modugno

Introduced by Domenico Modugno (in Italian). Received First Prize, San Remo (Italy) Festival of Music, 1958; the Grammy Award (NARAS), Song of the Year, 1958; for Best Popular Recording of the Year, 1958; and for Best Male Performance of the Year, 1958. This was the first year that the National Academy of Recording Arts and Sciences presented awards. Popular recording by Domenico Modugno (Decca). With English lyrics by Mr. Parish, it was re-introduceed as "Volare," again achieving success with Dean Martin's Capitol recording that sold more than a million records.   **640304-7**

Vote for Mr. Rhythm (1936)
Lyrics by Leo Robin, music by Ralph Rainger

Introduced by Martha Raye in the 1936 Paramount film *The Big Broadcast of 1937*.   **361029-5, 370208-4**

Wacky Dust (1938)
Lyrics by Stanley Adams, music by Oscar Levant

Introduced and recorded by Chick Webb and His Orchestra, vocal by Ella Fitzgerald (Decca). The "dust" is cocaine.   **380817-1**

Wait Till You See Her/Him (1942)
Lyrics by Lorenz Hart, music by Richard Rodgers

Introduced by Ronald Graham and chorus in the 1942 musical play *By Jupiter!*   **560829-9**

Wake Up and Live (1937)
Lyrics by Mack Gordon, music by Harry Revel

Introduced by Alice Faye and Jack Haley in the 1937 20th Century–Fox film *Wake Up and Live*.   **370324-2**

Walk Right In (1929)
Lyrics by Gus Cannon, music by Rosie Woods

Introduced by Gus Cannon's Jug Stompers (Victor).   **650326-1**

Walkin' by the River (1940)
Lyrics by Robert Sour, music by Una Mae Carlisle

Introduced by Una Mae Carlisle (Bluebird). Revived in 1952 by Ella Fitzgerald (Decca).   **520919-2**

Walkin' My Baby Back Home (1930)
Lyrics and music by Roy Turk and Fred E. Ahlert

Introduced and recorded by Harry Richman and His Orchestra (vocal by Richman) in 1930. Revived by Johnny Ray with a 1952 best-selling Columbia record. Sung by Donald O'Connor in the 1953 Universal-International film *Walkin' My Baby Back Home*.   **520607-3**

Walking in the Sunshine (1967)
Lyrics and music by Roger Miller

Introduced and recorded by Roger Miller (Stash).   **671220-4**

Warm All Over (1956)
Lyrics and music by Frank Loesser

Introduced by Jo Sullivan in the 1956 musical play *The Most Happy Fella*.   **621003-4**

Watch What Happens (Lola's Theme) (1960/1964)
French lyrics by Jacques Demy (1964), English lyrics by Norman Gimbel, music by Michel Legrand

Introduced by Marc Michel (dubbed by George Blanès) in the 1964 Franco-German film *The Umbrellas of Cherbourg*. Used earlier as an instrumental theme in the 1961 Franco-Italian film *Lola*. Introduced with English lyrics by Jean-Paul Vignon (Columbia). Recording by Tony Bennett (Columbia) attained such stature that when the soundtrack for the film was issued on CD, Mr. Bennett's recording was added as a bonus track.   **690200-4**

Water To Drink *see* **Agua de Beber**

Wave [Vou Te Contar] (1967)
Lyrics and music by Antonio Carlos Jobim

Introduced by Antonio Carlos Jobim on his album of the same title (A & M). This composition is one of Jobim's most popular, and has been performed and recorded by numerous jazz artists. Not to be overlooked is the 1969 version with vocals by Elis Regina on the Philips (later Verve) album *Aquarela do Brasil*.   **750717-4, 800917-6**

'Way Back Home (1935)

Lyrics and music by Al Lewis and Tom Waring

Introduced, featured on radio, and recorded by Fred Waring and His Pennsylvanians (Victor). Fred Waring ran a constest on his radio show each week asking for submissions of additional lyrics for this song. He would then have his singers perform the winning entries.   **491109-3**

The Way You Look Tonight (1936)

Lyrics by Dorothy Fields, music by Jerome Kern

Introduced by Fred Astaire in the 1936 RKO film *Swing Time*. Awarded the Academy (AMPAS) Award, Best Original Song, 1936. Fourteen weeks on "Your Hit Parade" in 1936, six as #1.   **500900-9, 630106-1**

We Can't Go On This Way (1938)

Lyrics and music Joe Bishop and Billy Butterfield

Introduced by Billy Butterfield, and covered by Ella for Decca on this recording.   **380503-5**

We Three [My Echo, My Shadow, and Me] (1940)

Lyrics and music by Dick Robertson, Nelson Colgane, and Sammy Mysels.

Introduced and recorded by The Ink Spots (Decca).   **650706-2**

We Three Kings of Orient Are (1863)

Lyrics and music by John Henry Hopkins, Jr.

Dr. Hopkins wrote the lyrics and music for this hymn around 1857 while serving as Rector of Christ Church in Williamsport, Pennsylvania. It was first published in 1863, and is one of the few American carols to achieve international reputation, being particularly popular in Britain.   **600715-4a, 670717-4**

We'll Be Together Again (1945)

Lyrics and music by Frankie Laine and Carl Fischer

Introduced and recorded by Frankie Laine (Mercury). Adopted by Mr. Laine as his signature theme song.   **571015-6**

Wee B. Doinit (1989)

Lyrics and music by Quincy Jones, Ian Prince, and Siedah Garrett

In 1989, Quincy Jonmes assembled a cast of hundreds to participate in the making of his new album *Back on the Block*. "Wee B. Doinit" is Track 5, an a capella groove number with Ella Fitzgerald, Sarah Vaughan, Al Jarreau, Bobby McFerrin, and Take 6.   **890000-1**

Well All Right! [Tonight's the Night!] (1939)

Lyrics and music by Frances Faye, Dan Howell, and Don Raye

A best-selling Decca record by The Andrews Sisters put this number on the charts for a brief period in 1939.   **390921-3**

What a Difference a Day Makes (1934)

English lyrics by Stanley Adams, Spanish lyrics and music by Maria Grever

Originally titled "What a Diff'rence a Day Made." Spanish title "Cuando Vuelva a Tu Lado." Reached # 1 on The Top Ten list in July, 1934.   **910000-1**

What a Friend We Have in Jesus (1868)

Lyrics by Joseph Scriven, music by Charles C. Converse

When asked about the composition of this hymn, Mr. Scriven, who was educated at Trinity College, Dublin, replied: "The Lord and I did it between us." He was a man of high character who, after a great sorrow, spent the rest of his life in a small Canadian community, there giving his services free to the poor. Mr. Converse's tune (Erie) complemented Mr. Scriven's words and vice versa. There are known throughout the world. Mr. Scriven wrote the poem in 1855. Mr. Converse set it to music in 1868.   **670200-2**

What Am I Here For? (1942)

Lyrics by Frankie Laine, music by Duke Ellington

Introduced and recorded as an instrumental by Duke Ellington and His Orchestra. Frankie Laine recorded the lyric version (Mercury).   **611114-1, 651018-1**

What Are You Doing New Year's Eve? (1947)

Lyrics and music by Frank Loesser

Introduced and recorded by Margaret Whiting (Capitol). This has become a standard performed at New Year's Eve party celebrations.   **600716-3**

What Can I Say After I Say I'm Sorry

see **After I Say I'm Sorry**

(Oh! Oh!) What Do You Know About Love? (1938)

Lyrics and music by Jerry Livingston and Mack David

This song was written for Judy Garland to perform in the 1938 MGM film *Love Finds Andy Hardy*. However, Mack Gordon and Harry Revel were contracted to supply the music, and although there is evidence that the song was recorded by Garland, it did not appear in the film. The Livingston-David team did not yet made a name for themselves, and so it is possible that Ella's recording of the number is the only one made.   **380503-2**

What Does It Take? (1951)

Lyrics by Johnny Burke, music by Jimmy Van Heusen

Introduced by Ella Fitzgerald on a Decca recording conducted by Sonny Burke.   **511126-2**

What Is There to Say? (1933)

Lyrics by E.Y. "Yip" Harburg, music by Vernon Duke

Written for a Billy Rose revue which never materialized. Introduced by Jane Froman and Everett Marshall in the 1934 revue *Ziegfeld Follies of 1934*.   **540329-3**

What Does It Take? (1951)

Lyrics by Johnny Burke, music by Jimmy Van Heusen

Introduced by Ella Fitzgerald on a Decca recording conducted by Sonny Burke.   **511226-2**

What Is There to Say? (1933)

Lyrics by E.Y. "Yip" Harburg, music by Vernon Duke

Written for a Billy Rose revue which never materialized. Introduced by Jane Froman and Everett Marshall in the 1934 revue *Ziegfeld Follies of 1934*.   **540329-3**

What Is This Thing Called Love? (1929)

Lyrics and music by Cole Porter

Introduced by Elsie Carlisle and danced by Tilly Losch, Toni Birkmayer, Galanova, and William Cavanaugh in the March, 1929, London production of the musical play *Wake Up and Dream*. Introduced in the U.S. by Frances Shelley and danced by Tilly Losch and Toni Birkmayer in December, 1929, when the production moved to New York.   **560209-8**

What Will I Tell My Heart? (1937)

Lyrics and music by Peter Tinturin, Jack Lawrence, and Irving Gordon

Introduced by Andy Kirk and His Clouds of Joy, vocal by Pha Terrell (Decca).   **571015-5, 780620-4**

What You Want wid Bess? (1935)

Lyrics by DuBose Heyward, music by George Gershwin

Introduced by Anne Wiggins Brown in Act II, Scene 2, of the folk opera *Porgy and Bess*. Gershwin composed this unrhymed song by giving a musical setting to some lines casually lifted from Heyward's libretto. The careful music structure has given it so definite a form, the absence of rhyme and the presence of unbalanced lines is unnoticed. Performed by Dorothy Dandridge (dubbed by Adele Addison) in the 1959 Columba film adaptation.   **570828-3**

What's Going On? (1971)

Lyrics and music by Renaldo Benson, Al Cleveland, and Marvin Gaye

Introduced and recorded by Marvin Gaye (Tamla).   **720602-5, 730705-10**

What's New? (1938)

Lyrics by Johnny Burke, music by Robert Haggart

Introduced and recorded by Bob Crosby and His Bobcats as an instrumental (Bob Haggart was bass player in the band, and Billy Butterfield had an outstanding trumpet solo.) Originally entitled "I'm Free." Bob Haggart later recorded it with Jess Stacy's Band (Varsity); and then with his own orchestra (Capitol), for which the song was the signature theme.   **571028-7**

What's the Matter with Me? (1940)

Lyrics by Al Lewis, music by Terry Shand

Introduced and recorded by Glenn Miller and His Orchestra, vocal by Marian Hutton (Bluebird).   **400122-8, 400126-4**

What's Your Story, Morning Glory? (1940)

Lyrics and music by Mary Lou Williams, Jack Lawrence, and Paul Webster

Introduced and recorded by Andy Kirk and His Clouds of Joy, with Mary Lou Williams at piano and doing the vocal. (Paul Webster was a trumpet player with several big bands, and is not to be confused with the lyricist whose middle name is Francis).   **581122-3**

Whatever Lola Wants (1955)

Lyrics and music by Richard Adler and Jerry Ross

Introduced by Gwen Verdon in the 1955 musical play *Damn Yankees*. Miss Verdon repeated her performance in the 1958 Warner Bros. film adaptation. Sung by Bebe Neuwirth in the 1994 Broadway revival.   **621002-2, 640800-10**

When a Woman Loves a Man (1934)

Lyrics by Johnny Mercer, music by Bernie Hanighen and Gordon Jenkins

Introduced by Gordon Jenkins and His Orchestra. The definitive recording is that of Billie Holiday in 1938 (Vocalion).   **641021-5**

When I Come Back Crying
(Will You Be Laughing at Me?) (1942)

Lyrics and music by Tot Seymour and Vee Lawnhurst

Introduced by Ella Fitzgerald and The Four Keys on this Decca recording.   **420311-2**

When I Get Low, I Get High (1936)

Lyrics and music by Marion Sunshine

Introduced and recorded by Chick Webb and His Orchestra, vocal by Ella Fitzgerald (Decca). **360407-5**

When It's Slumber Time Along the Swanee *see* **Slumber Time Along the Swanee**

When My Sugar Walks Down the Street (1924)

Lyrics and music by Gene Austin, Jimmy McHugh, and Irving Mills

Introduced and recorded by Gene Austin with Aileen Stanley (Victor). This was Jimmy McHugh's first song hit. **410731-3**

When Sunny Gets Blue (1956)

Lyrics by Jack Segal, music by Marvin Fisher

Popular recording by Johnny Mathis (Columbia). This is a jazz standard, with many vocal and instrumental recordings. **641022-3**

When the Hands of the Clock Pray at Midnight (1953)

Lyrics and music by Manny Kurtz

Introduced by Ella Fitzgerald with The Ray Charles Singers on this Decca recording. On the reverse was "Crying in the Chapel" which was on the popularity charts for four weeks, reaching #15. **530611-1**

When the Saints Go Marching In (1896)

Lyrics by Katherine E. Purvis, music by James M. Black

The song may have developed in the Bahama Islands. It was copyrighted by Black with the title "When the Saints Are Marching In." It was recorded in mid-November, 1923, by the (Elkins-Payne) Paramount Jubilee Singers on Paramount record 2073A. **560815-14**

When the Sun Comes Out (1940)

Lyrics by Ted Koehler, music by Harold Arlen

Introduced and recorded by Jimmy Dorsey and His Orchestra, vocal by Helen O'Connell (Decca). **600801-2**

When You're Smiling (1928)

Lyrics and music by Mark Fisher, Joe Goodwin, and Larry Shay

Introduced and recorded by King Oliver and His Orchestra (Victor). **580425-1, 580425-12, 580509-3**

When Your Lover Has Gone (1931)

Lyrics and music by E.A. Swan

Introduced by Joan Blondell in the 1931 Warner Bros. film *Blonde Crazy*. **611114-6, 620630-6, 750519-3, 890316-3**

Where Are You? (1936)

Lyrics by Harold Adamson, music by Jimmy McHugh

Introduced by Gertrude Niesen in the 1937 Universal film *Top of the Town*. The most popular recording is that of Frank Sinatra (Capitol). **680529-1e**

Where or When (1937)

Lyrics by Lorenz Hart, music by Richard Rodgers

Introduced by Mitzi Green and Ray Heatherton in the opening scene of the 1937 musical play *Babes in Arms*. Sung by Betty Jaynes and Douglas MacPhail and Judy Garland in the 1939 MGM film adaptation; and by Lena Horne in the 1948 MGM film *Words and Music*. **560831-4**

Whisper Not (1964)

Lyrics and music by Benny Golson and Leonard Feather

Introduced by Leonard Feather and His Orchestra. Ella liked the song (and Mr. Feather, who was a good friend) so much that when she recorded her last album for Verve, she included this song and insisted that the album title bear its name. **650625-2, 660720-2**

White Christmas (1942)

Lyrics and music by Irving Berlin

First publicly performed by Bing Crosby in a wartime show for the U.S. Armed Forces in the Philippines. Introduced by Bing Crosby and Marjorie Reynolds in the 1942 Paramount film *Holiday Inn*. Sung by Mr. Crosby in the 1946 MGM film *Blue Skies*, and again in the 1953 Paramount film *White Christmas*, which was inspired by the phenomenal success of the song. Estimated to be the world's most valuable popular song, with more than 200 million records sold to date. Awarded the Academy Award, Best Original Song, 1942. **531213-1, 600716-4, 600805-4**

Who? (1925)

Lyrics by Otto Harbach and Oscar Hammerstein II, music by Jerome Kern

Introduced by Marilyn Miller and Paul Frawley in the musical play *Sunny*. Sung by Anna Neagle and John Carroll in the 1941 RKO-Radio film version; and by Judy Garland as Marilyn Miller in the 1946 MGM film *Till the Clouds Roll By*. **660728-1a, 660729-1a**

Who Are You? (1940)

Lyrics by Lorenz Hart, music by Richard Rodgers

Introduced by Allan Jones in the 1940 Universal film *The Boys from Syracuse*. This was written especially for the film adaptation of the 1938 musical play. **411105-1**

Who Cares? (1931)

Lyrics by Ira Gershwin, music by George Gershwin

Introduced by William Gaxton and Lois Moran and ensemble in the 1931 musical play *Of Thee I Sing!*
590716-2, 830523-4

Who Walks In When I Walk Out? (1934)

Lyrics and music by Al Goodhart, Al Hoffman, and Ralph Freed

Introduced by Ray Noble and His Orchestra, vocal by Al Bowlly (Victor).   **511123-4**

Who Ya Hunchin'? (1939)

Music by Ella Fitzgerald and Chick Webb

Introduced by Chick Webb and His Orchestra in performance at the Roseland Ballroom, New York City. Broadcast on NBC radio during a performance in 1939, and recorded by RCA Victor for NBC Thesaurus transcriptions. Also broadcast by Ella Fitzgerald and Her Famous Orchestra in 1940.   **400304-6**

Who's Afraid? (Not I, Not I) (1954)

Lyrics by Jack Lawrence, music by Doris Tauber

Introduced by Tony Martin on an RCA recording, and covered by Ella on this Decca recording. **540325-4**

Who's Sorry Now? (1923)

Lyrics by Bert Kalmar and Harry Ruby, music by Ted Snyder

Introduced by Van and Schenck in vaudeville. Featured in the 1946 David L. Loewe Marx Brothers film *A Night in Casablanca*. Popular revival in 1957 by Connie Francis, at which time it reached "Your Hit Parade" for six weeks.   **600419-1**

Why Can't You Behave? (1948)

Lyrics and music by Cole Porter

Introduced by Lisa Kirk and Harold Lang in the 1948 musical play *Kiss Me, Kate!* Sung by Ann Miller in the 1953 MGM film adaptation.   **560207-7**

Why Don't You Do Right? (1942)

Lyrics and music by Joe McCoy

Introduced and recorded by Lil Green (Bluebird). Popular recordings by Benny Goodman and His Orchestra, vocal by Peggy Lee (Columbia).
530911-8, 531118-3, 560202-3, **860228-3**

Why Was I Born? (1929)

Lyrics by Oscar Hammerstein II, music by Jerome Kern

A blues written for and introduced by Helen Morgan in the 1929 musical play *Sweet Adeline*. Sung by Wini Shaw and reprised by Irene Dunne in the 1934 Warner Bros. film adaptation.   **610211-4a, 630106-4**

Willow, Weep for Me (1932)

Lyrics and music by Ann Ronell

Introduced and recorded by Paul Whiteman and His Orchestra, vocal by Irene Taylor (Victor). Featured in night club appearances, recorded by, and identified with Ruth Etting. Ronell dedicated the song to George Gershwin, "the only song ever dedicated to him," maintains Ronell, "and the only popular song published with a dedication line, a custom never observed in the popular music publishing field." (However, see "Sweet Sue, Just You.")
580810-15, **590325-2, 700104-1, 710507-2, 831000-2**

Winter Wonderland (1934)

Lyrics by Richard B. Smith, music by Felix Bernard

A perennial Christmas favorite with every singer and orchestra who has made a Christmas album. The 1950 Andrews Sisters Decca recording sold more than a million copies.   **600716-1**

Wishful Thinking (1940)

Lyrics by Leo Robin, music by Ralph Rainger

Introduced by Virginia Gilmore in the 1940 20th Century–Fox film *Tall, Dark and Handsome*. **410108-3**

Witchcraft (1957)

Lyrics by Carolyn Leigh, music by Cy Coleman

Originally written by Coleman and Leigh for an unproduced revue, the song was introduced by Gerry Matthews in Julius Monk's night-club revue *Take Five*. Popular recording by Frank Sinatra (Capitol).
580810-8, 580810-20, 580810-31, **610211-7**, 610518-20, 610519-2, 610520-9, 610520-31, 640203-9

With a Song in My Heart (1929)

Lyrics by Lorenz Hart, music by Richard Rodgers

Introduced by Lillian Taiz and John Hundley in the 1929 musical play *Spring Is Here*. Sung by Bernice Claire and Frank Albertson in the 1930 First National film adaptation. Sung by Susan Hayward (dubbed by Jane Froman) in the 1952 20th Century–Fox film *With a Song in My Heart*. The song was a special favorite of, and identified with, Jane Froman.   **560829-6**

Without Love (1954)

Lyrics and music by Cole Porter

Introduced by Hildegard Neff in the 1955 musical play *Silk Stockings*. Used instrumentally, but not sung, in the 1957 MGM film adaptation.   **720612-7**

Wives and Lovers (1963)

Lyrics by Hal David, music by Burt Bacharach

Inspired by the 1963 Paramount film *Wives and Lovers,* the song was introduced by Jack Jones with a Kapp recording that received the Grammy Award, Best Solos Vocal Performance, Male, 1963.

650626-1, **660208-8, 660222-2, 660720-11, 660728-3, 660729-3**

Woe Is Me (1938)

Lyrics by Eliot Daniel, music by Jack Lawrence

Introduced by Chick Webb and His Orchestra, vocal by Ella Fitzgerald (Decca).   **380818-2**

Would You Like to Take a Walk? (1930)

Lyrics by Mort Dixon and Billy Rose, music by Harry Warren

Introduced by Hannah Williams and Hal Thompson in the 1930 musical revue *Sweet and Low,* and retained for the 1931 Billy Rose musical revue *Crazy Quilt.*   **511123-3**

Yellow Man (1970)

Lyrics and music by Randy Newman

Introduced and recorded by Randy Newman on his 1970 Reprise album *12 Songs.*   **690526-3**

Yesterdays (1933)

Lyrics by Otto Harbach, music by Jerome Kern

Introduced by Faye Templeton in the 1933 musical play *Roberta.* Sung by Irene Dunne in the 1935 RKO film adaptation; by a chorus in the 1946 MGM film *Till the Clouds Rolls By*; and by Kathryn Grayson, and danced by Marge and Gower Champion, in the 1952 MGM film adaptation *Lovely to Love At.*   **630106-3**

The Yodelin' Jive (1939)

Lyrics and music by Hughie Prince and Don Raye

Introduced by Hughie Prince in performance and with a recording. Ella's version was the best around, but Decca opined that it was too puerile even for Ella.   **400000-3**

You Are the Sunshine of My Life (1973)

Lyrics and music by Stevie Wonder

Introduced and recorded by Stevie Wonder (Tamla).   **770714-10**

You'd Better Love Me (1964)

Lyrics and music by Hugh Martin and Timothy Gray

Introduced by Tammy Grimes in the musical play *High Spirits.*   **700520-7**

You Brought a New Kind of Love to Me (1930)

Lyrics by Irving Kahal, music by Pierre Norman and Sammy Fain

Introduced by Maurice Chevalier in the 1930 Paramount film *The Big Pond.*   **581123-12,** 610512-3

You Can Depend on Me (1932)

Lyrics and music by Charles Carpenter, Louis Dunlap, and Earl Hines

Introduced by recorded by Earl "Fatha" Hines and His Orchestra (Bluebird).   **620130-4**

You Can Have Him (1948)

Lyrics and music by Irving Berlin

Introduced by Mary McCarty and Allyn McLerie in the 1949 musical play *Miss Liberty.*   **580314-2**

You Can't Be Mine (and Someone Else's Too) (1938)

Lyrics and music by J.C. Johnson and Chick Webb

Introduced by Ella Fitzgerald and Her Savoy Eight, vocal by Ella Fitzgerald (Decca).   380503-3, **380503-4**

You Couldn't Be Cuter (1938)

Lyrics by Dorothy Fields, music by Jerome Kern

Introduced by Irene Dunne in the 1938 RKO film *Joy of Living.*   **630107-1**

You Do Something to Me (1929)

Lyrics and music by Cole Porter

Introduced by William Gaxton and Genevieve Tobin in the 1929 musical play *Fifty Million Frenchmen.*   **560208-2, 710721-2c**

You Don't Know My Mind (1923)

Lyrics by Samuel H. Gray and Virginia Liston, music by Clarence Williams

Introduced and first recorded by Virginia Liston.   **631029-1**

You Don't Know What Love Is (1941)

Lyrics and music by Don Raye and Gene DePaul

Introduced by Carol Bruce in the 1941 Universal film *Keep 'Em Flying.*   **411028-2,** 580810-30

You Go to My Head (1938)

Lyrics by Haven Gillespie, music by J. Fred Coots

Written in 1936, the song was refused publication by most leading publishers before Remick decided to take a chance with it. Introduced and recorded by Larry Clinton, vocal by Bea Wain. Ella used this song many times in a medley with "Goin' Out of My Head."

500900-3, **590325-1**, 660727-3a, **660728-8a,**
660729-7a, 680518-7a, 700520-10b, **730828-8**

(You Got Me) Singing the Blues see **Singing the Blues**

You Hit the Spot (1935)

Lyrics by Mack Gordon, music by Harry Revel

Introduced by Frances Langford, with the assistance of Jack Oakie and Mack Gordon, in the 1936 RKO-Radio film *Collegiate*.   **360219-2, 581122-1**

You Keep Coming Back Like a Song (1946)

Lyrics and music by Irving Berlin

Introduced by Bing Crosby in the 1946 MGM film *Blue Skies*. Nominated for an Academy Award, Best Original Song, 1946.   **580317-1**

You Leave Me Breathless (1938)

Lyrics by Ralph Freed, music by Frederick Hollander

Introduced by Fred McMurray and Harriet Hilliard in the 1938 Paramount film *Coconut Grove*.   **540330-4**

You Make Me Feel So Young (1946)

Lyrics by Mack Gordon, music by Josef Myrow

Introduced by Vera-Ellen (dubbed by Carol Stewart) and Frank Lattimore (dubbed by Del Porter) in the 1946 20th Century–Fox film *Three Little Girls in Blue*.   **590711-6**

You Showed Me the Way (1937)

Lyrics by Ella Fitzgerald, music by Benny Green, Teddy McRae, and Chick Webb

Introduced by Chick Webb and His Orchestra, vocal by Ella Fitzgerald (Decca).   **370324-4**

You Stepped Out of a Dream (1940)

Lyrics by Gus Kahn, music by Nacio Herb Brown

Introduced by Tony Martin in the 1940 MGM film *Ziegfeld Girl*.   **680528-2f**

You Took Advantage of Me (1928)

Lyrics by Lorenz Hart, music by Richard Rodgers

Introduced by Busby Berkeley and Joyce Barbour and ensemble in the 1928 musical play *Present Arms*. Performed by Lillian Tashman and Fred Santley in the 1930 RKO film adaptation *Leathernecking*. In the early 1930s, the Prince of Wales (later David, Duke of Windsor) was so delighted with Morton Downey's performance at the Café de Paris that he requested Downey repeat the song nine times.   **560831-6, 760130-3**

You Turned the Tables on Me (1936)

Lyrics by Sidney D. Mitchell, music by Louis Alter

Introduced by Alice Faye in the 1936 20th Century–Fox film *Sing, Baby, Sing*.   **471223-2, 570724-6, 730705-4**

You Won't Be Satisfied (Until You Break My Heart) (1945)

Lyrics and music by Freddie James and Larry Stock

Popular recordings by the orchestras of Les Brown, vocal by Doris Day (Columbia); Ella Fitzgerald and Louis Armstrong, with Bob Haggart's Orchestra; and by Perry Como with The Satisfiers (Victor).   **460118-1, 560815-12**

You'd Be So Nice to Come Home To (1942)

Lyrics and music by Cole Porter

Introduced by Don Ameche and Janet Blair in the 1943 Columbia film *Something to Shout About*. Nominated for an Academy Award, Best Original Song, 1943.   640203-1, **640729-18**

(If You Can't Sing It) You'll Have To Swing It see **Mr. Paganini**

You'll Never Know (1943)

Lyrics by Mack Gordon, music by Harry Warren

Introduced by Alice Faye in the 1943 20th Century–Fox film *Hello, Frisco, Hello*. Also sung by Miss Faye in the 1944 20th Century–Fox film *Four Jills in a Jeep*. Awarded the Academy Award, Best Original Song, 1943.   **550401-3**

Your Red Wagon (1947)

Lyrics by Don Raye, music by Richard M. Jones and Gene De-Paul

Based on a 1940 instrumental blues composition by Richard M. Jones, the song was given lyrics in 1947 and recorded by The Andrews Sisters (Decca).   **580701-1**, 580810-1

You're a Sweetheart (1937)

Lyrics by Harold Adamson, music by Jimmy McHugh

Introduced by Alice Faye and George Murphy in the 1937 Universal film *You're a Sweetheart*. Popular recording by Alice Faye (Brunswick). Sung by Frank Sinatra in the 1952 Universal film *Meet Danny Wilson*.   **680528-1f**

You're an Old Smoothie (1932)

Lyrics by Buddy DeSylva, music by Richard A. Whiting and Nacio Herb Brown

Introduced by Ethel Merman and Jack Haley in the

1932 musical play *Take a Chance*. This song was originally written for a show called *Humpty-Dumpty*, which proved such a dud that it closed out-of-town and the entire production scrapped. **581122-8, 581123-1**

You're Blasé (1932)

Lyrics by Bruce Sievier, music by Ord Hamilton

Introduced by Binnie Hale in the 1932 London production of the musical play *Bow Bells*. Popular recordings by the orchestras of Ambrose (Victor) and Jack Hylton (Brunswick). **571015-2, 730828-4**

You're Breaking In a New Heart (1947)

Lyrics and music by Ervin Drake and Jimmy Shirl

Introduced by Ella Fitzgerald with Bob Haggart and His Orchestra on this Decca recording.
470711-1, **470722-2**

You're Driving Me Crazy (1930)

Lyrics and music by Walter Donaldson

Originally called "What Did You Do to Me?" Mr. Donaldson turned it over to Guy Lombardo. Just before Lombardo was to introduce it, Donaldson telephoned him to change the title. Lombardo played the song on his radio program every night for a week, and within three days the sheet-music sales had exceeded 100,000 copies. Interpolated by Adele Astaire in the 1930 musical play *Smiles*, with Eddy Foy, Jr., and a chorus of girls.
520816-4, 610123-2, **610211-5, 610221-4, 610516-3,** 610518-8, 610520-1, **610825-2, 820204-3**

You're Gonna Hear from Me (1965)

Lyrics by Dory Langdon (Previn), music by André Previn

Introduced by Natalie Wood (dubbed by Jackie Ward) in the 1965 Warner Bros. film *Inside Daisy Clover*.
660406-2

You're Gonna Lose Your Gal (1933)

Lyrics by Joe Young, music by James V. Monaco

Popular recordings by Jan Garber and His Orchestra (Victor), and by Glen Gray and The Casa Loma Orchestra, vocal by Pee Wee Hunt (Brunswick). Sung by Doris Day and Gordon MacRae in the 1951 Warner Bros. film *Starlift*. **391012-1**

You're Laughing at Me (1937)

Lyrics and music by Irving Berlin

Introduced by Dick Powell in the 1937 20th Century–Fox film *On the Avenue*. **580317-4**

You're My Thrill (1933)

Lyrics by Sidney Clare, music by Jay Gorney

Introduced by Lya Lys in the 1933 Fox film *Jimmy and Sally*. **610622-5**

You're the Top (1934)

Lyrics and music by Cole Porter

Introduced by Ethel Merman and William Gaxton in the 1934 musical play *Anything Goes*. Sung by Bing Crosby and Ethel Merman in the 1936 Paramount film adaptation; by Ginny Simms and Cary Grant in the 1946 Warner Bros. film *Night and Day*; by Bing Crosby and Mitzi Gaynor in the 1956 Paramount film adaptation; and by Burt Reynolds, Madeline Kahn, Dulio del Prete and Cybil Shepard in the 1975 20th Century–Fox film *At Long Last Love*.
560208-6, 560327-3

You've Changed (1942)

Lyrics by Bill Cary, music by Carl Fisher

Popular recordings by the orchestras of Harry James, vocal by Dick Haymes (Columbia); Russ Case, vocal by Bill Farrell (MGM); and Harold Mooney, vocal by Connie Russell (Capitol). Sung by Diana Ross in the 1972 Paramount film *Lady Sings the Blues*.
650625-3, **660720-8, 670128-2, 670326-2, 790712-11**

You've Got a Friend (1971)

Lyrics and music by Carole King

Introduced and recorded by Carole King. James Taylor's recording was awarded the Grammy (NARAS) Awards for Best Vocal Performance, Best Solo Vocal Performance, and Best Contemporary Popular Vocal Performance (Male), 1971. Carole King was awarded the Grammy Award for Song of the Year (songwriter's award), 1971.
720602-4, *740411-7*

You've Got What Gets Me (1932)

Lyrics by Ira Gershwin, music by George Gershwin

Introduced by Eddie Quillan and Arlene Judge in the 1932 RKO-Radio film *Girl Crazy*, the first film version of the 1930 musical play, for which this song was especially written. **590107-5**

An "Album" of Songs Ella Recorded That You've Never Heard Her Sing

(Songs Ella Recorded That Have Never Been Released)

Am I Blue? (Clark-Akst) (610513-3)

Babalu (Russell-Lecuona) (530911-7)

Baby, Bye-Bye (Delafose) (660914-8)

Bernie's Tune (Miller-Stoller-Lieber) (560202-9)

The Birth of the Blues (DeSylva-Brown-Henderson) (530911-4)

The Boy Next Door (Blane-Martin) (500900-6)

Christmas Island (Moraine) (600715-5)

Dixie (Emmett) (531118-11b)

Ella's Blues (Fitzgerald) (640800-20)

Ella's Twist (Fitzgerald) (620630-27)

Fools Rush In (Mercer-Bloom) (560121-7a)

Glad To Be Unhappy (Hart-Rodgers) (560121-7b)

Hands Off the Man (The Flim Flam Man) (Nyro) (700124-3)

He's My Kind of Boy (unknown authors) (620630-1)

Hey, There! (Adler-Ross) (540918-2)

The Huckle-Buck (Alfred-Gibson) (500900-10)

I Don't Know Why (I Love You Like I Do) (Turk-Ahlert) (691023-1)

I Found a New Baby (Palmer-Williams) (610513-1)

I Had To Find Out for Myself (Lief-Sherwin) (530327-6)

I'll Remember April (Raye-Johnston-DePaul) (500900-4)

In the Mood (Razaf-Garland) (700105-1)

In the Wee Small Hours of the Morning (Hilliard-Mann) (610516-11)

It All Depends on You (DeSylva-Brown-Henderson) (560202-1)

It Had to Be You (Kahn-Jones) (620629-15)

It's a Good Day (Lee-Barbour) (520325-2)

The Lady's in Love with You (Loesser-Lane) (610518-1)

Little Boy (Bergman-Bergman-Mancini) (560202-16)

Once It Was All Right, Now... (Nyro) (700123-1)

One O'Clock Jump (Basie) (530911-9)

Oo-Bop-Sh'Bam (Fuller-Robets-Gillespie) (580810-29)

Pennies from Heaven (Burke-Johnston) (590325-6)

Run, Joe (Merrick-Willoughby-Jordan) (500900-5)

Salty Lips (Basie-Williams-Fitzgerald) (560625-3)

S'posin' (Razaf-Denniker) (530911-1)

Sweethearts on Parade (Newman-Lombardo) (531118-11a)

There Are Such Things (Baer-Adams-Meyer) (640304-5)

There! I've Said It Again (Evans-Mann) (640303-1)

They Pass by Singin' (from *Porgy and Bess*) (Heyward-Gershwin) (570819-4)

Timer (Nyro) (700124-3)

When Sunny Gets Blue (Segal-Fisher) (641022-3)

You're Gonna Hear from Me (Langdon-Previn) (660406-2)

Looking the list over, perhaps we should omit a couple, but what a great 2-CD album these would make! Write letters, write letters, write letters!

Appendices

A. They Wrote the Songs Ella Sings: The Lyricists and Composers

(L) = lyricist only

(C) = composer only

Ackers, Andrew Acquarulo (Andy) (1919–1978), composer
    (I'm Wearing) A New Shade of Blue

Ackley, Alfred Henry (1887–1960), composer-lyricist
    I Shall Not Be Moved

Adair, Thomas Montgomery (Tom) (b. 1913), lyricist
    Everything Happens to Me
    There's No You

Adam, Adolphe Charles (1803–1856), composer
    O Holy Night (Cantique de Nöel)

Adams, Stanley (b. 1907), lyricist
    Sing Me a Swing Song (and Let Me Dance)
    There Are Such Things
    Wacky Dust

Adamson, Harold (b. 1906), lyricist
    Everything I Have Is Yours
    I Didn't Mean a Word I Said
    It's a Wonderful World
    720 in the Books
    Thank Your Stars
    This Changing World
    Where Are You?
    You're a Sweetheart

Adler, Richard (b. 1921), composer-lyricist
    Hernando's Hideaway
    Hey, There!
    Steam Heat
    Whatever Lola Wants

Ager, Milton (1893–1979), composer
    Hard-Hearted Hannah (The Vamp of Savannah)

Ahbez, Eden (b. 1908), composer-lyricist
    Nature Boy

Ahlert, Fred E. (1892–1953), composer
    I Don't Know Why (I Love You Like I Do)
    Mean to Me
    There's Frost on the Moon
    Walkin' My Baby Back Home

Akst, Harry (1894–1963), composer
    Am I Blue?
    Guilty

Albrecht, Elmer (1901–1959), composer
    Elmer's Tune

Alexander, Van (Al Feldman) (b. 1915), composer-lyricist
    A-Tisket, A-Tasket
    Gotta Pebble in My Shoe (C)
    I Found My Yellow Basket

Alfred, Roy, lyricist
    The Huckle-Buck

Allen, Robert (b. 1927), composer-lyricist
    Gee, But I'm Glad To Know (That You Love Me)

Allen, Stephen Valentine Patrick William (Steve)
        (b. 1921), composer-lyricist
    Cutie Pants
    Oh, What a Night for Love!
    This Could Be the Start of Something Big

Alter, Louis (1902–1980), composer
    My Kinda Love
    You Turned the Tables on Me

Altman, Arthur (b. 1912), composer
    All or Nothing at All

Anderson, Leroy (1908–1975), composer
    Sleigh Ride

Anderson, Maxwell (1888–1959), lyricist
    September Song

André, Fabian (1910–1960), composer
    Dream a Little Dream of Me

Arlen, Harold [Hyman Arluck] (1905–1986), composer
    Ac-Cent-Tchu-Ate the Positive
    As Long As I Live
    Between the Devil and the Deep Blue Sea
    Blues in the Night
    Come Rain or Come Shine
    Ding-Dong! The Witch Is Dead
    Get Happy!
    Happiness Is (Just) a Thing Called Joe
    Hooray for Love
    I Gotta Right To Sing the Blues
    I've Got the World on a String
    Ill Wind
    It Was Written in the Stars
    Let's Fall in Love
    Let's Take a Walk Around the Block
    The Man That Got Away
    My Shining Hour
    One for My Baby (And One More for the Road)
    Out of This World
    Over the Rainbow
    (It's Only a) Paper Moon
    Sing, My Heart
    Stormy Weather
    That Old Black Magic
    This Time the Dream's on Me
    When the Sun Comes Out
Armatrading, Joan, composer-lyricist
    I Can't Lie to Myself
Armstrong, Louis Daniel (Satchmo) (1900–1971),
    composer-lyricist
    Ol' Man Mose
    Struttin' with Some Barbeque
Arnheim, Gus (1897–1955), composer-lyricist
    I Cried for You
    Sweet and Lovely
Austin, Gene (1900–1973), composer-lyricist
    When My Sugar Walks Down the Street
Austin, Lovie [Cora Calhoun] (1887–1972)
    Down-Hearted Blues
Bacharach, Burt F. (b. 1928), composer
    A House Is Not a Home
    I'll Never Fall in Love Again
    This Girl's/Guy's in Love with You
    Wives and Lovers
Baer, Abel (1893–1976), composer, lyricist
    Don't Wake Me Up
    My Mother's Eyes
    There Are Such Things
Bagdasarian, Ross (1919–1972), composer, lyricist
    Come On-a My House
Baker, Phil (1898–1963), composer
    Did You Mean It?

    Love and Kisses
Barbour, Dave, composer, lyricist
    It's a Good Day
Barefield, Eddie, composer
    Lindy Hoppers' Delight
Barouh, Pierre, lyricist
    A Man and a Woman (Une Homme et Une Femme)
Barris, Harry (1905–1962), composer
    I Surrender, Dear
Bartholemew, Dave (b. 1920), composer, lyricist
    I'm Walkin'
Basie, William (Count) (1904–1984), composer, lyricist
    Blue and Sentimental (C)
    Good Morning, Blues
    One O'Clock Jump (C)
    Party Blues
    Salty Lips
Bassman, George (b. 1914), composer
    I'm Getting Sentimental over You
Bates, Charles L. (1897–1937), lyricist
    Hard Hearted Hannah (the Vamp of Savannah)
Beal, Charles (Charlie) (b. 1908), composer, lyricist
    If You Only Knew
    Sugar Pie
Belle, Barbara [Barbara Belle Newman] (b. 1922),
    composer, lyricist
    A Sunday Kind of Love
Ben, Jorge (Jorge Duílio Menezes), composer
    Mas, Que Nada
Benjamin, Bennie (b. 1907), composer, lyricist
    Can Anyone Explain?
    I'll Never Be Free
Bennard, George (1873–1958), composer, lyricist
    The Old Rugged Cross
Benson, Renaldo, composer, lyricist
    What's Going On?
Bergantine, Borney (1909–1954), composer
    My Happiness
Bergman, Alan, lyricist
    Make Me Rainbows
Bergman, Marilyn Keith, lyricist
    Make Me Rainbow
Berk, Morty (1900–1955), composer, lyricist
    Tea Leaves
Berlin, Irving (Israel Baline) (1888–1989), composer,
    lyricist
    Alexander's Ragtime Band
    All by Myself
    Always
    Blue Skies
    Budella (Blue Skies)
    Change Partners
    Cheek to Cheek

Everybody Step
Get Thee Behind Me, Satan
Heat Wave
How About Me?
How Deep Is the Ocean
How's Chances
I Never Had a Chance
I Used To Be Color Blind
I'm Putting All My Eggs in One Basket
I've Got My Love To Keep Me Warm
Isn't This a Lovely Day (To Be Caught in the Rain)
It's a Lovely Day Today
Lazy
Let Yourself Go
Let's Face the Music and Dance
No Strings (I'm Fancy Free)
Now It Can Be Told
Pack Up Your Sins and Go to the Devil
Puttin' on the Ritz
Reaching for the Moon
Russian Lullaby
(Let's Go) Slumming on Park Avenue
The Song Is Ended
Supper Time
This Year's Kisses
Top Hat, White Tie and Tails
White Christmas
You Can Have Him
You Keep Coming Back Like a Song
You're Laughing at Me
Bernard, Felix (1897–1944), lyricist
   Winter Wonderland
Bernie, Saul, composer, lyricist
   Don't Cry, Cry-Baby
Bernier, Buddy (b. 1910), composer, lyricist
   Hurry Home
   This Time It's Real
Best, William, composer
   (I Love You) For Sentimental Reasons
Bigard, Albany Leon (Barney) (1906–1980), composer
   C-Jam Blues
   Mood Indigo
Bigelow, Robert Wilcox (Bob) (1890–1965), lyricist
   Hard Hearted Hannah (the Vamp of Savannah)
Biggs, Howard, composer, lyricist
   Melancholy Me
Bird, Bill, composer, lyricist
   Broadway
Bishop, Joe (1907–1976), composer, lyricist
   It's Foxy
   My Baby Likes to Be-Bop
Black, James E., composer
   When the Saints Go Marching In

Blackburn, John M. (b. 1913), lyricist
   Moonlight in Vermont
Blake, James Hubert (Eubie) (1883–1983), composer
   Memories of You
Blane, Ralph [Ralph Blane Hunsecker] (b. 1914), lyricist
   The Boy Next Door
   Have Yourself a Merry Little Christmas
   Someone Like You
Bliss, Philip Paul (1838–1876), composer, lyricist
   Let the Lower Lights Be Burning
Blitzstein, Marc (1905–1964), lyricist
   Mack The Knife (Moritat)
Block, Martin, composer, lyricist
   A New Moon and an Old Serenade
Bloom, Rube (1902–1976), composer
   Day In — Day Out
   Don't Worry 'Bout Me
   Fools Rush In
   Give Me the Simple Life
   I Can't Face the Music (Without Singing the Blues)
Bock, Jerrold (Jerry) (b. 1928), composer
   Too Close for Comfort
Boland, Clay A. (1903–1963), composer
   The Gypsy in My Soul
Boulanger, Georges, composer
   My Prayer
Bowman, Brooks (1913–1937), composer, lyricist
   East of the Sun and West of the Moon
Bradford, Parker, composer, lyricist
   (My Darling) Clementine
Bradshaw, Myron Carlton (Tiny) (1905–1958), composer,
   lyricist
   The Jersey Bounce (C)
   Later
Braham, Philip (1881–1934), composer
   Limehouse Blues
Brand, Oscar (b. 1920), composer, lyricist
   A Guy Is a Guy
Brecht, Bertolt Eugen Friedrich (1898–1956), lyricist
   Mack The Knife (Moritat)
Brent, Earl Karl (1914–1977), lyricist
   Angel Eyes
Brewster, Jimmy, composer, lyricist
   If I Give My Heart to You
Brooks, Harry (1895–1970), composer
   Ain't Misbehavin'
   Strictly from Dixie
Brooks, Jack (1912–1971), lyricist
   The Cricket Song
   Lonesome Gal
Brooks, Phillips (1835–1893), lyricist
   O Little Town of Bethlehem
Brooks, Pierce, composer, lyricist

Strictly from Dixie
Brooks, Shelton (1886–1975), composer, lyricist
    The Darktown Strutters' Ball
    Some of These Days
Brown, Frankie, composer, lyricist
    Born To Lose
Brown, Lester Raymond (Les) (b. 1912), composer
    Sentimental Journey
Brown, Lew [Louis Brownstein] (1893–1958), lyricist
    The Birth of the Blues
    Comes Love
    I'm the Lonesomest Gal in Town
    It All Depends on You
    Shine
    That Old Feeling
    The Thrill Is Gone
Brown, Nacio Herb (1896–1964), composer
    All I Do Is Dream of You
    I've Got a Feelin' You're Foolin'
    You Stepped Out of a Dream
    You're an Old Smoothie
Brown, Peter, composer, lyricist
    Sunshine of Your Love
Brown, Ray (b. 1926), composer
    No Sense
Bruce, John Symon Asher (b. 1943), composer, lyricist
    Sunshine of Your Love
Bryan, Tim, composer, lyricist
    If You Don't, I Know Who Will
Burke, Joe, composer
    My Favorite Song
Burke, Johnny (1908–1964), lyricist
    Chicago Style
    Here's That Rainy Day
    Imagination
    Like Someone in Love
    Misty
    Moonlight Becomes You
    Pennies from Heaven
    Polka Dots and Moonbeams
    What's New?
Burke, Joseph Francis (Sonny) (1914–1950), composer
    Black Coffee
    Midnight Sun
Burnett, Ernie (1884–1959), composer
    My Melancholy Baby
Burns, Ralph (b. 1922), composer
    Ah! Men! Ah! Women!
    Early Autumn
Burwell, Clifford R. (1898–1976), composer
    Sweet Lorraine
Caesar, Irving (b. 1895), lyricist
    I Want To Be Happy

Tea for Two
Cahn, Sammy [Samuel Cohen] (b. 1913), lyricist
    Bei Mir Bist du Schön
    Day by Day
    Dedicated to You
    Everybody's Wrong but Me
    If You Ever Should Leave
    The Impatient Years
    It's My Turn Now
    Just a Simple Melody
    Let It Snow! Let It Snow! Let It Snow!
    Love, You're Just a Laugh
    Pete Kelly's Blues
    Please Be Kind
    Saving Myself for You
    The Secret of Christmas
    Teach Me Tonight
    The Tender Trap
    Time After Time
    Until the Real Thing Comes Along
Caldwell, Anne [Anne Caldwell O'Dea] (1867–1936),
        lyricist
    I Know That You Know
Calloway, Cab, composer, lyricist
    (Hep! Hep!) The Jumpin' Jive
Campbell, James (Jimmy) (1903–1967),
        composer, lyricist
    If I Had You
    aaTry a Little Tenderness
Cannon, Gus (b. 1883), lyricist
    Walk Right In
Cannon, Hughie (1877–1912), composer, lyricist
    Bill Bailey, Won't You Please Come Home?
Capano, Francis Xavier (Frank) (1899–1956),
        composer, lyricist
    Tea Leaves
Care, Ralph, composer, lyricist
    I Need
Carey, William D. (Bill) (b. 1916), lyricist
    The Sun Forgot To Shine This Morning
    You've Changed
Carlisle, Una Mae (1918–1956), composer
    Walkin' by the River
Carmichael, Hoagland Howard (Hoagy) (1899–1981),
        composer, lyricist
    Georgia on My Mind
    Heart and Soul
    The Nearness of You
    Sing Me a Swing Song (and Let Me Dance)
    Skylark
    Star Dust
    Vagbond Dreams
Carney, Harry Howell (1910–1974), composer

Rockin' in Rhythm

Carpenter, Charles E. (b. 1912), composer, lyricist
  A Lover Is Blue
  You Can Depend on Me

Carr, Elizabeth, lyricist
  Lady Bug

Carr, Leroy (1899–1935), composer, lyricist
  How Long, How Long Blues
  In the Evening (When the Sun Goes Down)

Carson, Jenny Lou, composer, lyricist
  Foolish Tears

Carter, Bennett Lester (Benny) (b. 1907), composer
  Be-Bop Boogie
  Cow-Cow Boogie
  My Kind of Trouble Is You

Carter, Lou, composer, lyricist
  Detour Ahead

Carver, Wayman Alexander (1905–1967),
    composer, lyricist
  Swinging on the Reservation

Casey, Kenneth, Sr. (1899–1965), lyricist
  Sweet Georgia Brown

Cavanaugh, James, composer, lyricist
  Strictly from Dixie

Chaplin, Saul (b. 1912), composer, lyricist
  Bei Mir Bist Du Schön (L)
  Dedicated to You (C)
  Everybody's Wrong but Me (C)
  If You Ever Should Leave (C)
  It's My Turn Now (C)
  Just a Simple Melody (C)
  Love, You're Just a Laugh (C)
  Please Be Kind (C)
  Saving Myself for You (C)
  Until the Real Thing Comes Along

Charles, Jacques, lyricist
  My Man (Mon Homme)

Charles, Ray [Ray Charles Robinson] (b. 1930),
    composer, lyricist
  Hallelujah, I Love Him So

Chatman, Peter, composer, lyricist
  Every Day I Have the Blues

Chernis, Jay (Sir Jay) (b. 1906), composer
  Crying

Chessler, Deborah Shirley (b. 1923), composer, lyricist
  It's Too Soon To Know

Clapton, Eric (b. 1945), composer, lyricist
  Sunshine of Your Love

Clare, Sydney (1892–1972), lyricist
  Please Don't Talk About Me When I'm Gone
  You're My Thrill

Clark, Lester Leroy (Les) (1905–1959), lyricist
  Show Me the Way To Get Out of This World

Clarke, Grant, lyricist
  Am I Blue?

Cleveland, Al, composer, lyricist
  What's Going On?

Clifford, Gordon (1902–1968), lyricist
  I Surrender, Dear

Clinton, Larry (1909–1985), composer, lyricist
  The Dipsy Doodle
  Dodging the Dean
  An Empty Ballroom
  Molasses, Molasses
  My Reverie

Cobb, Arnett (Arnette Cleophus Cobbs) (b. 1918),
    composer, lyricist
  Smooth Sailing

Cochran, Dorcas, lyricist
  Again

Cochran, Hank, composer, lyricist
  Don't Touch Me
  It's Only Love

Cogane, Nelson (b. 1902), composer, lyricist
  Is There Somebody Else?
  We Three (My Echo, My Shadow and Me)

Colby, Robert, composer
  Baby

Cole, Nat "King" [Nathaniel Adams Coles] (1919–1965),
    composer, lyricist
  Because of Rain

Coleman, Cy [Seymour Kaufman] (b. 1929), composer
  The Best Is Yet To Come
  I've Got Your Number
  Witchcraft

Comden, Betty (b. 1915), lyricist
  Give a Little, Get a Little (Love)
  Just in Time
  There Never Was a Was a Baby Like My Baby

Connelly, Reginald (Reg), composer, lyricist
  If I Had You
  Try a Little Tenderness

Converse, Charles Crozat (1832–1918), composer
  What a Friend We Have in Jesus

Cooke, Charles L. (1891–1958), composer, lyricist
  I'm Up a Tree (C)
  Sing Song Swing

Coots, John Frederick (Fred) (1897–1985), composer
  Santa Claus Is Comin' to Town
  She's Tall, She's Tan, She's Terrific
  You Go to My Head

Coslow, Sam (1902–1982), composer, lyricist
  Mr. Paganini (You'll Have To Swing It)
  My Old Flame (L)
  A New Moon and an Old Serenade

Crane, Jimmie [Lloreto Fraieli] (b. 1910), composer, lyricist

If I Give My Heart to You
Creamer, Henry S. (1874–1930), lyricist
   After You've Gone
   If I Could Be with You
Cropper, Steve, composer, lyricist
   Knock on Wood
Crosby, Harry Lillis (Bing) (1904–1979), lyricist
   (I Don't Stand) A Ghost of a Chance (with You)
Dabney, Ford T. (1883–1958), composer
   Shine
Dameron, Tadley (Tad) (1917–1965), composer, lyricist
   Cool Breeze
Dant, Charles Gustave (Bud) (b. 1907), composer, lyricist
   If You Really Love Me
Dash, Julian (1916–1974), composer
   Tuxedo Junction
David, Hal (b. 1921), lyricist
   A House Is Not a Home
   I'll Never Fall in Love Again
   This Girl's/Guy's in Love with You
   Wives and Lovers
David, Mack (b. 1912), composer, lyricist
   Blue and Sentimental (L)
   Candy. (L)
   Dreams Are Made for Children (L)
   I Let a Tear Fall in the River (L)
   I'm Just a Jitterbug (L)
   I'm Just a Lucky So-and-So. (L)
   That's All, Brother
Davis, Benny (1895–1979), composer, lyricist
   All I Need Is You (C)
   (I Put) A Four Leaf Clover in Your Pocket (C)
   She's Tall, She's Tan, She's Terrific (L)
   To You
Davis, Jimmy, composer, lyricist
   Lover Man
Deane, Loryn, lyricist
   Mas Que Nada
Dee, Kool Moe, composer, lyricist
   Jazz Corner of the World
Dee, Sylvia (Josephine Proffitt Faison) (1914–1967), lyricist
   I Taught Him Everything He Knows
   I'm Thrilled
DeLange, Edgar (Eddie) (1904–1949), lyricist
   Darn That Dream
   Deep in a Dream
   Shake Down the Stars
   Solitude
DeLugg, Anne Renfer (b. 1923), composer
   The Beanbag Song
DeLugg, Martin (b. 1921), lyricist
   The Beanbag Song
de Moraes, Vinícius, composer, lyricist

   A Felicidade
   Agua de Beber [Water To Drink]
   The Girl from Ipanema [Garôta de Ipanema]
   He's/She's a Carioca [Ele é Carioca]
   How Insensitive [Insensatez]
   O Nossa Amor [Carnival Samba]
   Só Danço Samba [Jazz Samba]
   Somewhere in the Hills [Favela] [O Morro No Tem Vez]
Demy, Jacques (b. 1931), lyricist
   Watch What Happens [Lola's Theme]
Denniker, Paul, composer
   S'posin'
Dennis, Matt L. (b. 1914), composer
   Angel Eyes
   Everything Happens to Me
   Show Me the Way To Get Out of This World
dePaul, Gene (1919–1988), composer, lyricist
   Cow-Cow Boogie (C)
   He's My Guy
   I'll Remember April (C)
   Love That Boy (C)
   Teach Me Tonight (C)
   You Don't Know What Love Is
   Your Red Wagon (C)
de Roquemaure, Cappeau, lyricist
   O Holy Night (Cantique de Noël)
DeRose, Peter (1896–1953), composer
   All I Need Is You
   Deep Purple
   The Lamp Is Low
   A Marshmallow World
   The Starlit Hour
DeShannon, Jackie (b. 1944), composer, lyricist
   Put a Little Love in Your Heart
DeSylva, B.G. (Buddy), lyricist
   The Birth of the Blues
   It All Depends on You
   Somebody Loves Me
   You're an Old Smoothie
Dick, Dorothy [Dorothy Link] (b. 1900), lyricist
   Call Me Darling
Dietz, Howard (1896–1983), lyricist
   Along Together
   By Myself
   Moanin' Low
Dixon, Mort (1892–1956), lyricist
   Would You Like To Take a Walk?
Domino, Antoine, Jr. (Fats) (b. 1928), composer, lyricist
   I'm Walkin'
Donaldson, Walter (1893–1947), composer, lyricist
   (What Can I Say) After I Say I'm Sorry
   At Sundown

Little White Lies
Love Me or Leave Me (C)
Makin' a Whoopee (C)
You're Driving Me Crazy
Dorsey, James (Jimmy) (1904–1957), composer
I'm Glad There Is You
Dougall, Bernard, lyricist
I'll Be Hard To Handle
Dougherty, Dan (Doc) (1897–1955), composer, lyricist
I'm Confessin' (That I Love You) (C)
One Cigarette for Two
Drake, Ervin Maurice (b. 1919), composer, lyricist
Good Morning, Heartache
Perdido (L)
Something To Live For
You're Breaking In a New Heart
Drake, Milton (b. 1916), lyricist
Hotta Chocolata
Dreyer, Dave, composer, lyricist
Back in Your Own Back Yard
Dubin, Al (1891–1945), lyricist
I Only Have Eyes for You
Indian Summer
Lullaby of Broadway
Sweet and Slow
Duke, Vernon [Vladimir Dukelsky] (1903–1969),
     composer, lyricist
April in Paris (C)
Autumn in New York
Cabin in the Sky (C)
I Can't Get Started (with You)
I'm Not Complainin'
Our Love Is Here To Stay (C)
Taking a Chance on Love (C)
What Is There To Say? (C)
Dunlap, Louis (b. 1911), composer, lyricist
You Can Depend on Me
Duran, Dolores, lyricist
Don't Ever Go Away [Por Causa de Você]
Durham, Eddie (1909–1987), composer, lyricist
Good Morning, Blues
Dwight, John Sullivan (1813–1893), lyricist
O Holy Night [Cantique de Noël]
Ebb, Fred (b. 1932), lyricist
All That Jazz
Eckstine, Billy [Billy Eckstein] (1914–1993),
     composer, lyricist
Cool Breeze
I Want To Talk About You
Edwards, Michael [Michael Slowitzky] (1893–1962),
     composer
Once in a While
Egan, Raymond B., composer, lyricist

I Never Knew (I Could Love Anybody)
Eldridge, Roy, composer
Little Jazz
Eliscu, Edward (b. 1902), lyricist
Great Day!
More Than You Know
Ellington, Edward Kennedy (Duke) (1899–1974),
     composer, lyricist
All Too Soon
Azure
Basella [C-Jam Blues]
Bli-Blip
The Brown-Skinned Gal in a Calico Gown
C-Jam Blues
Caravan
Cotton Tail
Day-Dream
Do Nothin' Till You Hear from Me
Don't Get Around Much Any More
Drop Me Off in Harlem
Duke's Place [C-Jam Blues]
E and D Blues [E for Ella, D for Duke]
Everything but You
A Flower Is a Lovesome Thing
I Ain't Got Nothin' but the Blues
I Didn't Know About You
I Got It Bad (and That Ain't Good)
I Let a Song Go Out of My Heart
I Like the Sunrise
I Wanna Be a Rug-Cutter [I've Gotta Be a Rug-Cutter]
I'm Beginning To See the Light
I'm Gonna Go Fishin'
I'm Just a Lucky So-and-So
Imagine My Frustration
In a Mellow Tone [In a Mellotone]
In a Sentimental Mood
It Don't Mean a Thing (If It Ain't Got That Swing)
Just a-Sittin' and a-Rockin' [Just a-Settin' and a-Rockin']
Just Squeeze Me
Lost in Meditation
Love You Madly
Mood Indigo
Prelude to a Kiss
Rockin' in Rhythm
Rocks in My Bed
Satin Doll
Solitude
Sophisticated Lady
Take Love Easy
Things Ain't What They Used To Be
What Am I Here For?
Ellington, Mercer Kennedy (b. 1919), composer
The Greatest There Is

Things Ain't What They Used To Be
Ellington, Ray, composer
  Old Mother Hubbard
Ellis, Mitchell Herbert (Herb) (b. 1921),
    composer, lyricist
  Detour Ahead
Ellsworth, Robert H. (Bob), composer, lyricist
  Ella
Elman, Ziggy [Harry Finkelman] (1914–1968), composer
  And the Angels Sing
Emmerich, Robert D. (Bob) (b. 1904), composer, lyricist
  Hurry Home
  This Time It's Real
Emmett, Daniel Decatur (Dan) (1815–1904), composer,
    lyricist
  Dixie
Etaoin, N. ("Etaoin" and "Shrdlu" were typesetters'
    placeholders used where a word in a manuscript was
    indecipherable. This name was also used for composi-
    tions that were a collective effort where attribution to
    one writer would be impossible. Some jam numbers
    based on blues or standard harmonies were designated
    "traditional" when first released.)
Evans, Ray, composer, lyricist
  Silver Bells
Evans, Redd Louis (1912–1972), composer, lyricist
  The Frim Fram Sauce
  No Moon at All (L)
  There! I've Said It Again
Eyton, Frank (b. 1894), lyricist
  Body and Soul
Fain, Sammy (1902–1989), composer
  That Old Feeling
  You Brought a New Kind of Love to Me
Farley, Edward J. (b. 1904), composer
  The Music Goes 'Round and 'Round
Farrow, Johnny (b. 1912), composer
  (I'm Wearing) A New Shade of Blue
Faye, Frances, lyricist, composer
  Well All Right! [Tonight's the Night!]
Fernandez, Carlo, composer, lyricist
  Cielito Lindo
Fetter, Ted (b. 1906), lyricist
  Taking a Chance on Love
Feyne, Buddy (b. 1912), lyricist
  The Jersey Bounce
  Tuxedo Junction
Fields, Dorothy (1904–1974), lyricist
  Diga Diga Doo
  Exactly Like You
  A Fine Romance
  I Can't Give You Anything but Love
  I Must Have That Man

I Won't Dance
I'm in the Mood for Love
Lost in a Fog
On the Sunny Side of the Street
Pick Yourself Up
Remind Me
The Way You Look Tonight
You Couldn't Be Cuter
Fiorito, Ted (1900–1971), composer
  Then You've Never Been Blue
Fischer, Carl Theodore (1912–1954), composer, lyricist
  We'll Be Together Again
  You've Changed (C)
Fisher, Dan (b. 1920), composer, lyricist
  Good Morning, Heartache
Fisher, Doris (b. 1915), composer, lyricist
  Benny's Coming Home on Saturday
  Into Each Life Some Rain Must Fall
  That Old Devil Love
Fisher, Mark, composer, lyricist
  When You're Smiling
Fisher, Marvin (b. 1916), composer
  When Sunny Gets Blue
Fitzgerald, Ella (b. 1917), composer, lyricist
  Any Old Blues
  A-Tisket, A-Tasket
  Betcha Nickel
  Billie's Bounce
  Chew, Chew, Chew (Your Bubble Gum)
  Chewin' Gum
  The Greatest There Is (L)
  Happy Blues
  I Fell in Love with a Dream
  I Found My Yellow Basket
  It's Up to Me and You
  Joe Williams' Blues
  The Muffin Man
  No Sense (L)
  Oh Boy! I'm in the Groove
  Once Is Enough for Me
  Party Blues
  Please Tell Me the Truth
  Rough Ridin'
  Street Beater ("Sanford and Son" Theme)
  That Ringo Beat
  Who Ya Hunchin'?
  You Showed Me the Way (L)
Fletcher, Lucy, lyricist
  Sugar Blues
Floyd, Eddie, composer, lyricist
  Knock on Wood
Ford, Eugene, lyricist
  Rain

Forrest, George (Chet) (George Forrest Chichester)
    (b.1915), composer, lyricist
  It's a Blue World
Forster, B.Y., lyricist
  Lullaby of Birdland
Foster, Frank Benjamin (b. 1928), composer
  Shiny Stockings
Franklin, Dave, composer, lyricist
  A Man Wrote a Song
Freed, Arthur (1894–1973), composer, lyricist
  All I Do Is Dream of You (L)
  I Cried for You
  I've Got a Feelin' You're Foolin' (L)
Freed, Ralph (1907–1973), composer, lyricist
  Hawaiian War Chant
  Who Walks in When I Walk Out?
  You Leave Me Breathless (L)
  Young Man with a Horn (L)
Freedman, Max C. (1893–1962), composer, lyricist
  Tea Leaves
Freeman, Lawrence E. (Bud) (b. 1906), composer, lyricist
  Until the Real Thing Comes Along
Frigo, John Virgil (b. 1916), composer, lyricist
  Detour Ahead
Froeba, Frank, lyricist, composer
  (Hep! Hep!) The Jumpin' Jive
Fryberg, Mart (1890–1952), composer, lyricist
  Call Me Darling
Fuller, Walter Gilbert (Gil) (b. 1920), composer
  Manteca
  Oo-Bop-Sh'bam
  Ool-Ya-Koo [Royal Roost Bop Boogie]
Furber, Douglas (1885–1961), lyricist
  Limehouse Blues
Gabler, Milton (Milt) (b. 1911), lyricist
  In a Mellow Tone [In a Mellotone]
  L-O-V-E
Gabriel, Charles Hutchinson, Sr. (1865–1932), composer
  Brighten the Corner Where You Are
Gaines, Lee (Otho) (b. 1914), lyricist
  Just a-Sittin' and a-Rockin' [Just a-Settin' and a-Rockin']
  Just Squeeze Me
Gallop, Sammy (1915–1971), composer, lyricist
  Elmer's Tune
Gannett, William Channing (1840–1923), lyricist
  Sleep, My Little Jesus
Gannon, James Kimball (Kim) (1900–1974), composer,
    lyricist
  A Dreamer's Holiday (L)
  The Five O'Clock Whistle
  Make Love to Me (L)
  Mama, Come Home (L)
  Melinda, the Mousie (L)

Gardner, Nat, lyricist
  Love, You're Just a Laugh
Garland, Joe, composer
  In the Mood
Garner, Erroll Louis (1921–1977), composer
  Misty
Garrett, Siedah, composer, lyricist
  Wee B. Doinit
Gaskill, Clarence (1892–1947), lyricist
  I Can't Believe that You're in Love with Me
Gay, Byron (1886–1945), composer
  Four or Five Times
Gaye, Marvin Pentz (1939–1984), composer, lyricist
  What's Going On?
Geibel, Adam (1855–1933), composer
  Sleep, My Little Jesus
George, Don (b. 1909), composer, lyricist
  Everything but You (L)
  I Ain't Got Nothin' but the Blues (L)
  I'm Beginning To See the Light
Gershwin, George (1898–1937), composer
  All the Livelong Day
  Aren't You Kinda Glad We Did?
  (I've Got) Beginner's Luck
  Bidin' My Time
  Boy Wanted
  Boy! What Love Has Done to Me
  But Not for Me
  The Buzzard Song
  By Strauss
  Clap Yo' Hands
  Embraceable You
  Fascinating Rhythm
  A Foggy Day (in London Town)
  For You, for Me, for Evermore
  Funny Face
  "The Half of It, Dearie" Blues
  He Loves and She Loves
  Here Comes de Honey Man
  How Long Has This Been Going On?
  I Can't Be Bothered Now
  I Got Rhythm
  I Loves You, Porgy [I Wants To Stay Here]
  I Was Doing All Right
  I'm a Poached Egg
  I've Got a Crush on You
  Isn't It a Pity?
  Just Another Rhumba
  Let's Call the Whole Thing Off
  Let's Kiss and Make Up
  Looking for a Boy
  The Lorelei
  Love Is Sweeping the Country

Love Walked In
The Man I Love
Maybe
My Cousin in Milwaukee
My Man's Gone Now
My One and Only
Nice Work if You Can Get It
Of Thee I Sing
Oh, Dey's Fresh an' Fine [Strawberry Woman]
Oh! Doctor Jesus
Oh! Lady, Be Good!
Oh, So Nice!
Our Love Is Here To Stay
Porgy and Bess Medley
The Real American Folk Song (Is a Rag)
'S Wonderful
Sam and Delilah
Shall We Dance?
Slap That Bass
Somebody from Somewhere
Somebody Loves Me
Someone To Watch over Me
Soon
Stiff Upper Lip
Strike Up the Band!
Summertime
That Certain Feeling
There's a Boat dat's Leavin' Soon for New York
They All Laughed
They Can't Take That Away from Me
Things Are Looking Up
Treat Me Rough
What You Want wid Bess?
Who Cares?
You've Got What Gets Me
Gershwin, Ira [Arthur Francis Gershwin] (1896–1983),
    lyricist
All the Livelong Day
Aren't You Kinda Glad We Did?
(I've Got) Beginner's Luck
Bidin' My time
Boy Wanted
Boy! What Love Has Done to Me
But Not for Me
By Strauss
Cheerful Little Earful
Clap Yo' Hands
Embraceable You
Fascinating Rhythm
A Foggy Day (in London Town)
For You, for Me, for Evermore
Funny Face
"The Half of It, Dearie" Blues

He Loves and She Loves
Here Comes de Honey Man
How Long Has This Been Going On?
I Can't Be Bothered Now
I Can't Get Started (with You)
I Got Rhythm
I Loves You, Porgy [I Wants To Stay Here]
I Was Doing All Right
I'm a Poached Egg
I'm Not Complainin'
I've Got a Crush on You
Isn't It a Pity?
Just Another Rhumba
Let's Call the Whole Thing Off
Let's Kiss and Make Up
Let's Take a Walk Around the Block
Looking for a Boy
The Lorelei
Love Is Sweeping the Country
Love Walked In
The Man I Love
The Man that Got Away
Maybe
My Cousin in Milwaukee
My One and Only
My Ship
Nice Work if You Can Get It
Of Thee I Sing
Oh! Lady, Be Good!
Oh, So Nice!
Our Love Is Here To Stay
Porgy and Bess Medley
The Real American Folk Song (Is a Rag)
'S Wonderful
Sam and Delilah
Shall We Dance?
Slap That Bass
Somebody from Somewhere
Someone To Watch Over Me
Soon
Stiff Upper Lip
Strike Up the Band!
Summertime
That Certain Feeling
There's a Boat dat's Leavin' Soon for New York
They All Laughed
They Can't Take That Away from Me
Things Are Looking Up
Treat Me Rough
Who Cares?
You've Got What Gets Me
Gibbs, Arthur Harrington (1885–1956), composer
Runnin' Wild

Mountain Greenery
My Funny Valentine
My Heart Stood Still
My Romance
A Ship Without a Sail
Spring Is Here
Ten Cents a Dance
There's a Small Hotel
This Can't Be Love
Thou Swell
To Keep My Love Alive
Wait Till You See Him/Her
Where or When
Who Are You?
With a Song in My Heart
You Took Advantage of Me

Hastings, Thomas (1784–1872), composer
Rock of Ages

Hawkins, Erskine Ramsey (b. 1914), composer
Tuxedo Junction

Hawks, Annie Sherwood (1835–1918), lyricist
I Need Thee Every Hour

Hays, J.H. (Red), composer, lyricist
A Satisfied Mind

Hazelwood, Lee (b. 1929), composer, lyricist
These Boots Are Made for Walkin'

Heath, Walter Henry (Hy) (1880–1965),
        composer, lyricist
I Don't Want the World

Hebb, Bobby, composer, lyricist
Sunny

Hefti, Neal, composer
Li'l Darlin'
Oh, What a Night for Love!

Heindorf, Ray John (b. 1908), composer
Ella Hums the Blues
Pete Kelly's Blues

Hellman, Marco H. (b. 1878), lyricist
Four or Five Times

Henderson, Ray (1896–1970), composer
The Birth of the Blues
It All Depends on You
The Thrill is Gone

Hendricks, John Carl (Jon) (b. 1921), lyricist
Desafinado [Slightly Out of Tune]
A Night in Tunisia
One Note Samba [Samba de Uma Nota So]

Henry, S.R. [Henry Stern] (1874–1966), composer
By Heck

Herbert, Victor (1859–1924), composer
Indian Summer

Herman, Jerry (b. 1933), composer, lyricist
Hello, Dolly!

Herman, Reba Nell, composer, lyricist
A Kiss Goodnight

Herman, Woodrow Wilson (Woody)
        (1913–1987), composer
Early Autumn

Herst, Jerome P. (Jerry) (b. 1909), composer
So Rare

Herzog, Arthur, Jr., composer, lyricist
God Bless the Child
Some Other Spring (L)

Heyman, Edward (b. 1907), composer, lyricist
Body and Soul (L)
Heart of Mine
I Cover the Waterfront (L)
Out of Nowhere (L)

Heyward, Edwin DuBose (1885–1940), lyricist
The Buzzard Song
Here Comes de Honey Man
I Loves You, Porgy [I Wants to Stay Here]
My Man's Gone Now
Oh, Dey's Fresh an' Fine [Strawberry Woman]
Oh, Doctor Jesus
Porgy and Bess Medley
Summertime
What You Want wid Bess?

Higginbotham, Irene Evelyn [Irene Evelyn Higginbotham
        Padellan] (b. 1918), composer, lyricist
Good Morning, Heartache

Hill, William Joseph (Billy) (1899–1940),
        composer, lyricist
The Glory of Love

Hilliard, Bob (1918–1971), lyricist
In the Wee Small Hours (of the Morning)
Solid as a Rock
Somebody Bad Stole de Weddin' Bell
Stay with the Happy People

Hines, Earl Kenneth (Fatha) (1905–1983),
        composer, lyricist
You Can Depend on Me

Hirsch, Walter (b. 1891), lyricist
Baby, What Else Can I Do?
'Deed I Do

Hodges, Johnny (Rabbit) [Cornelius Hodge]
        (1907–1970), composer, lyricist
I'm Beginning to See the Light
Squatty Roo (C)

Hodgson, Red, lyricist
The Music Goes 'Round and 'Round

Hoffman, Al (1902–1960), composer, lyricist
Close to You (L)
Who Walks in When I Walk Out?

Holiday, Billie (Lady Day) [Eleanor Fagan] (1915–1959),
        composer, lyricist

Fine and Mellow
God Bless the Child
Holiday, James Edward (Jimmy) (b. 1934),
    composer, lyricist
  Put a Little Love in Your Heart
Holiner, Mann (1897–1958), composer, lyricist
  Until the Real Thing Comes Along
Hollander, Frederick (1892–1976), composer
  My Heart and I
  You Leave Me Breathless
Holofcener, Lawrence (Larry), lyricist
  Too Close for Comfort
Homer, Benjamin (Ben) (1917–1975), composer
  Sentimental Journey
Hopkins, Claude D. (b. 1906), composer
  Cryin' My Heart Out for You
Hopkins, John Henry, Jr. (1820–1891), composer, lyricist
  We Three Kings of Orient Are
Hopper, Harold S. (Hal) (1912–1970), composer
  There's No You
Horne, Hal, composer
  It's Only a Man
Houdini, Wilmoth [Frederick Wilmoth Hendricks]
    (1901–1973), composer, lyricist
  Stone Cold Dead in de Market
Howard, Bart [Howard Joseph Gustafson] (b. 1915),
    composer, lyricist
  Fly Me to the Moon
Howard, Carolyne [Caroline Horowitz] (b. 1908),
    composer, lyricist
  The Chesapeake and Ohio
Howard, Eddy (1914–1963), composer, lyricist
  Careless
  My Last Goodbye
Howard, Harlan (b. 1929), composer, lyricist
  The Chokin' Kind
  Evil on Your Mind
Howell, Dan, composer, lyricist
  Big Boy Blue
  Well All Right! [Tonight's the Night!]
Hubbell, Raymond (1879–1954), composer
  Poor Butterfly
Huddleston, Floyd Houston (b. 1919), lyricist
  Baby
Hudson, Will (b. 1908), composer
  The Organ Grinder's Swing
Hunter, Alberta (1897–1984), lyricist
  Down Hearted Blues
Ingraham, Edward Roy (b. 1895), composer
  No Regrets
Irwin, Gene (1916–1966), composer, lyricist
  The Five O'Clock Whistle
  Melinda, the Mousie (C)

Jackson, Michael (Mike) (1888–1945), composer, lyricist
  Knock Me a Kiss
Jacobs, Al T. (b. 1903), composer, lyricist
  If I Give My Heart to You
Jacobs, Jacob (1889–1977), lyricist
  Bei Mir Bist du Schön
Jacobson, Kenneth (Kenny), lyricist
  The Swingin' Shepherd Blues
Jacquet, Jean-Baptiste Illinois (b. 1922), composer
  Don'cha Go 'Way Mad
  Just When We're Falling in Love
  Robbins' Nest
Jaffe, Moe (1901–1972), lyricist
  The Gypsy in My Soul
James, Freddie, composer, lyricist
  You Won't Be Satisfied (Until You Break My Heart)
James, Harry Haag (1916–1983), composer, lyricist
  Everything but You (C)
  I'm Beginning to See the Light
Jenkins, Gordon Hill (1910–1984), composer, lyricist
  Goodbye
  When a Woman Loves a Man
Jobim, Antonio Carlos (Tom) (1927–1995), composer, lyricist
  A Felicidade (C)
  Agua de Beber [Water to Drink] (C)
  Bonita (C)
  The Girl from Ipanema [Garôta de Ipanema] (C)
  Desafinado [Off Key] [Slightly Out of Tune] (C)
  Dindi (C)
  Don't Ever Go Away [Por Causa de Você] (C)
  Dreamer [Viva Sonhando]
  He's/She's a Carioca [Ele é Carioca] (C)
  How Insensitive [Insensatez]
  Meditation [Meditação]
  O Nossa Amor [Carnival Samba]
  One Note Samba [Samba de Uma Nota Só]
  Photograph [Fotografia]
  Quiet Nights of Quiet Stars [Corcovado]
  Só Danço Samba [Jazz Samba] (C)
  Somewhere in the Hills [Favela] [O Morro No Tem
    Vez] (C)
  Song of the Jet [Samba do Avião]
  This Love I've Found [Só Tinha Que Ser Com Você]
  Triste
  Useless Landscape [Inútil Paisagem]
  Wave
Johnson, Edward (Ted) (1910–1961), composer
  The Jersey Bounce
  Even as You and I
Johnson, Haven, composer, lyricist
  My Last Affair
James C. Johnson (b. 1896), composer, lyricist
  Cryin' My Heart Out for You (L)

Rhythm and Romanc (C)
  You Can't Be Mine (and Someone Else's Too)
James P. Johnson (1891–1955), composer, lyricist
  Don't Cry, Cry-Baby
  If I Could Be with You (C)
Johnson, Jimmy, composer, lyricist
  That Was My Heart
Johnson, Pete K.H. (1904–1967), compoer, lyricist
  Cherry Red
Johnson, William (1912–1960), composer, lyricist
  Don't You Think I Ought to Know
  Tuxedo Junction
Johnson, Woodrow Wilson (Buddy) (1910–1984),
    composer, lyricist
  I Wonder Where Our Love Has Gone
  Since I Fell for You
Johnston, Arthur James (1898–1954), composer
  My Old Flame
  Pennies from Heaven
Johnston, Patricia, lyricist
  I Remember April
Jolson, Al, composer, lyricist
  Back in Your Own Back Yard
Jones, Bill, composer, lyricist
  Too Young for the Blues
Jones, David Hugh (b. 1900), compoers, lyricist
  Soldier Boy
Jones, composer, lyricist
  I Can't Stop Loving You
Jones, Henry (Hank) (b. 1918), composer, lyricist
  Ella's Contribution to the Blues (C)
  Rough Ridin'
Jones, Isham (1894–1956), composer
  I'll See You in My Dreams
  It Had To Be You
  On the Alamo
  The One I Love Belongs to Somebody Else
Jones, Quincy Delight, Jr., composer, lyricist
  Birdland
  Jazz Corner of the World
  Street Beater ("Sanford and Son" Theme)
  Wee B. Doinit
Jones, Richard Myknee (1892–1945), composer, lyricist
  Trouble in Mind
  Your Red Wagon (C)
Jordan, Louis, composer, lyricist
  Run, Joe, Run
Jurgens, Richard Henry (Dick) (b. 1910),
    composer, lyricist
  Careless
  Elmer's Tune
Kaempfert, Berthold (Bert), composer, lyricist
  L-O-V-E

Kahal, Irving (1903–1942), lyricist
  You Brought a New Kind of Love to Me
Kahn, Donald Gustave (b. 1918), composer
  A Beautiful Friendship
  The Silent Treatment
  Single-O
Kahn, Grace LeBoy (b. 1890), composer
  Dream a Little Longer
Kahn, Gustav Gerson (Gus) (1886–1941), lyricist
  Dream a Little Dream of Me
  Dream a Little Longer
  Guilty
  I'll Never Be the Same
  I'll See You in My Dreams
  I'm Through with Love
  It Had to Be You
  Love Me or Leave Me
  Makin' Whoopee
  On the Alamo
  The One I Love Belongs to Somebody Else
  You Stepped Out of a Dream
Kalmar, Bert (1884–1947), lyricist
  Thinking of You
  Three Little Words
  Who's Sorry Now?
Kander, John (b. 1927), composer
  All That Jazz
Kane, Big Daddy, composer, lyricist
  Jazz Corner of the World
Kaper, Bronislau (1902–1983), composer
  On Green Dolphin Street
Katz, William (Bill) (b. 1922), lyricist
  Duke's Place
  A Flower Is a Lovesome Thing
Keller, Jerry Paul (b. 1937), lyricist
  A Man and a Woman [Un Homme et Une Femme]
Kendis, James (1883-1946), composer
  (I Always Dream of) Billy
  Kennedy, Jimmy, lyricist
  Istanbul
  My Prayer
Kenny, Nick A. (1895–1975), lyricist
  Drop Me Off in Harlem
Kent, Arthur (b. 1920), composer
  I Taught Him Everything He Knows
Kenton, Stanley Newcomb (Stan) (1912–1979), composer
  And Her Tears Flowed Like Wine
Kern, Jerome David (1885-1945), composer
  All the Things You Are
  Bill
  Can't Help Lovin' Dat Man
  A Fine Romance
  I'll Be Hard To Handle

I'm Old Fashioned
Let's Begin
Only Make Believe
Pick Yourself Up
Remind Me
She Didn't Say "Yes"
The Song Is You
The Way You Look Tonight
Who?
Why Was I Born
Yesterdays
You Couldn't Be Cuter
King, Carole (b. 1942), composer, lyricist
   You've Got a Friend
King, Frank (Pee Wee) (b. 1914), composer, lyricist
   Tennessee Waltz
King, Jack, composer
   How Am I To Know?
Kitchings, Irene, composer
   Some Other Spring
Klages, Raymond W. (1888–1947), lyricist
   Just You, Just Me
Klenner, John, composer
   Just Friends
Koehler, Ted (1894–1973), lyricist
   As Long as I Live
   Between the Devil and the Deep Blue Sea
   Don't Worry 'Bout Me
   Get Happy!
   I Can't Face the Music (Without Singing the Blues)
   I Gotta Right to Sing the Blues
   I've Got the World on a String
   Ill Wind
   Let's Fall in Love
   Sing, My Heart
   Stormy Weather
   When the Sun Comes Out
Koffman, Moe (b. 1929), composer
   The Swingin' Shepherd Blues
Kramer, Alex Charles (1893–1955), composer, lyricist
   Candy (C)
   That's the Way It Is
Kress, Helmy (b. 1904), composer
   That's My Desire
Kuhn, Lee (1912–1955), composer, lyricist
   I Cried and Cried and Cried
Kuller, Sid C. (b. 1910), lyricist
   Bli-Blip
Kurtz, Emanuel (Manny) (b. 1911), lyricist
   In a Sentimental Mood
   No Nothing
Lai, Francis (b. 1933), composer
   A Man and a Woman [Un Homme et Une Femme]

Laine, Frankie [Frank Paul LoVecchio] (b. 1913), composer, lyricist
   We'll Be Together Again
   What Am I Here For? (L)
Lampl, Carl G. (1898–1962), composer
   Close to You
Landesman, Frances (Fran) (b. 1927), lyricist
   Spring Can Really Hang You Up the Most
Lane, Burton (b. 1912), composer
   Everything I Have Is Yours
   I Hear Music
   Necessity
   Old Devil Moon
   This Lady's in Love with You
Langdon, Dory [Dory Langdon Previn] (b. 1929), lyricist
   You're Gonna Hear from Me
Lange, Johnny (b. 1912), composer, lyricist
   Cry You Out of My Heart
   I Don't Want the World
Larkin, Joe, composer
   Even as You and I
Latouche, John (1917–1956), lyricist
   Cabin in the Sky
   Day-Dream
   Take Love Easy
   Taking a Chance on Love
Lawrence, Charles (b. 1905), composer
   And Her Tears Flowed Like Wine
Lawrence, Jack (b. 1912), composer, lyricist
   All or Nothing at All (L)
   All Over Nothing at All
   Big Boy Blue
   Deep in the Heart of the South
   If I Didn't
   Tenderly
   Vagabond Dreams
   What Will I Tell My Heart?
   What's Your Story, Morning Glory
   Who's Afraid? (Not I, Not I)
Layton, John Turner (1894–1978), composer
   After You've Gone
Lecuona, Margarita, composer, lyricist
   Babalu
Lee, Larry, composer, lyricist
   This Gun Don't Care
Lee, Lester, composer, lyricist
   I Want to Learn About Love
Lee, Peggy [Norma Delores Engstrom] (b. 1920), composer, lyricist
   I'm Gonna Go Fishin' (L)
   It's A Good Day
Lees, Gene (b. 1928), lyricist
   Bonita

Desafinado [Off Key]
Dreamer [Vivo Sonhando]
Quiet Night of Quiet Stars [Corcovado]
Song of the Jet (Samba do Avião)
Legrand, Michel Jean (b. 1932), composer
  Watch What Happens [Lola's Theme]
Leigh, Carolyn Paula (1926–1983), lyricist
  The Best Is Yet to Come
  I've Got Your Number
  Witchcraft
Leleiohaku, Prince William Pitt (0000–1877), composer
  Hawaiian War Chant
Lemare, Jules, composer, lyrcist
  Sweet and Lovely
Lengsfelder, Hans Jan [Harry Link] (1903–1979),
    composer, lyricist
  I've Got a Feelin' I'm Fallin' (C)
  Perdido (L)
  These Foolish Things (Remind Me of You) (C)
Lennon, John (1940–1980), composer, lyricist
  Can't Buy Me Love
  Got to Get You Into My Life
  A Hard Day's Night
  Hey, Jude
Leonard, Anita [Anita Leonard Nye] (b. 1922),
    composer, lyricist
  A Sunday Kind of Love
Lerner, Alan Jay (1918–1986), lyricist
  (It's) Almost Like Being in Love
  I Could Have Danced All Night
  I've Grown Accustomed to Her/His Face
  Show Me
Levant, Oscar (1906–1972), composer
  Wacky Dust
Leveen, Raymond [Raymond Ledeen] (b. 1893), lyricist
  Petootie Pie
Lewis, Al (1901–1967), composer, lyricist
  'Way Back Home
  What's the Matter with Me? (L)
Lewis, Samuel M. (1885–1959), lyricist
  Just Friends
  (On the) Street of Dreams
  Then You've Never Been Blue
Lewis, Morgan, composer
  How High the Moon
Lieber, Jerry, composer, lyricist
  Bernie's Tune
Lief, Max, lyricist
  I Had to Find Out for Myself
Liggins, Joe, composer, lyricist
  The Honeydripper
Lindsey, Mort (b. 1923), composer, lyricist
  Girl Talk

Lippman, Sidney (b. 1914), composer
  I'm Thrilled
Liston, Virginia, lyricist
  You Don't Know My Mind
Livingston, Fud (1906–1957), composer, lyricist
  I'm Through with Love
Livingston, Jay, composer, lyricist
  Silver Bells
Livingston, Jerry [Jerry Livingstone/Jerry Levinson]
    (1909–1987), composer, lyricist
  Blue and Sentimental (L)
  Close to You (L)
  Dreams Are Made for Children (C)
  I Let a Tear Fall in the River
  I'm Just a Jitterbug (C)
  A Little Bit Later On
  That's All, Brother
  Under a Blanket of Blue (C)
Loeb, John Jacob (1910–1970), composer, lyricist
  (I Put) A Four Leaf Clover in Your Pocket
  Love Marches On
  Seems Like Old Times
Loesser, Frank (1910–1969), composer, lyricist
  Baby, It's Cold Outside
  Guys and Dolls
  Heart and Soul (L)
  I Hear Music (L)
  I Said No (L)
  If I Were a Bell
  On a Slow Boat to China
  Somebody, Somewhere
  Spring Will Be a Little Late This Year
  This Lady's in Love with You (L)
  Warm All Over
  What Are You Doing New Year's Eve?
Loewe, Frederick (1901–1988), composer
  (It's) Almost Like Being in Love
  I Could Have Danced All Night
  I've Grown Accustomed to Her/His Face
  Show Me
Loman, Jules, lyricist
  Little Small Town Girl
Lombardo, Carmen (1903–1971), composer, lyricist
  Seems Like Old Times
  Sweethearts on Parade
Louchheim, Stuart F. (1892–1971), composer, lyricist
  Mixed Emotions
Loveday, Carroll (1898–1955), lyricist
  That's My Desire
Lowry, Robert S. (1826–1899), composer
  I Need Thee Every Hour
Lyman, Abe (1897–1957), composer
  (What Can I Say) After I Say I'm Sorry?

Did You Mean It? (L)
I Cried for You
Lyte, Henry Francis (1793–1847), lyricist
   Abide with Me
MacDonald, Ballard (1882–1935), lyricist
   Clap Hands! Here Comes Charlie!
   Somebody Loves Me
Mack, Cecil [Richard Cecil McPherson], lyricist
   Shine
Madeira, Paul [Paul Madeira Mertz] (b. 1904), lyricist
   I'm Glad There Is You
Madison, Paul, composer, lyricist
   Moon Ray
Magidson, Herbert Adolph (Herb) (1906–1986),
     composer, lyricist
   Gone with the Wind
   My Favorite Song
Malneck, Matty (1904–1981), composer
   Goody-Goody
   I'll Never Be the Same
   I'm Through with Love
   Stairway to the Stars
Mancini, Henry Nicole (1924–1994), composer
   Days of Wine and Roses
   Little Boy
Mandel, John Alfred (Johnny) (b. 1925), composer
   The Shadow of Your Smile
Mann, David A. (Dave) (b. 1916), composer
   In the Wee Small Hours (of the Morning)
   No Moon at All
   Solid as a Rock
   Somebody Bad Stole de Weddin' Bell
   There! I've Said It Again
Mann, Paul (b. 1910), composer
   Make Love to Me
Manning, Richard (Dick) (1912–1954), composer, lyricist
   I Still Feel the Same About You
Marbet, Rolf, composer, lyricist
   Call Me Darling
Marcus, Sol (1912–1976), composer, lyricist
   I Need
Marks, Gerald (b. 1900), composer
   All of Me
   Baby, What Else Can I Do?
Marks, John D. (Johnny) (1909–1985), composer, lyricist
   Rudolph, the Red-Nosed Reindeer
Marks, Walter (b. 1934), composer, lyricist
   I've Gotta Be Me
Marsala, Joe, composer, lyricist
   Don't Cry, Joe
Marsh, Roy, composer, lyricist
   I Never Knew (I Could Love Anybody)
Martin, Civilla Durfee (1868–1948), lyricist

   God Will Take Care of You
Martin, Hugh (b. 1914), composer
   The Boy Next Door
   Have Yourself a Merry Little Christmas
Martin, Walter Stillman (1862–1935), composer
   God Will Take Care of You
Marvel, Holt [Erich Masonvitz], lyricist
   These Foolish Things (Remind Me of You)
May, Billy, composer
   Somewhere in the Night
Mayfield, Curtis (b. 1942), composer, lyricist
   Hey, Little Girl
McAlpin, Vic, composer, lyricist
   Don't Let the Doorknob Hit You
McCartney, Paul (b. 1942), composer, lyricist
   Can't Buy Me Love
   Got to Get You Into My Life
   A Hard Day's Night
   Hey, Jude
McCoy, Joe (1905–1950), composer, lyricist
   Why Don't You Do Right?
McHugh, Jimmy (1894–1969), composer
   Diga Diga Doo
   Exactly Like You
   I Can't Believe that You're in Love with Me
   I Can't Give You Anything but Love
   I Didn't Mean a Word I Said
   I Must Have That Man
   I Won't Dance
   I'm in the Mood for Love
   Lost in a Fog
   On the Sunny Side of the Street
   Reach for Tomorrow
   When My Sugar Walks Down the Street
   Where Are You?
   You're a Sweetheart
McRae, Theodore (Ted, Teddy) (b. 1908),
     composer, lyricist
   Broadway
   Ding-Dong Boogie
   Lindy Hoppers' Delight (C)
   Take it from the Top (C)
   Traffic Jam (C)
   You Showed Me the Way (C)
Mellin, Robert, lyricist
   My One and Only Love
Melsher, Irving (1906–1962), composer, lyricist
   So Long
Mencher, T. Murray (b. 1904), composer
   I Want a Little Girl
   Oh, Yes, Take Another Guess
Mendelssohn-Bartholdy, Jakob Ludwig Felix
     (1809–1847), composer

Hark! The Herald Angels Sing
Mendonça, Newton, lyricist
  Desafinado
  Meditation [Meditação]
  One Note Samba [Samba de Uma Nota Só]
Mendoza y Cortez, Quirino, compoer, lyricist
  Cielito Lindo
Mercer, John Herndon (Johnny), composer, lyricist
  Ac-Cent-Tchu-Ate the Positive (L)
  And the Angels Sing (L)
  Baby Doll (L)
  Baby, Don't You Quit Now (L)
  Blues in the Night (L)
  Come Rain or Come Shine (L)
  Day In — Day Out (L)
  Days of Wine and Roses (L)
  Dream
  Early Autumn (L)
  Fools Rush In (L)
  Goody-Goody (L)
  I Remember You (L)
  I Thought About You (L)
  I'm Old Fashioned (L)
  Laura (L)
  Midnight Sun (L)
  My Shining Hour (L)
  One for My Baby (and One More for the Road) (L)
  Oops! (L)
  Out of This World (L)
  Satin Doll (L)
  Single-O (L)
  Skylark (L)
  Something's Gotta Give
  That Old Black Magic (L)
  This Time the Dream's on Me (L)
  Too Marvelous for Words (L)
  Trav'lin' Light (L)
  When a Woman Loves a Man (L)
Merrick, Walt, composer, lyricist
  Run, Joe
Merrill, Bob (b. 1921), lyricist
  Don't Rain on My Parade
  Lover's Gold
  People
Metzger, Rios, composer, lyricist
  One Cigarette for Two
Meyer, Charles (Chuck) (b. 1924), composer, lyricist
  Too Young for the Blues
Meyer, George W. (1884–1959), composer
  There Are Such Things
Meyer, Joseph (1894–1987), composer, lyricist
  Clap Hands! Here Comes Charlie!
  Hurry Home

Migliacci, Francesco, lyricist
  Volare [Nel Blu, Dipinto di Blu]
Miles, C. Austin (1868–1946), composer, lyricist
  In the Garden
Miller, Alton Glenn (1904–1944), composer
  Moonlight Serenade
Miller, Bernie, composer, lyricist
  Bernie's Tune
Miller, Roger, composer, lyricist
  Walking in the Sunshine
Miller, Seymour (Sy) (1908–1971), composer, lyricist
  Somebody Nobody Loves
Mills, Irving (1894–1985), composer, lyricist
  Azure (L)
  Blue Lou
  Caravan (L)
  I Let a Song Go Out of My Heart (L)
  If Dreams Come True (L)
  In a Sentimental Mood (L)
  It Don't Mean a Thing (if It Ain't Got That Swing) (L)
  Lost in Meditation (L)
  Prelude to a Kiss (L)
  Rockin' in Rhythm (C)
  Solitude (L)
  Sophisticated Lady (L)
  When My Sugar Walks Down the Street
Mitchell, Sidney D. (1888–1942), lyricist
  All My Life
  You Turned the Tables on Me
Mizzy, Vic (b. 1916), composer, lyricist
  Hotta Chocolata (C)
  If It Weren't for You
Modugno, Domenico (b. 1929), compoer, lyricist
  Volare [Nel Blu, Dipinto Di Blu]
Möhr, Josef (1792-1848), lyricist
  Silent Night
Moll, Billy, lyricist
  I Want a Little Girl
Monaco, James V. (1885–1945), composer
  I'm Making Believe
  Once Too Often
  Time Alone Will Tell
  You're Gonna Lose Your Gal
Monk, Thelonius Sphere (1917–1982), composer
  'Round Midnight ['Round About Midnight]
Monk, William Henry (1823–1889), composer
  Abide with Me
Montgomery, Robert (Bob), composer, lyricist
  Misty Blue
Montrose, Percy, composer, lyricist
  (My Darling) Clementine
Moore, Billy, Jr., composer, lyricist
  Santa Claus Got Stuck in My Chimney

Moore, Warren Thomas (Pete), composer, lyricist
Ooo, Baby, Baby
Moraine, Lyle L., composer, lyricist
Christmas Islande
Moret, Neil [Charles Neil Daniels] (1878–1943),
composer
He's/She's Funny That Way [I Got a
Woman/Man Crazy for Me]
Morgan, Carey (1885–1960), composer, lyricist
Rain
Morgan, Russ (1904–1969), composer, lyricist
So Long
Morris, Kenneth, composer, lyricist
Just a Closer Walk with Thee
Mundy, James R. (Jimmy) (1907–1983),
composer, lyricist
Don'cha Go 'Way Mad (C)
A Lover Is Blue
Trav'lin' Light (C)
Murray, James Ramsey (1841–1905), composer
Away in a Manger
Myers, Randy, composer, lyricist
Put a Little Love in Your Heart
Myers, Sherman, composer
Moonlight on the Ganges
Myrow, Josef [Joseph Myrow] (b. 1910),
composer, lyricist
Baby, Won't You Say You Love Me? (C)
The Five O'Clock Whistle
Keep Cool, Fool
Mama, Come Home (C)
Melinda, the Mousie (C)
You Make Me Feel So Young (C)
Mysels, Sammy (1906–1974), composer, lyricist
Is There Somebody Else?
We Three [My Echo, My Shadow, and Me]
Nash, Ogden (1902–1971), lyricist
Speak Low
Nieburg, Al J., lyricist
I'm Confessin' (that I Love You)
A Little Bit Later On
Under a Blanket of Blue
Nelson, Steve Edward (b. 1907), composer, lyricist
Frosty, the Snow Man
Nemo, Henry (b. 1914), composer, lyricist
I Let a Song Go Out of My Heart (L)
'Tis Autumn
Nero, Paul (1917–1958), composer
The Hot Canary
Nevins, Morty (b. 1917), composer
Lover's Gold
Newman, Charles (1901–1978), lyricist
Oh, Yes, Take Another Guess

Sweethearts on Parade
Newman, Lionel, composer
Again
Newman, Randy, composer, lyricist
I Wonder Why
Yellow Man
Nichols, Alberta (1898–1957), composer, lyricist
Until the Real Thing Comes Along
Nilsson, Harry, composer, lyricist
Open Your Window
Nix, Sally, composer, lyricist
I Can't Go on Without You
Noble, John Avery (Johnny) (1892–1944),
composer, lyricist
Hawaiian War Chant
Noble, Raymond (Ray) (1903–1978), composer, lyricist
I Hadn't Anyone Till You
The Very Thought of You
Norman, Pierre, composer
You Brought a New Kind of Love to Me
Norton, George A. (1880–1923), lyricist
Memphis Blues
My Melancholy Baby
Nyro, Laura, composer, lyricist
Hands Off the Man [The Flim Flam Man]
Timer
Ogden, Ina Duley, lyricist
Brighten the Corner Where You Are
Oliveira, Aloysio Louis (b. 1914), lyricist
Agua de Beber [Water to Drink]
Dindi
This Love That I've Found [Só Tinha Que
Ser Com Você]
Oliver, Melvin James (Sy) (1910–1988), composer, lyricist
'Tain't What You Do (It's the Way that You Do It)
That's Rich (C)
Olman, Abe (1888–1984), composer
Oh! Johnny! Oh! Johnny! Oh!
Pack, Lorenzo (b. 1916), composer, lyricist
Nowhere Guy
Petootie Pie (C)
Paley, Herman (1879–1955), composer
(I Always Dream of) Billy
Palmer, Jack, composer, lyricist
(Hep! Hep!) The Jumpin' Jive
I Found a New Baby
Paparelli, Frank (1918–1973), composer
A Night in Tunisia
Petootie Pie
Parish, Mitchell (1900–1992), lyricist
All I Need Is You
Deep Purple
Don't Be That Way

The Lamp Is Low
Mood Indigo
Moonlight Serenade
The Organ Grinder's Swing
Sleigh Ride
Sophisticated Lady
Stairway to the Stars
Star Dust
The Starlit Hour
Stars Fell on Alabama
Sweet Lorraine
Volare [Nel Blu, Dipinto Di Blu]
Parker, Charles Christopher, Jr. (Charlie)(Bird)
    (1920–1955), composer
  Billie's Bounce
Parker, Dorothy (1893–1967), lyricist
  How Am I to Know?
  I Wished on the Moon
Parker, Sol, composer
  This Love of Mine
Perkins, Frank S. (b. 1908), composer
  Stars Fell on Alabama
Persons, Ted, lyricist
  Things Ain't What They Used to Be
Peters, Ben, composer, lyricist
  Turn the World Around the Other Way
Peterson, Betty [Mrs. Louis Blasco] (b. 1918), lyricist
  My Happiness
Petkere, Bernice Naomi (b. 1906), composer, lyricist
  Close Your Eyes
  Lullaby of the Leaves (C)
Petrillo, James Caesar (1898–1963), composer
  Jim
Pierpont, James S. (1822–1893), composer, lyricist
  Jingle Bells [The One Horse Open Sleigh]
Pinkard, Maceo (1897–1962), composer, lyricist
  Sweet Georgia Brown (C)
  Them There Eyes
Pitts, Tom, composer, lyricist
  I Never Knew (I Could Love Anybody)
Pitts, William Savage (1830–1918), composer, lyricist
  The Church in the Wildwood
Plater, Robert (Bobby) (b. 1914), composer,
  The Jersey Bounce
Poll, Ruth (1899–1955), lyricist
  (I'm Wearing) A New Shade of Blue
Pollack, Ben (1903–1971), composer, lyrcist
  That's a-Plenty
Pollack, Channing (1880–1946), lyricist
  My Man [Mon Homme]
Pollack, Dave, composer
  Night Wind
Porter, Cole Albert (1891–1964), composer, lyricist

Ace in the Hole
After You — Who?
All of You
All Through the Night
Always True to You in My Fashion
Anything Goes
At Long Last Love
Begin the Beguine
C'est Magnifique
Do I Love You?
Don't Fence Me In
Down in the Depths (on the Ninetieth Floor)
Dream Dancing
Easy to Love
Ella's Twist [Too Darn Hot]
Ev'ry Time We Say Goodbye
From This Moment On
Get Out of Town
I Am in Love
I Concentrate on You
I Get a Kick Out of You
I Love Paris
I Love You
I've Got You Under My Skin
In the Still of the Night
It's All Right with Me
It's D'Lovely [It's De-Lovely]
Just One of Those Things
Let's Do It
Love for Sale
Miss Otis Regrets
My Heart Belongs to Daddy
Night and Day
Ridin' High
So in Love
So Near and Yet So Far
Too Darn Hot
What Is This Thing Called Love?
Why Can't You Behave?
Without Love
You Do Something to Me
You'd Be So Nice to Come Home To
You're the Top
Previn, André George (b. 1929), composer
  Like Young
  You're Gonna Hear from Me
Prima, Louis (1911–1978), composer, lyricist
  A Sunday Kind of Love
Prince, Hugh Durham (Hughie) (1906–1960),
    composer, lyricist
  Beat Me, Daddy, Eight to the Bar
  The Yodelin' Jive
Prince, Ian, composer, lyricist

Birdland
Wee B. Doinit
Purvis, Katherine E., lyricist
When the Saints Go Marching In
Quadling, Lew (b. 1908), composer, lyricist
Careless
Quenzer, Arthur L. (b. 1905), composer, lyricist
Moon Ray
Quinichette, Paul (b. 1921), composer, lyricist
Preview
Rainey, Gertrude Malissa Nix Pridgett (Ma) (1886–1939),
composer, lyricist
Heah Me Talkin' to Ya
See See Rider (C.C. Rider)
Rainger, Ralph (1901–1942), composer
Easy Living
Hello, Ma! I Done It Again
I Wished on the Moon
Moanin' Low
Thanks for the Memory
Vote for Mr. Rhythm
Wishful Thinking
Raksin, David John Sartain, Jr. (b.1912), composer
Laura
Raleigh, Ben, composer, lyricist
I Couldn't Stay Away
Laughing on the Outside (Crying on the Inside) (L)
Ram, Samuel Buck (b. 1907), composer, lyricist
Chew, Chew, Chew (Your Bubble Gum)
Have Mercy
Ramirez, Roger J. (Ram) (b. 1913), composer, lyricist
Lover Man
Randazzo, Teddy (b. 1937), composer, lyricist
Goin' Out of My Head
Randolph, Zilner Trenton (b. 1899), composer, lyricist
Ol' Man Mose
Rankin, Jeremiah Eames (1828–1904), lyricist
(God Be with You) Till We Meet Again
Raskin, Milton, lyricist
Somewhere in the Night
Raye, Don [Donald MacRae Wilhoite, Jr.] (b. 1909),
composer, lyricist
Beat Me, Daddy, Eight to the Bar
Cow-Cow Boogie (L)
He's My Guy
I'll Remember April (L)
Love That Boy (L)
Well All Right! (Tonight's the Night!)
The Yodelin' Jive
You Don't Know What Love Is
Your Red Wagon (L)
Razaf, Andy [Andrea Menentania Paul Razafkeriefo]
(1895–1973), lyricist

Ain't Misbehavin'
Cryin' Mood
Gee, Baby, Ain't I Good to You
Honeysuckle Rose
In the Mood
Knock Me a Kiss
Memories of You
S'posin'
Stompin' at the Savoy
Redman, Donald Matthew (Don) (1900–1964),
composer, lyricist
Gee, Baby, Ain't I Good to You
Redmond, John (b. 1906), lyricist
I Let a Song Go Out of My Heart
Redner, Lewis H. (1831–1908), composer
O Little Town of Bethlehem
Reed, L., lyricist
Holiday in Harlem
Reid, Don (b. 1914), composer, lyricist
I Still Feel the Same About You
Reid, Willis Wilfred (Billy) (b. 1910), composer, lyricist
It's a Pity to Say Goodnight
Reisfeld, Bert (b. 1906), composer, lyricist
Call Me Darling
Reitz, William J., composer, lyricist
Fairy Tales
Revel, Harry (1905–1958), composer
Goodnight, My Love
I Never Knew Heaven Could Speak
There's a Lull in My Life
Wake Up and Live
What Do You Know About Love?
You Hit the Spot
Reynolds, Ellis, lyricist
I'm Confessin' (that I Love You)
Rhodes, Jack, composer, lyricist
A Satisfied Mind
Rhodes, Stan (b. 1924), composer, lyricist
A Sunday Kind of Love
Rhythm, Doc, composer, lyricist
Keep Cool, Fool
Ricardel, Joe [Joseph A. Ricardello] (b. 1911),
composer, lyricist
The Frim Fram Sauce
Rich, Buddy, lyricist
Budella (Irving Berlin's "Blue Skies")
That's Rich
Richmond, Harry S. [Jessie Cavanaugh] (1895–1972),
lyricist
Desafinado [Slightly Out of Tune]
Riley, Michael (Mike) (b. 1904), composer
The Music Goes 'Round and 'Round
Rinker, Al (b. 1907), composer, lyricist

If You Really Love Me
Robbins, Everett, composer, lyricist
   'Tain't Nobody's Biz-Ness (If I Do)
Roberts, Allan (1905–1966), composer, lyricist
   Benny's Coming Home on Saturday
   Gee, But I'm Glad to Know (that You Love Me)
   I Want to Learn About Love
   Into Each Life Some Rain Must Fall
   That Old Devil Called Love
Roberts, Jay, composer
   Oop-Bop-Sh'bam
Roberts, Rhoda [Rhoda Ribot], lyricist
   The Swingin' Shepherd Blues
Roberts, Ruth (b. 1926), lyricist
   Duke's Place (C-Jam Blues)
   A Flower Is a Lovesome Thing
Robertson, Richard (Dick) (b. 1903), composer, lyricist
   Is There Somebody Else?
   We Three (My Echo, My Shadow and Me)
Robin, Leo (1899–1984), lyricist
   Easy Living
   Hallelujah!
   Hello, Ma! I Done It Again
   Hooray for Love
   It Was Written in the Stars
   My Heart and I
   Thanks for the Memory
   Vote for Mr. Rhythm
   Wishful Thinking
Robin, Sydney (Sid) (b. 1912), lyricist
   Flyin' Home
   Undecided
Robinson, William, Jr. (Smokey) (b. 1940),
     composer, lyricist
   Get Ready
   The Hunter Gets Captured by the Game
   Ooo, Baby, Baby
Rodgers, Richard (1902–1979), composer, lyricist
   Bewitched, Bothered and Bewildered (C)
   Blue Moon (C)
   A Blue Room (C)
   Dancing on the Ceiling (C)
   Dites-Moi (C)
   Ev'rything I've Got (Belongs to You) (C)
   The Gentleman Is a Dope (C)
   Give It Back to the Indians (C)
   Glad to Be Unhappy (C)
   Happy Talk (C)
   Have You Met Miss/Sir Jones? (C)
   Here in My Arms (C)
   I Could Write a Book (C)
   I Didn't Know What Time It Was (C)
   I Wish I Were in Love Again (C)

I'm Gonna Wash That Man Right Outta My Hair (C)
I've Got Five Dollars (C)
Isn't It Romantic? (C)
It Might as Well Be Spring (C)
It Never Entered My Mind (C)
Johnny One-Note (C)
The Lady Is a Tramp (C)
Little Girl Blue (C)
Lover (C)
Manhattan (C)
Mountain Greenery (C)
My Funny Valentine (C)
My Heart Stood Still (C)
My Romance (C)
No Other Love (C)
People Will Say We're in Love (C)
A Ship Without a Sail (C)
Spring Is Here (C)
Sunday (C)
The Sweetest Sound
Ten Cents a Dance (C)
There's a Small Hotel (C)
This Can't Be Love (C)
Thou Swell (C)
To Keep My Love Alive (C)
Wait Till You See Her/Him (C)
Where or When (C)
Who Are You? (C)
With a Song in My Heart (C)
You Took Advantage of Me
Roll, Ruth, composer, lyricist
   Because of Rain
Rollins, Walter E. (Jack), composer, lyricist
   Frosty, the Snow Man
Romberg, Sigmund (1887–1951), composer
   Lover, Come Back to Me
Rome, Harold Jacob (b. 1908), composer, lyricist
   Franklin D. Roosevelt Jones
Ronell, Ann, composer, lyricist
   Willow, Weep for Me
Rose, Billy (William Samuel Rosenberg) (1899–1966),
     lyricist
   Back in Your Own Back Yard
   Cheerful Little Earful
   Clap Hands! Here Comes Charlie!
   Great Day!
   I've Got a Feelin' I'm Fallin'
   It Happened in Monterey
   More Than You Know
   (It's Only a) Paper Moon
   Would You Like to Take a Walk?
Rose, Ed (1875–1935), lyricist
   Oh! Johnny! Oh! Johnny! Oh!

Rose, Fred (1897–1954), composer
'Deed I Do
Ross, Barney, lyricist
Crying
Ross, Edward (Milton Isadore Samuels) (b. 1904),
composer
Jim
Ross, Jerry (1926–1955), composer, lyricist
Hernando's Hideaway
Hey, There!
Matchmaker, Matchmaker (C)
Steam Heat
Whatever Lola Wants
Rothberg, Bob (1901–1938), lyricist
Night Wind
Rowles, Jimmy, composer
Baby, Don't You Quit Now
Rubens, Hugo (b. 1905), composer
Small Town Girl
Ruby, Harry (1895–1974), composer, lyricist
Give Me the Simple Life (L)
I'll Always Be in Love with You
Thinking of You (C)
Three Little Words (C)
Who's Sorry Now? (L)
Rushing, James Andrew (Jimmy) (1902–1972),
composer, lyricist
Good Morning, Blues
Ruskin, Harry (b. 1894), lyricist
I May Be Wrong (But I Think You're Wonderful)
Russell, Sidney Keith (Bob), lyricist
Babalu
Do Nothin' Till You Hear from Me
I Didn't Know About You
Just When We're Falling in Love
Ryan, Ben (Benny) (1892–1968), lyricist
M-I-S-S-I-S-S-I-P-P-I
No Nothing
One Cigarette for Two
Sacco, Anthony (Tony) (b. 1908), composer, lyricist
(When It's) Slumber Time Along the Swanee
Sampson, Edgar Melvin (1907–1973), composer, lyricist
Blue Lou
Don't Be That Way
I'll Chase the Blues Away
If Dreams Come True
Please Tell Me the Truth
Stompin' at the Savoy (C)
Under the Spell of the Blues
Shapiro, Ted, composer, lyricist
To You
Shrdlu, N.
"Shrdlu" "Etaoin" were typesetters' placeholders where

a word in a manuscript was indecipherable. This name was used for compositions that were a collective effort where attribution to one writer would be impossible. Some jam numbers based on blues or standard harmonies were designated "traditional" when first released.
Tauber, Doris (b. 1908), composer, lyricist
Them There Eyes
Who's Afraid? (Not I, Not I) (C)
Taylor, Irving, composer, lyricist
Ain't Nobody's Business but My Own
If It Weren't for You
Temperton, Rod, composer, lyricist
Birdland
Tennyson, Bill, composer
Rough Ridin'
Thiele, Robert (Bob) (b. 1922), lyricist
Duke's Place (C-Jam Blues)
A Flower Is a Lovesome Thing
Thomas, Joseph Lewis (Joe) (1909–1984), composer, lyricist
Melancholy Me
Thompson, "Sir" Charles Philip (b. 1918), composer
Just When We're Falling in Love
Robbins' Nest
Tierney, Harry Austin (1890–1965), composer
M-I-S-S-I-S-S-I-P-P-I
Tillman, Floyd (b. 1914), composer, lyricist
I Gotta Have My Baby Back
Tinturin, Peter (b. 1910), composer, lyricist
All Over Nothing at All
Big Boy Blue
Deep in the Heart of the South
(When It's) Slumber Time Along the Swanee
What Will I Tell My Heart?
Tizol, Vincente Martinez (Juan) (1900–1984), composer
Caravan
Lost in Meditation
Perdido
Tobias, Charles (1898–1970), lyricist
Comes Love
Gotta Pebble in My Show
Love Marches On
Tobias, Henry (Harry) (b. 1905), composer, lyricist
No Regrets (L)
Sweet and Lovely
Tomer, William Gould (1832–1896), composer
(God Be with You) Till We Meet Again
Toombs, Rudolph, composer, lyricist
Teardrops from My Eyes
Toplady, Augustus Montague (1740–1778), lyricist
Rock of Ages
Tormé, Melvin Howard (Mel) (b. 1925), composer, lyricist

Chew, Chew, Chew (Your Bubble Gum)
Chewin' Gum
Cryin' Mood (C)
Devoting My Time to You
Ella
Have Mercy (C)
Heart of Mine
Holiday in Harlem (C)
I Can't Stop Loving You
I Let a Tear Fall in the River
I'm Up a Tree (C)
If You Only Knew
It's Foxy
It's Wonderful
Once Is Enough for Me
Stompin' at the Savoy (C)
Strictly from Dixie
Sugar Pie
Swinging on the Reservation
That Was My Heart
Who Ya Hunchin'?
You Can't Be Mind (and Someone Else's, Too)
You Showed Me the Way (C)
Webster, Paul Francis (1907–1984), lyricist
Black Coffee
The Brown-Skinned Gal in a Calico
I Got It Bad (and That Ain't Good)
It's Only a Man
Like Young
The Shadow of Your Smile
Webster, Paul, composer, lyricist
What's Your Story, Morning Glory?
Weill, Kurt (1900–1950), composer
Mack The Knife [Moritat]
My Ship
September Song
Speak Low
Weinstein, Bobby, composer, lyricist
Goin' Out of My Head
Weiss, George David (b. 1921), composer, lyricist
Can Anyone Explain?
I'll Never Be Free
Too Close for Comfort (L)
Weiss, Stephan (b. 1899), composer
Make Love to Me
Welch, Ken, composer, lyricist
But Not Like Mine
Wells, Robert (Robert Wells Levinson) (b. 1922),
    composer, lyricist
(I Was) Born To Be Blue
The Christmas Song
It's Wonderful
Werner, Kay (b. 1918), composer, lyricist

Coochi-Coochi-Coo
I Got the Spring Fever Blues
I Want the Waiter (with the Water)
My Wubba Dolly
Rock It for Me
Werner, Sue (b. 1918), composer, lyricist
Coochi-Coochi-Coo
I Got the Spring Fever Blues
I Want the Waiter (with the Water)
My Wubba Dolly
Rock It for Me
Wesley, Charles (1707–1788), lyricist
Hark! The Herald Angels Sing
Weston, Paul [Paul Wetstein] (b. 1912), composer
Day by Day
Wettergreen, Melvin Richard (Mel) (b. 1909),
    composer, lyricist
Don't You Think I Ought to Know?
Whitefield, George (1714–1770), lyricist
Hark! The Herald Angels Sing
Whitfield, Norman, composer, lyricist
I Heard It Through the Grapevine
Whiting, George (1884–1943), lyricist
Rhythm and Romance
Whiting, Richard Armstrong (1891–1938), composer,
    lyricist
Guilty (C)
He's/She's Funny That Way [I Got a Man/Woman
    Crazy for Me] (L)
Too Marvelous for Words (C)
You're an Old Smoothie (C)
Whitney, Joan [Zoe Parenteau Kramer] (b. 1914),
    composer, lyricist
Candy (C)
That's the Way It Is
Wilder, Alec [Alexander Lafayette Chewilder]
    (1907–1980), composer, lyricist
Trouble Is a Man
Willemetz, Albert, lyricist
My Man [Mon Homme]
Williams, Charles Melvin (Cootie) (1908–1985),
    composer
'Round Midnight ['Round About Midnight]
Williams, Clarence (1893–1965), composer, lyricist
Baby, Won't You Please Come Home? (C)
Gulf Coast Blue
If You Don't, I Know Who Will
Jail House Blues
Royal Garden Blues
Sugar Blues (C)
You Don't Know My Mind (C)
Williams, Joseph Goreed (Joe), composer, lyricist
Lady Bug (C)

Party Blues

Salty Lips

Williams, John, composer

Make Me Rainbows

Williams, Mary Lou [Mary Elfrieda Scruggs] (1910–1981), composer, lyricist

What's Your Story, Morning Glory?

Williams, Paul, composer, lyricist

Ordinary Fool

Williams, Sandy, composer, lyricist

Devoting My Time to You

Williams, Spencer (1889–1965), composer, lyricist

Basin Street Blues

I Found a New Baby

Royal Garden Blues

Williams, Theodore, Jr. (Teddy), composer, lyricist

Soldier Boy

Willis, Richard Storrs (1819–1900), composer

It Came upon the Midnight Clear

Willoughby, Joe, composer, lyricist

Run, Joe

Wilson, Gerald, composer

Imagine My Frustration

Wilson, Neil C., lyricist

Cielito Lindo

Wodehouse, Pelham Granville (P.G.), lyricist

Bill

Wolf, Thomas J., Jr. (Tommy) (b. 1925), composer

Spring Can Really Hang You Up the Most

Wonder, Stevie [Stevland Morris], composer, lyricist

You Are the Sunshine of My Life

Wood, Guy B. (b. 1912), composer

My One and Only

Wood, Leo (1882–1929), lyricist

Runnin' Wild

Woode, William Henri (Henry) (b. 1909), composer, lyricist

Broadway

Woods, Harry MacGregor (1896–1970), composer, lyricist

Try a Little Tenderness

Woods, Hosie, composer

Walk Right In

Wright, Robert B., composer, lyricist

It's a Blue World

The Jersey Bounce

Wrubel, Allie (1905–1973), composer, lyricist

As You Desire Me

Gone with the Wind (L)

Wyche, Sid, composer, lyricist

Alright, Okay, You Win

Yellen, Jack (1892–1991), lyricist

Hard Hearted Hannah (the Vamp of Savannah)

Youmans, Vincent Millie (1898–1946), composer

Great Day!

Hallelujah!

I Know that You Know

I Want to Be Happy

More Than You Know

Tea for Two

Young, Lester, composer

Jumping with Symphony Syd

Young, James Oliver (Trummy) (1912–1984), composer, lyricist

A Lover Is Blue

'Tain't What You Do (It's the Way That'cha Do It)

Trav'lin' Light (C)

Young, Joseph (Joe) (1889–1939), lyricist

Lullaby of the Leaves

Then You've Never Been Blue

There's Frost on the Moon

You're Gonna Hear from Me

Young, Victor (1900–1956), composer

(I Don't Stand) A Ghost of a Chance (with You)

Love Is the Thing (So They Say)

Stella by Starlight

(On the) Street of Dreams

Sweet Sue, Just You

Yradier, Sebastian (1809–1865), composer, lyricist

Cielito Lindo

Yvain, Maurice (1891–1965), composer

My Man [Mon Homme]

Zaret, Hy, composer

Dedicated to You

Zolotow, Maurice, composer, lyricist

Ah! Men! Ah! Women!

B. They Play While Ella Sings: Ella's Musicians

Note: No attempt has been made to ascertain the true names of the musicians here listed. These are their professional names of choice.

Al Aarons, trumpet
  Count Basie and His Orchestra, 1963
  Orchestra conducted by Nelson Riddle, 1978, 1982
Don Abney, celeste, piano
  Orchestra conducted by Toots Camarata, 1955
  Small group accompaniment, 1955, 1956, 1957
Alex Acuña, drums
  Orchestra conducted by Eric Bulling, 1980
Pepper Adams, baritone saxophone
  Benny Goodman and His Orchestra, 1959
Bernard Addison, guitar
  Solo accompaniment, 1937
Manny Alabam, baritone saxophone
  Orchestra conducted by Sy Oliver, 1953
Napoleon "Snags" Allen, guitar
  Cootie Williams and His Orchestra, 1946
Shorty Allen, piano
  Randy Brooks and His Orchestra, 1945
Vernon Alley, bass
  Trio accompaniment, 1956
Laurindo Almeida, guitar
  Orchestra conducted by Sonny Burke, 1951
Trigger Alpert, bass
  Ella Fitzgerald and Her V-Disc Jumpers, 1945
  Bob Haggart and His Orchestra, 1946
Cat Anderson, trumpet
  Duke Ellington and His Orchestra, 1957, 1965, 1966, 1967
Stuart Anderson, tenor saxophone
  Randy Brooks and His Orchestra 1945
Richard Aplenalp, baritone saxophone
  Orchestra conducted by Gerald Wilson, 1969–1970
James Archey, trombone
  Ella Fitzgerald and Her Famous Orchestra, 1940

James Arkatov, cello
  Orchestra conducted by Nelson Riddle, 1959
Louis Armstrong, trumpet
  Bob Haggart and His Orchestra, 1946
  Dave Barbour and His Orchestra, 1951
  Orchestra conducted by John Scott Trotter, 1951
  JATP All-Stars, 1956
  Small group accompaniment, 1957
Victor Arno, violin
  Orchestra conducted by Nelson Riddle, 1959, 1963
George Arus, trombone
  Orchestra conducted by Jerry Gray, 1952
Bob Ashton, tenor and baritone saxophones
  Cootie Williams and His Orchestra (baritone), 1946, 1947
  The Chick Webb Orchestra (tenor), 1973
John Audino, trumpet
  Orchestra conducted by Nelson Riddle, 1964
Georgie Auld (1919-1990), tenor saxophone
  Benny Carter's Magnificent Seven, 1968
Robert Bain, guitar
  Orchestra conducted by Nelson Riddle, 1963, 1964
Taswell Baird, trombone
  Dizzy Gillespie and His Orchestra, 1947
Art "Artie" Baker, alto saxophone
  Orchestra conducted by Sy Oliver, 1951, 1953
Harold "Shorty" Baker, trumpet
  Duke Ellington and His Orchestra, 1957
Israel Baker, violin
  Orchestras conducted by Nelson Riddle, 1959, 1963; and by Billy May, 1961
Warren Baker, saxophones
  Orchestra conducted by John Scott Trotter, 1953, 1954
Butch Ballard, drums
  Cootie Williams and His Orchestra, 1946, 1947
Red Ballard, trombone
  Benny Goodman and His Orchestra, 1936

Dave Barbour (1912–1965), leader, guitar
    Orchestra, 1951
George Bardon, trumpet
    Randy Brooks and His Orchestra, 1945
Paul Bardon, alto saxophone
    Randy Brooks and His Orchestra, 1945
Eddie Barefield, clarinet, alto saxophone
    Ella Fitzgerald and Her Famous Orchestra, 1940
    Ella Fitzgerald with The Chick Webb Orchestra, 1940
    Small group accompaniment, 1941
    The Chick Webb Orchestra, 1973
Everett Barksdale, guitar
    Orchestra conducted by Sy Oliver, 1950, 1951, 1952, 1953
    Small group accompaniment, 1951
Kenny Barron, piano
    Small group accompaniment, 1989
Dallas Bartley, bass
    Louis Jordan and His Tympany Five, 1949
William "Count" Basie, leader, piano, organ
    Orchestra, 1956, 1963, 1971, 1972, 1979
Roland Bautista, rhythm guitar
    Orchestra conducted by Eric Bulling, 1980
Mario Bauza, trumpet
    Chick Webb and His Orchestra, 1933-1938
Victor Bay, violin
    Orchestra conducted by Nelson Riddle, 1959, 1963
Frank Beach, trumpet
    Orchestra conducted by Billy May, 1960
Bill Beason, drums
    Ella Fitzgerald and Her Famous Orchestra, 1940-1941
    Small group accompaniment, 1941
Heinie Beau, saxophones
    Dave Barbour and His Orchestra, 1951
Henry Beau, woodwinds
    Orchestra conducted by Billy May, 1961
Alex Beller, violin
    Orchestra conducted by Nelson Riddle, 1959, 1963
Louis Bellson, drums
    Small group accompaniment, 1957, 1974
    Duke Ellington and His Orchestra, 1965
    Benny Carter's Magnificent Seven, 1968
    Orchestras conducted by Gerald Wilson, 1969–1970;
        and by Nelson Riddle, 1978
    Duo accompaniment, 1978
    The JATP All-Stars, 1983
Max Bennett, bass
    Trio accompaniment, 1958, 1959
Norman Benno, oboe
    Orchestra conducted by Nelson Riddle, 1964, 1978
Irwin Berger, trumpet
    Benny Goodman and His Orchestra, 1959
Marty Berman, baritone saxophone
    Tommy Dorsey and His Orchestra, 1947

Milton Bernhart, trombone
    Orchestras conducted by Sonny Burke, 1951; by Jerry
        Gray, 1952; by Buddy Bregman, 1956; by Nelson Riddle,
        1959, 1964; and by Billy May, 1960, 1961
Eddie Bert, trombone
    Benny Goodman and His Orchestra, 1958
John Best, trumpet
    Orchestra conducted by Jerry Gray, 1952
Keter Betts, bass
    Small group accompaniment, 1965
    The Tee Carson Trio, 1968
    The Tommy Flanagan Trio, 1972, 1975, 1977
    The Tommy Flanagan Quartet, 1973, 1974
    The Ella Fitzgerald Trio, 1979, 1983
    The Jimmy Rowles Trio, 1981
Jerry Blake, clarinet, alto saxophone
    Teddy Wilson and His Orchestra, 1936
Stewart Blake, baritone saxophone
    Orchestra conducted by Sy Oliver, 1951
Sid Bloch, bass
    Tommy Dorsey and His Orchestra, 1947
Sandy Block, bass
    Orchestras conducted by Sy Oliver, 1951, 1952, 1953;
        and by Toots Camarata, 1955
    Small group accompaniment, 1951, 1952, 1953
Johnny Blowers, drums
    Small group accompaniment, 1943, 1944, 1951
    Orchestra conducted by Sy Oliver, 1950, 1951
Ray Bojorquez, tenor saxophone
    Orchestra conducted by Gerald Wilson, 1969-1970
Perry Botkin, guitar
    Orchestra conducted by John Scott Trotter, 1953, 1954
Eddie Bourne, drums
    Small group accompaniment, 1946
Nelson Boyd, bass
    Small group accompaniment, 1952
Will Bradley, trombone
    Bob Haggart and His Orchestra, 1947
    Orchestra conducted by Toots Camarata, 1955
Floyd Brady, trombone
    Ella Fitzgerald and Her Famous Orchestra
Buddy Bregman, leader, arranger
    Orchestra, 1956
Verlye Brilhart, harp
    Orchestra conducted by Billy May, 1961
Harry Brooks, trombone
    Randy Brooks and His Orchestra, 1945
Randy Brooks, leader, trumpet
    Orchestra, 1945
Dale Brown, clarinet, saxophones
    Orchestra conducted by Jerry Gray, 1952
Garnett Brown, trombone
    The Chick Webb Orchestra, 1973

John Brown, alto saxophone
    Dizzy Gillespie and His Orchestra, 1947
Lawrence Brown, trombone
    Duke Ellington and His Orchestra, 1965-1967
Ray Brown (b. 1926), double bass, Fender bass
    Small group accompaniment, 1947, 1953, 1954, 1956,
        1957, 1958, 1961, 1963, 1974, 1989
    The Ray Brown Trio, Quartet and Quintet,
        1948-1950, 1952, 1954
    Orchestras conducted by Sy Oliver, 1950; and by Gerald
        Wilson, 1969 1970
    The JATP All-Stars, 1950, 1953, 1954, 1956, 1957,
        1972
    Dave Barbour and His Orchestra 1951
Ray Brown, trumpet
    Count Basie and His Orchestra, 1979
Bobby Bryant, trumpet
    Orchestra conducted by Gerald Wilson, 1969-1970
Dennis Budamir, guitar
    Orchestra conducted by Gerald Wilson, 1969-1970
Eric Bulling, leader
    Orchestra, 1980
Mort Bullman, trombone
    Orchestra conducted by Sy Oliver, 1951, 1952
Larry Bunker, drums
    Orchestra conducted by Nelson Riddle, 1959
Ed Burke, trombone
    Cootie Williams and His Orchestra, 1944, 1946, 1947
Sonny Burke, leader, arranger
    Orchestra, 1949, 1951
Leroy Burnes, drums
    Benny Goodman and His Orchestra, 1958, 1959
Dave Burns, trumpet
    Dizzy Gillespie and His Orchestra, 1947
Ralph Burns (b. 1922), piano
    Count Basie and His Orchestra, 1956
Kenny Burrell, guitar
    Benny Goodman and His Orchestra, 1958, 1959
Garvin Bushell, clarinet, alto saxophone, soprano
        saxophone
    Chick Webb and His Orchestra, 1937-1939
    Ella Fitzgerald and Her Famous Orchestra, 1939, 1940
Joe Bushkin, piano
    Bob Haggart and His Orchestra, 1946
Bob Bushnell, bass
    Louis Jordan and His Tympany Five, 1950
Billy Butterfield, trumpet
    Bob Haggart and his Orchestra, 1946
    Benny Goodman and His Orchestra, 1958
Eddie Byrd, drums
    Louis Jordan and His Tympany Five, 1945
Ernie Caceres, baritone saxophone
    Bob Haggart and His Orchestra, 1947

Eddie Caine, alto saxophone
    Randy Brooks and His Orchestra, 1945
Red Callender (1916–1992), bass, tuba
    Orchestra conducted by Nelson Riddle, 1959
Toots Camarata, leader
    Orchestra and chorus, 1955
Pete Candoli, trumpet
    Orchestras conducted by Sonny Burke, 1951; by Buddy
        Bregman, 1956; and by Nelson Riddle, 1959
Frankie Capp, drums,
    Trio accompaniment, 1956
Ralph Carmichael, leader, arranger
    Orchestra, 1967
Harry Carney, clarinets, saxophones
    Duke Ellington and His Orchestra, 1957, 1965–1967
Tee Carson, pianist
    The Tee Carson Trio, 1968
Benny Carter, leader, alto saxophone
    The JATP All-Stars, 1953
    Orchestra, 1955
    Orchestras conducted by Nelson Riddle, 1959; and by
        Billy May, 1961
    Benny Carter's Magnificent Seven, 1968
    Small group accompaniment, 1989
Wayman Carver, flute/tenor saxophone
    Chick Webb and His Orchestra, 1934–1939
    Ella Fitzgerald and Her Famous Orchestra, 1939, 1940
Al Casamenti, guitar
    Orchestra conducted by Toots Camarata, 1955
Oscar Castro-Neves, rhythm guitar, solo
        acoustic guitar
    Orchestra conducted by Eric Bulling, 1980
George "Buddy" Catlett, bass
    Count Basie and His Orchestra, 1963
Sidney Catlett (1910–1951), drums
    Small group accompaniment, 1947
John Cave, French horn
    Orchestra conducted by Nelson Riddle, 1963, 1964
Henderson Chambers, trombone
    Orchestra conducted by Sy Oliver, 1950, 1951, 1953
Milton Chatz, baritone saxophone
    Bob Haggart and His Orchestra, 1946
Don Christlieb, bassoon
    Orchestra conducted by Nelson Riddle, 1978
Gene Cipriano, saxophones
    Orchestras conducted by Paul Weston, 1958; and by
        Nelson Riddle, 1964
Babe Clark, tenor saxophone
    Benny Goodman and His Orchestra, 1959
Chuck Clark, tenor saxophone
    Cootie Williams and His Orchestra, 1947
Mahlon Clark, clarinet
    Orchestra conducted by Nelson Riddle, 1978

Pete Clark, clarinet, alto saxophone
   Chick Webb and His Orchestra, 1932–1937
   Ella Fitzgerald and Her Famous Orchestra, 1940–1941
   The Chick Webb Orchestra, 1973
Arthur Clarke, tenor saxophone
   The Chick Webb Orchestra, 1973
Kenny Clarke, drums
   Small group accompaniment, 1941
Buck Clayton (1911–1991), trumpet
   Benny Goodman and His Orchestra, 1958, 1959
John Clayton, bass
   Count Basie and His Orchestra, 1979
James Cleveland, trombone
   Orchestra conducted by Gerald Wilson, 1969–1970
Al Cobb, trombone
   The Chick Webb Orchestra, 1973
Paul Cohen, trumpet
   Count Basie and His Orchestra, 1971, 1972, 1979
George "Sonny" Cohn, trumpet
   Count Basie and His Orchestra, 1963, 1971, 1972, 1979
Henry Coker, trombone
   Count Basie and His Orchestra, 1956, 1963
Buddy Cole (b. 1916), piano
   Orchestra conducted by John Scott Trotter, 1953, 1954
Cozy Cole, drums
   Teddy Wilson and His Orchestra, 1936
   Bob Haggart and His Orchestra, 1946
Rupert Cole, alto saxophone
   Cootie Williams and His Orchestra, 1944, 1946, 1947
Buddy Collette, woodwinds
   Orchestra conducted by Nelson Riddle, 1959, 1963,
      1964
John Collins (b. 1912), guitar
   The Ray Brown Quintet, 1950
   Orchestra conducted by Billy May, 1960
   Benny Carter's Magnificent Seven, 1968
Christopher Columbus, drums
   Louis Jordan and His Tympany Five, 1949
Joe Comfort, bass
   Orchestra conducted by Nelson Riddle, 1959, 1963, 1964
   The Jimmy Jones Trio, 1966
Chuck Connors, trombone
   Duke Ellington and His Orchestra, 1965–1967
Willie Cook, trumpet
   Duke Ellington and His Orchestra, 1957
Bob Cooper, tenor saxophone, oboe, English horn
   Orchestras conducted by Jerry Gray, 1952; by Buddy
      Bregman, 1956; and by Nelson Riddle, 1982
Buster Cooper, trombone
   Benny Goodman and His Orchestra, 1959
   Duke Ellington and His Orchestra, 1965, 1966
Sid Cooper, alto saxophone
   Orchestra conducted by Vic Schoen, 1945

Tommy Dorsey and His Orchestra, 1947
   Orchestra conducted by Sy Oliver, 1950, 1952
Ray Copeland, trumpet
   Orchestra conducted by Bill Doggett, 1962
Irving Cottler, drums
   Orchestra conducted by Nelson Riddle, 1964
Bob Cranshaw, bass
   The Jimmy Jones Trio, 1967
Jimmy Crawford, drums
   Orchestras conducted by Sy Oliver, 1950, 1951, 1952,
      1953; and by Toots Camarata, 1955
   Small group accompaniment, 1951, 1952, 1953
Wendell Culley, trumpet
   Count Basie and His Orchestra, 1956
Gail Curtis, tenor saxophone
   Tommy Dorsey and His Orchestra, 1947
Cutty Cutshall, trombone
   Orchestra conducted by Toots Camarata, 1955
Paulinho da Costa, percussion
   Orchestra conducted by Eric Bulling, 1980
Hank D'Amico, clarinet
   Orchestra conducted by Sy Oliver 1950
Bill Davis, piano, organ
   Louis Jordan and His Tympany Five, 1945, 1949
   Small group accompaniment, 1963
Carl Davis, saxophones
   Orchestra conducted by Bill Doggett, 1962
Eddie "Lockjaw" Davis, tenor saxophone
   Count Basie and His Orchestra, 1971
   The JATP All-Stars, 1972, 1983
   Small group accompaniment, 1974
Jackie Davis, organ
   Duo accompaniment, 1978
James Decker, French horn
   Orchestra conducted by Nelson Riddle, 1959, 1963, 1964
Barret Deems, drums
   Small group accompaniment, 1956
Buddy DeFranco, clarinet
   Orchestra conducted by Nelson Riddle, 1964
Karl DeKarske, trombone
   Orchestra conducted by Nelson Riddle, 1959
Frank De la Rosa, bass
   The Tommy Flanagan Trio, 1969–1971
Bill DePew, alto saxophone
   Benny Goodman and His Orchestra
Vincent DeRosa, French horn
   Orchestra conducted by Buddy Bregman, 1956
   The Marty Paich Dek-Tette, 1958
   Orchestra conducted by Nelson Riddle, 1959, 1963
Francisco DeSouza, bongos, congas
   Orchestra conducted by Gerald Wilson, 1969–1970
Henry De Vega, alto saxophone
   Orchestra conducted by Gerald Wilson, 1969–1970

Frank DeVol, leader, arranger
  Orchestra, 1957, 1958, 1959, 1960, 1964
Ed de Verteuil, baritone saxophone
  Cootie Williams and His Orchestra, 1944
Harry Dial, maraccas
  Louis Jordan and His Tympany Five, 1945
Harold Dicterow, violin
  Orchestra conducted by Nelson Riddle, 1959
Alvin Dinken, viola
  Orchestras conducted by Nelson Riddle, 1959; and by
    Billy May, 1961
Justin Ditullio, cello
  Orchestra conducted by Nelson Riddle, 1963
Eric Dixon, flute, tenor saxophone
  Count Basie and His Orchestra, 1963, 1971, 1972, 1979
Lucille Dixon, bass
  Orchestra conducted by Bill Doggett, 1962
Jerry Dodgion, saxophones
  Orchestra conducted by Bill Doggett, 1962
Bill Doggett, leader, piano, organ
  Small group accompaniment, 1943, 1944, 1945, 1951,
    1953
  Louis Jordan and His Tympany Five, 1950
  Ray Brown Quintet, 1952
  Orchestra, 1962
George Dorsey, clarinet, alto saxophone
  Ella Fitzgerald and Her Famous Orchestra, 1940, 1941
  Orchestra conducted by Sy Oliver, 1951, 1953
Tommy Dorsey, leader, trombone
  Orchestra, 1947
Jesse Drakes, trumpet
  The Lester Young Quartet, 1948
Art Drellinger, clarinet, tenor saxophone
  Bob Haggart and His Orchestra, 1946, 1947
David Allen Duke, flügelhorn
  Orchestra conducted by Nelson Riddle, 1982
Jack Dumont, saxophones
  Dave Barbour and His Orchestra, 1951
Modesto Duran, bongos, congas
  Orchstra conducted by Gerald Wilson, 1969–1970
Bobby Durham, drums
  The Tommy Flanagan Trio, 1972, 1975, 1977
  The Tommy Flanagan Quartet, 1974
  The Jimmy Rowles Trio, 1983
  The Ella Fitzgerald Trio, 1983
  Small group accompaniment, 1989
George Duvivier, bass
  Orchestras conducted by Leroy Kirkland, 1952; by Sy
    Oliver, 1953; and by Bill Doggett, 1962
Allen Eager (b. 1927), tenor saxophone
  The Ray Brown Quintet, 1948
Walter Edelstein, violin
  Orchestra conducted by Nelson Riddle, 1959

Harry Edison, trumpet
  The JATP All-Stars, 1950, 1956, 1972
  Orchestras conducted by Buddy Bregman, 1956; by
    Frank DeVol, 1957, 1958; by Marty Paich, 1966;
    and by Gerald Wilson, 1969–70
  Benny Carter's Magnificent Seven, 1968
  The JATP All-Stars, 1974, 1989
Roy Eldridge (1911–1989), trumpet
  The JATP All-Stars, 1949, 1953, 1954, 1956, 1957,
    1972, 1983
  Small group accompaniment, 1963, 1964
Duke Ellington, leader, piano
  Orchestra, 1957, 1965–1967
Mercer Ellington, trumpet
  Duke Ellington and His Orchestra, 1965–1967
Don Elliot, mellowphone
  Small group accompaniment, 1952
Herb Ellis, guitar
  Small group accompaniment, 1953, 1954, 1956–1959,
    1961, 1963
  The JATP All-Stars, 1953, 1954, 1956, 1957
  The Ray Brown Quartet, 1954
  Orchestras conducted by Frank DeVol, 1959; by Billy
    May, 1961; and by Gerald Wilson, 1969–1970
Ziggy Elman, trumpet
  Benny Goodman and His Orchestra, 1936
  Orchestras conducted by John Scott Trotter, 1953,
    1954; and by Nelson Riddle, 1959
Bob Enevoldsen, valve trombone, tenor saxophone
  The Marty Paich Dek-Tette, 1958
Ernie Englund, trumpet
  Randy Brooks and His Orchestra, 1945
Christine Ermacoff, cello
  Orchestra conducted by Nelson Riddle, 1982
Don Fagerquist, trumpet
  Orchestras conducted by Paul Weston, 1958; by Nelson
    Riddle, 1959, 1963; and by Billy May, 1960, 1961
  The Marty Paich Dek-Tette, 1958
Gilbert Falco, trombone
  Orchestra conducted by Nelson Riddle, 1964
Tony Faso, trumpet
  Orchestra conducted by Sy Oliver, 1950, 1951
Nick Fatool, drums
  Orchestra conducted by John Scott Trotter, 1953, 1954
Morey Feld, drums
  Bob Haggart and His Orchestra, 1947
Harry (Hal) Feldman, tenor saxophone
  Orchestras conducted by Vic Schoen, 1945; and by
    Toots Camarata, 1955
Vic Feldman, vibraphone
  Orchestra conducted by Gerald Wilson, 1969–1970
Sid Feller, leader, arranger
  Orchestra, 1967

Maynard Ferguson, trumpet
  Orchestra conducted by Buddy Bregman, 1956
Andy Ferretti, trumpet
  Bob Haggart and His Orchestra, 1947
Dave Filerman, cello
  Orchestra conducted by Nelson Riddle, 1959
The Firehouse Five + 2
  Orchestra conducted by John Scott Trotter, 1950
Arnold Fishkin, bass
  Small group accompaniment, 1951
Tommy Flanagan, piano
  Small group accompaniment, 1963, 1964, 1965, 1974
  Orchestra conducted by Gerald Wilson, 1969–1970
  The Tommy Flanagan Trio, 1969–1972, 1975, 1977
  The Tommy Flanagan Quartet, 1973, 1974
Med Flory, baritone saxophone, 1958
  The Marty Paich Dek-Tette, 1958
Frank Flynn, drums, percussion
  Small group accompaniment, 1954
  Orchestra conducted by Nelson Riddle, 1959, 1963, 1964
Jimmy Forrest, tenor saxophone
  Count Basie and His Orchestra, 1972
Frank Foster, tenor saxophone
  Count Basie and His Orchestra, 1956, 1963
  Duke Ellington and His Orchestra, 1957
Charlie Fowlkes, baritone saxophone
  Count Basie and His Orchestra, 1963, 1979
Frank Fowlkes, baritone saxophone
  Count Basie and His Orchestra, 1956
Panama Francis, drums
  Benny Carter's Magnificent Seven, 1968
Stan Freeman, piano
  Bob Haggart and his Orchestra, 1947
John Frosk, trumpet
  Benny Goodman and His Orchestra, 1959
Tommy Fulford, piano
  Chick Webb and His Orchestra, 1936–1939
  Ella Fitzgerld and Her Famous Orchestra, 1939–1941
  Small group accompaniment, 1941, 1942
Everett Gaines, tenor saxophone
  Cootie Williams and His Orchestra, 1946
Barry Galbraith, guitar
  Orchestra conducted by Toots Camarata, 1955
Otis Gamble, trumpet
  Cootie Williams and His Orchestra, 1947
Russ Garcia, leader, arranger
  Orchestra and Chorus, 1957, 1959
Jacques Gasselin, violin
  Orchestras conducted by Nelson Riddle, 1959; and by
    Billy May, 1961
Joe Gayles, tenor saxophone
  Dizzy Gillespie and His Orchestra, 1947
Herb Geller, alto saxophone

Orchestra conducted by Buddy Bregman, 1956
  Benny Goodman and His Orchestra, 1959
Charles Genduso, trumpet
  Orchestra conducted by Vic Schoen, 1945
Chuck Gentry, bass clarinet, bassoon, baritone saxophone
  Dave Barbour and His Orchestra, 1951
  Orchestras conducted by Sonny Burke, 1951; by Buddy
    Bregman, 1956; by Paul Weston, 1958; and by Billy
    May, 1961
Stan Getz, tenor saxophone
  JATP All-Stars, 1957, 1972
James Getzoff, violin
  Orchestra conducted by Nelson Riddle, 1959
Bobby Gibbons, guitar
  Orchestra conducted by Jerry Gray, 1952
Terry Gibbs, vibraphone
  Small group accompaniment, 1952
Ed Gilbert, tuba
  Orchestra conducted by Nelson Riddle, 1959
Ben Gill, violin
  Orchestras conducted by Nelson Riddle, 1959; and by
    Billy May, 1961
Dizzy Gillespie (1917–1993), leader, trumpet
  Orchestra, 1947
  The JATP All-Stars 1954
  Guest with Duke Ellington and His Orchestra, 1957
Felix Giobbe, bass
  Orchestra conducted by Vic Schoen, 1945
Ed Glover, trombone
  Cootie Williams and His Orchestra, 1944
Bernie Glow, trumpet
  Benny Goodman and His Quartet, Quintet, and
    Orchestra, 1958
Paul Gonsalves, tenor saxophone
  Duke Ellington and His Orchestra, 1957, 1965–1967
Benny Goodman, leader, clarinet
  Benny Goodman and His Orchestra, 1936, 1958, 1959
Harry Goodman, string bass
  Benny Goodman and His Orchestra, 1936
Irving Goodman, trumpet
  Tommy Dorsey and His Orchestra, 1947
Justin Gordon, woodwinds
  Orchestras conducted by Nelson Riddle, 1959; and by
    Billy May, 1960
Conrad Gozzo, trumpet
  Orchestras conducted by Jerry Gray, 1952; by Buddy
    Bregman, 1956; by Nelson Riddle, 1959; and by
    Billy May, 1961
Bill Graham, alto saxophone
  Count Basie and His Orchestra, 1956
Leonard Graham, trumpet
  Eddy Heywood and His Orchestra, 1947
  Small group accompaniment, 1947

Jewell Grant, woodwinds
    Orchestra conducted by Nelson Riddle, 1959
Ralph Grasso, guitar
    Orchestra conducted by Nelson Riddle, 1978
Jerry Gray, leader, arranger
    Orchestra, 1952
Bill Green, flute, clarinet
    Orchestra conducted by Nelson Riddle, 1978, 1982
Freddie Green, guitar
    Count Basie and His Orchestra, 1956, 1963, 1971,
       1972, 1979
Thurman Green, trombone
    Orchestra conducted by Gerald Wilson, 1969–1970
Urban "Urbie" Green, trombone
    Benny Goodman and His Orchestra, 1958, 1959
    Count Basie and His Orchestra, 1963
William Green, woodwinds
    Orchestras conducted by Nelson Riddle, 1959; and by
       Gerald Wilson, 1969–1970
Jack Greenberg, tenor saxophone
    Bob Haggart and His Orchestra, 1946
Elizabeth Greenschpoon, cello
    Orchestra conducted by Nelson Riddle, 1959
Al Grey, trombone
    Orchestra conducted by Sy Oliver, 1952
    Count Basie and His Orchestra, 1971, 1972
    The JATP All-Stars, 1989
    Small group accompaniment, 1989
Chris Griffin, trumpet
    Benny Goodman and His Orchestra, 1936
    Bob Haggart and His Orchestra, 1947
Robert Guy, trumpet
    Orchestra conducted by John Scott Trotter, 1953, 1954
Bob Haggart, bass
    Small group accompaniment, 1943, 1944, 1945
    The Lawson-Haggart Jazz Band, 1952
Corky Hale, harp
    Orchestra conducted by Buddy Bregman, 1956
Ed Hall, clarinet
    JATP All-Stars, 1956
Jim Hall, guitar
    Small group accompaniment, 1960
Larry Hall, trombone
    Tommy Dorsey and His Orchestra, 1947
John Halliburton, trombone
    Orchestras conducted by Sonny Burke, 1951; and by
       Jerry Gray, 1952
Jimmy Hamilton, clarinets, saxophones
    Duke Ellington and His Orchestra, 1957, 1965–1967
Earl Hardy, trombone
    Ella Fitzgerald and Her Famous Orchestra, 1940–1941
Bill Harris (1916–1973), trombone
    The JATP All-Stars, 1953

Dave Harris, saxophones
    Orchestra conducted by John Scott Trotter, 1953, 1954
Joe Harris, drums
    Dizzy Gillespie and His Orchestra, 1947
    The Tee Carson Trio, 1968
Stanley Harris, viola
    Orchestra conducted by Nelson Riddle, 1959
Chauncey Haughton, clarinet, alto saxophone
    Chick Webb and His Orchestra, 1937
    Ella Fitzgerald and Her Famous Orchestra, 1940
    The Chick Webb Orchestra, 1973
John Haughton, trombone
    Ella Fitzgerald and Her Famous Orchestra, 1940
Coleman Hawkins (1904–1969), tenor saxophone
    The JATP All-Stars, 1950, 1957
Roy Haynes, drums
    The Ray Brown Trio and Quintet, 1948, 1949
    Small group accompaniment, 1952
J.C. Heard (1917–1988), drums
    Small group accompaniment, 1947, 1953
    The JATP All-Stars, 1953
John Heard, bass
    Orchestra conducted by Nelson Riddle, 1978
Ernie Hecksher, leader
    Ernie Hecksher's Big Band, 1969
Al Hendrickson, guitar
    Orchestra conducted by Billy May, 1960
Heywood Henry, baritone saxophone
    The Chick Webb Band, 1973
Eddie Heywood, leader, piano
    Orchestra, 1947
Lloyd Hildebrand, bassoon
    Orchestra conducted by Nelson Riddle, 1964
Harry Hill, violin
    Orchestra conducted by Nelson Riddle, 1959
Art Hillery, organ
    Orchestra conducted by Nelson Riddle, 1982
Kenny Hing, tenor saxophone
    Count Basie and His Orchestra, 1979
William Hinshaw, French horn
    Orchestra conducted by Nelson Riddle, 1963, 1964
Johnny Hodges, alto saxophone
    Duke Ellington and His Orchestra, 1957, 1965–1967
Carl Hogan, guitar
    Louis Jordan and His Tympany Five, 1945, 1949
Bill Holcomb, saxophones
    Orchestra conducted by Sy Oliver, 1951, 1953
Mitch Holer, rhythm guitar
    Orchestra conducted by Eric Bulling, 1980
Bill Holman, tenor saxophone
    Marty Paich and His Dek-Tette, 1958
Milt Holland, percussion
    Orchestra conducted by Buddy Bregman, 1956

Frank Hooks, trombone
  Count Basie and His Orchestra, 1972
Claude Hopkins, leader
  Orchestra, 1944, 1945
Bob Horton, trombone
  Cootie Williams and His Orchestra, 1944, 1946
Al Howard, alto saxophone
  Orchestra conducted by Toots Camarata, 1955
Frank Howard, trombone
  Dave Barbour and His Orchestra, 1951
Joe Howard, trombone
  Orchestras conducted by John Scott Trotter, 1953,
    1954; and by Buddy Bregman, 1956
Paul Hubinon, trumpet
  Orchestra conducted by Gerald Wilson, 1969–1970
Peanuts Hucko, clarinet
  Ella Fitzgerald and Her V-Disc Jumpers, 1945
Jim Hughart, bass
  The Jimmy Jones Trio, 1966
  Orchestra conducted by Nelson Riddle, 1982
Bill Hughes, trombone, bass trombone
  Count Basie and his Orchestra, 1956, 1971, 1972, 1979
Barbara Jane Hunter, cello
  Orchestra conducted by Nelson Riddle, 1982
Bobby Hutcherson, vibraphones
  Orchestra conducted by Gerald Wilson, 1969–1970
Dick Hyman, piano, organ
  Orchestra conducted by Toots Camarata, 1955
  Small group accompaniment, 1958
Aaron Izenhall, trumpet
  Louis Jordan and His Tympany Five, 1945, 1949,
    1950
John Jackson, alto saxophone
  Cootie Williams and His Orchestra, 1946
Josh Jackson, tenor saxophone
  Louis Jordan and His Tympany Five, 1945, 1950
Milt Jackson, vibraphone
  Dizzy Gillespie and His Orchestra, 1947
Paul Jackson, rhythm guitar
  Orchestra conducted by Eric Bulling, 1980
Quentin Jackson, trombone
  Duke Ellington and His Orchestra, 1957
Jules Jacob, woodwinds
  Orchestras conducted by Nelson Riddle, 1959; and by
    Billy May, 1961
Dick Jacobs, tenor saxophone, orchestra bells
  The Ray Brown Quintet, 1952
  Orchestra conducted by Sy Oliver 1952
Illinois Jacquet (b. 1922), tenor saxophone
  Small group accompaniment, 1947
  JATP All-Stars, 1956, 1957
Harry James, trumpet
  Guest with Benny Goodman and His Quintet, 1958

Arnold Jarvis, piano
  Cootie Williams and His Orchestra, 1946
Jack Jeffers, trombone
  The Chick Webb Orchestra, 1973
Fred Jefferson, piano
  The Lester Young Quartet, 1948
Hilton Jefferson, alto saxophone
  Chick Webb and His Orchestra, 1938, 1939
  Ella Fitzgerald and Her Famous Orchestra, 1939, 1940
Gordon Jenkins, leader, arranger,
  Orchestra and chorus, 1949, 1954
Bill Jennings, guitar
  Louis Jordan and His Tympany Five, 1950
Jerry Jerome, tenor saxophone
  Orchestra conducted by Sy Oliver, 1950
Bobby Johnson, guitar
  Chick Webb and His Orchestra, 1937–1939
Eddie Johnson, tenor saxophone
  Cootie Williams and His Orchestra, 1947
  Louis Jordan and His Tympany Five, 1949
Edward Johnson, trombone
  Cootie Williams and His Orchestra, 1946, 1947
Gus Johnson, drums
  Small group accompaniment, 1958, 1959, 1960, 1961,
    1963, 1964, 1965
  Orchestra conducted by Bill Doggett, 1962
  The Jimmy Jones Trio, 1966
Howard Johnson, alto saxophone
  Dizzy Gillespie and His Orchestra, 1947
J.J. Johnson (b. 1924), trombone
  JATP All-Stars, 1957, 1983
  Orchestras conducted by Nelson Riddle, 1978; and by
    Gerald Wilson, 1969–1970
Money Johnson, trumpet
  Duke Ellington and His Orchestra, 1967
Plas Johnson, tenor saxophone
  Orchestras conducted by Nelson Riddle, 1959, 1963,
    1964; and by Billy May, 1960
Claude Jones, trombone
  Chick Webb and His Orchestra, 1934–1936
Dale Jones, bass
  Small group accompaniment, 1956
Eddie Jones, bass
  Count Basie and His Orchestra, 1956
Hank Jones (b. 1918), piano
  Small group accompaniment, 1947, 1950, 1951, 1952
  The Ray Brown Trio and Quintet, 1948, 1949, 1950,
    1952
  Orchestras conducted by Sy Oliver, 1950, 1951, 1952,
    1953; by Sonny Burke, 1951; by Leroy Kirkland,
    1952; by Jerry Gray, 1952; and by Bill Doggett, 1962
  The JATP All-Stars, 1950
  Dave Barbour and His Orchestra, 1951

Benny Goodman and His Orchestra, 1958, 1959
    Orchestra conducted by Bill Doggett, 1962
Harold Jones, drums
    Count Basie and His Orchestra, 1971
Herbie Jones, trumpet
    Duke Ellington and His Orchestra, 1965–1967
Jimmy Jones, piano
    Duke Ellington and His Orchestra, 1965
    The Jimmy Jones Trio, 1966, 1967
    Benny Carter's Magnificent Seven, 1968
Jo Jones (1911–1985), drums
    Small group accompaniment, 1957
Reunald Jones, trumpet
    Count Basie and His Orchestra, 1956
Thaddeus "Thad" Jones, trumpet
    Count Basie and His Orchestra, 1956
Louis Jordan, leader, alto saxophone, vocals
    Chick Webb and His Orchestra, 1937
    Louis Jordan and His Tympany Five, 1945, 1949
Taft Jordan, trumpet, vocalist
    Chick Webb and His Orchestra, 1933–1939
    Ella Fitzgerald and Her Famous Orchestra, 1939–1941
    Orchestras conducted by Sy Oliver, 1951, 1952, 1953;
        and by Bill Doggett, 1962
    Small group accompaniment, 1953
Knud Jorgensen, piano
    Small group accompaniment, 1961
Katherine Julyie, harp
    Orchestra conducted by Nelson Riddle, 1959, 1964
Stan Kane, drums
    Orchestra conducted by Leroy Kirkland, 1952
Armand Kaproff, viola
    Orchestras conducted by Nelson Riddle, 1959, 1963;
    and by Billy May, 1961
Dennis Karmazyn, cello
    Orchestra conducted by Nelson Riddle, 1982
Bernie Kaufman, alto saxophone
    Orchestra conducted by Vic Schoen, 1945
Connie Kay, drums
    JATP All-Stars, 1957
Norman Keenan, bass
    Cootie Williams and His Orchestra, 1946, 1947
    Count Basie and His Orchestra, 1971
Murray Kellner, violin
    Orchestras conducted by Nelson Riddle, 1959; and by
        Billy May, 1960
Ted Kelly, trombone
    The Lester Young Quartet, 1948
Stan Kenton, leader
    Orchestra, 1955
Barney Kessel (b. 1923), guitar
    Orchestra conducted by Buddy Bregman, 1956
    Small group accompaniment, 1956, 1964

Orchestras conducted by Frank DeVol, 1957; by Paul
    Weston, 1958, and by Nelson Riddle, 1964
Jerome Kessler, cello
    Orchestra conducted by Nelson Riddle, 1982
Lou Kievman, violin, viola
    Orchestras conducted by Nelson Riddle, 1959; and by
        Billy May, 1960
Al King, trombone
    Edde Heywood and His Orchestra, 1947
Jule Kinzler, flute
    Orchestra conducted by Buddy Bregman, 1956
Leroy Kirkland, leader, arranger, guitare
    Cootie Williams and His Orchestra (guitar), 1944
    Leroy Kirkland and His Orchestra, 1952
Don Kirkpatrick, piano
    Chick Webb and His Orchestra, 1935, 1936
John Kitzmiller, tuba
    The Marty Paich Dek-Tette, 1958
Harry Klee, flute, woodwinds
    Orchestra conducted by Nelson Riddle, 1959, 1963,
        1964, 1978
Manny Klein, trumpet
    Orchestra conducted by Nelson Riddle, 1959
Richard Klein, flügelhorn
    Orchestra conducted by Nelson Riddle, 1982
Al Klink, tenor saxophone
    Orchestras conducted by Sy Oliver, 1950, 1951; and by
        Toots Camarata, 1955
    Benny Goodman and His Orchestra, 1958
Irv Kluger, drums
    Orchestra conducted by Vic Schoen, 1945
Rene Knight, piano,
    Small group accompaniment, 1945, 1946
Arnold Koblentz, oboe, English horn
    Orchestra conducted by Buddy Bregman, 1956
Joe Koch, woodwinds
    Orchestra conducted by Nelson Riddle, 1959, 1963, 1964
George Koenig, alto saxophone
    Bob Haggart and His Orchestra, 1946
Ray Kramer, cello
    Orchestras conducted by Billy May, 1961; and by Nelson
        Riddle, 1963
Phil Kraus, vibraphone, percussion
    Orchestras conducted by Leroy Kirkland, 1952; and by
        Toots Camarata, 1955
    Benny Goodman and His Orchestra, 1959
Gene Krupa (1909–1973), drums
    Benny Goodman and His Orchestra
Edward Kusby, trombone
    Orchestra conducted by Billy May, 1961
Billy Kyle, piano
    Small group accompaniment, 1946
    JATP All-Stars, 1956

Abraham Laborie, bass
  Orchestra conducted by Eric Bulling, 1980
Paul Lajoie, string bass
  Randy Brooks and His Orchestra
John Lamb, bass
  Duke Ellington and His Orchestra, 1965, 1966
Harold Land, tenor saxophone
  Orchestra conducted by Gerald Wilson, 1969–1970
Ralph Lane, viola
  Orchestra conducted by Nelson Riddle, 1959
Mike Lang, keyboards
  Orchestra conducted by Eric Bulling, 1980
Ronnie Lang, alto saxophone
  Orchestra conducted by Nelson Riddle, 1959, 1963,
    1982
Robert La Marchina, cello
  Orchestra conducted by Buddy Bregman, 1956
Ellis Larkins, piano
  Solo accompanist, 1950, 1954, 1973
Hubert Laws, flute
  Orchestra conducted by Nelson Riddle, 1982
Yank Lawson, trumpet
  The Lawson-Haggart Jazz Band, 1952
The Lawson-Haggrt Jazz Band
  Orchestra, 1952
Cliff Leeman, drums
  The Lawson-Haggart Jazz Band, 1952
Jack Lesberg, bass
  Benny Goodman and His Orchestra, 1959
John Lesko, tenor saxophone
  Randy Brooks and His Orchestra, 1945
Stan Levey, drums
  Small group accompaniment, 1961, 1962
Walter Levinsky, alto saxophone
  Benny Goodman and His Orchestra, 1958
Lou Levy, piano, celeste
  Small group accompaniment, 1958, 1959, 1961
  The Marty Paich Dek-Tette, 1958
  Orchestras conducted by Frank DeVol, 1959; and by
    Billy May, 1961
Carroll Lewis, trumpet
  Orchestra conducted by Nelson Riddle, 1959, 1963,
    1964, 1978
John Lewis, piano
  Dizzy Gillespie and His Orchestra, 1947
Mel Lewis, drums
  The Marty Paich Dek-Tette, 1958
  Orchestra conducted by Nelson Riddle, 1959
Marvin Limonick, violin
  Orchestra conducted by Nelson Riddle, 1959
Ray Linn (1920–1997), trumpet
  Orchestra conducted by Buddy Bregman, 1956
Melba Liston, trombone

Orchestra conducted by Bill Doggett, 1962
Ulysses Livingston, guitar
  Ella Fitzgerald and Her Famous Orchestra, 1940, 1941
  Small group accompaniment, 1941
Joseph Livoti, violin
  Orchestra conducted by Nelson Riddle, 1959
Clyde Lombardi, bass
  Small group accompaniment, 1951
Johnny Long, leader
  Orchestra, 1944
Frank Lo Pinto, trumpet
  The Chick Webb Orchestra, 1973
Vic Lourie, claves
  Louis Jordan and His Tympany Five, 1945
Mundell Lowe, guitar
  Orchestra conducted by Bill Doggett, 1962
Hugo Lowenstern, saxophones
  Orchestra conducted by Sonny Burke, 1951
Dan Lube, violin
  Orchestras conducted by Nelson Riddle, 1959, 1963;
    and by Billy May, 1961
Lawrence Lucie, trumpet
  The Chick Webb Orchestra, 1973
Frank Ludwig, tenor saxophone
  Orchestra conducted by Sy Oliver, 1950
Edgar Lustgarten, cello
  Orchestras conducted by Buddy Bregman, 1956; by
    Nelson Riddle, 1959, 1963; and by Billy May, 1961
Machito's Rhythm, 1949
  Components unknown
Bernie Mackay, guitar
  Small group accompaniment, 1943, 1944, 1945
Arthur Maebe, French horn
  Orchestras conducted by Nelson Riddle, 1963; and by
    Gerald Wilson, 1969–1970
Virginia Majewski, viola
  Orchestra conducted by Billy May, 1961
Mickey Mangano, trumpet
  Orchestra conducted by Sonny Burke, 1951
Vito Mangano, trumpet
  Orchestra conducted by Nelson Riddle, 1959, 1963, 1964
Sonny Mann, drums
  Randy Brooks and His Orchestra, 1945
Shelley Manne, drums
  Benny Goodman and His Orchestra, 1959
  Orchestras conducted by Marty Paich, 1966; and by
    Nelson Riddle, 1982
Wendell Marshall, bass
  Small group accompaniment, 1957
Johnny Martell, trumpet
  Tommy Dorsey and His Orchestra, 1947
Dave Martin, piano
  Orchestra conducted by Sy Oliver, 1953

Robert L. Martin, cello
 Orchestra conducted by Nelson Riddle, 1982
Alex Mastren, trombone
 Tommy Dorsey and His Orchestra, 1947
Carmen Mastren, guitar
 Tommy Dorsey and His Orchestra, 1947
Julian Matlock, clarinet
 Orchestra conducted by Paul Weston, 1958
Matty Matlock, saxophones
 Orchestra conducted by Johns Scott Trotter, 1953, 1954
George Matthews, trombone
 Chick Webb and His Orchestra, 1938, 1939
 Ella Fitzgerald and Her Famous Orchestra, 1939–1941
 The Chick Webb Orchestra, 1973
Billy May, leader, arranger, trumpet
 Orchestra, 1960, 1961, 1991
Wendell Mayhew, trombone
 Orchestra conducted by John Scott Trotter, 1953, 1954
Carlton McBeath, trumpet
 Orchestra conducted by Sonny Burke, 1951
John McConnell, trombone
 Ella Fitzgerald and Her Famous Orchestra, 1940, 1941
Clarence McDonald, keyboards
 Orchestra conducted by Eric Bulling, 1980
Murray McEachern, trombone
 Benny Goodman and His Orchestra, 1936
Lou McGarity, trombone, violin
 Ella Fitzgerald and Her V-Disc Jumpers, 1945
 The Lawson-Haggart Jazz Band, 1952
 Benny Goodman and His Orchestra, 1958
John McGhee, trumpet
 Small group accompaniment, 1943, 1944, 1949
Larry McGuire, trumpet
 Orchestra conducted by Gerald Wilson, 1969–1970
Matthew McKay, trumpet
 Dizzy Gillespie and His Orchestra, 1947
Al McKibbon (b. 1919), bass
 Dizzy Gillespie and His Orchestra, 1947
Dale McMickle, trumpet
 Orchestras conducted by Toots Camarata, 1955; and
  by Nelson Riddle, 1959
Fraser McPherson, leader, tenor saxophone
 The Fraser McPherson Big Band, 1968
Dave McRae, baritone saxophone
 Orchestra conducted by Sy Oliver, 1951, 1953
Ted (Teddy) McRae, baritone saxophone, tenor
  saxophone
 Chick Webb and His Orchestra, 1936–1939
 Ella Fitzgerald and Her Famous Orchestra, 1939–1941
 Teddy Wilson and His Orchestra, 1936
 Small group accompaniment, 1941
Bob Merrill, trumpet
 Cootie Williams and His Orchestra, 1946, 1947

Joe Meyer, flügelhorn
 Orchestra conducted by Nelson Riddle, 1982
Wilfred Middlebrooks, bass
 Small group accompaniment, 1960, 1961, 1962
 Orchestra conducted by Billy May, 1961
Charles "Butch" Miles, drums
 Count Basie and His Orchestra, 1979
Jackie Mills (b. 1922), drums
 Trio accompaniment, 1956
George "Pete" Minger, trumpet
 Count Basie and His Orchestra, 1971, 1972, 1979
Grover Mitchell, trombone
 Count Basie and His Orchestra, 1963
Oliver Mitchell, trumpet
 Orchestra conducted by Sonny Burke, 1951
Red Mitchell, drums
 Orchestra conducted by Frank DeVol, 1957
Toots Mondello, alto saxophone
 Bob Haggart and His Orchestra, 1947
Abe Most, clarinet, alto saxophone
 Tommy Dorsey and His Orchestra, 1947
 Orchestras conducted by Buddy Bregman, 1956; and
  by Nelson Riddle, 1964
Lamont Moten, bass
 Small group accompaniment, 1946
Earl Murphy, trombone
 Ella Fitzgerald and Her Famous Orchestra, 1941
Ralph Mussilo, trumpet
 Orchestra conducted by Vic Schoen, 1945
Vido Musso, tenor saxophone
 Benny Goodman and His Orchestra, 1936
Ray Nance, trumpet, vocals
 Duke Ellington and His Orchestra, 1957, 1966
Dick Nash, trombone
 Orchestra conducted by Nelson Riddle, 1959, 1963, 1964
Ted Nash, trombone, flute, tenor saxophone
 Orchestras conducted by Buddy Bregman, 1956; by
  Paul Weston, 1958; by Nelson Riddle, 1959, 1963; and
  by Billy May, 1960
George Neikrug, cello
 Orchestra conducted by Nelson Riddle, 1959, 1963
Larry Neil, trumpet
 Dave Barbour and His Orchestra, 1951
Alex Neimann, viola
 Orchestra conducted by Nelson Riddle, 1963
Ralph Neimann, viola
 Orchestra conducted by Nelson Riddle, 1959
Erno Neufeld, violin
 Orchestras conducted by Nelson Riddle, 1959, 1963;
  and by Billy May, 1961
Joe Newman, trumpet
 Count Basie and His Orchestra, 1956, 1963
Frank Newton, trumpet

Teddy Wilson and His Orchestra, 1936
George Nicholas, tenor saxophone
    Dizzy Gillespie and His Orchestra, 1947
Red Nichols, trumpet
    Orchestra conducted by John Scott Trotter, 1950,
        1953, 1954
Richard Noel, trombone
    Orchestras conducted by Nelson Riddle, 1959, 1978;
        and by Billy May, 1960
Benny Norton, trombone
    Teddy Wilson and His Orchestra, 1936
Red Norvo, leader, vibraphone
    Benny Goodman and His Quintet, 1958
    Red Norvo and His Jazz Group, 1959
James Nottingham, trumpet
    Orchestras conducted by Sy Oliver, 1952, 1953; and by
        Toots Camarata, 1955
Freddie Ohms, trombone
    Bob Haggart and His Orchestra, 1947
Sy Oliver, leader, arranger
    Orchestra, 1949, 1950, 1951, 1952, 1953
Ray Orr, trumpet
    Dizzy Gillespie and His Orchestra, 1947
Anthony Ortega, flute, piccolo
    Orchestra conducted by Gerald Wilson, 1969–1970
Marty Paich, leader, arranger
    The Marty Paich Dek-Tette, 1958
    Orchestra, 1959, 1962, 1964–1966
Remo Palmieri, guitar
    Ella Fitzgerald and Her V-Disc Jumpers, 1945
Charlie Parker (1920–1955), alto saxophone
    The JATP All-Stars, 1949, 1950
Joe Pass, guitar
    The Tommy Flanagan Quartet, 1973, 1974
    Orchestras conducted by Eric Bulling, 1980; and by
        Nelson Riddle, 1982
    Small group accompaniment, 1974
    Solo accompaniment, 1973, 1976, 1983, 1986, 1991
Tom Patton, trumpet
    Orchestra conducted by Jerry Gray
Cecil Payne, flute, baritone saxophone
    Dizzy Gillespie and His Orchestra
    Count Basie and His Orchestra, 1971
Percival "Sonny" Payne, drums
    Count Basie and His Orchestra, 1956, 1963
Sylvester Payne, drums
    Cootie Williams and His Orchestra, 1944
    Small group accompaniment, 1946
Curtis Peagler, alto saxophone
    Count Basie and His Orchestra, 1971, 1972
Bob Peck, trumpet
    Bob Haggart and His Orchestra, 1947
Niels-Henning Ørsted Pedersen

The JATP All-Stars, 1983
Tommy Pederson, trombone
    Orchestra conducted by Nelson Riddle, 1959, 1963,
        1964
Beverley Peer, string bass
    Chick Webb and His Orchestra, 1936–1939
    Ella Fitzgerald and Her Famous Orchestra, 1939–1941
    Small group accompaniment, 1941
    The Chick Webb Orchestra, 1973
Ralph Peña, bass
    Orchestra conducted by Nelson Riddle, 1959
Judy Perett, cello
    Orchestra conducted by Nelson Riddle, 1982
Andy Peretti, trumpet
    Tommy Dorsey and His Orchestra, 1947
Robert Perissi, French horn
    Orchestra conducted by Nelson Riddle, 1964
Bill Perkins, tenor saxophone
    Orchestra conducted by Marty Paich, 1966
Danny Perri, guitar
    Bob Haggart and His Orchestra, 1946, 1947
Ermit V. Perry, trumpet
    Cootie Williams and His Orchestra, 1944, 1946, 1947
Richard Perry, leader, arranger
    Orchestra, 1969
Ron Perry, tenor saxophone
    Orchestra conducted by Jerry Gray, 1952
Oscar Peterson, piano
    The JATP All-Stars, 1953, 1957, 1983
    Small group accompaniment, 1954, 1956, 1957, 1958,
        1961
    Solo accompaniment, 1983
Flip Phillips, tenor saxophone
    Small group accompaniment, 1949
    The JATP All-Stars, 1949, 1950, 1953, 1954, 1956, 1957
Bobby Plater, flute, alto saxophone
    Count Basie and His Orchestra, 1971, 1972, 1979
Carl Poole, trumpet
    Orchestra conducted by Sy Oliver, 1951
Lee Pope, tenor saxophone
    Cootie Williams and His Orchestra, 1944
Al Porcino, trumpet
    The Marty Paich Dek-Tette, 1958
Johnny Potaker, piano
    Tommy Dorsey and His Orchestra, 1947
Benny Powell, trombone
    Count Basie and His Orchestra, 1956, 1963
Buddy Powell, piano
    Cootie Williams and His Orchestra, 1944
Frank Powell, alto saxophone
    Cootie Williams and His Orchestra, 1944
Jimmy Powell, alto saxophone
    Eddy Heywood and His Orchestra, 1947

David Pratt, cello
  Orchestra conducted by Nelson Riddle, 1963
André Previn, leader, arranger
  Orchestra, 1955
  Guest with Benny Goodman and His Orchestra, 1959
George Price, French horn
  Orchestra conducted by Nelson Riddle, 1964
Jesse Price, drums
  Ella Fitzgerald and Her Famous Orchestra
James Priddy, trombone
  Orchestras conducted by Sonny Burke, 1951; by Jerry
    Gray, 1952; and by Nelson Riddle, 1959
William Pritchard, trombone
  Orchestra conducted by Vic Schoen, 1945
Bernie Privin, trumpet
  Orchestra conducted by Sy Oliver, 1950, 1951, 1952
Russell Procope, clarinets, saxophones
  Duke Ellington and His Orchestra, 1957, 1965–1967
Carl Pruitt, bass
  Cootie Williams and His Orchestra, 1944
William "Keg" Purnell, drums
  Eddie Heywood and His Orchestra, 1947
Janet Putnam, harp
  Orchestra conducted by Toots Camarata, 1955
Emil Raddochia, percussion
  Orchestra conducted by Nelson Riddle, 1964
Don Rader, trumpet
  Count Basie and His Orchestra, 1963
Lou Raderman, violin
  Orchestras conducted by Nelson Riddle, 1959, 1963;
    and by Billy May, 1961
Don Raffell, saxophones
  Orchestra conducted by Sonny Burke, 1951
Junior Raglan, bass
  Small group accompaniment, 1946
Roger "Ram" Ramirez, piano,
  Ella Fitzgerald and Her Famous Orchestra, 1940
Irving Randolph, trumpet
  Ella Fitzgerald and Her Famous Orchestra, 1940, 1941
Billy Rauch, trumpet
  Bob Haggart and His Orchestra, 1947
Clarence "Gene" Redd, trumpet
  Cootie Williams and His Orchestra, 1946, 1947
Waymon Reed, trumpet, flügelhorn
  Count Basie and His Orchestra, 1971, 1972
Kurt Reher, cello
  Orchestra conducted by Nelson Riddle, 1959, 1963
Allan Reuss, guitar
  Benny Goodman and His Orchestra
Fortunatus "Flip" Ricard, trumpet
  Count Basie and His Orchestra, 1963
Buddy Rich (1917–1987), drums, vocals
  Ella Fitzgerald and Her V-Disc Jumpers, 1945

Small group accompaniment, 1947, 1956
The Ray Brown Trio, 1949
The JATP All-Stars, 1950, 1954
The Ray Brown Quartet, 1954
Emil Richards, vibraphone
  Orchestra conducted by Billy May, 1961
Boomie Richman, tenor saxophone
  Tommy Dorsey and His Orchestra, 1947
Bill Richmond, drums
  Orchestra conducted by Nelson Riddle, 1959
Christopher Riddle, bass trombone
  Orchestra conducted by Nelson Riddle, 1978
Nelson Riddle, leader, arranger
  Orchestra, 1959, 1963, 1972, 1978, 1982
Lawrence Rivera, bongos
  Orchestra conducted by Sy Oliver, 1953
George Roberts, bass trombone
  Orchestras conducted by Buddy Bregman, 1956; by
    Nelson Riddle, 1959, 1963, 1964; and by Billy May,
    1960
Gale Robinson, flügelhorn
  Orchestra conducted by Nelson Riddle, 1982
Paul Robyn, viola
  Orchestras conducted by Nelson Riddle, 1959, 1963;
    and by Billy May, 1961
Alex Rodriguez, trumpet
  Orchestra conducted by Gerald Wilson, 1969–1970
Mickey Roker, drums
  The Ella Fitzgerald Trio, 1979
Art Rollini, tenor saxophone
  Benny Goodman and His Orchestra, 1936
Hale Rood, trombone
  Benny Goodman and His Orchestra, 1959
Nathan Ross, violin
  Orchestras conducted by Nelson Riddle, 1959, 1963;
    and by Billy May, 1961
John Rotella, clarinet, saxophones
  Orchestra conducted by Jerry Gray, 1952
Jimmy Rowles, piano
  Orchestras conducted by Marty Paich, 1966; and by
    Nelson Riddle, 1982
  The Jimmy Rowles Trio, 1981
Tommy Rowles, drums
  Orchestra conducted by Sonny Burke, 1951
Ernie Royal, trumpet
  Orchestra conducted by Bill Doggett, 1962
Marshall Royal, clarinet, flute, alto saxophone
  Count Basie and His Orchestra, 1956, 1963
  Orchestras conducted by GeraldWilson, 1969–1970;
    and by Nelson Riddle, 1982
Sid Rubin, tenor saxophone
  Orchestra conducted by Vic Schoen, 1945
Louis Ruggiero, trumpet

Orchestra conducted by Vic Schoen, 1945

Misha Russell, violin, concertmaster
Orchestras conducted by Buddy Bregman, 1956; by
Nelson Riddle, 1959; and by Billy May, 1961

Babe Russin (1911–1984), trombone, tenor saxophone
Orchestras conducted by Paul Weston, 1958; and by
Nelson Riddle, 1964

Hammond Russum, saxophones
Orchestra conducted by Sonny Burke, 1951

Jack Ryan, bass
Orchestra conducted by Paul Weston, 1958

Eddie Safranski, bass
Orchestra conducted by Toots Camarata, 1955

Lester Salomon, flügelhorn
Orchestra conducted by Toots Camarata, 1955

Joe Sample, organ, electric piano
Orchestra conducted by Gerald Wilson, 1969–1970

Edgar Sampson, alto saxophone, arranger
Chick Webb and His Orchestra, 1932–1936

John Sanders, trombone
Duke Ellington and His Orchestra, 1957

Russ Sanders, bass
Benny Goodman and His Orchestra, 1958

Gerald Sanfino, alto saxophone
Benny Goodman and His Orchestra, 1959

Frank Saracco, trombone
Orchestras conducted by Sy Oliver, 1951, 1953; and by
Toots Camarata, 1955

Jack Satterfield, trombone
Bob Haggart and His Orchestra, 1947
Orchestra conducted by Sy Oliver, 1953

Joseph Saxon, cello
Orchestra conducted by Nelson Riddle, 1963

Hymie Schertzer, alto saxophone, tenor saxophone
Benny Goodman and His Orchestra, 1936, 1958, 1959
Bob Haggart and His Orchestra, 1947
Orchestras conducted by Sy Oliver, 1951; and by Toots
Camarata, 1955

William Schiöpffe, drums
Small group accompaniment, 1961

Sol Schlinger, baritone saxophone
Benny Goodman and His Orchestra, 1958

Vic Schoen, leader, arranger
Orchestra, 1945

Gordon Schoneberg, oboe
Orchestra conducted by Nelson Riddle, 1978

Seymour Schoneberg, oboe
Orchestra conducted by Nelson Riddle, 1964

Wilbur Schwartz, clarinet, soprano saxophone, alto
saxophone
Orchestras conducted by Buddy Bregman, 1956; by
Nelson Riddle, 1959, 1963, 1964, 1978, 1982; and by
Billy May, 1960

George Seaberg, trumpet
Orchestra conducted by Nelson Riddle, 1963, 1964

Al Sears, tenor saxophone
Ella Fitzgerald and Her V-Disc Jumpers, 1945

Emmet Sergeant, cello
Orchestra conducted by Nelson Riddle, 1963

Doc Severinsen, trumpet
Benny Goodman and His Orchestra, 1958

Frederick Seykora, cello
Orchestra conducted by Nelson Riddle, 1982

Seymour Shaffer, trumpet
Bob Haggart and His Orchestra, 1947

Wilmer Shakesnider, reeds
Orchestra conducted by Bill Doggett, 1962

Bud Shank, flute, clarinet, soprano saxophone, alto
saxophone
Orchestra conducted by Buddy Bregman, 1956
The Marty Paich Dek-Tette, 1958

Sidney Sharp, violin
Orchestra conducted by Nelson Riddle, 1963

Arvell Shaw, bass
Benny Goodman and His Quintet, 1958

Norris Shawker, drums
Bob Haggart and His Orchestra, 1947

Tommy Shepard, trombone
Orchestra conducted by Nelson Riddle, 1963, 1964

Bill Shepherd, trombone
Dizzy Gillespie and His Orchestra, 1947

Shorty Sherock (1915–1980), trumpet
*Early in his career, Mr. Sherock's name was also spelled
"Cherock."*
Orchestra conducted by Nelson Riddle, 1959, 1963,
1964, 1978

Jimmy Shirley, guitar
Small group accompaniment, 1946

Eddie Shomer, baritone saxophone
Randy Brooks and His Orchestra, 1945

Paul Shure, violin
Orchestra conducted by Nelson Riddle, 1959

Ward Silloway, trombone
Orchestra conducted by Toots Camarata, 1955

John Simmons, bass
Small group accompaniment, 1947

Sam Simmons, tenor saxophone
Ella Fitzgerald and Her Famous Orchestra, 1940, 1941

Lonnie Simmons, tenor saxophone
Ella Fitzgerald and Her Famous Orchestra, 1941

Barbara Simons, viola
Orchestra conducted by Nelson Riddle, 1959, 1963

Jesse Simpkins, bass
Louis Jordan and His Tympany Five, 1945

Zoot Sims, tenor saxophone
Benny Goodman and His Orchestra, 1958

Orchestras conducted by Frank DeVol, 1964; and by
Eric Bulling, 1980
Small group accompaniment, 1974
The JATP All-Stars, 1983
Buck Skalak, woodwinds
Orchestra conducted by Nelson Riddle, 1959
Eleanor Slatkin, viola
Orchestras conducted by Nelson Riddle, 1959, 1963;
and by Billy May, 1961
Felix Slatkin, violin, concertmaster
Orchestra conducted by Nelson Riddle, 1959, 1963
Cliff Smalls, piano
The Chick Webb Orchestra, 1973
Allen Smith, trumpet
Benny Goodman and His Orchestra, 1959
Charlie Smith, drums
The Ray Brown Trio and Quintet, 1948, 1950
Small group accompaniment, 1951
George Smith, clarinet
Orchestra conducted by Nelson Riddle, 1964
Nolan Smith, trumpet
Count Basie and His Orchestra, 1979
Paul Smith, piano, celeste
Orchestras conducted by Buddy Bregman, 1956; by
Nelson Riddle, 1959, 1963, 1964, 1978; by Frank
DeVol, 1957; by Paul Weston, 1958; and by Billy
May, 1960
Small group accompaniment, 1956, 1960, 1962
Solo accompaniment, 1960
The Ella Fitzgerald Trio, 1979, 1983
Stuff Smith, violin
Small group accompaniment, 1956
William Smith, woodwinds
Orchestra conducted by Nelson Riddle, 1964
Willie Smith (1910–1967), alto saxophone
The JATP All-Stars, 1953
Johnny Spence, leader, arranger
Orchestra, 1964
Marshall Sosson, violin,
Orchestra conducted by Nelson Riddle, 1959, 1963;
and by Billy May, 1961
Jess Stacy, piano
Benny Goodman and His Orchestra, 1936
Lennie Stanfield, string bass
Teddy Wilson and His Orchestra, 1936
Bobby Stark, trumpet
Chick Webb and His Orchestra, 1934–1939
Ella Fitzgerald and Her Famous Orchestra, 1939, 1940
Bill Stegmeyer, clarinet, alto saxophone
Bob Haggart and His Orchestra, 1946
The Lawson-Haggart Jazz Band, 1952
Lou Stein, piano
The Lawson-Haggart Jazz Band, 1952

Maurice Stein, alto saxophone
Orchestra conducted by Buddy Bregman, 1956
Nancy Stein, cello
Orchestra conducted by Nelson Riddle, 1982
Joseph Stepansky, violin
Orchestra conducted by Billy May, 1961
Haig Stephens, bass
Small group accompaniment, 1945
Phil Stephens, bass
Orchestra conducted by John Scott Trotter, 1953, 1954
David Sterkin, viola
Orchestra conducted by Nelson Riddle, 1959
Tommy Stevenson, trumpet
Cootie Williams and His Orchestra, 1944
Sonny Stitt, alto saxophone
JATP All-Stars, 1957
Ann Stockton, harp
Orchestra conducted by Nelson Riddle, 1963
Alvin Stoller, drums
Tommy Dorsey and His Orchestra, 1947
Dave Barbour and His Orchestra, 1951
Orchestras conducted by Jerry Gray, 1952; and by
Buddy Bregman, 1956
Small group accompaniment, 1956
JATP All-Stars, 1956
Orchestras conducted by Paul Weston, 1958; by Nelson
Riddle, 1959, 1963; and by Billy May, 1960, 1961
Bob Stone, bass
Orchestra conducted by Jerry Gray, 1952
Nat Story, trombone
Chick Webb and His Orchestra, 1936–1939
Ella Fitzgerald and Her Famous Orchestra, 1939, 1940
Billy Strayhorn, piano, arranger
Duke Ellington and His Orchestra, 1957
Fred Stulce, clarinet
Orchestra conducted by Paul Weston, 1958
Phil Sundell, saxophones
Orchestra conducted by John Scott Trotter, 1953, 1954
Nick Tagg, piano
Small group accompaniment, 1947
Mel Tait, tenor saxophone
Orchestra conducted by Sy Oliver, 1953
Paul Tanner, trombone
Orchestra conducted by Sonny Burke, 1951
Grady Tate, drums
The Jimmy Jones Trio, 1966
Billy Taylor, bass
Eddie Heywood and His Orchestra, 1947
Les Taylor, reeds
Orchestra conducted by Bill Doggett, 1962
Rudy Taylor, drums
The Ray Brown Quintet, 1952
Sam Taylor, tenor saxophone

Cootie Williams and His Orchestra, 1944, 1946
Orchestra conducted by Sy Oliver, 1952, 1953
Tommy Tedesco, guitar
Orchestra conducted by Nelson Riddle, 1982
Clark Terry, trumpet
Duke Ellington and His Orchestra, 1957
Small group accompaniment, 1974, 1989
Orchestra conducted by Eric Bulling, 1980
The JATP All-Stars, 1983
Howard Terry, bassoon
Orchestra conducted by Nelson Riddle, 1964
Toots Thielemans, harmonica
Orchestra conducted by Eric Bulling, 1980
Ed Thigpen, drums
The Tommy Flanagan Trio, 1969–1971
Count Basie and His Orchestra, 1972
Alexander Thomas, trombone
Orchestra conducted by Gerald Wilson, 1969–1970
Bill Thomas, string bass
Chick Webb and His Orchestra, 1935
Whitey Thomas, trumpet
Orchestra conducted by Jerry Gray, 1952
Sir Charles Thompson, organ
Small group accompaniment, 1947
Pee Wee Tinney, guitar
Cootie Williams and His Orchestra, 1947
Juan Tizol, trombone
Orchestra conducted by Nelson Riddle, 1959
William Tole, trombone
Orchestra conducted by Gerald Wilson, 1969–1970
Sol Train, trombone
Tommy Dorsey and His Orchestra, 1947
George Treadwell, trumpet
Cootie Williams and His Orchestra, 1944, 1946
Bobby Tricarico, bassoon
Orchestra conducted by Nelson Riddle, 1978
Joe Triscari, trumpet
Orchestras conducted by Nelson Riddle, 1959; and by
Billy May, 1960
John Scott Trotter, leader, arranger
Orchestra, 1949, 1950, 1951, 1952, 1953, 1954
Terry Trotter, keyboards
Orchestra conducted by Eric Bulling, 1980
John Trueheart, banjo, guitar
Chick Webb and His Orchestra, 1929–1939
Teddy Wilson and His Orchestra, 1936
Ella Fitzgerald and Her Famous Orchestra, 1939–1940
Ray Tunia, piano
Cootie Williams and His Orchestra, 1947
Small group accompaniment, 1947, 1953
Apollo Theater Orchestra, 1954
The Ray Brown Quartet, 1954
The JATP All-Stars, 1954

Tommy Turk (1928–1981), trombone
The JATP All-Stars, 1949,
Charles Turner, trumpet
Orchestra conducted by Nelson Riddle, 1978
Danny Turner, flute, alto saxophone
Count Basie and His Orchestra, 1979
Lloyd Ulyate, trombone
Orchestra conducted by Buddy Bregman, 1956
Dick Vance, trumpet
Chick Webb and His Orchestra, 1938, 1939
Ella Fitzgerald and Her Famous Orchestra, 1939–1941
The Chick Webb Orchestra, 1973
William Vandenberg, cello
Orchestra conducted by Nelson Riddle, 1963
Ted Vesely, trombone
Orchestra conducted by John Scott Trotter, 1953, 1954
Gerald Vinci, violin
Orchestras conducted by Nelson Riddle, 1959, 1963;
and by Billy May, 1961
Eddie Vinson, alto saxophone
Cootie Williams and His Orchestra, 1944
Freddie Waits, drums
The Tommy Flanagan Quartet, 1973
Melvin Wanzo, trombone
Count Basie and His Orchestra, 1971, 1972, 1979
Billy Watrous, trombone
Orchestra conducted by Nelson Riddle, 1978, 1982
John Watson, trombone
Count Basie and His Orchestra, 1971
Julius Watson, trombone
Cootie Williams and His Orchestra, 1947
Ernest Watts, flute, piccolo
Orchestra conducted by Gerald Wilson, 1969–1970
Champ Webb, woodwinds
Orchestra conducted by Nelson Riddle, 1959
Chick Webb, leader, drums
Chick Webb and His Orchestra, 1929–1939
Ben Webster, tenor saxophone
The JATP All-Stars, 1953
Small group accompaniment, 1956
Orchestra conducted by Frank DeVol, 1957
Duke Ellington and His Orchestra, 1966
Paul Webster, trumpet
Orchestra conducted by Sy Oliver, 1950, 1951
Moe Wechsler, piano
Orchestra conducted by Vic Schoen, 1945
Buddy Weed, piano
Ella Fitzgerald and Her V-Disc Jumpers, 1945
Frank Wess, tenor saxophone, flute
Count Basie and His Orchestra, 1956, 1963
Bob West, bass
Benny Carter's Magnificent Seven, 1968
Harold "Doc" West (1915–1951), drums

Chick Webb and His Orchestra, 1938
Paul Weston, leader, arranger
    Orchestra, 1958
Riley Weston, clarinet, saxophones
    Orchestra conducted by Jerry Gray, 1952
George Wettling, drums
    Small group accompaniment, 1945
Hy White, guitar
    Small group accompaniment, 1945, 1947
    Orchestras conducted by Vic Schoen, 1945; and by
        Leroy Kirkland, 1952
Joe Wilder, trumpet
    Orchestra conducted by Bill Doggett, 1962
Cootie Williams, leader, trumpet
    Orchestra, 1944, 1946, 1947
    Duke Ellington and His Orchestra, 1965–1967
Daniel Williams, alto saxophone
    Cootie Williams and His Orchestra, 1947
Elmer Williams, tenor saxophone
    Chick Webb and His Orchestra, 1929–1936
    Ella Fitzgerald and Her Famous Orchestra, 1941
Francis "Franc" Williams, trumpet
    The Chick Webb Orchestra, 1973
Fred Williams, tenor saxophone
    Orchestra conducted by Sy Oliver, 1951
John C. Williams, baritone saxophone
    Count Basie and His Orchestra, 1972
Sandy Williams, trombone
    Chick Webb and His Orchestra, 1934–1939
    Ella Fitzgerald and Her Famous Orchestra, 1939, 1940
Stu Williamson, trumpet
    Orchestra conducted by Marty Paich, 1966
Dennis Wilson, trombone
    Count Basie and His Orchestra, 1979
Gerald Wilson, leader, arranger
    Orchestra, 1969–1971
Teddy Wilson, leader, piano
    Orchestra, 1936
    Benny Goodman and His Quintet, 1958

Mike Wimberly, trombone
    Orchestra conducted by Gerald Wilson, 1969–1970
Kai Winding, trombone
    The Ray Brown Quintet, 1948
    Orchestra conducted by Bill Doggett, 1962
Mike Wofford, piano
    Small group accompaniment, 1989
Mitchell "Booty" Wood, trombone
    Count Basie and His Orchestra, 1979
Jimmy Woode, bass
    Duke Ellington and His Orchestra, 1957
    Small group accompaniment, 1961
Britt Woodman, trombone
    Duke Ellington and His Orchestra, 1957
    Orchestras conducted by Bill Doggett, 1962; and by
        Gerald Wilson, 1969–1970
Phil Woods, reeds
    Orchestra conducted by Bill Doggett, 1962
Sam Woodyard, drums
    Duke Ellington and His Orchestra, 1957, 1966
    The Jimmy Jones Trio, 1967
Elmon Wright, trumpet
    Dizzy Gillespie and His Orchestra, 1947
Lammar Wright, trumpet
    Cootie Williams and His Orchestra, 1944
Larry Wright, saxophones
    Orchstra conducted by John Scott Trotter, 1953, 1954
Bill Yancey, bass
    Small group accompaniment, 1963, 1964
Milt Yaner, alto saxophone
    Orchestra conducted by Sy Oliver, 1950, 1951, 1952
Lester Young (1909–1959), tenor saxophone
    The Lester Young Quartet, 1948
    The JATP All-Stars, 1949, 1957
Trummy Young (1912–1984), trombone
    JATP All-Stars, 1956
Zeke Zarchey, trumpet
    Benny Goodman and His Orchestra, 1936

...And They Sang with Ella

The Andy Love Quintet, 1947
Louis Armstrong, 1946, 1951, 1956, 1957
Bing Crosby, 1949, 1950, 1951, 1952, 1953, 1954
The Day Dreamers, 1947
The Delta Rhythm Boys, 1945, 1946
   Carl Jones, first tenor
   Traverse Crawford, second tenor
   Kelsey Pharr, baritone
   Otho Gaines, bass
Four Hits and a Miss, 1950
The Four Keys, 1942
   Bill Furness, piano, vocals
   Slim Furness, guitar, vocals
   Peck Furness, bass, vocals
   Ernie Hatfield, drums, vocals
Benny Goodman, 1958, 1959
The Hi-Lo's, 1959
   Eugene Puerling, leader
   Robert Morse
   Clark Burroughs
   Dan Shelton
The Ink Spots, 1943, 1945, 1959
   Bill Kenny, countertenor
   Ivory "Deke" Watson, tenor
   Charles Fuqua, baritone
   Orville "Hoppy" Jones, bass and talking chorus
     (1943, 1945)

Herb Kenny, bass and talking chorus (1959)
Louis Jordan, 1936, 1945, 1949
Peggy Lee, 1959
Charles Linton, 1936
The McGuire Sisters, 1958
   Christine McGuire
   Dorothy McGuire
   Phyllis McGuire
The Mills Brothers, 1937, 1949
   Donald Mills, second tenor
   Harry Mills, baritone
   Herbert Mills, first tenor
   John Mills, Sr., bass
Ray Nance, 1966
The Ray Charles Singers, 1951–1952
Buddy Rich, 1947
Edgar Sampson
Frank ...... .58, 1959
   ...arks, 1951
   Gilda Maiken, lead
   George Becker, lead
   Jackie Gershwin, first tenor
   Joe Hamilton, second tenor
   Earl Brown, baritone
The Song Spinners, 1944
Jo Stafford, 1958

C. Ella's Movies

Ella Fitzgerald appeared in four feature-length films. Her roles were never great ones, and although the films are all but forgettable, her images on screen are always remembered. Aware that she was no great beauty in the mold of a Lena Horne or a Dorothy Dandridge, she was embarrassed to be fawned over and excessively admired as if she were. Ella was her Voice; her Voice was Ella. People came to see and hear her sing. No performer has ever exhibited more than she such exultant joy of singing to an audience, whether on a concert stage, in a recording studio, or on a movie soundstage. That is what you feel when you see her on screen (and in person), that she loves to have you love to watch and hear her sing. Those little chuckles you hear when the applause begins are her expressions of the pleasure she feels that you have enjoyed her performance. She simply loved to sing, living to sing; for when she was not planning, rehearsing, or performing, she found her freedom to relax difficult to enjoy. From the day that Chick Webb took her to Yale and allowed her to sing at a prom, she lived only to perform.

RIDE 'EM, COWBOY

Universal Pictures. Produced by Alex Gottlieb. Directed by Arthur Lubin. Screenplay by True Boardman and John Grant. Adaptation by Harold Shumate, from an original story by Edmund L. Hartmann. Cinematographer, John W. Boyle. Film editor, Phillip Cahn. Art Director, Jack Otterson. Choreographer, Nick Castle. Musical Director, Frank Skinner. Released 7 February 1942. 86 minutes.

The Players

Duke	Bud Abbott
Willoughby	Lou Costello
Robert (Bronco Bob) Mitchell . .	Dick Foran
Anne Shaw	Anne Gwynne
Alabam Brewster	Johnny Mack Brown
Sam Shaw	Samuel S. Hinds
Jake Rainwater	Douglass Dumbrille
Pete Conway	Richard Lane
Martin Manning	Charles Lane
Moonbeam	Jody Gilbert
Ace Henderson	Morris Ankrum
Dotty Davis	Mary Lou Cook
Ruby	**Ella Fitzgerald**
Tom, Dick, and Harry	The Merry Macs

(Judd, Ted, and Joe McMichael, Mary Lou Cook)
The Hi Hatters
The Buckaroos Band
The Ranger Chorus of Forty
The Congoroos

The film is, as one critic described it, "unutterable piffle from fade-in to fade-out," but Abbott and Costello, playing a pair of peanut and hotdog vendors who end up on a dude ranch as cowhands, turned it into another top-grossing smash for Universal, their seventh. Singing Cowboy Dick Foran as a western novelist and Anne Gwynne as the ranch owner's daughter provide the romantic interest. What separates this from other Abbott and Costello films is the unusual quality of the musical talent appearing. Ella Fitzgerald as a featured singer (her screen debut) does a rousing version of her own "A-Tisket, A-Tasket. There are also some good Don Raye–Gene DePaul songs. Dick Foran warbles "Give Me My Saddle" and the film's biggest hit, "I'll Remember April," crafted with Patricia Johnston, became an instant and enduring standard. The Merry Macs do a few numbers as well, including "Wake Up, Jacob," "Beside the Rio Tonto," and "Rockin' 'n' Reelin'" (with Ella). The Congoroos contributed "Cow Cow Boogie." Originally a lavish production number featuring Ella, the song was considered to lengthen the film unreasonably, and though it was filmed in its entirety, it was cut before release (remember, these were the days of double features). If you look sharply, you will see Dorothy Dandridge doing the jitterbug as one of The Congoroos.

Hey, you guys at Universal, how about a "director's cut"?

PETE KELLY'S BLUES

Warner Bros. Produced by Jack Webb for Mark VII, Ltd. Directed by Jack Webb. Screenplay by Richard L. Breen. Cinematographer, Hal Rosson (CinemaScope, WarnerColor). Film Editor, Robert M. Leeds. Production Designer, Harper Goff. Art Director, Field Gray. Set Decorator, John Sturtevant. Costumes, Howard Shoup. Makeup, Gordon Bau. Musical Director, Ray Heindorf. Released 28 July 1955. 95 minutes.

The Players

Pete Kelly . . . . Jack Webb
Fran McCarg . . . . Edmond O'Brien
Ivy Conrad . . . . Janet Leigh
Rose Hopkins . . . . Peggy Lee
Al Gannaway . . . . Lee Marvin
George Tenell . . . . Andy Devine
Maggie Johnson . . . . **Ella Fitzgerald**
Joey Firestone . . . . Martin Milner
Cigarette Girl . . . . Jane Mansfield
Rudy . . . . Than Wynn
Bedido . . . . Herb Ellis
Guy Bettenhouser . . . . . . John Dennis
Cootie Jacobs . . . . Mort Marshall
Squat Henchman . . . . Nesdon Booth
Dako . . . . William Lazarus
Cornetist . . . . Dick Cathcart
Clarinetist . . . . Matty Matlock
Trombonist . . . . Moe Schneider
Saxophonist . . . . Eddie Miller
Guitarist . . . . George Van Eps
Drummer . . . . Nick Fatool
Pianist . . . . Ray Sherman
Bass Player . . . . Jud de Naut
Waiter in Rudy's . . . . . . Snub Pollard
Featured Members of The Tuxedo Band   Joe Venuti,
                                        Harper Goff,
                                        Perry Bodkin
The Israelite Spiritual Church Choir of New Orleans

Jack Webb directs, produces, and stars in this interesting tale of jazz and gangsters in prohibition-era Kansas City. Opening with the funeral of a black cornet player (Peggy Lee sings "Oh, Didn't He Ramble" by W.C. Handy and Bob Cole), the film moves on to show how Pete Kelly's Big Seven is threatened when gangster O'Brien decides to diversify his operation by extorting agent fees from the musicians. Webb and his boys try to stand up to him, but when drummer Milner is killed, Webb opts for revenge, and after a shootout in a nightclub, O'Brien's gunman crashes through the ceiling on to the dance floor, taking with him the huge revolving mirrored globe. Webb's direction is craftsman-like and exciting in a blunt way, but his performance is stiff and hardly different from his Joe Friday character in the **Dragnet** movie and TV series. Miss Leigh supplies the romantic angle as an empty-headed Scott Fitzgerald species who chases the hero. Mr. O'Brien's gangster, for all his talent, is little more than cardboard. Peggy Lee, as his alcoholic mistress, is surprisingly effective as a singer on the skids whom he eventually beats into insanity, a performance that garnered her an Academy Award nomination. The best performance comes from Lee Marvin as Webb's faithful wise-cracking best friend. Ella Fitzgerald contributes with a small supporting turn and three numbers: "Hard Hearted Hannah" (Jack Yellen, Milton Ager, Bob Bigelow and Charles Bates), "Ella Hums the Blues" (Ray Heindorf), and the title tune, "Pete Kelly's Blues" (Sammy Cahn and Ray Heindorf) which would become indelibly identified with her. Another reason to check out this late movie perennial is the impressive collection of top jazzmen, such as Matty Matlock, Moe Schneider, and George van Eps. Webb's cornet playing was dubbed by Dick Cathcart. The film has a certain edge of realism and unsentimentality not usually found in films about jazz before this time (the bars where the band plays are crowded and smoky, and the drinks are probably overpriced), and the music is good. It's possible that most early jazz outfits such as Pete Kelly's Big Seven lived in terror of greedy underworld gangs and sorely needed a superman-leader to run interference. Although the script alludes to band bookings and competition, the dialogue generally ranges from flip to jailhouse. Peggy Lee's other vocal contributions, performed in fine style, include "He Needs Me" and "Sing a Rainbow" (Arthur Hamilton), written especially for the film, and "Somebody Loves Me" (George and Ira Gershwin), "I Never Knew" (Gus Kahn and Ted Fiorito), "Sugar" (Maceo Pinkard, Sidney Mitchell and Edna Alexander), "Bye Bye, Blackbird" (Mort Dixon and Ray Henderson), and "What Can I Say After I Say I'm Sorry" (Walter Donaldson-Abe Lyman). Note Jayne Mansfield's cigarette girl, and Herb Ellis in a small role.

ST. LOUIS BLUES

Paramount Pictures. Produced by Robert Smith. Directed by Allen Reisner. Screenplay by Robert Smith and Ted Sherdeman (based on the life and music of W.C. Handy). Cinematographer, Haskell Boggs (in VistaVision). Film Editor, Eda Warren. Music Director, Nelson Riddle (music based on themes and songs by Handy). Art Directors, Hal Pereira and Roland Anderson. Costumes by Edith Head. Special Effects, John P. Fulton. Released 4 April 1958. 93 minutes.

The Players

W.C. Handy . . . . Nat "King" Cole
Gogo Germaine . . . . Eartha Kitt
Aunt Hager . . . . Pearl Bailey
Blade . . . . Cab Calloway
Ella Fitzgerald . . . . **Herself**
Bessie May . . . . Mahalia Jackson
Elizabeth . . . . Ruby Dee
Charles Handy . . . . Juano Hernandez
W.C. Handy as a boy . . . . . Billy Preston
Musicians . . . . Teddy Buckner,
Barney Bigard,
George "Red" Callender,
Lee Young,
George Washington

Nat "King" Cole is W.C. Handy, a musically gifted young man oppressed by his fundamentalist minister father (Juano Hernandez) into feeling that it is sinful to write jazz and popular songs. "There's only two kinds of music, the Devil's and the Lord's," Papa roars, and with that he snatches the cornet from the boy's hands and throws it under a passing wagon's wheels. The lad falls on his knees in fearful misery. True, the lad turns from little Billy Preston into the adult Nat "King" Cole, and does much of his later repining in a sitting position on a piano stool. In that position he is able to let his fingers flow over the keys and pick out such compositions as "Careless Love" and "Yellow Dog Blues." He also throws his troubled head back against the comforting tummy of Eartha Kitt, a nightclub singer who advocates the Devil's music, in competition with Ruby Dee, who's for the Lord's. Tragedy strikes when psychosomatic blindness sets in, but Cole eventually overcomes this. But he really doesn't snap out of it until his unrelenting father finally comes to New York and hears a performance of his famous composition, "St. Louis Blues," done by a symphony orchestra and Miss Kitt in Aeolian Hall. Then papa embraces son and in proud surrender the Devil's music wins. The thing to do is just ignore the narrative interruptions and enjoy the concert of some great black stars, all of whom sparkle. Cole's voice is at its lyrical best, and there are fine performances by Cab Calloway, Mahalia Jackson and Ella Fitzgerald. Watch for future pop star Billy Preston playing Handy as a child. What's really significant about *St. Louis Blues* is its almost exclusive use of black talent. Up to this time, blacks had been ignored or mistreated by Hollywood from the beginning of the movie industry, and an all-black cast of this quality was a rarity. Ella Fitzgerald, unfortunately, is limited to only one number, "Beale Street Blues" (W.C. Handy), but the sequence is a shining gem. Other songs include "Hesitating Blues," "Chantez les Bas," (W.C. Handy); "Careless Love" (based on folk music by Handy with lyrics by Spencer Williams and Martin

Koenig); "Morning Star," "'Way Down South Where the Blues Began," "Mr. Bayle," "Aunt Hagar's Blues" (W.C. Handy, lyrics by Tim Brymn); "They That Sow" (hymn), and "Going To See My Sarah" (spiritual).

LET NO MAN WRITE MY EPITAPH

Columbia Pictures. Produced by Boris D. Kaplan. Directed by Phillip Leacock. Screenplay by Robert Presnell, Jr. (adapted from a novel by Willard Motley). Cinematographer, Burnett Guffy. Music by George Duning. Edited by Chester W. Schaeffer. Released 16 September 1960. 105 minutes.

The Players

Judge Bruce Mallory Sullivan . . . Burl Ives
Nellie Romano . . . . Shelley Winters
Nick Romano . . . . James Darren
Barbara Holloway . . . . Jean Seberg
Louie Ramponi . . . . Richard Montalban
Flora . . . . **Ella Fitzgerald**
Max . . . . Rudolph Acosta
Grant Holloway . . . . Philip Ober
Fran . . . . Jeanne Cooper
Goodbye George . . . . Bernie Hamilton
Wart . . . . Walter Burke
Magistrate . . . . Francis DeSales
Nick, as a child . . . . Michael Davis
Eddie . . . . Dan Easton
Mike . . . . Nesdon Booth
Whitey . . . . Roy Jenson
Barney . . . . Joel Fricano
Lee . . . . Joe Gallison

An occasionally moving but rather mild film has been culled from the pages of Willard Motley's novel, and it's pretty good, everything considered. Remember *Knock on Any Door*, also from Mr. Motley's pen? Here again is the drama of youth caught in the hard environment of a Chicago slum area. Principally because of the earnest, restrained acting and the realistic photography of a run-down urban neighborhood, the film projects a persuasive intimacy as it examines a group of social vagrants, who are drawn to a sturdy, ambitious lad, played by Mr. Darren, and his emotional, widowed mother, Miss Winters. The story centers on their relationship as the pianist son tries to sidestep the tougher neighborhood elements and the stain of an executed father to make it to the concert hall. Simultaneously, Miss Winters, in trying to protect her son (no mama's boy, by the way) succumbs to an insidious mobster (Mr. Montalban, an excellent villan for a change) who blandly enslaves her with dope. The frowsy, good-hearted woman goes to pieces, and her performance with Mr.

Darren in their showdown over narcotics is a fine, ugly scene with real urgency. To this, add a nice girl (the excellent Miss Seberg) who loves the young hero, and a handful of friendly, tawdry neighborhood "characters" (Burl Ives, Rudolph Acosta, Jeanne Cooper, Walter Burke, and Bernie Hamilton) who amble in and out. Yet the picture rarely attains unified strength, since the spectator feels all along that everything will turn out right — and it does, almost mathematically. The best thing about the whole operation is that the movie people finally had the good judgment to allot that great lady of song, Ella Fitzgerald, a brief acting chore, and that is precisely what she does. As a tired "junkie" beating out a living as a nightclub pianist-singer, she delights us with a dozen standards (when you can hear her over the hubub) as only she can sing them, in addition to an especially poignant "Reach for Tomorrow," written especially for the film by Paul Francis Webster and Jimmy McHugh, a sort of a Narcotics Anonymous hymn. For this, hail Columbia (Pictures).

D. Do-It-Yourself
Ella Fitzgerald Song Books

On 28 October 1992, President Bush signed into law the Audio Home Recording Act (Title 17, Chapter 10, U.S. Code), which legalizes first-generation copying for personal use of commercially produced and marketed material with consumer recording devices. The Home Recording Rights Coalition maintains an Internet Web site, www.hrrc.org, that has the complete text of the Act and answers questions concerning consumer's rights on this topic. They may also be reached by telephone at 1-800-282-8273.

Tim had lunch with Uncle Jack, whom he visited occasionally, and afterward rumbled through the more than a thousand CDs his uncle had collected over the years. He chose ten, telling Uncle Jack that he would return them next week. Stopping off at Kinko's, he gave instructions to the clerk for the reproduction of one of his own small paintings, the text, chose a heavy slick paper stock, and was off to CeeDee's. There, he surrendered his driver's license and was supplied with a ten-disc magazine, a blank compact disc, and a jewel box, which he chose over the cardboard sleeve. Placing the CDs into the magazine in an already determined order, he inserted the magazine into the copier, punched in record and track numbers, 50 tracks in all, pressed the "Record" button, and two minutes later the new CD ejected. He reinserted the CD, pressed the "Play" button, and with earphones scanned briefly for quality and to check that the correct tracks had been recorded. Satisfied, he pressed the "Burn" button, and the tracks were permanently bonded into the new CD, now uneraseable. Placing it carefully in the jewel box, he passed the clerk a twenty,

got his change along with his license, and then back to Kinko's for the "liner notes" and the tray card. In his car, he paused briefly to assemble the whole thing, smiled at the beautiful reproduction of his art, and checked the text of his gift to Grandma Ellen. The cover read, "Happy Birthday and Happy New Millennium, Grandma, from Your Loving Grandson, Tim." He would present it to her this evening at dinner when all the family gathered to celebrate Ellen's birthday anniversary, January 1, and beginning of the new millennium, 2001. All her very favorite favorites were on the CD, and since her eyesight had begun to fail she read less, listening to music by the hour, and Tim could see her rocking and smiling as she listened to the selections he had chosen for her. But he had a lot to do and all this had taken the better part of an hour.

Whether you use this new technology, or resort to the old-fashioned cassette tapes, it is still lawful to reproduce a copyrighted work for your own personal use, even as a gift.

For your own listening pleasure, you might want to assemble a few Ella Song Books, choosing your own favorites without having to resort to changing magazines and punching in track numbers all the time.

Here, then, are some suggestions. Please note that after each title there is a DRN, a suggestion by the editor. Consult Part Three, **The Songs Ella Sings: An Annotated Index**, for other choices.

Ella Fitzgerald Sings the Complete Ella Fitzgerald Song Book

Whose songs better to begin **The Complete Ella Fitzgerald Song Books** than with those of Miss Fitz herself. With the success of "A-Tisket, A-Tasket" in 1938, she felt that her talents as composer-lyricist might give her another hit. None ever quite exceeded the popularity of "A-Tisket, A-Tasket," but a few did make the charts. In 1940 she became one of the youngest members of the American Society of Composers, Authors and Publishers (ASCAP). Lyrics and music by Ella Fitzgerald unless otherwise indicated. An as yet unreleased recording is also listed — a hint to producers.

Any Old Blues, 730705-14
A-Tisket, A-Tasket (with Al Feldman), 380501-1
Basella (m. Duke Ellington's "C Jam Blues"), 790712-11
Betcha Nickel (with Chick Webb), 390629-1,
Chew, Chew, Chew (Your Bubble Gum) (with Buck Ram, Dick Vance and Chick Webb), 390302-6
Chewin' Gum (with Buck Ram and Chick Webb), 400304-4
Deedle-De-Dum, 400509-1
Ella Hums the Blues (m. Ray Heindorf), 550503-3
Ella's Blues (never released). Introduced and recorded at a Tokyo concert in 1953.
Ella's Contribution to the Blues (m. Henry William "Hank" Jones, Jr.), 520919-2
The Greatest There Is (m. Mercer Ellington), 520811-2
Happy Blues, 740411-6
I Fell in Love with a Dream (with Skye and Goldsmith), 400509-4
I Found My Yellow Basket (with Al Feldman), 381006-4
It's Up to Me and You, 680501-1
Joe Williams' Blues, 610211-15
The Muffin Man, 410108-5
No Sense (m. Ray Brown), 580314-4
Oh Boy! I'm in the Groove, 39092-1
Once Is Enough for Me (with Chick Webb), 390302-1

Party Blues (with William "Count" Basie and Joseph Goreed "Joe" Williams), 560625-5
Please Tell Me the Truth (with Edgar Sampson), 390818-3
Rough Ridin' (with William Henry "Hank" Jones, Jr. and William J. "Bill" Tennyson, Jr.), 520104-2,
Shiny Stockings (l. Jon Hendricks, m. with Frank B. Foster), 630716-1
Spinnin' the Webb (instr) (with J.C. Johnson) 380503-6
Street Beater ("Sanford and Son" Theme)(m. Quincy Jones), 060272-12
That Ringo Beat, 641023-1
Who Ya Hunchin' (instr) (with Chick Webb), 400304-6
You Showed Me the Way (m. Benny Green, Teddy McRae, and Chick Webb), 370324-4

ASCAP credits Ella with four other titles, none of which she ever recorded!

The Devil Sat Down and Cried (with Walter Bishop). Recorded by Harry James.
Just One of Those Nights (with Josef Myrow and Lupin Fein). Recorded by Dick Haymes.
Oh, Boy, I'm in the Groove (no recording known to editor)
Oh, But I Do (with Kenneth Watts). Recorded by King Cole Trio.

The Complete Ella Fitzgerald Sings the Johnny Mercer Song Book

John Herndon ("Johnny") Mercer (b. 18 November 1909, Savannah, Georgia; d. 25 June 1976, Los Angeles, California) was one of filmdom's most popular and prolific lyricists (and composer, upon occasion). He is credited with more than 1000 lyrics, not a few of them set to his own music. An excellent biography is *Our Huckleberry Friend: The Life, Times, and Lyrics of Johnny Mercer*, by Bob Bach and Ginger Mercer (Lyle Stuart, N.J., 1982).

Academy Awards nominations (* indicates winner):

1942 "Dearly Beloved," from **You Were Never Lovelier**
1943 "My Shining Hour," from **The Sky's the Limit**
"That Old Black Magic," from **Star Spangled Rhythm**
1944 "Long Ago and Far Away," from **Cover Girl**
1945 "Ac-Cent-Tchu-Ate the Positive," from **Here Come the Waves**
1946 *"On the Atchison and Topeka and the Santa Fe," from **The Harvey Girls**
1955 "Something's Gotta Give," from **Daddy Long-Legs**
1961 *"Moon River," from **Breakfast at Tiffany's**
1962 *"Days of Wine and Roses," from **Days of Wine and Roses**

Ella recorded thirty of Mercer's songs, some more than once:

Ac-Cent-Tchu-Ate the Positive, (m. Harold Arlen), 600801-6
And the Angels Sing (m. Ziggy Elman), 650326-7
Baby Doll (m. Harry Warren), 511126-1
Baby, Don't You Quit Now (m. Jimmy Rowles), 890320-2
Blues in the Night (m. Harold Arlen), 610114-2
Come Rain or Come Shine (m. Harold Arlen), 610116-5
Day In — Day Out (M. Rube Bloom), 640728-3
Days of Wine and Roses (m. Henry Mancini), 860223-7
Dream (m. Johnny Mercer), 641019-6
Early Autumn (m. Ralph Burns-Woody Herman), 641019-5
Fools Rush in (m. Rube Bloom), 560121-7a (in medley)
Goody Goody (m. Matty Malneck), 361105-1
I Remember You (m. Victor Schertzinger), 641021-4
I Thought About You (m. Jimmy Van Heusen), 571015-9
I'm Old Fashioned (m. Jerome Kern), 630105-1

Laura (m. David Raksin), 641021-2

Midnight Sun (m. Lionel Hampton-Sonny Burke), 580425-3

My Shining Hour (m. Harold Arlen), 610115-2

One for My Baby (m. Harold Arlen), 610114-5

Oops! (m. Harry Warren), 511123-2 (duet with **Louis Armstrong**)

Out of This World (m. Harold Arlen), 610116-6

Satin Doll (m. Billy Strayhorn), 560904-12

Single-O (m. Donald Kahn), 641020-4

Skylark (m. Hoagy Carmichael), 641020-3

Something's Gotta Give (m. Johnny Mercer), 641021-3

That Old Black Magic (m. Harold Arlen), 650326-4

This Time the Dream's on Me (m. Harold Arlen), 610115-4

Too Marvelous for Words (m. Richard Whiting), 641021-1

Trav'lin' Light (m. Jimmy Mundy-James "Trummy" Young) 641019-1

When a Woman Loves a Man (m. Bernie Hanighen-Gordon Jenkins), 641021-5

The Complete Ella Abraça Jobim/ The Antonio Carlos Jobim Song Book

Antonio Carlos Brasileiro de Almeida ("Tom") Jobim (b. Rio de Janeiro, Brazil, 25 January 1927; d. New York City, 8 December 1994) is often called "the father of the bossa nova," his fame arising from his compositions featured in the Brazilian film, **Orfeu Negro** (**Black Orpheus**), which gained international prominence in 1959 when it won the Grand Prize at the Cannes Film Festival. His talents as a composer, lyricist, and singer brought him stardom on the concert stage, and his recordings were best sellers for more than thirty years. His television appearance with Sinatra and Ella, "Frank Sinatra + Ella + Jobim," was a highlight of his career (available on home video). Jobim wrote several hundred published songs, a goodly portion for which he also wrote lyrics. Ella recorded only 22 of his songs, but these are the diamonds.

Lyricists and, in some cases, co-composers are given in parentheses.

A Felicidade (Vinícius de Moraes), 800917-3

Agua de Beber [Water To Drink], (Engl. Norman Gimbel, Port. Vinícius de Moraes), 800918-1

Bonita (Ray Gilbert and Gene Lees), 800919-3

The Girl from Ipanema [Garôta de Ipanema] (Engl. Norman Gimbel, Port. Vinícius de Moraes), 810318-1

Desafinado [Slightly Out of Tune/Off Key] (Engl. "Slightly Out of Tune," Jon Hendricks and Jessie Cavanaugh (pseudonym of Harry S. Richmond); Engl. "Off Key" Gene Lees, Port. Newton Mendonça), 810318-2

Dindi (Engl. Ray Gilbert, Port. Aloysio de Oliveira), 800919-1

Don't Ever Go Away [Por Causa de Você] (Engl. Ray Gilbert, Port. Dolores Duran), 810320-2

Dreamer [Vivo Sonhando] (Engl. Gene Lees, Port. Jobim), 800917-1

He's/She's a Carioca [Ele/Ela é Carioca] (Engl. Ray Gilbert, Port. Vinícius de Moraes), 810318-3

How Insensitive [Insensatez] (Engl. Norman Gimbel, Port. Vinícius de Moraes), 800919-2

Meditation [Meditação] (Engl. Norman Gimbel, Port. Newton Mendonà), 810726-12

O Nosso Amor [Carnival Samba] (Vinícius de Moraes), 710721-4c (in medley)

Once I Loved [Amor Em Paz] (Engl. Ray Gilbert, Port. Vinícius de Moraes), 730828-2

One Note Samba [Samba de Uma Nota Só] (Engl. (two versions) Jobim/Jon Hendricks, Port. Newton Mendonça), 800919-4

Photograph [Fotografia] (Eng. Ray Gilbert, Port. Jobim), 800919-5

Quiet Nights of Quiet Stars [Corcovado] (Engl. Gene Lees, Port. Jobim), 800918-2

Só Danço Samba [Jazz Samba/I Only Dance the Samba] (Vinícius de Moraes), 670430-3

Somewhere in the Hills [Favela] [O Morro No Tem Vez] (Engl. Ray Gilbert, Port. Vinícius de Moraes), 810319-1

Song of the Jet [Samba do Avião] (Engl. Gene Lees, Port. Jobim), 810320-1

This Love That I've Found [Só Tinha Que Ser Com Você] (Louis Oliveira), 800923-1

Triste (Jobim), 800919-6

Useless Landscape [Inútil Paisagem] (Engl. Ray Gilbert, Port. Aloysio de Oliveira), 800919-3

Wave (Jobim), 800917-2

Ella Fitzgerald Sings the Fred Astaire Song Book

Fred Astaire (b. Frederick Austerlitz 10 May 1899 in Omaha, Nebraska; d. Los Angeles, 22 June 1987) was one of the most popular and beloved stars both on stage and in movies. He is best known for the eleven films he made with Ginger Rogers, although the list of his dancing partners in other films reads like a list of Hollywood's most beautiful ladies, Lucille Bremer, Leslie Caron, Joan Caulfield, Cyd Charisse, Joan Crawford, Joan Fontaine, Judy Garland, Paulette Goddard, Rita Hayworth, Audrey Hepburn, Joan Leslie, Eleanor Powell, Jane Powell, and Vera-Ellen. His films introduced some of our most popular standards, for the composers and lyricists who wrote especially for him included Irving Berlin, the Gershwins, Cole Porter, Jerome Kern, Arthur Freed and Johnny Mercer, to mention a few. Ella recorded 57 songs either introduced by or closely associated with Fred Astaire, and they make a truly wonderful Song Book.

Recommended reading are Fred Astaire's biography, *Steps in Time* (1979, DaCapo Press, New York); *Astaire, the Biography*, by Tim Satchell (1987, Hutchinson, London); and *Astaire Dancing: The Musical Films*, by John E. Mueller (1985, Knopf, New York).

After You — Who? (from **The Gay Divorce**, 1933), 780213-2

All of You (from **Silk Stockings**, 1957), 560209-9

Baby Doll (from **The Belle of New York**, 1952), 511126-1

Begin the Beguine (from **Broadway Melody of 1940**, 1939), 560208-3

Beginner's Luck (from **Shall We Dance**, 1937), 590105-10

Blue Skies (from **Blue Skies**, 1946), 580318-5

By Myself (from **The Band Wagon**, 1953), 860228-12

Change Partners (from **Carefree**, 1938), 580317-6

Cheek to Cheek (from **Top Hat**, 1935), 580318-3

Clap Yo' Hands (from **Funny Face**, 1957), 590107-3

Dream (from **Daddy Long Legs**, 1955), 641019-6

Dream Dancing (from **You'll Never Get Rich**, 1941), 780213-1

Fascinating Rhythm (from **Lady, Be Good!**, 1924), 590318-5

A Fine Romance (from **Swing Time,** 1936), 630105-2

A Foggy Day (from **A Damsel in Distress**, 1937), 590105-6

Funny Face (from **Funny Face**, 1927)

"The Half of It, Dearie" Blues (from **Lady, Be Good!**, 1924), 590715-5

He Loves and She Loves (from **Funny Face**, 1927), 590105-9

Heat Wave (from **Blue Skies**, 1946), 580318-2

How Long Has This Been Going On? (from **Funny Face**, 1957), 590105-5

I Can't Be Bothered Now (from **Damsel in Distress**, 1937), 590318-1

I Concentrate on You (from **Broadway Melody of 1940**, 1939), 560209-4, 560327-4

I Used To Be Color Blind (from **Carefree**, 1938), 580314-1

I Won't Dance (from **Roberta**, 1935), 611227-2

I'll Be Hard To Handle (from **Roberta**, 1935), 630105-3

I'm Old Fashioned (from **You Were Never Lovelier**, 1942), 630105-1

I'm Putting All My Eggs in One Basket (from **Follow the Fleet**, 1936), 580313-4

Isn't This a Lovely Day (To Be Caught in the Rain) (from **Top Hat**, 1935), 580313-1

Let Yourself Go (from **Follow the Fleet**, 1936), 580319-2

Let's Begin (from **Roberta**, 1935), 630107-3

Let's Call the Whole Thing Off (from **Shall We Dance**, 1937), 590326-6

Let's Face the Music and Dance (from **Follow the Fleet**, 1936), 580318-7

Let's Kiss and Make Up (from **Funny Face**, 1927), 590326-9

Limehouse Blues (from **Ziegfeld Follies**, 1946), 400125-2

My One and Only (from **Funny Face**, 1927), 590326-1, 620410-3

My Shining Hour (from **The Sky's the Limit**, 1943), 610115-2

Nice Work If You Can Get It (from **A Damsel in Distress**, 1937), 590326-3

Night and Day (from **The Gay Divorce**, 1932), 560327-1

Oh, Lady, Be Good! (from **Lady, Be Good!** 1924), 590108-4

One for My Baby (from **The Sky's the Limit**, 1943), 610114-5

Oops! (from **The Belle of New York**, 1952), 511123-2 (duet with **Louis Armstrong**)

Pick Yourself Up (from **Swing Time**, 1936), 611115-1

Puttin' on the Ritz (from **Blue Skies**, 1946), 580318-9

'S Wonderful (from **Funny Face**, 1927), 590716-1

Shall We Dance (from **Shall We Dance**, 1937), 590715-1

Slap That Bass (from **Shall We Dance**, 1937), 590107-2

So Near and Yet So Far (from **You'll Never Get Rich**, 1941), 720612-5

Something's Gotta Give (from **Daddy Long Legs**, 1955), 641021-3

Stiff Upper Lip (from **Damsel in Distress**, 1937) 590717-3

They All Laughed (from **Shall We Dance**, 1937), 590326-10

They Can't Take That Away from Me (from **Shall We Dance**, 1937), 590105-4

Things Are Looking Up (from **A Damsel in Distress**, 1937), 590717-2

Three Little Words (from **Three Little Words**, 1950), 410108-1

Top Hat, White Tie and Tails (from **Top Hat**, 1935), 580319-3

The Way You Look Tonight (from **Swing Time**, 1936), 630106-1

Who Cares? (from **Of Thee I Sing**), not used in an Astaire film, but he had a hit record with Benny Goodman, 1938), 590716-2

Without Love (from **Silk Stockings**, 1957), 720612-7

Ella Fitzgerald Sings the Judy Garland Song Book

Judy Garland (b. Frances Ethel Gumm, Grand Rapids, Minnesota, 10 June 1922; d. London, England, 22 June 1969) became a show business legend at 17, when she clicked the heels of her ruby slippers in the M-G-M movie, **The Wizard of Oz**, and landed in the hearts of an entire generation of film-goers. The daughter of vaudeville performers, she was on the stage from the age of five, and a star at 16. She was awarded a special Academy Award in 1939 "for her outstanding performance as a screen juvenile." She made 32 films, most of them musicals, but, unable to stand the pace of her own success, her life ended in tragedy. "If I'm such a legend, why am I so lonely?" she once said. Biographies include **The Other Side of the Rainbow**, by Mel Tormé; **Judy Garland**, by David Shipman; and **Judy Garland — World's Greatest Entertainer**, by John Fricke.

These are a few of the songs associated with Judy Garland, Ella's tribute:

After You've Gone (from **For Me and My Gal**, 1942), 620130-1

Bidin' My Time (from **Girl Crazy**, 1943), 590105-8

The Boy Next Door (from **Meet Me in St. Louis**, 1944), 500900-6

But Not for Me (from **Girl Crazy**, 1943), 590326-5

By Myself (from **I Could Go On Singing**, 1963), 860228-12

Ding-Dong! The Witch Is Dead (from **The Wizard of Oz**, 1939), 600802-4

Embraceable You (from **Girl Crazy**, 1943), 590108-1

Franklin D. Roosevelt Jones (from **Babes on Broadway**, 1941), 381006-1

Get Happy! (from **Summer Stock**, 1950), 600802-1

Have Yourself a Merry Little Christmas (from **Meet Me in St. Louis**, 1944), 600716-5

I Cried for You (from **Babes in Arms**, 1939), 600414-5

I Got Rhythm (from **Girl Crazy**, 1943), 590105-2

I Wish I Were in Love Again (from **Words and Music**, 1948), 560828-2

Johnny One-Note (from **Words and Music**, 1948), 560828-4

The Man That Got Away (from **A Star Is Born**, 1954), 600801-5

My Melancholy Baby (from **A Star Is Born**, 1954), 600414-1

The One I Love Belongs to Somebody Else (from **Everybody Sing**, 1938), 610123-6

Over the Rainbow (from **The Wizard of Oz**, 1939), 610115-4

Sam and Delilah (from **Girl Crazy**, 1943), 590716-5

Stompin' at the Savoy (Judy's first record for Decca, 12 June 1936, coincidentally recorded exactly one year after Ella's first Decca record.)

Strike Up the Band! (from **Strike Up the Band!**, 1940), 590716-4

Where or When (from **Babes in Arms**, 1939), 560831-4

Ella Fitzgerald Sings the Complete George and Ira Gershwin Song Book

George Gershwin (b. 26 September 1898, New York City; d. 11 July 1937 in Hollywood, California) and Ira Gershwin (b. 6 December 1896, New York City; d. 17 August 1983, Beverly Hills, California) hardly need an introduction to music lovers anywhere in the world. From 1917 to 1933, there was not a theatre season on Broadway that did not present eagerly awaited new songs from the Gershwins. By 1933, however, the musical film became a be-all, end-all Hollywood phenomenon, and the Gershwins were summoned frantically with offers of fat salaries and long-term contracts. They didn't give it a second thought, because (1) there was no such thing as a flop when it came to a Hollywood musical — even the worst of them made money, and (2) many of the stars of their Broadway productions had already deserted the theater with the promise of perfect weather every day of the year, fabulous mansions with tennis courts and swimming pools, orange trees in their back yards, and contracts that would assure them immortality.

What may be overlooked by some Gershwin aficionados is that they did not always work together. There is a small roster of George's songs with other lyricists, and, of course, after his death, Ira continued to write lyrics with a many composers, including his dead brother, whose music collection revealed a number of discarded melodies to which Ira immediately sat down and wrote lyrics and peddled them to delighted Hollywood producers, coming up on one occasion with an all-Gershwin musical.

Ella recorded 75 songs by the Gershwins, including those written with other lyricists/composers. There are, however, three collections devoted entirely to the Gershwins: a 78 r.p.m. set made up of four singles, **Ella Sings Gershwin**, for Decca (1900); **Ella Fitzgerald Sings the George and Ira Gershwin Song Book**, for Verve (1959). The first, a collection of eight tracks, appears on compact disc as the first eight selections on the GRP Decca Jazz CD **Pure Ella**. The second is arguably the greatest work that Ella (and Norman Granz) ever produced, 56 titles, a couple of which had never been previously recorded, with peerless arrangements and a superb orchestra led by Nelson Riddle — "who could ask for anything more." Sitting on the sidelines was Ira, who rewrote some of his lyrics especially for Ella, and who was heard to remark on one occasion, "I didn't know how good our songs were until I heard Ella sing them." The third is the justly famous incomparable collection of songs from **Porgy and Bess** with the great Louis Armstrong. Altogether these six CDs contain 68 different titles (some are duplicated).

I will not burden the reader with these titles found elsewhere in this book (cf. LPD-20, LPD-55, and LPD-57). The handful of other Gershwin tunes recorded by Ella at various times in her career are listed herewith.

Highly recommended reading are *The Gershwin Years: George and Ira*, by Edward Jablonski (3rd Ed., 1996, DaCapo Press, New York), *Gershwin: Rhapsody in Blue* by David Schiff (1997, Cambridge University Press, London), and *The Complete Lyrics of Ira Gershwin* by Gershwin and Robert Kimball (1993, Knopf, New York).

All songs are by George and Ira Gershwin, unless otherwise indicated.

All the Livelong Day (and the Long, Long Night), 641019-2

I Can't Get Started with You (Ira Gershwin-Vernon Duke), 550401-4

I'm a Poached Egg (Without Toast), 641019-3

I'm Not Complainin' (Ira Gershwin-Vernon Duke), 390818-4

Let's Take a Walk Around the Block (Ira Gershwin-E.Y. Harburg-Harold Arlen, 600802-4

The Man That Got Away (Ira Gershwin-Harold Arlen), 540917-2

My Ship (Ira Gershwin-Kurt Weill), 830323-5

The Complete Ella Sings Broadway

Ella Sings Broadway, a 1962 Verve album contained Ella's versions of thirteen hits from great Broadway musicals, but she recorded a host of others that appeared here and there on other albums throughout the years. Listed below are the Broadway shows in alphabetical order and Ella's recorded tributes, along with a my favorite versions. "Broadway" is, of course, used here in its broadest sense, to include not only "off-Broadway," but also wherever a musical show opened its doors.

A to Z (various, 1922)
Limehouse Blues, 400125-1

Allegro (Hammerstein-Rodgers, 1947)
The Gentleman Is a Dope, 611115-2

Americana (various, 1929)
My Kinda Love (Trent-Alter), 581122-5
America's Sweetheart (Hart-Rodgers, 1931)
I've Got Five Dollars, 560821-3
Anything Goes (Cole Porter, 1934)
All Through the Night, 560208-4
Anything Goes, 560208-9
I Get a Kick Out of You, 560209-1
You're the Top, 560209-2
As Thousands Cheer (Irving Berlin, 1933)
Heat Wave, 580318-2
How's Chances?, 580314-3
Suppertime, 580317-2
Babes in Arms (Hart-Rodgers, 1937)
I Wish I Were in Love Again, 560828-2
Johnny One-Note, 560828-4
The Lady Is a Tramp, 560821-2
My Funny Valentine, 560830-9
Where or When, 560831-3
Beggar's Holiday (Latouche-Ellington, 1947)
Take Love Easy, 730828-1
Bells Are Ringing (Comden-Green-Styne, 1956)
Just in Time, 650514-1
Betsy (Hart-Rodgers, 1926)
Blue Skies (Irving Berlin), 580318-5
Between the Devil (Dietz-Schwartz, 1937)
By Myself, 860228-12
Big Boy (DeSylva-Brown-Henderson, 1925)
It All Depends on You, 560202-1
Bow Bells (Sevier-Hamilton, 1932)
You're Blasé, 571015-2
The Boys from Syracuse (Hart-Rodgers, 1938)
This Can't Be Love, 560821-1
Brigadoon (Lerner-Loewe, 1947)
(It's) Almost Like Being in Love, 621004-1
By Jupiter! (Hart-Rodgers, 1942)
Everything I've Got (Belongs to You), 560904-15
Wait Till You See Her, 560829-9
Cabaret (Ebb-Kander, 1966)
Cabaret, 690617-4
Cabin in the Sky (Latouche-Duke, 1940)
Taking a Chance on Love, 540214-2
Call Me Madam (Irving Berlin, 1950)
It's a Lovely Day Today, 580318-8
Can-Can (Cole Porter, 1953)
C'est Magnifique, 720609-12
I Am in Love, 560207-5
I Love Paris, 560207-2
It's All Right with Me, 560207-7
Carnival in Flanders (Burke-Van Heusen, 1953)
Here's That Rainy Day, 650326-4
The Cat and the Fiddle (Harbach-Kern, 1931)
She Didn't Say "Yes", 630107-2

Chicago (Ebb-Kander, 1975)
"All That Jazz," 890322-1
"(I'm) My Own Best Friend," 741018-2
"Roxie," 741018-1
A Connecticut Yankee (Hart-Rodgers, 1927)
My Heart Stood Still, 560830-2
Thou Swell, 560829-2
To Keep My Love Alive (from 1943 revival), 560829-7
Cotton Club Parade (various, 1932)
I've Got the World on a String (Koehler-Arlen),
600801-8
Cotton Club Parade of 1933 (various, 1933)
Stormy Weather (Koehler-Arlen), 610114-4
Cotton Club Parade of 1934 (various, 1934)
As Long As I Live (Koehler-Arlen), 581123-2
Ill Wind (Koehler-Arlen), 610114-7
Cotton Club Parade (3rd Edition (various, 1937)
He's Tall, He's Tan, He's Terrific (Davis-Coots),
371210-2
Cotton Club Parade of 1939 (various, 1939)
Don't Worry 'Bout Me (Koehler-Bloom), 790216-2
Damn Yankees (Adler-Ross, 1955)
Whatever Lola Wants, 621002-2
A Dangerous Maid (Gershwin-Gershwin, 1921)
Boy Wanted, 590715-4
Dearest Enemy (Hart-Rodgers, 1925)
Here in My Arms, 560830-5
DuBarry Was a Lady (Cole Porter, 1939)
Do I Love You?, 560207-3
Earl Carroll's Vanities (10th Edition) (various, 1932)
I Gotta Right To Sing the Blues, 610114-3
Earl Carroll's Vanities (various, 1940)
The Starlit Hour (Parish-DeRose), 400126-3
Ever Green (Rodgers-Hart, 1930)
Dancing on the Ceiling, 560831-2
Fiddler on the Roof (Harnick-Ross, 1964)
Matchmaker, Matchmaker, 650626-2
Fifty Million Frenchmen (Cole Porter, 1929)
You Do Something to Me, 560208-2
Finian's Rainbow (Harburg-Lane, 1946)
Necessity, 541120-1 (duet with Frank Sinatra)
Ol' Devil Moon, 550427-3
The Five O'Clock Girl (Kalmar-Ruby, 1927)
Thinking of You, 680529-1f
Flying Colors (Dietz-Schwartz, 1932)
Alone Together, 611114-2
Follow Me! (Rose-Olman, 1916)
Oh! Johnny! Oh! Johnny! Oh!, 400124-4
Funny Face (Gershwin-Gershwin, 1927)
Funny Face, 590318-4
He Loves and She Loves, 590107-3
Let's Kiss and Make Up, 590326-9
My One and Only, 590326-1

'S Wonderful, 590716-1
Funny Girl (Merrill-Styne, 1964)
  Don't Rain on My Parade, 650626-4
  People, 640407-3
The Garrick Gaieties (Hart-Rodgers, 1925)
  Manhattan, 560829-3
  Mountain Greenery, 560828-3
The Gay Divorce (Cole Porter, 1932)
  After You — Who?, 780213-2
  Night and Day, 560327-1
George White's Scandals of 1924 (various, 1924)
  Somebody Loves Me (DeSylva-MacDonald-Gershwin), 590107-5
George White's Scandals (various, 1926)
  The Birth of the Blues (DeSylva-Brown-Henderson), 530911-4
George White's Scandals of 1931 (various, 1931)
  The Thrill Is Gone (Brown-Henderson), 830322-10
Girl Crazy (Gershwin-Gershwin, 1930)
  Bidin' My Time, 590105-8
  Boy! What Love Has Done to Me, 590715-3
  But Not for Me, 590326-5
  Embraceable You, 590108-4
  I Got Rhythm, 590105-2
  Sam and Delilah, 590716-5
  Treat Me Rough, 590716-3
The Girl Friend (Hart-Rodgers, 1926)
  A Blue Room, 560831-2
Golden Rainbow (Walter Marks, 1967)
  I've Gotta Be Me, 730705-7
Great Day! (Rose-Eliscu-Youmans, 1929)
  More Than You Know, 571015-3
Guys and Dolls (Frank Loesser, 1950)
  Guys and Dolls, 621002-3
  If I Were a Bell, 581122-6
Heads Up! (Hart-Rodgers, 1929)
  A Ship Without a Sail, 560830-3
Hello, Dolly! (Jerry Herman, 1963)
  Hello, Dolly!, 710518-7
Hi, Diddle, Diddle (various, 1934)
  Miss Otis Regrets (Cole Porter), 560207-11
Hit the Deck! (Robin-Grey-Youmans, 1927)
  Hallelujah!, 371217-4
Hot Chocolate (various, 1929)
  Ain't Misbehavin' (Razaf-Waller-Brooks), 630716-4
I Married an Angel (Hart-Rodgers, 1938)
  Spring Is Here, 560830-8
I'd Rather Be Right (Hart-Rodgers, 1937)
  Have You Met Miss Jones?, 560830-4
Innocent Eyes (various, 1929)
  Hard Hearted Hannah (Bigelow-Bates-Yellen-Ager), 550503-1
Jubilee! (Cole Porter, 1935)

Begin the Beguine, 560208-3
  Just One of Those Things, 560207-9
Jumbo (Hart-Rodgers, 1935)
  Little Girl Blue, 560815-5
  My Romance, 560830-1
Jump for Joy (Fuller-Webster-Ellington, 1941)
  Bli-Blip, 570627-4
  The Brown-Skinned Gal in a Calico Gown, 651000-11
  I Got It Bad (and That Ain't Good), 570704-2
Kiss Me, Kate! (Cole Porter, 1948)
  Always True to You in My Fashion, 560208-5
  So in Love, 560208-1
  Too Darn Hot, 560207-10
  Why Can't You Behave?, 560207-1
Knickerbocker Holiday (Anderson-Weill, 1938)
  September Song, 600419-5
Ladies First (Gershwin-Gershwin, 1918)
  The Real American Folk Song (Is a Rag), 590718-6
Lady, Be Good! (Gershwin-Gershwin, 1924)
  Fascinating Rhythm, 590318-5
  Oh! Lady, Be Good!, 590108-7
Lady in the Dark (Gershwin-Weill, 1941)
  My Ship, 830323-5
Leave It to Me (Cole Porter, 1938)
  Get Out of Town, 560207-12
  My Heart Belongs to Daddy, 540330-3
Let's Face It (Cole Porter, 1941)
  Ace in the Hole, 560208-7
Lew Leslie's Blackbirds of 1928 (various, 1928)
  Diga Diga Doo (Fields-McHugh), 400125-4
  I Can't Give You Anything but Love (Fields-McHugh), 560815-10
  I Must Have That Man (Fields-McHugh), 410731-2
Lew Leslie's Blackbirds of 1930 (various, 1930)
  Memories of You (Razaf-Blake), 640303-4
Lew Leslie's International Revue (various, 1930)
  Exactly Like You (Fields-McHugh), 610521-6
  On the Sunny Side of the Street (Fields-McHugh), 531104-1
Life Begins at 8:40 (Harburg-Gershwin-Arlen, 1934)
  Let's Take a Walk Around the Block, 600802-4
The Little Show (various, 1929)
  Can't We Be Friends? (Warburg-Swift), 581124-6
  Moanin' Low (Dietz-Rainger), 531213-1
Load of Coal (various, 1929)
  Honeysuckle Rose (Razaf-Waller), 630716-1
Me and Juliet (Hammerstein-Rodgers, 1953)
  No Other Love, 621003-2
Mexican Hayride (Cole Porter, 1943)
  I Love You, 560207-2
The Midnight Follies (various, 1916)
  M-I-S-S-I-S-S-I-P-P-I (Hanlon-Ryan-Tierney),

500509-1

Mike Todd's Peep Show (various, 1950)
Stay with the Happy People (Hilliard-Styne), 500503-1

Miss Liberty (Irving Berlin, 1948)
You Can Have Him, 580314-2

Mr. Wonderful (Holofcener-Weiss-Bock, 1956)
Too Close for Comfort, 560815-6

The Most Happy Fella (Frank Loesser, 1956)
Somebody Somewhere, 621003-1
Warm All Over, 621003-4

Murray Anderson's Almanac (various, 1929)
I May Be Wrong (but I Think You're Wonderful (Ruskin-Sullivan), 580509-2

The Music Box Revue of 1921 (Irving Berlin, 1921)
Everybody Step, 380609-3

The Music Box Revue of 1922 (Irving Berlin, 1922)
Pack Up Your Sins and Go to the Devil, 380609-1

Music in the Air (Hammerstein-Kern, 1932)
The Song Is You, 671113a

My Fair Lady (Lerner-Loewe, 1956)
I Could Have Danced All Night, 560815-3
I've Grown Accustomed to His Face, 590325-3
Show Me, 611004-3

The Nervous Set (Landesman-Wolf, 1955)
Spring Can Really Hang You Up the Most, 610123-3

New Faces of 1936 (various, 1936)
My Last Affair (Johnson), 361118-1

The New Moon (Hammerstein-Romberg, 1928)
Lover, Come Back to Me, 530911-3

The New Yorkers (Cole Porter, 1930)
Love for Sale, 560208-8

The 9:15 Revue (various, 1930)
Get Happy!, 600802-1

No, No, Nanette (Caesar-Youmans, 1924)
I Want To Be Happy, 371217-1
Tea for Two, 630716-2

No Strings (Rodgers, 1962)
The Sweetest Sounds, 640407-4

Of Thee I Sing (Gershwin-Gershwin, 1931)
Love Is Sweeping the Country, 590718-2
Of Thee I Sing, 590318-2
Who Cares?, 590716-2

Oh, Kay! (Gershwin-Gershwin, 1926)
Clap Yo' Hands, 590108-1
Maybe, 500912-4
Someone To Watch Over Me, 590326-2

Oklahoma! (Hammerstein-Rodgers, 1943)
People Will Say We're in Love, 540329-6

On Your Toes (Hart-Rodgers, 1936)
Glad To Be Unhappy, 560202-11
There's a Small Hotel, 560829-4

One Touch of Venus (Nash-Weill, 1943)

Speak Low, 830321-1

Out of This World (Cole Porter, 1950)
From This Moment On, 560207-8

The Pajama Game (Adler-Ross, 1954)
Hey, There!, 540918-2
Steam Heat, 621001-3

Pal Joey (Hart-Rodgers, 1940)
Bewitched, Bothered and Bewildered, 560829-8
I Could Write a Book, 560830-10

Pardon My English (Gershwin-Gershwin, 1932)
Isn't It a Pity?, 590718-5
The Lorelei, 590326-8
My Cousin in Milwaukee, 590717-1

Paris (Cole Porter, 1928)
Let's Do It, 560208-11

Paris Qui Jazz (various, 1921)
My Man [Mon Homme] (Willehetz-Charles-Pollack-Yvain), 640304-3

Porgy and Bess (Gershwin-Heyward-Gershwin, 1935)
Bess, You Is My Woman Now, 570819-5 (duet with Louis Armstrong)
The Buzzard Song, 570828-4
Here Comes de Honey Man, 570828-6
I Got Plenty o' Nuttin', 570818-3 (duet with Louis Armstrong)
It Ain't Necessarily So, 570818-4 (duet with Louis Armstrong)
I Wants to Stay Here (I Loves You, Porgy), 580509-2
My Man's Gone Now, 570828-2
Oh, Dey's So Fresh and Fine [Strawberry Woman], 570827-7
Oh, Doctor Jesus, 570828-5
Summertime, 580810-10 (duet with Louis Armstrong)
What You Want Wid Bess?, 570828-3

Present Arms (Hart-Rodgers, 1928)
You Took Advantage of Me, 560831-5

Promises, Promises (David-Bacharach, 1964)
I'll Never Fall in Love Again, 690526-3

Red Hot and Blue (Cole Porter, 1936)
Down in the Depths (on the Ninetieth Floor), 720609-6
It's D'Lovely [It's De-Lovely], 560208-6
Ridin' High, 560207-6

Rhythmania (various, 1931)
Between the Devil and the Deep Blue Sea (Koehler-Arlen), 610116-1

Roberta (Harbach-Dougall-Kern, 1933)
I'll Be Hard To Handle, 630105-3
Let's Begin, 630107-3
Yesterdays, 610106-3

Rosalie (Gershwin-Gershwin, 1928)
How Long Has This Been Going On?, 590105-5

St. Louis Woman (Mercer-Arlen, 1946)

Come Rain or Come Shine, 770714-4
The Seven Lively Arts (Cole Porter, 1944)
   Ev'ry Time We Say Goodbye, 560207-4
Show Boat (Hammerstein-Wodehouse-Kern, 1927)
   Bill, 530911-2
   Can't Help Lovin' Dat Man, 630106-2
The Show Is On (various, 1936)
   By Strauss (Gershwin-Gershwin), 590717-6
Silk Stockings (Cole Porter, 1955)
   All of You, 560209-9
   Without Love, 720609-13
Simple Simon (Hart-Rodgers, 1930)
   Ten Cents a Dance, 560828-1
Sing Out the News (various, 1938)
   Franklin D. Roosevelt Jones, 381006-1
South Pacific (Hammerstein-Rodgers, 1949)
   Dites-moi, 621003-4
   Happy Talk, 490428-1
   I'm Gonna Wash That Man Right Outa My Hair,
     490428-2
Spread It Abroad (various, 1935)
   These Foolish Things (Remind Me of You)
     (Marvel-Strachey-Link), 5709295
Spring Is Here (Hart-Rodgers, 1929)
   With a Song in My Heart, 560829-6
Strike Up the Band! (Gershwin-Gershwin, 1930)
   Soon, 590105-1
   Strike Up the Band!, 590716-4
Sweet Adeline (Hammerstein-Kern, 1929)
   Why Was I Born?, 630106-4
Sweet and Low (various, 1930)
   Cheerful Little Earful (Gershwin-Rose-Warren),
     590108-2
   Would You Like To Take a Walk
     (Dixon-Rose-Warren), 511123-3
Take a Chance (DeSylva-Whiting-Brown, 1932)
   You're an Old Smoothie, 581122-8
The Three-Penny Opera (**Dreigroschenoper** (Brecht-
  Blitzstein-Weill, 1928)

Mack The Knife (Moritat), 600213-10
Thumbs Up! (Vernon Duke, 1935)
   Autumn in New York, 570723-3
Tip Toes (Gershwin-Gershwin, 1925)
   Looking for a Boy, 590326-7
   That Certain Feeling, 590714-2
Too Many Girls (Hart-Rodgers, 1939)
   Give It Back to the Indians, 560828-5
   I Didn't Know What Time It Was, 560829-5
Treasure Girl (Gershwin-Gershwin, 1928)
   I've Got a Crush on You, 590108-5
   Oh, So Nice!, 590717-4
Two for the Show (various, 1940)
   How High the Moon (Hamilton-Lewis), 560202-7
Two on the Aisle (Comden-Green-Styne, 1951)
   Give a Little, Get a Little (Love), 510718-4
Very Warm for May (Hammerstein-Kern, 1939)
   All the Things You Are, 630107-5
Wake Up and Dream (Cole Porter, 1929)
   What Is This Thing Called Love?, 560209-4
Walk a Little Faster (Harburg-Duke, 1932)
   April in Paris, 580509-1
What Makes Sammy Run? (Ervin Drake, 1964)
   Something To Live For, 660914-5
Whoopee! (Kahn-Donaldson, 1928)
   Love Me or Leave Me, 580810-14
   Makin' Whoopee, 581124-8
Will o' the Wisp (Irving Berlin, 1927)
   The Song Is Ended, 580318-4
Yokel Boy (Tobias-Brown-Step, 1939)
   Comes Love, 570423-9
You Never Know (Cole Porter, 1938)
   At Long Last Love, 720612-3
Ziegfeld Follies of 1934 (various, 1934)
   What Is There To Say?, 540329-3
Ziegfeld Follies of 1936 (various, 1936)
   I Can't Get Started (with You) (Gershwin-Duke),
     550401-4

Ella Fitzgerald Sings the .... Song Book

The foregoing were just a few suggestions. Using Part Three, the annotated index, you will discover a host of others whom you may wish to honor with their own Song Books:

Ella Fitzgerald Sings the Hammerstein and Rodgers
Song Book
The Complete Ella Fitzgerald Sings the Duke Elling-
ton Song Book
Ella Fitzgerald Sings the Frank Sinatra Song Book
Ella Fitzgerald Sings the Jule Styne Song Book
Ella Fitzgerald Sings the Sammy Cahn Song Book
Ella Fitzgerald Sings the Mitchell Parish Song Book
Ella Fitzgerald Sings the Vernon Duke Song Book

Ella Fitzgerald Sings the Leo Robin and Ralph
Rainger Song Book
Ella Fitzgerald Sings the Alan Jay Lerner and Freder-
ick Loewe Song Book
Ella Fitzgerald Sings the Al Dubin and Harry Warren
Song Book
Ella Fitzgerald Sings the Frank Loesser Song Book

...and many more!

E. Some Recommended Reading

ELLA BIOGRAPHIES

Ella Fitzgerald: A Biography of the First Lady of Jazz/Includes an Authoritative Discography by Phil Schaap, by Stuart Nicholson (Victor Gollancz, London, 1993). American edition published by Charles Scribner's Sons, New York, 1994)

First Lady of Song: Ella Fitzgerald for the Record, by Geoffrey Mark Fidelman (Carol Publishing Company, New York, 1994)

Ella: The Life and Times of Ella Fitzgerald, by Sid Colin (Elm Tree, London, 1986)

Ella Fitzgerald: A Life Through Jazz, by Jim Haskins (New English Library, London, 1991)

Ella Fitzgerald, by Bud Kliment (Chelsea Press, New York, 1988, and Melrose Square Publishing Co., Los Angeles, 1989)

Ella: Ein Bildband, by R. Ambor (Hamburg, Germany, 1961) (in German)

Ella Fitzgerald, by Alain Lacombe (Limon, Montpelier, France, 1989) (in French)

Ella Fitzgerald: Sein Leben, Sein Musik, Seine Schallplatten, by Rainer Nolden (Waalkirchen, Germany, 1986) (in German)

Ella Fitzgerald: Ein Porträt, by Jimmy Jungerman (Wetzlar, Germany, 1960) (in German)

COMMENTARY

The Ella Fitzgerald Companion: Seven Decades of Commentary, by Leslie Gourse (Schirmer Books, New York, 1998)

DISCOGRAPHY

Eminent in the field of jazz discography is Tom Lord's compilation, **The Jazz Discography**, which will finally comprise 26 volumes, as well as supplementary volumes updating material (to the year 2000). There will also be the volumes **Musicians Index** and **Tunes Index** following publication of the final volume. Twenty volumes are now published, and a recent note from Tom indicates that the last volume should be published early in 2000. Jazz artists are listed alphabetically, thus:

Vol. 1 ISBN 1-881993-00-0 A Touch of the Sun — Tallulah Bankhead
Vol. 2 ISBN 1-881993-01-9 Billy Banks — Christer Boustedt
Vol. 3 ISBN 1-881993-02-7 Lillian Boutte — Dick Cathcart
Vol. 4 ISBN 1-881993-03-5 Philip Catherine — Tony Dagradi
Vol. 5 ISBN 1-881993-04-3 Nils-BertilDahlander — Dutch Dixie Devils
Vol. 6 ISBN 1-881993-05-1 Dutch Swing College Band — Axel Fischbacher
Vol. 7 ISBN 1-881993-06-X Clare Fischer — Janos Gonda
Vol. 8 ISBN 1-881993-07-8 Nat Gonella — Everett Harp
Vol. 9 ISBN 1-881993-08-6 Billy Harper — Claude Hopkins
Vol. 10 ISBN 1-881993-09-4 Duncan Hopkins — Doug Jernigan
Vol. 11 ISBN 1-881993-10-8 Jeff Jerolamon — Billy Kirsch
Vol. 12 ISBN 1-881993-11-6 Kiruna Swing Sextet — Mark Lewis
Vol. 13 ISBN 1-881993-12-4 Meade Lux Lewis — Steve Masakowski
Vol. 14 ISBN 1-881993-13-2 Miya Masaoka — Sid Millward
Vol. 15 ISBN 1-881993-14-0 Bob Milne — Martha Nelson
Vol. 16 ISBN 1-881993-15-9 Oliver Nelson — Paradise City Jazz Band
Vol. 17 ISBN 1-881993-16-7 Paradise Club Band — Roy Powell
Vol. 18 ISBN 1-881993-17-5 Seldon Powell to Rimaak
Vol. 19 ISBN 1-881993-18-3 Sammy Rimington to Janne Schaffer
Vol. 20 ISBN 1-881993-19-1 Wolfgang Schalk to Holly Slater
Vol. 21 ISBN 1-881993- John Slaughter to Straight Line Jazz Ensemble
Vol. 22 ISBN 1-881933-
Vol. 23 ISBN 1-881933-

Mr. Lord appears to have have researched every possible source to produce the most complete jazz discography ever compiled. Approximately 35 to 40 percent of the sessions listed have never before appeared in print. Even though **The Jazz Discography** is in most libraries, many serious collectors purchase copies of their own. Mr. Lord's world-wide distributor is **North Country Distributors**, Cadence Building, Redwood, New York 13679, U.S.A. Telephone: (315) 287-2852/Fax: (315) 287-2860/E-Mail: cjb@cadencebuilding.com). The price is $60 U.S., including postage world-wide. For a brochure, contact North Country Distributors or use their website at www.cadencebuilding.com.

ELLA'S FELLAS: THEIR BIOGRAPHIES AND AUTOBIOGRAPHIES

Harold Arlen: Happy with the Blues, by Edward Jablonski (Doubleday and Co., New York, 1961, and Da Capo Press, New York, 1986)

Horn of Plenty (Louis Armstrong), by Robert Goffin (Allen, Towne & Heath, New York, 1947)

Louis Armstrong, by Genie Iverson (Thomas Y. Crowell, New York, 1976)

Louis Armstrong, A Self-Portrait, by Louis Armstrong (Eakins Press, New York, 1971)

Louis Armstrong: Ambassador Satchmo, by Jean Gay Cornell (Dell, New York, 1972)

Louis Armstrong, an American Genius, by James Lincoln Collier (Oxford University Press, New York, 1985)

Louis Armstrong Diaries, by Louis Armstrong (Institute of Jazz Studies, Rutgers University, Newark, New Jersey, 1987)

Louis Armstrong, His Life and Times, by Mike Pinford (Universe Books, New York, 1987)

Louis: The Louis Armstrong Story, by Max Jones (Da Capo Press, New York, 1988)

Louis' Children, by Leslie Gourse (William Morrow, New York, 1984)

Satchmo, by Louis Armstrong (Prentice Hall, New York, 1954)

Satchmo, by Gary Giddins (Doubleday, New York, 1988)

Trumpeter's Tale (Louis Armstrong), by Jeanette Eaton (William Morrow, New York, 1955)

With Louis and the Duke, by Barney Bigard (Oxford University Press, New York, 1988)

As Thousands Cheer: The Life of Irving Berlin, by Lawrence Bergreen (Viking Press, New York, 1990)

Irving Berlin, by Michael Freedland (Stein and Day, New York, 1974)

Nat King Cole, by James Haskins (Stein and Day, New York, 1984)

Nat King Cole: An Intimate Biography, by Maria Cole (William Morrow, New York, 1971

Nat "King" Cole, His Voice and Piano, by Charles Garrod (Joyce Record Club Publications, Zephyrhills, Florida, 1987)

Straighten Up and Fly Right (Nat King Cole), by Klaus Teubig (Scarecrow Press, Metuchen, New Jersey, 1989)

Unforgettable (Nat "King" Cole), by Leslie Gourse (St. Martin's Press, New York, 1991)

Bing, by Charles Thompson (David McKay Company, New York, 1976)

Bing Crosby, by Barbara Bauer (Pyramid, New York, 1977)

Bing Crosby, the Hollow Man, by Donald Shepherd and Robert F. Slatzer (St. Martin's Press, New York, 1981)

Call Me Lucky, by Bing Crosby (Simon and Schuster, New York, 1953)

The Crosby Years, by Ken Barnes (St. Martin's Press, New York,

Beyond Category: The Life and Genius of Duke Ellington (Simon and Schuster, New York, 1993)

A Journey to Greatness: The Life and Music of George Gershwin, by David Ewen (Henry Holt and Co., New York, 1956)

A Gershwin Companion: A Critical Inventory and Discography, 1916–1984, by Walter Rimer (Popular Culture, Ink., Ann Arbor, Michigan, 1991)

Gershwin: His Life and Music, by Charles Schwartz (Da Capo Press, New York, 1979)

The Gershwin Years, by Edward Jablonski and Lawrence Stewart (Doubleday and Co., Garden City, New York, 1958/1973)

The Gershwins, by Robert Kimball and Alfred Simon (Bonanza Books, New York, 1973)

Lyrics on Several Occasions, by Ira Gershwin (Alfred A. Knopf, New York, 1959)

BG on the Record: A Bio-Discography of Benny Goodman, by D. Russ Connor and Warren W. Hicks (Arlington House, New Rochelle, New York, 1969)

Jerome Kern: His Life and Music, by Gerald Boardman (Oxford University Press, New York/London, 1980)

Cole Porter: A Biography, (Dial Press, New York, 1977)

The Complete Lyrics of Cole Porter, edited by Robert Kimball (Alfred A. Knopf, New York, 1983)

Richard Rodgers Fact Book (with Supplement), (Lynn Farnol Group, Inc., New York, 1968)

The Rodgers and Hammerstein Story, by Stanley Green (The John Day Co., New York, 1963)

Rodgers and Hart: Bewitched, Bothered and Bedevilled, by Samuel Marx and Jan Clayton (G.P. Putman's Sons, New York, 1976)

Some Enchanted Evenings: The Story of Rodgers and Hammerstein, by Deems Taylor (Harper and Brothers, New York, 1953)

The Sound of Their Music: The Story of Rodgers and Hammerstein, by Frederick Nolan (Walker and Co., New York, 1978)

The Compleat Sinatra, by Albert I. Lonstein (Cameron Publications, Ellensville, New York, 1970)

Frank Sinatra, by John Howlett (Courage Books, Philadelphia, 1980)

Frank Sinatra, My Father, by Nancy Sinatra (Doubleday, Garden City, New York, 1985)

Frank Sinatra, Ol' Blue Eyes, by Norm Goldstein (Holt, Rinehart and Winston, New York, 1982)

The Frank Sinatra Scrapbook, by Richard Peters (St. Martin's Press, New York, 1983)

His Way (Frank Sinatra), by Kitty Kelley (Bantam Books, New York, 1986)

Rat Pack Confidential, by Shawn Levy (Doubleday, Garden City, New York, 1998)

Sinatra, by Robin Douglas-Home (Grosset & Dunlap, New York, 1962)

Sinatra, by Alan G. Frank (L. Amiel Publishing, New York, 1978)

Sinatra, by Tony Sciacca (Pinacle Books, New York, 1976)

Sinatra: An American Classic, by John Rockwell (Rolling Stone Press, New York, 1984)

Sinatra and His Rat Pack, by Richard Gehman (Belmont Books, New York, 1961)

Sinatra and the Great Song Stylists by Ken Barnes (Ian Allen, London, 1972)

Sinatra in His Own Words, by Frank Sinatra (W.H. Allen, London, 1979)

The Sinatra Sessions, 1939–1980, by Ed O'Brien (Sinatra Society of America, Dallas, 1980)

Sinatra, the Entertainer, by Arnold Shaw (Delilah Press, New York, 1982)

Sinatra the Singer, by Stan Britt (MacMillan London, London, 1989)

THE WORLD OF ELLA'S MUSIC: SOME INTERESTING READING

Amateur Night at the Apollo, by Ralph Cooper, with Steve Dougherty (HarperCollins, New York, 1990)

American Musicians: 56 Portraits in Jazz, by Whitney Balliett (Oxford University Press, New York, 1986)

American Singers, 27 Portraits in Song, by Whitney Balliett (Oxford University Press, Oxford/New York, 1988

Billie's Blues (Billie Holiday), by John Chilton (Da Capo Press, New York, 1989)

Combo, USA (Billie Holiday), by Rudi Blesh (Chilton Book Co., Philadelphia, 1971)

From Satchmo to Miles, by Leonard Feather (Da Capo, New York, 1972; reprinted 1984)

I Had the Craziest Dream, by Helen Forrest with Bill Libby (Coward, McCann & Geoghegan, New York, 1982)

The Jazz Singers: From Ragtime to the New Wave, by Bruce Crowther and Mike Pinfold (Poole, New York, 1986)

Jazz Singing: America's Great Voices from Bessie Smith to Bebop and Beyond, by Will Friedwald (Charles Scribner's Sons, New York, 1990)

Lady Sings the Blues, by Billie Holiday (Lancer Books, New York, 1956)

Lena: An Autobiography, by Lena Horne with Richard Schickel (Doubleday, Garden City, New York, 1986)

Lena: A Personal and Professional Biography, by James Haskins and Kathleen Benson (Stein and Day, New York, 1984)

Mabel Mercer, by James Haskins (Atheneum, New York, 1987)

Queen of the Blues (Dinah Washington), by James Haskins (William Morrow, New York, 1987)

Showtime at the Apollo, by Ted Fox (Da Capo Press, New York, 1983)

Stormy Weather: The Music and Lives of a Century of Jazzwomen, by Linda Dahl (Pantheon Books, New York, 1984)

This for Remembrance, by Rosemary Clooney (Playboy Press, New York, 1977)

MORE INTERESTING READING

All the Years of American Popular Music, by David Ewen (Prentice-Hall, Englewood Cliffs, New Jersey, 1977)

American Popular Song, by Alec Wilder (Oxford University Press, Oxford/London, 1972)

Anything Goes: The World of Popular Music, by David Dachs (Bobbs-Merrill, Indianapolis/New York, 1964)

Art Tatum: A Guide to His Recorded Music, by Arnold Laubich and Ray Spencer (Scarecrow Press, Metuchen, New Jersey)

Benny Carter: A Life in American Music, by Morroe Berger, Edward Berger, and James Patrick (Scarecrow Press, Metuchen, New Jersey, 1982)

The Best of the Music Makers, by George T. Simon (Doubleday, Garden City, New York, 1979)

Bibliographical Dictionary of American Music, by Charles Eugene Claghorn (Parker Publishing Co., West Nyack, New York, 1973)

The Big Band Almanac (rev. ed.), by Leo Walker (Da Capo Press, New York, 1978)

The Big Bands, by George T. Simon (Collier Books/ Macmillan, New York, 1974)

Big Band Jazz, by Albert McCarthy (Putnam's, New York, 1974)

Black Beauty, White Heat: A Pictorial History of Classic Jazz, 1920–1950, by Frank Driggs and Harris Lewine (William Morrow, New York, 1982)

Black Women and American Bands and Orchestras, by D. Antoinette Handy (Scarecrow Press, Metuchen, New Jersey, 1981)

Broadway on Record: A Directory of New York Cast Recordings of Musical Shows, 1931–1986, by Richard Chigley Lynch (Greenwood Press, Westport, Connecticut)

Brown Sugar: Eighty Years of America's Black Superstars by Donald Bogle (Harmony Books, New York, 1980)

Concise Biographical Dictionary of Singers, by Karl Josef Kutsch and Leo Riemens, 1962. Translated, expanded, and annotated by Harry Earl Jones. (Chelton Book Co., Fresno, California, 1969)

The Dance Band Era, by Albert McCarthy (Chilton, Philadelphia, 1972)

Discovering Great Jazz, Stephen M. Stroff (Newmarket Press, New York, 1991)

The Encyclopedia of American Music, by Edward Jablonski (Doubleday, Garden City, New York, 1981)

The Encyclopedia of Jazz in the Sixties, by Leonard Feather (Horizon Press, New York, 1966)

The Encyclopedia of Jazz in the Seventies, by Leonard Feather and Ira Gitler (Horizon Press, New York, 1976)

The Faber Companion to 20th-Century Popular Music, by Phil Hardy and Dave Laing (Faber and Faber, London/Boston, 1990)

Famous Black Entertainers of Today, by Raoul Abdul (Dodd, Mead & Co., New York, 1974)

The Great American Popular Singers, by Henry Pleasants (Simon and Schuster, New York, 1985)

Hendersonia: The Music of Fletcher Henderson and His Musicians: A Bio-Discography, by Walter C. Allen (Walter C. Allen, Highland Park, New Jersey, 1973)

A History of Popular Music, by David Ewen (Barnes and Noble, New York, 1961)

The Hit Parade, 1920–1955dd, by Don Tyler (William Morrow/Quill, New York, 1985)

The Illustrated History of Jazz, by Brian Case and Stan Britt (Harmony Book, New York, 1968)

I've Heard Those Songs Before: The Weekly Top Ten Tunes for the Last 50 Years, by Elston Brooks (Morrow Quill Paperbacks, New York, 1981)

Jazz, by Dean and Nancy Tudor (Libraries Unlimited, Inc., Littleton, Colorado, 1979)

Jazz: A History of the New York Scene, by Samuel Charters and Leonard Kunstadt (Doubleday & Co., New York, 1962)

Jazz: A Listener's Guide, by James McCalla (Prentice-Hall, Englewood Cliffs, New Jersey, 1982)

The Jazz Book: From New Orleans to Rock and Free Jazz (4th rev. ed.), by Joachim Berendt. Translated by Dan Morgenstern and Helmut and Barbara Bredigkeit (Lawrence Hill & Co., New York, 1975)

Jazz Masters of the Forties, by Ira Gitler, 1966. Reprint. (Collier Books, New York, 1974)

Jazz Masters of the Thirties, by Rex Stewart (Da Capo Press, New York, 1980)

Jazz on Record: A Critical Guide to the First 50 Years, 1917–1967, by Albert McCarthy, et al. (Hanover Books, London, 1968)

Jazz Pearls by William Van Eyle (Published by the author, Oudkarspel, Holland) (3102 jazz tunes, listed in date order from 1902 to December 1974)

Jazz Records, 1897–1942 (4th rev. and enlarged ed)(2 vols.), by Brian Rust (Arlington House, New Rochelle, New York, 1978)

The Jazz Tradition, by Martin T. Williams (Oxford University Press, Oxfordshire, 1983)

Modern Jazz: The Essential Records, by Max Harrison, et al. (Aquarius Books, London, 1975)

The New Edition of the Encyclopedia of Jazz, by Leonard Feather (Horizon Press, New York, 1960)

The 101 Best Jazz Albums: A History of Jazz on Records, by Len Lyons (William Morrow, New York, 1980)

The Penguin Encyclopedia of Popular Music, edited by Donald Clarke (Viking Penguin, London, 1989)

A Pictorial History of Jazz: People and Places from New Orleans to the Sixties, by Orrin Keepnews and Bill Grauer (2nd ed.) (Bonanza, New York, 1981)

Pop Memories 1890–1954: The History of American Popular Music by Joel Whitburn (Record Research, Menomonee Falls, Wisconsin, 1986)

Popular Culture and American Life, by Martin W. LaForse (Nelson-Hall, Chicago, 1981)

The Real Jazz, Old and New, by Stephen Longstreet (Greenwood Press, New York, 1969)

The Sights and Sounds of the Swing Era, 1935–1955, by George T. Simon (Galahad Books, New York, 1971)

Singers and the Song, by Gene Lees (Oxford University Press, Oxford/New York, 1987)

The Story of Jazz, by Michael Stearns (New American Library, New York, 1958)

The Street That Never Slept: New York's Fabled 52nd Street, by Arnold Shaw (Coward, New York, 1971)

Swing Out: Great Negro Jazz Bands, by Gene Fernett (Pendell, Midland, Michigan, 1970)

Tin Pan Alley, by David A. Jasen (Donald I. Fine, New York, 1988)

TV and Studio Cast Musicals on Record: A Discography of TV Musicals and Studio Recordings of Stage and Film Musicals, by Richard Chigley Lynch (Greenwood Press, Westport, Connecticut, 1900)

V-Discs: A History and Discography, by Richard S. Sears (Greenwood Press, Westport, Connecticut, 1980)

V-Discs: First Supplement, by Richard S. Sears (Greenwood Press, Westport, Connecticut, 1986)

We Don't Play Requests: A Musical Biography/Discography of Buddy Rich, by Doug Meriweather, Jr. (Creative Communications Corporation, Baltimore, Maryland, 1984)

Who's Who of Jazz: Storyville to Swing Street, by John Chilton (Chilton, Philadelphia, 1972) (Reprinted by Time-Life Records Special Edition, Chicago, 1978)

The Wonderful Era of the Great Dance Bands, by Leo Walker (Doubleday, Garden City, New York, 1964)

The World of Swing, by Stanley Dance (Charles Scribner's Sons, New York, 1974)

Index

This is an index to names, songs, albums, people, and places mentioned in the introductory essays and other front matter. The reader seeking more particular information, such as recording data for a song or the contents of a certain album, should turn to one of the following sections.